The Macmillan
HISTORY
OF THE
WORLD

Enameled 13th-century
French reliquary casket

Silver-mounted
Argentinian
gourd cup

Argentinian silver
drinking vessel

African Tuareg
camel saddle

Ceremonial
shield from
New Guinea

17th-century statue of
Tibetan god, Vajvapani

Modern
Nigerian vessel
with guinea
fowl decoration

Late 18th-century Japanese
hanging sword and scabbard

Algerian
cloak pin

Seventh-century
Bolivian sacred
jaguar vessel

14th-century British
chimney pot
decoration

The Macmillan

HISTORY

OF THE

WORLD

PLANTAGENET SOMERSET FRY

Ninth-century
Scottish scabbard
protector

Macmillan
C A N A D A

A DORLING KINDERSLEY BOOK

Senior Editor Gillian Denton	**Senior Art Editor** Gillian Allan
Project Editors Miriam Farbey, Claire Gillard	**Art Editors** Sarah Ponder, Mark Regardsoe, Rachael Foster
Editors Djinn von Noorden, David Pickering	**Designer** Clare Archer

Bronze fifth-century
Etruscan warrior

Gold and copper
Colombian figure

Managing Editor Simon Adams
Production Susannah Straughan
Picture Research Clive Webster
U.S. Editor Charles A. Wills

*The author wishes to acknowledge the indispensable assistance
of the team at Dorling Kindersley in this project, without
whom this work would simply not have been possible.*

Consultants

DR. CHRISTOPHER ABEL, Senior Lecturer in Latin American History, University College London

DR. DAVID G. C. ALLAN, Curator-Historian, RSA (retired), Visiting Lecturer in History, University of Connecticut Overseas Programme

DR. ROBIN BIDWELL, for 20 years Secretary/Librarian of the Middle East Centre, Cambridge University, where he also taught modern Arab history

DR. GORDON DANIELS, Reader in History, University of Sheffield

DR. R. HALPERN, Lecturer in American History, University College London

GEORGE HART, Education Service, British Museum

DR. JOHN HENDERSON, Fellow, Wolfson College, Cambridge University

CATHERINE KEY, Department of Anthropology, University College London

ANN KRAMER, University of Sussex

PROFESSOR BRUCE P. LENMAN, Professor of Modern History, University of St. Andrews

MICHAEL LOEWE, Faculty of Oriental Studies, Cambridge University

JAMES LUPTON, Researcher, Latin American History; has taught at University of London and Universidad de los Andes, Bogota, Colombia

GORDON MARSDEN, Editor, *History Today*

ANNE PEARSON, Education Officer, British Museum

PROFESSOR A. D. ROBERTS, School of Oriental and African Studies, University of London

DR. HELEN WALLIS OBE, formerly Map Librarian, the British Library

KYRIL ZINOVIEFF (AKA FITZLYON), Russian historian

U.S. Consultants

DR. STUART LAZARUS, Learning Design Associates, Inc., Columbus, Ohio

RUTH MACAULAY, Head of History Department, Lincoln School, Providence, Rhode Island

First published in Great Britain in 1994 by
Dorling Kindersley Limited,
9 Henrietta Street, London WC2E 8PS
First Canadian edition published by Macmillan Canada 1994

Copyright © 1994 Dorling Kindersley Limited, London
Text copyright © 1994 Plantagenet Somerset Fry

Canadian Cataloguing in Publication Data

Fry, Plantagenet Somerset, 1931–
  The Macmillan history of the world

Canadian ed.
Includes index
ISBN 0-7715-9047-4

1. World history - Juvenile literature.
I. Title

D20.F78 1994   j909   C94-930647-9

Colour reproduction by Colourscan, Singapore
Printed and bound in Italy by A. Mondadori Editore, Verona

Brazilian macaw feather hairpin

AUTHOR'S FOREWORD

The world is nearly six billion years old. Yet the story of people like us, *Homo sapiens sapiens*, or modern humans, who have existed for only about 100,000 years, takes up nearly the whole of this book. This is because we are looking not at geological movements and prehistoric beasts of skyscraper height, but at the development of our own species from inarticulate savages to sophisticated technicians. There are several ways of looking at our history. We can see it as a dreary record of attempts by big, strong peoples to dominate smaller ones, or as an account of groups of humans solving problems – political, social, and economic – in similar ways. When you have read this book, perhaps you will develop your own theories. Of all animals, only humans control their environment and development. Yet how far have we advanced? We can explore space and split the atom, but we still have widespread slavery, racial discrimination, and injustice. Despite thousands of years of war, we have only just begun to see that there are other ways to resolve conflicts. Some recent examples are enormously encouraging. It is for the next generation to multiply these efforts and make them work by knowing a little more about how and why earlier peoples found it so difficult.

Indian water beast frieze

Seljuk bowl

North American Hopi pot

EDITORS' NOTE

THE BOOK IS DIVIDED into five regions: Africa, Asia, Europe, the Americas, and Oceania (Australasia, Papua New Guinea, and the Pacific islands). Russia is seen as a part of Europe and, with its empire, becomes the Soviet Union from 1917 to 1991. For the sake of clarity, the modern names of countries, cities, rivers, and other geographical features have generally been used, both in the text and on the maps, large and small. Where the old names are more appropriate to the passage, however, they have been retained, notably in colonial contexts, as have particular names, such as Persia, which are especially well known. On the small maps, which focus on specific areas, a flexible policy has been adopted to help the reader.

For example, occasionally, as in the cases of Germany and Italy, countries may be referred to as one entity before unification has occurred. The pinyin spelling is used for most Chinese names, but other spellings have been kept where they have become generally accepted. As far as people's names are concerned, English versions (such as William for Wilhelm) are used throughout the book. Where dates are given in parentheses after a person's name they are birth and death dates, except in the cases of certain monarchs whose reign dates are more relevant to the passage. Measurements, such as the distances of conquests, are given in imperial, with the metric measurements in parentheses afterward.

CONTENTS

Seventh-century north Indian Buddhist statue

17th-century Indian dagger

Egyptian ewer

Moluccan shield

Native American doll

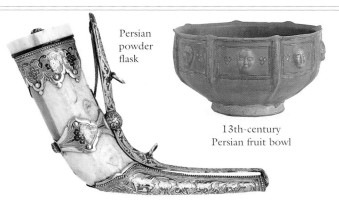
Persian powder flask

13th-century Persian fruit bowl

Gilded brass Benin armlet

18th-century French linstock

Ming Chinese food dish

HOW THIS BOOK WORKS

The Macmillan History of the World starts with the origins of life on earth and ends in the 1990s. It is a visual journey into the past. The time span of the book is divided into 20 chapters, and a fully illustrated map introduces the most important events of each period. A specially designed timechart follows, which pinpoints key developments and events in the cultures of each continent. Key events are then described in chronological order, continent by continent.

In every chapter, feature pages explore fascinating aspects of the daily life, religion, and civilizations of the period. Photographs, paintings, maps, and illustrations bring each subject vividly to life. Any topic can be found easily by looking in the comprehensive index. Difficult words are explained clearly in the glossary, and illustrated reference pages, packed with up-to-date information, include a detailed section on Canadian national history.

A WORLD MAP opens every chapter, providing a visual overview of the period. The projection gives equal prominence to each continent. Artwork illustrations show scenes from the crucial events of the period, and labels enable the reader to locate the important empires, countries, and cities of the time. A general introduction summarizes the main political, social, and cultural themes of the period.

Artwork scene locates a key event covered in detail in the chapter

Introduction relates the developments of the period to the whole course of history

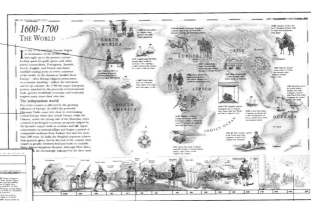

Each continent is color-coded throughout the book for easy identification

1st symbol 1 beside a date indicates an invention or discovery

Small globe locates the continent

Entry is illustrated with a photograph of an artefact of the period

Timeline crosses each page, containing a colored timebar that highlights the chapter's time period

Asterisk indicates that this event is described in the continent section

An illustrated scroll unrolls to reveal major events and civilizations

The faint area beyond the scroll's end indicates the future passage of time

AN ILLUSTRATED COMPARATIVE TIMECHART follows the world map. Arranged in continental order, it lists major events and developments in chronological order. It enables the reader to see at a glance what was happening in every part of the world at any one time. The key events that will be described in detail later in the chapter are indicated by an asterisk *.

KEY EVENTS PAGES follow the timechart. They are organized continent by continent in the order first established by the timechart. The events appear in the continent sections in chronological order, headed by their dates. Special feature pages describe aspects of everyday life and culture essential to understanding the events. Small fact boxes provide extra information, such as key date lists and concise biographies.

Date-led entry provides concise details of significant events

Modern photograph of historic building shows how the past is still present today

Map shows the extent of states and colonies; other maps locate empires, trade routes, and physical features

Specially commissioned photograph of a museum object brings history to life on the page

ABBREVIATIONS

Some words are abbreviated, or shortened. This list explains them.

cm	centimeter
m	meter
km	kilometer
sq	square
in	inch
ft	foot
yd	yard
c.	circa, used before a date, means "about"
BC	before Christ
AD	"anno Domini": in the time after Christ's birth
MYA	million years ago

Key date box lists the crucial dates of the subject, both inside and outside the chapter's time period, and briefly describes each development

Information box provides absorbing details on an intriguing aspect of the event; biography box (top) reviews the life and achievements of a major figure

Artwork reconstructs a scene from daily life; points of particular interest are comprehensively annotated

CHAPTER 1

570 MYA – 40,000 BC

INTRODUCTION TO HUMAN HISTORY

Female ammonite fossil

LIFE ON EARTH

How did our universe begin? Scientists believe that millions of years ago the universe formed in a colossal explosion they call the Big Bang. Within seconds this fireball expanded and cooled from fantastic temperatures into the universe we know. Zillions of particles cooled from the superhot gas created by the explosion and started to swirl toward one another by the universal force of gravity. The particles formed stars and planets. On one of these planets – earth – life began some 4,600 million years ago (MYA).

Archimedes' screw
Carboniferous bryozoa were tentacled creatures that inhabited the seabed in colonies. In this bryozoan *Archimedes* the screw-shaped central skeleton provided a home to the colony members.

Supercontinent Pangaea
Today we have five continents, but this has not always been the case. Continents move, fuse, and break apart over huge periods of time. During the Carboniferous period all the continents were fused together to form one vast supercontinent called Pangaea.

The Paleozoic era (570–245 MYA)

The earth was born some 4,600 MYA. The first simple life forms, like bacteria and algae, appeared around 3,500 MYA. During the last 570 million years more complex creatures evolved. This time span is divided into three eras: the Paleozoic (old life), Mesozoic (middle life), and Cenozoic (recent life), which are themselves divided into shorter periods or epochs (see timechart below). The Paleozoic era began with the appearance of jawless fish and invertebrates (creatures without a backbone). Later, as jawed fish, sharks, and giant scorpions hunted the seas, amphibians (creatures who live on land and in water) ventured onto land, where they lived in swamps. Some evolved into reptiles. The Paleozoic era drew to a close as half the world was covered in ice, resulting in extinctions.

Fossil cone cross-section
Lepidostrobus are cigar-shaped cones. They come from trees that were up to 130 ft (40 m) tall.

Skeleton of a carnivore
An amphibian, *eryops* grew up to 7 ft (2 m) in length and had sharp teeth for eating meat.

Cambrian 570–510 MYA	Ordovician 510–440 MYA	Silurian 440–410 MYA	Devonian 410–360 MYA	Carboniferous 360–290 MYA

Paleozoic era

570 MYA	500 MYA	450 MYA	400 MYA	350 MYA	300 MYA

Dragonfly fossil
This Jurassic dragonfly fell into stagnant mud and was preserved. Mud provided the perfect conditions for fossilization, which is how this rare fossil of such a delicate animal came to be.

The Mesozoic (245–65 MYA)

After the mass extinctions at the end of the Paleozoic, the Mesozoic era, known as the Age of Reptiles, opened with an explosion of new life forms. Reptiles evolved on the land (into mammals and dinosaurs), in the water (as crocodiles and frogs), and even took to the air as pterosaurs. Ichthyosaurs swam in the sea with belemnites and ammonites, and flowering plants and small mammals appeared on land. During the Jurassic period dinosaurs spread far and wide. Some of the smaller ones evolved into the first birds. Dinosaurs continued their reign for most of the Mesozoic era but came to a sudden end 65 MYA. This mass extinction may have been the result of a giant meteorite crashing into the earth and covering it with dust.

New oceans
During the Mesozoic the ice sheets melted, releasing lots of water. The Tethys sea grew, and new oceans were formed. Pangaea broke into several smaller continents.

Bird skull
Fossils of birds such as *Prophaethon* are rare. This skull clearly shows a long gull-like beak which indicates that *Prophaethon* was probably a seabird.

Cenozoic era (65 MYA–present)

When the dinosaurs died out, mammals quickly took their throne, increasing in variety not only on land, but also in the air (bats) and sea (whales and dolphins). In Australia, isolated from the other continents, a whole new kind of pouched mammal evolved, called marsupials (like the kangaroo). Other additions included the first primates (monkeys and apes) and saber-toothed cats in the Oligocene epoch. During the Miocene, new species of antelope, deer, cattle, and primates appeared, and the forerunners of humankind arose in Africa.

Long neck
Barosaurus was a colossal giraffelike dinosaur. It used its long neck to browse off treetops which other dinosaurs could not reach. *Barosaurus* traveled in herds, probably as a defense against faster predators.

Ape ancestry
An early Miocene ape, *Proconsul* lived in the forests of East Africa and evolved into apes, such as gibbons and gorillas, and humans.

Cenozoic globe
Continents and oceans became more familiar. India collided with Asia, creating the Himalayas. South and North America joined c.3.4 MYA.

Permian 290–245 MYA	Triassic 245–208 MYA	Jurassic 208–146 MYA	Cretaceous 146–65 MYA	Paleocene 65–56.5 MYA	Eocene 56.5–35.4 MYA	Oligocene 35.4–23.3 MYA	Miocene 23.3–5.2 MYA	Pliocene 5.2–1.8 MYA	Pleistocene 1.8 MYA–40,000 BC
	Mesozoic era					Cenozoic era			
250 MYA	200 MYA	150 MYA	100 MYA		50 MYA			40,000 BC	

DEVELOPMENT OF MARINE LIFE

Life began in the oceans more than 600 MYA. The first tiny creatures were made up of only one cell. Over millions of years more complex animals appeared made up of many cells. The main records of ancient marine life are fossils, the remains of animals and plants buried in the ground and preserved naturally for millions of years. By examining fossils, scientists have discovered that for a long time most marine animals were invertebrates (they had no skeleton) and built shells as armor for their soft bodies. The first vertebrates (animals with backbones) were fish, which appeared in the Ordovician period (510–440 MYA), increasing in variety and abundance during Devonian times (410–360 MYA), when sharks began hunting the seas. Since then, many kinds of marine animals have appeared and disappeared, each adding to the amazing variety of life in the seas and oceans.

Burgess shale worm
This worm was one of the earliest multicellular life forms, living on the seabed over 500 MYA. Fossilization usually preserves only bony skeletons, but fossilized worms and other soft-bodied invertebrates have been found in a deposit, called the Burgess shale, in Canada. The fossils included trilobites, animals with flat bodies and horny shells, and primitive crustaceans, animals with jointed external skeletons and antennae.

Shell with flap
This fossil shell and the creature it housed is known as *Platystrophia*. It lived on the seabed, feeding on plankton, during the Ordovician period. It had a horseshoe-shaped flap used to beat water, containing food and oxygen, into its shell. *Platystrophia* belongs to the phylum Brachiopoda, whose members were very common in the Ordovician period. More than 30,000 fossil species have been identified, but only 300 of these species still exist today.

Arm waver
Sea lilies, such as *Sagenocrinites*, are plantlike organisms which live on the seabed. Extinct species are sometimes called stone lilies. *Sagenocrinites* has a mouth on its upper surface and uses its waving arms to collect food. It is a member of the crinoid family, very common in the Silurian period (440–410 MYA). There are only 80 living species, but 2,000 fossil forms have so far been identified.

FOSSIL FORMATION

Dead animal sinks to seabed and is buried by sediment layers

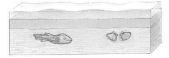
Lower sediment layers turn to rock; animal's remains harden

Rock is folded and eroded

Fossil is exposed on the surface

The bodies of dead animals and plants usually were eaten or rotted away. Occasionally, hard parts, such as shells, bones, and teeth, were buried quickly in sediment, such as sand or mud. The seabed provided the best conditions for this. Over millions of years, the sediment turned to rock. During this time, the minerals that made up the hard parts of the animal turned to stone, forming fossils. Movements of the earth twisted and buckled the surface so that rock from under the sea became the tops of mountains. As mountains were eroded, fossils could be found close to the surface of the soil.

Living fossil
Some animals today, such as the coelacanth fish, are very similar to their fossil ancestors. The first coelacanth fossils date to the Devonian period, when huge numbers of fish appeared, but the coelacanth was most common in Triassic times (245–208 MYA). It was thought by scientists to have become extinct 50 MYA until, in 1938, a steely-blue coelacanth, 4.9 ft (1.5 m) long, weighing 125 lbs (57 kg), was caught by fishermen off the coast of South Africa. More than 60 specimens have been caught since. The fish has lobed fins which can be used as limbs and lives at the bottom of very deep water, where it feeds on other fish.

Swimming predator

Goniatites was a type of mollusk that lived during the Carboniferous period (360–290 MYA). Mollusks, such as snails and slugs, have a fleshy body that is usually protected by a shell. They are common throughout the fossil record and are divided into three groups, or families. *Goniatites* belongs to the cephalopod family which use jet propulsion for swimming, as though it were a mini-submarine. Many modern cephalopod species no longer have shells. They include some of the fastest, largest invertebrates, such as the squid, which can travel as quickly as a car can, 30 mph (48 km/h).

Animal flowers

The numbers of sea lilies greatly increased during the Mesozoic era (245–65 MYA), and varieties without stems first appeared. This sea lily retained the long stem and had branching arms for catching food.

Arms spread out to fan small particles of food to mouth

Long stem attached animal to hard surface

Long beak contained sharp, cone-shaped teeth for meat eating

Dragon of the seas

Ichthyosaurus was a giant creature of Mesozoic times. It was a reptile, but looked like a fish and was superbly adapted to life in the water. It had a powerful tail like a shark's, used "arms" as steering paddles, and had a flexible backbone for moving easily through the water. It came to the surface to breathe.

Underwater clubber

Marine life greatly diversified during the Cretaceous period (146–65 MYA), and the ancestors of many modern groups can be traced back to this time. *Tylocidaris* is a primitive sea urchin that became common in the Cretaceous period. It had many club-shaped arms which it used to beat off predators and to guide small animals into its central mouth. Heart urchins, which are related to sea urchins but do not have any arms, also became common at this time.

Mouth

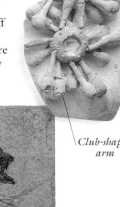

Club-shaped arm

Limestone contains well-preserved skeleton

Dominant fish

Sparnodus is an example of the "modern" type of bony fish, the teleosts. Teleosts first appeared in the Cretaceous period and over the next ten million years became (and still are) the most common bony fish in both salt and fresh water. The wide variety includes the slow, inactive flatfish and the speedy swordfish and marlin.

Powerful predator

The magnificent *Carcharodon* (great white shark) rarely attacks humans.

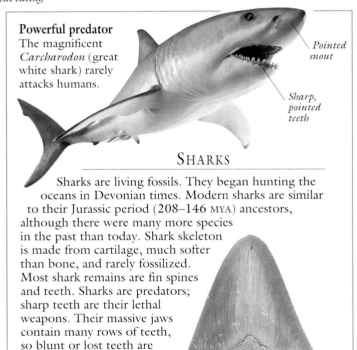

Pointed snout

Sharp, pointed teeth

SHARKS

Sharks are living fossils. They began hunting the oceans in Devonian times. Modern sharks are similar to their Jurassic period (208–146 MYA) ancestors, although there were many more species in the past than today. Shark skeleton is made from cartilage, much softer than bone, and rarely fossilized. Most shark remains are fin spines and teeth. Sharks are predators; sharp teeth are their lethal weapons. Their massive jaws contain many rows of teeth, so blunt or lost teeth are quickly replaced.

Big tooth

Carcharodon teeth from the Pliocene era (5.2–1.8 MYA) are as long as 4.3 in (11 cm). The whole shark was 40 ft (12 m) long.

EVOLUTION OF LAND ANIMALS

For millions of years life existed only in the oceans. Then, during the Silurian period (440–410 MYA), mossy plants began to live in damp areas near the water. This enabled plant-eating arthropods (animals with jointed external skeletons) to appear and survive on land, and they in turn became food for the first meat-eating arthropods to live out of the water. As the land became covered in thick vegetation during Devonian times (410–360 MYA) amphibians, the ancestors of frogs, left the oceans. They developed lungs for breathing in air and strong limbs for walking. Insect members of the arthropod family, such as spiders, dragonflies, and cockroaches, also evolved. Amphibians and reptiles, scaly-skinned animals that appeared on land 300 million years ago, spent most of their time in water, until reptiles developed eggs that could be laid on dry land. Since then, the land has been home to a massive variety of fascinating creatures including dinosaurs, birds, mammals, and eventually human beings.

Plant food
There was no life on land until Devonian times, when the first plants to emerge included *Archaeopteris,* which grew to 60 ft (18 m) tall. It belonged to the progymnosperms plant group, the forerunners of the gymnosperms, woody plants that protect seeds in a cone. Plants provided shelter and food for the first land animals.

Early creepy-crawlies
Remains of spiderlike forms have been found from the Devonian period, when the first insects appeared on land. The first easily recognizable spiders are from the Carboniferous period (360–290 MYA) and included *Grephorus* (right). Spiders have changed very little since these early times. Like modern species, *Grephonus* had spinnerets, organs which give out silken thread for weaving webs, in which unfortunate prey is trapped.

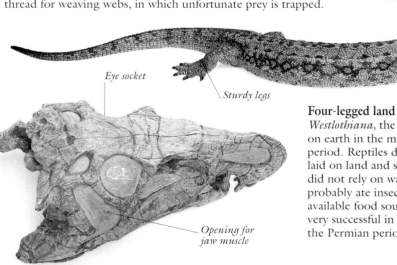

Eye socket

Sturdy legs

Tips of upper teeth formed curve like scalpel blade

Head twisted to saw off flesh

Four-legged land animal
Westlothiana, the earliest-known reptile, appeared on earth in the middle years of the Carboniferous period. Reptiles developed eggs that could be laid on land and so were the first animals that did not rely on water for survival. They probably ate insects, which were a readily available food source. Reptiles became very successful in the dry conditions of the Permian period (290–245 MYA).

Opening for jaw muscle

Dinosaur ancestor
Riojasuchus was a reptile living in the Triassic period (245–208 MYA). It was a small, lizardlike animal with sharp teeth set into sockets for eating meat. It belonged to a group of reptiles, the thecodonts, which walked on hind legs and had powerful tails. They were probably the ancestors of dinosaurs and crocodiles.

King dinosaur
Dinosaurs ruled the land for millions of years, from the Triassic period to the end of the Cretaceous period (146–65 MYA). *Tyrannosaurus rex* was king of them all. It was the largest meat-eating animal ever to live on land, nearly 40 ft (12 m) wide and 20 ft (6 m) tall standing on its rear legs. *Tyrannosaurus* had huge curved teeth, massive jaws, and lethal talons on its toes. It probably trailed migrating herds of duckbilled and horned dinosaurs, picking off the young and the weak.

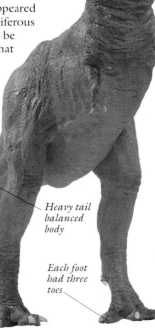

Heavy tail balanced body

Each foot had three toes

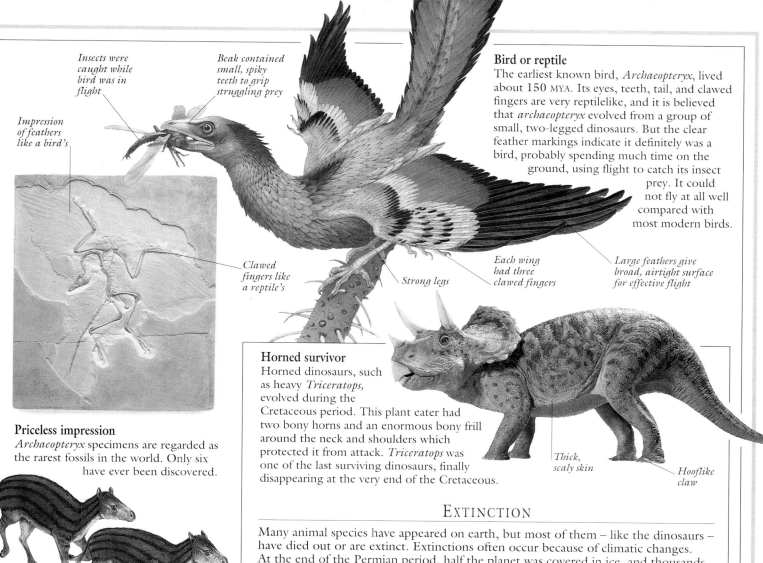

Insects were caught while bird was in flight

Beak contained small, spiky teeth to grip struggling prey

Impression of feathers like a bird's

Clawed fingers like a reptile's

Strong legs

Each wing had three clawed fingers

Large feathers give broad, airtight surface for effective flight

Bird or reptile

The earliest known bird, *Archaeopteryx*, lived about 150 MYA. Its eyes, teeth, tail, and clawed fingers are very reptilelike, and it is believed that *archaeopteryx* evolved from a group of small, two-legged dinosaurs. But the clear feather markings indicate it definitely was a bird, probably spending much time on the ground, using flight to catch its insect prey. It could not fly at all well compared with most modern birds.

Priceless impression

Archaeopteryx specimens are regarded as the rarest fossils in the world. Only six have ever been discovered.

Horned survivor

Horned dinosaurs, such as heavy *Triceratops*, evolved during the Cretaceous period. This plant eater had two bony horns and an enormous bony frill around the neck and shoulders which protected it from attack. *Triceratops* was one of the last surviving dinosaurs, finally disappearing at the very end of the Cretaceous.

Thick, scaly skin

Hooflike claw

EXTINCTION

Many animal species have appeared on earth, but most of them – like the dinosaurs – have died out or are extinct. Extinctions often occur because of climatic changes. At the end of the Permian period, half the planet was covered in ice, and thousands of species died out in the harsh conditions. Dinosaurs became extinct 65 MYA, at the end of the Cretaceous period. This may have been due to a meteorite crashing into the earth, covering it with dust, causing widespread destruction.

Herbivores with hooves

Hyracotherium was the first horse, appearing in the late Paleocene period (65–56.5 MYA) in North America and Europe. It was a surprisingly small animal, a mere 9.75 in (25 cm) high, that ran on four-toed feet. It lived in forests, feeding on soft leaves. *Hyracotherium* evolved into the modern horse and related animals, such as the zebra.

Baby silverback

The first mammals (animals with warm blood and a hairy body whose young drink their mothers' milk) appeared in Triassic times. The first primates, mammals that grasp with their hands, appeared 32 MYA. Since then, primates have appeared in many different shapes and sizes. Monkeys, apes, and humans are all primates but are adapted to quite different lives. Monkeys are adapted to swinging in trees; this baby silverback gorilla is more at home on the ground.

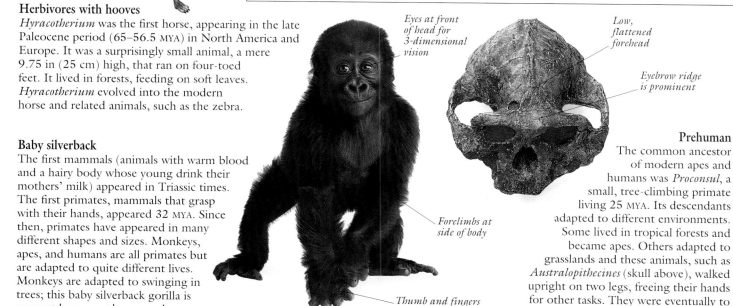

Eyes at front of head for 3-dimensional vision

Forelimbs at side of body

Thumb and fingers add dexterity

Low, flattened forehead

Eyebrow ridge is prominent

Prehuman

The common ancestor of modern apes and humans was *Proconsul*, a small, tree-climbing primate living 25 MYA. Its descendants adapted to different environments. Some lived in tropical forests and became apes. Others adapted to grasslands and these animals, such as *Australopithecines* (skull above), walked upright on two legs, freeing their hands for other tasks. They were eventually to evolve into human beings.

HUMAN ANCESTRY

Fossil evidence shows us that, by 4 MYA, the human evolutionary line had become distinct from those of other primates. Humans and their most recent ancestors are called hominids. There is only one species of hominid alive today – humans – but 2 MYA ago there lived at least three, and maybe six or more, different species. Fossils of these first hominids have been found only in East and South Africa and can be divided into two main groups: *Australopithecines* ("southern ape"), which had a small brain and large cheek teeth, and *Homo*, which had a larger brain and small cheek teeth. All hominids were bipedal (they walked on two legs) and probably lived in bushland or woodland savannah. *Homo habilis* was the first tool-making hominid. The first hominids to leave Africa were *Homo erectus* ("upright man"). They had bigger bodies and brains than their immediate ancestors, used more varied tools, and knew how to use fire. Eventually *Homo erectus* evolved into *Homo sapiens*, which in turn became *Homo sapiens sapiens* – modern humans.

Laetoli footprints
More than 3.5 MYA a volcano erupted at a place called Laetoli in East Africa, spewing hot lava across the land. Many animals walked through the cooling lava, including three *Australopithecines* – two adults and a child – who left this trail of footprints. The fossilized footprints were found in 1978 and are a very important discovery because they proved that the *Australopithecines* were walking on two legs.

The first Lucy
The *Australopithecine* shown here has been named Lucy after The Beatles song, *Lucy in the Sky with Diamonds,* which was playing in the excavators' camp at the time Lucy was discovered. Lucy has taught us a great deal about *Australopithecines* because we have the remains of 40 percent of her skeleton. Lucy lived in Hadar, East Africa, around 3 MYA. She was small and walked on two legs like a human, but her legs were short, like those of an ape. Lucy probably walked with slightly bent knees, and it is thought that she spent some time climbing trees, perhaps to sleep, find food, or to avoid predators. Lucy had a small brain, like a chimpanzee, a long low skull, and powerful jaws. Her hard teeth enabled her to eat a varied vegetarian diet. *Australopithecines* may have used rocks and sticks for daily tasks such as cracking nuts.

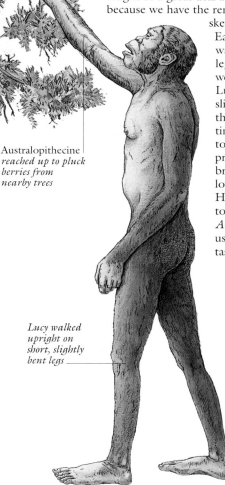

Australopithecine reached up to pluck berries from nearby trees

Lucy walked upright on short, slightly bent legs

FOSSIL REMAINS AT OLDUVAI GORGE

Olduvai Gorge (seen below), in the Serengeti Plain of northern Tanzania, East Africa, is famous for its hominid fossils. It was once a lush lake environment which attracted many animals, including hominids. Today it is a canyon 328 ft (100 m) deep and 31 miles (50 km) long. Fossil remains of *Australopithecines*, *Homo habilis*, and *Homo erectus* have been found here as well as some of the oldest known stone tools. These were quite simple, and were probably used to cut meat and prepare plant foods. Tool marks have been found on some bones.

Louis Leakey
It was Louis and his wife Mary Leakey's work that proved Africa to be the home of our earliest ancestors. The first East African *Australopithecine* was found by them at Olduvai Gorge in 1959. Later, the first *Homo habilis* fossil was found.

Handy man

This is a model of the earliest commonly accepted species of *Homo*, *H. habilis*. It lived at the same time as the *Australopithecines* in South and East Africa, from 2.3 MYA to about 1.8 MYA. The first *Homo* fossils were found at Olduvai Gorge, alongside the first stone tools. Hence this hominid was christened *Homo habilis*, meaning "handy man." The brain size of *Homo habilis* was greater than in the *Australopithecines*, but much smaller than in humans. Like the *Australopithecines*, *Homo habilis* was short and had curved fingers and long arms, which suggest that they were also treeclimbers. *Homo habilis* was replaced by, or evolved into, *Homo erectus*.

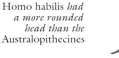

Homo habilis had a more rounded head than the Australopithecines

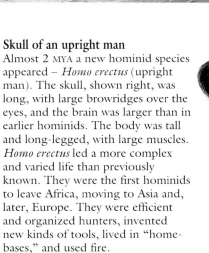

Homo habilis fashioned tools from stone

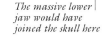

Saber-toothed cat

This saber-toothed cat, *Smilodon*, was one of the most ferocious animals that lived at the same time as the hominids. It had distinctive 6 in (15 cm) long teeth that it used to slice into its prey. Many people believe that hominids lived in groups as a defense against predators. The small *Australopithecines* would have been most vulnerable and may have climbed up trees to escape falling victim to *Smilodon*. *Smilodon* became extinct during the Pleistocene epoch.

Homo erectus had a thick skull, with a sloping forehead and large eyebrow ridge

Skull of an upright man

Almost 2 MYA a new hominid species appeared – *Homo erectus* (upright man). The skull, shown right, was long, with large browridges over the eyes, and the brain was larger than in earlier hominids. The body was tall and long-legged, with large muscles. *Homo erectus* led a more complex and varied life than previously known. They were the first hominids to leave Africa, moving to Asia and, later, Europe. They were efficient and organized hunters, invented new kinds of tools, lived in "home-bases," and used fire.

The massive lower jaw would have joined the skull here

This hand ax has an uneven surface where it has been chipped away

Hand ax

Homo erectus used larger tools than those used by earlier hominids, such as hand axes, picks, and cleavers. These tools, which are called bifaces, were made from stone which was cut away on two sides. The teardrop-shaped hand ax above is typical of this new technology, which is known as Acheulean. Hand axes were heavy tools with sharp cutting edges, probably used as axes or knives. They were good for chopping bone, meat, and wood and also for cutting through tough hide, such as an elephant's.

First fire

It is impossible to know when hominids began to use fire since fires often occur naturally and early hominids probably made use of this. However, we know that *Homo erectus* was a fire user. In the Zhoukoudian caves in China, burned bones and stones, thick ash beds, and charcoal have been found, showing that fire was being used 500,000 years ago. In the cooler climate of Eurasia, fire would have provided much-needed warmth. It could also be used for cooking and warding off predators.

THE NEANDERTHALS

The Neanderthals, *Homo sapiens neanderthalensis,* whose existence was first discovered in the Neander valley in Germany in 1856, were a kind of primitive people who lived in Ice Age Europe and western Asia between 120,000 and c.35,000 years ago. They were strong, heavily muscled people who lived in caves or outdoor shelters to escape the cold, harsh environment. The Neanderthal way of life may have been very similar to that of our own species, *Homo sapiens sapiens,* and although there can be no proof, it is possible that they were using language effectively. The Neanderthals were the first known people to bury their dead and to care for their sick and elderly. It is known from archeological evidence that one Neanderthal male survived with a crushed eye socket and a withered arm due to the help of other group members. The Neanderthals gradually died out as modern humans appeared in Asia and Europe.

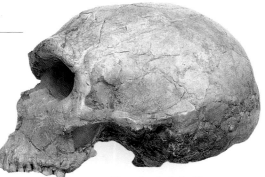

Neanderthal skull
This skull clearly shows the large browridges typical of the Neanderthals.

Flint tools and weapons
Neanderthals revolutionized flint working; they split sharp flakes from a single flint to use as tools and weapons.

Possible ritual items such as rings of animal horns were sometimes placed with the body

Graves were quite shallow

Burial ceremonies
Some Neanderthals buried their dead, marking and even mourning the loss of a community member. The deaths of children were often marked with a ceremonial burial.

Cooked meat was sometimes placed in the grave

1 A flint flake was broken from a piece of flint with a stone and roughly shaped

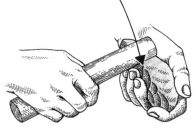

2 The flint flake was refined into a tool or weapon with a bone or stone hammer

3 The weapon or tool could be further refined by paring the flint's surface with a sharp stone or bone

CHARLES DARWIN 1809–82

Charles Darwin was a British naturalist who in 1859 wrote an important book titled *The Origin of Species.* Darwin had realized that animals and plants change over long periods of time because they compete for food and mates. He proposed that the "best" or "fittest" creatures survive, and those alive today are the result of millions of years of evolution; this he called natural selection. Darwin caused a furor in 19th-century England by applying his theories to humans; the discovery of Neanderthal fossils proved that humans are also the product of evolution.

CHAPTER 2

40,000 – 5000 BC

EARLY PEOPLE

Stylized bone mammoth from the Ice Age

40,000-5000 BC
THE WORLD

A T THE BEGINNING of this long period of time, recognizably modern humans (*Homo sapiens sapiens*) populate many parts of the world, even building boats to sail across the shallow waters that separate Southeast Asia from Australia. Some 35,000 years ago, for reasons that are still not clear, Neanderthals die out; *Homo sapiens sapiens* is the only human species resourceful enough to survive an Ice Age, which at its coldest, around 20,000 years ago, lowers sea levels by 300 ft (100 m). By c.13,000 BC the first settlers cross the icy land bridge that then connects Siberia to Alaska, beginning the long migration that by c.9000 BC takes them as far as Patagonia on the extreme tip of South America.

The birth of art

No one knows why early people decorated their environment, but this period sees the world's first art. In Europe, Africa, and Australia, people decorate caves with lively representations of animals. Later they carve human and animal figures from bone. Early people live by hunting and gathering their food, moving from place to place in order to eat. The beginnings of crop cultivation, the later creation of farms, and the domestication of wild animals allow people to settle in one place. Villages and then towns spring up. By the end of this period, the world's first civilizations begin to emerge.

c.20,000 BC Mastodons, related to mammoths and elephants, roam North America

c.9000 BC Hunter-gatherers in the great plains of North America hunt bison

c.7000 BC Early farmers grow crops in Mexico

c.9000 BC Hunter-gatherers make stone tools in Peru

NORTH AMERICA

SOUTH AMERICA

ATLANTIC OCEAN

PACIFIC OCEAN

Mississippi

Andes

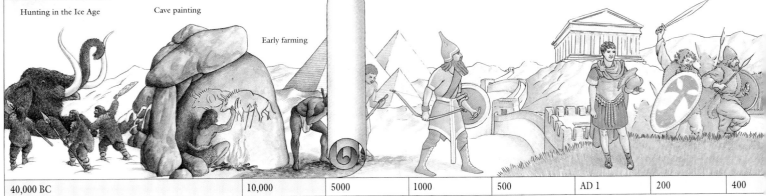

Hunting in the Ice Age

Cave painting

Early farming

| 40,000 BC | | 10,000 | 5000 | 1000 | 500 | AD 1 | 200 | 400 |

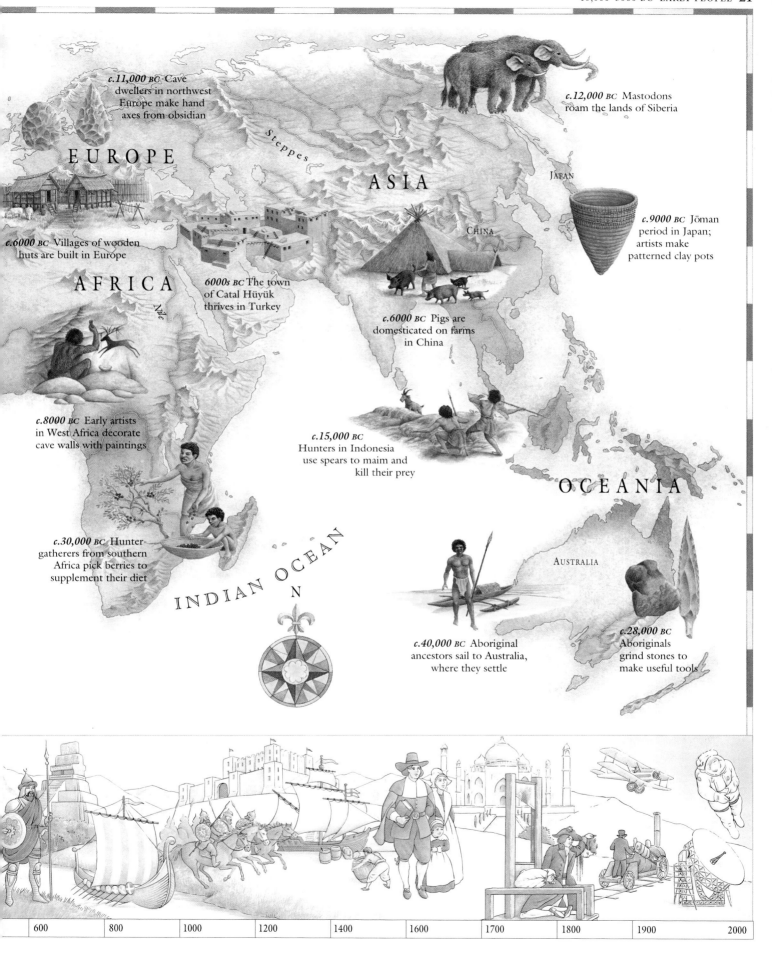

c.11,000 BC Cave dwellers in northwest Europe make hand axes from obsidian

c.12,000 BC Mastodons roam the lands of Siberia

EUROPE

Steppes

ASIA

JAPAN

c.9000 BC Jōman period in Japan; artists make patterned clay pots

CHINA

c.6000 BC Villages of wooden huts are built in Europe

AFRICA

6000s BC The town of Catal Hüyük thrives in Turkey

Nile

c.6000 BC Pigs are domesticated on farms in China

c.8000 BC Early artists in West Africa decorate cave walls with paintings

c.15,000 BC Hunters in Indonesia use spears to maim and kill their prey

OCEANIA

c.30,000 BC Hunter-gatherers from southern Africa pick berries to supplement their diet

AUSTRALIA

INDIAN OCEAN

N

c.40,000 BC Aboriginal ancestors sail to Australia, where they settle

c.28,000 BC Aboriginals grind stones to make useful tools

| 600 | 800 | 1000 | 1200 | 1400 | 1600 | 1700 | 1800 | 1900 | 2000 |

40,000 BC

30,000 BC

AFRICA

c.40,000 Modern humans have already evolved*

c.35,000 Simple counting device found in South Africa

c.34,000 Hunter-gatherers occupy areas of Lesotho and Zambia

c.33,000 Small tools decorated with quartz stone made in Zaire

Ostriches were part of the diet of early hunter-gatherers in Lesotho and Zambia

c.24,000 Oldest rock paintings in Apollo site in Namibia

Drawings of horses, bison, and wild cattle dominated the cave walls

ASIA

Stone flakes have been chipped from these tools

c.40,000 Small stone tools found in Israel

c.38,000 Evidence of human life in limestone caves in northern Borneo

EUROPE

c.38,000 Cro-Magnon man reaches Europe from Africa

Cro-Magnon villagers performing daily tasks

c.24,000 European hunter-gatherers begin to make permanent houses with clay roofs

c.23,000 First clay statuettes made by hunter-gatherers

c.21,000 Ivory boomerang made in Poland; earliest in Europe

c.20,000 Paintings decorate caves in Lascaux, France, and in Altamira, Spain

Stylized terra-cotta figurine from eastern Europe

Engraved bone from Laugerie Basse in France, showing a human figure chasing a bison

AMERICAS

OCEANIA

c.40,000 Aboriginals arrive in Australia*

c.40,000 Rock engravings made in Australia

c.38,000 Waisted axes crafted in New Guinea

Rock engravings, Australia

c.28,000 Aboriginals grind stones to make ax blades in northern Australia

c.24,000 World's earliest human cremations carried out in Australia

Aboriginal man grinding stone into an ax blade

20,000 BC

c.18,000 Hunter-gatherers settle in Zaire

c.13,000 Terra-cotta figures made in Algeria, North Africa

Fruit eaten by early Mediterranean peoples

Bag used by hunters for carrying snares and small animals

c.17,000 Earliest wild cereal gathered near Lake Kinneret (Sea of Galilee)

c.13,000 Hunter-gatherers in Asia hunt animals for food to survive*

c.11,000 Caves are used as dwellings in Fukui, near Nagasaki in Japan

Wild emmer, an early domestic wheat, can still be found in the Levant

c.16,000–c.10,000 Huts with mammoth bone roofs built in Europe, especially in western Russia

c.11,000 Obsidian first used for tools by cave dwellers in Greece

Mammoth bone hut, Siberia

c.13,000 First crossings to America over Bering Strait made by hunter-gatherers*

c.11,000 Early humans arrive in Chile

Second molar tooth of a giant mastodon

c.18,000–c.11,000 Occupation of Kutikina Cave, southern Tasmania; users of stone tools

c.17,000 First rock paintings in Australia

Kutikina Cave in Australia provided shelter for early people

10,000 BC

c.10,000 General advance in stone tool technology in several parts of Africa

c.8000 Hunter-gatherers paint human figures on rock in North Africa

c.7000 Fishing communities emerge in Sahara region, North Africa

c.6000 Cattle domesticated in the Sahara region

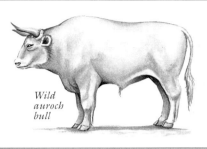

Wild auroch bull

c.10,000 Farming begins in Asia: domestication of animals*

c.9000 Jōmon period in Japan

c.8000 Settlement of Jericho; construction of dwellings

c.8000 Earliest mud-brick buildings in western Asia

c.7000 Farming in western Asia

c.6500 Farming in Indus valley

6000s First towns thrive including Catal Hüyük in Turkey*

c.6000 Millet grown in Yellow River valley, China; domestication of pigs

c.6000 Mesopotamia: canal irrigation of fields

c.5000 Yellow River settlements in China import jade from Siberia

c.5000 Rice cultivation along Yangtze River valley in China

Pottery vessel made during the Jōmon period in Japan

Millet was widely cultivated in Mesopotamia

c.8000 Shellfish becomes an important source of protein for European coastal dwellers

c.6500 Earliest cereal farming in southeast Europe

c.5000 Earliest copper and gold metalworking in Europe

Oysters were gathered and eaten by coastal villagers in Europe

c.9000 Clovis hunter-gatherers in the Great Plains of North America begin to hunt bison

c.7500 The world's earliest-known cemetery found in Arkansas, North America

c.7000 Earliest crops grown in Mexico

c.6500 Grain crops grown in Peru, South America

Bison roamed the Great Plains of North America

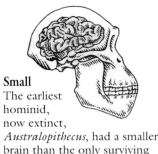

Small
The earliest hominid, now extinct, *Australopithecus*, had a smaller brain than the only surviving hominid, *Homo sapiens sapiens*.

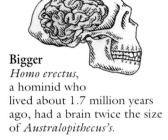

Bigger
Homo erectus, a hominid who lived about 1.7 million years ago, had a brain twice the size of *Australopithecus's*.

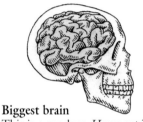

Biggest brain
This is a modern *Homo sapiens sapiens* skull. Its brain capacity is in the range of 1200–1600 ml, nearly three times as that of *Australopithecus*.

c.40,000 BC
The spread of modern humans

The first early humans, *Homo sapiens*, appeared in Africa and Europe about 500,000 years ago. They had larger, more rounded skulls than their *Homo erectus* ancestors, although they retained the projecting browridges and other *Homo erectus* features. In Europe these early *Homo sapiens* evolved into the Neanderthals, while in Africa and East Asia there were different trends. Some experts believe that the African *Homo sapiens* were the ancestors of all modern humans (*Homo sapiens sapiens*) and that they replaced the Neanderthal and East Asian peoples. Others believe that the three types of *Homo sapiens* in Africa, Europe, and East Asia each developed independently into different "races" of *Homo sapiens sapiens*. Whichever is true, by 40,000 BC fully modern humans had populated many parts of the globe, even building boats to arrive in Australia. They had learned to produce art, and bone and stone artifacts and had developed complex burial and farming practices.

Thoroughly modern
This early *Homo sapiens sapiens* (modern human) skull has small teeth and a tall, rounded braincase. *Homo sapiens neanderthalensis*, or Neanderthal humans, had much heavier features. They had a protruding jaw, a backward-sloping forehead, and a prominent browridge.

Point where spine joins base of skull

Jaw is small

Early humans used whatever materials came to hand, however unusual, to build their homes

Mammoth jaws weighed down animal hides and stopped them from tearing in the wind

Roof arches were made from curved mammoth tusks

Teeth are crowded together and directly below brow

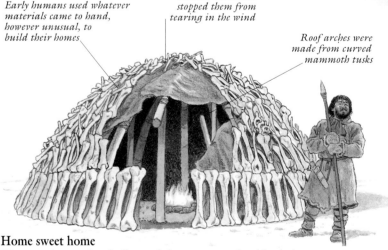

Home sweet home
Homo sapiens sapiens built much larger, more durable shelters than their predecessors. The most common homes were probably made from wooden posts covered with animal hides. Caves provided ready-made shelter in many places. Between 18,000 and 12,000 years ago, these amazing huts in Mezhirich in Ukraine were built from mammoth bone because wood was scarce.

Counting the notches
Several pieces of engraved wood and carved bones were found in Border Cave in South Africa. Archeologists believe that they were simple counting devices. Instruments such as these were probably used in Africa as long as 37,000 years ago. This baboon fibula (lower leg bone) has 29 parallel notches carved on it. It is similar to the wooden calendar sticks that are still used by some Khoisan clans living in southwestern Africa.

Fibula has 29 parallel incised notches

40,000 BC		10,000	5000	1000	500		200	400

c.40,000 BC
Aboriginals' ancestors settle Australia

Australia was colonized by *Homo sapiens sapiens* (modern humans) from Southeast Asia by c.40,000 BC. At that time Indonesia was a continuous land mass linked to Asia, and New Guinea was joined to Australia, so the people walked most of the journey, sailing distances as short as 60 miles (100 km) probably on rafts or in canoes. The settlers, ancestors of today's Aboriginals (the word *Aboriginals* means "inhabitants from earliest times"), at first stayed mainly near the coasts and developed an economy based on fishing. They also hunted animals and gathered fruit and vegetables. The first inland settlements were probably in the southern lakelands, between the Darling and Murray rivers. Inland Aboriginals may have controlled their local environment using the "firestick" method, in which the edges of an area were burned, limiting the distance animals foraged so they could be more easily hunted. By c.30,000 BC Aboriginals used sharpened stone axes to clear trees and make room for settlements. In c.10,000 BC rising seas flooded coastal sites, forcing more Aboriginals inland.

Creation story
According to Aboriginal religion, many great spirits journeyed across the earth when it was barely formed, creating the mountains, rivers, and trees, as well as the first Australians. The places made by these "ancestral" spirits are holy. Perhaps the most famous is massive Uluru (Ayers Rock), in the very center of the country.

Rock art
About 40,000 years ago Aboriginals began to etch circles, dots, arcs, and pictures of humans and animals onto rocks. These rock paintings were probably among the first works of art. Aboriginals today think the images were drawn by their earliest ancestors and represent the great spirits that created these first people.

Wanderers' resting place
Aboriginals moved from camp to camp, staying at each until the local food supply was depleted. The type of temporary shelter they built varied with the habitat and season. In cold climates they made huts of branches or rocks, often near lakes, where food was plentiful. In hot, dry areas they made grass windbreaks, staying at each for as little as a week because food was scarce. Aboriginals built stone hearths near their shelters for warmth, light, and cooking, and to scare off wild animals.

Dugout bark canoes were probably used for fishing and sailing

Edge-ground axes were one of the first examples of ground stone tools

Shelters were made of slabs of bark over a wooden frame

HUNTING AND GATHERING

Settlers encountered animals they had known in Asia, such as crocodiles. They also saw for the first time strange creatures such as giant kangaroos, 10 ft (3 m) tall; ferocious, doglike Tasmanian tigers, and rhinoceroslike *Diprotodons* (all now extinct). For food, they fished, trapped shellfish and turtles, hunted kangaroos, wallabies, and hairy-nosed wombats, and gathered nuts, fruits, and yams. In c.16,000 BC the climate became drier. Vast expanses of grasslands turned to desert. Some Aboriginals adapted to the desert environment, traveling great distances between camps close to food and water. They passed the whereabouts of the camps onto fellow Aboriginals in songs.

Kangaroo
Skillful hunters tracked kangaroos over rocky ground by following their light footprints.

Food search
Mussels (right) were gathered easily; bogong moths (above) could only be caught in certain seasons on mountains.

c.13,000 BC
Settlers cross Bering Strait into North America

At various times throughout early history, vast ice caps and huge glaciers covered much of northern Europe, Asia, and North America. These cold periods, known as Ice Ages, occurred roughly every 100,000 years and were followed by warmer periods of about 20,000 years each. The last Ice Age began around 110,000 BC and was mostly over by c.13,000 BC. Because so much water was frozen, sea levels fell by about 300 ft (90 m). As a result, continents previously separated by the oceans were linked, and there was a bridge of land across the Bering Strait between northeast Russia and Alaska. Hunter-gatherers who had settled in Asia began to move south in about 13,000 BC, crossing into what is now Alaska and the Yukon in North America. After c.12,000 BC, the Bering Strait flooded over again, cutting off the Asians from their homeland. So they continued to spread southward through North America and then into South America, reaching as far south as Patagonia in Argentina and Chile by about 9000 BC.

Moving south
The changing climate displaced vegetation, so that cold-weather species of trees such as this silver birch spread south into much of Europe.

Mammoth
As humans migrated and settled across the world, their artistic talents evolved. This stylized mammoth with large tusks curving around its head was carved out of an animal's shoulder blade. Mammoths were common until the end of the Ice Age.

☐ Area covered by ice
--- Extended land mass above sea level

Cold world
The shape of the world was very different 10,000 years ago. This map shows the amount of land visible above sea level during the last Ice Age. The arrows on the round map show human movement across the Bering Strait land bridge.

Glaciers move at a rate of up to 13–16 ft (4–5 m) per day

The sharp ridge between glaciers is called an arête

Ice at the center of the glacier always moves faster than ice at the sides

As the ice flows around a sharp bend or over a ridge, it splits to form deep cracks called crevasses

Antlers could span up to 11.5 ft (3.5 m)

As big as a horse
This deer-like *Megaceros* roamed the countryside during the last Ice Age.

River of ice
A valley glacier is a large mass of ice that forms on land and moves slowly downhill under its own weight. During the Ice Ages, these glaciers dramatically changed the shape of the landscape. The moving ice scoured and polished underlying rock, forming many of today's valleys and mountains.

ROCK ART

Even the earliest human beings, around 40,000 BC, produced paintings, engravings, and sculptures. The pictures were cut or painted on rocks or on the walls of caves where people lived. Sculptures were usually human or animal figures made of antlers, bone, ivory tusks, or stone. Dyes for painting were derived from stone and seem to have been discovered very early. No one is quite sure why the artworks were carried out, but it was probably for a variety of motives: possibly as part of religious practices, or to record something of the environment in which early people worked and played, or even just for fun. Some depictions of animal movements were so lifelike that they must have been the result of many hours of careful study. Early art appears in many parts of the world including Africa, Asia, Australia, and Europe, but so far no evidence of early art in the Americas has been found. The oldest known art forms were painted by the Aboriginals in Australia.

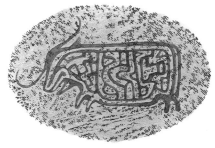

Bhimbekta bison
Rock art in cave shelters at Bhimbekta in India was flourishing well before 11,000 BC. Paintings are either abstract outlines or filled in, like this bison.

Making paint

Cave artists made pigments by grinding minerals to a powder and then mixing them with water. Red pigment was derived from hematite (iron oxide or red ochre), white from kaolin or chalk, and black was either manganese dioxide or charcoal. Some communities heated minerals to produce new colors. Most minerals used for pigments were readily available and collected locally, although some must have been mined. Ochre mines discovered in Africa were first worked around 42,000 years ago.

Kaolin

Charcoal
Hematite

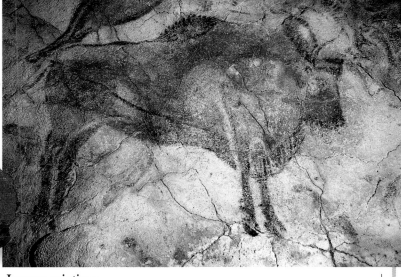

Animal art
This animal painting from a rock shelter at Ingaladdi in the Northern Territory in Australia dates to after the last Ice Age. The best-preserved Australian rock art, painted by Aboriginals, dates from this time.

Lascaux paintings
Among the most famous paintings in Europe are these from the Lascaux caves in southwest France. They were made by Cro-Magnon people over many centuries, and those that have survived are thought to date from c.15,000–10,000 BC. They consist of paintings of bulls, cows, deer, and horses. Schoolboys wandering in the caves in 1940 first stumbled across the paintings.

Lighting the way
How artists lit their caves is still a puzzle. Most artists probably used torches and lamps made from flat stones holding burning lumps of fat. This lamp from Lascaux is extremely rare, since only 300 lamps have been identified as dating to the 25,000 years of cave art.

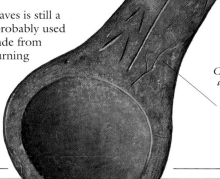

Carvings decorate handle of lamp

c.13,000 BC
Hunter-gatherers kill for a living

Homo sapiens sapiens had to hunt for food in order to survive. The men hunted a variety of animals, according to where they lived, such as horses, bison, reindeer, elk, and woolly mammoths, while the women and children gathered fruit and nuts. There were important advances in hunting techniques as the last Ice Age came to an end in about 13,000 to 10,000 BC. Wooden spearthrowers were devised to increase a spear's range and penetration, deer-antler harpoons made effective implements for stabbing fish, and in c.10,000 BC bows and arrows were introduced. These developments occurred in many places throughout the world, such as Siberia, Czechoslovakia, southern Africa, Japan, Egypt, Spain and France, Persia, and Alaska and Canada. Overexploitation of many species of large mammals, such as woolly mammoths, saber-toothed cats, and wild asses, by the skillful human hunters probably caused their final extinction.

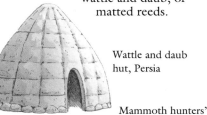

Multipurpose tool
The hand ax, invented by *Homo erectus* 2 MYA, was still used by hunter-gatherers in c.13,000 BC. It was an effective implement for butchering meat and cutting animal skins.

Tusks were used in constructing shelters

Closing in for the kill
Men hunted woolly mammoths in groups. First they ambushed and wounded their prey. Then they followed it until it collapsed and moved in to complete the slaughter.

The wounded mammoth could take days to die

Hunters used spears strapped to long wooden shafts to maim their prey

A mammoth kill provided enough meat to feed a group for several months

SHELTER FROM THE STORM

During the harsh, cold winter months, hunter-gatherers lived in caves, but when the milder weather arrived, they built shelters outside. Hunter-gatherers in Ice Age Europe and Russia built huts with frames made of mammoth bones and timber props, covering them with animal hides. In Persia and India, after about 10,000 BC, huts began to be built from stone blocks covered with wattle and daub, or matted reeds.

Wattle and daub hut, Persia

Mammoth hunters' dwelling, Russia

A woman's task
Groups of women and young children went on gathering expeditions while the men were out hunting. Armed with flint axes and digging sticks, they set out daily to fill their leather bags and reed baskets with nuts, berries, roots, and other edible foods such as birds' eggs, lizards, and honey.

These bark "plates" were used to collect berries and nuts

c.10,000 BC
The first farmers cultivate crops

The retreat of the last Ice Age (from c.13,000–c.10,000 BC) released huge amounts of water in many parts of the world and produced climate changes, such as plentiful and regular rainfall, which helped to make desert land more fertile. Before long, people learned how to domesticate animals and farm fields. This major advance in people's control over their food resources occurred very rapidly in a region stretching from Turkey across the eastern Mediterranean coast and Mesopotamia to the Zagros Mountains in Persia. In about 10,000 BC hunter-gatherers found that if they planted cereal seeds in watered fields, they would grow into new cereal crops the next year. The earliest farms began to appear in western Asia in about 9000 BC. Farmers also learned how to select wild animals and breed them in captivity to give birth to more domestic types. Domesticated sheep first appeared in Iraq in about 8700 BC, and pigs are first recorded in Turkey in c.7200 BC. The farmers learned to store food, and this meant they no longer needed to move each year to keep themselves and their families clothed and fed. Within 1,000 years small farming settlements had grown into larger ones, and the first seeds of civilization began to emerge.

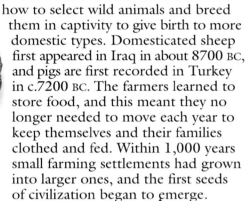

Making sparks
Early people discovered how to make fire using iron pyrite, a naturally occurring mineral compound containing sulfur. When the iron pyrite was struck with a flint, a spark was produced which, when it fell on dry grass, could be fanned into a flame. Fires were made to cook meat, to keep warm, and to scare away dangerous wild animals.

Iron pyrite

Flint

Grinding grain
The new farmers harvested their grain and used it to make beer, or ground it into flour. This type of stone quern, or hand mill, was in use about 4000 to 6000 years ago. Grain was placed on the flat surface and ground into flour with the smooth lump of sandstone.

Plant taming
By 8000 BC people living in western Asia relied more and more on domestic crops. Wild einkorn is the forerunner of early domestic wheat and can still be found in parts of western Asia. The domestic version has larger seeds and a tough stalk, which requires threshing for seed dispersal.

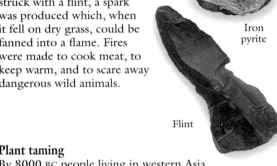

Wild einkorn

Domestic einkorn

Walls were made of sunbaked mud bricks

A fence enclosed the farmstead and kept wild animals out

Poles were covered with reeds and straw and spread with mud to form a roof

Dough was rolled out on a stone slab to make flat bread cakes

An early farmhouse
An early farmstead contained several mud brick dwelling houses, courtyards for milking cattle, a well for drawing water, ovens for cooking food and firing pottery, and shrines for worshiping the gods.

Wood was gathered to stoke the fire

The points of spears were hardened in the flames of an outside fire

| 800 | | 1200 | 1400 | 1600 | 1700 | 1800 | 1900 | 2000 |

6000s BC
The first towns thrive

Some farmers in western Asia learned how to grow surplus crops and began to trade them with their neighbors. As their settlements prospered, they built permanent homes from durable materials such as stone or mud brick. They arranged the houses so that families could easily contact each other and organized communal services, such as roads, shops, and drains. Two of these first towns were Catal Hüyük in Turkey and Jericho in Israel. Catal Hüyük was situated by a river on a fertile plain. It consisted of many tightly packed mud brick houses. More than six thousand people lived there by the 6000s BC. The economy was based on agriculture, cattle breeding, and trade. Among the crops were cereals, peas, almonds, and crab apples. The people also mined local obsidian (volcanic rock) to make into cutting tools.

Fertility figure
This female figure was one of many stone and clay sculptures made at Catal Hüyük. Her big stomach suggests pregnancy, and she probably represents a goddess of motherhood or sexuality.

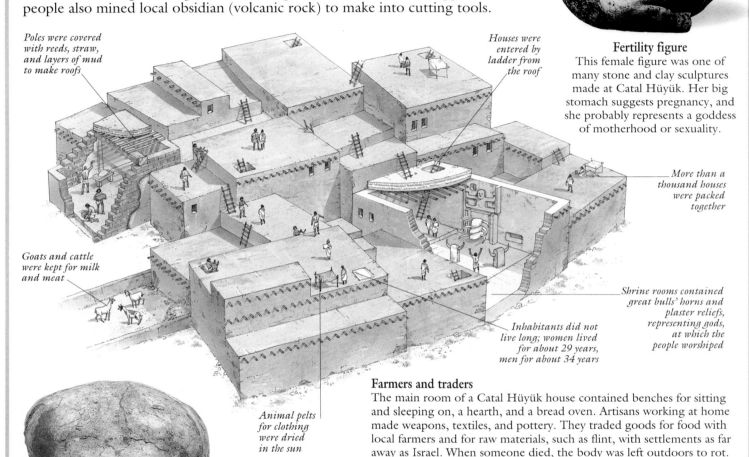

Poles were covered with reeds, straw, and layers of mud to make roofs

Houses were entered by ladder from the roof

More than a thousand houses were packed together

Goats and cattle were kept for milk and meat

Shrine rooms contained great bulls' horns and plaster reliefs, representing gods, at which the people worshiped

Inhabitants did not live long; women lived for about 29 years, men for about 34 years

Animal pelts for clothing were dried in the sun

Life after death
This Jericho woman's skull had been deliberately stretched while the woman lived. After death, the skull was covered in plaster, and cowrie shells were placed in the eye sockets. Skulls were probably used in rituals.

Farmers and traders
The main room of a Catal Hüyük house contained benches for sitting and sleeping on, a hearth, and a bread oven. Artisans working at home made weapons, textiles, and pottery. They traded goods for food with local farmers and for raw materials, such as flint, with settlements as far away as Israel. When someone died, the body was left outdoors to rot. The skeleton was then buried under benches in house rooms or in shrine rooms, decorated with wall paintings, where people prayed to their mysterious gods.

Great tower of Jericho
In c.8000–7000 BC farmers built a settlement of mud-brick houses on stone floors, which were entered at ground level. They raised a massive defensive stone wall around their town, about 10 ft (3 m) thick, and 13 ft (4 m) tall, broken at one point by a circular tower 30 ft (9 m) wide. Roving bands of hunters who preferred nomadic life to town life traded their catch with Jericho people in return for cereal crops or domestic animals, such as sheep.

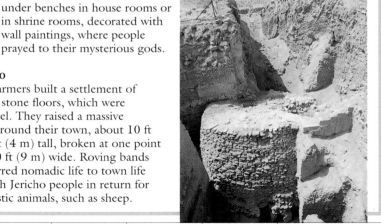

CHAPTER 3

5000 – 1200 BC

THE FIRST CIVILIZATIONS

Ancient Egyptian heart scarab

5000-1200 BC
THE WORLD

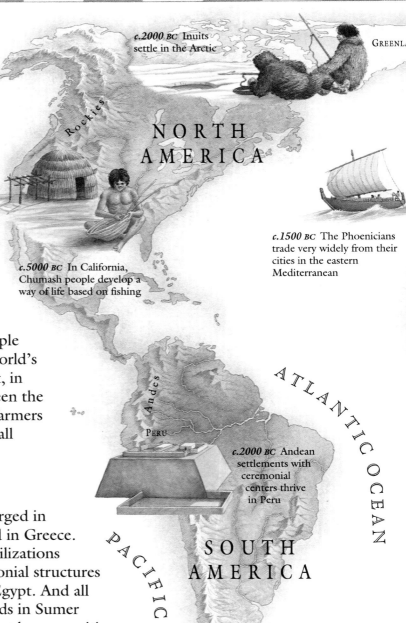

I N 5000 BC, MOST PEOPLE in the world live by hunting and gathering their food. Small villages of settled farmers do exist in China, India, the Nile valley, the eastern Mediterranean, parts of Europe, and central and South America, but most of the world's population are still essentially nomadic. Over the next 3,000 years, a major transformation occurs. The development of farming allows more people to settle in towns and cities. As a result, the world's earliest civilizations begin to emerge. The first, in Sumer, grows up in the fertile farmland between the Tigris and Euphrates rivers. Soon afterward, farmers along the banks of the Nile begin to build small towns that eventually come together in about 3100 BC to create the kingdom of Egypt.

A more settled world

By 1200 BC, major civilizations have also emerged in China, along the banks of the Indus river, and in Greece. Although very different in character, these civilizations have much in common. All build large ceremonial structures and richly furnished tombs, most notably in Egypt. And all conduct trade with their neighbors, which leads in Sumer to the development by merchants of the earliest known writing system in the world. But not everyone lives in settled conditions by the end of this period. In the Americas, most of Africa, Europe, and Asia, and the whole of Oceania, the traditional nomadic way of life continues uninterrupted.

c.2000 BC Inuits settle in the Arctic

GREENLAN

NORTH AMERICA

Rockies

c.1500 BC The Phoenicians trade very widely from their cities in the eastern Mediterranean

c.5000 BC In California, Chumash people develop a way of life based on fishing

Andes

PERU

c.2000 BC Andean settlements with ceremonial centers thrive in Peru

ATLANTIC OCEAN

PACIFIC OCEAN

SOUTH AMERICA

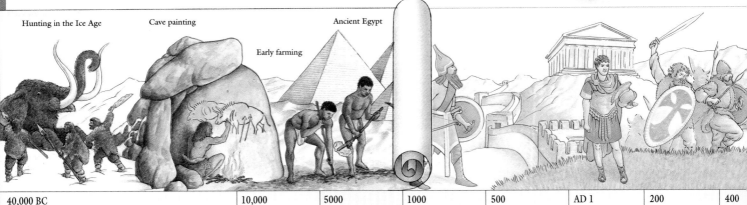

Hunting in the Ice Age   Cave painting   Early farming   Ancient Egypt

| 40,000 BC | | 10,000 | 5000 | 1000 | 500 | AD 1 | 200 | 400 |

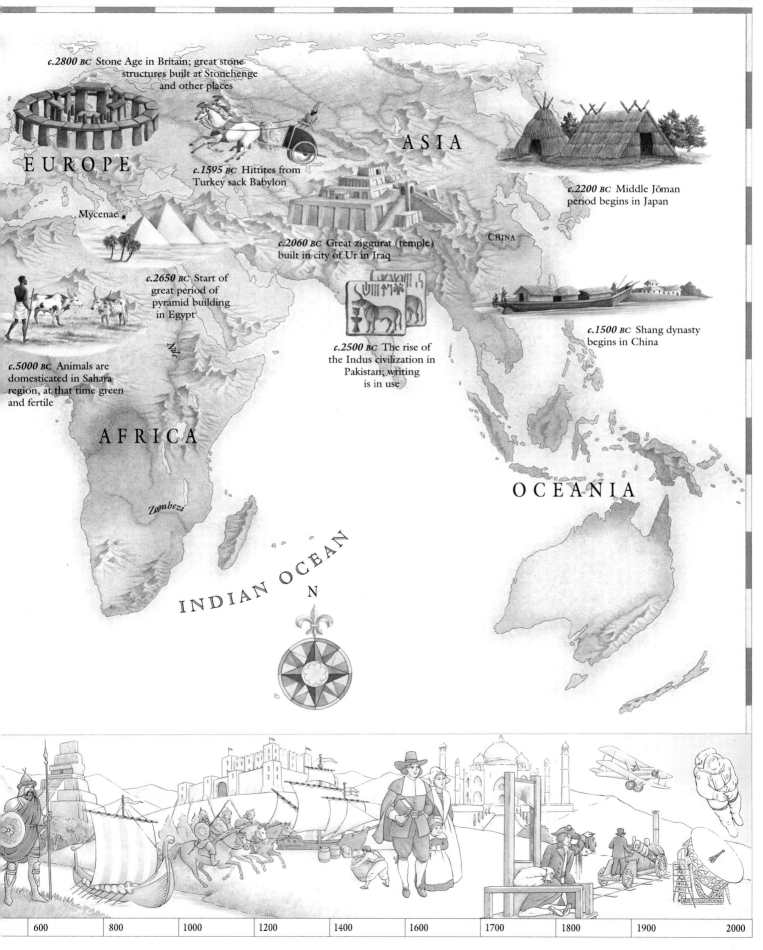

c.2800 BC Stone Age in Britain; great stone structures built at Stonehenge and other places

ASIA

c.1595 BC Hittites from Turkey sack Babylon

EUROPE

c.2200 BC Middle Jōman period begins in Japan

Mycenae

CHINA

c.2060 BC Great ziggurat (temple) built in city of Ur in Iraq

c.2650 BC Start of great period of pyramid building in Egypt

c.1500 BC Shang dynasty begins in China

c.5000 BC Animals are domesticated in Sahara region, at that time green and fertile

c.2500 BC The rise of the Indus civilization in Pakistan; writing is in use

Nile

AFRICA

Zambezi

OCEANIA

INDIAN OCEAN

N

| 600 | 800 | 1000 | 1200 | 1400 | 1600 | 1700 | 1800 | 1900 | 2000 |

5000 BC

4000 BC

AFRICA

c.5000 Village communities in Egypt grow wheat and barley and herd domestic animals

c.4500 Pottery made in Nubia (modern Sudan)*

Peoples living in the Saharan regions were skilled artists; this detail is from a cave painting at Tassili in Algeria

c.4000 Farming peoples in the Sahara region domesticate animals*

c.4000 The sail is first used on boats on the Nile in Egypt

c.4000 Coastal peoples make pottery in Ghana, West Africa

c.3500 Naqada culture begins in Egypt

c.3200 Earliest hieroglyphic script in Egypt

c.3100 King Menes unites Upper and Lower Egypt*

This flint knife was made in Naqada

ASIA

c.5000 First examples of rice cultivation in China

c.5000 Stone Age settlements emerge in China

c.5000 First towns established in Sumer, western Asia*

c.5000 Copper first used in Mesopotamia

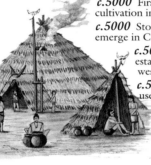

Stone Age people in China lived in wattle and mud huts with conical roofs

c.4000 City of Eridu in Mesopotamia (Iraq) expands

c.3500 Foundation of city of Ur in Mesopotamia

c.3500 Appearance of cuneiform script in Sumer

c.3100 Byblos city founded on eastern Mediterranean coast

c.3100 Experimental bronzework in Mesopotamia

Cuneiform script was an adaptable form of writing used by a variety of peoples

EUROPE

c.5000–4000 Gumelnitsa culture emerges in Romania

c.5000 Farming villages emerge in southern France

c.5000 Karanova settlement established in Bulgaria

c.4500 Vinca copper culture begins in former Yugoslavia

This shard, with its distinctive pattern, is about 6,000 years old, and comes from Romania

c.4000 First passage graves built in western Europe at Carnac, northwest France

c.4000 Farmers first begin to cultivate crops in the British Isles

c.3350 Jordhoj graves constructed in Denmark

The heaviest rock at Fairies Rock in France weighed 50 tons (50,800 kg)

c.3300 Passage graves for communal burial built at Los Millares, Spain

c.3200 Newgrange passage grave built in Ireland*

AMERICAS

c.5000 Corn first cultivated in Mexico

c.5000 Cochise culture flourishes in southwestern North America

c.5000 Chonchorros people in northern Chile begin settlements

c.5000 Development of Chumash way of life in California

The Chumash people built large plank canoes for fishing

c.3750 Chilca Monument valley settlement based on maritime economy begins in Peru

c.3500 The llama is first used as a pack animal in Peru

c.3500 Haida culture begins on northwest coast of Canada

c.3500 Fishing villages flourish along the Peruvian coast, South America

c.3500 Cotton introduced as a crop in Peruvian coastal villages

A carved jade fish; artists living on the coasts of Peru were often inspired by marine life

OCEANIA

c.5000 Aboriginal peoples live peacefully in Australia

3000 BC

c.2650 Start of great period of pyramid building; construction of pyramid of Zoser, Egypt
c.2600 Building of pyramid of Khufu (Cheops), Egypt
c.2500 Building of the Sphinx at Giza to guard the way to the pyramid of the pharaoh Khafre

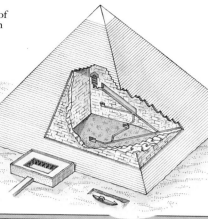

The bodies of deceased pharaohs were laid to rest in burial chambers inside pyramids

c.3000 Wheel appears in Mesopotamia
c.3000 The plough is first used in China
c.3000 Neolithic age begins in southeast Asia
c.2700 King Gilgamesh reigns at Uruk in Sumer
c.2500 Writing first appears in the Indus civilization
c.2500 Rulers in Ebla, in western Syria, trade with Mediterranean peoples
c.2500 Rise of Indus civilization in Pakistan
c.2300 Sargon II of Akkad dominates Sumer
c.2200 Middle Jōmon period begins in Japan

This flame-shaped pottery is an example of Jōmon ware

c.3000 Bronze Age begins in Crete
c.3000–2500 First stone temples erected in Malta
c.3000 Neolithic village of Skara Brae built in Orkney, Scotland*
c.2800 Structures built at Stonehenge, in England, possibly for rituals celebrating seasonal festivals
c.2500 Beaker culture, originating in the Low Countries where drinking vessels found in the graves of warriors gave it its name, reaches France
c.2200 Beginning of Bronze Age in Ireland

This bronze bull was made in Sybrita in central Crete

Maize was widely grown in this period

c.2500 Paloma site in Chilca river valley on Peruvian coast is abandoned
c.2500 Corn becomes staple diet throughout Central America
c.2100 Corn grown in Andean highlands, South America

2000 BC

c.1786 Rule of the Hyksos, migrants from Palestine, in Egypt
c.1550 Ahmose I drives the Hyksos out of Egypt*
c.1379–1362 Reign of King Akhenaton in Egypt
c.1290 Ramesses II reasserts Egyptian power*

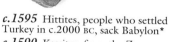

This lotus-design tile was found at King Akhenaton's capital in Egypt

Rulers in places like Babylonia, Anatolia, and Assyria exchanged gifts like this gold figurine of a Hittite king

c.2000 Afanasievo Neolithic culture begins in southern Siberia
c.2000 End of Sumerian power in Mesopotamia
c.1790–1750 Reign of King Hammurabi of Babylonia*

c.1595 Hittites, people who settled Turkey in c.2000 BC, sack Babylon*
c.1590 Kassites, from the Zagros Mountains in Iran, seize Babylonia
c.1500 Shang kingdom flourishes in China*
c.1500 Cuneiform (wedge-shaped symbols) script appears in Asia Minor
c.1500 Kassites take over the region of an Indus civilization already stricken by flood and earthquake
c.1400 First alphabet-type script devised by the Phoenicians
c.1380 Suppiluliumas I becomes king of the Hittites
c.1200s Tradition of Hebrew Exodus from Egypt*

c.2000–700 Bronze Age in Scotland
c.2000 Minoan palace civilization begins to flourish in Crete; island inhabitants develop an original style of painted pottery, with bird and fish designs
c.1600 Beginnings of Mycenaean power in Aegean
c.1500 Collapse of Minoan civilization in Crete
c.1250 Building of Lion Gate at Mycenae

This Mycenaean jar bears an octopus motif

This Olmec jade necklace with a human head motif was worn by a member of the ruling class

c.2000 Inuits settle the Arctic; they hunt caribou and seals for food*
c.2000 Andean settlements with ceremonial centers thrive in Peru*
c.1800 Ceremonial platform sites are built at Kotosh, Peru
c.1800 Ceremonial center raised at El Paraiso, near Lima, Peru
c.1500 First gravel platforms built at Olmec site, San Lorenzo, Mexico
c.1400 Development of farming and village life, Copan, Honduras
c.1350 Settlement begins at San Jose Mogote, southern Mexico

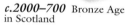

| 600 | 800 | 1000 | 1200 | 1400 | 1600 | 1700 | 1800 | 1900 | 2000 |

5000-1200 BC AFRICA

Egypt was the first civilization in Africa, beginning in the fourth millennium BC along the banks of the River Nile. It lasted to the end of this period and beyond and was marked by dynasties of rulers, massive tomb building projects, a system of government, the evolution of a hieroglyphic script, and the development of bronze technology. At the same time, crop growing and animal breeding communities flourished in parts of the Sahara in North Africa.

One ruler, one kingdom
Menes united the kingdoms of Upper and Lower Egypt. He built a capital at Memphis.

Egyptian writing
Egyptians learned about writing from Sumer and began to develop their own hieroglyphic script. Words were formed by pictures, with extra signs to make the meanings clear.

c.4000 BC
Saharan farming communities

Between c.4000 BC and c.2000 BC the Sahara area of North Africa was not the desert it is today. Much of the region had a wet climate and there were wide grasslands on which people grazed cattle and other livestock. Farming flourished and was probably as productive and efficient as Egyptian farming along the banks of the Nile. Then, some time before 2000 BC, there was a change in climate. The regular wet periods every year began to get shorter, with the result that the land became more difficult to farm, until it was impossible for the communities to continue their previous lifestyle. Many farmers moved away, some to Egypt, some farther east into Asia, while others moved farther south.

c.3100 BC
Menes unites Egypt

The Nile valley was the second place in the world, after Sumer, where people began to establish communities. The great river provided everything that was needed to create settlements: food, water, communications, and transport. From c.5000 BC, small towns grew up along its banks, and canals were dug from the river to irrigate the fields. After many centuries of division, the two kingdoms of Upper and Lower Egypt were united in c.3100 BC under a pharaoh (ruler), Menes, who built a capital at Memphis. The first two Egyptian dynasties lasted from c.3100–2686 BC. During the third dynasty (to 2613 BC) kings began to be buried in pyramids.

Stone bowl
Farming people living in the Sahara crafted elegant stone bowls like this one.

Wall painting
Among the Saharan farming people there were many talented artists. They engraved and painted the walls of caves with scenes showing wild, and later, domestic animals. The rock painting shown above was executed in a cave at Tassili, in Algeria.

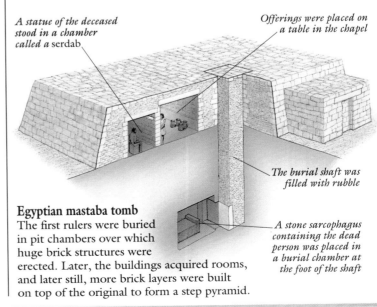

A statue of the deceased stood in a chamber called a serdab

Offerings were placed on a table in the chapel

The burial shaft was filled with rubble

A stone sarcophagus containing the dead person was placed in a burial chamber at the foot of the shaft

Egyptian mastaba tomb
The first rulers were buried in pit chambers over which huge brick structures were erected. Later, the buildings acquired rooms, and later still, more brick layers were built on top of the original to form a step pyramid.

THE AFTERLIFE IN ANCIENT EGYPT

Ancient Egyptians believed in life after death and wanted their souls to live forever. So they devised a way of preserving dead bodies by embalming, or mummifying, them. The embalmed body was put in a coffin to protect it and to keep in the spirit. At first only pharaohs were mummified, but by around 2300 BC the privilege was extended to anybody who could afford it. By this time, too, bodies were being placed inside double coffins, the inner one in the shape of the mummy and the outer one a simple rectangular box. The first pyramids were built in a series of steps which represented a huge staircase for the pharaoh to climb to join the sun god in the sky. Later pyramids evolved smooth, sloping sides. The coffins of pharaohs were placed inside sarcophagi (stone boxes), which were buried deep inside the pyramids.

Chambers were built to relieve the weight of bricks from above

King's burial chamber

A gallery led into the burial chamber

Mortuary temple

Causeway linked temples

Egyptian cat goddess
Cats, which were sacred to the goddess Bastet, were mummified when they died.

A pharaoh's resting place
A funeral boat transported the dead body up the Nile to a valley temple, from where it was carried along a causeway to the pyramid. Then the body was borne up a passage into the heart of the pyramid, and laid to rest in the royal burial chamber.

Royal burial tombs at Giza
The pyramids at Giza were built between 2550 and 2470 BC. The most famous one is that of King Khufu, which was 486 ft (148 m) tall and is estimated to contain 2,300,000 blocks of stone.

The ancient art of mummification

The word *mummy* is of Arabic origin and means "pitch-preserved body." All the internal organs were removed from the dead body, except for the heart, which was believed to control thought and action, both of which were needed in the afterlife. Next the body was washed with spices and palm wine, covered with natron salts (a drying agent and antiseptic), and left to dry out. Then the body was packed with linen and spices to restore it to shape, and coated with resins to make it waterproof. Finally, the mummy was wrapped in long linen bandages and placed in a coffin. The whole process could take more than two months to complete.

Protective clothing
The mummy case shielded the mummy from tomb robbers and was also regarded as a substitute body and a house for the dead person's spirit. Around 650 BC, a woman called Seshepenmehit was buried in these coffins (one inside the other).

Storage jars
The mummy's internal organs were stored in four jars. These containers were adorned with the heads of gods or of the dead person.

c.1550 BC
Ahmose I drives the Hyksos out of Egypt

Around 1785 BC Egypt was in a state of anarchy, with one pharaoh at Thebes being challenged by other rulers, particularly from the Hyksos, a people from Asia who had settled in the Nile Delta. They provided a dynasty of pharaohs that ruled from c.1650 BC and intimidated the Theban pharaohs. Then in c.1550 BC a Theban pharaoh, Ahmose I, defeated the Hyksos and drove them out of Egypt. Ahmose went on to expand his empire south to Nubia and east into Canaan (Israel). He set up firm government in Egypt and built temples to Egyptian gods in Thebes and elsewhere. Ahmose was succeeded by a line of great pharaohs. In c.1353 BC Amenhotep IV came to the throne. A religious reformer, he tried to change Egyptian belief in many gods to a one-god faith, worshiping only the sun god Aton. He changed his name to Akhenaton and founded a city, Akhetaton, midway between Thebes and Memphis. After his death in c.1335 BC the worship of many gods was restored, and Thebes was revived as Egypt's capital.

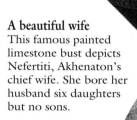

A beautiful wife
This famous painted limestone bust depicts Nefertiti, Akhenaton's chief wife. She bore her husband six daughters but no sons.

Bronze weapons
The Hyksos influenced Egyptian craftsmanship in fields such as weaponry. These Hyksos ax heads are made of bronze.

Chariot in stone
This stone relief showing an Egyptian riding in a horse-drawn chariot is from Ramesses II's temple in Abydos, Upper Egypt.

TUTANKHAMEN

Tutankhamen was Akhenaton's son by a secondary wife. He succeeded to the Egyptian throne as a young boy in c.1333 BC and ruled for only nine years. His great tomb, in the Valley of the Kings at Thebes, remained undiscovered until 1922 when it was found by the English Egyptologist, Howard Carter, and the Earl of Carnarvon. In the antechamber to the tomb was an amazing collection of ancient artifacts. Tutankhamen's golden throne, shown below, was among the many treasures unearthed.

c.1290 BC
Ramesses II reasserts Egyptian power

Akhenaton's obsession with changing Egypt's religion led him to neglect the empire, which was for a time in great danger from outside attack. The decline continued after his death, but in c.1290 BC a new pharaoh, Ramesses II, reasserted Egyptian power. He warred against Syria and Palestine and even challenged the Hittites from Anatolia (Turkey). Around 1285 BC Ramesses's forces fought a great battle against a Hittite army under King Muwattalis in Syria. The battle ended in a stalemate and King Muwattalis maintained power over northern Syria.

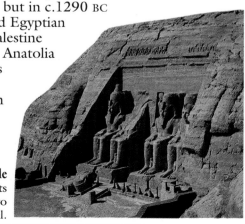

Rock-cut temple
Ramesses initiated many building projects during his reign. Shown here is one of two rock-cut temples he had built at Abu Simbel.

Epic figure
This cup shows a bearded figure wrestling with a bull, or perhaps two lions. It probably illustrates a Mesopotamian story about Gilgamesh, king of Uruk. The story describes Gilgamesh's adventurous journey to find eternal life.

5000-1200 BC ASIA

The first civilization, Sumer, developed in western Asia in about 5000 BC. After 3000 BC other civilizations emerged in the region, such as Babylonia, the Hittite Empire, which pioneered ironworking, and trading cities on the East Mediterranean coast. In about 2500 BC, cities grew up along the Indus River; by 1500 BC the Shang dynasty ruled a civilization in the Yellow River valley in China.

c.5000 BC
First cities founded in Sumer

In about 5000 BC, farmers settled the fertile land between the Tigris and Euphrates rivers in southern Mesopotamia (Iraq), known as Sumer. They dug a network of canals branching off the rivers to water barley, linseed, and other crops, and kept pigs, oxen, and sheep. Sumerians traded surplus food for metals, tools, and vessels with peoples as far away as present-day Afghanistan and Pakistan. They built villages, then towns and cities. Some major cities, called city-states, came to control surrounding lands. The leading city-state from 2700 BC until 2300 BC was Ur. City-states contained temples; temple priests grew powerful and acted as rulers. Some built great ziggurats, or temple towers. From c.2330 BC to c.2275 BC Sargon, king of Akkad, north of Sumer, built an empire from Syria to the Persian Gulf, uniting all the Sumerian cities under his control.

Warring cities
Every Sumerian city was on a river or joined to one by a canal. Merchants sailed these waterways to the Persian Gulf and beyond. The cities often fought over water and land rights. In the south, Ur and Lagash frequently allied to fight Umma. The cities suffered constant attacks by local mountain peoples, and the nomads of the Arabian Desert.

Foundation cone
In Ur, brick cones were placed in walls to record the foundation of a building. Sumerians also used colored cones to decorate ziggurats by pressing them into plaster walls in regular patterns.

Sargon of Akkad
Sargon, whose name means "the king is just," was a fruit grower, then cupbearer to a local ruler before becoming king of Akkad. Akkad thrived on trade, and Sargon conquered lands in order to police trade routes and stop local rulers from exacting tolls. His empire was held together by the threat of his armies. It is said that 5,400 of his soldiers ate with him every day.

THE EARLIEST WRITING

By c.3500 BC Sumerians had invented the first script. They scratched pictures that represented words or sounds onto clay tablets with reed pens, often to record business transactions. The pens produced a wedge shape, and the script came to be called cuneiform (*cuneus* in Latin means "wedge"). After a time, pictures were drawn sideways and simplified. Only 200–300 were in constant use. They were written in a straight line rather than a column and were read from left to right.

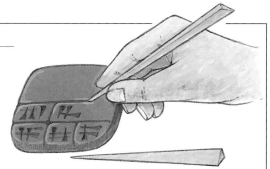

Tablet and pen
Cuneiform was complex, so it was usually only specially trained scribes who wrote on tablets.

| 600 | 800 | 1000 | 1200 | 1400 | 1600 | 1700 | 1800 | 1900 | 2000 |

INDUS CIVILIZATION

The Indus River valley in modern Pakistan was very fertile. Farmers from further west moved there in about 2500 BC. They dug canals to control and distribute floodwater, making farming more productive. River settlements grew into cities, the largest at Harappa, Mohenjo-daro, and Lothal. Harappa was probably the most powerful and exercised some control over the others. Harappa and Mohenjo-daro were over 1 sq mile (2 sq km) in area. Each had a raised citadel containing temples, a centrally heated public bathhouse, granaries, and halls. Indus cities were built according to a grid system: each of the main streets was parallel. Streets were lined with terraced houses, many two storeys high. Houses were built of bricks, and people used bitumen on walls and roofs to keep out damp. Indus plumbing was the most advanced in the world. Large houses had wells for drinking and bath water, and a drainage system. The cities thrived for nearly 1,000 years, but in c.1700 BC they were devastated by earthquakes and floods. Kassite people of the northwest later invaded and allowed the cities to decay further.

Proud ruler?
This stone sculpture was found in the ruins of Mohenjo-daro. Archeologists think that it may represent a god or priest-king. Indus sculptors made figures from terra-cotta, as well as stone.

Widespread early settlements
Archeologists have found nearly 100 Indus settlements within an area of about 1,100 miles (1,770 km) from north to south. The Indus civilization probably covered a larger area than did Mesopotamia and Egypt put together.

Bull seal
Thousands of seals 1 sq in (6 sq cm) in size were found at Mohenjo-daro, carved with animals and symbols of an as-yet undeciphered form of writing. Seals may have been used to label cotton bales and bags of grain. Indus seals have been found in Iraq, showing that trade routes linked the Indus civilization with Mesopotamia.

Citadel was built on an artificial mound of mud and mud bricks

Windows and wooden balconies faced onto courtyards

Mats were laid on flat roofs for people to rest on

Paved main roads ran from north to south

Palm trees provided shade from the hot sun

Mohenjo-daro
As many as 40,000 people may have lived in Mohenjo-daro. The perfectly straight main streets were up to 33 ft (10 m) wide, crammed with craft stalls and workshops. Side streets were narrower, and small alleys wound between housing blocks.

DRAINAGE

The people of Mohenjo-daro built the world's first drainage system. Houses had bathrooms and toilets. Water and sewage ran out of them through pipes (right) into drains, which ran under the streets. Manhole covers were placed over drains at intervals, allowing municipal cleaners to climb down and clear blockages. Waste finally went to disposal points outside the city.

Cast in stone
This black basalt pillar, found at Susa in southern Iran, has the most complete surviving set of Hammurabi's laws inscribed beneath a carving of Hammurabi himself. The 282 laws cover a wide range of subjects such as property, rent, and medical treatment. The most famous aspect of the law code is the establishment of the principle of "an eye for an eye." This means that personal injuries should be punished by the victim inflicting the same injury on the offender.

c.1790 BC
Hammurabi rules Babylon

After 2000 BC the people living in and around the city of Babylon (south of Baghdad) in Mesopotamia grew powerful. The greatest Babylonian king, Hammurabi, sixth of their ruling dynasty, reigned between c.1790 BC and c.1750 BC. He conquered the lands of Sumer and Akkad and brought them into a strong Mesopotamian empire, whose capital was an enlarged Babylon. He governed well, introducing social reforms and establishing a code of laws. The laws were recorded on stone pillars and clay tablets, and Hammurabi's code is the world's oldest surviving law code. Some laws seem harsh today, but they were mostly fair, and it is clear from them that Hammurabi was determined not to allow the mighty to oppress the weak.

c.1595 BC
Hittites sack Babylon

The Hittites settled in Turkey before 2000 BC around a capital at Hattushash. One of their first kings, Hattusilas I (1650–1620 BC), invaded Syria. His successor Mursilis I pressed farther south and sacked Babylon (c.1595 BC), but he was killed soon afterward, and his conquests lost. By c.1380 BC the Hittites were ruled by their greatest king, Suppiluliumas, who built an empire that briefly rivaled Egypt. He invaded Syria and took control almost to Canaan (modern Israel). His descendant, Muwattalis, remained unbeaten in a fierce battle with Egyptian pharaoh Ramesses II at Kadesh (c.1300 BC). Hittite power collapsed under the onslaught of the Aegean sea peoples c.1200 BC.

Bronze king
Sculptures of kings carrying building materials in baskets have been found in Babylonian temple foundations.

Hittite and Babylonian empires
Hittite kings kept control of their territories by appointing family members as governors of the provinces. Babylonian kings usually negotiated terms with local rulers. All treaties of this time were written in Akkadian on clay tablets.

Chariot was light enough to be picked up by one man

Archers were equipped with powerful bows and bronze-tipped arrows

Hittite warriors wore iron armor

Chariots were pulled by a team of horses specially trained to stay calm and gallop swiftly into the fiercest fighting

Chariot charges into battle
The Hittites became a major power largely through their military skill, particularly the development of the horse-drawn battle chariot.

IRONWORKERS

It is not certain exactly where or when people began to produce iron, but the first civilization to use it on a large scale was the Hittite Empire, probably by c.1500 BC. Iron was made from iron ore, mined and then heated with charcoal in a process of repeated warming, quenching, and hammering to get it ready for making into tools or weapons. The Hittites kept iron technology secret, and use of the metal only spread several centuries later. Ironworkers also produced steel, made from iron and carbon.

Bloom of iron
Heated iron ore formed a spongy lump, or bloom, which was hammered into shape while hot.

c.1500 BC
Shang kingdom of China

An early form of civilization to emerge in China, perhaps from c.2200 BC, is called Xia (or Hsia), after the Xia dynasty of kings who may have ruled at this time. It was centered in the Yellow River valley. Archeologists have found that Xia farmers used stone tools. The kings of the Shang dynasty were based near modern Anyang from c.1700 BC, and the civilization over which they presided flourished by c.1500 BC. Chinese people learned how to use bronze, making it into sacred vessels, fittings for the newly invented chariot, and weapons of war. Shang people also made silk textiles and used a sophisticated writing system. Their buildings, which may have included temples, were made with compressed earth, timber, and mud bricks. Shang people worshiped their kings' ancestors as gods. Large royal tombs included treasures buried with the dead and the remains of humans and animals sacrificed to keep a dead king company. The Zhou (or Chou) warrior race took power from the Shang by c.1045 BC.

Bronze halberd blade
Bronze was cast in molds made from several sections that fitted together precisely. This enabled Shang crafts-workers to make very large vessels for religious rituals, as well as small vessels for daily use, tools, and weapons. The halberd was the chief Chinese weapon at this time.

Shang China
The power of Shang rulers was centered in the Yellow River valley, but they exercised influence to the southeast as far as the Yangtze River. Shang methods of metalworking and writing spread through the area.

Oracle bones
Shang people tried to predict the future. One method involved heating the shoulder bones of oxen or turtle shells. Hot metal tools were then pressed on the bone, which cracked, and the nature of the cracks led prophets to make forecasts. Official clerks engraved signs representing questions and answers on bones and shells. These are the earliest records of Chinese writing.

Ten commandments
This scene from the film *The Ten Commandments* shows the Hebrews leaving Egypt. The Bible story describes how Moses received ten commandments, or laws, from God during the journey. Jews believe the Hebrews were their ancestors and try to live by the same laws today.

1200s BC
Hebrews' Exodus from Egypt

Hebrews were nomadic farmers and mercenaries. Some settled in Canaan by 1400 BC. In the reign of Egyptian pharaoh Ramesses II (c.1304–1237 BC) many foreigners in Egypt seem to have emigrated to Canaan, among them the Hebrews. A Bible story tells the circumstances of the Hebrews' travels, although there is no archeological evidence to prove them. The story describes how Egyptian Hebrews had been enslaved and ill-treated. One Hebrew leader, Moses, appealed to Ramesses to be allowed to take his people to Canaan. Eventually, Ramesses gave in, and the Hebrews began a journey, known as the Exodus, across the Sinai desert. After years of wandering, they reached Canaan and, led by Moses' successor, Joshua, conquered it.

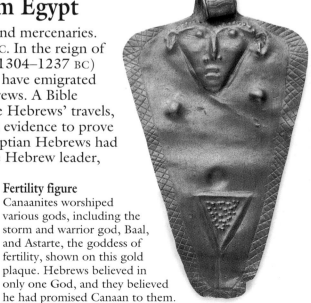

Fertility figure
Canaanites worshiped various gods, including the storm and warrior god, Baal, and Astarte, the goddess of fertility, shown on this gold plaque. Hebrews believed in only one God, and they believed he had promised Canaan to them.

| 40,000 BC | | 10,000 | 5000 | 1000 | 500 | AD 1 | 200 | 400 |

MEDITERRANEAN TRADERS

Many peoples lived on the fertile coast of the eastern Mediterranean in present-day Syria, Lebanon, and Israel. They grew cedar wood (used for building), corn, and olives and produced oil, wine, and cloth, which they traded with Crete, Egypt, Cyprus, and cities as far away as Troy on the coast of western Turkey. They founded coastal cities, such as Ugarit (c.4000 BC) and Byblos (c.3000 BC), both of which lasted for centuries as trade centers, as well as inland trading towns, such as Ebla (c.3000 BC). Over 15,000 clay tablets from Ebla have been found, inscribed with cuneiform writing recording the city's activities: the exporting of cloth, the taxation of imports, and the amount of gold and silver received by the king in tribute from smaller towns. In about 1500 BC new cities were built on the eastern Mediterranean coast that became centers of commercial power, the greatest being Tyre and Sidon. The region was named "Phoenicia," from the Greek word for "purple," as the cities were famous for an expensive process of dyeing fabric purple.

Chain of cities
Phoenician cities stood on a narrow coastal strip now divided between Syria, Lebanon, and Israel, central to trade routes from Turkey and Crete to Mesopotamia.

TROY
Nine successive cities were built at Troy (founded c.2700 BC) as one after another was destroyed by disaster or invasion. One may be the city described by the Greek poet, Homer. In the *Iliad*, Homer tells how the Greeks besieged Troy and took it by a trick (c.1200 BC). They made a wooden horse, left it outside Troy, and sailed off. Curious Trojans pulled the horse into the city. That night Greek soldiers hidden in the horse crept out and opened Troy's gates. The Greek army, which had returned, entered and sacked the city. Above is a modern replica of the horse.

Ugarit merchant's seal
Traders had personal seals and used them as companies use trademarks today. They attached their seals to goods to identify them and guarantee quality. Buyers preferred products with a famous trader's seal. Poor traders may have copied well-known seals to deceive buyers into taking goods from them.

Bustling Phoenician port
Phoenicians sold agricultural goods, but their prosperity rested on trading manufactured luxury items: fine glassware, delicately carved ivory, and exquisite gold and silver ornaments. Raw materials were imported, as were slaves, ebony, and Egyptian paintings, which were resold for a profit by shrewd Phoenician merchants. Purple textiles came to be associated with the most exalted ranks: the emperors of Rome wore deep purple tunics.

Galleys crafted from cedar logs carried fabulous cargoes all over the Mediterranean

Phoenician navigators learned how to use the North Star to guide ships at night

Large ships could carry two banks of rowers, one on each side, for greater speed

600	800	1000	1200	1400	1600	1700	1800	1900	2000

Metalworking began in Europe in c.5000 BC. Farming began to prosper, and large stone structures were erected in many parts of the continent, long before pyramids were built in Egypt. People began to use bronze tools in Crete in c.3000 BC, and before c.2000 BC bronze technology had spread across western Europe to the British Isles, where it lasted until c.500 BC. The Minoan civilization on the island of Crete flourished for hundreds of years before an earthquake weakened it, and in c.1450 BC, it fell to the growing might of the Mycenaean civilization from mainland Greece.

Tomb sites and stone circles
England, Ireland, Scotland, and France have some of the most fascinating sites in Europe.

c.3200 BC

Newgrange passage grave

The most extraordinary creations of the New Stone Age communities were tombs hewn from massive stones. They were widespread where suitable stone was to be found, and their purpose was to house the dead communally and sometimes over several generations. One of these was the passage grave at Newgrange in Ireland, built c.3200 BC, not long after the chamber tomb at Maes Howe in Orkney, Scotland. These are some 600 years older than the first Egyptian pyramids. Burials in passage graves were common in many parts of Europe. Sites such as Jordhoj in Denmark (c.3300 BC), Los Millares in Spain (c.3300–3000 BC), and Mané Karnaplaye in France (c.3500–3300 BC) were among the most important.

Grave goods
Beautiful objects were buried in the graves with the bodies. This gold dress fastener was found in Ireland.

Newgrange
Newgrange consists of a round mound of earth, in which there is a central chamber. It is reached through a narrow passage, lined with huge stone slabs.

c.3000 BC

The village of Skara Brae

Skara Brae, a Neolithic village in Orkney off the coast of Scotland, was built in about 3000 BC. It was discovered by chance in AD 1850, after a terrible storm shifted huge quantities of sand from the shore where the buildings had lain covered for centuries. The village has about ten small houses made of local stone. Flat stones were used for walls and larger slabs for flooring. The furniture had stone bases or was cut into the walls. Tools and utensils were also made of stone or sometimes bone. No wood was available because there are no trees on Orkney.

STANDING STONES

From c.4000 BC Neolithic and early Bronze Age peoples in western Europe, especially in northwest France and Britain, built huge circles and avenues of large standing stones called megaliths. These megaliths were placed either individually upright, or as two uprights with a third stone laid horizontally on top. The stones were spaced out according to mathematical or astronomical plans, but no one knows for certain what these plans of circles and avenues were. They may have been meeting places for widely scattered farming communities. They could also have had religious purposes. It is likely that at the site of the megaliths there would have been funerary rituals, offerings, celebrations on feast days, and soothsaying ceremonies when priests or wise men looked into the future or tried to discover the cause of a disaster. It is also extremely likely that sacrifices, both of animals and humans, took place inside these mysterious circles.

Carnac
The stone avenues and circles at Carnac in France, which date from c.2400 BC, were probably used to observe the stars.

Stonehenge
This stone circle in southern England was constructed in c.2800 BC. It may have been used as a center for rituals celebrating seasonal festivals.

THE DRUIDS

Druids were powerful priests in Celtic Gaul (France) and Britain. Druids performed religious ceremonies in the stone circles, centuries after they were raised. The Romans often tried to suppress the Druids, but interest in the cult has frequently been revived.

Barrows

During the same period as the standing stones, people were often buried in collective graves. These graves came in various forms, and in England they were usually long chambers covered with earth to form mounds, called barrows. Inside, the chambers were lined with megaliths, small boulders, or timber planks. Some barrows were round because they were for one important burial only, perhaps for a chief. Small groups of round barrows have been found, which may have served as a graveyard for a whole dynasty. The size of the barrows and the communal nature of the burials suggest that the builders were becoming increasingly socially organized. Archeologists now think that these burial places were not simply tombs, but holy places where ancestors were worshiped. Remains, such as skulls or bones, were taken by tribal priests for "magical" ceremonies intended to benefit the living. Offerings were laid at the entrances to the barrows, including pots containing food and drink for the afterlife.

West Kennet barrow
West Kennet barrow in Wiltshire, England, is one of the most impressive barrows in Europe. The huge stones which formed the walls and roofs can still be seen today. Two ditches were dug alongside each other to provide the soil for the barrow mound, which was raised between them. The mound, which is over 330 ft (100 m) long, took about 15,700 hours to build. It was likely that West Kennet was intended to be used many times and as a burial place for groups of people rather than individuals. When West Kennet barrow was excavated in the 1950s, the bones of 46 people were discovered inside.

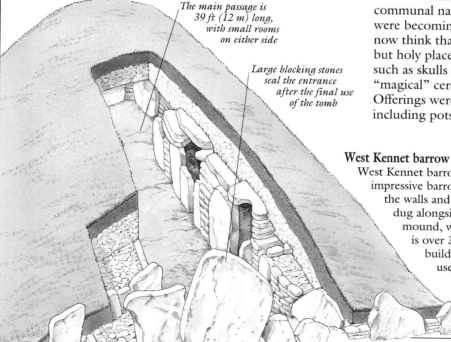

The main passage is 39 ft (12 m) long, with small rooms on either side

Large blocking stones seal the entrance after the final use of the tomb

| | 1200 | 1400 | 1600 | 1700 | 1800 | 1900 | 2000 |

PALACE CIVILIZATIONS

The Minoan civilization flourished c.3000–1450 BC, on the island of Crete in the Mediterranean Sea. It took its name from Minos, a legendary king of Crete. The Minoans became rich by trading across the eastern Mediterranean. They used their wealth to develop towns and ports; later, they built palaces of great beauty. Minoan civilization went into a sudden decline after 1500 BC.

In c.1450 BC the Mycenaeans from the Plain of Argos in eastern Greece invaded and settled Crete. They took over and developed the Minoans' trade, palaces, and art. Their own most famous monuments were their vast royal tombs and the citadel of Mycenae. Mycenaean civilization fell in the 12th century BC.

Knossos remade
The most famous of all the Minoan palaces was at Knossos (left); parts of it have been restored.

Slaying the Cretan beast
Greek legend told how each year Athenian children were sacrificed to a Cretan monster called the Minotaur, which was half-man, half-bull. It lived in a maze called the Labyrinth. A young prince of Athens, Theseus, eventually killed the beast.

Minoan glory
By 2000 BC, the Minoans' influence had spread over the eastern Mediterranean. Over the next 300 years, they produced fine pottery and metalwork in gold and bronze and invented a more advanced form of writing to replace their earlier pictorial script. They built palaces, at Knossos, Mallia, Phaestos, and Zakro. After c.1700 BC, their civilization reached its height, but about 200 years later it collapsed. It is possible that a massive earthquake on the nearby island of Thera (now Santorini) caused a tidal wave, destroyed most of the Minoans' ships, and damaged their palaces and cities.

Knossos-made
Knossos palace was almost like a small town. Many artefacts, like this cup, were made there. It had a series of courtyards, with workshops for craftspeople, and residential quarters.

IN MINOS' KINGDOM
English archeologist Sir Arthur Evans (1851–1941) discovered the biggest and most famous of the Minoan palaces at Knossos in 1894. He dug there for several years and the remains of the colossal building with its hundreds of rooms amazed the world. He even restored some of the palace so that it was possible to get some idea of what it was like when it was new. The remains of the lavish buildings, built in stone and mud brick, decorated in brightly colored frescoes and stucco reliefs, are evidence of the skill of Minoan architects, engineers, and artists.

Taking the bull by the horns
In Greek legend, the god Zeus fell in love with a princess called Europa. He turned into a white bull and swam to Crete with her on his back. They had three sons, one of whom was Minos, who became the king of Crete. The Minoans thought of the bull as a sacred animal, and daring bull sports became a way of worshiping it. This bronze figure shows a boy somersaulting over a bull's horns.

| 40,000 BC | | 10,000 | 5000 | 1000 | 500 | AD 1 | 200 | 400 |

The Mycenaeans

The Mycenaeans lived on the Plain of Argos in eastern Greece. Their era of greatness began c.1600 BC. At this time they started to build towns with defensive walls, as at Tiryns, Pylos, and Mycenae. The city of Mycenae was dominated by a huge citadel on a hill with a magnificent stone entrance, the Lion Gate, begun in the 13th century. After Minoan civilization fell, the Mycenaeans occupied Crete and took over the Minoan sea trade. They founded colonies at Rhodes and Cyprus and sailed to the western Mediterranean, trading with Sicily and Italy. They changed Minoan script into a form of Greek for their own use. Mycenae was invaded more than once in the 12th century BC and finally collapsed as a civilization when the city was destroyed c.1120 BC. The cause of the destruction is unknown.

Rise and fall

Seaborne trade made the Minoans and Mycenaeans rich, and their great palaces were a wonder of the early Mediterranean, but by 1100 BC their glory was only a memory. During the course of the 12th century BC, amid vast disturbances of which we know little, the Mycenaean civilization was destroyed. Greece entered a dark age which lasted nearly 300 years.

A continuing tradition

This clay bull's head was used as a ritual sprinkler at religious ceremonies. There are small holes in the mouth to let the water escape. Although these sprinklers are sometimes in the shape of other animals, bulls are the most common. Mycenae borrowed much from Minoan art of all kinds. Its metalwork was chiefly bronze and gold. Crafts workers made gold masks, and strong bronze vessels, armor, and weapons.

A shape to please a king

The shape of this graceful drinking cup, with its long stem, was invented by the Mycenaeans. Mycenaean artists, including potters, often worked for the king and had their workshops close to the palace.

This drinking cup is decorated with stylized cuttlefish

The mask of Agamemnon

Five of the royal persons buried in the shaft graves of Mycenae wore funeral masks of beaten gold. When Schliemann removed one of the masks, for a moment he could see the dried face of the corpse beneath before it disintegrated. The mask shown here was thought by Schliemann to belong to Agamemnon, the legendary king of Mycenae at the time of the Trojan War. Schliemann was wrong, as the mask seems to have belonged to an earlier time, 1550–1500 BC, but the name he gave it persists.

TREASURE TROVE

German archeologist Heinrich Schliemann (1822–90) searched for many years for the site of ancient Troy. In 1870 he found it, near the Mediterranean coast of modern Turkey. Four years later he found a fabulous hoard of golden treasure there (which later mysteriously vanished during World War II). Then he excavated the city of Mycenae, where, in 1876, he found gold jewelry dating from c.1550 BC.

| 600 | 800 | 1000 | | 1600 | 1700 | 1800 | 1900 | 2000 |

5000-1200 BC AMERICAS

Food cultivation was thriving in Mexico by the beginning of this period, and settlements began to appear in southwestern North America. Later, settlements were also being established in the Arctic regions of Canada and the Bering Strait islands. In South America, fishing and cotton industries flourished along the coast. Inland, corn was grown and became the staple diet throughout Mexico and central America. In the last centuries of the period, ceremonial centers were built in Peru and Mexico.

A model home
This model of a reindeer skin tent is typical of the type of dwelling inhabited by peoples living below the Arctic Circle where the climate is milder.

Inuit kayak
Inuits moved about the icy Arctic waters in skin-covered boats. Open boats were called umiaks, and closed ones, like the one shown above, were called kayaks.

c.2000 BC
Inuits colonize the Arctic

Prehistoric peoples probably existed in the Arctic from c.8000 BC. More advanced cultures appeared in c.2000 BC. One was the Arctic Small Tool people, possibly descended from Siberians of northeast Russia, who had crossed from Asia to North America over the Bering Strait when it had been a land bridge in the last Ice Age. They settled as far east as Greenland by c.2000 BC and later split into subcultures, known as *Inuit* but later grouped by Europeans under the term *Eskimo*. The Arctic climate, with its long dark hours, shaped the Inuit way of life. They lived by hunting animals such as caribou, whales, and seals.

Snow knife
In very cold areas, Inuits lived in igloos. They used knives to cut blocks of snow to make the igloos. This knife is decorated with figures of animals, hunters, and houses.

Spindle of spun cotton

c.2000 BC
Andean settlements thrive in Peru

There were hunter-gatherers in the Andean region of South America as long ago as c.6000 BC. By about 3500 BC many villages flourished on the Peruvian coast where the main industry was fishing. Farther inland, other communities practiced farming, grew cotton and later corn, and quarried stone from the Andean mountains for building and for making jewelry. Irrigation skills enabled larger areas to be farmed, and by c.2000 BC there were many sizeable settlements. Some of these settlements had substantial buildings, centers of religious ritual or important public works. A huge pyramid was built at El Paraiso, near Lima, in c.1800 BC, with rock from nearby hills.

Reedwork basket
Women wove cloth from cotton grown in the fields. They were often buried with their work baskets.

Dyed cotton thread

Ear-shaped vessel
Andean pottery was often modeled in the shape of the fruit and vegetables that were grown. Corn was a staple crop.

40,000 BC	10,000	1000	AD 1	400	800	1200	1600	1800	2000

CHAPTER 4

1200 – 500 BC

TRADERS AND WARRIORS

Carved ivory plaque of Assyrian priest

1200-500 BC
THE WORLD

S OME OF THE WORLD'S major civilizations begin to grow during this period. In South America, the Chavin people build a sophisticated religious and trading center, while to their north, the Olmecs develop the first civilization in central and northern America. In Europe, the city states of the Etruscans, Greeks, and later the Romans all develop advanced societies. The Phoenicians grow into a major maritime trading empire in the Mediterranean, while in Asia, the Assyrian Empire declines in the face of Babylonian power. The entire region eventually falls to the world's greatest power, the mighty Persian empire. All these differing societies prosper through trade and commerce; many maintain power through military efficiency.

Technology and culture

Before 2000 BC, the first ironworking experiments are carried out in the eastern Mediterranean. For centuries, the use of iron is limited, but by 700 BC it has become common in Europe, India, and China. The availability of iron ore revolutionizes hunting and farming. The adoption of an alphabet in Greece in about 800 BC is similarly revolutionary – for the first time in Europe, a popular literary culture develops. Theater becomes one of the most popular forms of entertainment in the new Greek democracy.

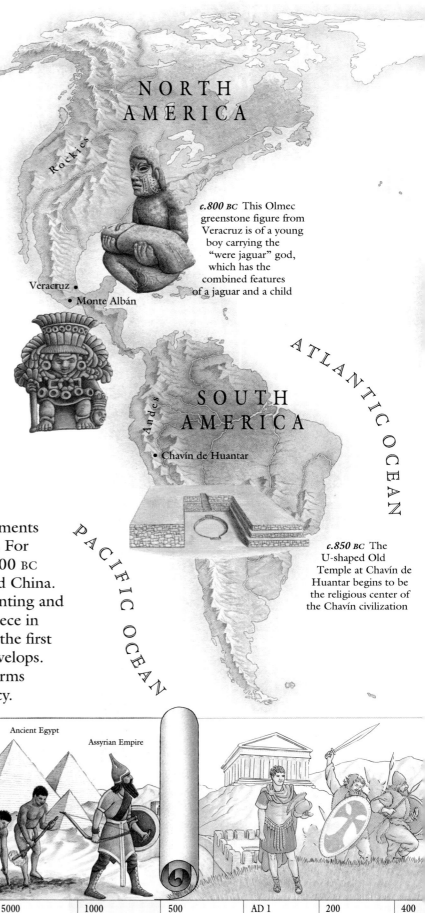

NORTH AMERICA

Rockies

Veracruz

Monte Albán

c.800 BC This Olmec greenstone figure from Veracruz is of a young boy carrying the "were jaguar" god, which has the combined features of a jaguar and a child

ATLANTIC OCEAN

SOUTH AMERICA

Andes

Chavín de Huantar

c.850 BC The U-shaped Old Temple at Chavín de Huantar begins to be the religious center of the Chavín civilization

PACIFIC OCEAN

Hunting in the Ice Age

Cave painting

Early farming

Ancient Egypt

Assyrian Empire

| 40,000 BC | | 10,000 | 5000 | 1000 | 500 | AD 1 | 200 | 400 |

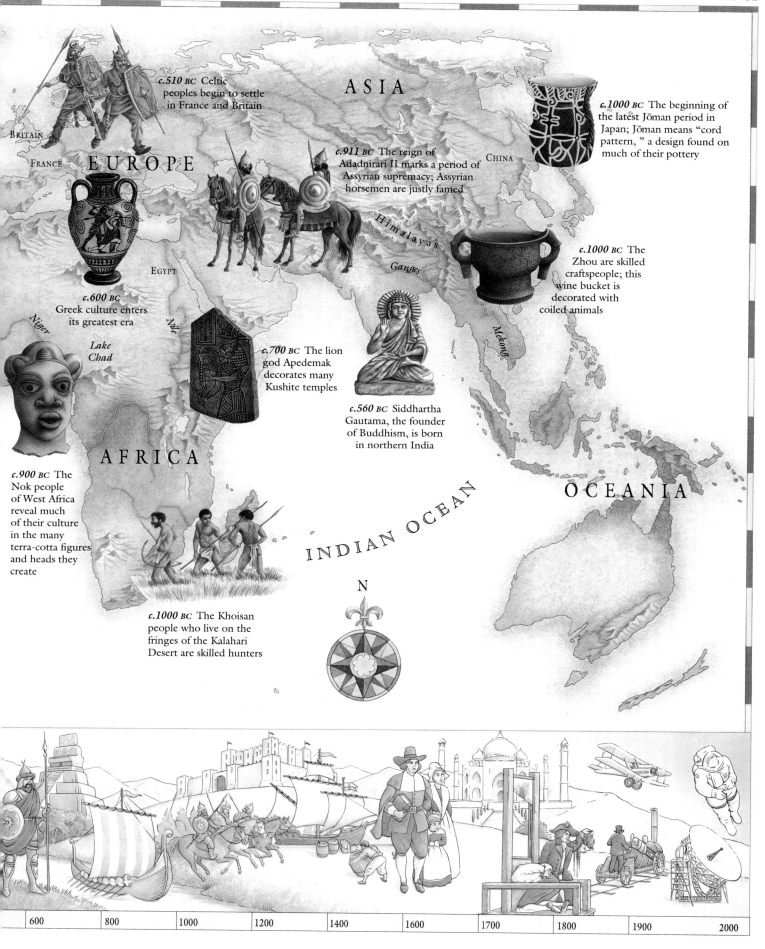

ASIA

c.510 BC Celtic peoples begin to settle in France and Britain

BRITAIN

FRANCE

EUROPE

c.911 BC The reign of Adadnirari II marks a period of Assyrian supremacy; Assyrian horsemen are justly famed

CHINA

c.1000 BC The beginning of the latest Jōman period in Japan; Jōman means "cord pattern," a design found on much of their pottery

Himalayas

Ganges

EGYPT

c.600 BC Greek culture enters its greatest era

Niger

Nile

c.1000 BC The Zhou are skilled craftspeople; this wine bucket is decorated with coiled animals

Mekong

Lake Chad

c.700 BC The lion god Apedemak decorates many Kushite temples

c.560 BC Siddhartha Gautama, the founder of Buddhism, is born in northern India

c.900 BC The Nok people of West Africa reveal much of their culture in the many terra-cotta figures and heads they create

AFRICA

OCEANIA

c.1000 BC The Khoisan people who live on the fringes of the Kalahari Desert are skilled hunters

INDIAN OCEAN

N

600 800 1000 1200 1400 1600 1700 1800 1900 2000

1200 BC

1025 BC

Nok terra-cotta life-size head

AFRICA

c.1200 Yams are grown in West Africa

c.1182–51 Reign of Pharaoh Ramesses III of Egypt, who defends his lands from attacks of Libyans and Mediterranean peoples

c.1085–945 Government of Egypt passes to pharaohs in north

c.1000 Priest-kings of Thebes in Egypt become virtually independent of pharaohs

c.900 Nok people of Nigeria work with terra-cotta

c.900 Kushite kingdom in Sudan thrives; capital established at Napata*

Egyptian courtiers used wooden throwsticks to catch birds; this one had no practical use but was carried during court ceremonies

ASIA

c.1200 Greeks destroy city of Troy on coast of western Turkey after ten-year war

c.1100–c.900 First Assyrian civilization of northern Mesopotamia (Iraq) declines

1045 Kingdom of Zhou established in China*

Clay vase showing scene from the Iliad, a poem by Homer

c.1000 Beginning of Banki (Latest Jōmon) culture in Japan

c.1000 Emergence of Dong Son civilization in Southeast Asia

c.970–35 Reign of Solomon, king of Israel; he builds a great temple in Jerusalem

c.911–891 Reign of King Adadnirari II of Assyria; late Assyrian civilization revives*

853 Battle of Qarqaar: Assyrian king Shalmaneser III defeated by kings of Israel and Damascus

Assyrian art and architecture were magnificent, but the empire is remembered for its brutality; Shalmaneser III boasted that he devastated over 250 enemy cities

EUROPE

c.1120 City of Mycenae destroyed; Mycenaean civilization comes to an end

Thousands of small terra-cotta figures in the form of women have been found at Mycenaean sites; they may represent a fertility goddess

c.1000–800 Greeks establish colonies on some Aegean islands

c.1000 Early iron age begins in Italy

c.900–800 Revival of trade in the Mediterranean

Vine leaves, grapes, and smiling faces decorate this gold Etruscan headband

900 State of Sparta in southern Greece founded by Dorians

c.900 Peoples at Hallstatt in Austria mine salt; they go on to use a variety of iron objects, including swords and harnesses

900–700 Geometric art appears in Greece

Arms held up as though woman is worshiping

Long skirt

AMERICAS

Sculpted heads on the temple at Chavín de Huantar perhaps represent priests being transformed into jaguar gods

c.1200 Rise of Olmec civilization on coast of Gulf of Mexico*

c.1200 Chavín culture grows up at Cerro Sechin on central Peruvian coast

c.1100 Olmec culture flourishes around center at San Lorenzo

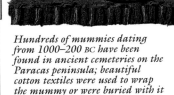

Hundreds of mummies dating from 1000–200 BC have been found in ancient cemeteries on the Paracas peninsula; beautiful cotton textiles were used to wrap the mummy or were buried with it

c.1000 Olmec city at Cuicuilco, west of San Lorenzo, expands

c.1000 La Venta becomes major Olmec center

c.900 People on Paracas peninsula in Peru develop ceremonial center

c.900 Chavín culture grows around Chavín de Huantar in Peruvian Andes

OCEANIA

c.1200 Aboriginals' peaceful culture continues in Australia

850 BC

814 Phoenician traders of eastern Mediterranean coast found colony at Carthage in Tunisia*

c.800 Cereal production continues in Ethiopia

c.770 Kushite rulers of Sudan lead armies against Egypt and establish ruling dynasty there

c.700 Iron tools and weapons are made in Egypt

This gravestone is from a Phoenician graveyard in Carthage

675 BC

671 Egypt overrun by Assyrians of northern Mesopotamia

c.650 Greeks found colony at Cyrene in North Africa

c.600 Nok people of Nigeria begin to mine iron*

c.600 Carthaginian expedition explores southward from North Africa by sea and possibly circumnavigates Africa

525 Cambyses, king of Persia, conquers Egypt

This gate is part of a great Kushite temple, center of royal prestige and power, dedicated to the Kushites' four-armed lion god, Apedemak

771 Zhou capital moved east near to Luoyang

721–04 Reign of Sargon II of Assyria

c.720 Sargon II conquers Israel

704–681 Sennacherib rules Assyria

c.689 Sennacherib invades Babylonia and sacks city of Babylon

Assyrian prince Assurnadin-Sumi, ruler of Babylonia from 699–94, had pictures of gods carved on this boundary stone to gain their protection

c.625 Babylon reemerges as major power in western Asia

612 Assyrian capital, Nineveh, sacked by Babylonians and Medes*

c.605 Nebuchadrezzar II becomes king of Babylonia*

586 Nebuchadrezzar II conquers Judah and exiles Jews to Babylonia*

c.560–c.482 Life of Indian religious teacher Siddhartha Gautama, founder of Buddhism

557–29 Reign of Cyrus the Great, founder of Persian empire

539 Cyrus captures Babylon*

The gold figures on this Persian silver bowl have the head of Egyptian god Bes

c.800 Etruscan people begin to set up citystates in westcentral Italy*

776 First Olympic Games held in Greece

c.753 Rome founded on river Tiber in Italy*

c.735 Greeks found colony at Syracuse in Sicily

Back of a Celtic mirror decorated with swirls

616–578 Reign of Etruscan king Tarquinius Priscus at Rome

590s Solon, chief magistrate of Athens, introduces laws in Greece abolishing enslavement of debtors

The eyes on this sixth-century BC Greek cup were thought to give life and power to the object

578–35 Reign of Servius Tullius at Rome; he builds wall around city

509 Roman republic founded; Brutus becomes one of two consuls, or elected magistrates jointly exercising authority

508 Cleisthenes, Athenian politician, introduces democratic reforms to Greece

c.850 Peruvians make pilgrimages to worship the Smiling God in the temple at Chavín de Huantar*

c.700 Olmecs abandon San Lorenzo

At Tlatelolco, near present-day Mexico City, hundreds of Olmec burials contained white, ceramic baby figures wearing caps

c.600 In Mexico, Oaxaca culture grows stronger than Olmec civilization

c.550 Oaxaca establish center at Monte Albán in southeast Mexico

Temples at Monte Albán contain stone slabs depicting male figures, who may have been slain captives

| 600 | 800 | 1000 | 1200 | 1400 | 1600 | 1700 | 1800 | 1900 | 2000 |

Pyramids of Meroë
Kush was much influenced by Egypt, but it also gradually developed its own distinctive culture.

1200-500 BC AFRICA

In West Africa, people of the Nok culture used iron and introduced new artistic styles in pottery and other artifacts. Phoenicians from the eastern Mediterranean founded colonies along the North African coastline to boost trade, most famously at Carthage in Tunisia. In the northeast, the Kushites of Nubia ruled Egypt for a century, then moved south to base themselves at Meroë.

c. 900 BC
Kushite civilization revives

South of ancient Egypt was the land of Nubia (now Sudan). From about 2000 BC to about 1600 BC it was dominated by Egypt. The area of Upper Nubia came to be known as Kush. During the period a rich and individual culture developed in the region of Kerma, and for a time the Kushites enjoyed some independence. From about 1500 BC to 900 BC Nubia was reoccupied by Egypt, and Kush was overrun, but then Egypt began to lose control, Kush enjoyed a revival, and a capital was set up at Napata, north of the fourth cataract of the Nile. Between about 770 BC and 716 BC two Kushite rulers led armies against Egypt, brought down the ruling dynasty and established their own dynasty, which ruled to about 671 BC. As Kushite power in Egypt declined, the focus of Kushite civilization gradually moved southward, coming to center on the city of Meroë. At this time, ironworking began in Kush; Meroë had good supplies of iron ore and timber.

The land of Kush
As Kushite civilization developed, it became more independent of Egyptian ideas and beliefs.

Meroë's pottery and metalwork are renowned.

Hunters used bows, arrows, and spears

Everyone worked together to build huts

THE KHOISAN

By 1000 BC Khoisan-speaking peoples had lived in various regions of Africa below the equator and in the southwest in and around the Kalahari Desert for thousands of years. Khoisan people were hunters, not crop growers. They used stone tools and hunted with bows using arrows tipped with stone heads. They may already have had knowledge of ironworking when Bantu-speaking peoples from Cameroon began to move into their territory after 100 BC, when they also began to herd sheep and cattle. Gradually, most of the Khoisan peoples were absorbed by the Bantu, but some, especially those on the edges of the Kalahari, continued on their own. Several thousand still live in the region today.

Ingenious people
The Khoisan store water in ostrich eggs and coat the tips of their arrows with poison.

The art of the hunter
The Khoisan have produced amazing rock paintings, with paint made from clay, ochre, and gypsum, mixed with grease or blood, applied with feathers, hair, or bones, and carried in horn pots.

40,000 BC		1000	500	AD 1	200	400

Glorious glass
The Phoenicians were skilled glassmakers, creating objects like this beautiful vase.

814 BC
Phoenicians found Carthage

The Phoenicians had founded trading cities along the eastern Mediterranean coast in the years c.1500–1000 BC in what is now Lebanon. In the last years of this period, they began to sail westward to explore the other coastlines of the Mediterranean. They did so to expand trade and thus bolster the prosperity of their cities, because their coastal strip was not wide or fertile enough to feed the Phoenician people. In 814 BC, they founded Carthage in Tunisia. Carthage quickly expanded into the largest city and trading center along the North African coast, west of Egypt, linking the trade between the African interior and the Mediterranean world. By c.600 BC, the population of Carthage had greatly expanded, and it became rich and independent enough to break away from Phoenician control. People in Carthage built their own ships and organized expeditions, and a Carthaginian admiral is said to have sailed around Africa during this time.

Travel and trade
As well as Carthage, the many colonies set up by the Phoenicians included Utica (Tunisia,) Leptis Magna (Libya), and Mogador (Morocco). Their extensive traveling and trading, however, eventually brought the Phoenicians into conflict with the Greeks, and later the Romans.

Give and take
The Phoenicians traded throughout the Mediterranean. This beautifully carved ivory, showing a woman wearing an Egyptian-style wig, was made by a Phoenician crafts worker and comes from the first Assyrian capital, Nimrud.

c.600 BC
Nok people mine iron

The Nok people lived in Nigeria in West Africa. In about 600 BC, this agricultural community began to mine iron ore and smelt iron in shallow pit furnaces with cylindrical clay walls. Named after the village in which many terra-cotta figurines were found, the Nok people made arrowheads, knives, spearheads, and ax and hoe blades with which to clear and farm the tropical forest. They were also skilled at producing stone tools. Much is revealed about the Nok people's way of life through their pottery figures and sculptures. For example, they wore beads for jewelry, and their axes had wooden handles. The Nok culture probably came to an end in about AD 200–300, but many of its features, especially its artistic styles in pottery and other artifacts, appear in later West African cultures, particularly the Ife culture.

Plateau settlers
The Nok culture was centered in the Jos plateau in northern Nigeria, about 100 miles (160 km) north of the river Benue.

Terra-cotta head
Many Nok terra-cotta figurines were found during tin-mining operations near Jos. Several figurines, such as this terra-cotta head, had elaborate hairstyles and holelike eyes.

| 600 | 800 | 1000 | 1200 | 1400 | 1600 | 1700 | 1800 | 1900 | 2000 |

Assyrian tile
This decorative tile shows Ninurta, goddess of love.

1200-500 BC ASIA

This period saw the rise and fall of the Assyrian Empire, while neighboring Babylonia enjoyed a few decades of dominion over West Asia. This ended when Cyrus the Great of Persia founded the Persian Empire and conquered Babylonia. In China, fighting feudal lords kept the country divided, while Japan adopted crop farming and was influenced by Chinese and Korean ideas and craft skills.

1045 BC
Zhou dynasty begins in China

In about 1045 BC the rulers of the kingdom of Zhou took over from the Shang rulers. The new leaders had come from the west, and for the next three centuries their rule is known as the Western Zhou. In 771 BC they were forced to move their capital east; a number of independent leaders arose in various parts of the country, sometimes adopting their own titles of kingship, sometimes maintaining loyal links with those of Zhou. In the Warring States period, (481–221 BC), seven major kingdoms were often fighting each other, and the kings of Zhou, who survived until 256 BC, had little power. But the Zhou period has always been regarded as a blessed age of happiness.

Jingle bells
Bronze jingling bells such as this one were worn by the horses of noblemen. Horses were sometimes buried with their owner.

Belt buckle
The Zhou were skilled artists. This silver buckle comes from the Ordos region of northwestern China.

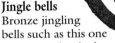

HINDUISM

Around 1500 BC, the Indus civilization in India was invaded by the Aryans, nomads from central Asia. Their earliest records are four sacred books called the Vedas – the years from 1500 to 500 BC are called the Vedic Age. Aryan society had four great divisions, or classes. The highest class, or *varna*, was the priests and scholars, then the soldiers, then the farmers and merchants, and finally the lowest class, who served the upper ones. By the later Vedic period, the religion of the conquered peoples had combined with the traditions of the Vedas to form early Hinduism. This was a very different religious tradition, and its social unit, the caste, was far smaller and more exclusive than the *varna*. An important aspect of Hinduism is *karma*, a belief that people are affected by what they did in previous lives and what they will do in the future. The three most important Hindu gods are Brahma the creator, Vishnu the preserver, and Shiva the destroyer, who rules over life and death.

A god for all seasons
Krishna is one of the most popular of all Hindu gods, and images of him appear everywhere in India. An incarnation of Lord Vishnu, Krishna is portrayed in legends as intensely human. This charming, handsome god was a naughty baby and child who grew up to become a passionate lover and victor over evil.

River Ganges
The Ganges, the chief river in India, is considered sacred to the Hindus. A bath in its waters is believed to wash away all earthly sins.

| 40,000 BC | | 10,000 | 5000 | 1000 | 500 | AD 1 | 200 | 400 |

Fine flower
The Assyrians enjoyed art. This ivory plaque shows an Assyrian priest holding a lotus flower stem.

911 BC
King Adadnirari II ascends Assyrian throne

The kingdom of Assyria had existed in Mesopotamia since at least 2000 BC. During the tenth century BC, the Assyrian kings began expanding their territory to secure their boundaries and to gain control of trade routes. Over the next 200 years, Assyrian armies continued their conquests, until, at its height, the new Assyrian Empire stretched from the borders of Egypt to the Persian Gulf and northward almost to Mount Ararat. The ascent in 911 BC of King Adadnirari II to the Assyrian throne marked a period of Assyrian supremacy; the Assyrians celebrated new territorial gains by building huge palaces and carved intricate stone tablets charting their exploits. Many Assyrian warrior kings ruled with such force and violence, however, that several subject states rebelled. Internal disorder and military failures in the 620s led to the breakup of the empire, and Assyria was eventually invaded and conquered by the Medes and Babylonians in 612 BC.

Man of war
Tiglath-Pileser III (745–27 BC) was an Assyrian warrior king. His armies conquered parts of Syria, Palestine, and Armenia and annexed Babylonia. He brought the Assyrian kingdom under royal control and appointed Assyrian rulers to govern the conquered lands.

THE JŌMAN PERIOD

The Jōman period began in Japan in about 9000 BC and lasted until at least 300 BC. It was one of the first, and by far the longest, culture in early Japanese history. The period is called Jōman from the word meaning "cord pattern," which decorates the pottery first made by Jōman people around 7000 BC. For much of this long period, the people lived in small settlements on the coast, at river mouths, or at the bottom of mountains. Their homes were huts half sunk in the ground, with roofs made from branches and leaves. The coastal villagers survived on mussels, oysters, and other shellfish for their basic diet, while mountain dwellers hunted mammals and gathered berries and nuts. Although the people grew vegetables and millet crops, rice was not cultivated until the very end of the period, when the Jōman finally gave way to the Yayoi period.

Terra-cotta jewels
Beautifully molded terra-cotta earrings such as these were made about 500 BC.

THE FIRST EMPEROR OF JAPAN

The *Kojiki* (Record of Ancient Things), a collection of three volumes of early Japanese legends and historical facts, written in Chinese characters, was completed around AD 712. It mentions an emperor who came from the southeastern part of Kyushu, southwest Japan, and led a migration of his people northeastward. The emperor was called Jimmu-tenno (divine warrior emperor). Jimmu claimed to be a descendent of the sun goddess Amaterasu. In the fifth century BC, the Yamato clan established power in south central Honshu, around what is now Kyoto. The Yamato clan leader declared his descent from Jimmu-tenno, who was regarded in Japanese tradition as the first emperor of Japan.

Polished pots
These lacquered earthenware pots date from c.700 BC. By this time there is evidence of Chinese influence on Jōman culture, mainly from Chinese bronze articles, which the Jōman people copied in their pottery.

| 600 | 800 | 1000 | 1200 | 1400 | 1600 | 1700 | 1800 | 1900 | 2000 |

612 BC
Nineveh is destroyed

After the death in battle of the great Sargon II of Assyria (721–04 BC), his son, Sennacherib (704–681 BC), built a huge palace at the capital city of Nineveh. Sennacherib sacked Babylon in 689 BC but was killed eight years later by his son, Esarhaddon, who rebuilt the city. Esarhaddon's son, Ashurbanipal (668–27 BC), was the last great Assyrian king. He was both a successful general and a patron of the arts, and initiated many great building projects. By the time of his death in 627 BC Assyria had become a powerful state. Almost immediately, Babylonia broke free from Assyrian rule and joined with other subject states to conquer Assyria once and for all. In 612 BC, after a three-month siege, Nineveh and other cities were sacked. A great, though brutal, civilization was at an end.

Assyrian soldiers wore conical helmets

The sack of Babylon
This stone relief was carved in the seventh century BC. It shows Assyrian soldiers escorting loot and captives from the city of Babylon.

Babylonians wrote using cuneiform script, which was made up of wedge-shaped characters

Etched in clay
This Mesopotamian clay barrel records restoration work on the temple of the sun god, Shamash, in Sippar, by Nebuchadrezzar II.

c.605 BC
Nebuchadrezzar II rules Babylonia

After Assyria's fall, the Babylonian king, Nabopolassar (626–05 BC), attempted to expand his kingdom into an empire. He sent an army, led by his son, Nebuchadrezzar II, to fight the Egyptians, defeating them at Carchemish and thereby winning Syria. Nebuchadrezzar succeeded his father in 605 BC and reigned for more than 40 years. He enlarged the city of Babylon with a magnificent new avenue, the Sacred Way, rebuilt a temple to the Babylonian god, Marduk, and raised a palace for himself which he had flanked by the famous hanging gardens. Although archeologists have found no traces of these gardens, they may have been built on different levels over arches so that the greenery cascaded downward. Nebuchadrezzar also had the Tower of Babel enlarged, a fine ziggurat of nine storeys built in order to reach heaven.

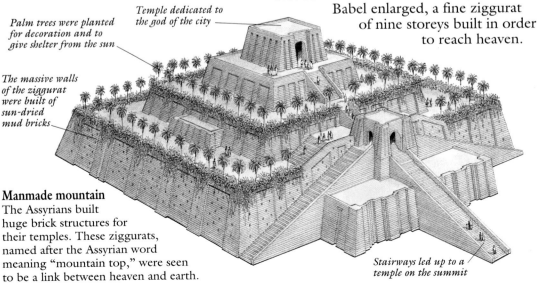

Temple dedicated to the god of the city

Palm trees were planted for decoration and to give shelter from the sun

The massive walls of the ziggurat were built of sun-dried mud bricks

Manmade mountain
The Assyrians built huge brick structures for their temples. These ziggurats, named after the Assyrian word meaning "mountain top," were seen to be a link between heaven and earth.

Stairways led up to a temple on the summit

The gates of Ishtar
Nebuchadrezzar II built a fine new gate in the city wall. Named after Ishtar, goddess of love, the gate rose 50 ft (15 m) above the north entrance to Babylon.

40,000 BC		10,000	5000	1000	500	AD 1	200	400

586 BC
The Babylonian Captivity

For several years, Nebuchadrezzar II of Babylonia had to contend with Jewish rebellion in Judah (in southern Palestine). Three times he put the Jews down, and in 586 BC, after a 16-month siege, he captured their capital, Jerusalem. The city was destroyed, along with the great temple of Solomon. Nebuchadrezzar forced most of the surviving Jews to travel to Babylonia as prisoners, where they were reduced to slavery. This exodus to Babylonia is known as the Babylonian Captivity, and it was the first time that Jewish people in large numbers were scattered in foreign territory. Those that remained in Judah were peasant farmers who were allowed to work the land, but town life in Judah almost vanished. The land of Judah became easy prey to neighboring peoples who moved in to settle. They clashed with the peasant farmers, and there was further conflict when the Babylonian Jews returned to their former homeland. Nebuchadrezzar led another campaign against Egypt and is said to have gone mad in later years, dying in 562 BC.

Rare beast
This bronze stag from Kish in Babylonia dates to 750–650 BC, one of the few sculptures from Babylonia to have survived.

Lapis lazuli necklace
Found in a Kish grave, this necklace is made of lapis from Afghanistan and etched cornelian from Pakistan.

539 BC
Babylon falls to Cyrus of Persia

The Medes, Indo-Europeans living in northern Iran who helped the Babylonians conquer Assyria in 612 BC, ruled several peoples in lands nearby. Their armies had strong detachments of archers who were often a decisive influence in battle. Among their subject peoples were the Persians, who occupied land in the southwest. The Persian rulers were descended from an Iranian king, Achaemenes, and so the dynasty is called the Achaemenid. In 557 BC a young king, Cyrus II (the Great), came to power. In c.550 BC he mobilized his people to throw off Median rule and built a Persian Empire which was to become the ruling power in western Asia for two centuries. He went on to invade Babylonia, taking Babylon in 539 BC. One of his first acts was to free the Jews made captive by Nebuchadrezzar in 586 BC. Cyrus turned the small town of Pasargadae into a splendid capital for his empire. Cyrus died in 529 BC during a campaign.

A conqueror's coin
The rich kingdom of Lydia, in western Turkey, was the first country to produce coins. In 547 BC Cyrus II conquered and annexed Lydia. This coin bears Cyrus's image.

Queen Tomyris looks on while Cyrus's head is immersed in blood

Revenge of a bloodthirsty queen
Although Cyrus is recorded as dying while on campaign, Greek historian Herodotus tells a different tale. He relates how a subject queen, Tomyris, avenged herself cruelly on Cyrus for his campaigns. She had his head cut off and then plunged it into a cup filled with blood, saying, "You thirsted for blood; here you are."

BUDDHISM

Buddhism is the faith that stems from the teachings of Siddhartha Gautama (c.560–c.482 BC), a noble from north India. His early life had been luxurious and sheltered, but when he reached the age of 29, Siddhartha ventured out into the real world. In a single day, he encountered a sick man, an old pauper, and a dead man. This affected him deeply, and he decided to give up his wealthy but useless existence and search for the true meaning of life, spending the next few years as a beggar. In about 528 BC, as he sat beneath a Bodhgaya tree in a village called Bihar, he suddenly found the enlightenment he had been seeking and understood the riddle and source of suffering. He dedicated the rest of his long life to teaching, passing on his ideas to those who would listen. He did not claim to be a god, but after his death his followers formed a new religion to worship him and to spread his ideas. This new faith came to be called Buddhism, from the Indian word *Buddha*, meaning "the enlightened."

Toshogu shrine, Japan
Some Buddhist temples house relics of Buddha, such as robes or a sandal. Worshipers burn incense and leave offerings of fruit and flowers at the shrine. Today there are more than 300 million Buddhists, mainly in Asia, split between the simpler Hinayana form and the more complex Mahayana variety.

The enlightened one
Many images of Buddha exist. This huge statue is from the Shive Dagon pagoda in Rangoon, an early Buddhist site in Burma.

Tibetan monks
The chief Tibetan monks were called lamas. They were not allowed to drink or to get married.

Monks wore simple robes

Birth of Buddha
Dating from the second to third century AD, this wooden plaque illustrates the birth of Buddha.

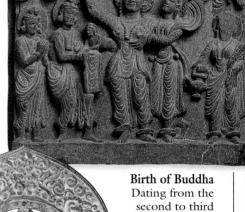

Tibetan prayer wheel
Buddhism in the more elaborate Mahayana (Greater Vehicle) form reached Tibet in the late seventh century AD. Tibetan Buddhists attach written prayers to prayer wheels. The act of spinning the wheel is believed to "say the prayer."

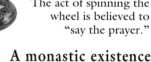

A monastic existence
Buddhist monasteries for monks, and similar institutions for nuns, grew up in India and other parts of Asia. Buddhist monks had to renounce most of their possessions, keeping only their saffron robes, a needle, razor, water strainer, and a begging bowl to beg for food each day. They lived a life of careful discipline, devoting their time to teaching, meditation, and prayer. Some Buddhist monasteries became centers of learning, where monks and nuns studied medicine and looked after the sick and the aged in their communities.

Three main civilizations flourished in this period: the Greeks, the Etruscans, and later, the Celts. The Greek civilization, which developed from c.900 BC, was based on city-states, the most powerful at Athens and Sparta. The Etruscans, too, built a civilization based on an alliance of city-states. Rome was also founded in this period.

Dangerous games
The Romans may have got the idea of chariot racing from the Etruscans.

Etruscan warrior
Etruscan sculpture and bronzework are admired greatly. The strange, remote sense of design is unique.

c.800 BC
The Etruscans

In the eighth century BC the Etruscan people emerged as a civilization of city-states in west-central Italy. Their origins are uncertain, and their language has still not been properly deciphered. Their artistic achievements were remarkable. Their tombs, in particular, were treasure houses. For a long time they dominated west-central Italy and vied with the Latin people of central Italy over possession of the settlement at Rome on the banks of the river Tiber. The Etruscans were not united, however, but a collection of city-states in loose alliance, so the growing power of Rome could target one city after another and take them over. Eventually, after a long decline, the Etruscans were absorbed into the Roman state.

Etruscan fresco
The Etruscans were renowned for their art and architecture. They had a deep influence on Rome, especially on its religion, architecture, and engineering.

c.753 BC
The birth of the "Eternal City"

The Romans dated the foundation of their capital, Rome, on the river Tiber, as 753 BC. By that date several communities, mainly Etruscans and Latins, had settled in the area, and they soon joined together to form one community. Roman tradition said that there were seven kings in succession, the first being the city's founding father Romulus. Some were Latin, some Etruscan, including Tarquinius Superbus. He was a tyrant who involved Rome in expensive wars, terrorized the citizens, and governed so badly that a conspiracy was formed to remove him. After he was driven out, traditionally in 509 BC, the Romans decided they had had enough of kings and formed a republic, to be run by two consuls, each elected for one year's service.

Where it all began
Tiber island (left) marks an ancient crossing place over the river. Bronze Age people were living there as early as 1500 BC – the earliest traces of humans on the site of Rome.

THE CHILDREN OF THE WOLF

In legend, twins Romulus and Remus were abandoned as infants by the Tiber, saved from death by being suckled by a she-wolf, then rescued by shepherds. Romulus went on to build Rome naming it after himself. Romulus was in fact a Latin chief, possibly chosen as Rome's first king (753 to 716 BC).

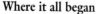

600	800	1000	1200	1400	1600	1700	1800	1900	2000

THE ANCIENT GREEKS

After the fall of the Mycenaeans, Greece did not develop into one united country but grew into an association of city-states that were often at war with each other. The largest and most powerful was the warrior state of Sparta, while Athens became the commercial and cultural center. Around 700 BC, the Greeks began to expand beyond Greece and the Aegean Islands. By the late 500s BC, the new Persian Empire posed a serious threat to the Greeks, which temporarily united the warring city-states against the enemy. Despite these difficulties, the Greeks produced a glorious culture that has had a profound effect on civilization right through to the present day.

Greek slave
This little bronze statue of an African slave boy holding a shoe shows how Greek society depended on slaves.

Power and politics

People in Athens in around 600 BC were controlled by rich landowners. Some landowners who ruled Athens were known as tyrants. In about 590 BC, a city lord called Solon introduced a radical reform program. The tyrants were driven out by the people, who acquired power and freedom. This new government was the beginning of democracy. The Assembly was the center of political life, where citizens could vote and take part in state decisions.

The Elgin Marbles
Lord Elgin brought these marble sculptures from the Parthenon to England in 1815.

The Parthenon
Around 447 BC, the Athenian statesman Pericles ordered the Parthenon to be built on the summit of the Acropolis. It was dedicated both as a temple to the goddess of wisdom, Athena, and also to celebrate Athens's role as leader of Greece against the Persians. The sculptures which decorated it were by the great sculptor Phidias. The Parthenon still dominates the city of Athens today.

SCHOOL FOR THOUGHT

The Greeks were great thinkers. Philosophy, or "love of wisdom," was something that involved all aspects of life, including religion and science. Early Greek thinkers were concerned with ideas about the physical world. The religious thinker Pythagoras and his fellow philosophers also believed that souls could be reborn in other bodies (reincarnation). Philosophy and the arts were also part of religion. Hymns celebrated the mystery of life and explained the origins of the gods. The Greeks made lovely objects both as offerings to the gods and also for their own use.

Deep in thought
This beautiful fresco by the Italian artist Raphael (1483–1520) shows the two great Greek philosophers Aristotle and Plato.

The expansion of Greece

In the eighth century BC, the Greeks began to establish trading posts beyond their own boundaries, in places as far away as the Nile Delta. These trading posts, or colonies, were modeled on the cities from which the colonists had come. They had the same form of government, and the cities were built with much the same street plans. After starting with help from the "mother" state, the colonies soon opened markets and set up their own industries. Several places, such as Syracuse in Sicily, went on to become major trading centers. Some colonies were very rich; it was rumored that roosters were banned from the town of Sybaris in southern Italy so that the residents would not be woken up too early in the morning.

Gold griffin head

Greek colonization

Colonies were established in places with good harbors and agricultural land. Syracuse on the island of Sicily was founded in the 730s. Byzantium on the Bosphorus was founded c.650.

Games and sport

Sport and games were very important to the Greeks. The most prestigious sporting event was the Olympic Games, which were held every four years in honor of the chief god Zeus at Olympia. The scene above shows athletes competing in the pentathlon, an event which included discus and javelin throwing, jumping, wrestling, and running. Discipline in sport was strict, and breaking the rules was severely punished.

Vases and vessels

The ancient Greeks produced a variety of fine pottery, including plates, bowls, vases, and cups. Most were painted with scenes from daily life, legends, or religious subjects. This vase shows one of the 12 labors of Heracles, a Greek hero. Another vase sold at a London auction for more than $3 million in 1993.

Monuments to the gods

Greek life was dominated by religion, so the temples of ancient Greece were the biggest and most beautiful buildings. Decorative sculptures in the form of friezes and statues, many of which can still be seen today, adorned the temples. Greek sculptors were masters in the art of portraying the human form and have influenced sculpture ever since. This beautiful bronze charioteer is at the temple of Apollo at Delphi, where chariot races were held at a nearby stadium in the god's honor. The charioteer is still holding the reins of his horses, even though they have long since disappeared.

Animal bowl
Artists living at Chavín de Huantar produced large quantities of ceramics, many inspired by animals, which they traded throughout Peru.

🌎 *1200-500 BC* AMERICAS

Two great civilizations arose in this period. These were the Chavín people in South America, who built a sophisticated ceremonial center at Chavín de Huantar in the central Andes, and the Olmecs in central Mexico, a highly artistic people who flourished for 600 years, notably at San Lorenzo and La Venta. Toward the end of the period, other cultures emerged, like the Paracas in Peru, influenced by the Chavín people, and the Oaxaca in Mexico, who inherited some Olmec characteristics.

c.1200 BC
Olmec civilization advances

The Olmec civilization is believed to have been the first civilization in North and central America. It began about 1500 BC as a cluster of villages in the swampy Veracruz lowlands fronting the Mexican Gulf.
Around 1200 BC the villages merged into larger settlements, with ceremonial centers flanked by public buildings, houses, and shops.
One of the main centers was at La Venta. Located near a coastal estuary, La Venta was rich in food crops and salt and supported a wealthy community of fishers, farmers, traders, and skilled artisans. They lived in pole and thatch dwellings on top of earth mounds and ate corn, fish, and turtles. Stone for building special monuments had to be imported from the Tuxtla Mountains, in the northwest, and was transported on enormous rafts by river to the sites.

Seated figure
This carved figure has the slanted eyes, flat nose, and thick lips characteristic of much Olmec art.

Greenstone mask
This Olmec mask, dating from 300 BC–AD 300, was probably too heavy to wear and may have been a funerary offering.

Pigeon toes
More than 200 finely worked stone sculptures have been recovered from Chavín de Huantar. This stone stela is carved with a warrior figure brandishing a stick in one hand and holding a small hand shield in the other. It is a typical example of the style of art found in and around Chavín de Huantar.

c.850 BC
Chavín people worship the Smiling God

The Chavín civilization began in South America in the 1200s BC and lasted until c.300 BC. Named after the major site excavated at Chavín de Huantar, which lies in a small valley on the eastern slopes of the Peruvian Andes, it was notable for its strong artistic styles, which spread around much of the Andes region. The Chavín de Huantar site itself dates from c.850 BC. A great religious center, its main feature was a huge stone U-shaped temple containing galleries and chambers connected by stairs and ramps. At the heart of the temple was a sacred space filled by a massive stone sculpture, a human body with the face of a cat, called the Lanzon, or Smiling God. Chavín de Huantar is thought to have been a pilgrimage site for people from all over Peru.

CHAPTER 5

500 BC – AD 1

THE GROWTH OF EMPIRES

Head of a Persian man from Persepolis carved in stone

500 BC–AD 1
THE WORLD

MANY GREAT THINKERS are alive at the start of this period – Buddha in India, Confucius in China, and Pythagoras, Socrates, Plato, and Aristotle in Greece. Together they have a profound effect on the thinking and religious beliefs of the world. In Greece, the philosophers contribute toward a system of government – democracy, which is based on rule by the people expressed through elected representatives – which, some 2,500 years after its foundation, becomes the most common form of political organization in the world today.

Great empires

While Greece is organized into small city states, much of the world consists of large and powerful empires. The Persian Empire reaches its height in the 480s, but it is finally conquered by Alexander the Great, who in 13 years carves out a huge empire that stretches from Greece in the west to India in the east. In this period, China becomes a united empire for the first time, and Rome emerges as the most powerful state in Europe. By the end of the period, more than half of the world's population – 150 million people out of an estimated total of 250 million – live in just three empires, the Roman in Europe, the Parthian in western Asia, and the Han in China. Smaller empires of the Maya in Central America, and the Moche in Peru, also begin to emerge at this time.

c.100 BC People living around the Bering Sea make beautiful ivory objects

NORTH AMERICA

Rockies

c.500 BC The Adena people build large burial mounds as communal graves

c.480 BC Carthaginian admiral Hanno explores along the coast of Africa

Andes

SOUTH AMERICA

PERU

c.500 BC The Oculate Being appears on materials woven and embroidered by the Paracas people of Peru

ATLANTIC OCEAN

PACIFIC OCEAN

Hunting in the Ice Age
Cave painting
Early farming
Ancient Egypt
Assyrian Empire
Great Wall of China
Classical Greece

| 40,000 BC | | 10,000 | 5000 | 1000 | 500 | AD 1 | 200 | 400 |

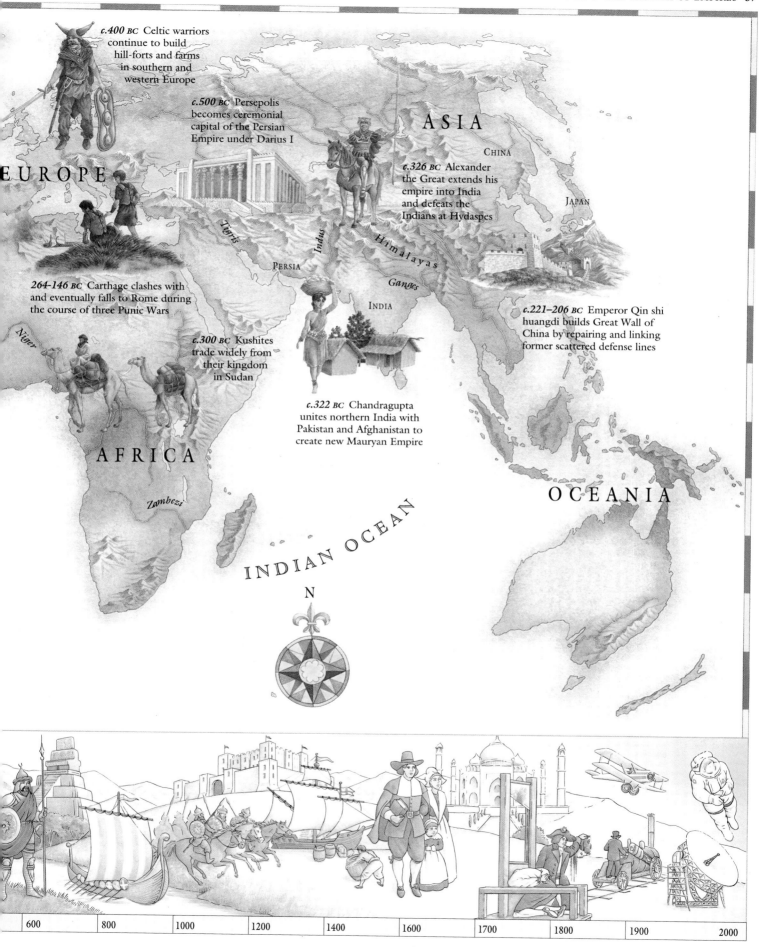

c.400 BC Celtic warriors continue to build hill-forts and farms in southern and western Europe

c.500 BC Persepolis becomes ceremonial capital of the Persian Empire under Darius I

ASIA

CHINA

EUROPE

c.326 BC Alexander the Great extends his empire into India and defeats the Indians at Hydaspes

JAPAN

Tigris

Indus

Himalayas

PERSIA

Ganges

264-146 BC Carthage clashes with and eventually falls to Rome during the course of three Punic Wars

INDIA

c.221–206 BC Emperor Qin shi huangdi builds Great Wall of China by repairing and linking former scattered defense lines

Niger

c.300 BC Kushites trade widely from their kingdom in Sudan

c.322 BC Chandragupta unites northern India with Pakistan and Afghanistan to create new Mauryan Empire

AFRICA

Zambezi

OCEANIA

INDIAN OCEAN

N

| 600 | 800 | 1000 | 1200 | 1400 | 1600 | 1700 | 1800 | 1900 | 2000 |

500 BC

375 BC

AFRICA

Egyptian ceremonial ax with openwork head

c.500 Semitic people from southern Arabia migrate to Eritrea and Ethiopia; they trade ivory, spices, and incense

c.480 Voyage of Carthaginian admiral Hanno along West African coast

Copper arrowheads from Mauritania in the western Sahara

c.400 Copper smelting begins in Mauritania, western Sahara; sharp arrowheads were made

332 Alexander the Great conquers Egypt

305 Founding of the Ptolemaic dynasty in Egypt; Ptolemy II builds great library in Alexandria

c.300 Kushite kingdom expands; Kushites open up trade contacts eastward, southward, and westward, from Meroë, Sudan*

285 Ptolemy rules Egypt jointly with his son*

ASIA

c.500 Darius I of Persia (521–486) improves government and communications in his empire; starts to build king's highway from Ephesus to Susa*

Carved in stone, people bearing offerings to the king of Persia ascend the steps of the royal palace at Persepolis

336–323 Conquests of Macedonian ruler Alexander the Great

c.322 Chandragupta founds the Mauryan Empire in India

c.300 Yayoi civilization develops in Japan*

c.265 Mauryan ruler Ashoka conquers Kalinga*

A silver-gilt drinking horn from the Persian Empire

EUROPE

490 Athenian Greeks defeat Persian attack at Battle of Marathon

480 Persian fleet of King Xerxes annihilated at Salamis

c.460 Perikles elected leader of popular party and governs Athens to 429

449 The Roman republic grows in power; 12 tables drawn up – earliest Roman code of laws*

431–404 Great Peloponnesian War between Athens and Sparta*

390 Brennus, Gaulish chief, sacks city of Rome

This coin shows Themistokles, an Athenian leader

264–241 First Punic War; Rome defeats Carthage and takes most of Sicily

Greek soldiers were called hoplites from the word hoplon meaning shield; only wealthy men could afford the expensive armor and weapons

AMERICAS

c.500 Paracas culture flourishes in Peru*

c.500 Adena people in Ohio reach peak of their civilization; start building large burial grounds as communal graves*

c.450 Specialized woodworking tools appear along northwest coast of Canada and Alaska

c.400 Site at Tiahuanaco near Lake Titicaca in Bolivia first occupied by farming families

c.325 End of La Venta, center of Olmec culture in Mexico

Nazca people in Peru were great potters and weavers; this pot shows a woman holding a spindle in one hand

From Peru, a Moche stirrup-spout vessel in the form of a frog

c.300 Beginning of later burial mound period of Hopewell culture of North America

c.300 End of Chavín culture in Peru

c.300 Moche civilization begins on northern coast of Peru

c.300–100 The growing city of Teotihuacan comes to dominate the Valley of Mexico

OCEANIA

c.500 Aboriginal culture continues to develop in Australia

250 BC

202 Hannibal is defeated at Zama in Tunisia by the Romans*
146 Carthage is destroyed

Ships in Carthage harbor were controlled from the admiralty building

c.250 Arsaces I founds the Parthian kingdom on the edge of Persia; it becomes the Parthian Empire in second century BC
221 Zheng, king of Qin, adopts the title Qin shi huangdi, first emperor of China*
202 Beginning of western Han dynasty in China (to AD 9)*
171 Mithradates I becomes Parthian emperor*

This Chinese figure was made for a funeral during the time of the Han dynasty

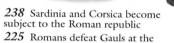

238 Sardinia and Corsica become subject to the Roman republic
225 Romans defeat Gauls at the Battle of Telamon in northern Italy
218–201 Second Punic War between Rome and Carthage
216 Roman army annihilated by Hannibal at Battle of Cannae
212 Romans besiege and take Syracuse in Sicily; mathematician Archimedes is killed in siege
207 Battle of the Metaurus in Italy; Romans defeat relief force coming to the aid of Hannibal
197 Battle of Cynoscephalae in northern Greece; Romans defeat Philip V of Macedon
147–146 Rome takes over Macedon and brings Greece under Roman rule

The bronze Roman statuette on the right shows the goddess of victory holding a crown of laurel leaves

c.200 Beginning of early classic period of Maya civilization in Central America
c.200 Beginning of Nazca culture in southern Peru

A greenstone mask from Teotihuacan; the Teotihuacan culture grew to be the most influential in Central America

125 BC

30 Cleopatra, last Ptolemaic ruler of Egypt, commits suicide; Egypt becomes Roman province

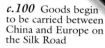

An Egyptian glass tube for eye paint, with its applicator

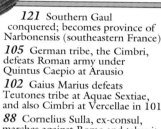

c.100 Goods begin to be carried between China and Europe on the Silk Road
63 Romans conquer Judah (in modern Israel)*

This miniature bronze altar comes from the Phoenician city of Byblos; once an important port, Byblos declined and was only a minor town in the Roman period

121 Southern Gaul conquered; becomes province of Narbonensis (southeastern France)
105 German tribe, the Cimbri, defeats Roman army under Quintus Caepio at Arausio
102 Gaius Marius defeats Teutones tribe at Aquae Sextiae, and also Cimbri at Vercellae in 101
88 Cornelius Sulla, ex-consul, marches against Rome and takes it
73–71 Massive but unsuccessful slave revolt in Italy, led by Spartacus, against Roman government and army
60 The first triumvirate, consisting of Crassus, Pompeius, and Caesar, rules Rome*
59 Julius Caesar becomes consul
58–50 Julius Caesar's conquest of Gaul extends Roman Empire in western Europe

This Roman Samian ware bowl was made in a factory in France and then exported to England

45 After civil war, 49–45, Julius Caesar is master of the Roman world but is then assassinated in 44; further civil war follows*
31 Octavian, Julius Caesar's great nephew, finally ends civil wars by decisive victory at Battle of Actium
27 Octavian becomes first emperor of Rome as Augustus

c.100 Beginning of pioneer period of Hohokam culture, especially at the Snaketown site in Arizona
c.100 Emergence of the first Anasazi culture in southwestern United States

The design on the left shows flute players; it comes from a Hohokam bowl from Snaketown

Beasts of burden
This Kushite carving showing elephants comes from Musawaret es-Sofra.

Carthage was a great military and commercial force, but centuries of power came to an end after its army under Hannibal failed to take Rome. In the Sudan, the Meroitic civilization extended its trade links. Meanwhile, Egypt fell to Alexander the Great, and the Ptolemaic dynasty took over until Egypt was defeated by Rome and became a province. The Iron Age spread throughout Africa.

c.300 BC
Kushite kingdom expands

Before 300 BC, the Kushite people of the Sudan had relied on Egypt for much of their trade. Around 300 BC, the Kushites changed their seat of government to the southerly city of Meröe and began to open up new trading routes. The gradual expansion of their kingdom allowed the Kushites to develop an increasingly separate culture from that of Egypt. Over the years, the Kushites modified Egyptian hieroglyphics into a complex, and so far untranslated, script. Meröe grew into a major city, with temples, palaces, and houses. This culture was known as Meroitic. Meroitic rulers, who were regarded as demigods, were buried in pyramidlike graves, which were similar to those used by the Egyptians.

Temple guardians
As the Meroitic culture grew increasingly powerful, the Kushites began to place more importance on their own gods rather than those of the Egyptians. One of the most prominent Meroitic gods was the lion-god Apedemak. Here he is engraved on the wall of the temple complex at Naga.

285 BC
Ptolemy II rules Egypt jointly with his father

After Alexander the Great died in 323 BC, the rule of Egypt passed to one of his generals, the Macedonian Ptolemy. In 305 BC Ptolemy became king of Egypt and moved his capital to Alexandria on the Mediterranean coast, where it became a great center of trade and scholarship. From 285 BC he ruled jointly with his son, Ptolemy II, who went on, after his father's death in 282 BC, to further strengthen the country's commerce. Ptolemy III continued to consolidate the power of the dynasty, but his successors were weak. The Ptolemaic dynasty ended when a joint Egyptian and Roman fleet under Mark Antony was defeated by Octavian, Caesar's heir, at the Battle of Actium in 31 BC.

CLEOPATRA

Cleopatra, queen of Egypt, was the last of the Ptolemaic dynasty. She was famed for her beauty and intelligence. Both Julius Caesar and Mark Antony courted her. In 30 BC Cleopatra committed suicide, supposedly from a snakebite, after Antony's defeat at Actium. In the film *Caesar and Cleopatra*, based on Shaw's play, she is played by the actress Vivien Leigh.

The marble tower was 427 ft (130 m) high

The light from a fire in the base of the tower was reflected out to sea by bronze mirrors

Lighting the way
The imposing Pharos lighthouse in Alexandria harbor was built between 297–280 BC to overcome the navigational hazards of the low-lying Egyptian coastline. The Pharos lighthouse was counted among the Seven Wonders of the Ancient World. It was completed by Ptolemy II who ruled Egypt between 285–246 BC and erected many other splendid structures and buildings in Alexandria.

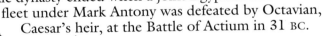

40,000 BC		10,000	5000	1000	500	AD 1	200	400

Carthaginian coin
This silver coin was made to pay Carthaginian troops during the Punic Wars. The emblem of Carthage was a horse, shown here as Pegasus.

202 BC
Hannibal defeated at Battle of Zama

After failing to defeat the Greeks in the Mediterranean in the fifth century BC, the Carthaginians turned to expand westward along the north coast of Africa. Then, in the third century BC, Carthage clashed with Roman might, and three major wars were fought (in 264–241 BC, 218–201 BC, and 149–146 BC). In the first Carthaginian (or Punic) War, the Carthaginians lost supremacy at sea. Then, in the 230s, Hamilcar Barca, a leading general, took an army into Spain to extend the Carthaginian empire further into Europe. His son-in-law, Hasdrubal, founded the city of New Carthage (modern Cartagena) in Spain in about 226 BC. Hasdrubal was killed in 221 BC and Hamilcar's son, Hannibal (c.247–183 BC), became commander in Spain. In 218 BC the second Punic War began. Hannibal took an army up the Spanish east coast into Gaul (France) and across the Alps to try to reach Rome itself. Over the next 15 years, despite winning many battles, he failed to defeat Rome. He returned to Africa and, in 202 BC at Zama, about 100 miles southwest of Carthage, a Roman army under Cornelius Scipio routed him. Harsh terms were imposed on Carthage afterward.

Grisly offering
The Carthaginians performed a ceremony in which they sacrificed live babies to their sun god, Baal-Hammon. The remains of the child were then placed in an urn and put in a burial chamber such as this one.

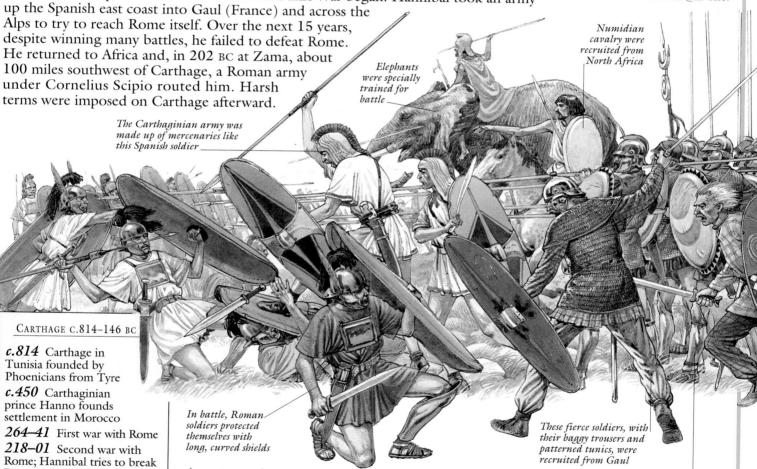

Elephants were specially trained for battle

Numidian cavalry were recruited from North Africa

The Carthaginian army was made up of mercenaries like this Spanish soldier

In battle, Roman soldiers protected themselves with long, curved shields

These fierce soldiers, with their baggy trousers and patterned tunics, were recruited from Gaul

Marching forward in tight formation, with long lances at the ready, Carthaginian soldiers were barelegged with short red tunics and shiny bronze helmets

CARTHAGE c.814–146 BC

c.814 Carthage in Tunisia founded by Phoenicians from Tyre

c.450 Carthaginian prince Hanno founds settlement in Morocco

264–41 First war with Rome

218–01 Second war with Rome; Hannibal tries to break Rome's Mediterranean power

216 Hannibal wins crushing victory over Romans at Cannae

202 Battle of Zama; Romans defeat Hannibal

183 Death of Hannibal

149–46 Third war with Rome; Carthage destroyed 146

A great general
Hannibal was a splendid leader. He took 30,000 men and some 40 elephants across the Alps into Italy, losing many men and most of the elephants on the way. But he defeated one Roman army after another. His greatest victory was at Cannae in 216 BC: 60,000 Romans were killed or taken captive. This left Rome defenseless, but his army was tired and did not attack the city. Hannibal ravaged much of Italy over the next 13 years but fought no major battles, because the Carthaginian government failed to support him. Nineteen years after his defeat at Zama, he committed suicide rather than surrender himself to the Romans.

| 600 | 800 | 1000 | 1200 | 1400 | 1600 | 1700 | 1800 | 1900 | 2000 |

500 BC-AD 1 ASIA

This was a time of major change for the continent. The kingdom of Persia grew into the most powerful empire in western Asia, the Mauryan dynasty gained control of central and western India, and Prince Cheng united China, appointing himself first emperor. Many important inventions were made in China during the rule of the Han dynasty that followed Cheng. In the 330s and 320s BC, military leader Alexander the Great conquered huge parts of western Asia.

King or nobleman?
The Persian man in this stone carving wears a crown that looks as if it is made of feathers but is actually pleated fabric. His rank is unknown.

c.500 BC
King's highway built in Persia

Cyrus the Great of Persia died in 529 BC. By then, he had founded an empire and organized its government, dividing the lands into satrapies, or provinces, with common customs. One of his greatest successors was Darius I (521–486 BC), who extended the empire's borders to northern India in the east and Turkey in the west, increasing the number of satrapies from 23 to 31. His ambitious building program included the construction in c.500 BC of a 1,500 mile (2,400 km) highway from Susa in modern Iran to Ephesus in Turkey, with stations at intervals in which fresh horses for royal messengers were stabled. In 499 BC Greek settlements in Turkey rebelled, aided by mainland Greek cities, including Athens. Darius managed to restored order and, in 490 BC, sent an army to punish Athens. It was defeated at Marathon, near Athens, by a force of Athenians half the size, sparking off the Persian Wars between Greece and Persia. Darius's successor, Xerxes, burned Athens in 480 BC, but later that year his fleet was sunk in the sea battle of Salamis. Xerxes returned to Asia, leaving the Greeks independent.

Glamorous goat
This silver goat is said to come from the palace of Darius I in the city of Persepolis, his ceremonial capital, near present-day Shiraz in Iran.

Priest of fire
Persians worshiped many gods associated with nature, social and economic relationships, and ideas such as truth and justice. Priests of the fire god, such as the one on this gold plaque, carried a bundle of twigs, or barsom, which was used to feed a sacred fire.

Vast empire united
The Persian Empire, the largest the world had seen, stretched from North Africa, through southern Asia, to India. Rulers improved roads to link distant lands and introduced standard weights and coins. Most were tolerant, allowing their subjects religious freedom.

Government center
The stairways at Persepolis were carved with pictures of courtiers, warriors, and foreign rulers bearing tributes of precious metals and elephant tusks. Much palace business, such as dispensing food rations to officials, was recorded by scribes on clay tablets.

PERSIAN EMPIRE 550–330 BC

550 Cyrus becomes first effective king of Persia

539 Cyrus captures Babylon

529 Death of Cyrus

525 Cyrus's son, Cambyses, invades Egypt

521–486 Reign of Darius I

499–479 Persian Wars between Greeks and Persians

c.479 Persians scrap plan to conquer Greece after Greeks defeat them at Marathon (490) and Salamis (480)

358–336 After decline, Persian power revives under two kings, Artaxerxes III and Arses

334–330 Darius III defeated in three battles by Alexander the Great; Alexander makes Persia a part of his empire

| 40,000 BC | | 10,000 | 5000 | 1000 | 500 | AD 1 | 200 | 400 |

Holes may represent the eyes of rice gods

Dotaku were up to 4 ft (1.2 m) tall

Stakes were not decorated

Dotaku

Yayoi people made bell-shaped bronze objects, or dotaku, decorating them with pictures of the natural world, hunting, farming, and fishing. Some pictures show buildings which resemble later shrines and farm houses. Dotaku were possibly mounted on stakes during ceremonies.

c.300 BC
Yayoi culture develops in Japan

Merchants and settlers from mainland Asia arrived on the island of Kyushu in western Japan in about 300 BC, and their influence spread eastward. Their culture is named after one settlement, Yayoi, in Tokyo. They brought with them Chinese methods of rice farming, irrigation, and metalworking. Yayoi people introduced both bronze and iron to Japan at the same time, making metal tools, weapons, and vessels. Yayoi people also introduced the potter's wheel, and their pottery includes some of the earliest figures of Japanese people, animals, and houses. They buried their dead in funerary urns, stone tombs, or wooden coffins. Some large tombs held many fine objects, suggesting they belonged to nobles who controlled large workforces.

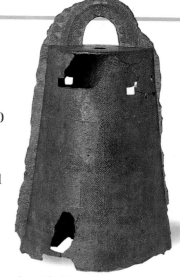

Mysterious "bells"
Dotaku were sometimes found buried in groups, in mounds on the edge of rice fields, or in hill slopes.

c.265 BC
Ashoka captures Kalinga

In c.322 BC a revolt broke out in the Punjab (in northwest India and Pakistan) against the governors appointed by its recent conqueror, Alexander the Great. It was led by nobleman Chandragupta Maurya, who made the first proper attempt to create an Indian nation, incorporating all of north India in what is called the Mauryan Empire. He built a strong central government and maintained a well-paid army, beating off an invasion by Alexander's former general, Seleucus, in 305 BC. A peace treaty fixed a frontier along the Hindu Kush mountain peaks. His son expanded the empire southward, and Chandragupta's grandson, Ashoka took a small kingdom, Kalinga, around 265 BC. Ashoka was so appalled by the suffering involved that he became a devout Buddhist and pursued a policy of peace toward nearby states. Missionaries were sent to convert peoples of Burma and Sri Lanka to Buddhism.

Hero of the people
Ashoka's laws were carved on pillars, topped by sculptures. The four lions in this sculpture are now India's national emblem. The laws aimed to curb poverty and insecurity, and included the provision of roads, rest houses, and wells. Ashoka reduced his army and sent officials to the regions to settle complaints with regard to the needs of local people. A strict vegetarian, he forbade the killing of many animal species.

Map labels: Hindu Kush · Punjab · MAURYAN EMPIRE · Pataliputra · Magadha · Burma · Kalinga · Bay of Bengal · Arabian Sea · Sri Lanka

First Indian empire
Chandragupta seized Magadha, the main state of northeast India, at the same time taking the Punjab. He made Pataliputra his capital. Victory over Seleucus gained him much of modern Pakistan and Afghanistan. His son gained control over most of southern India.

Colossal female
Mauryans excelled in the arts of sculpting and polishing stone. They sculpted huge stone female figures, called "yakshis," representing fertility spirits, that show their ideal of feminine beauty.

Terracotta army
Qin shi huangdi ordered the sculpting of life-size statues of an entire army. More than 7,000 uniformed terra-cotta warriors, no two faces the same, were painted brilliant colors and armed with actual weapons. Clay charioteers and horses were attached to real chariots. The clay army was buried around the tomb of the first emperor in battle formation to protect his spirit.

221 BC
China's first empire

During the Warring States period (c.485–221 BC), the rule of China was divided between seven major kingdoms and some smaller states, including that of Zhou. These kingdoms fought one another and took each other's lands until, in 221 BC, the king of Qin succeeded in defeating all his rivals and formed China's first united empire. Adopting the title Qin shi huangdi, or First Emperor of Qin, from which the name China is derived, he set about organizing the land and its people so as to coordinate their work, put down crime, and create a dependable and well-disciplined army. He took stern measures to implement the laws and to establish a unified system of writing, weights and measures, and currency.

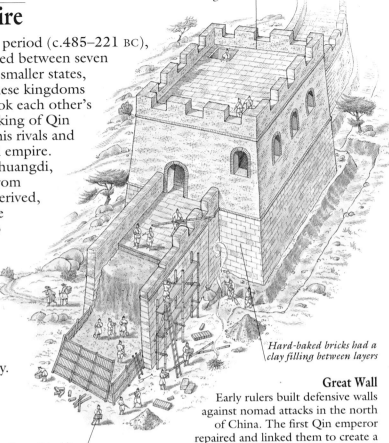

Watchtowers provided shelter from crossfire during attacks

Hard-baked bricks had a clay filling between layers

Conscript soldiers and lawbreakers were forced to build the wall

Great Wall
Early rulers built defensive walls against nomad attacks in the north of China. The first Qin emperor repaired and linked them to create a Great Wall, with offshoots, nearly 4,000 miles (6,400 km) long.

Empire enlarged
Han rulers extended the borders of Qin shi huangdi's empire to take in Korea and parts of Vietnam. The early Han rulers made their capital in the west, at Chang'an, and are therefore known as the "Western Han." Most people lived in the north of China.

Great Wall of China

• Chang'an

Extent of the Qin Empire

Extent of Han Empire

South China Sea

202 BC
Han dynasty dominates China

The death of the first emperor of Qin in 210 BC was soon followed by civil war, until a family named Liu set up the Han dynasty in Qin's place. Many of Qin's methods of government were continued and in the next two centuries were further developed in the hope of strengthening China's unity and protecting Chinese territory against invaders from the north. From 100 BC Chinese merchants were often able to carry silks along a trade route, known as the Silk Route, through central Asia to western Europe.

CONFUCIUS c.551–479 BC

Officials of the Han dynasty were taught to respect the teachings of the great Chinese philosopher Confucius. He believed that people could be taught to behave themselves as members of a well-ordered community rather than as individuals seeking their own gains. After an unsuccessful career in public life, he set up a school to teach pupils to treat their parents, the aged, and others with respect and kindness. His pupils recorded his sayings in a famous book, *The Analects*.

Ready for dinner
These lacquered bowls were full of food when buried with senior officials and noblemen, or their wives, of the Han period.

40,000 BC		10,000	5000	1000	500	AD 1	200	400

171 BC
Mithradates I becomes Parthian king

Alexander the Great invaded Persia in 334–330 BC, and after his death it was ruled by Seleucus, one of his generals. In c.250 BC a tough leader from central Asia, Arsaces, founded a kingdom called Parthia in eastern Persia. A relative, Mithradates I, came to the Parthian throne in 171 BC and stayed in power for 33 years. He set out to conquer the vast domains ruled by the great Persian emperor, Darius I, over 300 years previously. In a series of campaigns (c.160 BC–140 BC) Mithradates conquered the lands between the Caspian Sea and the Persian Gulf, and eastward to India's frontiers. He built a military camp on the Tigris River, facing the city of Seleucia, and the two merged into a city, Ctesiphon, which became Parthia's capital. Mithradates died in 138 BC but his Arsacid dynasty ruled for 300 years. Parthia remained a major power much longer. Greek culture, which had spread through Persia after Alexander's conquest, was replaced by a revived Persian culture.

Parting shot
Devastatingly effective Parthian mounted archers could even shoot backwards as they rode (a "Parthian shot"), giving them enormous advantage in battle.

63 BC
Romans conquer Judah

In 198 BC Antiochus the Great, the king of the Syrian-based Seleucids, took control of the state of Judah in Israel. He tried to impose Greek culture and religion on the Jewish people. The Jews retained a measure of independent government through their high priests, some of whom broke Jewish law to impress the Seleucids. In 168 BC Jews wanting a strictly religious state of their own revolted, led by Judas the Maccabee and his brothers. They took Judah's capital, Jerusalem, set up a ruling dynasty, and held power until 63 BC when the Romans annexed Judah, retaining Maccabean Hyrcanus as puppet ruler. In 37 BC the Romans made Hyrcanus's half-Jewish minister, Herod, king of Judah, and the state became known as Judea.

Wailing Wall
The remodeled temple was magnificent but was virtually destroyed when the Romans sacked Jerusalem in AD 70 to suppress a Jewish revolt. For centuries Jews could only enter Jerusalem once a year to pray at the remaining temple wall, the Wailing Wall, and grieve for their lost city.

Last stand at Masada
The Maccabees built Masada, a fortress on a ridge in the barren mountains south of Jerusalem. Herod developed Masada into a palace stronghold, with heated baths, extensive storerooms, and a synagogue. After his death the palace was disused, but the last survivors of the sack of Jerusalem escaped there. They held out for three years against Roman attacks. When the Romans finally broke through in AD 73, they found the defenders and their families had killed themselves rather than be captured.

HANUKAH
When the Maccabees' army swept into Jerusalem, they found the temple vandalized, and a statue of a Greek god on the altar. Judas the Maccabee rededicated the temple to the Jewish God in a solemn ritual, lighting a menorah, or seven-branched candlestick. He ruled that every year, starting the same day, Jews must celebrate a festival of dedication, called Hanukah. They should burn lights for eight days, adding a new light every night, and sing praise and thanks to God.

Jewish symbol
To Jews in all ages, in good and bad times, the Maccabees' story showed that no force could crush those who fought to practice their religion freely and live the way they chose. The menorah is the symbol of this struggle and triumph. This one stands in Jerusalem today.

ALEXANDER THE GREAT

Alexander the Great had a remarkable career. In 13 years, beginning at the age of 23, he expanded his Greek kingdom into an empire that reached as far as India. Son of Philip II of Macedon (382–336 BC), Alexander served in his father's campaigns and was already admired for his courage and leadership when he took over the army. He set out to fulfill his father's aim to free the Greek states from Persian rule, and from 334–330 BC he conquered Syria, Turkey, Phoenicia, Persia, and Egypt (333–332 BC), where he founded the city of Alexandria. He continued into India but had to return to Persia to quash a revolt. Alexander died on his way home in 323 BC. His empire was divided up among his leading generals.

Babylonian coin
This coin shows Alexander on horseback attacking two Indian warriors.

Alexander's empire
By the time of Alexander's death, his empire reached from Macedon to the Indus River in the east, and he was still planning conquests. He settled Greeks in new cities to strengthen his control over conquered lands, and encouraged marriage between Greeks and Asians.

Alexander (356–323 BC)
Alexander the Great was a great general and had an extremely powerful personality. Many of Alexander's troops looked upon him as a god. He was always up at the front in battle, whether on foot or on his great black horse, Bucephalus. He was frequently wounded in battle and was always ready to share hardships and discomforts with his men, as well as the spoils of victory. He died of a fever at the age of 33.

Aristotle (384–322 BC)
Aristotle was himself a pupil of the Greek philosopher, Plato.

ALEXANDER'S TUTOR

In his youth, Alexander had the best education his father could arrange. He was taught at the Macedonian court by Aristotle, the great Athenian philosopher, who managed to instil in him a great enthusiasm for the free expression of ideas. Alexander eagerly encouraged Greek art and culture during his reign.

The Battle of Issus
In 333 BC Alexander's army won a victory against the Persians, led by Darius III, at the Battle of Issus in Syria. The victory marked a turning point in the great clash between Europe and Asia and is commemorated in the largest surviving mosaic from ancient times (a detail is shown above), found at Pompeii in 1831.

| 40,000 BC | | 10,000 | 5000 | 1000 | 500 | AD 1 | 200 | 400 |

In this period Greece, and later Rome, thrived and imposed their civilizations upon much of the continent. Greece was taken over in the fourth century by its neighbor, Macedon, under Philip and his son, Alexander. The Romans destroyed Carthaginian power and took control of the Mediterranean. Finally, Julius Caesar conquered Gaul (France) and made Rome the dominant power throughout Europe.

449 BC
The growth of the republic of Rome

The Roman republic's idea of electing two new consuls each year was meant to prevent elected leaders from becoming dictatorial. Magistrates were chosen on the same basis, to assist the consuls, thus encouraging more people to share in the city's affairs. This system worked well initially, but then conflict arose between the patricians (the aristocracy), who had all the top jobs, and plebeians (the common people), who wanted more say. In 449 the plebeians won the right to elect tribunes (representatives), who were to share in the making of laws. Later, these tribunes could block measures introduced by the senate (government) by calling out, "Veto" ("I forbid it"). A slave class, mainly men captured in war, had almost no rights at all.

A Roman citizen
A toga was the mark of Roman citizenship. By the time of the empire, togas were worn only on important occasions.

Roman Empire
The Romans consolidated their power by building a road network across Italy, expanding trade, and opening up contacts overseas, especially in Greece, the eastern Mediterranean, and North Africa.

The togas of magistrates and other officials had purple borders

� 200 BC	▪ 133 BC	☐ AD 1

PERIKLES

Perikles (c.490–29 BC) was leader of Athens from 461–29 BC. An honest and upright man, he earned a strong reputation for political skill. In the Great Peloponnesian War, he appealed to the pride and patriotism of the Athenian people, and pursued the war vigorously. He died in a serious plague in 429 BC.

431 BC
The Great Peloponnesian War

The city-states of Ancient Greece often fought each other. Rivalry between Athens and Sparta, the two most important city-states, continued to grow, and culminated in 459 BC in the First Peloponnesian War (named after the Peloponnesus, the peninsula that forms the southern part of Greece in which Sparta and its allies were located). The result of the war was a victory for Sparta. Fifteen years later, in 431 BC, Athenian aggression against Corinth, one of Sparta's allies, sparked off the Second, or Great, Peloponnesian War, which lasted until 404 BC, when Athens, having had its entire fleet of ships destroyed in a single battle at Aegospotami the previous year, finally surrendered following a siege.

Athens versus Sparta
The two sides were fairly evenly matched in the Peloponnesian Wars. The Spartan army, with its fierce and much feared infantry, were stronger on land, while for a time the Athenian navy dominated the sea.

600	800	1000	1200

THE CELTS

People called Celts were dwelling in central Europe by about 500 BC. They were highly skilled in horsemanship and had an advanced knowledge of ironworking. Fierce, proud warriors who loved fighting and feasting, the Celts held great banquets, often lasting several days, to drink and celebrate their victories. They were also artistically gifted, and many stunning examples of their metalwork can still be seen today. The Celts had no writing system. Instead, they committed their history to memory, passing it on verbally through poetry and dialogue. Celts lived in Gaul and in parts of Spain where they set up farms and large, well-protected hill-forts, and related peoples lived in the British Isles. Their unruly and disorganized armies, however, never succeeded in overcoming the formidable force of the highly trained Roman legions.

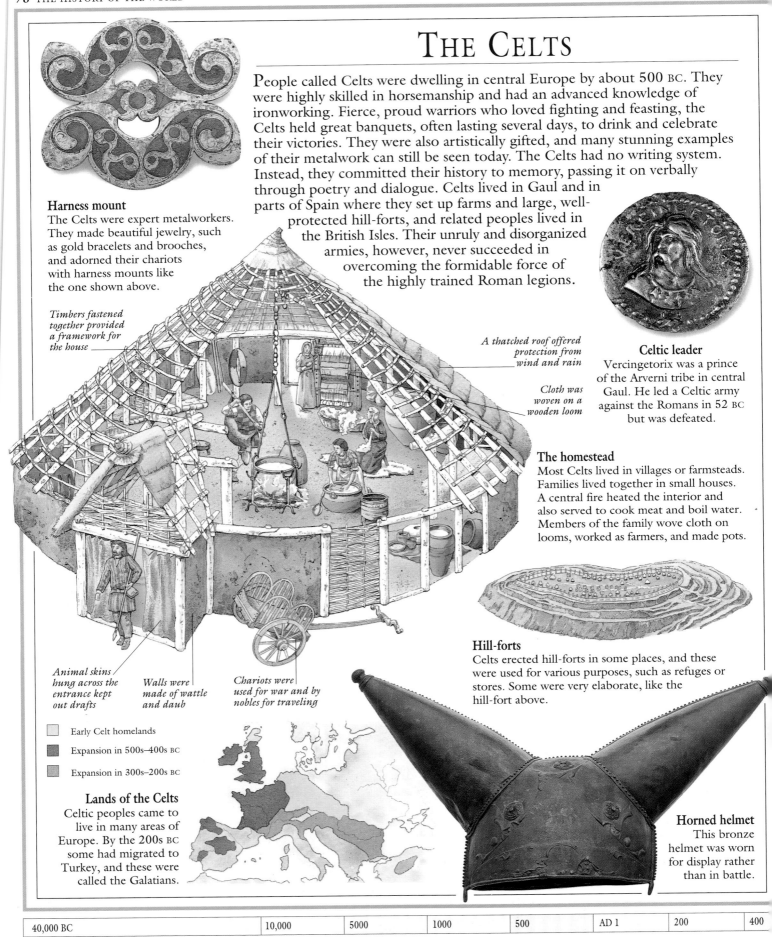

Harness mount
The Celts were expert metalworkers. They made beautiful jewelry, such as gold bracelets and brooches, and adorned their chariots with harness mounts like the one shown above.

Timbers fastened together provided a framework for the house

A thatched roof offered protection from wind and rain

Cloth was woven on a wooden loom

Celtic leader
Vercingetorix was a prince of the Arverni tribe in central Gaul. He led a Celtic army against the Romans in 52 BC but was defeated.

The homestead
Most Celts lived in villages or farmsteads. Families lived together in small houses. A central fire heated the interior and also served to cook meat and boil water. Members of the family wove cloth on looms, worked as farmers, and made pots.

Animal skins hung across the entrance kept out drafts

Walls were made of wattle and daub

Chariots were used for war and by nobles for traveling

Hill-forts
Celts erected hill-forts in some places, and these were used for various purposes, such as refuges or stores. Some were very elaborate, like the hill-fort above.

Early Celt homelands

Expansion in 500s–400s BC

Expansion in 300s–200s BC

Lands of the Celts
Celtic peoples came to live in many areas of Europe. By the 200s BC some had migrated to Turkey, and these were called the Galatians.

Horned helmet
This bronze helmet was worn for display rather than in battle.

40,000 BC		10,000	5000	1000	500	AD 1	200	400

60 BC
The First Triumvirate is formed in Rome

In 109 BC Italy was threatened by barbarian forces from Gaul and Germany. Several Roman armies were defeated. An ex-consul of humble birth, Gaius Marius, was re-elected, mobilized fresh armies, and completely destroyed the barbarians at Aquae Sextiae (102 BC) and Vercellae (101 BC). He entered politics but was unused to opposition, and in 88 BC was driven from Rome by the aristocrat L. Cornelius Sulla. Sulla strengthened senatorial powers and left to wage wars in Asia Minor.

Winning several victories, he came home in 82 BC to become dictator, an office with absolute power, but retired in 79 BC. Chaos followed as politicians competed for power. Finally, in 60 BC, three men united to restore order. They were Marcus Crassus, a wealthy financier with political ambitions, Gnaeus Pompeius, and a young man, Julius Caesar, destined to become one of the great men of the ancient world. They formed the First Triumvirate (rule by three men), with Caesar becoming consul in 59 BC.

THE ROMAN ARMY

For centuries the Roman army was made up of working men who gave their services voluntarily for particular wars. The first professional army was founded in c.104 BC. In Caesar's time the army consisted mainly of legions, the main first-line troops, all of whom were Roman citizens. Each legion had some 5,000 infantry and cavalry, together with mainly medical men, craftsmen, and others. Legionaries wore helmets and carried tall shields, and were armed with short swords and javelins.

Roman sword
The short sword, with its wooden or bone grip and double-edged blade, was an extremely effective stabbing weapon.

JULIUS CAESAR

80 BC First military service, in Turkey, where he wins civic crown for personal bravery

60 BC Caesar, with Gnaeus Pompeius and Marcus Crassus, forms First Triumvirate and is elected consul for 59 BC

58–50 BC Caesar campaigns in and conquers Gaul

49 BC Caesar crosses into Italy and precipitates civil war

45 BC Caesar appointed dictator for life

March 15 44 BC Caesar is assassinated in Rome

Julius Caesar
Caesar was a gifted orator, writer, soldier, and politician. In battle he displayed superb powers as commander, strategist, and organizer. He could sometimes be unscrupulous in the pursuit of his own interests.

45 BC
Caesar is master of the Roman world

As consul, Caesar introduced constructive reforms. Then, in a superbly masterminded eight-year campaign (58–50 BC), he conquered all Gaul and made it a Roman province. In 49 BC he returned home to receive rewards for his devoted troops and honor for himself, but he found himself declared a public enemy. So he marched on Rome, drove out his opponents, and became dictator. By 45 BC he was master of the Roman world. He continued to introduce reforms, such as updating the calendar, reshaping Roman law, and making the senate more democratic. Caesar was assassinated in 44 BC. Mark Antony, his friend, together with Octavian, his great-nephew and adopted son, avenged Caesar's death, and many leading Romans were killed. By 31 BC Octavian had become master of the Roman world, and in 27 BC he took the name Augustus, meaning "revered."

The assassination of Caesar
In 44 BC some senators plotted to murder Caesar, and on March 15 they stabbed him to death. But by murdering him they ensured his ideas would live, for his adopted son, Octavian, completed his work.

Friend of Caesar
In 31 BC Mark Antony quarreled with Octavian and fought him at the battle of Actium, which Antony lost. This portrait of Mark Antony is from a seal ring.

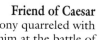

500 BC-AD 1 AMERICAS

New farming methods emerged in North America through the cultivation of locally grown plants. This new way of growing food, rather than gathering it, allowed the Adena people to flourish along the Ohio River valley. In Peru in South America, the development of the artistic Paracas culture marked an important transition between the earlier Chavín and later Nazca cultures.

Paracas vessel
Elaborate ceramics, such as this vessel in the shape of a trophy head, were often placed in graves with the dead for use in the next world.

Oculate Being
With its large eyes and extra limbs, this supernatural creature appears on many Paracas objects, including clothes and masks.

c.500 BC

Paracas culture flourishes in Peru

Between about 500 BC and AD 200, the rich and varied Paracas culture flourished on an isolated windswept spit of land south of Lima in Peru. The Paracas had a varied agriculture, cultivating corn, beans, peanuts, sweet potatoes, and yucca. They were superb embroiderers and weavers, using advanced techniques unknown elsewhere. Over 100 different shades of color have been identified on clothes discovered over 2,000 years later. Embroidered designs include human figures, birds, cats, foxes, and demons. The Paracas followed elaborate mummification and burial rituals. Dead bodies may have been dried or smoked to preserve them and placed in underground chambers along with textiles, false heads, and pottery items.

Desert tree
Carved into the desert hillside by the Paracas people, this candelabralike tree still overlooks the entrance to the modern Paracas harbor.

Smoke hole

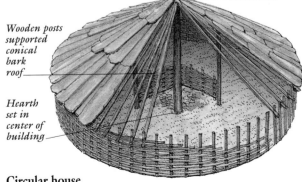

Wooden posts supported conical bark roof

Hearth set in center of building

Circular house
Adena houses were circular, ranging from 13–32 ft (4–10 m) in diameter. The walls were formed by closely spaced posts and a wickerwork type of paneling.

c.500 BC

Adena culture constructs burial mounds

Based along the Ohio River valley in the present-day United States, the people of the Adena culture subsisted on hunting, gathering, and some plant cultivation. They grew corn, beans, gourds, and sunflowers, and formed small communities in groups of dwellings. The Adena were the first people in the North American Midwest to build large earthen mounds in which important people were buried. These mounds hid simple clay-lined basins as well as large log tombs in which the bodies lay. Among the objects interred with the dead were copper bracelets, carved stone tablets, and tobacco pipes previously used for smoking.

40,000 BC		10,000	1000	AD 1	400	800	1200	1600	1800	2000

CHAPTER 6

1 – 400

THE DECLINE
OF THE ANCIENT WORLD

Roman horse armor

1-400
THE WORLD

THREE OF THE GREAT EMPIRES that dominate the classical world – the Han, Parthian, and Roman – fall apart during this period, leading to instability throughout Asia and Europe. In China, the end of the Han dynasty is marked by the division of the empire into three separate kingdoms, while the Parthian Empire is overthrown by the Sassanid dynasty, which strengthens Persian power and threatens Roman control of the region. Rome itself begins a long period of decline that leads to the splitting of the empire into halves and the creation of an eastern empire based on Constantinople. The new Christian religion becomes the official imperial religion.

The rise of new empires

As old empires decline, new empires are gradually created. In India, the Gupta dynasty bring peaceful and intelligent rule to the country, creating the most powerful nation in Asia. A golden age of art and literature flourishes. On the other side of the world, the Moche in Peru and the people of Tiahuanco in the Andes mountains develop artistically rich societies. In Central America, the Maya flourish, creating a highly developed, literate society that is mathematically and scientifically well in advance of anything known in Europe at the time.

NORTH AMERICA

c.100–200 The Hopewell culture flourishes in eastern North America

c.250 The Maya civilization of Central America enters its greatest age

c.100 On the Peruvian coast, the Moche civilization site at Sipan is begun

SOUTH AMERICA

ATLANTIC OCEAN

PACIFIC OCEAN

c.100 Beside Lake Titicaca, the city of Tiahuanaco begins to grow; its people travel over the lake on reed rafts

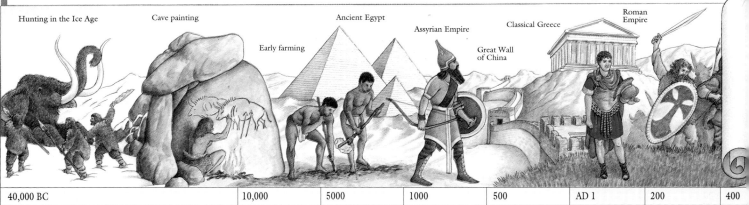

Hunting in the Ice Age

Cave painting

Early farming

Ancient Egypt

Assyrian Empire

Great Wall of China

Classical Greece

Roman Empire

| 40,000 BC | 10,000 | 5000 | 1000 | 500 | AD 1 | 200 | 400 |

180 After the death of Emperor Marcus Aurelius, the 150 years of Pax Romana, or "Roman peace," are over, and Rome's armies see battle more often

360s Huns from central Asia first invade Europe

ASIA

c.33 Jesus Christ, Jewish religious leader and founder of Christianity, dies by crucifixion in Israel

Leptis Magna

25 Eastern Han dynasty begins its rule in China

193 By command of Roman emperor Septimius Severus, imposing buildings are erected to beautify his hometown of Leptis Magna in Libya

Ganges

226 The Sassanid dynasty comes to power in Persia

c.350 In Sudan, the Kushite civilization of Meroe ends, possibly brought down by invasion from the kingdom of Aksum

376 The reign of Chandragupta II in India sees the Gupta Empire's greatest days

AFRICA

OCEANIA

c.300–400 Bantu peoples in southeast Africa grow cereal crops and begin to farm herds of cattle

INDIAN OCEAN

N

| 600 | 800 | 1000 | 1200 | 1400 | 1600 | 1700 | 1800 | 1900 | 2000 |

AD 1

100

AFRICA

17–24 Revolt of Tacfarinas, Numidian leader, against Roman government in North Africa

40 Mauretania (now northern Morocco and northwestern Algeria) annexed by Rome

61–63 Roman force explores the Nile Valley up into Sudan

c.100 Aksum becomes capital of major state in Eritrea northern Ethiopia

115 Revolt of Jewish community in Cyrenaica (northeastern Libya) against Roman administration

193–211 Libyan Septimius Severus is emperor of Rome*

The Roman amphitheater at Thysdrus (now El Djem) in Tunisia could seat 50,000 people

This Roman soldier's helmet protects head, face, and neck

ASIA

9–23 Rule of Wang Mang as emperor of China

25 Eastern Han dynasty begins its rule over China*

c.33 Jesus Christ, Jewish religious leader, crucified

c.50 Buddhism reaches China

Pottery storage jars like this were used in Israel and other countries

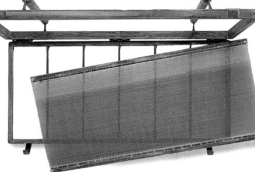
Paper mold; the papermaker dips the mold in and out of the vat and shakes it to settle the pulp on the mesh

☐ **c.105** Paper invented in China, perhaps by Cai Lun

☐ **c.120** In China Zhang Heng introduces the seismograph

c.120–62 Kushan king Kanishka rules large areas of northern India, Pakistan, Afghanistan, and central Asia

184–205 In China, rebellion by members of Yellow Turban sect greatly weakens Han dynasty

c.190 Rise of Hindu Chola kingdom near Tanjore, southern India

EUROPE

14 Death of Roman emperor Augustus*

43 Roman emperor Claudius invades Britain

60–61 Rebellion of Boudicca, queen of the Iceni, against Romans in Britain

64 Great Fire of Rome

68–69 Civil war in Roman Empire after Emperor Nero dies

c.80 Completion of Colosseum amphitheater in Rome

Romans enjoyed watching gladiators, usually slaves or criminals, fight in the Colosseum

116–17 Roman Empire reaches its greatest extent, under emperor Trajan (98–117)

122–38 Hadrian's Wall built to defend province of Britain

166–67 Roman Empire devastated by plague

180 Death of emperor Marcus Aurelius; end of Pax Romana*

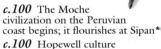
This pickax (now restored) was used by Roman soldiers

AMERICAS

c.1 El Mirador in northern Guatemala, perhaps the greatest early Maya city, is at its height

c.1 The growing city of Teotihuacan in the Valley of Mexico has a population of more than 40,000 people

c.50 Nazca culture flourishes in coastal Peru; the Nazca create vast, enigmatic lines and patterns in the desert

c.100 The Moche civilization on the Peruvian coast begins; it flourishes at Sipan*

c.100 Hopewell culture flourishes on upper Mississippi

c.100 Mogollon culture develops in southwestern United States; interesting painted pottery is produced*

c.100–200 Monte Alban center in Oaxaca, Mexico, at greatest extent of its power

Nazca arts are famous, including textiles, metalwork, and, most of all, their painted pottery

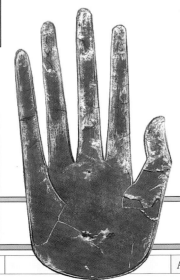
This artwork shows a larger-than-life hand, cut out of the mineral mica, found in a mound at a Hopewell site in Ohio, in the northeastern United States

OCEANIA

200

c.200 Roman emperor Septimius Severus strengthens frontier defenses in North Africa with chain of forts and long ditches

238 Revolt in Africa against Roman rule begins half century of unrest

This African adze is designed for shaving bark off poles for fences, huts, and ladders

Haniwa, clay objects such as this horse, were placed on grave mounds in Japan

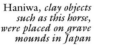

295–300 Emperor Diocletian reorganizes local government in North Africa

220 End of Han dynasty in China, followed by Three Kingdoms and Jin dynasty

226 End of Parthian power in Persian Empire: beginning of Sassanid dynasty under Ardashir I (226–41)*

260 Shapur I of Persia defeats Roman Emperor Valerian in battle; Valerian captured

212 Roman citizenship formally extended to all freeborn people within the empire

235–84 Long period of civil war and chaos in Roman Empire

271–76 Building of Aurelian walls around Rome

284–305 Diocletian is emperor of Rome; major reforms; forms "tetrarchy" of four emperors to rule the empire together*

Diocletian was a Roman soldier who made himself emperor in 284; he restored order and reformed the systems of government of the Empire

Maya writing, stamped on pottery here, bears no resemblance to any other known writing

c.200–375 First period of major construction at city of Tiahuanaco, near Lake Titicaca in Bolivia

c.250 In Guatemala, Honduras, and eastern Mexico, classic period of Maya civilization begins

300

c.300–400 Bantu cereal-cultivators in southeast Africa begin to develop herds of cattle

c.330–40 Beginning of conversion of kingdom of Aksum in Ethiopia-Eritrea to Christianity by Bishop Frumentius

c.350 End of Kushite civilization at Meroe; it is possibly brought down by invasion from kingdom of Aksum

397 Berber prince Gildo begins a major rebellion against Roman emperor Honorius*

A coin of the Libyan Roman emperor Septimius Severus; the wealth of Libya then came largely from wheat and olive oil

A Yue ware burial model of a dog in a pen, from China

c.320 Rise of Gupta Empire in Ganges Valley, India

360 Embassy from King Meghavarna of Sri Lanka reaches Gupta court; religious monument for Sri Lankan visitors is built

376 Beginning of reign of Chandragupta II; golden Gupta age

386 Beginning of era of north-south division in China (to 589)

399 Chinese Buddhist historian, Fa-hien, begins his journey through India

313 Christianity tolerated throughout Roman Empire

324 Constantine becomes sole emperor (western emperor in 312)

330 New city of Constantinople (now Istanbul) inaugurated on site of ancient Greek city of Byzantium in European Turkey

360s First invasions of Europe by Huns from central Asia

378 Romans defeated at Adrianople by Visigoths; Emperor Valens killed

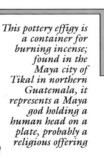

This pottery effigy is a container for burning incense; found in the Maya city of Tikal in northern Guatemala, it represents a Maya god holding a human head on a plate, probably a religious offering

This fragment of gold glass shows a family with the early Christian chi (X)-rho(P) symbol (made from the first letters of Christ's name in Greek)

c.375–600 City of Tiahuanaco continues to develop; eventually, 50,000 people live there

c.378 Rivalry between leading Maya cities Tikal and Uaxactún ends in invasion and capture of Uaxactún by Tikal, which goes on to great prosperity

c.300 Beginning of early eastern Polynesian culture

Small canoes such as this were used by the Polynesians for voyages between neighboring islands and for fishing; the main hull is made from a hollowed-out log

Central and southern Africa experienced the benefits of a developing iron technology, and certain areas also engaged in greater trading activities. The kingdom of Aksum, in the northeast, adopted the Christian religion in the fourth century, following the conversion of its king. The northern coastal areas of the continent, largely under Roman dominion, grew prosperous through trade and also produced one of the greatest of all Roman emperors, Septimius Severus.

Portrait on a coin
Septimius Severus was born in the city of Leptis (in modern Libya) and rose to become Roman emperor from 193 to 211.

Lion mosaic
North Africa became noted for its superb mosaics during the "Roman" period. Animals were a popular subject, like this realistic portrayal of a lion, from a fourth-century mosaic in Tunisia.

193

Septimius Severus is emperor of Rome

When the Romans destroyed Carthage in 146 BC, its land came under their control. They absorbed nearby states, and by the end of the first century AD Roman North Africa reached from Morocco, east to the Nile delta in Egypt. New cities were built, and trade and agriculture boomed. By the second century North Africa was supplying Rome with nearly two-thirds of its annual grain needs. The high point of Romanization was reached when a North African-born soldier, Septimius Severus, became emperor of Rome in 193. He donated money to developing cities, and planned to extend Roman citizenship to free men throughout the empire.

Roman ruins in Africa
The amphitheater at El Djem, in Tunisia, was built by the Romans in the third century.

c.397

Gildo revolts against Roman rule

In the 380s the Roman emperor Theodosius I (379–95) appointed a Berber chief, Gildo, as Count of Africa, effectively making him head of the Roman administration of the province of Africa. He ruled like a tyrant and in 397 decided to break links with Rome, cutting off African supplies of grain to Italy on which the Romans had depended for centuries. So the Romans sent an army of Gauls to Africa to remove the tyrannical Gildo from power. They defeated him, and he tried to escape by ship off the African coast but was captured and put to death.

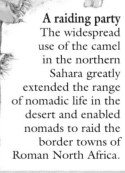

A raiding party
The widespread use of the camel in the northern Sahara greatly extended the range of nomadic life in the desert and enabled nomads to raid the border towns of Roman North Africa.

40,000 BC		10,000	5000	1000	500	AD 1	200	400

1-400 ASIA

The Parthian Empire in western Asia declined, and in the third century a new dynasty, the Sassanids, took over and revived Persian power, posing a serious threat to Roman Asian interests. Early in the same century, the restored Han dynasty of China fell after two centuries of weak rule. The Gupta dynasty in India flourished in the late fourth century.

Watchtower with moat
Tall towers were a popular feature of Chinese architecture in the Han period. They were built as lookout posts or pavilions, often with decorated roofs.

25
Eastern Han dynasty

The Western Han dynasty in China was brought to an end in 9 by Wang Mang, a relative by marriage of the last emperor. He was overthrown in 23, and in 25 the Han dynasty began to rule again. The capital was moved eastward from Chang'an to Luoyang, and the dynasty is known as the Eastern Han. Although not a prosperous time, this period witnessed some important inventions, including paper (c.105) and porcelain. The dynasty fell in about 220 following a civil war.

Dragons and toads
In c.120 Zhang Heng invented the seismograph, an instrument to indicate the features of earthquakes. During a tremor the dragons would open their jaws, releasing balls into the mouths of the toads below.

"TUMULUS PERIOD" IN JAPAN

In the third century, the Yayoi culture in Japan experienced a number of changes. The Iron Age was established, which led to better tools and more productive agriculture. More effective weapons and armor helped a growing aristocratic class to become more powerful, and the horse was domesticated, which allowed warriors to fight on horseback. Much of this change occurred in western central Japan, where elaborate burial sites for emperors and other important people were built in the form of chambers, constructed with enormous stone blocks, and covered by immense earth mounds, or tumuli, some reaching 120 ft (37 m) tall. The dead person was surrounded by his arms, spears, and mirrors. His helmet was placed near his head, with funerary pottery and pearl necklaces at his feet. Clay tomb models, called *haniwa*, were planted in the earth around the tumulus to protect the deceased from evil spirits.

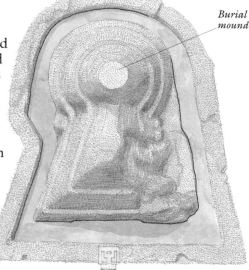

Burial mound

Keyhole burial mound
Tumuli for burying the dead were originally barrow-shaped; later they became round or square and finally some took the form of a keyhole. Each mound had a stone burial chamber containing one or more coffins and was surrounded by a water-filled moat.

Food for the dead
Model platters and bowls were placed inside the tombs. They were intended for use by the deceased in the next world.

CHRISTIANITY

In the first century AD Israel was ruled by the Romans, against the wishes of its people. Some looked to their God to send a leader to set them free. Then, about AD 30, a carpenter called Jesus began to preach. His teachings were popular, and he acquired many followers. But the religious leaders of the Jews felt threatened and had him tried (as a political danger) by the Roman governor, Pontius Pilate. He was found guilty and crucified around AD 33. Jesus' followers believed that he was the Messiah, or "Chosen one" – in Greek, "the Christ," from which derives the name of his religion. One man who at first regarded Jesus' teachings as unacceptable, then suddenly became converted, was a learned Jewish tentmaker from Tarsus in Turkey whose name was Saul. Better known to Christians as St. Paul, he gave the rest of his life to spreading the new faith and became one of its greatest leaders. At the time of Jesus' death, few people thought much about his crucifixion except his followers, who believed that he had risen from the dead. But before long his teachings were being spread around the Roman world, and in AD 313 Christianity was officially tolerated in the Roman Empire.

The symbol of Christianity
The Romans nailed the most serious criminals to crosses to die, so a cross was seen as a symbol of shame until Christ died on one. Then the cross became the symbol of the Christian faith.

The Bible
The Bible is Christianity's holy book. It contains the Old Testament – the Jewish scriptures – and the New Testament, written in the first century AD. Christians believe that the Bible is "the word of God."

THE STORY OF JESUS

Jesus was an Israeli Jew, born into a poor family living in the region of Galilee in northern Israel. He worked as a carpenter until he was in his 30s, when he gave up work and began to devote all of his time to preaching and healing the sick, traveling around the country on foot. Before long he had many disciples (followers) and picked twelve to be an inner circle, the apostles. His most famous teaching is called the Sermon on the Mount. It sets out a new code of behavior for men and women, based on love for God and for all people. He angered the Jewish establishment and they persuaded the Roman governor, Pontius Pilate, to put him on trial. It was a mockery; even Pilate is supposed to have said that he could find no fault in Jesus. But such was the clamor for his death that Pilate handed him over for crucifixion. Some of his followers who visited his tomb afterward claimed that he rose from the dead and later ascended to heaven.

Stained glass window
Christians think that Jesus (left, as a baby) was born in a stable in Bethlehem, not far from Jerusalem in Israel, while his parents were on a journey.

A church in Jerusalem
Because Christians call the groups of people who follow Jesus "the Church," the buildings built for them to meet in are called churches. They are often laid out in the shape of a cross. Some are tiny, some are vast and beautiful.

The last supper

On the night before he died, Jesus had a last supper with his disciples at which he shared bread and wine with them. Ever since then, Christians have shared bread and wine in a ceremony called the Eucharist, or Holy Communion. *Eucharist* is Greek for "thanksgiving." Usually, priests share the bread and wine with congregations in church during a service. This picture of the last supper is by the great Italian artist Leonardo da Vinci (1452–1519).

Communion cup
Christians practice the ceremonies of baptism and communion, following Jesus' instructions to do so. These ceremonies, and some others, are called sacraments.

The divisions of Christianity

The history of Christianity has been characterized by centuries of division among its believers, with persecutions, martyrdoms, bloodshed, and much else done in the name of God. Even before Emperor Constantine granted toleration to Christians in the Roman Empire in 313, groups had broken away from mainstream belief, and these multiplied as time went on. For many centuries, Christianity was divided into two main groups: the Roman Catholic church in western Europe, headed by the Pope in Rome, and the Eastern Orthodox, centered on Constantinople and dominated by the Byzantine emperor until 1453, when Constantinople fell to the Turks and the eastern church leadership was taken over by the Russians in Moscow. Then, in Europe, various reformers, such as Luther and Calvin, broke away from the authority of the Pope in Rome. They and their followers came to be known as Protestants. They were forerunners of the evangelical groups of the 17th and 18th centuries and the Protestant churches of today. This process continues, so that there are many different churches. In spite of all these divisions, Christianity has spread to almost every country on earth. Today, about 30 percent of the world's people call themselves Christian.

The water of baptism
In a Christian baptism, water symbolizes the spiritual cleansing of the believer's soul. This baptism is taking place in Mozambique in Africa. Christianity is spreading fastest in sub-Saharan Africa and in Asian countries such as China and South Korea.

Pope John Paul II
The head of the Roman Catholic church, which numbers 900 million people, is the Pope, based in Rome.

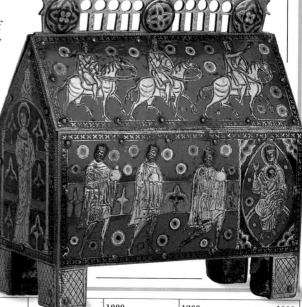

A casket made to hold relics
In the Roman Catholic and Eastern Orthodox traditions, Christians who have been especially close to God may be named saints after they die. Many Christians ask them for help, believing that the saints can ask God to aid others. Certain objects called relics are thought to have healing power because they are linked to saints, or to Jesus, or his mother Mary.

| 600 | 800 | 1000 | 1200 | 1400 | 1600 | 1800 | 1900 | 2000 |

c.224
Ardashir founds Sassanid dynasty in Persia

In 248 BC, the nomadic Parthian people entered Persia where they established a powerful empire. Around 224 AD, the last Parthian king was killed by one of his soldiers, Ardashir, a member of the noble Sassanid family. Ardashir seized the Parthian throne and founded the Sassanid dynasty and empire. He rebuilt the ancient Persian Empire by conquering neighboring territories, and Persia became a major threat to Roman interests in Asia. The Sassanid court at the city of Ctesiphon subsequently became the focus for a brilliant culture. Scholars studied medicine, astronomy, and philosophy. Arts and crafts flourished, and games like chess and polo became popular. King Shapur I, Ardashir's son, erected fine buildings and may have ordered the construction of the great palace at Ctesiphon, the remains of which can still be seen today. The Sassanid dynasty finally collapsed with the onslaught of the Muslim Arabs around 642.

Leopard on a lead
This fragment of Egyptian tapestry dates from the sixth century. It shows two hunters, each holding a leopard on a lead. Leopards were often captured by the Sassanids and used for hunting wild animals.

Defeat of the Roman emperor
Ardashir's son Shapur I was probably the most outstanding of the Sassanid rulers. He is well remembered for his defeat and capture of the Roman emperor Valerian at the Battle of Edessa in 260. This famous stone relief shows Valerian kneeling before Shapur's horse and begging for mercy.

The Sassanids hunted lions, as well as wild boar and other game

ZOROASTRIANISM

Zoroastianism is an ancient religion based on the teachings of the sixth century BC Persian prophet, Zoroaster. It was the state religion of three successive Persian dynasties, the Achaemenid, the Parthian, and the Sassanid. According to Zoroaster, humans are free to choose between good – the wise lord Ahura Mazda – and the spirit of ultimate evil – Angra Mainyu. In their emphasis on the idea of heaven and hell, resurrection and final judgment, the teachings of Zoroaster have had a profound effect on later religions such as Judaism, Christianity, and Islam. Many Zoroastrians left Iran in the eighth century and settled in northwest India, where they are still known as Parsis. Today, Zoroastrianism is practiced all over the world.

King coin
This coin was issued by the Sassanid king Hormizd II, who reigned between 302–309.

Fire temple
Zoroastrians believe that fire is linked with purity. This fire temple of the Sassanid period is at Takht-i Saulaiman, in modern western Iran. The complex housed a sacred fire and was built around a deep lake at the top of a small hill.

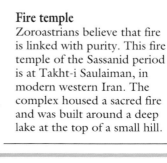

The pursuits of kings
Hunting was a favorite sport of kings. Special hunting parks were laid out, where the king and his nobles enjoyed the pleasures of the chase. This beautiful silver dish shows a royal lion hunt. It might have been used at a banquet during the Sassanid Empire.

THE GUPTA DYNASTY

After the disintegration of the Kushan Empire, northern India was made up of a number of independent kingdoms and republics. In 320, Chandragupta I (not to be confused with the Mauryan ruler of six centuries earlier), ruler of the kingdom of Magadha, enlarged his empire by conquering neighboring territories and by marrying a princess from a powerful clan. His son Samudragupta, carried the conquests further north and east, opening up immense trade potential. Chandragupta II, who ruled from 376–415, was a great patron of the arts, and it was under his intelligent rule that India became the greatest Asian country of its time. Successive Gupta kings maintained their great empire, which began to crumble only after the death of the last Gupta king in 467.

Extending the empire
The Gupta kings ruled most of India from their heartland in the kingdom of Magadha. The Guptas ran the empire as a group of semi-independent kingdoms which owed them allegiance.

Seat of learning
A large number of fine universities flourished during the Gupta age. The Buddhist university at Nalanda, shown here, attracted students from all over Asia. At institutions such as these, Indian scholars studied and taught divinity, philosophy, and medicine.

Surya
The sun god Surya was a god from the Vedic age (1500–500 BC). During the Gupta period, however, Surya came to represent the Buddha as the sun that illuminates the universe. This sandstone statue of Surya as Buddha comes from the Mathura area.

Makara
The fabulous, half-aquatic Makara was one of the most popular mythical animals in Indian art. This stone relief formed part of a frieze on one of many brick temples built in northern India during and after the Gupta period.

Ajanta caves
Over 30 Buddhist cave temples and monastic halls were carved into the Ajanta hills in the northwest Deccan in India, over a period of a thousand years. This palace scene is one of many frescoes painted during the Gupta age, which appear all over the temple complex.

Glory of the Guptas
The age of the Guptas is often called a "golden age." Architecture, literature, and art thrived during this calm and plentiful time. Many wonderful palaces and temples were built, including the stupa (a domed shrine) at Sarnath, where Buddha gave his first lectures. Kalidasa, one of India's greatest poets and playwrights, wrote his best verse during the time of Kumaragupta (415–55). Music and dance developed into their classical Indian forms, and elaborate Hindu and Buddhist sculptures became models for later Indian art. The Sanskrit language was firmly established, and used not only for religious purposes, but also as a medium for a classical literature, understood by educated elites all over India.

Queen Juno

Romans subjects were allowed to worship any god as long as they also paid homage to the official state gods and to the genius, or guardian spirit, of the emperor. King of the state gods was Jupiter. His wife, Juno, is seen in this clay figure enthroned with her symbol, the peacock. People made sacrifices of food, drink, and animals to seek the gods' favor.

1-400 EUROPE

These centuries saw the growth of the Roman Empire, as the Romans brought their unique culture to a huge area of Europe. But before 400 the empire was clearly too large. Emperor Diocletian divided it into two more manageable parts; Emperor Constantine moved the capital to Constantinople (Istanbul) in the east. But frontiers were often attacked by foreigners eager for Rome's wealth.

c.14

Peace and prosperity for Rome

During his long reign (27 BC–AD 14) Emperor Augustus brought peace and order to the Roman Empire. He secured the boundaries at the rivers Rhine, Danube, and Euphrates, posting legions of troops along each frontier. He continued the reforming work begun by his great-uncle Julius Caesar, erecting fine new buildings in Rome and organizing road construction. The period between the rule of Augustus, who died in AD 14, and the death of Marcus Aurelius in 180, is often called the Pax Romana (Roman peace), a time in which few major disturbances jolted the feeling of security within the empire's borders, despite some dramatic events, such as a great fire at Rome in 64 that destroyed much of the city. Some of the emperors who succeeded Augustus were outstanding. Trajan (97–117) waged successful wars against Rome's enemies. Hadrian (117–138) limited the empire's size to keep it manageable, extensively touring the provinces to ensure they were well governed.

In the triclinium, or dining room, people reclined on couches as they ate

Marble columns lined walkways in the elegant garden, or peristyle

Wealthy Romans ate great delicacies, such as ostrich, flamingo with dates, and roast parrot

Emperor Augustus

Augustus (right) was given the powers of an absolute monarch, but he presented himself as the preserver of republican traditions. He treated the Senate, or state council, with great respect and successfully reduced the political power of the army by retiring many soldiers, but giving them land or money to keep their loyalty. Augustus also tried to encourage more devotion to family life among his subjects.

Town house

Bustling cities were the heart of Roman life. A town hall and marketplace, or forum, lay at their center. Culture and entertainment thrived in schools, libraries, theatres, and public baths. Most people lived in poor-quality rented housing on streets with shops and inns. Blocks of apartments five stories high, without water or adequate drainage, were covered in graffiti. Wealthy Romans, by contrast, lived in a private town house, or *domus*. They bought slaves, often captives taken in wars, to do household tasks.

40,000 BC		10,000	5000	1000	500	AD 1	200	400

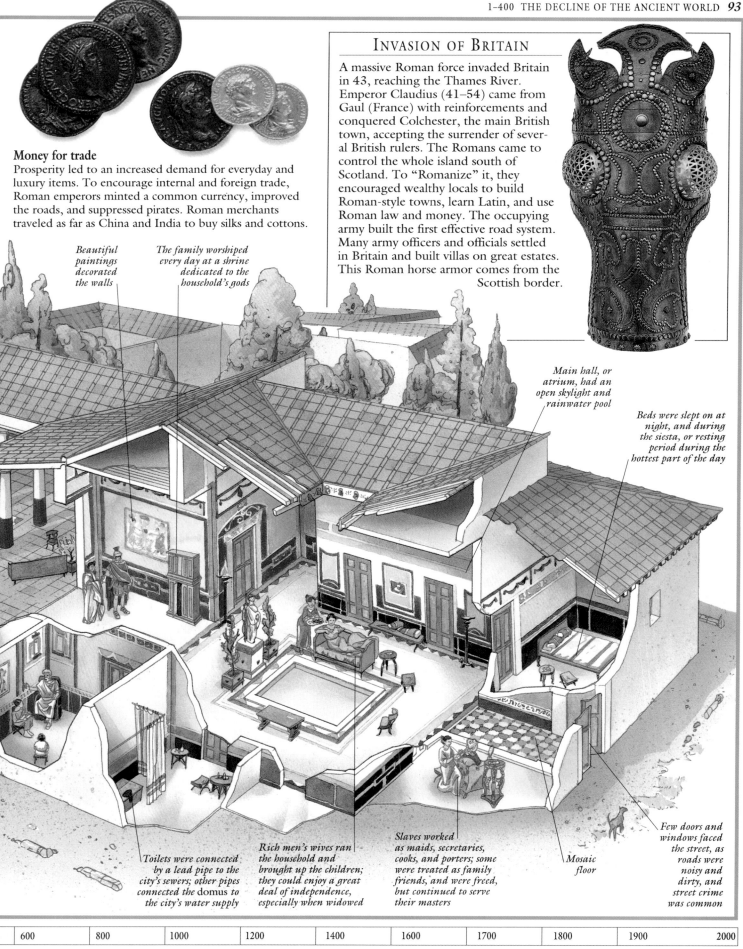

Money for trade

Prosperity led to an increased demand for everyday and luxury items. To encourage internal and foreign trade, Roman emperors minted a common currency, improved the roads, and suppressed pirates. Roman merchants traveled as far as China and India to buy silks and cottons.

INVASION OF BRITAIN

A massive Roman force invaded Britain in 43, reaching the Thames River. Emperor Claudius (41–54) came from Gaul (France) with reinforcements and conquered Colchester, the main British town, accepting the surrender of several British rulers. The Romans came to control the whole island south of Scotland. To "Romanize" it, they encouraged wealthy locals to build Roman-style towns, learn Latin, and use Roman law and money. The occupying army built the first effective road system. Many army officers and officials settled in Britain and built villas on great estates. This Roman horse armor comes from the Scottish border.

Beautiful paintings decorated the walls

The family worshiped every day at a shrine dedicated to the household's gods

Main hall, or atrium, had an open skylight and rainwater pool

Beds were slept on at night, and during the siesta, or resting period during the hottest part of the day

Toilets were connected by a lead pipe to the city's sewers; other pipes connected the domus to the city's water supply

Rich men's wives ran the household and brought up the children; they could enjoy a great deal of independence, especially when widowed

Slaves worked as maids, secretaries, cooks, and porters; some were treated as family friends, and were freed, but continued to serve their masters

Mosaic floor

Few doors and windows faced the street, as roads were noisy and dirty, and street crime was common

600	800	1000	1200	1400	1600	1700	1800	1900	2000

At the baths
News, views, and gossip about emperors and politicians were exchanged at public baths. These elaborate buildings had progressively hotter rooms that were dry, like a sauna, or humid, like a Turkish bath, as well as cold plunge pools and heated swimming pools. Floors were raised on pillars to allow hot air from fires to pass under them, and heat the pools and rooms. After their bath, people could play ball-games in the yard, have a massage, or buy snacks. Men and women bathed separately.

180
Roman Empire begins decline

The death of Roman emperor Marcus Aurelius in 180 marked the end of a long period of peace and stability within the empire. His son and heir, Commodus, was totally unfit to rule, spending most of his time pursuing his favorite pastimes, such as competing in contests with professional gladiators. He was strangled by a wrestler in 192 and left no obvious heir. After a power struggle, an African-born general, Septimius Severus, became emperor in 193 and reigned well for 18 years. After his death more than 40 people, one after another or simultaneously, seized the throne in nearly 80 years. Some emperors lasted only a few months before being murdered or deposed. During this period of instability, European and Asian enemies challenged Rome's power on many occasions. In 260 Emperor Valerian was defeated by the Persians at the Battle of Edessa in Turkey. He was forced to crawl on his hands and knees before the Persian king and was then thrown into a Persian prison.

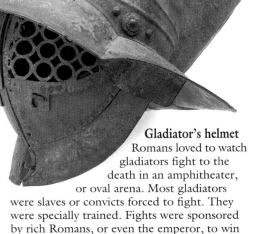

Gladiator's helmet
Romans loved to watch gladiators fight to the death in an amphitheater, or oval arena. Most gladiators were slaves or convicts forced to fight. They were specially trained. Fights were sponsored by rich Romans, or even the emperor, to win popularity. A wounded gladiator could ask for mercy. If the crowd supported him, he was spared; if they turned their thumbs down and shouted "Iugula!" the victor killed him.

284
Diocletian restores order

Diocletian was almost 40 when, in 284, he was chosen to be emperor by the Roman army he commanded in Turkey. He immediately had to deal with invasions and rebellions, and in 286 he decided the empire was too large for one person to rule alone. He divided it into two, a western half controlled by Maximian, the general in command of Gaul (France), and an eastern half controlled by himself. In 292, two more commanders, Constantius and Galerius, were chosen to rule subsections. These deputies were given the title Caesar, while Diocletian and Maximian held the title Augustus. Order was restored for a time. Diocletian set up his government at Nicomedia, in Turkey, realizing that the most wealthy and vital part of the empire lay in the east. He stabilized the empire's finances and reorganized the army and law. In 305 he retired "to grow cabbages," as he said, in his native Croatia.

On the road
One of the most durable aspects of the empire was its roads, first made by and for the army, although much used by imperial messengers and traders. Brilliantly surveyed and engineered, they took the most direct route, often running perfectly straight. Expertly constructed bridges carried them through hills and across rivers.

Board of emperors
This statue shows Diocletian and his co-emperors united as one. The two junior and two senior emperors are sculpted identically to prove their equality.

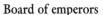

40,000 BC		10,000	5000	1000	500	AD 1	200	400

BYZANTINE CIVILIZATION

Diocletian was succeeded in 305 by his co-rulers, Constantius and Galerius. Constantius soon died, and Constantine, his son, took power over the whole Roman Empire by 324. That year Constantine moved the capital from Rome to the town of Byzantium in the eastern empire, founding what is called the Byzantine Empire, which lasted until 1453. In six years, he built a fine new city at Byzantium, later called Constantinople. He had granted toleration to Christians in 313, and Constantinople was a city of Christian worship and great churches. Constantine died in 337. Of his successors, only Theodosius I (388–395) kept control of the whole empire. When he died, it was divided between his sons into east and west. The west was ravaged by invaders, but in the east Byzantine civilization thrived under two excellent emperors: Theodosius II (408–50) built a great wall to protect Constantinople; Anastasius I (491–518) overhauled the empire's finances.

Emperor Constantine
An imaginative politician, Constantine realized the commercial potential of a new center in the eastern empire. Constantinople, on the border of Europe and Asia, became the crossing point for trade routes between the two continents, and grew extremely rich.

Plight of the poor
To support the army and luxurious court, Constantine followed Diocletian's policy of high taxation. If the wealthy still bought ornate jewels, most people became poorer. Big cities, the centers of traditional Roman life, declined as artisans and merchants were poverty-stricken. Farmers could not escape heavily taxed farms, as the law demanded they stay on the land to ensure the food supply.

Semiprecious stone pendants hang from gold brooch

Cameo, or profile of owner's head

New Rome
The official name of Constantinople was New Rome, formally founded by Constantine in May 330 amid great celebrations, including spectacular games in the new stadium. Treasures from all over the empire, like the gold figure above, decorated new buildings. The citizens preserved Greek and Roman culture: Greek books filled the libraries, and magistrates practiced Roman law.

Christian art
Constantinople was a Christian city from the time of its foundation, and the emperor was regarded as head of the Christian church. Religion was central to Byzantine life. People sought the church's blessing for many everyday activities, and all art, architecture, and entertainment was intended to glorify God. Popular Byzantine art forms, such as the mosaic, were widely copied. This gilded mosaic from Venice shows the biblical hero, Noah.

Objects of devotion
Representations of Christ and of the Virgin Mary in sculpture or painting were worshiped in churches, public places, and at home. The artists did not try to make these "icons" look original but copied conventional poses and colors most beautifully.

1-400 Americas

Many civilizations flourished in the Americas during this period. In the 200s the Maya people of Mexico and parts of Central America began a great age of expansion and cultural development. Nearby, the hilltop city of Monte Albán in Mexico, the great Oaxaca center, reached the peak of its power and importance. In South America the Moche civilization settled in a new site on the Peruvian coast at Sipan, one of the richest archeological sites in South America. At Tiahuanaco in Bolivia, many impressive public buildings were begun at this time.

Pottery treasures
Moche potters created one of the finest ceramic traditions in the world. These red clay figurines were found at Sipan.

c.100
The Moche flourish at Sipan

The Moche civilization controlled a strip of some 250 miles (400 km) along the north coast of Peru. They were skilled farmers and cut canals to irrigate their land, kept their water channels clean, and introduced fertilizers in the form of guano (bird excrement). They became rich and built pyramidlike structures called *huacas*. The largest of these was the Huaca del Sol, which stood more than 135 ft (41 m) high. One huaca was built at Sipan on the coast. The Moche were very great artists. Their amazing pottery was produced without a potter's wheel, and they were the first South American potters to produce clay objects from molds. Their knowledge of gold metal working was amazingly advanced. In 1987 the tomb of two lords was uncovered in the pyramid at Sipan, together with many gold objects.

Man and beast
Very vivid images of Moche life appear on bottles and jugs, like this one of a jaguar attacking a man. Most Moche pottery is decorated with red, white, or earth-colored designs, and the subject matter ranges from gods to owls and serpents.

Monster fish
This scene taken from a Moche vase shows a priest or demon struggling with a fish monster.

Mourning bowls
Clan ancestors and mythical beings decorated the bowls.

c.100
The Mogollon potters

The Mogollon were farming people living chiefly in the highlands of the southwestern United States. They were neighbors of the Anasazi people. They lived in villages in houses built half underground with roofs made of stone and mud. The Mogollon were famous for their superb painted pottery, and the best potters, usually women, were the Mimbres potters who lived along the banks of the Mimbres River in New Mexico. Their bowls were highly valued and were often buried with their owners. During burial, a hole was punched in the bottom of the bowl, perhaps to release the spirits of the painted figures.

40,000 BC	10,000	1000	AD 1	400	800	1200	2000

CHAPTER 7

400 - 800

RELIGIOUS WORLDS

Tomb guardian from the Chinese Tang dynasty

400-800
The World

FOUR RELIGIOUS TRADITIONS dominate the world between 400 and 800. In Asia, Hinduism, the world's oldest religion, remains the principal faith in India, while Buddhism, a newer Indian religion, continues to spread throughout China and reaches into Japan. In Europe, Christianity struggles to survive outside the Byzantine Empire, as barbarian peoples move from Central Asia and overrun the western Roman Empire. These people worship their own gods, but gradually Christian missionaries begin to convert them and reestablish Christianity as the major European religion.

A new religion

In the early 600s, a new religion, Islam, begins in Arabia. Inspired by their new faith, the Arabs set out both east and west to conquer and convert as much of the world as possible. As they move toward India and across North Africa, they create brilliant civilizations with great centers of art and learning, which influence the culture of the people they conquer. Not all the world is affected by these four religions. In the Americas, people practice their own religions and build magnificent, huge, temple-pyramids and ceremonial centers to their gods. Much of Africa, too, continues to follow old religious beliefs and practices.

ALASKA

c.500 Thule people from Siberia in Asia reach Alaska

NORTH AMERICA

Mississippi

500s Hopewell people living along the banks of the Mississippi River build many burial mounds

MEXICO

MAYA EMPIRE

432 St. Patrick introduces Christianity to Ireland; he is also credited with driving all snakes from its shores

c.600 The Maya use a complex form of picture writing; they also develop an advanced calendar

c.650 The Pyramid of the Sun is the center of the civilization of Teotihuacan in Mexico; this civilization is the mightiest in the Americas before the Spanish conquest

Andes

PERU

BOLIVIA

SOUTH AMERICA

ATLANTIC OCEAN

PACIFIC OCEAN

c.600 The god of the Gateway of the Sun in Tiahuanaco is made from andesite and sandstone; these materials are used to make many sculptures

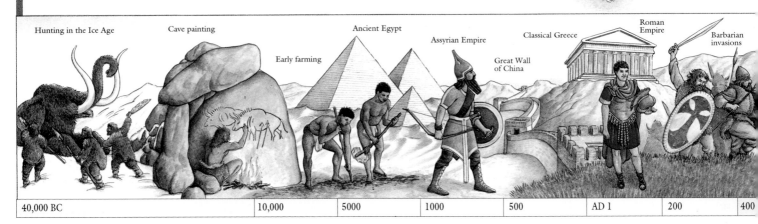

Hunting in the Ice Age · Cave painting · Early farming · Ancient Egypt · Assyrian Empire · Great Wall of China · Classical Greece · Roman Empire · Barbarian invasions

40,000 BC		10,000	5000	1000	500	AD 1	200	400

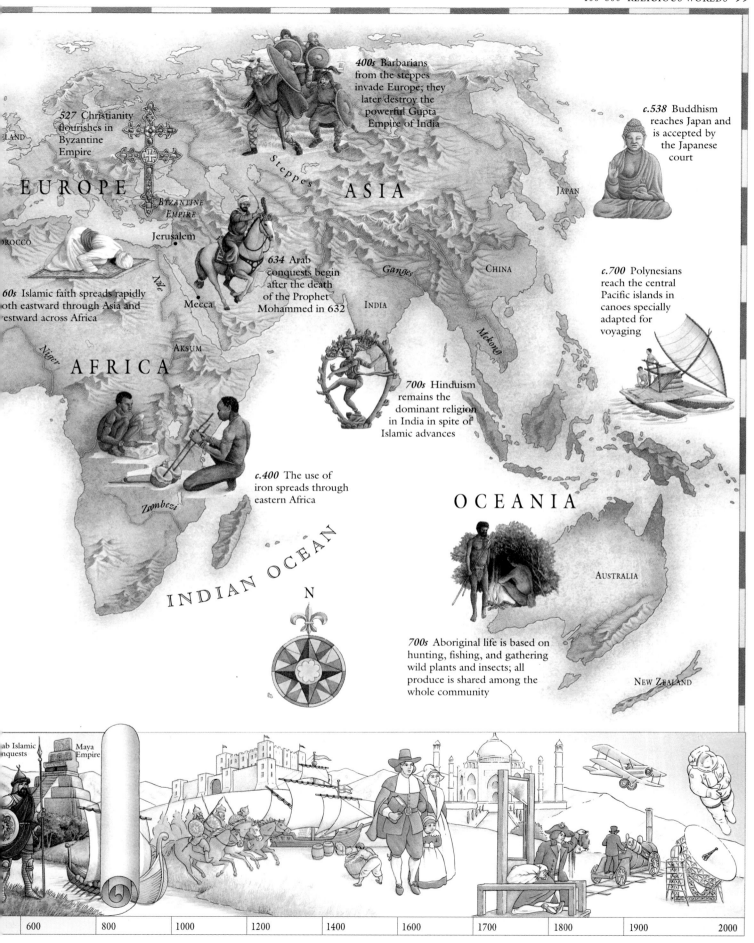

400s Barbarians from the steppes invade Europe; they later destroy the powerful Gupta Empire of India

c.538 Buddhism reaches Japan and is accepted by the Japanese court

527 Christianity flourishes in Byzantine Empire

EUROPE

Byzantine Empire

ASIA

JAPAN

Jerusalem

Steppes

634 Arab conquests begin after the death of the Prophet Mohammed in 632

CHINA

Ganges

INDIA

Nile

Mecca

Mekong

c.700 Polynesians reach the central Pacific islands in canoes specially adapted for voyaging

60s Islamic faith spreads rapidly oth eastward through Asia and estward across Africa

Niger

AKSUM

AFRICA

700s Hinduism remains the dominant religion in India in spite of Islamic advances

c.400 The use of iron spreads through eastern Africa

Zambezi

OCEANIA

INDIAN OCEAN

N

AUSTRALIA

700s Aboriginal life is based on hunting, fishing, and gathering wild plants and insects; all produce is shared among the whole community

NEW ZEALAND

ab Islamic nquests

Maya Empire

| 600 | 800 | 1000 | 1200 | 1400 | 1600 | 1700 | 1800 | 1900 | 2000 |

400

500

AFRICA

c.400 Use of iron spreads through eastern Africa

c.400 Christianity in the Aksum Empire in northeastern Africa becomes more widespread*

In 800 Christianity was flourishing in Aksum; this illustration from a contemporary manuscript shows a lively Noah's Ark

c.500 The Ghanaian Empire becomes most important power in West Africa*

525 King Kaleb of Aksum conquers Yemen in southern Arabia; he builds many churches

c.550–600 Nubians in Sudan, northeastern Africa, become Christian

Aksum was a rich nation and its king lived in some style; this crown studded with precious stone

ASIA

Padmapani was an Indian god worshiped during the rule of the Gupta dynasty; he was known as the lotus bearer

c.400 Gupta Empire grows until it stretches across the whole width of India

489 Large Buddhist temples built in China; Buddhists also use cave temples

The style of this sleeping Japanese Buddha was influenced by Korean Buddhist art

[1] **c.500** Indian mathematicians introduce the zero (0)

c.500–15 The Huns, a nomadic central Asian people, destroy the powerful Gupta Empire of India

c.538 Buddhism reaches Japan, and slowly spreads throughout the country*

570 Mohammed, the Prophet of Islam, is born in Mecca

580s Wen di, the first Sui emperor, reunites divided Chinese empire

595 Indian mathematicians use decimal system

EUROPE

410 Alaric the Goth, king of the Germanic tribe of Visigoths, sacks Rome*

432 St. Patrick introduces Christianity to Ireland

445 Attila the Hun attacks western Europe

c.450 Saxons from Germany begin to invade Britain

451 Attila defeated at Châlons*

476 Germanic invader Odoacer expels Romulus Augustus, last emperor of Rome, and takes control of the city

This beautiful eagle-shaped fibula or brooch was made by the Visigoths

527–65 Reign of Justinian, Byzantine emperor; he tries to reunite the eastern and western branches of the Christian church which are bitterly divided*

529 St. Benedict founds a monastery at Monte Cassino, south of Rome

529–34 Justinian's Codes of Law

552–53 Monks smuggle silkworms to Constantinople from China; start of important Byzantine silk industry

563–97 St. Columba comes from Ireland to spread Christian religion in Scotland

597 Mission of St. Augustine to England to convert the Anglo-Saxons to Christianity*

Justinian (right) built the church of Hagia Sophia in Constantinople (below); it later became a mosque, and minarets (slender towers) were added

AMERICAS

This Zapotec urn from Mexico contains the ashes of the dead; urns were placed inside the tomb

c.400 Zapotec state with its capital at Monte Alban flourishes in southern Mexico

OCEANIA

Thule people traveled by canoe

c.500 Thule people move into Alaska

c.500 Hopewell culture in northern America builds elaborate burial mounds, makes pottery, and uses iron weapons

500s Polynesians, originally from southeast Asia, settle in Hawaiian Islands and Easter Island

500s Polynesians continue to navigate eastward*

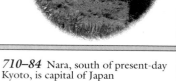

600

640–41 Caliph Omar, a successor to Mohammed as Islamic leader, conquers Egypt

c.640–711 Arabs, carrying the Muslim faith, expand across northern Africa

642 Arabs erect first mosque in al-Fustat, new capital of Muslim Egypt

652 Christian Nubians and Arabs in Egypt agree that Aswan on Nile should mark southern limit of Arab expansion

697–98 Arabs destroy Byzantine city at Carthage in North Africa; new city of Tunis built nearby

The Grand Canal in China provided a major trading route

c.605–10 Chinese build Grand Canal to link Yangtze with Chang'an

618 Tang dynasty begins in China*

626 Tang court adopts Buddhism

632 Death of Mohammed

634 Beginning of the Arab Empire*

645–784 Japanese court imitates Chinese form of government

646–700 Political and social reforms (Taika) take place in Japan

c.650 Revelations of Mohammed are written; they become the Koran

661–750 The Muslim Omayyads rule in Damascus, Syria

c.600 Beginning of an important period of art and literature in Ireland

c.602 Slavic tribes begin settlement of the Balkans

664 Synod of Whitby in England; Roman Christianity chosen in preference to Celtic teachings

c.670 Syrian chemist, Callinicus, invents Greek fire, a highly inflammable liquid used by the Byzantine army in battle; first used in the battle of Cyzicus c.673

c.675 Bulgars, nomadic people from the Russian steppes, settle in lands south of the Danube

The Book of Kells written c.800 was so called because it was kept at St. Columba's abbey at Kells in Ireland; it is one of the finest illuminated manuscripts of the period

Fragment of a Maya jade pendant

The Maya Pyramid of the Magician at Uxmal in the Yucatan peninsula of Mexico

c.600 Tiahuanaco civilization begins in Bolivia*

c.600 Height of Maya civilization

c.600 Rise of Huari in Peru*

c.650 Hopewell people established along the upper Mississippi River*

c.650 Teotihuacan in Mexico thrives as an important trade center*

700

c.788 Idris, Arab chief, becomes ruler in Morocco

The city of Moulay Idris in Morocco is named for the eighth-century Arab chieftain

This warrior on horseback is a good example of Tang pottery; the arts flourished during the Tang period

710–84 Nara, south of present-day Kyoto, is capital of Japan

711 Omayyads conquer Sind and found first Muslim state in India

751 Arabs win battle of Talas River, Central Asia; Islam comes to China

762 Abbasid dynasty ruling Iraq makes Baghdad its capital*

786–809 Reign of Harun–al–Rashid, greatest Abbasid ruler

794 Heian-kyo (Kyoto) becomes capital of Japan

794–1185 Heian period in Japan; increased independence from China

715 Muslim forces conquer most of Spain; only the mountainous north, home of the Basque people, remains independent

732 Charles Martel, king of the Franks, defeats Muslims at Poitiers in France, stopping Muslim advance northward

768 Charlemagne becomes king of the Franks*

784–96 Offa, king of Mercia in central England, builds defensive dike between England and Wales

787 Vikings make their first raids on the coasts of Britain

This painting in St. Alban's cathedral, England, shows Offa, king of Mercia

A Teotihuacan stone face; it could be a ritual mask or part of an incense burner

c.700 Rise of Mississippi culture in the Mississippi river basin; flat-topped mounds built as temple bases

c.700–900 In eastern Arizona, Pueblo people live in houses above ground for the first time

c.750–800 Collapse of Teotihuacan civilization in Mexico

Polynesian peoples believed that every occupation was looked after by a god or spirit; this wooden canoe god from the Cook Islands was thought to bring good fortune to fishermen

c.700 Easter Islanders begin to build stone platforms which form part of ceremonial enclosures

c.700 First Polynesians settle in the Cook Islands

| 600 | 800 | 1000 | 1200 | 1400 | 1600 | 1700 | 1800 | 1900 | 2000 |

400-800 AFRICA

Slaying the dragon
Murals illustrating scenes from the Bible and episodes from the lives of saints were a common feature of churches in the area. This mural, from a church near Lake Tana to the west of Lalibela, shows St. George slaying the dragon.

No single society dominated the history of Africa during this period. In the northeast, the powerful kingdom of Aksum spread Christianity throughout the region and grew rich from trade across the Red Sea. In the 600s Muslim Arab armies invaded the north coast and started to spread the new religion of Islam. Further south, across the Sahara, the powerful West African kingdom of Ghana prospered. Arab writers later called Ghana "the land of gold" because of its fabulous wealth. In the far south, less developed countries flourished as their peoples became increasingly skilled in the working of iron to make tools and weapons.

400s

Christianity grows in the Aksum Empire

The Aksum Empire, on the borders of the Red Sea in northeast Africa, was founded in the second century. The people of Aksum originally worshiped their own gods, but in the early 300s one of their rulers, King Ezana, became Christian. By the end of the 400s, most of the country had adopted the new religion, which then spread

slowly to neighboring countries. Christianity has flourished in the area ever since, and many remarkable churches were built, most notably that of St. George in Lalibela which was hewn from solid rock. Aksum was a major trading state, and traded as far afield as Egypt, Arabia, Persia, and India. The empire remained the most powerful state in the region until the mid-600s, when it went into decline as a result of the expansion of Arab Islamic influence.

Mural in the rock
This mural was cut into the rock face of an Ethiopian church near Lake Tana.

c.500

The rise of Ghana

The kingdom of Ghana lay between the Upper Niger and Senegal rivers in West Africa. Its prosperity came chiefly from the gold mined in its valleys. This was exported in the form of gold dust, first to local tribes, and later across the Sahara caravan routes, in return for copper, cotton, and salt. The Ghanaian capital was at Kumbi Saleh, a city of two linked towns. Powerful kings lived in the royal palace there and were buried with food and drink on its grounds in earth mounds.

Stone obelisk
More than 100 obelisks (stelae) were erected at Aksum. Carved from single stone slabs, some were up to 100 ft (30 m) high. Many of them remain today, but only one of the giant ones still stands. They were probably royal burial monuments.

40,000 BC		10,000	5000	1000	500	AD 1	200	400

400-800 ASIA

Arab coin
The silver dirham was widely used in the Muslim world. This example was minted at Bukhara in Central Asia.

Migration and religious expansion dominated Asia at this time. In the fifth century, Huns from the icy wastes of Mongolia poured out of their homelands toward Europe and also to other parts of Asia, in search of new places to settle. They destroyed the Gupta kingdom of India and threatened China. Two centuries later, Arab armies began to spread the Islamic faith, and in so doing created an empire that stretched from the edge of France in Europe to the borders of western China.

c.538

Buddhism reaches Japan

Chinese-style capital at Nara
In the early eighth century, the Japanese built a new capital city at Nara. It was modeled closely on the Chinese capital at Chang'an. Palaces and temples were erected, and new Chinese-style furniture filled the rooms.

During the fifth century, China began to exert great influence on its close neighbor, Japan. Chinese scholars taught the Japanese to read and write Chinese, and the Japanese adopted a modified form of Chinese as their official language. The height of Chinese influence came in about 538, when Buddhist monks from China convinced the Japanese court to adopt Buddhism as the official religion of the country. The old temples were swept away and new Buddhist temples were erected in their place. In about 640, the emperor Kotoku introduced the Taika Reforms to reorganize the government along Chinese lines. Slavery was abolished, universities founded, and a civil service established. By 800, almost every aspect of Japanese life was influenced by the Chinese.

618

Tang dynasty begins in China

Bullock and cart
Porcelain, a ceramic material made from different clays, is first known from the Tang period. This glazed earthenware ornament is a typical example of Tang porcelain.

The stable government of the Tang dynasty took the place of the Sui dynasty in 618. The years that followed saw many new inventions. Printing on paper using moveable wood type was introduced, and book production flourished. It was also a great period for literature and the arts, in particular ceramics, porcelain, and sculpture, so that it is sometimes called China's "Golden Age." As China's power and wealth increased, Chinese culture spread to Japan, Korea, southeast Asia, and Tibet.

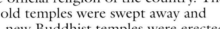

Tang tomb guardian
This hybrid figure, half human, half beast, was one of a pair that guarded the burial chamber of a person of high rank.

634
The Arab Empire

Mohammed, the Prophet of Islam, encouraged his followers to convert as much of the world as possible to the new faith. When he died in 632, Abu Bakr, his father-in-law, took the title of caliph (successor or ruler) and became the chief defender of Islam. By 634, when he died, the conquest of Arabia was complete. But it was under the next caliph, Omar, that conquests which were to change the world began in earnest. New Islamic dynasties were set up, including the Omayyad dynasty in Syria, one of the most important, which was founded in 661. Its capital at Damascus became the center of an Islamic empire that soon stretched from Morocco to India. The Omayyads held power until 750, when they were replaced by descendants of Mohammed's uncle, the Abbasid dynasty, who then ruled for more than 500 years.

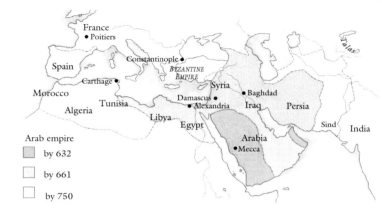

Arab empire
- by 632
- by 661
- by 750

The empire grows

By Mohammed's death in 632, Islam had spread throughout much of Arabia. His successors completed the conquest of the country and went on to invade Egypt. By 670, they had expanded westward as far as Algeria in North Africa and northward to Iraq, Syria, and Persia. Arab armies from North Africa invaded Spain and France but were utterly defeated at Poitiers in 732 by the Frankish ruler, Charles Martel. Meanwhile, other armies had overrun large parts of Asia, including western India. By 751, following a victory at Talas River, the Islamic Empire stretched from the borders of France almost to the edge of China in Asia.

Dome of the Rock

This famous mosque in Jerusalem was begun by Caliph Omar. It is said that the rock inside marks the spot from which Mohammed the Prophet ascended into the heavens in a vision.

ARAB CONQUESTS

632 Death of Mohammed

634 Abu Bakr, first caliph, completes conquest of Arabia

635–42 Caliph Omar's army captures Damascus and conquers Syria and Egypt

642 Arabs complete conquest of Persia

670 Arabs invade Tunisia, part of the Byzantine Empire

698 Arabs capture Carthage

711 Omayyads set up Muslim state in Sind, India

711 Muslim armies invade Spain from North Africa; most of Spain overrun by 715

732 Abd-al-Rahman, ruler of Spain, invades France but is defeated at Poitiers by Frankish ruler Charles Martel

751 Arabs defeat Chinese army at Battle of Talas River in central Asia

Arab army in action

Mounted on dromedary camels or horses, the Arab cavalry fought with lances and swords. They used camels to travel over huge distances very quickly without stopping for food or water, as they and their camels were used to the hot, dry climate of the desert. Horses were more agile in close combat.

Trading places

As the Arab Empire expanded, opportunities for trade improved greatly, and merchants were able to ride their camels safely along routes that ran from Morocco to India. In this manuscript illustration, two Arab merchants are arriving at a village, where they will stop, rest, and barter goods with villagers before continuing on their way.

| 40,000 BC | | 10,000 | 5000 | 1000 | 500 | AD 1 | 200 | 400 |

762
Baghdad becomes capital

Descendants of Mohammed's family overthrew the Omayyads in 750 and founded the Abbasid caliphate. In 762 they moved the capital from Damascus to Baghdad and built a beautiful, walled city. Baghdad became the prosperous center of a huge trading empire. Goods were carried to and from Basra, on the Persian Gulf, where ships from many places unloaded gold, ivory, furs, and carpets, and loaded up camphor, copper, amber, and jewelry. Baghdad was also a center of learning, with a university and many schools.

HARUN AL-RASHID

Harun al-Rashid was the fifth Abbasid caliph to govern from Baghdad. He reigned from 786–809, during which time he extended the Abbasid Empire and defeated the Byzantine emperor Nicephorus I in battle. Harun's renown spread far beyond his own empire. He corresponded with Charlemagne, the Frankish king, sending him an elephant, and exchanged ambassadors with the Tang emperor of China. He is seen here taking a steam bath.

Abbasid wedding feast

Extravagant nuptial celebrations sometimes took place at the Abbasid court. Although the wedding itself was a simple contractual agreement, the festivities afterwards were extremely lavish. On one occasion, it is said, hundreds of pearls were showered from a golden tray upon the happy couple. Male and female guests always attended separate parties.

Baghdad mosque
The Shalia mosque, with its elaborate dome and minaret, is a typical example of Islamic architecture. During Harun's reign, Baghdad became the artistic center of the Muslim world.

Dancing girls bearing wine sang and entertained guests

Male guests sat crosslegged on rugs eating and chatting. The bride and groom were not present but met each other for the first time in the bridal chamber, after the festivities ended

ARABIAN NIGHTS

The lavish setting of Harun al-Rashid's court was the inspiration for the Arabian Nights, a series of 1,001 anonymous tales written at a later date in Arabic. The overall plot concerns the efforts of a woman to keep her husband, the legendary king of Samarkand, from killing her by telling him a different tale every night for 1,001 nights. The magic genie shown here figures in many of the tales.

Men wore turbans, as it is Islamic custom to cover the head

THE WORLD OF ISLAM

In the early seventh century, Arab peoples were not united in any way. Some farmed the land, others traded across the desert in camel-drawn caravans, and they all worshiped different gods. Then, in about 610, an Arab merchant named Mohammed revealed a new religion, Islam, which means "submission to the will of God." There are many representations of Mohammed, but Islamic tradition forbids the showing of his face, so he is sometimes portrayed wearing a veil. Mohammed's influence grew throughout Arabia, and after his death in 632, his followers, whom he called Muslims, continued to spread the faith. They soon conquered Persia, Syria, Egypt, and Mesopotamia. By 750, the Muslim Empire stretched from India to Spain and down to the Sahara in Africa. Today, Islam is one of the world's largest religions, with more than 800 million followers of all races, colors, and nations.

Symbol of Islam
Countries with majority Muslim populations, such as Turkey and Pakistan, use the crescent and star, the symbol of Islam, on their flags.

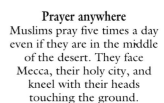

Prayer anywhere
Muslims pray five times a day even if they are in the middle of the desert. They face Mecca, their holy city, and kneel with their heads touching the ground.

MOHAMMED THE PROPHET

Mohammed was born in Mecca around 570. He became a merchant and during his business life met many people of different religions whose beliefs he thought were wrong. About 610 he gave up his daily work and went into the mountains to meditate. There he had a vision that the Angel Gabriel instructed him to preach a new faith centered on one true God, Allah. He went among his own people, teaching and delivering his message, but he was driven out of Mecca in 622 by officials who felt threatened by him. He went north to Medina where he attracted many supporters. In 630 he returned to Mecca and conquered it. He died two years later in Medina.

A special place
Most Muslim households have a copy of the Koran, and many Muslims have boxes specially made to keep it safely. This elaborate box is decorated in ivory and mother-of-pearl. The lid's shape echoes the shape of the domes of mosques.

The Koran
The Koran is the holy book of Islam. Muslims believe it contains the direct word of Allah as revealed to his prophet Mohammed. A Koranic quotation is always qualified by the words "saith Allah." The Koran is probably the most widely read of all books, for besides its religious function, most Muslims learn to read Arabic from it.

The holy city
Mecca, where Mohammed the Prophet was born, is the holiest city in the Islamic world. Muslims try to visit Mecca at least once during their lifetime to worship at the Kaaba shrine. This shrine contains the Black Stone, believed to have been brought to Mecca centuries before by Abraham, the reputed forefather of the Arab people. Pilgrims to Mecca walk around the Kaaba shrine seven times in homage.

Guide for life
It is the duty of all Muslims to study the Koran. The word *Koran* comes from the Arabic word meaning recitation. School children have to learn passages from the book by heart and recite them. Apart from an official Turkish version, no authorized translation exists, although there are unauthorized translations in several languages. At Cairo's El Azhar University, the largest Muslim university in the world, the Koran is the basis of the curriculum. Muslims believe that if they follow the teachings of the Koran, their lives will be holier.

Sunni city
Idris, a descendant of Mohammed, ruled Morocco from his capital at Fez. This Koranic school in Fez is a center of Sunni belief today.

SUNNIS AND SHI'ITES
When Mohammed died in 632, he left a daughter, Fatima, but no son, and he did not name anyone to succeed him. A great argument broke out among his followers. Some, known as Shi'ites, thought that only the descendants of Fatima and her husband Ali should succeed Mohammed. Another faction, who became known as Sunnis, believed that any follower of Islam should be eligible. The argument soon became political as well as religious, and to this day it has not been settled.

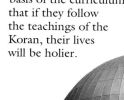

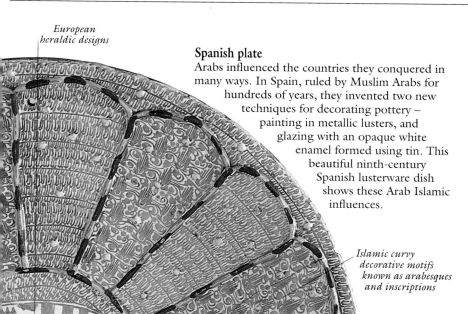

European heraldic designs

Spanish plate
Arabs influenced the countries they conquered in many ways. In Spain, ruled by Muslim Arabs for hundreds of years, they invented two new techniques for decorating pottery – painting in metallic lusters, and glazing with an opaque white enamel formed using tin. This beautiful ninth-century Spanish lusterware dish shows these Arab Islamic influences.

Islamic curvy decorative motifs known as arabesques and inscriptions

Religious center
The earliest Islamic building to survive in its original form is the mosque of the Dome of the Rock in Jerusalem. It is one of the most sacred places on earth for three of the world's great religions – Islam, Judaism, and Christianity. Muslims believe that the site of the Dome of the Rock was the stopping place for the Prophet on his journey to heaven.

| 600 | 800 | 1000 | 1200 | 1400 | 1600 | 1700 | 1800 | 1900 | 2000 |

400-800 EUROPE

For much of this period Europe was filled with turmoil. Barbarians (from the Latin *barbarus* meaning "strange") invaded and destroyed the Roman Empire and broke up the unity of Europe. One unifying force remained – Christianity. New states emerged with Christian rulers, such as the Frankish kingdom in France. But as these kingdoms were established, Europe was threatened by two non-Christian forces. From the south, Arab armies invaded Spain and France in the name of Islam, while from the north, Viking raiders attacked Christian towns and settlements.

410
The sack of Rome

At the end of the fourth century, various eastern peoples, in search of wealth and new lands to settle, took advantage of the weakness of the Roman Empire and began to pour over its long eastern border. In 410 a Visigothic army commanded by their king, Alaric, laid siege to Rome, then the world's mightiest city. After the city had been reduced to near starvation, discontented citizens opened the gates and the Visigoths entered Rome.

Barbarian buckle
Northern Italy was settled by the Lombards, a barbarian people from the north of Germany. They were remarkable crafts workers and made elaborate jewelry of gold and precious stones such as this buckle.

THE LEGEND OF ARTHUR

When Jutes, Angles, and Saxons overran most of southern England in the 400s, a British commander called Artorius (Arthur) won great battles against them. Little is known about him, but in the 12th century, a Welsh chronicler, Geoffrey of Monmouth, created the famous legend of King Arthur and his knights of the Round Table, who traveled around the country performing courageous deeds. This painting by James Archer (1824–1904) portrays King Arthur's death.

Visigoths plunder Rome
Early in his life Alaric, the son of a Visigothic king, volunteered for the Roman army and rose to the rank of commander. He resigned when he became king of the Visigoths. Several times, the Roman emperor Honorius tried to bribe him not to attack Rome, but he never paid the bribes, so Alaric attacked the city in 410. The Visigoths roamed the streets for three days, pillaging and burning. But Alaric was a Christian convert, and he ordered his army not to molest women, destroy churches, or steal Christian objects. On the whole his orders were obeyed, and so Rome was not totally destroyed.

451
Attila defeated at Châlons

The Huns were of Mongolian origin. At the end of the fourth century, they swept out of their Asian lands and invaded Europe. Under their great leader Attila, they settled on the shores of the Danube and from there they attacked Gaul and Italy. In 451 a combined army of Romans, Goths, and Franks defeated the Huns at Châlons in Gaul. When Attila died in 453, the Hunnish empire disintegrated, but their movement westward had, in turn, dislodged other barbarian peoples from their homes, and soon Vandals, Lombards, and others were roaming over western Europe. In 455 Rome was sacked by Vandals led by Genseric, and in 476 the last Western Roman emperor, Romulus Augustus, was deposed and his throne taken by a German chief Odoacer. It was the end of the Western Roman Empire.

Attila the Hun
Contemporary Christian writers describe Attila as "the scourge of God." In an Italian film, the Huns' leader was played by Anthony Quinn.

Spanish gold
The Visigoths were not just warriors – they were also skilled crafts workers. This gold cross was found in Toledo in Spain.

Barbarian invasions 350–600
For centuries, barbarian peoples had challenged the Roman frontiers. The poor economies of some tribes, like the Goths and Vandals, forced them to find new lands to plunder and settle. During the great invasions of the period, migrations of whole populations took place, some people traveling thousands of miles.

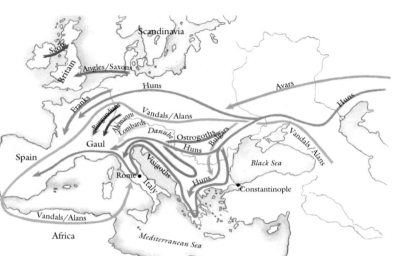

The Sutton Hoo treasure
Anglo-Saxon kings and lords were often buried in their ships which had been dragged onto land. They were surrounded by treasures to take with them to the afterlife. In Sutton Hoo in England, a ship grave was found filled with beautiful ornaments made both in England and abroad. This reconstructed helmet probably came from Sweden.

THE DARK AGES?

Tradition has it that when the Western Roman Empire collapsed, Europe slid into a Dark Age of barbarism in which all beauty and learning were destroyed. But although some things were lost, art and learning did survive in Europe, and flourished particularly strongly in Ireland. St. Patrick had converted Ireland to Christianity in the years 432–c.461. As the new religion became firmly established, crafts workers and scholars came from all over Europe to study in Irish monasteries. Artists produced fine objects in gold and silver encrusted with precious stones and metal and stone sculptures. Monks copied out important works in wonderfully illuminated manuscripts, such as the Book of Kells. Irish priests and scholars traveled all over Europe, founding schools, monasteries, and cathedrals, which in their turn became centers of art and learning.

The Hunterston brooch
This beautiful silver gilt Irish brooch was made c.700.

Center of commerce
The Byzantine Empire
flourished commercially. Its
importance was shown in the
prestige enjoyed by its currency.
Byzantine gold coins (bezants)
retained their purity and value
for some 700 years.

527
Justinian rules empire

After the collapse of the Western Roman
Empire, the Byzantine Empire in the east
continued to thrive. Its capital,
Constantinople, was protected from
barbarian invasions by huge fortifications
of walls and towers. In 527, the devoutly
Christian Justinian I became emperor. He
wanted to create a vast Christian empire by
bringing the Western and Eastern empires
together. He partly succeeded when his
armies conquered North Africa and much
of Italy. He reorganized the empire's legal
system, which influenced European law
for centuries. Justinian died in 565.

The power behind the throne
Justinian's wife, Theodora, was a strong
woman who greatly influenced her husband.
This mosaic is in a church in Ravenna, for a
time the Byzantine capital of Italy.

Justinian's empire
Justinian directed his armies
against the barbarian kingdoms
in order to achieve his aim of
uniting the Eastern and Western
Christian empires. He also
sought to keep a shaky peace
with Persia, which periodically
threatened the eastern borders of
his empire. By his death in 565,
Justinian's empire stretched
across North Africa and reached
from Spain to Persia.

Hagia Sophia
The church of Hagia Sophia is the
greatest building of the Byzantine
Empire. Hagia Sophia means
"Holy Wisdom." It was begun
by Justinian in 532 and became a
mosque in the 16th century when
Arabic medallions were added to
the interior and minarets to the
exterior. Today it is a museum.

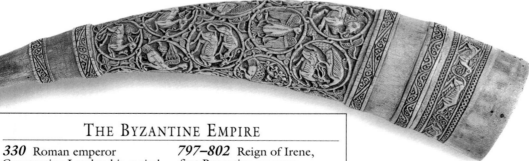

THE BYZANTINE EMPIRE

330 Roman emperor
Constantine I makes his capital
Constantinople, built on site
of older city of Byzantium

***c.*412** Emperor Theodosius
II constructs protective walls
around Constantinople

527–65 Reign of Justinian I

529–33 Justinian introduces
his Codes of Law which
reform legal system

532–37 Justinian builds
church of Hagia Sophia

674–78 Arabs besiege
Constantinople by land and
sea but fail to take it; use of
Greek fire at sea saves city

797–802 Reign of Irene,
first Byzantine empress

963–1025 Reign of Basil II,
known as Bulgaroctonus, or
slayer of the Bulgars

1054 Christian church in
Constantinople breaks with
church in Rome

1071 Seljuk Turks defeat
Byzantine army at Manzikert

1204 Crusaders from western
Europe sack Constantinople

1341–54 Major civil war in
Byzantine Empire

1453 Ottoman Turks
capture Constantinople;
end of Byzantine Empire

Hunting horn
This carved Byzantine ivory
horn was found in southern
Italy. Byzantine crafts workers
were greatly influenced by
earlier Greek and Roman art.

Ornate binding
The only people who could read
or write in the Byzantine Empire
were monks and scholars. Books
were prized and were often
covered with gold and precious
stones to show their worth.

40,000 BC		10,000	5000	1000	500	AD 1	200	400

597

St. Augustine travels to England

When the Angles, Saxons, and Jutes settled in southern England in the fifth and sixth centuries, they brought their own gods with them. Before long, Christianity, introduced by the Romans, had disappeared. In Rome in about 590, Pope Gregory I noticed some blond child slaves in the streets. Told they were English (Angles), he is said to have exclaimed: "They may be Angles, but they look like angels." The story goes that as a result of this encounter, he appointed Augustine, head of a Roman monastery, to take forty monks to England to reconvert the people to Christianity. In 597 Augustine landed in England and was welcomed by King Ethelbert of Kent. Although the missionaries encountered strong opposition among the Anglo-Saxons, the king was sympathetic to Augustine's mission and agreed to be baptized a Christian. Very soon, many of the English followed him.

Slave market
In the time of Pope Gregory, slavery still thrived in Rome. It was not restricted to any single age or class of person; anyone could be forced into slavery. At this time, a slave with a kind master could be better off than a free person. The poorest people lived in appalling circumstances. Gregory tried to improve their lot.

768

Charlemagne rules the Franks

After the fall of Rome, western Europe split into several kingdoms, such as that of the Franks in Gaul (France). In 711 Arab invasions threatened the new nations. Arab armies from Spain entered France, but the Frankish ruler, Charles Martel, defeated them at Poitiers in 732, saving both France and most of western Europe from Arab dominance. In 768 Charlemagne, Charles's grandson, became king of the Franks. His chief concern was to spread Christianity. He was a great military leader, and by extending his domains he also widened the Christian religion. He welcomed all scholars to his court, encouraged education, helped the monasteries, and improved the legal system.

Charlemagne's empire
On the death of Charlemagne in 814, his empire stretched from Denmark to the Spanish border and down to Rome. His capital was Aachen, also called Aix-la-Chapelle.

Christmas coronation
For several years, Charlemagne supported Pope Leo III in his efforts to rid Italy of the Lombards (barbarian invaders) and other factions opposed to the pope. At the pope's request, Charlemagne visited him in Rome in December 800. While the devout Charlemagne was praying at St. Peter's altar on Christmas Day, Pope Leo crowned him emperor of the Romans, the first Holy Roman Emperor, and paid him homage. In this way, the pope was showing the importance of the West, and rejecting the Eastern Byzantine Empire.

Frankish brooch
Although Charlemagne was probably illiterate, he respected art and learning and encouraged crafts workers to settle and work in his lands.

THE FRANKISH EMPIRE
c.400 Franks settle Gaul
451 Frankish Roman forces defeat Attila the Hun at Châlons
481 Clovis becomes Frankish king
732 Charles Martel defeats Arabs at Poitiers
768 Charlemagne becomes king of the Franks
778 Basques of northern Spain defeat Charlemagne at Roncesvalles
800 Charlemagne becomes first Holy Roman Emperor
814 Death of Charlemagne

600	800	1000	1200	1400	1600	1700	1800	1900	2000

Tiahuanaco bowl
Pottery was skillfully
made and lightweight
so it could be carried
on the backs of
llamas on its way to
the market.

 # *400-800* AMERICAS

T hroughout the Americas, settled
civilizations grew and prospered. They
had much in common with each other,
growing abundant crops of corn and sweet
potatoes, and rearing animals for wool and
meat. They also mined gold, silver, and
copper from the nearby hills, which they
made into beautiful objects or traded
with their neighbors. Trade improved
communications between different
civilizations, but travel throughout the two continents
was hard, for walking was the main form of transport.

c.600

The growth of Tiahuanaco and Huari

Two empires began to flourish in Peru and Bolivia in South America
at this time. One was centered at Tiahuanaco, near Lake Titicaca in
Bolivia. The other, the Huari Empire, was based in northern Peru. For
many years these empires were linked, sharing a similar style of art and
possibly also a religion. Together they controlled the whole Andean
region. Tiahuanaco, with its huge stone ceremonial buildings, was
probably the religious center of
the joint empire, which was
governed from Huari. It is
estimated that more than
100,000 people lived in Huari
City when the empire was at its
height in the ninth century.
Both empires were destroyed
in the tenth century.

Gateway of the Sun
This huge doorway was carved from a single
stone slab. It led to the Kalasasaya, the main temple
enclosure at Tiahuanaco. Above the doorway stands
the Gateway God, wearing a headdress of puma
heads. From his belt hangs a row of
human faces, possibly the heads of
sacrificial victims.

*Tail spout
linked to head
by bridge
handle*

Squat god
The people of Tiahuanaco made
many pottery representations of
their gods, like the painted figure
seated in its square tray.

Clay jaguar
This vessel of painted pink pottery is in
the form of a standing jaguar with a spout at the back.
It may have been used to store oil for anointing purposes.
The jaguar was important in many South American religions.

Ponce monolith
Named after the Bolivian archeologist who worked most
at Tiahuanaco, this sandstone sculpture stands just inside
the Kalasasaya. The masklike face with square, staring eyes
is often seen in Tiahuanaco art.

c.650
The society of the Hopewell

The Hopewell people lived along the banks of the upper Mississippi River from about 300 BC to around AD 700. They were named after Captain Hopewell, on whose land some thirty burial mounds were discovered in the 19th century. The Hopewell people adopted many customs from the Adena people, particularly in burying their dead. Ordinary Hopewell people were cremated, but the wealthy were buried in tombs with several chambers which were filled with grave goods. The Hopewell people lived peacefully and prosperously. They grew corn on a wide scale and appear to have had an organized government with hereditary rulers. Their culture gradually faded around AD 700.

Shaman
Communal tasks such as erecting burial mounds for the dead were organized by people called shamans.

Copper bird
The Hopewells imported copper, silver, shells, and alligator teeth from all over North America to make burial goods for the tombs of the dead.

c.650
The city of Teotihuacan prospers

Teotihuacan, on the central plateau of Mexico, reached its greatest extent in the period c.250–650. It was vast, covering some 8 sq miles (21 sq km). Over 100,000 people lived there. No one really knows who they were, or even where they came from. Much of their city was painted, and many temples were adorned with gold. Situated close to a source of obsidian (a dark green glassy volcanic rock), Teotihuacan was able to trade the stone to the Mayas, who used it to make sacrificial knives. Agriculture in nearby swamplands provided huge quantities of corn and beans. The city declined after about 650, and in about 750 it was destroyed.

Cast   Mold

Crafts center
This figurine was cast in one of the city's many workshops, where skilled craftspeople also made tools and weapons which were used for trade.

Grid system
Teotihuacan was made up of 600 pyramids, 500 workshop areas, a marketplace, 2,000 apartment compounds, and numerous squares, all laid out on a grid plan. In the center a 5-mile (8-km) long ceremonial avenue lined with shrines and tombs, called the Street of the Dead, led to the Citadel, where the Temple of Quetzalcoatl stood.

WRITING ON THE WALL
Paintings on the walls of shrines and houses in Teotihuacan show evidence of quite complicated hieroglyphics, or picture writing. The two natural assets of corn and water, which were important to the farmers of the dry highlands, are major themes in this writing. Other pictures illustrate religious beliefs.

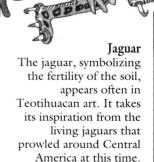

The feathered serpent
Quetzalcoatl was the earliest known god of Mexico. He was known as the civilizing god and was opposed to human sacrifice.

Jaguar
The jaguar, symbolizing the fertility of the soil, appears often in Teotihuacan art. It takes its inspiration from the living jaguars that prowled around Central America at this time.

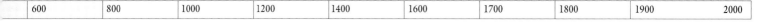

THE MAYA EMPIRE

The Maya of central Mexico were a brilliant people, creating a highly organized civilization that lasted from c.300 BC to around AD 1500. Each Maya city had its own ruler and a ceremonial center where worship of the gods and human sacrifice took place. The rulers of these separate city-states often fought each other. They fought for prisoners to offer up as sacrifices to please their gods. From the third century to about 800, the Maya undertook a great building program and created large cities containing temple pyramids, palaces, ball courts, and community houses. Outside the cities many Maya people were farmers. They cleared forest land and grew corn, vegetables, tobacco, and cocoa, and kept turkeys, ducks, and bees in hives made from hollowed logs. The farm produce fed the country people and also supported the urban dwellers. The basic item of diet was corn, but the Maya also ate beans, chili peppers, and meat stews.

Funerary vessel
This vessel was probably used to store the ashes of the dead.

Rabbit writer
This illustration, taken from an eighth-century painted vase, shows the rabbit god as a scribe. He holds a brush pen in one hand and writes on a manuscript with jaguar-skin covers.

Temple at Palenque
Built during the reign of Chan-Bahlum II around 683, the Temple of the Foliated Cross stands at the ceremonial center of the Maya city of Palenque in southern Mexico.

Maya Empire
At its height, from the fourth to the tenth century, the empire of the Maya stretched from the northern plains of the Yucatán peninsula of Mexico to the lush tropical jungle of Petén in Guatemala. The civilization spread first into the central lowlands, then up into the Yucatán peninsula. It flourished in the north up until the 16th century. The Maya Empire was made up of many independent city-states, of which Palenque, Copán, and Tikal, and later Chichén Itzá and Uxmal, were among the most powerful.

Writing and the calendar

The Maya were the first people in America to develop an advanced form of pictorial writing, or hieroglyphics. They wrote in books made from the bark of trees or carved their writing, or glyphs, on tombs, buildings, and stelae. The writing system was controlled by a caste of scribes of very high rank, who had their own patron deities, including Itzamna, the Creator God and legendary inventor of writing, and the Monkey Man gods. The Maya were also highly skilled astronomers and mathematicians. They invented two calendars. One was a highly accurate yearly calendar of 365 days, based on the orbit of the earth around the sun. The other, of 260 days, was a sacred calendar used to foretell the future and avoid bad luck. Only priests trained in astrology could read it, and people would consult them before an important event, such as a birth or marriage. If a child was born on an unlucky day, his naming ceremony could be postponed until a luckier date.

Standing stone
This intricately carved stela at Copán in Honduras shows the head and hands of a Maya ruler. He is surrounded by glyphs which record events in his life.

Temples and religion

Religious ceremonies played a central part in
Maya life. Many of the city-states were governed
by priests as well as lords. The style of the temple-
pyramids, the most important buildings in the
cities, may have been copied from the temples
at Teotihuacan. Leading men were often buried
inside them. In the 1950s, a stone-lidded
sarcophagus was found at the Temple of the
Inscriptions at Palenque. Inside were the
bones of a man. He was wrapped in a cotton
shroud and covered with jade and mother-
of-pearl ornaments, indicating his
importance during his lifetime.

Pottery for the dead
This funerary urn, decorated with skulls
and a cat motif, dates from the 800s or
900s. Maya crafts materials included
wood, bone, shell, jade, flint,
obsidian, and pottery.

Temple of the Giant Jaguar
This temple stands on top of
a 145-ft-high (44-m) stepped
pyramid at Tikal. Tikal was
the largest Maya city. Fifty
thousand people may
have lived there
during the eighth
and ninth
centuries.

Cutting tool
All Maya stone tools
were made from obsidian, the
greenish glass which the Maya
traded from Teotihuacan. This sharp
blade may have been used to cut human
flesh during bloodletting ceremonies.

THE CULT OF THE JAGUAR

The Maya, like the people of Teotihuacan and many other
South American cultures, worshiped the mysterious jaguar,
or cat god. In the Maya civilization, he was the master of
the underworld and the symbol of bravery in war. The
Maya worshiped many other gods, too. They believed
that they could please their
gods by making offerings of
human blood. They could
either cut themselves, collect
the blood, and offer it to a
god, or they could make
human sacrifices. Bloodletting
was thought to be purifying.
Sometimes, several people
would be killed and placed near
the body of a great man who
was buried in a temple-pyramid
so that their spirits could guard
his in the afterlife.

Bloodletting ceremony
The jaguar cult leader holds a
torch above his wife, who pulls a
thorny rope through her tongue
to make the blood flow faster.

Bloodbowl
This jaguar-shaped bowl from
Guatemala, part of the Maya
Empire, may have been used to
collect blood offerings.

Jolly jaguar
This simple clay vase is decorated
with a complex jaguar motif.

400-800 OCEANIA

D uring this period, Polynesian sailors reached almost every island in eastern Polynesia. They settled on some of them and grew sweet potatoes, coconuts, bananas, and taros (plants with large edible roots) in well-irrigated fields. After about 700, Easter Island settlers built stone platforms used for religious ceremonies.

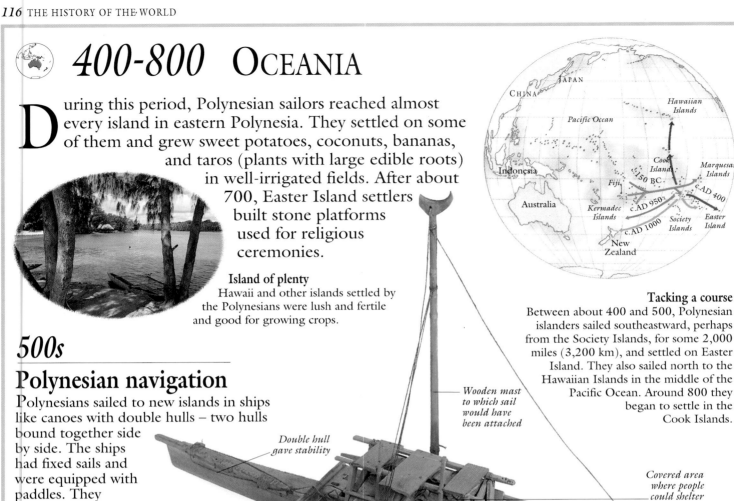

Island of plenty
Hawaii and other islands settled by the Polynesians were lush and fertile and good for growing crops.

Tacking a course
Between about 400 and 500, Polynesian islanders sailed southeastward, perhaps from the Society Islands, for some 2,000 miles (3,200 km), and settled on Easter Island. They also sailed north to the Hawaiian Islands in the middle of the Pacific Ocean. Around 800 they began to settle in the Cook Islands.

500s

Polynesian navigation

Polynesians sailed to new islands in ships like canoes with double hulls – two hulls bound together side by side. The ships had fixed sails and were equipped with paddles. They carried men, women, children, animals, and useful plants and seeds to help them start new lives on the islands they reached. Polynesian navigators were extremely skilled. They navigated vast distances by observing the movements of the stars, calculating wave patterns, and working out wind changes.

Double hull gave stability

Wooden mast to which sail would have been attached

Covered area where people could shelter

THE *KON-TIKI* EXPEDITION

Norwegian explorer and scientist Thor Heyerdahl believed the Polynesians were South American peoples who migrated from South America to the Pacific islands in the 800s. Other experts thought Polynesians came much earlier to the Pacific, sailing from Indonesia and New Guinea. Heyerdahl set out to prove his idea. In 1947, he built a balsawood raft, the *Kon-Tiki*, and sailed it from Callao in Peru toward the Pacific islands. He reached the Tuamotu Islands in eastern Polynesia 101 days later. This showed that the journey could have been made by Native Americans, but did not prove that this was where the Polynesians came from. Most historians today still believe they came east from Indonesia.

Thor sails the Pacific
Kon-Tiki was based on the rafts Heyerdahl believed the native South Americans used.

Double canoe
In 1976, the *Hokule'a*, a replica of a Polynesian double canoe, set sail from Hawaii, heading southward. It carried 17 people and food and animals similar to those the Polynesians would have had. It reached Tahiti in the Society Islands, 3,000 miles (4,800 km) away, 35 days later. This expedition helped to show how the Polynesians had voyaged across the Pacific more than 1,000 years ago.

40,000 BC	10,000	1000	AD 1	400	800	1200	1600	1800	2000

CHAPTER 8

800 – 1000

NEW NATIONS

Jewel made for Alfred the Great of England

800-1000
THE WORLD

T HE BREAK UP of empires in Africa, Asia, and Europe in the ninth century heralds the foundation of new dynasties. In Asia, Tang China divides into small warring states, and in northern India, too, new states form under pressure from Arab invasion. In Europe, the mighty Frankish empire of Charlemagne crumbles, and Viking raiders from Scandinavia, and later the Hungarian Magyars, threaten much of western Europe.

The old and the new

North Africa remains under Arab control, but some Muslims break away from the influence of the Abbasids at Baghdad. A new Islamic dynasty, the Fatimids, comes to power in Egypt. In West Africa, the wealthy state of Ghana is still the dominant power, but there is room for other, smaller cultures like that at Igbo-Ukwu in Nigeria to flourish. In the Americas, the brilliant Maya civilization of Mexico continues to prosper in the north, while the Toltec people build amazing new centers near by in the Valley of Mexico.

Order and unity

By the year 1000 order has been restored in much of the world. The Song dynasty rules in China, the Khmers build a splendid new kingdom in southeast Asia, and both preside over magnificent cultural achievements. Strong rulers like Otto the Great of Germany and Vladimir of Kiev control the new nations of Europe.

NORTH AMERICA

GREENLA

c.986 Viking explorer Eric the Red founds a colony in Greenland

c.800 The Hohokam play rough ball games in specially created courts

MEXICO

c.900 In the Toltec civilization, people are regularly offered as sacrifices to their gods

c.891 Monks begin to write the history of England in the *Anglo-Saxon Chronicle*

Andes

Amazon

SOUTH AMERICA

ATLANTIC OCEAN

PACIFIC OCEAN

N

Hunting in the Ice Age

Cave painting

Early farming

Ancient Egypt

Assyrian Empire

Great Wall of China

Classical Greece

Roman Empire

Barbarian invasions

| 40,000 BC | | 10,000 | 5000 | 1000 | 500 | AD 1 | 200 | 400 |

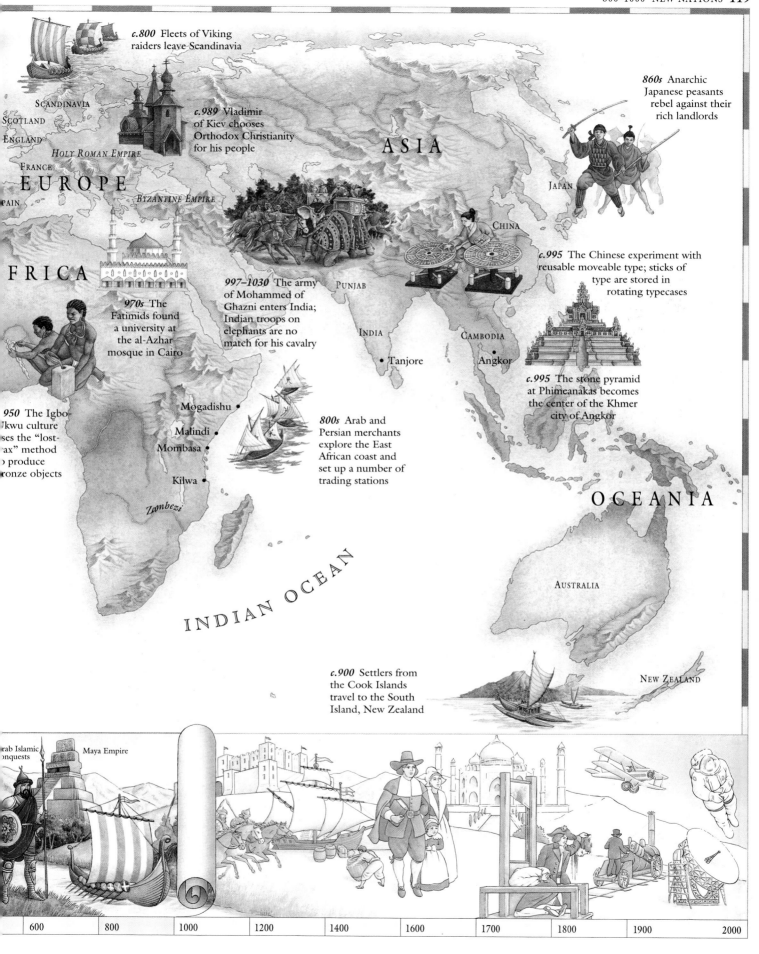

c.800 Fleets of Viking raiders leave Scandinavia

SCANDINAVIA
SCOTLAND
ENGLAND
FRANCE
EUROPE
SPAIN

Holy Roman Empire

Byzantine Empire

AFRICA

ASIA

JAPAN

CHINA

c.989 Vladimir of Kiev chooses Orthodox Christianity for his people

860s Anarchic Japanese peasants rebel against their rich landlords

c.995 The Chinese experiment with reusable moveable type; sticks of type are stored in rotating typecases

970s The Fatimids found a university at the al-Azhar mosque in Cairo

997–1030 The army of Mohammed of Ghazni enters India; Indian troops on elephants are no match for his cavalry

PUNJAB

INDIA

• Tanjore

CAMBODIA

Angkor

c.995 The stone pyramid at Phimeanakas becomes the center of the Khmer city of Angkor

950 The Igbo-Ukwu culture uses the "lost-wax" method to produce bronze objects

Mogadishu •

Malindi •

Mombasa •

Kilwa •

Zambezi

800s Arab and Persian merchants explore the East African coast and set up a number of trading stations

OCEANIA

INDIAN OCEAN

AUSTRALIA

NEW ZEALAND

c.900 Settlers from the Cook Islands travel to the South Island, New Zealand

Arab Islamic Conquests   Maya Empire

600   800   1000   1200   1400   1600   1700   1800   1900   2000

800

850

AFRICA

800–909 Aghlabid dynasty rules in Tunis on the coast of North Africa; the rulers set up a colony in Sicily (827–902) and invade southern Italy

c.800–c.950 Christian empire in Ethiopia continues after the decline of Aksum

c.800s Arabs and Persians explore East African coast and set up trading stations at Malindi, Mombasa, Kilwa, and Mogadishu

Ships bound for Africa sailed from Arabia and Persia, laden with exotic goods

868 Ahmad ibn-Tulun, Egyptian noble of Turkish descent, breaks away from Abbasid caliphate and sets up Tulunid dynasty in Egypt

The Tulun mosque in Cairo is named after the founder of the Tulunid dynasty

ASIA

802 King Jayavarman II of Khmer people of Cambodia founds Angkorian dynasty which becomes center of Khmer life*

813–33 Rule of Abbasid caliph Al–Mamun; he sets up a House of Wisdom in Baghdad that becomes the most important school in the Arab world

820s Persian mathematician Musa al-Chwarazmi develops algebra

845 Buddhism banned in China

In 844–45 Japanese monk and chronicler Ennin witnessed the government's violent moves to rid the country of Buddhism

This eleven-headed Japanese god made of sandalwood dates from the Fujiwara period

850s Arabs perfect astrolabe

858 Beginning of Fujiwara clan's control of Japanese emperors

866 Fujiwara Yoshifusa (804–72) becomes regent over child emperor Seiwa*

868 The *Diamond Sutra*, the oldest printed book still in existence, is produced by wood block printing in China

886–1267 Chola dynasty rules much of south India from capital at Tanjore

887 Fujiwara Mototsune (836–91) becomes chief advisor to the Japanese emperor

889 Khmers start to build capital city at Angkor, Cambodia

EUROPE

800 Pope crowns Charlemagne Emperor of Rome on Christmas Day in St. Peter's Church, Rome

c.800 First castles built in western Europe

809–17 War between the Byzantine Empire and the Bulgars – Khan Krum of Bulgaria defeats Byzantines in 811 and kills their emperor

814 Death of Charlemagne

841 Vikings found Dublin on east coast of Ireland

This bronze statue shows Charlemagne, the great military leader, on horseback

c.843 Charlemagne's Frankish empire breaks up

843 Kenneth Mac Alpin creates kingdom of Scotia and becomes first king of Scotland (dies c.859)*

This silver bowl forms part of a Pictish treasure buried in the Shetlands, Scotland

844–78 Rule of Rhodri Mawr, first prince of all Wales

c.860 Vikings rule at Novgorod in Russia

862 Vikings are invited by eastern Slavic and Finnish tribes of north Russia to rule them

871–99 Reign of Alfred the Great of England

878 Alfred defeats Danes under Gudrum at Ethandune; Treaty of Wedmore divides England between Alfred and Danes*

885–86 Vikings raid Paris in France

c.891 Monks write the history of England in *Anglo-Saxon Chronicle*

A Viking warrior may have used this brooch to fasten his heavy overcloak

According to legend, King Alfred burned some cakes while resting in a peasant woman's hut; his ignorance of cooking helped her to guess his true identity

AMERICAS

This Maya flint is called an "eccentric" because its use is unknown. Such objects were placed in graves as offerings to the gods

c.850 Maya civilization in the southern lowlands of Mexico collapses; many cities are abandoned

c.890 Huari Empire begins to collapse in Peru

OCEANIA

c.800 Hohokam people expand settlements and enlarge houses*

900

c.900 Kasar Hausa (Hausaland), a fertile region on the lower Niger River in West Africa, prospers due to increasing trade and industry

Hausa traders exchanged foodstuffs locally and traveled long distances eastward to neighboring states

This Tang horse is made from jade

906–07 Collapse of Tang dynasty in China after many years of war; for the next 50 years, China is divided into many warring states

907–26 Khitan Mongols under Ye-lu a-pao-chi conquer inner Mongolia and several districts of northern China

935 Koryo state founded in western central Korea

941 Fujiwara Tadahira becomes civil dictator in Japan

c.900 Magyars, nomadic people from Central Asia, invade Europe

910 Benedictine Abbey of Cluny begun in Burgundy, France

911 Rollo, Viking chief, settles in Normandy, France

912–61 Rule of Abd-ar-Rahman III, Omayyad caliph of Cordoba, Spain; during his peaceful reign he develops arts and industry, such as paper making

936–73 Reign of Otto the Great, king of Germany; he is crowned Holy Roman Emperor in 962*

937 Athelstan of England defeats large army of Scots, Irish, and Danes at battle of Brunanburh, northern England

942–50 Record of Welsh law is written down on the orders of Hywel Dda, Prince of all Wales

This elaborate knife was part of the regalia of the Holy Roman Emperor; it was not used as a weapon but was worn for display

c.900–c.1000 Maya power in northern Mexico begins to fade

c.900–c.1100 Pueblo settlements in North America; inhabitants build circular rooms with wall benches

c.900–c.1150 Hohokam culture flourishes in Arizona and New Mexico

c.900 Toltecs build capital at Tula, Mexico*

919–1130 Pueblo peoples live at Pueblo Bonito, Chaco Canyon, New Mexico

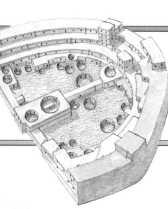

At its peak in the 12th century Pueblo Bonito housed 1,200 people

This shell necklace is from the Cook Islands; such ornaments were worn by chiefs and their families

c.900 First settlers from the Cook Islands, ancestors of the Maoris, reach the South Island, New Zealand

950

c.950–1050 Igbo-Ukwu culture thrives in eastern Nigeria*

969 Fatimid dynasty, descendants of Mohammed's daughter, Fatima, expand from Tunis and conquer Egypt from Tulunid dynasty; they build Cairo*

970s Fatimids build Al-Azhar University in Cairo, one of the world's first universities

This beautifully carved ivory panel was used as an inlay for a piece of Fatimid furniture

People of Igbo-Ukwu cast bronze ornaments, such as this shell with a leopard

960 Sung dynasty reunifies China*

962 Alptigin, Turkish warrior slave, seizes Afghan fortress of Ghazni and founds Ghaznavid dynasty

970 Paper money introduced by Chinese government

983 1,000 chapter encyclopedia, Taiping Yulan, produced in China

985 Chola king Rajaraja I (985–1014) conquers Kerala in south India, and Sri Lanka in 1001

997–1030 Reign of Mohammed of Ghazni, grandson of Alptigin; he invades India 17 times*

This red sandstone panel, made in central India during the Chola period, depicts Kurera, the god of wealth, seated on a bull

955 Otto defeats Magyars at battle of Lechfeld, near Augsburg, and defeats Slavs at Rechnitz

963 Mieszko I founds kingdom of Poland; he is succeeded by Boleslav I, who makes it an independent state

976–1025 Reign of Basil II, Byzantine emperor who defeats Bulgarians in 1014*

978 Vladimir becomes Grand Prince of Kiev

c.986 Eric the Red, Viking explorer, sets up a colony in Greenland

Hugh Capet, shown greeting a bishop, was so-called because of the short cape he wore when he was a lay abbot of St. Martin de Tours

987–96 Reign of Hugh Capet, first Capetian king of France

c.989 Vladimir, Grand Prince of Kiev, chooses Orthodox Christianity as the official religion for his people

Eric the Red sailed to Greenland in a sturdy wooden Viking boat similar to these

990s Toltec people take over Chichén Itzá

| 600 | 800 | 1000 | 1200 | 1400 | 1600 | 1700 | 1800 | 1900 | 2000 |

Egyptian textile
Egyptian weavers were famous for producing gorgeous textiles, which they sold to Europe.

800-1000 AFRICA

The Abbasid Empire in North Africa disintegrated in this period, but the area was still dominated by Islam. A rebel Shi'ite dynasty, the Fatimids, grew powerful in the northwest and overran Egypt. In West Africa, the Ghana Empire increased its wealth through its gold trade with North Africa, and other smaller cultures grew up, such as Igbo-Ukwu.

c.950

Igbo-Ukwu culture thrives

In 1938, a farmer in the Nigerian town of Igbo-Ukwu dug up some bronze bowls. When the area was later excavated, a burial chamber was found containing bronze, iron, and copper objects, masses of beads, and a human skeleton. The bronze objects had been made by the "lost wax" method. A wax model, mostly covered in clay, was heated. Molten wax ran out of the uncovered part, and molten bronze was poured in. The clay was broken away when the bronze hardened. These skillfully crafted objects showed that a fascinating culture existed at Igbo-Ukwu in about 950. Historians do not know much about it, but they believe its citizens were equals and elected a ruler, judge, or army commander.

Copper crown
Beaded armlet
Copper balls held a stool
Elephant tusk

A ruler's burial?
The finds in the chamber show that a fully dressed corpse was buried seated on a stool. The man was obviously of great importance, as among the findings was a crown. Historians think he might have been a ruler similar to an Eze Nri, a title used in the region until the beginning of the present century.

Cairo city gates
The Fatimid caliphs built a splendid city at Cairo. The Great Gates are among the grandest Fatimid buildings which can be seen today.

Painted plate
The Fatimids used animals as symbols in their art. The gazelle stood for beauty, grace, and a loved one.

969

Fatimids conquer Egypt

The Fatimid dynasty was founded in Tunisia in 909 by Ubaydullah (al-Mahdi), a Shi'ite leader who claimed descent from Mohammed's daughter, Fatima. He aimed to overthrow the Abbasid Empire and become master of all Islam. With an army of local mountain tribesmen, the Berbers, he conquered all of Arab North Africa from Morocco to the edge of Egypt by 914. His great-grandson invaded Egypt in 969. A new town, al-Qahirah, or Cairo, was built, which became capital of the Fatimid Empire. Among the buildings was the great al-Azhar mosque. The Fatimid Empire gradually declined after 1100. Many of the African provinces declared independence, and possessions were lost in Syria and Palestine. Saladin, a Kurdish general in Egypt, became a politician and overthrew the Fatimids in 1171.

Fatimid astrolabe
Fatimid Cairo became a major center for scientific studies, particularly astronomy.

40,000 BC		10,000	5000	1000	500	AD 1	200	400

Brahma
This Khmer monument shows three of the four heads of the important Hindu god Brahma.

800–1000 ASIA

The mighty Arab empire reached its greatest extent during the 750s. By 900 it was breaking up as new dynasties such as the Ghaznavids seized power and concentrated on setting up independent states. China, too, split into a number of states and was not reunited until the Sung dynasty took control in 960. Japan and Cambodia broke away from Chinese influence and developed new national identities.

The wheel on the palm of each hand of this little Buddha symbolizes Buddhist teaching

802

Khmer Empire founded

The Khmer people of Cambodia built their first state on the southern Mekong River. Called Funan, and much influenced by India, it was overrun in the late 500s by another Khmer state, Chenla. In 802 the young king Jayavarman II founded the Angkorian dynasty which he made the center of Khmer life and religion. He and his successors were worshiped as gods and built cities with massive temple complexes. For many years, the Khmer capital was at Roluos on a flood plain, until in about 900, Jayavarman's great nephew built a new capital a short distance away which he called Angkor. The god-kings built advanced irrigation schemes and created an empire which lasted until after 1300.

Preah Ko
The temple of Preah Ko was built near Roluos. There were two rows of towers, the front row devoted to the king's male ancestors and the back row to the female.

Many gods
In Cambodia, the religions of Buddhism and Hinduism, and worship of the king and his ancestors, coexisted peacefully.

The Heian shrine
In 794, Heian-Kyoto became the capital of Japan. The Heian period saw a breakaway from Chinese influence. This shrine shows the Chinese-style palace buildings of the earlier period.

866

The regency of Yoshifusa

In 858 a child, Seiwa, became Japanese emperor. Previously, a member of the royal family had been appointed regent for a child-emperor but Yoshifusa, a member of the powerful Fujiwara clan, wanted power. Although he was the child's grandfather, he was not a member of the royal family. In 866 he removed his opponents and established himself as regent (*sessho*). He continued in power even after Seiwa came of age. Yoshifusa's nephew Mototsune succeeded him and became the first regent for an adult emperor and the first civil dictator (*kampaku*). From this time, the imperial family retreated into isolation while the country was governed by successive administrations headed by military or civilian rulers.

Enthronement of an emperor
Seiwa was only nine or ten years old when he became emperor but he still had to undergo the elaborate ritual of enthronement. The ceremony and even the clothes the emperor wears have changed little since Seiwa's day.

Sung pillow
This ceramic pillow comes from Hebei, a province of northern China. Hard pillows were common in China.

960

Sung emperor rules China

In the eighth century, three events weakened the Tang dynasty of China. The first was the battle of Talas River in 751 when Chinese forces were defeated by Arab armies. The second was an uprising by General An Lushan which resulted in the abdication of the emperor. The third event was a surprise invasion by Tibetans who occupied the Tang capital of Chang'an in 763. By the early tenth century, China was divided into small states. In 960 a general in one of the states became the first Sung emperor under the title of Taizu. He introduced reforms in army and government, ensuring that promotion depended on merit. Trade increased between provinces, and wealthy merchants became patrons of artists. Taizu and his successors regained much territory lost to the Tang, restoring China to her former greatness.

Heavenly being
In Buddhism, a Bodhisattva is an enlightened person who selflessly helps others attain enlightenment. This Bodhisattva was made in China during the Sung dynasty.

FOOTBINDING

During the Sung dynasty, and for centuries after, most well-off young girls had their feet bound. This deforming torture, which made walking difficult, prevented women from leaving their husbands.

997

Mohammed rules Afghan Empire

In 962 Alptigin, a Turkish slave-soldier employed by the Samanid rulers of Persia, rebelled and seized the Afghan city of Ghazni. He created a Muslim dynasty, which he and his son-in-law Subaktigin expanded until they ruled a large part of Asia. In 997 the greatest Ghaznavid ruler, Mohammed, succeeded Subaktigin. He spent most of his reign leading armies against neighboring states. He is said to have made 17 expeditions into India, where the divided Hindu rajas (rulers) were easy prey. Mohammed added Indian elephant forces to his feared cavalry. In the name of Islam, he killed his opponents by the hundreds of thousands and plundered treasuries and temples. On one raid 50,000 Hindus were massacred and a great shrine was destroyed. Mohammed used his spoils to enrich Ghazni with universities, libraries, and a cultured court life. After his death in 1030, his empire was threatened by the growing power of Seljuk Turks and gradually declined.

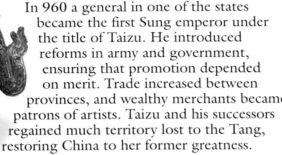

The Ghaznavid Empire
At its height under Mohammed in the late 900s and early 1000s, the Ghaznavid Empire stretched from the Caspian Sea in the west to the Punjab in northern India in the east.

Light for the rich
This Ghaznavid oil lamp, made of bronze, is heavily carved. Only the rich of Mohammed's empire had light in their homes. The poor had no form of lighting at all, so they rose and retired with the sun.

Last resting place
The tomb of Mohammed in his capital city Ghazni is a magnificent resting place for the bloody warrior of central Asia.

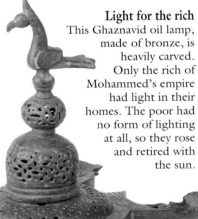

| 40,000 BC | | 10,000 | 5000 | 1000 | 500 | | 200 | 400 |

Pictish bracelet
This Scottish bracelet was found buried under a chapel, hidden from Viking raiders.

800-1000 EUROPE

The unity of western Europe under Charlemagne began to break down after his death in 814. Many small states emerged, ruled by great landowners with private armies. Politically divided, western Europe fell prey to fierce invaders. Viking raids continued, reaching far inland. Magyars from Hungary and Romania looted Germany, northern Italy, and France.

Some leaders fought off invaders by creating powerful kingships. Otto, king of Germany, crushed the Magyars at the Battle of Lechfield, near Augsburg, in 955. In Britain, Vikings were defeated by strong rulers who forged the kingdoms of Scotland, Wales, and England.

Britain besieged
Viking raids on Britain (routes shown by blue arrows) were fought off by forceful kings who united their countries against the invaders. In the north, Kenneth Mac Alpin dominated Scotland; in the west, Rhodri Mawr ruled much of Wales. Alfred, king of southern England, was overlord of Vikings in the Danelaw.

First Scottish king
At the time of his death in 859, Kenneth was undisputed master of the new kingdom of Scotia, north of the river Forth.

843
Scotland is united

In the late 830s Scotland was made up of several kingdoms, including Pictish kingdoms in the east and north, and Dalriada in the west. Dalriada's king was Kenneth Mac Alpin. He aimed to build one Scottish nation to resist Viking attacks. In 841 he drove the Vikings from Dalriada, then invaded the Pictish kingdoms and routed them there. He became king of the Picts in 843. In the west, Rhodri Mawr (the Great), prince of Gwynedd, fought off Viking invaders and English armies, making himself supreme ruler over much of Wales. With him, the idea of a dynasty of Welsh rulers was born.

Coronation stone
Kenneth made his capital at Scone, in the Pictish kingdom. He took there the Stone of Destiny, on which Dalriadan kings were crowned. It is now in the Coronation Chair in Westminster Abbey.

878
Alfred defeats the Vikings

By the ninth century, the most powerful kingdom in England was Wessex in the southwest. Alfred became the king of Wessex in 871. For the next few years, he fought off the Vikings, and finally routed the main Viking army at the Battle of Ethandune in 878. By 886 Alfred had also captured London and was recognized as the king of all England. The Viking leader, Guthrum, was allowed to keep the northern half of England, called the Danelaw, but had to recognize Alfred as his overlord. The only English king ever to be called "The Great," Alfred reformed Saxon law and promoted a revival in learning, founding schools and employing scholars. Alfred commissioned the compilation of the famous *Anglo-Saxon Chronicle*, a history of the people of England.

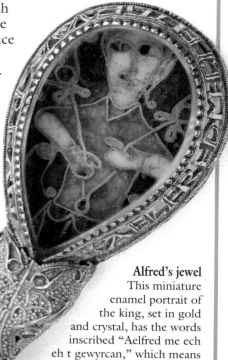

Alfred's jewel
This miniature enamel portrait of the king, set in gold and crystal, has the words inscribed "Aelfred me ech eh t gewyrcan," which means "Alfred ordered me to be made."

THE VIKING WORLD

Arm ring
The Vikings excelled at metalwork. Animal heads decorate this silver arm ring.

When barbarians invaded Europe between 350 and 550, some of them settled in Scandinavia. By 700, their descendants, the Vikings, lived in separate groups in Norway, Sweden, and Denmark, and were rich through trade and agriculture. They had developed efficient government. Members of local communities voted at assemblies, called "things," to decide laws and judge crimes. Criminals could be made into slaves for farms in Scandinavia or for sale abroad. As the population increased, farmland grew scarce. Around 800, adventurous Vikings left their homes to find new lands. Warriors raided the coasts of Britain, Ireland, and France, terrifying the inhabitants. Merchants sailed on long voyages, opening new trade routes, and reaching new places across uncharted seas.

Comb
Viking crafts workers made everyday items from natural products. This comb is made from bone and antler.

Viking women carried the farm keys to show they were in charge while their husbands went raiding

Sword hilt
This intricately wrought handle held a sword. Viking men treasured their weapons. They fought furiously in battles, raids, and duels. The fiercest fighters were called "berserkers."

At home on the farm
Most Viking families and their slaves lived on farms. They worked hard to produce everything they needed. They grew barley and oats, which were made into bread and porridge, and bred cattle, sheep, goats, pigs, and poultry. Fish were caught from nearby lakes and seas. Most Vikings lived in a long, rectangular farmhouse, or longhouse. Inside, the farmer's wife and her slaves cooked over the fire that heated and lit the dark room. Iron tools made in the farm's forge were kept in chests. People sat on high-backed chairs or three-legged stools at trestle tables. At night, they slept on wooden beds or earth benches.

Lords of the seas
Vikings sailed vast distances to raid and to trade. Merchants shipped goods all over Europe and western Asia, making the first known voyages to Iceland, Greenland, and North America. Other Vikings plundered foreign coasts, especially Britain, France, and northwest Europe. Many settled where they raided, becoming farmers or crafts workers. Iceland was colonized in the 860s.

Ready for work
Before work, Viking women pinned an apron to their dresses with brooches such as these. They ran the household, cooking and spinning. They shared their husband's wealth, and could own land in their own right.

| 40,000 BC | | 10,000 | 5000 | | 1000 | 500 | AD 1 | 200 | 400 |

Food bowl

This bowl was carved from Norwegian soapstone. Cooking equipment was often made from this soft stone.

Lamp

Fish-oil lamps, hung with rope from the ceiling, lit the windowless longhouse.

Merchant adventurers

Viking merchants sold jewelry, furs, leather, and slaves to the Arab world and Byzantium, in return for bronze, glass, silverware, pottery, and textiles. After 800 they began to build towns in land conquered by raiders, such as Dublin in the 840s, and in lands they traveled through to open new trade routes. Swedish traders in western Asia founded Kiev and Novgorod, the first Russian states, in the 860s.

Silver coins

These two silver coins from Baghdad in Iraq were found in a Viking grave in Sweden. They show how far merchants traveled to find new markets.

Lead weights

Viking merchants decided how much an item was worth by weighing it against lead weights.

Scales

Traders used scales to weigh precious metals, like gold and silver, which were used as cash.

Gabled roofs were covered with thatch

Barns contained dried and smoked fish for winter

Farmers tilled their fields with ox-drawn ploughs, or ards

Keels ran underneath the whole length of the boat

Knorrs were loaded with farm produce and metalwork for trade

Longship prows were carved with dragon heads to terrify enemies

Expert shipbuilders

Most Vikings lived near the coast. They were the best shipbuilders in Europe. They built sturdy ships, or knorrs, to carry cargo, and longships, or langskips, for raiding and fishing. Hulls, made from overlapping planks, were so shallow that a boat could land on a beach or be rowed up river. A mast and sail were made in sea winds. By 800 the Vikings had adopted the keel, a plank running along the bottom of a boat, which kept it stable in the rough seas.

Rune stone

The Vikings thought that runes had supernatural associations. Here they are engraved on a picture stone illustrating a story about Odin.

WRITING AND STORYTELLING

The letters of the Viking alphabet are called runes. Everyday messages were carved in runes on wood, metal, and stone. Some rune stones told stories from Viking history. One tells of Vikings, called Varangians, who served as royal guards to the Byzantine emperor. The skill of storytelling was important in Viking life. Poets, or skalds, repeated aloud the battles and adventures of Viking heroes. They recited legends about their gods, such as Odin, god of battle and death, and Thor, ruler of the sky. Many of these stories were later written down. They are known as sagas. Most of them were composed in Iceland centuries after the events.

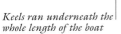

600	800	1000	1200	1400	1600	1700	1800	1900	2000

962
Otto crowned Holy Roman Emperor

Lands of an empire
This map shows the lands of the Holy Roman Empire in 987.

Imperial crown
As Holy Roman Emperor, Otto I claimed to lead all European Christians.

The empire of Charlemagne broke up into small states after his death in 814. Central and western Europe, already plagued by Viking raids, became the target of Magyar invaders from Hungary and Romania. They seemed unstoppable. Otto the Great became king of Germany in 936. In 955 he routed the Magyars near the River Lech in south Germany, ending their threat to western Europe. This victory gave him enough support for election as Emperor of the Holy Roman Empire, and he was crowned in 962. Soon afterward, he was made king of Italy, although local Italian princes continuously opposed his rule.

HOLY ROMAN EMPIRE

800 Charlemagne, king of the Franks, crowned first Emperor of the Romans

840 Charlemagne's son and heir Louis dies; empire split into three

962 Otto, king of Germany, crowned Holy Roman Emperor

1200s Conflict rages between popes and emperors for political leadership of western Europe

1273 Rudolf, duke of Austria, is first of Hapsburg dynasty to become emperor

1519 Under Charles V, Holy Roman Empire becomes part of worldwide Hapsburg empire

1648 Peace of Westphalia recognizes independence of all the states of the Holy Roman Empire

1806 Francis II gives up the title of Holy Roman Emperor, ending the empire

976
Basil II becomes Byzantine ruler

During the long reign of Basil II (963–1025), the Byzantine Empire reached its greatest heights since the time of Justinian. Basil was crowned at the age of five, sharing the throne with army commanders; in 976 he became sole emperor.

To increase his power, he confiscated the estates of great landowners and gave top jobs to loyal but less wealthy men. In 990 he started a campaign to stem the growing power of the Bulgarians under Tsar Samuel. In 1014 Basil decisively defeated Samuel at the Battle of Balathista. He then turned his attention to the west, defeating an army of Italians and Normans in 1018. By his death, Byzantium stretched from Italy to the Euphrates River in Iraq.

The "Bulgar Slayer"
After the Battle of Balathista, Basil ordered thousands of Bulgarian prisoners to be blinded before sending them home to Samuel. The shock killed the tsar.

An audience with Vladimir
Vladimir heard Jewish, Muslim, and here, Byzantine Christian scholars before choosing a religion.

978
Vladimir I becomes Grand Prince

Swedish Viking traders, led by Rurik, founded Russia in the 860s. They built settlements at Novgorod and Kiev, which were united by Oleg, Rurik's successor. Oleg's grandson Vladimir became Grand Prince of Kiev in 978. To make Russia more European, he decided to adopt a state religion. He chose Byzantine Christianity over Islam, it is said, so that he and his people could continue drinking alcohol. From then on, Byzantine art and law deeply influenced Russian culture. Vladimir extended Russian territory in the west and founded new towns.

Turtle dish
Large quantities of red and buff colored decorated pottery were produced in Hohokam workshops. The dish shown above bears a turtle motif.

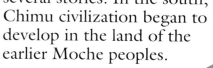

The warlike Toltecs moved in alongside the Mayas of central America in this period, blending many aspects of Mayan culture with their own. In the north, Hohokam people thrived using skillful farming techniques. Neighboring Pueblo peoples built interconnecting houses of several stories. In the south, the Chimu civilization began to develop in the land of the earlier Moche peoples.

Weaving
The patterns on Hohokam textiles were influenced by artists of Mexican civilizations.

c.800

Hohokam people prosper

The Hohokam were based in southern Arizona from c.100 BC to c.AD 1400. Most of the people lived in the fertile Gila River valley. About 800 they expanded their settlements - the largest is now called Snaketown - and were much influenced by civilizations to their south in Mexico. This can be seen in their pottery, weaving, and the ball courts they built to play Mexican ball games. After 1400 the sites were abandoned. Archeologists still do not know why the people disappeared, so they have named the culture "Hohokam," meaning "those who have vanished."

Artist's palette
This stone tray may have been used to mix pigments for body painting. Hohokam people painted their bodies for games and religious ceremonies. The tray might also have been filled with water and used as a mirror.

FIRST ACID ETCHINGS

The Hohokam invented etching with acid. They etched shells obtained through trade with west coast tribes. Pitch was painted on shells in the shape of an animal. The shell was soaked in a weak acid solution, which ate away the unpainted shell surface, leaving a raised design underneath the pitch.

Houses were built of wattle and daub, set in shallow pits

The Hohokam grew large quantities of maize

Etched shell pendant
This shell was etched using the acidic juice of the saguaro cactus fruit, found in the Arizona desert.

Expert irrigationists
The irrigation canals that Hohokam farmers dug to water their fields enabled them to grow two crops a year, one in the spring when melted winter snow swelled the river, and another in late summer when heavy rains fell. Their crops included corn, tobacco, beans, and cotton.

Hohokam farmers used mats of woven fiber to dam the canals. These served to divert the flow of water from one area of land to another

Tlaloc vase
This vase depicts Tlaloc, the Toltec god of rain and water, and also sometimes of war.

c.900

Toltecs build capital at Tula

The Toltecs were nomadic people of Central America. In the eighth century they settled Mexico Valley, where they farmed and worshiped Quetzalcoatl, or "Feathered Serpent," a man-god. By the 900s they dominated much of central Mexico under their ruler, Mixcoatl. His son, Topiltzin, founded the Toltec capital at Tula, some 37 miles (60 km) north of Mexico City. Tula soon became a city of between 30,000 and 60,000 people. At its height it covered about 13 square miles (34 square km) and housed many temples and palaces. At the end of the tenth century, a dispute broke out between Quetzalcoatl's followers, led by Topiltzin, and another man-god. Topiltzin and his people were driven from the city. They went east and settled at the Maya city of Chichén Itzá, where they erected buildings which combined Toltec and Mayan architectural styles.

Chacmool at Chichén Itzá
The Toltecs carved stone figures, called chacmools, of warriors lying on their backs. These figures had bowls on their chests which were used to receive the hearts of sacrificial victims.

Toltec temple pyramid
This temple pyramid at Chichén Itzá is a mixture of Toltec and Mayan styles. It is an immense structure of four stepped sides rising to a temple at the top.

THE WARRIOR CULT

Contrary to the later Aztec view of the Toltecs as a wise, good, and peaceful people, they were in fact a fierce and warlike community. Their capital at Tula, chosen for its excellent defensive position on a cliff overlooking a river, was the center from which its leaders ruled forcefully. By a series of military conquests, they expanded the Toltec Empire across much of central Mexico during the 11th and 12th centuries. They also fought frequently among themselves and used their prisoners as human offerings to the gods. Tula itself was attacked in 1168 by fierce nomads from the north. As the people fled from the burning city, palaces and temples were ransacked and stone statues representing warriors were pushed to the ground. The Toltec capital was completely destroyed, and the civilization came to an end.

Pearly fighter
This figure of a coyote warrior from Tula is decorated with mother of pearl.

Standing warriors
The Toltecs erected a massive temple to Quetzalcoatl at Tula, with rows of figures called "atlantes" (shown left) standing on the roof. These huge stone warriors were thought to guard the temple.

40,000 BC	10,000	1000	AD 1	400	800	1200	1600	1800	2000

CHAPTER 9

1000 – 1200

MONKS AND INVADERS

A Chimu double whistling jar from Peru

1000-1200
THE WORLD

EUROPEAN CHRISTIANS and Muslims in western Asia are at war for much of the period. These wars are called the Crusades. Although religion is the chief motivating force, the main aim of those involved is to obtain more territory. In Europe, the feudal system, based on land ownership and military service, governs every aspect of daily life.

Western empire declines

In North Africa, there are upheavals in the Muslim world. Ghana loses its dominance in West Africa to Almoravids from the north. The Zagwe dynasty displaces the Aksumite dynasty in Ethiopia and encourages the growth of Christianity. In Central Africa, Bantu farming peoples found new kingdoms.

Building and expansion

Across the Atlantic, cultures and civilizations rise and fall. Pueblo people in North America build remarkable villages in the shelter of the cliffs of the southwest. The powerful Chimu people expand from their capital at Chan Chan and dominate much of South America. In the Pacific, Polynesians make long voyages in open boats to found new settlements, particularly in New Zealand.

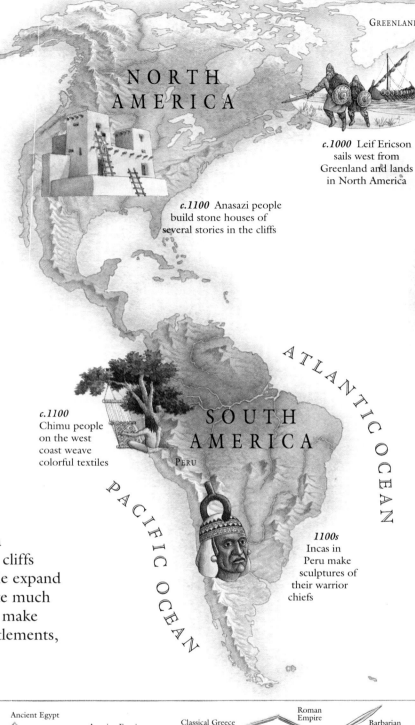

GREENLAND

NORTH AMERICA

c.1000 Leif Ericson sails west from Greenland and lands in North America

c.1100 Anasazi people build stone houses of several stories in the cliffs

c.1100 Chimu people on the west coast weave colorful textiles

SOUTH AMERICA

PERU

ATLANTIC OCEAN

PACIFIC OCEAN

1100s Incas in Peru make sculptures of their warrior chiefs

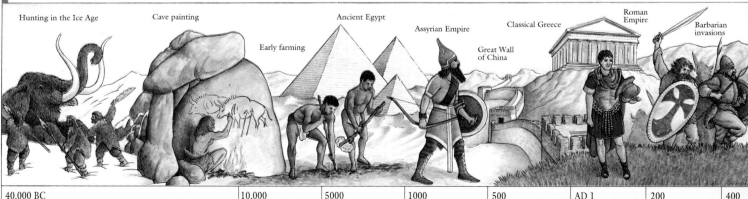

Hunting in the Ice Age

Cave painting

Early farming

Ancient Egypt

Assyrian Empire

Great Wall of China

Classical Greece

Roman Empire

Barbarian invasions

| 40,000 BC | | 10,000 | 5000 | 1000 | 500 | AD 1 | 200 | 400 |

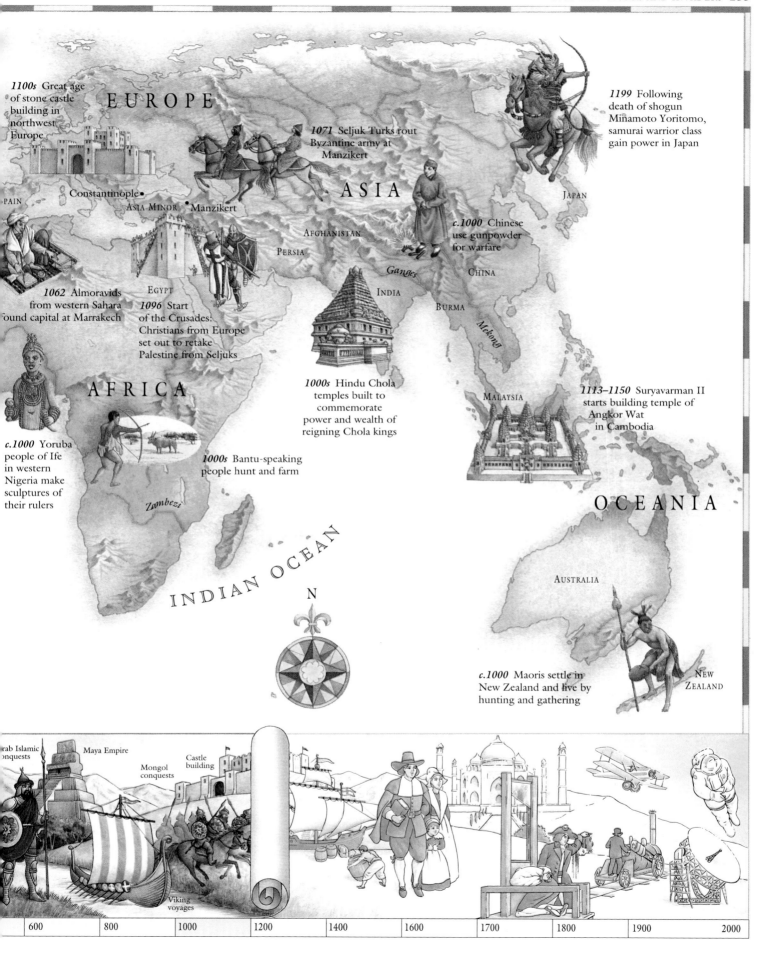

1100s Great age of stone castle building in northwest Europe

EUROPE

1071 Seljuk Turks rout Byzantine army at Manzikert

ASIA

1199 Following death of shogun Minamoto Yoritomo, samurai warrior class gain power in Japan

JAPAN

Constantinople•

ASIA MINOR • Manzikert

SPAIN

AFGHANISTAN

PERSIA

c.1000 Chinese use gunpowder for warfare

CHINA

1062 Almoravids from western Sahara found capital at Marrakech

EGYPT

1096 Start of the Crusades: Christians from Europe set out to retake Palestine from Seljuks

Ganges

INDIA

BURMA

Mekong

1000s Hindu Chola temples built to commemorate power and wealth of reigning Chola kings

AFRICA

c.1000 Yoruba people of Ife in western Nigeria make sculptures of their rulers

1000s Bantu-speaking people hunt and farm

Zambezi

MALAYSIA

1113–1150 Suryavarman II starts building temple of Angkor Wat in Cambodia

OCEANIA

INDIAN OCEAN

N

AUSTRALIA

c.1000 Maoris settle in New Zealand and live by hunting and gathering

NEW ZEALAND

Arab Islamic conquests

Maya Empire

Mongol conquests

Castle building

Viking voyages

| 600 | 800 | 1000 | 1200 | 1400 | 1600 | 1700 | 1800 | 1900 | 2000 |

1000

1050

AFRICA

1000s Bantu-speaking peoples set up kingdoms in southern Africa

1000s Kingdoms of Takrur and Gao flourish in West Africa due to gold trade

1021–35 Reign of Fatimid Caliph Al-Zahir marks start of decline of Fatimid power

Bantu farmers herded cattle across much of Africa

c.1050s Culture of Yoruba people of Ife flourishes in Nigeria in West Africa; it survives until 1400s

1050s–1146 Almoravids, Berber Muslims from western Sahara, take over Morocco, Algeria, and part of Muslim Spain; they invade Ghana in 1076 and establish power there

1062 Almoravids found capital at Marrakech★

Yoruba artists at Ife made beautiful sculptures of early rulers

ASIA

Illustration from Tale of Genji *shows two ladies of the court*

1 **c.1000** Chinese perfect gunpowder and begin to use it in warfare

c.1008–20 Japanese court lady Murasaki Shikibu writes the famous novel, *Tale of Genji*

1014 Rajendra I becomes ruler of the Cholas, who dominate much of India★

1044 Anawrata takes power in Burma; he builds a large empire, strengthens his army, and founds a dynasty of able rulers

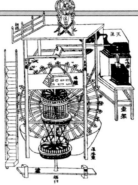

Chinese clocks relied on power from a water wheel to work bells and gongs which sounded the hours

1065 Muslim Seljuk Turks invade Asia Minor

1071 Seljuks defeat Byzantine army at Battle of Manzikert; they capture Jerusalem in 1076★

1 **c.1090** Mechanical clock, driven by water, built in Kaifeng (China's capital city)

1096 Christian rulers from Europe go on First Crusade to retake Palestine from Seljuks

1099 Crusaders capture Jerusalem, in Palestine★

EUROPE

c.1000–c.1200 Italian towns, including Rome, Florence, and Venice, become city-states

1020s Boleslav I of Poland creates a powerful state

1000–38 Rule of Stephen, first of Arpad dynasty of Hungary; he accepts Christianity for his people

1014 Brian Boru, High King of all Ireland, defeats Vikings at Battle of Clontarf but is killed after victory★

1016–35 Reign of Canute, Viking king of England, Denmark, Norway, and Sweden

1019–54 Yaroslav the Wise, ruler of Kiev in Russia, unifies many Russian principalities

King Canute's reign was marked by good government and prosperity

1034 Scotland becomes united down to present border with England

1035–66 Normandy in north of France grows powerful

1037 Spanish kingdoms of Castile and Leon unite★

Spurs helped the Norman knights to control their horses in battle

1054 Split between Catholic church of Rome and Orthodox Christian church of Byzantium

1066 William, Duke of Normandy, defeats Harold of England at Battle of Hastings★

1072–91 Norman armies conquer Sicily

1077 Pope Gregory expels Holy Roman Emperor Henry IV from church; Henry pleads forgiveness, but conflict between Empire and Papacy continues into 12th century

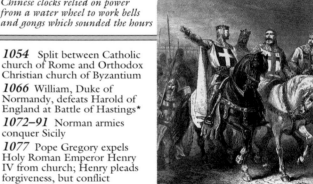

Noblemen leading First Crusade set out on road to Jerusalem

1086 Survey of England by order of William I is recorded in Domesday Book★

1098 Monastery founded at Citeaux in France; start of Cistercian order of monks

AMERICAS

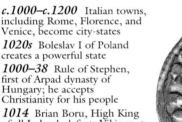

Sweet potato thrives in tropical rainforests of Peru

c.1000 Farmers in Peru grow potatoes and corn for food

c.1000 Leif Ericson reaches America★

OCEANIA

c.1000 Maori people settle on North Island, New Zealand★

c.1000 Polynesians begin to build stone temples

Maoris ate birds and plants, and made sharp hooks to catch fish

Polynesians sailed in strong canoes to find new islands; this canoe prowboard features a bird and waves

40,000 BC		10,000		1000	500	AD 1	200	400

1100

c.1100 Ghana Empire in West Africa declines

c.1100 Katanga in Zaire in central Africa probably founded

1147 Almohads, Berber Muslims opposed to Almoravids, seize Marrakech and go on to conquer Almoravid Spain, Algeria, and Tripoli*

Berber traders sold precious metals, ivory, and slaves from West Africa to Europe

1113–50 Reign of Suryavarman II of Cambodia; he starts building temple complex of Angkor Wat

1 **c.1120** Chinese play cards with painted decks

1147–49 Christian armies of Second Crusade defeated by Turks in Asia Minor and abandon siege of Damascus

Bronze nagas, or serpents, decorate the Hindu temple of Angkor Wat

c.1115–42 French scholar Peter Abelard makes Paris center of religious learning

1115–53 Career of Bernard of Clairvaux, whose abbey becomes most important monastery in Europe

1119 Bologna University founded in Italy; Paris University, in France, is founded in 1150

1124–53 David I rules Scotland

1132–44 St. Denis Abbey, the first Gothic church, built by Abbot Suger in Paris

1139–85 Alphonso I becomes first king of Portugal

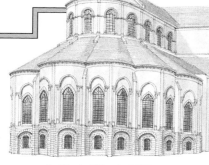

St. Denis Abbey in 1200

c.1100 Height of Chimu civilization at Chan Chan, on the northwest coast of Peru*

c.1100 Anasazi people in North America build cliff dwellings at Mesa Verde, Chaco Canyon, and Canyon de Chelly*

1100s Rise of Incas in Peru; they were farmers led by warrior chiefs

1100–1200 Hohokam people of Arizona, North America, begin to build platform mounds

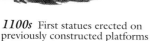

Incas kept leaves of coca plants in pouches; they chewed them with lime to release the drug, cocaine

1100s First statues erected on previously constructed platforms in Easter Island

1100s Beginnings of organized societies in Hawaiian Islands

1100s Earliest settlements by Polynesians in Pitcairn Island

Maori shell trumpet

1150

1150s Zagwe dynasty rules in Ethiopian highlands

1171 Saladin, Muslim warrior and commander in Egyptian army, overthrows Fatimid dynasty

1173 Saladin declares himself sultan of Egypt

This Persian portrait shows Sultan Saladin

Yoritomo was head of a samurai, or warrior, family

c.1163 Birth of Genghis Khan, creator of Mongol Empire

1173–93 Saladin overcomes Palestine and Syria, taking Damascus

1180s Decline of Chola kingdom

1186–87 Last Ghaznavid ruler deposed by Mohammed of Ghur, Muslim founder of an empire in North India

1187 Saladin defeats Christians at Hattin and takes Jerusalem*

1192 Truce between Christian Richard I of England and Muslim Saladin ends Third Crusade*

1192 In Japan, Minamoto Yoritomo becomes shogun after long civil war ends with his victory*

1152–90 Reign of powerful Holy Roman Emperor Frederick I, called Barbarossa ("red beard")

1154–89 Reign of Henry II Plantagenet of Anjou as king of England; he reforms law and government

1171–72 Henry II invades Ireland and is accepted as its lord

1180–1223 Philip II Augustus rules France, conquering Angevin lands in the west

1190 Teutonic Order of Knights, a military society, set up in Germany to defend Christian lands in Palestine and Syria

Beautiful bronze of the Hindu god, Vishnu, made by a Chola artist

The most impressive building at Tula was a four-tiered temple pyramid

c.1150 End of Hopewell culture in North America

1170s Mexican Toltecs' capital at Tula overthrown by fierce Chichimec nomads from the northern desert

c.1180 Toltecs driven out of Chichén Itzá

c.1190 End of first period in which flat-topped mounds built as bases for temples in Mississippi

c.1150 Maoris begin to settle in the river mouth areas in the north of the South Island, New Zealand, notably at Wairau Bar

| 600 | 800 | 1000 | 1200 | 1400 | 1600 | 1700 | 1800 | 1900 | 2000 |

1000-1200 AFRICA

In Africa, this period was one of rising and falling empires. During the mid-11th century Muslim Berbers, the Almoravids, grew powerful in the northwest. They invaded the Ghana Empire, which had dominated West Africa for centuries. The Almoravids were conquered in the 1140s by another Berber religious movement, the Almohads. In East Africa, the Fatimid dynasty in Egypt was overthrown by a great warrior, Saladin, who went on to unite parts of the African and Asian Muslim world.

The Berbers
Berber people were the first inhabitants of northwest Africa. After the Arab invasions of the 600s, they became Muslims. Some lived a nomadic life; others were farmers.

Marrakech
Huge markets, or bazaars, sprang up in Marrakech as merchants brought back goods from all over the Almoravid Empire. The city's streets teemed with businessmen and their slaves, traders, artisans, servants, and beggars.

c.1062
Marrakech is founded

In the western Sahara, a tribe of devoutly religious Muslim Berbers began a holy war to reform their neighbors. They founded a capital at Marrakech in about 1062, which became one of the greatest cities in North Africa. The Berbers' general, Abu Bakr, took an army of followers, called Almoravids, south to invade the Ghana Empire. They seized the capital, Kumbi, in 1076. Abu Bakr's cousin, Yusuf ibn Tashfin, expanded Almoravid rule across North Africa and went to Spain to defeat Christian armies threatening Spanish Muslims. By 1100 all Muslim Spain was part of the Almoravid Empire.

1147
Almohads seize Marrakech

The Almoravid Empire in North Africa and Spain did not last long. In the 1120s, another religious movement of Berbers, the Almohads, formed in Morocco. They accused the Almoravids of living too well in Spain. Their leader, Ibn Tumart, organized them into a strong army. Under Caliph Abd-al-Mumin, they took Marrakech from the Almoravids in 1147 and went on to conquer all Morocco and Muslim Spain. By 1163 Abd-al-Mumin had become ruler of northeast Africa as far as Tripoli in Libya. The Almohads dominated Spain for about 60 years but were defeated in 1212 by Alfonso VIII at the Battle of Las Navas de Tolosa.

Alcazar Palace
Since the eighth-century Arab invasions, Muslim Spain had been a great center of Islamic civilization. Almoravid and Almohad rulers continued to fund colleges and libraries with revenues from taxation, and build palaces, such as the Alcazar in Seville. Most were tolerant toward Christian and Jewish subjects.

Almohad banner
The Almohads raised their banners in battle to fight for the stricter observance of Muslim law. Ibn Tumart set an example to his followers by smashing their wine bottles and pulling his general's wife off her horse for not wearing a veil.

| | 10,000 | 5000 | 1000 | 500 | AD 1 | 200 | 400 |

1000-1200 Asia

Story bowl
Seljuk artists painted bowls as though they were pages from a book. This bowl has letters around the rim, and a picture of warriors on horseback.

This was the age of conquests by Seljuk Turks in western Asia, threatening the Byzantine Empire. They seized the holy places in Palestine where European Christians went on pilgrimage. Byzantium and Europe responded with Crusades, military expeditions to drive out the Turks. In southern India, the Chola kingdom grew strong and extended its naval power over the southeast Asian seas. In Japan, the Fujiwara family's dominance was ended by the rising Minamoto family.

1014

Rajendra I becomes Chola ruler

The Cholas were a Hindu people of southeast India. After 880 they conquered much of southern India, the island of Sri Lanka, and lands to the north as far as the Ganges River. Rajendra I became Chola king in 1014. He sent merchant fleets on trading expeditions to new waters. The Chola navy took control of the eastern sea trade route between the Arabs and China. Chola merchants grew rich. They began to use coins instead of barter, or exchange. They set up guilds, whose members made rules to govern business practice. Chola rule was popular among peasants: village assemblies were left free to manage their own affairs.

Temple city
Rajendra I built a temple at Tanjore, his capital, which housed hundreds of people, including 400 dancing girls. It was used as a shelter in times of emergency.

Chola art
Rich Chola merchants commissioned new buildings and works of art. Their artists made famous bronzes of gods and goddesses.

1071

Seljuks attack Byzantine Empire

Arms advantage
Seljuk warriors balanced on their stirrups to shoot arrows from a safe distance. The Byzantine heavy lancers (left above) found the Seljuks' clever evasiveness a major problem.

In the mid-11th century, a tribe of wandering Muslim Turks, the Seljuks, moved down from central Asia, defeated the Afghan Ghaznavids, pressed on into Persia, and reached Baghdad. They were welcomed by the Abbasid caliph, who made their leader, Tughril Beg, into his regent, with the title of sultan. Tughril was succeeded by his nephew Alp Arslan. Alp invaded Asia Minor and Armenia. In 1071 he won a crushing victory over the Byzantine army at the Battle of Manzikert and captured the emperor, who was later released. Seljuks began to settle in large numbers throughout Asia Minor. The Greek language and the Christian religion were gradually replaced in the region by the Turkish language and Islam.

The Rubaiyat
Some of the most outstanding Persian artists and thinkers lived at the time of Seljuk rule. Omar Khayyam (c.1050–c.1123), a mathematician and royal astronomer, devised a new calendar. He also wrote a famous sequence of poems, *The Rubaiyat*.

600	800	1000	1200	1400	1600	1700	1800

1099

Crusaders take Jerusalem

After the Seljuk Turks overran Palestine in the late 11th century, they began to attack Christians on pilgrimage to holy places. This angered both the eastern and western Christian churches. The Byzantine emperor appealed for help in resisting Seljuk oppression. In 1095 the Pope called for a crusade, or holy war, against Muslim Turks. Thousands of ordinary people responded. A wandering preacher, Peter the Hermit, led the People's Crusade to the East, but they were slaughtered by Seljuks in Asia Minor. In 1096 an official European force joined with a Byzantine army in Constantinople. Some of the leaders were inspired by religious faith, but others wanted to increase their territory and wealth. They conquered Seljuk lands in Asia Minor and Syria. In 1099 they took Jerusalem.

Godfrey of Bouillon
A leader of the First Crusade, Frenchman Godfrey of Bouillon, became Christian king of Jerusalem in 1099.

Massacre at Jerusalem
The crusaders broke into Jerusalem in July 1099, after a five-week siege. They stole the city's treasures and killed all the inhabitants, Jews and Muslims alike.

1187

The Battle of Hattin

Surrounded by Muslims in a harsh land, the Europeans did not keep their Asian conquests for long. Fully armored Christian knights, struggling in the heat, made easy targets for swift Muslim mounted archers. In 1144 the Muslims retook Edessa in Asia Minor. A second crusade from Europe to win back Edessa foundered on the long journey eastward. Those soldiers who reached Asia Minor were destroyed by Turks. In Palestine, Christian rulers competed for power, organizing their resources with the defense of their own territory in mind. In the 1170s Syrian and Egyptian Muslims united under a great warrior, Saladin. In 1187, at the Battle of Hattin, he routed the Christians and took Acre and Jerusalem. In 1189 Richard I of England, German emperor Frederick I Barbarossa, and Philip II of France led a third crusade to the East. In 1191 Richard recaptured Acre.

Hospitaller knight

Templar knight

Christian lands in Asia
The Crusaders who stayed in the Holy Land founded four small principalities in the conquered lands. The new Christian lands were together called Outremer.

Soldier monks
In 1118 a band of knights who protected Christian pilgrims in Palestine became monks, called Templars. Templars differed from most monks as they remained warriors. In battle, they wore distinctive white robes with red crosses. Another order of monks who were also soldiers were the Knights Hospitallers. These military orders grew rich and powerful.

Impregnable stronghold
Crusaders built huge fortresses to guard the routes through their Asian lands. The mighty Krak des Chevaliers (left) in Syria housed hundreds of Hospitaller knights and their servants.

Assassins

A small fierce group of Shi'ite Muslims attacked Sunni Seljuks as well as Christians. They were called "assassins" from the Arabic word *hashshashun*, meaning smoker of hashish. They placed a sharp knife on a victim's pillow, then returned to assassinate him.

1192
Christian and Muslim truce

In 1192 Richard I of England came within a few hours' march of taking Jerusalem. At that moment, his troops refused to go any further; they were desperately short of food and water and were worn out. Richard had to retreat.

Helmet
This German crusader's helmet is decorated with cross-shaped strips to show its wearer's Christian faith.

He refused even to look toward Jerusalem, saying, "My eyes shall not see it if my arm may not reconquer it." In despair, Richard sought a truce with Saladin. He took the extraordinary step of offering his Christian sister in marriage to the great sultan's Muslim brother. Richard and Saladin made a treaty in November 1192, by which the Christians could keep control of their coastal towns, and Christian pilgrims were guaranteed safe journeys to holy places. Despite all the efforts of crusaders and decades of conflict, most of Palestine remained in Muslim hands.

SALADIN 1138–93

Saladin was an ideal warrior, reputed to be brave, honorable, and just. Born in Iraq of Kurdish ancestry, he became a commander, then chief minister in Fatimid Egypt. He overthrew the Fatimids in 1171 and conquered Syria and part of North Africa. His combined forces almost completely expelled the crusaders from Outremer. A cultured and generous man, Saladin patronized scholars, founded schools, and funded public services such as hospitals.

1192
Yoritomo becomes shogun

By the mid-12th century, Japanese emperors at Kyoto had lost power to the Fujiwara family. Civil war broke out involving the Fujiwara and two leading families from the warrior class, or samurai, the Taira and the Minamoto. In 1160 Kiyomori, leader of the Taira clan, seized power from the Fujiwara, but in 1185 the Taira were defeated by the Minamoto clan at the Battle of Dan No Ura. Yoritomo, head of the Minamoto, set up a military government in the name of the emperor at Kamakura. In 1192 the emperor gave him the important title of shogun (great general).

Homage to the shogun
Yoritomo was first of a series of military shoguns. Here he receives homage from some of his most high-ranking samurai.

THE SAMURAI

The warrior class, or samurai, probably first emerged in Japan in the ninth century. Local officials in the north and east, far away from the imperial court, began to employ small bands of mounted archers and swordsmen to maintain order. By the 11th century these warrior lords, their families and retainers had begun to control whole provinces. The Minamoto and the Taira became the most powerful samurai families in Japan. After Minamoto Yoritomo became shogun in 1192, he used his samurai retainers to enforce law and order. Top loyal warriors were made constables in each province, and samurai stewards were sent to manage large areas of land. This remained the basic pattern of Japanese government for many centuries afterward.

| 600 | 800 | 1000 | 1200 | 1400 | 1600 | 1700 | 1800 | 1900 | 2000 |

1000-1200 EUROPE

Trade increased in Europe during this period due in part to the Crusades, which involved all levels of society in Christian Europe against a common foe, Islam. New roads which crossed borders and advances in ship building also encouraged commercial enterprise. Nations became more stable under strong royal rulers and were reinforced by feudalism. Many new monastic orders started up, which encouraged Church reform. There were great advances in learning, and Europe's first universities, Bologna and Paris, were founded.

The death of Brian
As the Vikings fled from Clontarf, one of them saw Brian near a tent and cut him down.

1014

The Battle of Clontarf

Up to about 1000, Ireland was divided into several warring kingdoms. This had made it easy for the Vikings to establish themselves in many areas. In 1002 Brian Boru, king of Munster, made himself High King over all Ireland. Brian spent much of his reign consolidating this position. In 1013 Vikings who had settled in the Dublin area joined with discontented lords to challenge his authority. The two sides met in 1014 at Clontarf near Dublin. The Irish triumphed, although Brian was killed. The threat of Viking dominance over Ireland was at an end.

Royal visit
In 1006 Brian visited Armagh. He distributed gold, some of it paid to him as tribute (the name Boru means "taker of tributes"). While there, he caused to be added to the ninth-century *Book of Armagh* a note of his visit as "Emperor of the Irish."

Eagle illustration in the *Book of Armagh*

EL CID 1043–99

During his attempts to conquer Muslim Spain after 1072, Alfonso VI was helped by one of his most powerful nobles, Rodrigo Díaz de Vivar, known as El Cid ("Cid" from the Arabic *Sayyid* meaning "lord"). This Castilian-born warrior led raids into Muslim territory as far south as Cadiz. Although brave, he was untrustworthy and in 1081 fell out with Alfonso and offered his services to a Muslim leader. Díaz performed great deeds and earned himself the name El Cid Campeador (Champion). Later, reconciled to Alfonso, he captured Muslim Valencia and held it for five years until his death. Despite his inconstancy, today El Cid is one of Spain's national heroes.

Hollywood hero
In 1961 Charlton Heston played El Cid in a fanciful but hugely popular film.

1037

Spanish kingdoms unite

At the beginning of the 11th century, the Spanish peninsula was divided between the Muslim states in the center and south and several Christian kingdoms in the north. In 1037 Fernando of Castile completed the conquest of the neighboring kingdom of León begun by his father. It was not until 1072 that Fernando's son Alfonso VI felt sufficiently secure in his inheritance to challenge the Muslim supremacy of the south. This conflict continued for another 400 years until the last Muslim kingdom, Granada, was conquered in 1492.

The kingdoms of Spain
By 1150 most of north and central Spain was Christian. However, many Muslims remained in Aragon, and there were some Christians living in the south. By the 1300s only the very far south centered around Granada remained under Muslim control.

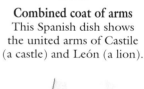

Combined coat of arms
This Spanish dish shows the united arms of Castile (a castle) and León (a lion).

León · Navarre · Christian Spain · Castile · Aragon · Portugal · Valencia · Andalusia · Granada · *Mediterranean Sea*

CHURCH LIFE

Christian religious belief and practice dominated everyday lif thousands of men and women devoted their whole lives to th studying, and praying in monasteries and nunneries. These m helped people outside their communities, nursing the sick and the poor. Many churches were built for people to worship in. The largest were cathedrals containing the official throne of the bishop of the area.

Easter lamb crozier
The lamb in this crozier (bishop's crook) stands for the salvation of the faithful, while the serpent represents the jaws of Hell.

Monasteries
A monastery was a group of buildings arranged around a cloister. They housed religious communities of monks (and in some cases, nuns) who were guided by a set of rules originally laid down by St. Benedict in the sixth century.

Dormitory where monks slept

Cloisters

Abbey church was the center of monastic life

Herb garden for food and medicine

Orchard

Frater or dining hall where monks had their meals

Infirmary or hospital where monks cared for the sick

Travelers often stayed in monasteries

Santiago de Compostela
St. James's remains made this cathedral in Spain a place of pilgrimage.

MONASTIC ORDERS
Men and women who chose to devote their lives to Christianity often became monks or nuns and entered monasteries or religious houses for women (nunneries). The first monastic order, the Benedictine, was founded by St. Benedict in Italy, in 529. The monks' way of life was regulated by a strict set of rules. As conditions in Europe changed, new orders were created, following basically the same rules. These included the Cluniacs (910), Carthusians (1084), the Cistercians (1098), and Gilbertines (1131). Newer orders were founded in the 13th century, such as the Franciscans and Dominicans; these were not closed orders.

Pilgrimages
Many Christians used to make long journeys by land and sea to sacred places which held relics of Jesus Christ or early saints. They hoped to receive forgiveness for sins or cures for illnesses. Some places, like Rome where both St. Peter and St. Paul were believed to be buried, were especially popular.

Norman lance
and arrows

1066

The Battle of Hastings

When King Edward the Confessor of England died in 1066, he left no heir but had promised his throne to William, Duke of Normandy in France. However, the English lords did not want a foreigner as king, so they offered the throne to Harold, Earl of Wessex. William was furious and, after some months spent assembling a large army, set sail from Normandy, reaching Hastings the next day. Harold and his army were in the north of England and marched over 250 miles (400 km) south in a few days, arriving hungry and exhausted. They put up a brave fight but the Normans triumphed, and Harold was slain. William was crowned king. The Normans poured in and took over the country, changing the course of English history. England was never conquered by foreign forces again.

The Bayeux tapestry

This amazing record of events leading to the Battle of Hastings is embroidered needlework made up of 72 story panels. It was created on the orders of Odo, Bishop of Bayeux, and half-brother to William. This panel shows a soldier, once considered to be Harold, with an arrow in his eye. The tapestry is now in Bayeux in northwest France.

William the Conqueror

William was the illegitimate son of Robert, Duke of Normandy. After his conquest, he divided England among his Norman lords and spent much of the rest of his reign putting down scattered English resistance. This portrait is from the 13th-century *Great Chronicle* of Matthew Paris. The church William holds in his hand represents his control of the church.

THE FEUDAL SYSTEM

Feudalism emerged in eighth-century Europe as a stabilizing force in the period of disorder that followed the collapse of the Roman Empire. In order to control their realms efficiently, kings leased land, known as a fief, to vassals (powerful lords) in return for an oath of loyalty and an agreement to carry out military service on request. The lords divided their land into manors (estates) which they in turn leased to their vassals, who were lesser nobles or knights. These lesser vassals swore their oaths of loyalty and military obedience to their lord but were also bound to the king, who was overlord of everyone. All land was ultimately held by the king. The lowest level of all society were the serfs (or slaves) who worked on the land. William the Conqueror introduced a particularly efficient form of feudalism to England. Types of feudalism were also practiced in some Asian countries.

Feudal tree

This 14th-century illustrated manuscript shows the feudal structure with the king at the top.

1086

English land survey takes place

In 1085, to find out how much income he could raise from his kingdom by taxation, William I (the Conqueror) ordered a nationwide survey of England (excepting the counties in the far north) to record the value, population, extent, state of cultivation, ownership, and tenancy of the land. The regions were divided up and commissioners appointed for each area. Citizens had to answer, under oath, questions about the state of their lands both at the time of the survey and in 1066. The results of the survey, completed in 1086, were written in the Domesday Book.

Domesday Book

The book was divided into two volumes, one covering the richest counties of Essex, Suffolk, and Norfolk, and the other covering the remaining counties. The book is shown on a replica of the chest in which it was kept.

CASTLES

Castles in Europe were first built in the eighth century and continued to be built until at least 1600. Castles were fortified residences for kings and lords. Because nobles were often warring with each other and with the king, and there was no general force of law and order, it was necessary for lords to be able to defend their domains. Castles were made of timber or stone. Many timber castles consisted of a large mound of earth with a wooden tower on the summit where the lord and his family lived. The tower stood inside or just outside a timber-walled enclosure. These were called motte-and-bailey castles.

Great Tower
The White Tower at the Tower of London in England was one of the first great stone towers in the country. William the Conqueror began building it in 1078.

Siege engine
This mangonel, operated by torsion (twisting) of ropes, threw stones against castle walls.

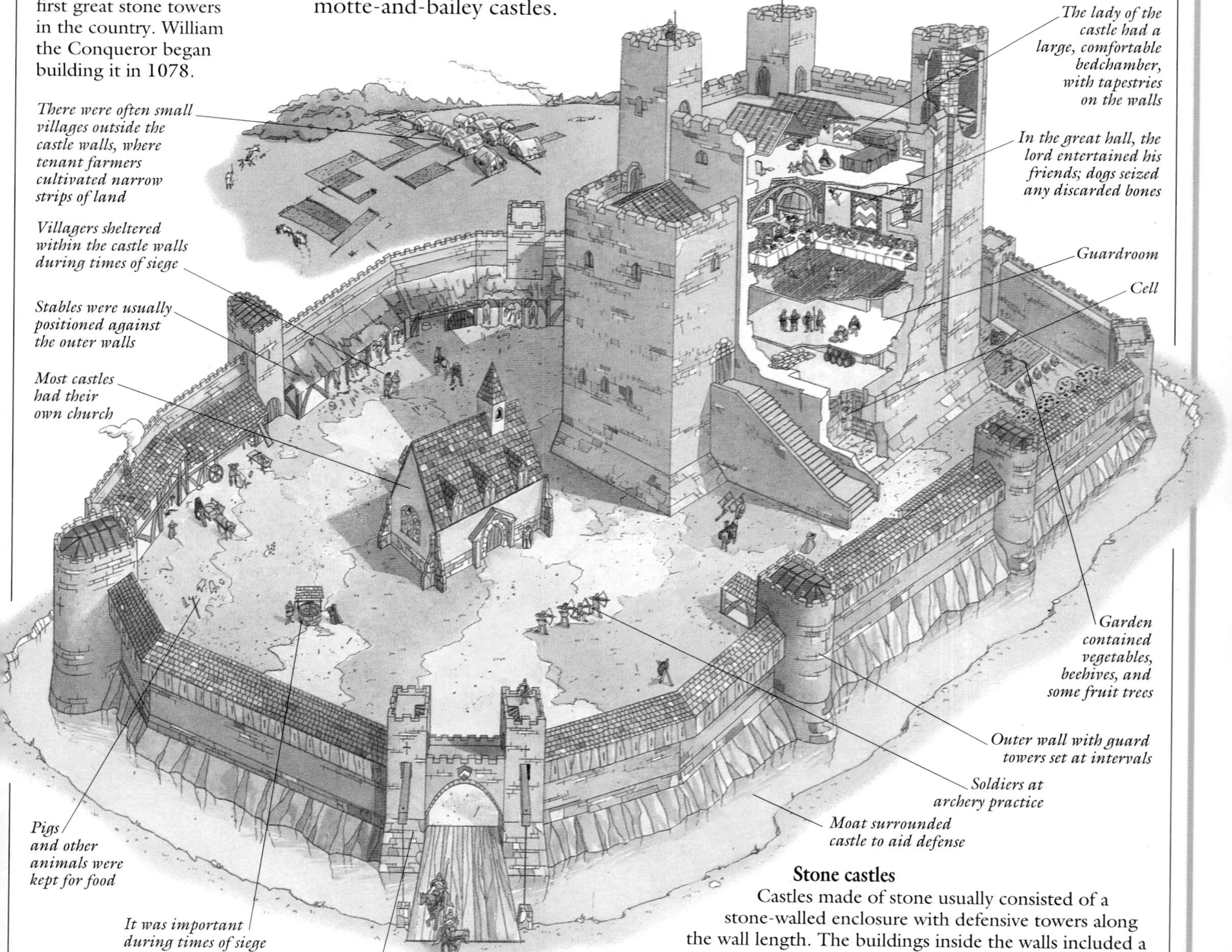

The lady of the castle had a large, comfortable bedchamber, with tapestries on the walls

In the great hall, the lord entertained his friends; dogs seized any discarded bones

There were often small villages outside the castle walls, where tenant farmers cultivated narrow strips of land

Villagers sheltered within the castle walls during times of siege

Stables were usually positioned against the outer walls

Most castles had their own church

Guardroom

Cell

Garden contained vegetables, beehives, and some fruit trees

Outer wall with guard towers set at intervals

Soldiers at archery practice

Moat surrounded castle to aid defense

Pigs and other animals were kept for food

It was important during times of siege to have a water supply within the walls

Gatehouse and drawbridge

Stone castles
Castles made of stone usually consisted of a stone-walled enclosure with defensive towers along the wall length. The buildings inside the walls included a residential great tower often several stories high. Some smaller buildings were built against the encircling walls.

600	800	1000	1200	1400	1600	1700	1800	1900	2000

1000-1200 AMERICAS

Leif's huts
The Icelandic sagas say Leif and his crew set up temporary huts in North America before building permanent houses. None remain today.

Narth America was visited by Viking adventurers from Greenland, who sailed to Newfoundland and explored the coast, possibly as far south as Chesapeake Bay. In the southwest, Pueblo people built houses in the cliffs, and further east the Mississippi people erected flat-topped mounds for temples. The Chimu came to power in South America, dominating the whole northern Andes region.

The voyage
Leif Ericson and his crew of 35 set sail from their settlement in Godthabfjord, on the west coast of Greenland, and landed on the North American continent. There they explored a number of sites, which Leif named Helluland, Markland, and Vinland. Vinland may have been located in northern Newfoundland.

c.1000

Leif Ericson reaches America

Leif Ericson was the son of Eric the Red, who reached Greenland. Around 1000 Leif set sail from his Viking settlement in Godthabfjord. He was looking for a strange land seen by another Viking mariner on a previous voyage. He finally landed in North America. After exploring, Leif returned to Greenland. In the 1960s, remains of a Viking settlement were found in northern Newfoundland. They dated back to about 1000, showing that Vikings visited America five centuries before Columbus.

Expert weaving
The Chimu were skillful weavers. This detail from a painted textile shows a figure standing beneath a serpent, a common Chimu motif.

c.1100

Chimu capital at Chan Chan

The Chimu occupied land along the Peruvian coast beside the northern Andes mountains. They may have descended from the earlier Moche people in the same area. By the 11th century, the Chimu had created a powerful state called Chimor, based at a capital, Chan Chan, and ruled over by lords and priests. Chan Chan was well supplied with food from irrigated farmland nearby. In the early 1100s, huge rain storms ruined these fields, and new land had to be found. So the Chimu conquered neighboring territories, and a system of roads was built to link each new farm to the city.

Double whistling jar
Thousands of potters worked at Chan Chan. The fish design on this blackware jar may have been inspired by the fishing industry that thrived on the Chimu coast.

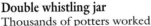
Walls were made of mud bricks

Chimu capital
Chan Chan covered 8 sq miles (20 sq km). It contained several giant rectangular enclosures, in which Chimu lords lived with their entourage. Outside the enclosures were humble mud dwellings for the poorer people.

40,000 BC		10,000	5000	1000	500	AD 1	200	400

c.1100

The Anasazi cliff-dwellers

The Anasazi people, whose name means "the ancient ones," were Native American settlers who based themselves in the southwest of North America from about 700. Over the years they developed a kind of dwelling made up of interconnecting mudbrick rooms stacked in layers on top of each other. These rooms grew to form small villages or towns, called pueblos. Around 1100 the Anasazi moved into the hills, possibly for protection from enemies, and began to build pueblos of stone in the shelter of overhanging cliffs. On the cliff tops, they grew corn and other crops in irrigated fields. Anasazi artists made pottery and other beautiful objects from precious stones including turquoise.

The territory of "the ancient ones"
The Anasazi were based in the "four corners" area where the four states of Arizona, Colorado, New Mexico, and Utah join. Major sites included Mesa Verde, Chaco Canyon, and Canyon de Chelly.

Walls built into cliff face

Ladders could be pulled up for defense purposes

Keyhole-shaped entrance

Walls of kiva were painted with murals

Circular wall bench

Cliff palace
The Mesa Verde cliff palace was begun around 1100. It had several hundred living rooms and was fortified against attack.

Geometric mug
Anasazi women made pottery by hand, as the potter's wheel was not known in America at this time. They coiled ropes of clay on top of each other to form bowls, mugs, and other utensils.

Ceremonial chamber
In front of their cliff houses the Anasazi built circular ceremonial rooms called *kivas*, with fitted wall benches that ran right around the inside walls. These rooms were for men only and were used for local assemblies, prayer meetings, and even as classrooms for students.

600	800	1000	1200	1400	1600	1700	1800	1900	2000

1000-1200 OCEANIA

Polynesians continued to settle Pacific islands. Among the most important were people from the Cook Islands and Austral Islands who sailed to the North and South Islands of New Zealand, the largest uninhabited islands in the Pacific. In Australia, Aboriginals continued to live as hunter-gatherers, undisturbed by outside influences.

Tattoo artist
The Maoris tattooed their faces and bodies by carving into the flesh with sharpened stones. Important people had many tattoos, as this was a sign of high standing in the community.

c.1000

Maoris settle in New Zealand

Around 1000 a group of Polynesians sailed many hundreds of miles in open boats to settle on the two large islands of New Zealand, the North and South Islands. They brought with them crops they had grown on their previous island settlements, such as sweet potatoes, yams, taros, and gourds. Only the sweet potato grew well. In New Zealand, they found other sources of food, including the moa bird, shell fish, and an edible fern. It is thought that the South Island people lived as fishing and gathering people right up to the visit to the island by Captain James Cook in 1769. On the North Island, the sweet potato was more successfully grown, but eventually the harvested crop rotted each season. So the Maoris dug underground pits to store the potatoes at a steady temperature in order to keep them fresh. In this way they learned how to become self-sufficient farmers.

Moa bird
The moa was a large bird, growing up to 10 ft (3 m) tall. It could not fly but ran very fast on two strong legs, often pursued by Maoris who killed it for its meat. Finally they hunted it into extinction.

War canoe
Maori canoes were among the largest watercraft in the world until the 18th century. Made from single logs up to 100 ft (30 m) in length, each canoe took up to 100 warriors to paddle its huge bulk through the water.

Canoe bailer
This wooden bailer has a head carved at the base of the handle. Carving was believed by the Maoris to be a semisacred task through which the gods expressed their will.

Elaborately carved prow

Greenstone neck pendant

Lucky charm
This *hei tiki*, or neck pendant, was worn to bring good luck or to keep evil spirits away. It is carved from greenstone, a hard kind of jade found on South Island.

CHAPTER 10

1200 – 1400

CONQUEST AND PLAGUE

Mongol warrior's quiver

1200-1400
THE WORLD

ONE MAN and his family dominate Asia and Europe during this period – Genghis Khan, founder of the Mongol Empire. From Korea in the east to Kiev in the west, nobody is left untouched by the invasions of his fierce Mongol armies. Even China is conquered. Also in this period, the Ottomans emerge as a major power in Turkey, threatening the Byzantine Empire. Europe and Asia are later devastated by the Black Death, a bubonic plague that kills one third of the population of Europe. Yet despite these major disasters, contacts between the two continents flourish; Europeans visit China, and new trade routes are opened up across the Asian continent.

New empires

In those parts of the world untouched by either the Mongols or the Black Death, some important new civilizations grow up. In West Africa, the gold-rich state of Mali grows prosperous through trade across the Sahara desert. Across the Atlantic, the Mississippi people of North America construct huge platform mounds for temples and houses. To their south, the Aztecs build sprawling towns in Central America. The Chimu expand their coastal kingdom in northern Peru, while in the Andes, the Incas strengthen their grip on the lands around their mountain capital at Cuzco.

NORTH AMERICA

Rockies

MEXICO

c.1200 Thousands of people live on and around mounds in the Mississippi town of Cahokia

1241 North German cities form a league, or Hansa, to protect the trading interests of their merchants and fleets

1300s Warrior knights are an important elite in Aztec society, and the jaguar knights are among the most powerful

1300s Inca people of Peru become highly skilled stonemasons and builders

Andes

PERU

• Cuzco

SOUTH AMERICA

ATLANTIC OCEAN

PACIFIC OCEAN

Hunting in the Ice Age

Cave painting

Early farming

Ancient Egypt

Assyrian Empire

Great Wall of China

Classical Greece

Roman Empire

Barbarian invasions

40,000 BC		10,000	5000	1000	500	AD 1	200	400

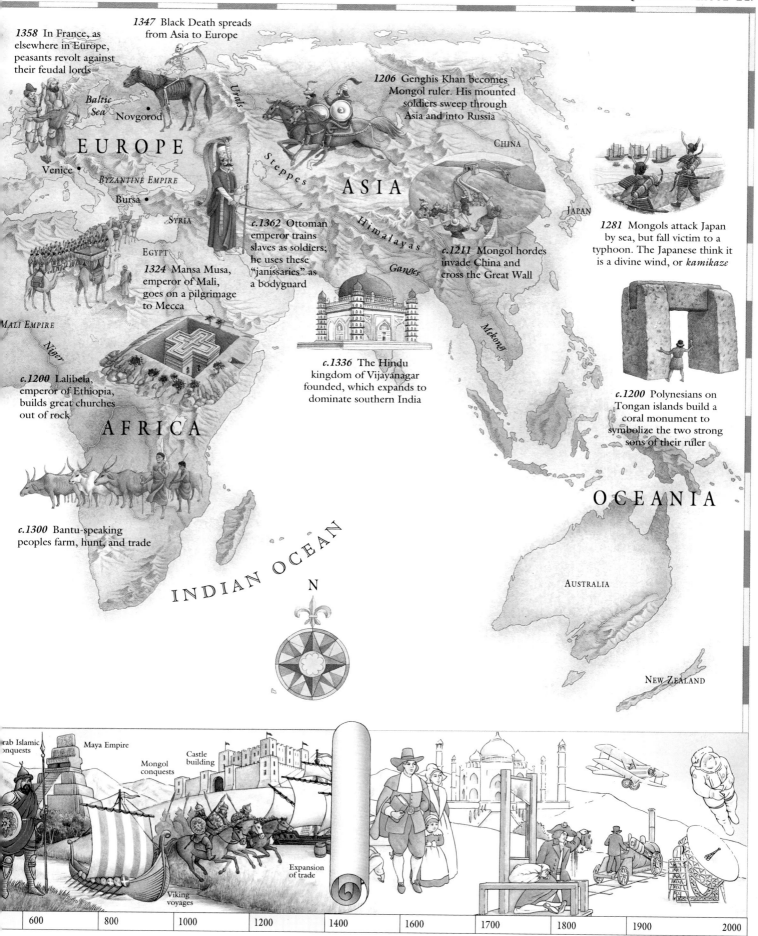

1358 In France, as elsewhere in Europe, peasants revolt against their feudal lords

1347 Black Death spreads from Asia to Europe

Baltic Sea

Novgorod

Urals

EUROPE

Venice

BYZANTINE EMPIRE

Bursa

SYRIA

EGYPT

Steppes

ASIA

Himalayas

Ganges

CHINA

JAPAN

1206 Genghis Khan becomes Mongol ruler. His mounted soldiers sweep through Asia and into Russia

1281 Mongols attack Japan by sea, but fall victim to a typhoon. The Japanese think it is a divine wind, or *kamikaze*

c.1362 Ottoman emperor trains slaves as soldiers; he uses these "janissaries" as a bodyguard

1324 Mansa Musa, emperor of Mali, goes on a pilgrimage to Mecca

c.1211 Mongol hordes invade China and cross the Great Wall

MALI EMPIRE

Niger

c.1200 Lalibela, emperor of Ethiopia, builds great churches out of rock

c.1336 The Hindu kingdom of Vijayanagar founded, which expands to dominate southern India

Mekong

c.1200 Polynesians on Tongan islands build a coral monument to symbolize the two strong sons of their ruler

AFRICA

c.1300 Bantu-speaking peoples farm, hunt, and trade

OCEANIA

INDIAN OCEAN

N

AUSTRALIA

NEW ZEALAND

Arab Islamic conquests | Maya Empire | Mongol conquests | Castle building | Expansion of trade | Viking voyages

600 | 800 | 1000 | 1200 | 1400 | 1600 | 1700 | 1800 | 1900 | 2000

1200

1250

AFRICA

c.1200–30 King Lalibela of Ethiopia responsible for churches cut from rock

1218 Ayyubid Empire breaks up but Ayyubids rule Egypt to 1250

c.1220 City-state of Kilwa in Tanzania increases in prosperity

c.1230 Hafsid monarchy takes over from Almohads in Tunisia and acquires much trade across the Sahara desert

c.1235 Great warrior leader Sun Diata founds Mali Empire in West Africa; it expands under his rule*

Trade across the Sahara flourished; camels were the most reliable form of transport in the waterless wastes

c.1250 Kanem kingdom in Lake Chad region begins to break up into rival factions

1250 Last Ayyubid ruler in Egypt murdered; Mamluks, soldiers from central Asia employed by Ayyubids, seize power and found military state*

1260–77 Mamluk commander Baybars takes over as sultan of Egypt

This candlestick was made by craftspeople in Mamluk Egypt

ASIA

c.1203 Hojo family rules Japan after Minamoto Yoritomo's death

1206 Former Turkestan slave Aibak founds new sultanate of Delhi in north India

1206 Mongol Empire founded by Genghis Khan*

1229 Christians regain Jerusalem but lose it in 1244

This Persian manuscript shows Genghis Khan in his tent or yurt

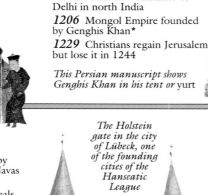

This Persian tile is decorated with a dashing horseman; the Mongol founders of the kingdom of Persia were famous for their horsemanship

1256 Hulagu, grandson of Genghis Khan, founds Mongol kingdom of Persia

1260 Khubilai, grandson of Genghis, becomes Great Khan*

1260 Battle of Ain Jalut – Mongols, under Hulagu, halted by Mamluks in Palestine

1271 Venetian explorer Marco Polo sets out for China*

1281 Mongols driven away from Japan by *kamikaze*, the divine wind*

EUROPE

1209 St. Francis of Assisi founds Franciscan religious order

1212 Almohads defeated by Christians at battle of Las Navas de Tolosa

1215 English King John seals Magna Carta, giving more power to barons*

1240 Russian Alexander Nevsky defeats Swedes at great battle on the Neva River*

1241 Lübeck and Hamburg form a Hansa (association) for trade and mutual protection; beginning of Hanseatic League*

1249 University College, first college of Oxford University, England, founded

The Holstein gate in the city of Lübeck, one of the founding cities of the Hanseatic League

c.1254 Explorer Marco Polo born in Venice

1262 Iceland and Greenland come under Norwegian rule

1273 Rudolph I becomes first Hapsburg ruler of Austria

1282–84 Edward I of England conquers Wales

1284 Peterhouse, first college of Cambridge University, founded in England

⬜ *1284* Sequins coined in Venice, Italy

⬜ *c.1290* Invention of spectacles in Italy

1291 Three Swiss cantons join together to begin struggle for independence from Hapsburgs

The great explorer Marco Polo is here dressed in the costume of a Tatar

AMERICAS

This simple earthenware statuette comes from the Cuzco region of Peru

c.1200 Cahokia in North America, city of temple mounds, at its height*

c.1200 Incas in Peru centered around growing settlement of Cuzco

c.1200–50 Complexes of apartment blocks and circular kivas built at Cliff Canyon and Fewkes Canyon, Colorado

This Maya funerary urn contains the complete skeleton of a baby

c.1250s Chimu people expand their empire along northern coast of Peru

c.1250s Maya revival: following collapse of Chichén Itzá, a new capital is built at Mayapán

OCEANIA

c.1200 Tui Tonga monarchy builds coral platform for ceremonial worship on island of Tonga in South Pacific

This Tongan ceremonial paddle made of a hard wood was sometimes also used as a weapon

c.1250 Beginnings of intensive valley irrigation schemes in Hawaiian Islands

| 40,000 BC | | 10,000 | 5000 | 1000 | 500 | AD 1 | 200 | 400 |

1300

1300 Ife culture of West Africa produces famous brasses

1324 Emperor of Mali, Mansa Musa, goes on a pilgrimage to Mecca, Arabia

1348 Egypt devastated by plague, called Black Death

This 14th-century map shows the pilgrimage of Mansa Musa to Mecca

1350

c.1350 Kingdom of Great Zimbabwe in southern Africa thrives on gold trade

1352–53 Ibn Battuta, Berber scholar, travels across Africa and writes an account of all he sees

1380s Foundation of Kongo kingdom in Congo river mouth region of Zaire, Central Africa

Fishing played an important part in Mali life

The magnificent tomb near Delhi of the murdered founder of the Tughluq dynasty, Ghiyas-ud-din Tughluq

c.1300 Osman I founds Ottoman dynasty in Turkey*

1321 Tughluq dynasty founded in Delhi*

1335–38 Ashikaga Takauji, Japanese general, rebels against emperor and becomes first of the Ashikaga shoguns

1336 Hindu empire of Vijayanagar in India founded by Harihara I becomes center of resistance to Islam*

1350 Last Hindu Javanese kingdom of Majapahit begins to spread in southeast Asia

1368 Mongols driven out of China; Zhu Yuanzhang founds Ming dynasty

c.1390 Ottoman Turks complete conquest of Asia Minor

1398 Tamerlane sacks Delhi*

The Ming dynasty was famous for its patronage of the arts; this little bronze figure is of an immortal and is the symbol of old men

---

1308 Papal court moves to Avignon; Great Schism follows

1314 Scots defeat English at Battle of Bannockburn*

1337 Edward III of England claims French throne – 100 Years War (1337–1453) begins*

1346 English defeat French at Battle of Crécy

1347 Bubonic plague or Black Death reaches Europe*

Edward III of England and his son, the Black Prince, won several battles in the 100 Years War

1358 Jacquerie revolt; peasant uprising north of Paris, France*

1370 Geoffrey Chaucer writes first book, *Book of the Duchess*

1373 Treaty of Anglo-Portuguese friendship; the English and Portuguese are still allies today

1381 Peasants' Revolt in England led by Wat Tyler*

1389 Christian Serbs defeated by Ottoman Turks at Kossovo in Serbia

1397 Kalmar Agreement unites three Scandinavian kingdoms of Denmark, Norway, and Sweden

A gathering of discontented peasants; living conditions in much of Europe were so bad that separate revolts sprang up in many countries

---

c.1300 Incas begin to expand their empire throughout the central Andes

c.1325 Aztecs found city of Tenochtitlan (now Mexico City) on an island in Lake Texcoco*

This Aztec carved wooden drum was used for ceremonial purposes, possibly as an accompaniment to sacrificial ceremonies

c.1370 Acamapitchtli chosen king of Aztecs

c.1390s Viracocha becomes eighth Inca ruler; an Inca myth tells how he traveled to the Pacific and never returned*

Although most Incas traveled on foot, Inca royalty and nobility were often transported in litters in considerable style

---

c.1300 Hawaiian peoples start to develop class structure as a result of economic growth through agriculture

c.1300 Stone temple complexes, or "marae," erected in Rarotonga, Cook Islands, and on Moorea Island in the Society Islands

c.1300 Huge stone statues erected on Easter Island*

The stone statues of Easter Island were sometimes built in the craters of extinct volcanoes

c.1350 Maoris flourish on the North Island, New Zealand; first terrace-type fortifications, called *pa*, built

This ceremonial carved adze from New Zealand was carried by a man of high rank

| 600 | 800 | 1000 | 1200 | 1400 | 1600 | 1700 | 1900 | 2000 |

1200-1400 AFRICA

In West Africa, the once-powerful kingdom of Ghana was displaced in the 13th century by the new kingdom of Mali. The people of Mali continued to profit by the caravan trade across the Sahara to and from North Africa. In Egypt, the Ayyubid dynasty was overthrown by the Mamluks, who were formerly soldiers in the employ of the Ayyubids. In Ethiopia, there was a revival of fortune under the great Zagwe ruler, Lalibela. Christianity flourished and many churches were built. Further south, by the end of the 1300s, the Kongo kingdom had arisen on the Congo River in Zaire.

Cavalrymen
This manuscript, produced c.1348, shows Mamluk cavalrymen exercising their horses.

c.1235

The Mali Empire founded

As the Ghana Empire declined, it was taken over and ruled by two of its subject peoples, first the Susa and then the Keita. In the 1230s, the Keita were ruled by a great warrior king, Sun Diata. He founded a new West African kingdom in Mali. Mali became much larger than Ghana and all earlier kingdoms, expanding north, south, and west and taking control of the caravan trade centers of the southern Sahara such as Timbuktu and Gao. Sun Diata converted to Islam and his most famous successor, Mansa Musa (1312–37), went on a pilgrimage to Mecca. By 1337, the Mali Empire was one of the great African empires. A tolerant legal system made Mali a rich and peaceful land.

Mali
During the 14th century, Mali exported gold from the Niger and Senegal river valleys into North Africa.

Heart of an empire
Kirina was one of the towns on the Niger which formed the heart of the Mali Empire. The small grain stores here are raised on stones to keep the grain dry and away from rats.

Mamluk mace
The Mamluks founded a military aristocracy which produced strong generals and an efficient army.

1250

Mamluks seize power in Egypt

The Ayyubid sultanate of Egypt founded by Saladin was overthrown in 1250 by the Mamluks. *Mamluk* was the Arab word for "owned," for the Mamluks were originally slaves employed as soldiers by Muslim rulers. In 1258 the Muslim world was stunned by the Mongol seizure of Baghdad.

In 1260 the Mongol leader Hulagu sent an army against Egypt, but it was utterly defeated at the battle of Ain Jalut in Palestine. One of the Mamluk commanders, Baybars, a Turkish slave, subsequently seized power and made himself sultan. He was a great leader and organized important building works, irrigation schemes, and an efficient postal service.

The Mamluk Empire
The Mamluk Empire became rich through their domination of the silk and spice routes of Syria and Palestine.

Mosque lamp
Under Sultan Baybars, the Mamluks created many beautiful objects. Their rule declined in the late 1300s through greed and corruption at court.

40,000 BC		10,000	5000	1000	500	AD 1	200	400

1200-1400 ASIA

Asia in this period was dominated by the Mongol conqueror Genghis Khan and his family, but some of the continent stayed free from their control. In Asia Minor, a Turkish leader, Osman, founded the Ottoman kingdom. The Muslim sultans of Delhi ruled much of north India, but Vijayanagar in the south remained independent.

Proud horseman
Genghis Khan's military might was based on the speed and ferocity of his mounted archers.

Admired archers
Mongol cavalrymen carried a bow, two quivers, and about 30 arrows. The most skilled rode to the furthest Mongol lands to bring back news about enemies and the concerns of border people.

Mongol quiver

The Mongol Empire
The different parts of the empire gradually became independent. Khubilai did not control the Ilkhanate of Persia or the Khanate of the Golden Horde in southern Russia.

RULE OF THE MONGOLS

1167 Birth of Genghis Khan in Mongolia

1206 Mongol tribes confirm Genghis as Great Khan, or ruler

1211 Mongol troops enter China

1215 Beijing besieged and falls to Genghis Khan

1227 Death of Genghis; his son Ogödei succeeds

1260 Khubilai is elected Great Khan

1279 Khubilai recognized as ruler of all China

1294 Death of Khubilai

1368 Mongols driven from China by Ming forces

1395 Tamerlane, descendant of Genghis Khan, invades large parts of southern Russia

1398 Tamerlane takes Delhi

1402 Tamerlane defeats Ottomans at Ankyra

1405 Death of Tamerlane

1206

The rule of Genghis Khan

The Mongols were nomads of central Asia. In 1206 their bravest leader, 44-year-old Temuchin, was chosen as khan, or ruler, and took the name Genghis, or Lord Absolute. He aimed to conquer the world. In 1211 his armies entered China and in 1215 captured Zhongdu, later called Peking and now known as Beijing. They then overran central Asia, Afghanistan, and much of Persia. By the time of Genghis's death in 1227, as he himself said, it took almost a year to ride from one end of his empire to the other and back. His successors soon conquered southern Russia and briefly invaded eastern Europe. They defeated the divided states of northern Russia and exacted tribute from them.

1260

Khubilai is elected Great Khan

Genghis's family continued to expand the Mongol Empire. They conquered Iraq and the rest of Persia. One grandson, Khubilai, was elected Great Khan in 1260. He moved to Beijing in China, crushed the Song dynasty in the south, and was recognized as ruler of all China in 1279. Khubilai was a statesman as well as a warrior. He ordered the building of long roads to connect far-flung parts of his empire. He organized charity for the sick and food supplies in case of famine.

Traveling home
Mongols lived in circular tents, or *yurts*. Women moved them from place to place in wagons.

| 600 | 800 | 1000 | 1200 | 1400 | 1600 | 1700 | 1800 | 1900 | 2000 |

1271
Marco Polo travels to China

In 1271 Niccolo and Maffeo Polo, two brothers from Venice in Italy, set off for China with Niccolo's 17-year-old son, Marco. They traveled via Palestine, Persia, central Asia, and across the Gobi desert in Mongolia, reaching the court of Khubilai Khan in Beijing in 1274. The Europeans were made welcome by the great Mongol emperor, who took a liking to young Marco. He sent him on many missions to distant parts of his vast empire, even making him governor of a province. The Polos spent 17 years in China, finally returning to Venice in 1295. They brought with them a fortune in precious stones, and fabulous tales of the wealth and magnificence of China. Marco's account of his travels astonished European readers.

Warm welcome
This painting shows the Polo family arriving at the court of Khubilai. The artist has portrayed the Khan as a European king.

The cost of success
In civil wars, soldiers were rewarded with captured lands, but after the kamikaze wind successes, there were no prizes to give out. This led to unrest and governmental collapse.

Those men who struggled ashore were cut down by Japanese soldiers

1281
Typhoon saves Japan

When he became emperor of China, Khubilai Khan adopted many Chinese characteristics and grew to love the country he had conquered, yet he always wanted to extend Mongol power. In 1274 he launched a fleet against Japan, but much of it was destroyed by a storm. In 1275 he sent envoys to demand Japan's complete submission. The Japanese killed the envoys, so in 1281 Khubilai sent another fleet carrying some 150,000 troops to attack Japan. The Japanese managed to hold off the invaders for seven weeks. At this point a typhoon struck the Mongol force and destroyed over half of it. The Japanese called these welcome storms *kamikaze* or divine winds.

c.1300
The birth of the Ottoman Empire

Osman I
The Ottoman dynasty ruled in an unbroken line for more than 600 years.

The Ottoman Empire
In 1326, the empire occupied only a small part of Turkey. By 1400 it covered some 167,000 sq miles (433,000 sq km).

As Mongol power in Asia began to decline toward the end of the 13th century, new principalities were created in lands taken from the Byzantine Empire. Each was ruled by a "beg" or prince. Among the first was Osman (or Othman), who in about 1300 founded the principality of Osmani (or Ottoman) in the northeast of Turkey. He gradually expanded the new state and introduced Islamic ideas of law and government. In 1317 he began the siege of the fortified city of Bursa which took nearly nine years to capture. After its fall, Bursa became the Ottoman capital. Osman died in 1326.

Black Sea
Constantinople
Sea of Marmara
• Bursa
OTTOMAN EMPIRE
Sakarya

JANISSARIES

Around 1362 the Ottomans raised an elite corps of foot-soldiers recruited from slaves. The corps was strengthened by the introduction of child tribute, levied on non-Muslim subjects of the Ottoman Empire.

1321

The rise of the Tughluqs

At the end of the 13th century, the Muslim sultanate of Delhi spent many years defeating the Mongols, but fell into chaos after 1316. In 1321 the nobles elected a Turkish general with an Indian mother as sultan. He was Ghiyas-ud-din Tughluq, who founded the Tughluq dynasty. He planned and encouraged construction and agricultural developments before being murdered by his son Mohammed, under whom the Tughluq Empire reached its greatest extent. By the time of his death in 1351, his tyranny had provoked widespread revolt in the provinces. His successor, Firoz Shah, held the core Tughluq territories together and organized a great building program, founding several new cities, but at his death in 1388 the empire again disintegrated.

Murderous building
Mohammed bin Tughluq erected a splendid pavilion to welcome his father home from a military campaign. However, the pavilion was designed to collapse when struck by elephants passing in parade. It did so. Ghiyas-ud-din Tughluq was killed and his son succeeded.

Madurai temples
The rulers of Vijayanagar were responsible for building a number of large Hindu temples lavishly decorated with paintings and sculpture.

1336

Hindus resist Islam

Even under the vigorous Tughluqs, Muslim forces were never successful in conquering all India. A new Hindu state in the south, Vijayanagar, founded by five brothers, became the center of resistance to Islam. The eldest brother, Harihara I, created a well-organized civil service which ran the growing empire and a strong army to defend it. The city of Vijayanagar, built as the capital, was full of gorgeous palaces and temples, designed in a unique style. The empire lasted until the mid 1500s.

Tamerlane
Tamerlane, a Muslim, was a gifted general. He indulged in a policy of terrorism against those peoples who resisted him.

1398

The sack of Delhi

By the mid 1300s, the Mongol Empire had largely broken up. Then in 1369, Timur "Leng" ("the lame"), known as Tamerlane, made himself ruler of Samarkand. Claiming descent from Genghis Khan, he set out to re-create the great khan's empire. With an army of superb horsemen, he conquered Persia, Iraq, Syria, Afghanistan, and part of Russia. In 1397 he invaded India, attacking the Tughluq Empire. He sacked Delhi in 1398, killing most of its people. His last goal was China, but he died on the way there in 1405.

Tamerlane's empire in 1397
In 1397, Tamerlane set out for Delhi, which was the key to eastern Asia.

Tomb tile
This 14th-century glazed tile reputedly came from the tomb of a Mongol lord, Buyan Kuli Khan. Such tiles adorned the tombs of rulers in Samarkand.

600	800	1000	1200	1400	1600	1700	1800	1900	2000

1200-1400 EUROPE

T he Asian conquests of Genghis Khan and his family opened up trade routes to Europe, and merchants benefited from expanding trade between the two continents. Commercial towns in northern Europe joined together to form the Hanseatic League, controlling trade in the Baltic and North Sea. Fervor for the Crusades faded as Christians were driven out of western Asia once and for all by the Ottoman Turks. In 1348 the Black Death devastated most of the continent, and deteriorating living conditions led to revolts by working people in England and France.

Silver collar
This collar, made in the second half of the 15th century in Holland, is believed to have been worn by leaders of a Confraternity of Archers.

Sealing ceremony
After much haggling with the barons, King John stamped the Magna Carta with his royal seal, to show he agreed to their demands.

1215

King John and the Magna Carta

During the reign of King John of England (1199–1216), serious disagreements broke out between the monarchy and the barons. The barons wanted more involvement in the government of the country, while the king tried to keep all the power for himself. A number of defeats for the king in France, and quarrels with the Church, made his position weaker, and on June 15, 1215, at Runnymede in southern England, the barons presented him with the Magna Carta, or the Great Charter, a list of demands to which they made him agree. But the Pope, Innocent III, absolved John from his oath to grant the demands, because he believed that no anointed monarch should be made to sign away his rights.

The Great Charter
Only a few of the 63 demands in the Magna Carta promised anything for the common people.

1240

The Battle of the Neva

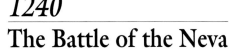

In the early 13th century, Russia west of the Ural mountains consisted of several states including Novgorod, Vladimir, and Kiev. Between 1237 and 1240 Mongols overran much of Russia. In 1240 Novgorod was invaded by a Swedish army. Alexander, Prince of Novgorod, defeated the Swedes in a great battle on the river Neva, and two years later repelled an invading German-led army. He then made a peace treaty with the Mongol leader, Batu. These three events ensured that Alexander's realm was safe from foreign rule for the foreseeable future.

Nevsky's helmet
Alexander's victory on the river Neva earned him the title Nevsky and made him one of Russia's greatest national heroes.

The Hanseatic cog was a broad-beamed, flat-bottomed cargo ship, with a stern platform, well suited to trading in northern waters

1241

The Hanseatic League

During the 12th century, there was an expansion of trading along the north German coast and its rivers, especially the Rhine and the Elbe. At the same time, Germans began to settle further eastward toward Poland, opening up more markets. Among the earliest trade towns to flourish were Hamburg on the Elbe River and Lübeck on the Baltic Sea. In 1241 the two towns formed an association, or *hansa*, for mutual protection. Soon they were joined by other towns, and by the early 14th century a commercial and defensive alliance, later called the Hanseatic League, was well established. By the mid-14th century, it included some seventy towns, from Bruges in Flanders to Novgorod in Russia. This powerful league was chiefly commercial, to protect members' trading interests, as there was no strong German national government able to guarantee safety for trade. Normally, the league was not involved in war, but in the reign of Waldemar IV of Denmark (1340–77), it had to fight twice against his attempts to interfere with the league.

Leading city
Lübeck was a thriving trading center. Representatives from other Hanseatic towns met there to discuss trade policies and rules.

Towns and trade routes
The Hanseatic towns of northern Europe controlled trade in both the North and Baltic Seas.

CRAFT GUILDS

Guilds were groups of merchants or craftspeople created to protect members and their families. Craft guilds were formed to control wages and prices, to train apprentices and to maintain high standards of work. The pupil of a gunmaker made these tiny pistols as a test of his capability.

Pistols shown life-size

Maritime trading scene
Hanseatic ports were busy places. Here boats loaded and unloaded their cargoes, and merchants exchanged goods in the open marketplace.

Central covered marketplace

Individual market stalls sold food, cloth, leather, and other goods

600	800	1000	1200	1400	1600	1700	1800	1900	2000

Monymusk reliquary
A wooden casket in the shape of a Celtic chapel, the Monymusk reliquary was carried into battle at Bannockburn by the Scottish Abbot of Arbroath Abbey. The Declaration of Arbroath, signed in 1320, demanded recognition of Scottish independence.

1314
The Battle of Bannockburn

Ever since the early 1000s, English kings had yearned to conquer Scotland and take it over. Then, in 1296, the English king Edward I defeated Scottish armies and ruled Scotland directly. When Edward died in 1307, one Scottish claimant to the throne, Robert Bruce, began a campaign to drive the English out of Scotland. He captured castles, ambushed armies, and finally, in 1314, faced the English army, led by Edward II, at Bannockburn in central Scotland. The Scottish army won the battle, and Scotland's independence was assured for over 300 years, although it was some years before England formally recognized it.

On the battlefield
Although outnumbered three to one, Robert Bruce's superior military leadership enabled the Scots to defeat the English on the field at Bannockburn.

1337
100 Years War

Edward III became king of England in 1327. He believed he also had a claim to the French throne, but it was already occupied by Philip VI. In 1337 Edward declared war on France. This started the 100 Years War, which was to continue on and off until 1453. In 1346 Edward took an army across the English Channel to France, where he won a great victory over Philip at Crécy. In 1360 Edward gave up his claim to the French throne in return for possession of land in the west of France, but the war continued because Henry V of England later renewed the claim to the French throne.

100 Years War armor
Made from about 50,000 iron links, this chain mail vest weighed 20 lbs (9 kg).

SECRET WEAPON

The longbow, which was developed in Wales in the 1200s, revolutionized land warfare. It could pierce armor at a range of 200 yards (180 m) and could be reloaded much more quickly than the earlier crossbow, which had to be wound up before each shot. The English victory at Crécy was largely due to their use of the longbow. The French lost more than 10,000 men in the battle, the English less than 200.

100 YEARS WAR

1337 Edward III declares war on France

1346 Edward III routs French army at Crécy

1356 Black Prince wins great victory over France at Poitiers; French king, John II, captured

1374–1415 Long intervals of peace interrupted by occasional minor battles and coastal raids

1415 Henry V of England (1413–22) renews English claim to French throne, declares war, and defeats French at Agincourt

1420 Treaty of Troyes makes Henry heir to French throne; he marries Katherine, daughter of French king, Charles VI

1422 Henry V dies; war with France renewed

1429 French led by Joan of Arc defeat English at Orléans and Pataye

1431 Joan of Arc burnt at stake by English; French begin to push English out

1449 Normandy recaptured by French

1453 End of 100 Years War: French victory at Châtillon (1452) leaves only Calais in English hands

The Black Prince
One of Edward's commanders was his 16-year-old son, who was called the Black Prince because he always wore black armor. He won his spurs at the battle of Crécy.

40,000 BC		10,000	5000	1000	500	AD 1	200	400

Plague carrier
The plague was spread by fleas that lived on rats. The fleas then transferred to humans when the rats died.

1347

Black Death reaches Europe

The Black Death was an infection of bubonic plague. It began in the foothills of the Himalayas in India in the late 13th century and spread along trade routes with great rapidity. It reached China in the 1330s and struck with devastating ferocity in the Byzantine Empire in 1347. In Constantinople it was called the "Great Dying" and was soon taken to European cities such as Venice, which traded with the Byzantine Empire. By 1351 the disease, which affected rich and poor alike, had spread over most of Europe. The plague killed about one third of the total European population.

How the plague spread

Within a year of reaching the Byzantine Empire, the Black Death had spread to Italy, France, Spain, and Britain, and by 1351 Russia, too, was affected. Milan, Poland, Belgium, a small part of southwest France, and eastern Germany remained unaffected.

Death visits a plague victim
Contemporary illustrations often depicted the Black Death as a skeleton strangling its victim. Symptoms of the plague included skin turning black and high fever, and most people who caught it died. Doctors were unable to find any cure for the dreadful disease.

FRENCH PEASANT LIFE

This detail from a French tapestry shows peasants hard at work pressing grapes to make into wine. The expressions on their faces are full of discontent and contrast sharply with the superior looks of their richly dressed employers. The Jacquerie revolt, a peasant uprising that occurred north of Paris in 1358, was mainly a class war between the peasants and the nobles. The peasants were weary of the inequality of their situation and rose up, killing many nobles and their families. Repression followed, and many peasants were slaughtered.

1381

English peasants rebel

After the Black Death, there was a shortage of labor because so many workers had died. The survivors had to work harder, but their wages remained the same. This made them resentful; when the government in England introduced a new tax, the peasants decided to rebel. They marched to London to petition the 14-year-old king, Richard II, raiding and burning houses on the way. The young king met the rebels, spoke to their leader, Wat Tyler, and agreed to their demands. Meanwhile, other rebels had broken into the king's residence, sacked his rooms, and murdered the Archbishop of Canterbury and the Lord Treasurer. When the king met the peasants again the next day, a quarrel broke out. Wat Tyler was killed. The tax was abandoned and many rebels pardoned, but the king soon went back on his promises.

The protest march
Wat Tyler, an ex-soldier, led thousands of angry peasants from southern England to London to appeal to the king. Thousands more came from eastern England and joined with Tyler's force. This picture shows the two groups meeting. Wat Tyler stands on the left, and the central figure on the horse is John Ball, a priest who supported the peasants' cause.

600	800	1000	1200	1400	1600	1700	1800	1900	2000

Mound bottle
This bottle, shaped as a mother and child, comes from Cahokia.

1200-1400 AMERICAS

In North America in this period, great towns and ceremonial centers were built around the Mississippi, the most important at Cahokia in Illinois and Moundville in Alabama. In Central America, the Valley of Mexico was settled by Aztec nomads who, in about 1325, founded the city of Tenochtitlan on islands in Lake Texcoco, which was to grow into the capital of their empire. Further south, in Peru, Inca people who had settled in the Cuzco area and created a capital there, began to expand their empire. Their rulers grew powerful and by 1400 had conquered neighboring lands.

c.1200

Mounds built at Cahokia

A typical Mississippi settlement consisted of many rectangular flat-topped mounds used as bases for wooden temples and the houses of important people. The mounds were grouped around squares or beside wide streets. The largest settlement was probably Cahokia, in southern Illinois, which had over 100 mounds. The largest of these was Monk's Mound, over 98 ft (30 m) high. The structure of Cahokian society is not certain, but the people were probably ruled by chiefs, who were worshiped as gods. Elaborate tombs of some chiefs have been excavated. One was buried with 20,000 shell beads. Corpses nearby show that his family and servants were killed and buried with him.

Mound cross-section
Early European settlers in America carelessly dug up the mounds in Mississippi, destroying vital evidence of what was in them and how they were made. This painting shows the 19th-century archeologist Dr. Montreville Dickenson, who directed a painstaking investigation of some 1,000 mounds. It clearly shows the layers of earth, the skeletons, and grave goods that were uncovered by his cautious workers.

Mound builders carried the earth in baskets

Monk's Mound

Wooden fence around central square

Conch and other shells were crushed and added to clay to strengthen it

Each family made their own pots and tools to use and trade

Farmers hunted deer with a bow and arrow

Life in Cahokia
Most of the people of Cahokia were farmers. They lived in wattle and daub houses around the mounds and in villages along river banks where the soil was most fertile. They grew corn, beans, and pumpkins, which they tilled with hoes. Each household stored most of their surplus crops in a pit outside their home. Some surplus crops were taken into the city where they were redistributed to government officials and crafts workers or to foreign traders in return for mica, copper, and shells.

c.1325

Aztecs found Tenochtitlan

The Aztecs were a wandering people who arrived in the Valley of Mexico in the 13th century. They settled on two marshy islands in the south of Lake Texcoco. Energetic farmers, they floated large baskets full of earth into the marshland to create fertile raised fields called "chinampas." Then they planted trees to keep the artificial plots in place. In the 1320s they began to build a city, Tenochtitlan, on one of the islands. The site was divided into four quarters, within which were separate districts for each family group. Tenochtitlan's first ruler was a priest-king called Tenoch, who is thought to have died in about 1370. To protect their new settlement from attack, the Aztecs forged alliances with powerful leaders of local warring tribes, sometimes offering their services as mercenaries. Tenochtitlan slowly grew into a huge capital city, with over 250,000 inhabitants.

Tenochtitlan: place of the cactus

In Aztec legend, the war god gave priest-leaders a sign, an eagle on a cactus, to show them where to build Tenochtitlan. This Aztec book page shows the city with this symbol at its crossroads. The cactus fruits are red and in the shape of hearts torn from those sacrificed in the city center to feed the war god.

Aztec calendar stone
Aztec farmers needed to know when to plant and harvest. They divided a 365-day year into 18 months of 20 days each, and a further five days which were very unlucky. Calendar stones had a picture for every day.

1390s

Viracocha becomes Inca ruler

In the 12th century, some Native Americans moved down the Peruvian mountains to settle in the Cuzco valley. They were farmers and crafts workers, with few territorial ambitions. Soon a dynasty of rulers emerged, each with the name "Sapa Inca," meaning "the unique Inca." In the 1390s Hatun Tapac became Sapa Inca, taking the name of his people's supreme god, Viracocha Inca. Viracocha was the first Inca empire builder. He absorbed some of his neighbors' lands and increased his prestige by making alliances with strong local rulers. He gave top jobs in army, government, and religion to his family or associations under his control. He and his descendants came to be thought of as living gods. Those entering their presence bowed, wore no shoes, and carried a pack on their backs to show their lowly position.

Feather headdress and shirt

An Inca's clothes showed position in society. Sapa Incas wore the finest materials, threaded with gold, covered with bright feathers of tropical birds.

Stored in mountain snow
Potatoes were a staple part of the Inca's diet. They freeze-dried any surplus in case of a famine. These potatoes are over 500 years old.

Rope sandal
Men and women shared the tasks of farming. They needed strong shoes in the rough mountain terrain.

| 600 | | 1200 | 1400 | 1600 | 1700 | 1800 | 1900 | 2000 |

1200-1400 OCEANIA

I n the Polynesian Islands, a dynasty of kings, the Tui Tonga,
began to rule on the island of Tongatapu. Maoris on the
North Island, New Zealand, expanded their settlements.
Far to the east, on Easter Island, Polynesians erected huge
statues on the stone platforms which their predecessors had
been building along the coast since about 1100, or even earlier.

Top-knot style
Many statues still wore their top-
knots when Europeans first
visited, centuries later.

1 V-shaped
stone
sledge tied
to front of
statue with
rope

2 Team of men pulled rope,
which moved wooden
support forwards,
causing statue to
swing along
underneath it

*Statue tied to wooden
support with rope*

c.1300

Statues erected on Easter Island

Easter Island is on the eastern edge of Polynesia, hundreds of miles from its nearest
neighbor. It was settled by Polynesians in the sixth century. They lived on locally
grown sweet potatoes, taro, bananas, and gourds, and kept chickens and pigs. They
also built rectangular platforms, called *ahu*, along the coasts. But the great age
of Easter Island monuments and statues was much later, around 1300, when the
islanders built hundreds of *ahu* and raised massive carved statues on them. The
platforms were huge and smooth on their
seaward side where waves splashed continually
on the stone surface. One platform was 148 ft
long (45 m) and supported fifteen
statues. No one knows why the
statues were built, but they may
have had religious significance.

3 A ramp was built in front of
the *ahu*, and the statue was
moved to the top. Its huge
weight helped it to drop down
into place on the *ahu*

*Sledge protected
front of statue as it
was dragged along
the ground*

*Lever helped to
prise statue into
an upright
position on
the platform*

*Ropes controlled
fall of statue
over the edge
of the ramp*

Ahu

Standing statues
Most of the statues on Easter Island
were carved in stone quarries inside
extinct volcanic craters. Statue shapes
were cut in the rock face. When
finished on all sides except for a
holding ridge at the back, the ridge
was chipped away, the statues were
lowered to the ground and polished.
Then they were moved to the
platforms where they were set up,
singly or in rows. Many had top-
knots, cylindrical disks of dark red
stone cut from another quarry.

Vital statistics
The Easter Island statues are
huge, ranging from 10 to 40 ft
(3 to 12 m) in height, and very
heavy. The largest statue so far
found weighs 85 tons. It is
extraordinary to think that the
Polynesians carved these
colossal works of art in the
quarries and then dragged
them considerable distances
by hand to the stone platforms
along the coast where many
of them still stand today.

40,000 BC	10,000	1000	AD 1	400	800	1200	1600	1800	2000

CHAPTER 11

1400 – 1500

THE EXPANSION
OF KNOWLEDGE

Wood carving of a French school

1400-1500
THE WORLD

D URING THE 15TH CENTURY, the course of history begins to change as entire continents and civilizations cease to develop in isolation from each other. The African trade with Asia and Europe, the voyages of Chinese merchants across the Indian Ocean in search of precious raw materials, the gradual Portuguese exploitation of sea routes to India, and, at the end of the century, the voyage of Columbus across the Atlantic, all bring the peoples of the world into increasing contact with each other. For the first time in history, an international economy begins to develop.

The Renaissance

In Europe, the renaissance in art and the revival of learning, which began in the south in the late 13th century, spreads throughout the continent. It is helped by increased wealth and by the introduction of moveable-type printing, which enables information to be spread more quickly.

The Americas

The American continent remains aloof from the developments that are affecting the rest of the world. In Central America, the Aztecs, a powerful and very hard-working people, build a vast empire, while to their south, the Incas, equally powerful and extremely well organized, rule over about a third of the South American continent.

1400s Navigators set sail from Portugal to find new routes to Asia

1492 Genoese explorer Christopher Columbus sails across the Atlantic and reaches the Caribbean

1400s The Aztec capital, Tenochtitlan, expands on its island in Lake Texcoco, Mexico

1400s The Incas use llamas for transport and also trade them with other peoples

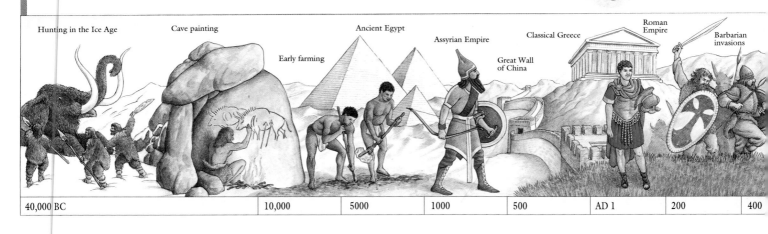

Hunting in the Ice Age

Cave painting

Early farming

Ancient Egypt

Assyrian Empire

Great Wall of China

Classical Greece

Roman Empire

Barbarian invasions

| 40,000 BC | | | 10,000 | 5000 | 1000 | 500 | AD 1 | 200 | 400 |

EUROPE

RUSSIA

1462 Ivan III becomes ruler of Russia

Moscow •

ASIA

c.1460 China exports Ming pottery

JAPAN

KOREA

1467 The Onin civil war, a dispute over shogunal succession, begins in Japan

1419–50 Reign of Korean King Sejong; he introduces an official script

NGLAND

FRANCE

SPAIN

1429 Joan of Arc leads France against the English at Orléans

1453 Ottomans take Constantinople

1411–42 Indian sultan Ahmad Shah of Gujarat builds city of Ahmadabad

Nile

ARABIA

Jedda •

1431 The Ming fleet reaches Arabia

INDIA

THAILAND

1431 The Ming fleet sets off from Nanking to collect tribute from other countries

• Gao

1400s Africa does prosperous trade with Asia and Europe

1432 Ming ships reach ports on the east coast of Africa

SRI LANKA

Malindi •

AFRICA

1498 Vasco da Gama reaches India and meets the ruler of Calicut

OCEANIA

• Sofala

c.1450 Great Zimbabwe is at the height of its power

INDIAN OCEAN

c.1400 The people of Tonga erect burial mounds for their dead

Cape of Good Hope

1497 Portuguese navigator Vasco da Gama rounds the Cape of Good Hope and sails on to India

ab Islamic onquests

Maya Empire

Mongol conquests

Castle building

Expansion of trade

Viking voyages

| 600 | 800 | 1000 | 1200 | 1400 | 1600 | 1700 | 1800 | 1900 | 2000 |

1400

1425

AFRICA

1400s Gold from mines in Zimbabwe is exported to Asia via Sofala on the east coast*

c.1400 Engaruka community farms land in Tanzania*

c.1420 Portuguese sailors begin to explore west coast of Africa

1420s Songhai people in Gao region, West Africa, begin raids on Mali Empire

This bird was carved in Zimbabwe

c.1430 Sultans of Kilwa on east African coast begin grand building program

1434–68 Reign of Christian emperor Zera Yacub in Ethiopia; he expands church and promotes great monasteries

The Great Mosque at Kilwa was extended in the 15th century

ASIA

"Fo" dog is a Chinese guardian figure

1402 Tamerlane, Mongol conqueror from central Asia, defeats Ottomans at battle of Ankyra in Turkey

c.1403–09 Encyclopedia of over 20,000 chapters, the *Yongle dadian*, compiled in China

1405–33 Chinese Muslim, Zheng He, makes seven voyages westward to collect tribute for Ming emperors

1411–42 Reign of Indian sultan Ahmad Shah of Gujarat, who builds splendid capital city of Ahmadabad*

1419–50 Korea prospers under King Sejong; he introduces official Korean script*

1420–21 Chinese Ming capital moves from Nanjing to Beijing

This Thai figurine in white glazed stoneware dates from around the reign of King Trailok

1430s Collapse of Khmer Empire in southeast Asia; Angkor Wat abandoned after being sacked by Thai army in 1431

1431–33 Zheng He makes his seventh and final voyage; he sails as far as the east coast of Africa*

1448–88 Thailand expands under King Trailok; he brings about major administrative and legal reforms*

1449–74 Rule of shogun Ashikaga Yoshimasa in Japan

EUROPE

1403 Ghiberti sculpts human bodies in realistic style for bronze doors of Florence baptistry, heralding the Renaissance

1415 John Hus, Bohemian religious reformer, burned at stake

1417 End of Great Schism in Catholic church; a single pope elected in Rome

This coin, made in honor of John Hus, bears his portrait

1429 Joan of Arc leads French forces against occupying English army at Siege of Orléans

1431 Joan of Arc is burned at the stake by the English

1430s Gutenberg, a German metalworker, experiments with printing using moveable type

1447 Casimir IV of Poland unites Polish kingdom with Grand Duchy of Lithuania

Johannes Gutenberg (1397–1468) invented a method of making type from molten metal

AMERICAS

Mississippian art often featured figures with weeping eyes, as does this vase

c.1400 Pueblo people abandon northern sites and gather in large towns

1400s Expansion of Aztec Empire in Mexico*

1400s Inca Empire enters period of expansion*

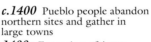

The Aztecs made large quantities of distinctive patterned and painted pots

1426–40 Aztecs at Tenochtitlan form "Triple Alliance" with neighboring cities of Texcoco and Tlacopan; emperor Itzcoatl reorganizes state to concentrate power in his hands

c.1438 Inca emperor Viracocha dies; his successor Pachacuti expands Inca Empire north to Ecuador

1440s Incas build great fortress at Cuzco

1440–68 Reign of Aztec emperor Montezuma I; he and his warriors conquer large areas of eastern Mexico, taking many people prisoner

OCEANIA

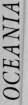

c.1400 Tonga people build major ceremonial center at Mu'a, on the largest island in the Tongatapu Group, South Pacific Ocean*

1400s Widespread cultivation of wet taro in Hawaiian Islands

Taro, a starchy root vegetable, was prepared outside the home

40,000 BC		10,000	5000	1000	500	AD 1	200	400

1450

c.1450 Building at Great Zimbabwe, southern Africa, at its height

1462 Sonni Ali becomes ruler of the Songhai and goes on to build an empire*

The center of Songhai life was the village

c.1460 Imperial porcelain works at Jingdezhen in China successfully export Ming pottery abroad

1463–79 War between Ottoman Turks and Venetians; Turks eventually triumphant*

1467–77 Onin War in Japan, a civil war beginning as a conflict over shogunal succession, ends Ashikaga shogunate's authority*

Ming statuettes of laughing boys

1453 Ottomans besiege and capture Constantinople, ending Byzantine Empire*

☐1 **1453** End of 100 Years War; English expelled from all France except Calais*

1455–56 First Bible printed in Europe by Gutenberg

1456 Hungarians under nobleman John Hunyadi storm Belgrade and drive out Turks

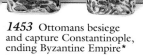

These 15th-century French pattens were worn over shoes to protect them from mud

This sculpture of St. Sebastian is a striking example of the art of the Renaissance in northern Europe

1462–1505 Reign of Ivan III (the Great), Grand Prince of Muscovy*

1466 Birth of Erasmus, Dutch scholar and leader of revival of learning in northern Europe

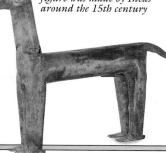

This gold and silver llama figure was made by Incas around the 15th century

c.1450 Inca city of Machu Picchu built on high ridge above Urubamba River in Peru

1455 Huge temple built to Aztec war god Huitzilopochtli in Tenochtitlan

1470s Collapse of Chimu culture in northern Peru

1471–93 Emperor Topa Inca expands Inca Empire into Bolivia, Chile, and Argentina

1473 Tenochtitlan absorbs neighboring Aztec city, Tlatelolco

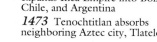

1475

1482 Portuguese explore Congo river estuary

1491 Ruler of Kongo kingdom baptized as Christian by Portuguese

1483 Ashikaga Yoshimasa completes building of the Silver Pavilion temple, or Ginkakuji, at Kyoto in Japan

1488 First major Ikko-ikki, or uprising of Ikko Buddhists, in Japan

1488 Ming emperors order rebuilding of Great Wall to defend China from northern invaders

1492 Sikander Lodi, sultan of Delhi (1489–1517), annexes Bihar and moves his capital to Agra to facilitate conquest of Rajasthan

Portuguese explorers sailed to Africa in carracks such as these

The Temple of the Silver Pavilion got its name from Ashikaga Yoshimasa's plan to cover it in silver

1478–92 Rule of Renaissance art patron, Lorenzo de Medici

1479 Crowns of Aragon and Castile in Spain united under Ferdinand and Isabella

1480 Spanish Inquisition introduced to uncover heresy

1485 Henry VII becomes first Tudor king of England and Wales after defeat of last Plantagenet king Richard III at the Battle of Bosworth

The Spanish Inquisition tortured Jews and Muslims cruelly

1492 Christian Spanish capture Granada in Spain from Muslims

1492 Christopher Columbus lands on Bahama Islands, Cuba, and Hispaniola; he is first European to reach Americas since Vikings

1497–99 Portuguese Vasco da Gama rounds Cape of Good Hope, South Africa, and sails on to India

1498 Italian religious reformer, Savonarola, burned at stake

1486–1502 Rule of Aztec emperor Ahuitzotl; Aztec Empire at height of power in Mexico

This beautiful Aztec statue is of the god of flowers; he is seen here standing on top of a temple

1400-1500 AFRICA

The rich Mali Empire in West Africa was taken over by the Songhai people, whose growing strength also affected the neighboring Hausa states and Kanem-Bornu. Also in the west, the two large towns of Timbuktu and Jenne were important centers of trade with Europe and Asia. To the east, in Tanzania and Kenya, several local cultures flourished, notably at Engaruka, where irrigation farming was practiced. The gold-producing Zimbabwe civilization in southern Africa reached its most powerful extent and huge urban enclosures of stone were built.

Shell money
The Africans used cowrie shells as a form of currency.

c.1400

The Engaruka people

The Engaruka were a self-supporting farming community in northern Tanzania, about 100 miles (160 km) west of Kilimanjaro. As the land was on a steep slope, they had to build drystone platforms to level it off before building on top of them. Beside the settlements, which covered up to 8 sq miles (20 sq km), the Engaruka terraced the hillsides in order to grow crops. These fields were supported by stone walls, and irrigated by directing water along stone-lined canals from the river Engaruka. The settlements have been excavated since the 1960s, and evidence shows that the site was occupied for many years. It is not clear how the Engaruka culture came to an end, but it may have been affected by a long period of drought that made it impossible to continue farming.

1462

Sonni Ali becomes ruler of Songhai

The land of the Songhai people of West Africa adjoined that of the rich Mali Empire. The Songhai started to raid Mali land in the early 1400s and by the middle of the century had become a serious threat. Under their ruler, Sonni Ali (1462–92), they overran large areas in the eastern Mali Empire. This land became the Songhai Empire. Sonni Ali was a military commander and spent much of his reign campaigning. He strengthened the new empire by taking over and developing the main trade centers in Mali, such as Timbuktu and Jenne, as well as expanding his own capital of Gao. Having overrun much of Mali, he aimed to preserve its best features and develop them under better management. He died in 1492 and was succeeded by his son, who within the year was displaced by one of Sonni's leading generals, Askia Mohammed Turré.

River empire
The Songhai were situated around the bend of the Niger River in West Africa.

Crops included millet and corn

Thatched roofs were probably woven from tall grasses growing nearby

Living quarters
The Engaruka people lived in circular houses made of timber, mud, and thatch, and built stone walls around the settlements to keep out intruders.

Commercial capital
The Songhai capital at Gao was an important trade center which controlled trade across the Sahara.

The outside wall was 16 ft (5 m) thick at the base, and 32 ft (9·75 m) tall

1400s
Great Zimbabwe

In about the ninth century, crop-farming and livestock-rearing people living in the wide Zimbabwe plateau between the Zambezi and Limpopo rivers in southern Africa learned how to extract gold from nearby mines. Soon they were trading it beyond their immediate neighbors, and by the 1200s Zimbabwe gold, and also copper, were being exported across the Indian Ocean to Asia, in return for a variety of goods, such as Chinese porcelain. The Zimbabwean rulers prospered from this trade and created a rich and powerful empire. In the 1100s they began to build large stone enclosures called *mazimbabwe*. By around 1450 the settlement at Great Zimbabwe reached its greatest extent, when massive walls and a huge tower were added to the main enclosure. By this time, it had become a major religious, political, and trading center.

The ruler and his entourage lived in round thatched houses inside the enclosure

Stone dwelling
The main enclosure at Great Zimbabwe was built over a period of about 400 years. It was later abandoned, possibly because the surrounding land was no longer fertile enough to maintain the inhabitants.

The stone conical tower was solid all the way through

Soapstone bird
Birds carved from soapstone were mounted on columns which stood in an enclosure outside the palace of Great Zimbabwe. One of these birds became the national symbol of Zimbabwe when the country gained its independence from Britain in 1980.

A chevron pattern decorated part of the outside wall

Rooofless remains
None of the oval enclosures at Great Zimbabwe appear to have had roofs. The site was originally covered in large boulders, some of which were incorporated into the buildings. Others were split into building blocks and used to form walls.

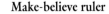

Make-believe ruler
The mythical Emperor Mutota is said to have expanded his territory away from Great Zimbabwe during the 15th century.

AFRICAN TRADE

The African continent is rich in natural resources such as gold, copper, and salt. During the 15th century, African merchants exported such goods to Arabia, India, China, and Europe, in return for luxury goods such as porcelain and silk. The ancient Ghana Empire in the west, and its successors, the Mali and the Songhai empires, thrived by trading gold, which by the 15th and 16th centuries was in great demand in Europe. The gold arrived there via Muslim traders in North Africa, who transported it on camel trains across the Sahara. To the south, Zimbabwe prospered from trading gold and copper, which were exported via the port of Sofala as far as India and China. In the later 15th century, Portuguese explorers sailed around the African coast, opening the way for the Portuguese in the 16th century to establish trading stations up the east coast. Contact with Europe also led to an increase in the slave trade.

Ruins in Africa
Merchants from Asia may have stayed at the town of Gedi on the east coast of Africa on their way to do business in the interior.

FOREIGN RELATIONS
Envoys from Africa traveled abroad bearing gifts to foreign rulers with whom they wished to maintain good trade relations. This envoy is taking a giraffe as a gift to the Chinese emperor.

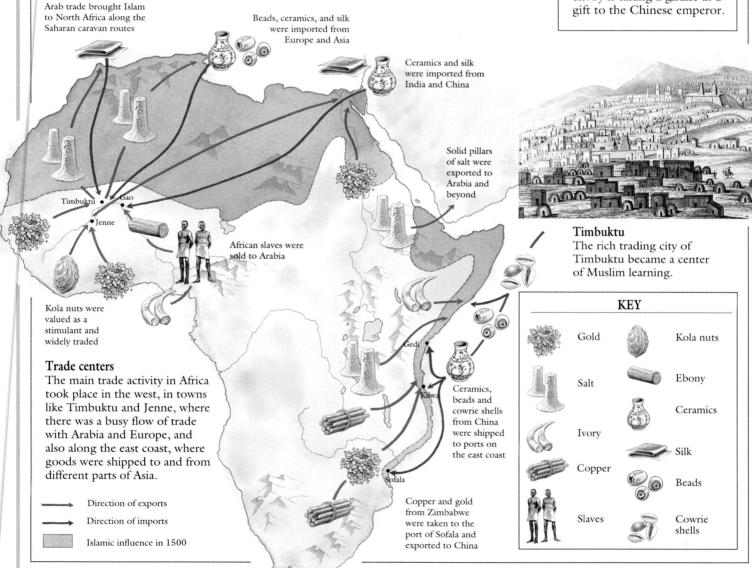

Arab trade brought Islam to North Africa along the Saharan caravan routes

Beads, ceramics, and silk were imported from Europe and Asia

Ceramics and silk were imported from India and China

Solid pillars of salt were exported to Arabia and beyond

African slaves were sold to Arabia

Kola nuts were valued as a stimulant and widely traded

Timbuktu · Gao

Jenne

Gedi

Kilwa

Sofala

Ceramics, beads and cowrie shells from China were shipped to ports on the east coast

Copper and gold from Zimbabwe were taken to the port of Sofala and exported to China

Timbuktu
The rich trading city of Timbuktu became a center of Muslim learning.

Trade centers
The main trade activity in Africa took place in the west, in towns like Timbuktu and Jenne, where there was a busy flow of trade with Arabia and Europe, and also along the east coast, where goods were shipped to and from different parts of Asia.

→ Direction of exports

→ Direction of imports

▨ Islamic influence in 1500

KEY

Gold		Kola nuts	
Salt		Ebony	
Ivory		Ceramics	
Copper		Silk	
Slaves		Beads	
		Cowrie shells	

1400-1500 ASIA

When Mongol aggression in Asia subsided, individual countries began to reassert their independence. China rebuilt its old power and began to spread its influence further afield. In Thailand, reforms were introduced which were to last for centuries. The Yi dynasty in Korea patronized an era of learning. To the east, Japan was disturbed by civil wars. In India, the sultanate of Delhi declined rapidly and provinces remote from the center became independent under local Muslim dynasties.

Korean royal tombs
These statues from the Chim Jon royal tombs near Seoul, South Korea, date from the 15th century.

1411
Ahmad Shah founds Ahmadabad

The Delhi sultanate in India, ruled by the Tughluqs since 1320, began to break up in the 1390s into smaller independent sultanates. In 1401 Zafar Khan, the last governor appointed by the Delhi sultans, proclaimed his independence. In 1411 he was succeeded by his grandson, Ahmad Shah. Ahmad ruled sternly but fairly, and trade prospered. He founded a new capital at Ahmadabad where he built one of India's finest cities. Much of his reign was taken up with increasing his territory. His undefeated armies were composed of soldiers who were paid half in cash and half in plots of land, which gave them a stake in their own country. Ahmad Shah died in 1442.

Exquisite window
This carved stone window is from an Ahmadabad mosque.

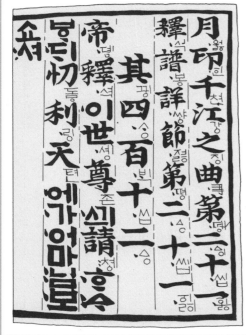

1419
King Sejong rules Korea

For many years, Korea was a semi-independent province of China. In the 1250s the Mongols invaded Korea and took over the monarchy, holding power for over a century. Around 1354 a Korean army chief, Yi Song-gye, led a successful revolt against the Mongols, and returned Korea to Chinese rule. Then, in 1392, he overturned the ruling Chinese Koryo dynasty. He founded the Yi dynasty and set up his capital at Kyon-Song, or present-day Seoul. In 1419, a relative of his, Sejong, became king of Korea and ruled for 32 years. Sejong was a great patron of learning. During his reign, a new official Korean alphabetic script, known as "Han'gul," was introduced, and he also showed great interest in the development of movable-type printing. In addition to his contribution to learning, Sejong was successful in stopping Japanese piracy along the Korean coasts.

Patron of learning
King Sejong was an enthusiastic reformer and encouraged many intellectual pursuits.

Royal poetry
This poem was written by King Sejong for his deceased wife, Queen Sohon, in 1447.

600	800	1000	1200	1400	1600	1700	1800	1900	2000

Dinner plate
This Ming household dish would have been used to serve food.

1431
The seventh voyage of Zheng He

The Ming dynasty encouraged the opening up of China, and Zheng He (1371–1433) did much to achieve this. A Chinese Muslim by birth, he was appointed commander of the Ming fleet by the emperor, Yong Le. Between 1405 and 1433, Zheng He led seven expeditions westward into the Indian Ocean, calling at numerous ports to collect tribute from the countries over which China considered it had power and to extend Chinese influence abroad. On his travels he carried goods such as gold, porcelain, silks, and spices for trading. Following the emperor's death in 1424, Zheng He made one final voyage, possibly the grandest of all. He set sail from Nanking, the first Ming capital, in 1431 and traveled as far as Jedda on the Red Sea, where he formed good relations with the local Muslims, helped by his own Muslim origins. He sent ships on to visit ports on the east coast of Africa, such as Mogadishu and Malindi, and finally returned to China in 1433, where he died.

Third Ming emperor
Emperor Yong Le (1402–24) was an all-powerful ruler. He enlarged the Chinese empire considerably during his reign.

THE MING DYNASTY 1368–1644

The Ming period began in 1368 when Hong Wu, a Chinese peasant who had led revolts against the Mongols, set up a new dynasty at Nanking and finally drove out the Mongols. He revived Chinese self-confidence and national pride, a significant achievement after years of Mongol rule, and began to restore China's power over its neighbors. He also established good government and ensured a long period of peace and prosperity. Much was done to make Chinese society more equal: slavery was abolished, large estates were confiscated and redistributed among the poor, and higher taxes were raised from the rich. Meanwhile, a strong army was maintained to deal with foreign attacks, and the Great Wall was repaired and strengthened. Hong Wu was succeeded by a grandson in 1398, and future emperors continued the good works he had begun.

Chinese junk
The Ming fleet was made up of flat-bottomed cargo-carrying junks.

Wooden slats kept sails flat

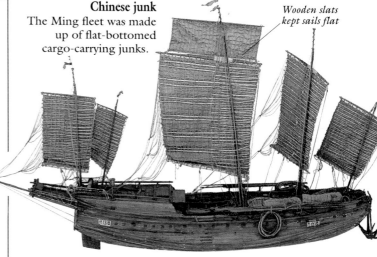

Roof decoration
Emperor Yong Le sponsored the arts, and so the Ming period was a creative one. This beautiful horse ridge tile would have been used to adorn a roof.

Ports of call
Zheng He's early expeditions took him to southeast Asia, Sri Lanka, and India. He later visited Arabia and the east coast of Africa.

1448
King Trailok reforms Thailand

In the 12th and 13th centuries, the part of southeast Asia known today as Thailand consisted of small states that vied with each other for control of the fertile central lowlands. In the mid-14th century, the kingdom of Ayutha was founded in the south. It grew to take in part of the coveted lowlands and came to be known as Siam. In 1448 King Trailok came to the Siamese throne. He was a great administrator, whose legal reforms lasted until the mid-19th century. He organized the administration in a practical way, into military and civilian divisions, with departments for local government, finance, and law. He also split Siamese society into classes, each of which had a given amount of land for every one of its members. Even the poorest people had some land, so no-one went hungry. Much of Trailok's reign was taken up with wars with northern states. As his empire grew, he moved his capital north to P'itsanulok. Trailok died in 1488, having appointed his son "second king," an office that lasted until the middle of the 19th century.

Bronze Buddha
Buddhism had become the dominant religion in Thailand by the 15th century. Many images of Buddha were made.

Thai treasure
This beautiful gold elephant is encrusted with semiprecious stones.

1463
Turco-Venetian conflict

Venice was a city-state in northern Italy. Founded in about the sixth century, it prospered through vigorous trading with Asia and the use of an increasingly powerful navy. From 1100 onward, the Venetians set up outposts in the eastern Mediterranean and became the most important power in the region. In the 15th century the Ottoman Turks challenged Venetian trading power. A great war broke out in 1463, which lasted for 16 years. The Ottomans finally triumphed, after at one time reaching almost to the center of Venice. Peace was made in 1479, in which Venice was allowed to keep some of its outposts in the eastern Mediterranean but had to pay to the Ottoman sultan a large amount of money every year.

Lethal weapon
This Italian war hammer, dated 1490, was used in battle against the Ottomans.

Merchant city
Pilgrims often stopped in Venice on their way to the Holy Land.

1467
Onin War in Japan

There had been many internal wars between feudal lords under the Ashikaga shoguns of Japan up to the mid-15th century. Lords gained more control over their lands and the lives of those living there. This led to peasant uprisings. By 1467 Ashikaga shogun Yoshimasa felt unable to cope with the disorders and retired. Two rival clans, the Hosokawa and the Yamana, claimed the right to nominate one of their own clan as successor, and fighting began in the capital of Kyoto. The Onin War lasted on and off for ten years. In 1473 the claimants died, and a member of the Hosokawa clan acted as deputy shogun until 1493, when wars broke out again.

| 600 | 800 | 1000 | 1200 | 1400 | 1600 | 1700 | 1800 | 1900 | 2000 |

 # *1400-1500* EUROPE

Several powerful kingdoms developed empire-building ambitions during this century. France, Spain, Portugal, and England all began to look overseas, as the desire for increased prosperity encouraged exploration to uncharted lands for new natural resources and trading ventures. Explorers tried to find more efficient routes to old trading partners in Asia. At the same time there was a revival of learning and a rush of creative energy which produced the great artistic achievements known as the Renaissance.

Peace-time riches
France emerged from the 100 Years War a rich and successful country. This page from a religious book painted for the Duke of Berry, son of the French king, displays the wealth of the nobility at the time.

1453

English driven from France

In 1414, after a lull of several years in the conflict of the 100 Years War, Henry V of England renewed his claims to the French throne and in 1415 defeated the French at the battle of Agincourt. In 1420 Henry was made heir to the French throne but died in 1422, leaving English control of France seriously weakened. The great victories of Joan of Arc, and even more the manner of her death at the hands of the English, fired the patriotism of the French, who began to win back huge areas of France. By 1453 only Calais remained under English control. The 100 Years War was over. The French king Louis XI was determined on a united and prosperous France and subdued strong local leaders like the Duke of Burgundy. By 1480 nearly all France was under the king's authority.

Jean Seberg playing Joan of Arc in *Saint Joan*, 1957

It was vital for French forces to take English strongholds on the river banks

The English controlled the crucial river approaches to the city

JOAN OF ARC 1412–31

Joan of Arc (Jeanne d'Arc) was the daughter of a farmer. When she was about 16, she claimed that saints had told her in a vision to lead the French against the English. She persuaded the heir to the French throne, the Dauphin Charles, to let her command a force, relieved the besieged city of Orléans, defeated another English force at Patay. In 1430 she tried to regain Paris but was captured by a Burgundian army, and handed to the English regent, the Duke of Bedford. She was burned as a witch in Rouen on May 30, 1431. Joan was canonized as a saint in 1920.

The Siege of Orléans
In 1429 the siege had dragged on for seven months. Joan of Arc saw clearly that the English did not have the troops to end it quickly. By replenishing the garrison through a gap in the siege lines, raising French morale, and undertaking a furious assault on a stronghold, she ensured a rapid victory, which was a turning point in French fortunes in the 100 Years War.

Strategic site
Constantinople occupied a vital position between the Mediterranean and Black Seas. Control of the Golden Horn, the water in the middle of the picture, was the key to its defense. It offered a sheltered harbor near the weakest stretch of the sea wall.

1453
The fall of Constantinople

The Byzantine Empire had been in decline for a long time. By 1450 the empire consisted only of Constantinople and small areas to the west. In 1451 a new Ottoman sultan, Mohammed II, came to power. He was a very great military commander and tactician. He wanted to make Constantinople the capital of his expanding empire. Constantinople had often been besieged by various foes but had managed to withstand them all because of its commanding position between the straits of Bosporus and the Black Sea, and its huge sea defenses. But in 1453 Mohammed used a battery of siege guns against Constantinople. After a heavy bombardment for about eight weeks, an Ottoman army of some 80,000 men stood before the Romanus gate to the city. It soon fell, but once inside the Ottomans met fierce resistance led by the emperor himself, Constantine XI, who died fighting. His death heralded the collapse of the city and the end of the Byzantine Empire.

Mohammed II
Mohammed II was a broad-minded and cultured leader.

Roumeli Hissar
This castle was built by Mohammed II at the narrowest point of the Bosporus, thus cutting off Constantinople from food and naval aid from its allies in western Europe.

The Kremlin
The citadel of a Russian city was called a *kremlin*. Ivan III ordered the re-building of the Moscow Kremlin buildings in a suitably grand style. In the mid 1500s, after a fire, Ivan IV restored the small Kremlin Cathedral of the Annunciation (seen here in the foreground).

ICONS

Icons were images of holy persons or events, usually painted in oil on a wooden panel. For the Russian Orthodox Church, icons were an important part of holy worship. The monk Andrei Rublyov (1370–1430) was one of the greatest Russian icon painters. His painting of the Archangel Michael was possibly painted for the Annunciation Cathedral.

1462
Ivan III becomes Grand Prince

In the 1200s, much of Russia was overrun by the Mongols, who set up a kingdom on the Volga River, which was called the Khanate of the Golden Horde. Its people were known as Tatars. Only the Russian state of Muscovy held out against them. By the 1400s, Tatar power had waned and Muscovy extended its authority over neighboring smaller states. In 1462, Ivan III succeeded as Grand Prince of Muscovy and continued to expand his land. The Tatars viewed this expansion with alarm and in 1480 marched against the Muscovite capital of Moscow but were unable to capture it. Ivan declared himself the "Tsar of all the Russias" (*Tsar* from the Latin *Caesar*, the title of Roman emperors). By 1500 Russia had become one of the great powers of Europe.

No shining armor
Russian knights wore leather armor and carried bows just like their Tatar forebears.

| 600 | 800 | 1000 | 1200 | 1400 | 1600 | 1700 | 1800 | 1900 | 2000 |

THE RENAISSANCE

Beautiful books
This intricately designed letter is taken from a 15th-century northern Italian choir book.

In 14th-century Italy, there was a rebirth (renaissance) of interest in the art, architecture, and literature of ancient Greece and Rome. Scholars realized the importance of this knowledge and tried to reconcile Greek and Roman ideas with Christian beliefs. There was more emphasis on the significance of human life on earth and less on the possibilities of an afterlife. Artists began to try to represent the human form with greater realism and accuracy, even when painting Christ and the saints. In literature, too, great Italian poets, such as Dante (1265–1321) and Petrarch (1304–74), began to explore human nature. These new movements spread from Italy throughout Europe. As the absolute authority of the Church was challenged, rulers began to emphasize their own power. They paid artists to produce magnificent paintings, sculptures, and buildings to celebrate their importance. Many of these are now regarded as among the greatest works of European art. The artists began to be acknowledged as important figures in society. Although much of their work was not seen by ordinary people at that time, today millions of people from all over the world can appreciate its significance and beauty in churches and museums.

City-states
During the Renaissance, Italy was made up of several regions. Wealth and power lay largely with a few city-states such as Genoa, Pisa, and Venice, and later Milan and Florence, which were successful self-governing centers of commerce. As the wealth of the states grew, so did the desire to display it. Governments commissioned buildings, paintings, and sculptures which used new techniques and covered adventurous new subjects.

16th-century helmet from Milan

Classical inspiration
Sandro Botticelli (1444–1510), one of the artists who helped to decorate the Sistine chapel in the Vatican, worked mainly in Florence under the patronage of Lorenzo de' Medici. The myths of ancient Greece and Rome were a rich source of inspiration for Renaissance artists, and Botticelli produced several paintings based on legends. In this painting, *Primavera* (Spring), he tells the story of the nymph Chloris (right), pursued by the wind god, Zephyr, who transforms her into Flora, goddess of spring.

The d'Estes
The d'Este family were dukes of Ferrara in northeastern Italy. Their court became a center for new thought and learning.

PATRONS

The Italian nobility wanted great works of art to advertise their wealth and importance. The Viscontis and Sforzas of Milan, the Gonzagas of Mantua, and the rich and powerful Medicis of Florence all commissioned great buildings, sculptures, and beautiful paintings from artists like Titian, Botticelli, Breughel, and Michelangelo.

The Medicis of Florence
The Medicis, and especially Lorenzo de' Medici (left), patronized many great artists.

40,000 BC		10,000	5000	1000	500	AD 1	200	400

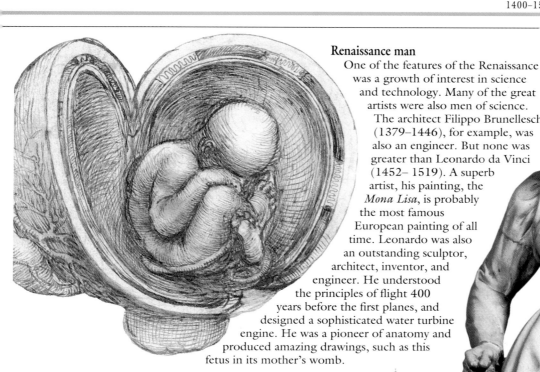

Renaissance man

One of the features of the Renaissance was a growth of interest in science and technology. Many of the great artists were also men of science. The architect Filippo Brunelleschi (1379–1446), for example, was also an engineer. But none was greater than Leonardo da Vinci (1452–1519). A superb artist, his painting, the *Mona Lisa*, is probably the most famous European painting of all time. Leonardo was also an outstanding sculptor, architect, inventor, and engineer. He understood the principles of flight 400 years before the first planes, and designed a sophisticated water turbine engine. He was a pioneer of anatomy and produced amazing drawings, such as this fetus in its mother's womb.

Florence cathedral

The huge dome of the Cathedral of Santa Maria del Fiore, designed by the architect Brunelleschi and built between 1420 and 1436, dominates the center of Florence. The cathedral itself was built over a period of 165 years from 1296. Many famous artists worked on it, including the painter Giotto. Renaissance architects borrowed a variety of forms from Greek and Roman style, including domes, columns, and cornices.

STATECRAFT

Niccolo Machiavelli

The Renaissance encouraged new thought and ideas. Niccolo Machiavelli (1469–1527) was a Florentine diplomat, historian, and political philosopher who wrote about statecraft. His book *Il Principe* (The Prince) was a summary of how he believed a state should be governed. Rulers should always do what was beneficial for their state, using force if necessary. Decisions should be made to fit situations, not based on a fixed set of rules or theories. Machiavelli is regarded by some people as the founder of modern political science.

Flesh and blood

In ancient Greece, sculptors like Phidias gloried in the accurate representation of the human form. Renaissance sculptors resurrected their beliefs. Michelangelo Buonarroti (1475–1564) was one of the greatest figures of the Renaissance. Painter, sculptor, and architect of genius, sculpture was the art form he loved best. This powerful sculpture is of St. Proculus. Michelangelo created it in 1494–95, while living for a year in Bologna, in northern Italy. The details of the figure are astonishing, and in realism and grandeur the statue rivals the sculpted heroes of ancient Greece.

| 600 | 800 | 1000 | 1200 | 1400 | 1600 | 1700 | 1800 | 1900 | 2000 |

NORTHERN REVIVAL

Lübeck altarpiece
Wood carving flourished during the northern Renaissance. This carving was done in Germany c.1480–90.

As the Renaissance spread throughout Europe, it took on a more religious character. Northern scholars, like those in Italy, looked to the past to find out how best to live in the present. But they looked more to early Christianity and less to ancient Greece and Rome. They learned ancient Greek and Hebrew in order to study the Bible in its original languages and campaigned against corruption in church and public life. They rebuilt education around their new ideas, seeing its purpose more in character development than in practical training. Their approach is known as humanism. Flemish painters brought a new kind of detailed realism to painting. Printing was revolutionized by Gutenberg in Germany in the late 1430s, and by 1500 more than 200 European cities had printing presses. This meant that new ideas could spread with much greater speed and impact, as the Reformation was to show.

Picture by Albrecht Dürer, a great German artist

ERASMUS 1466–1536

The Dutch scholar Desiderius Erasmus led the new humanism. He taught and wrote across Europe, advancing education and theology. In books such as *In Praise of Folly*, he mocked church abuses and used humor to guide his readers toward a better life.

Imagination's landscapes
The Dutch painter Hieronymus Bosch (c.1450–1516) united a most fantastic imagination with detailed and exact clarity of style.

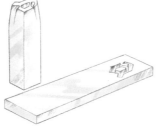

1 In the first stage of typecasting, a hard metal punch, carved with a letter, was hammered into a soft metal to make a mold.

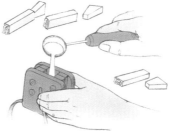

2 The mold was placed in a holder. A ladle was used to pour molten metal, a mixture of tin, lead, and antimony, into the mold to form a piece of type.

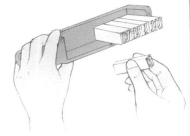

3 The type was arranged into words on a small tray called a composing stick. The letters had to be arranged upside down and right to left.

The printer's workshop
About 1438 the German metalworker Johannes Gutenberg invented typecasting, a method of making movable type – single letters on individual blocks – out of molten metal. In 1455 he printed a copy of the Bible which was the first large printed book made in Europe. The printers seen here are setting type and using the press in Gutenberg's workshop. Printed pages are hanging up for the ink to dry. Printing made books far cheaper and more widely available. This meant that knowledge could be spread farther and faster and preserved more reliably. Poor people who couldn't read gathered to hear books and pamphlets, often lavishly illustrated, read aloud.

PORTUGUESE NAVIGATION

In the 15th century, Europeans began to look for sea routes to Asia, hoping to obtain its goods more cheaply than by the ancient land routes. The Portuguese led the way. After winning their independence from Spain in 1385, they began to expand, attacking Muslim North Africa and Muslim fleets at sea. King Joao I appointed his son Prince Henry to organize voyages of discovery. In 1444 Henry's sailors reached the Senegal River in West Africa. By 1471, they had reached Ghana. In 1482–84 Diego Cäo's expedition came to the Congo River in Zaire. Bartholomeu Diaz rounded the Cape of Good Hope at the southern tip of Africa in 1487–88. Ten years later Vasco da Gama sailed up Africa's east coast; in 1500 Pedro Cabral landed in Brazil. Both were on their way to India.

The world unknown
In the 100 years after this 15th-century world map was made, European knowledge of geography advanced more than in the previous 1,000 years.

Henry the Navigator
Prince Henry the Navigator (1394–1460) was the moving spirit behind the great Portuguese discoveries. Though no great sailor himself, he founded a school of navigation in 1416 at Sagres on the southwest tip of Portugal. He sent expeditions out at least once a year to explore the African coast.

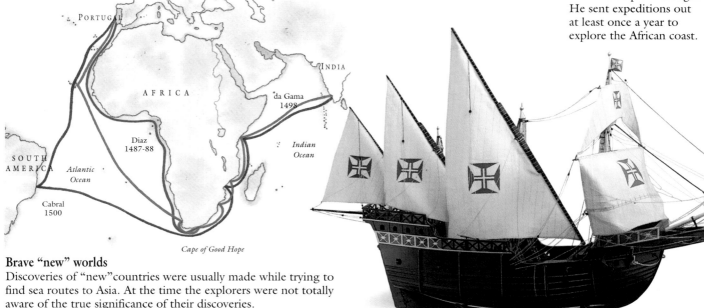

Brave "new" worlds
Discoveries of "new" countries were usually made while trying to find sea routes to Asia. At the time the explorers were not totally aware of the true significance of their discoveries.

COLUMBUS

Spain also looked overseas. In 1492 Christopher Columbus (1451–1506) persuaded the king and queen of Spain to finance a voyage across the Atlantic. He landed in the Caribbean. On later voyages he went on to reach Central and South America.

Ship of discovery
Most early Portuguese explorers sailed in caravels. They were longer and narrower than previous ships, easier to maneuver with a greater spread of sail, and better able to withstand storms. They had large holds capable of carrying the substantial cargoes needed for long voyages. Portuguese sailors also benefited from improved maps, astrolabes, and navigational training, largely thanks to Prince Henry the Navigator.

VOYAGES

1416 Prince Henry founds school of navigation
1444 Expedition reaches Senegal River
1472 Lopo Gonçalves crosses the Equator
1482–84 Cäo reaches mouth of Congo River
1487–88 Diaz rounds Cape of Good Hope
1497–98 Vasco da Gama rounds Cape of Good Hope and arrives in India
1500 Cabral reaches Brazil and sails on to India

Codex Aubin
The Aztecs used a pictographic code to communicate. Pictographs were painted on strips of paper (codex) made from birch bark.

1400-1500 AMERICAS

The Aztecs in Mexico had greatly expanded their empire and their capital city of Tenochtitlan. They built incredible temples and palaces but fought constant wars with neighboring peoples to take prisoners to be used as sacrificial victims in religious ceremonies. However, the Aztecs were then surrounded by peoples bent on revenge. The Incas in Peru built a splendidly managed empire which they controlled by using runners to carry messages along a sophisticated road system.

The Aztec Empire in 1500
In 1500, the Aztec Empire consisted of more than 10 million citizens and was overlord of a large area of Mexico, much of it conquered lands.

1400s
The rise of the Aztecs

In 1426 the Aztec king, Itzcoatl, formed an alliance with the adjacent states of Texcoco and Tlacopan and overthrew their powerful neighbors, the Tapanecs. Before long the Aztecs were rulers of a vast empire. They were great traders and operated a network of trade caravans controlled by a merchants' guild, the *pochteca*. They also built splendid pyramids, palaces, and temples. The temple at Tenochtitlan was the absolute center of the empire and a holy place. After a military campaign, sacrifices were made there, sometimes as many as 20,000 in one day.

Eagle knight
Aztec warriors were divided into military orders; the most prestigious were the jaguar and eagle knights. Warriors wore jaguar pelts or eagle feathers and were among the most privileged people in Aztec society.

RELIGIOUS CEREMONY

The Aztecs believed that they lived in the world of the "Fifth Sun" and that one day this world would be destroyed. To postpone this evil day, their gods, and in particular the mighty sun god Huitzilopochtli, had to be kept content and fed daily. Aztecs believed that it was their sacred duty to provide the sun god with *chalchiuhuatl*, a precious form of nectar found in human blood. Without the blood, they thought the whole universe would cease to function. To the Aztecs, the human heart was the symbol of life itself, and Huitzilopochtli needed to be fed both blood and human hearts so that he would not wreak his anger on the Aztec people. Feeding the sun was the warriors' business. Their continual conquest of neighboring peoples in the search for more victims to feed their god was regarded as a quest of honor; they were empire building in the name of Huitzilopochtli.

Nourishing the sun
This contemporary painting by Aztec artists shows the presentation of human hearts to Huitzilopochtli.

40,000 BC		10,000	5000	1000	500	AD 1	200	400

1400s
The Inca Empire

In the 1430s the Inca kingdom was invaded by a neighboring state which attacked the capital, Cuzco. The old ruler, Viracocha Inca, handed over the defense of his realm to his son Yupanqui, who took the name Pachacuti. Pachacuti repelled the invader and over the next three decades reformed the government and improved Cuzco. Pachacuti and his successors also greatly increased the empire to include parts of Chile, Bolivia, and Ecuador. The Inca Empire was very well run. There was a hierarchy of nobles, provincial governors, and officials, all headed by the Sapa Inca. The central administration controlled the building of new towns and monitored the use of natural resources. Even the art and pottery conformed to a single set of styles dictated by Cuzco.

Machu Picchu

This Inca city was built in the mid-15th century on a high plain between the peaks of two mountains in the Andes, above the Urubamba River. It consisted of agricultural terraces and complex stone buildings set in an extraordinarily beautiful and dramatic position.

Road runners

Although the Incas had not invented a wheel, Inca rulers controlled their vast domains by developing a massive road network over some very inaccessible terrain covering some 19,000 miles (30,000 km). The government kept in close touch with provincial and local officials by means of relays of couriers or runners. Small offices were placed along the roads some 1.5 miles (2.5 km) apart, at which runners waited to take messages, instructions, reports, and so on, further down the line. An order could be carried as far as 150 miles (241 km) in a day.

Golden feather

This golden feather was probably part of an elaborate ceremonial headdress. Gold was often buried with the dead. Inca rulers were considered to be immortal, and their bodies were mummified. Their riches and property were administered by their heirs. The mummies "entertained" through their heirs and attended all important ceremonies.

Inca territory

During the reign of Pachacuti's son Topa Inca (1471–93), the Inca Empire expanded greatly. Topa conquered territory in Bolivia and northern Chile, and his successor gained land in Ecuador.

Runners trumpeted their arrival at road stations on a conch shell

There were many hanging bridges in the Inca Empire, supervised by an official called a chaca suyoyoc

QUIPUS

The Incas had no writing. They stored information such as statistics, lists, and even historical records on a string and knot device called a quipu. The strings, which hung from a cord or set of cords, were colored according to the type of information. The positions of the knots provided details, which could be quite complex, usually in the form of numbers. The interpreters of the quipus (scribes) were also expected to memorize additional details.

Double canoe
Craft like this one were used by Polynesians for their annual migrations between different island groups. During the rest of the year, the craft would often be split and used as two single canoes.

Polynesia continued to be cut off from the rest of the world, but this did not arrest the development of some of its islands. There were already advanced societies in Samoa, Tonga, the Society Islands, including Tahiti, the Hawaiian Islands, and the Tuamotu archipelago. In Tonga, the Tui Tonga dynasty, which had ruled for more than two centuries, spread its influence over parts of Polynesia beyond the Tonga Islands.

c.1400
Tui Tonga build ceremonial center at Mu'a

Polynesians first settled on the Tonga group of islands in the South Pacific Ocean as early as about 1300 BC. They lived around the edge of a large lagoon in the north of the largest island of Tongatapu. It was a long time before a ruling hierarchy developed in the islands, but by about AD 1200 the Tui Tonga dynasty, based in the Mu'a district of northeast Tongatapu, ruled the whole group. Around 1400, they built their main ceremonial center at Mu'a. This was surrounded by a defensive ditch and bank and enclosed many platforms on which were erected houses for chiefs, their families, and servants. Tonga was one of the few Polynesian island groups to have a society with a top class that held authority over everyone else. Council meetings among the top class were accompanied by special ceremonies where a potent root-based drink called *kava*, which had a drowsy effect, was drunk. Around 1500 the political leadership passed to another dynasty. This in turn gave way to the Tui Kanokupolu dynasty, which still rules Tonga today.

Neck adornment
This necklace was made by sticking seeds from a tropical plant onto a wooden base with breadfruit gum. It was probably worn by chiefs on ceremonial occasions.

Cuttlefish lure
Covered with cowrie shells to attract its prey, this lure was used by Tongan fisherfolk to attract small fish such as cuttlefish. They also caught larger fish, such as sharks and tuna.

Market place
Farmers went to the local market place to sell their produce, mainly bananas, sweet potatoes, copra (dried coconut), tapioca, yams, and breadfruit (a white fruit with a breadlike texture). The fertile soil and tropical climate of Tonga were good for agriculture.

CHAPTER 12

1500 – 1600

THE GREAT RULERS

Gold Benin leopard mask

1500-1600
THE WORLD

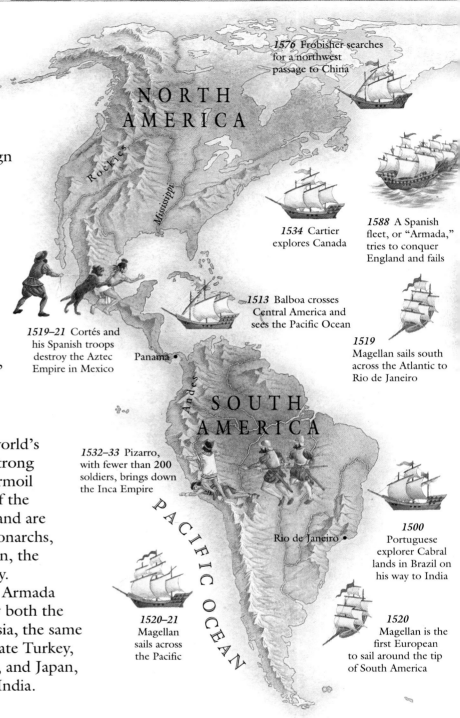

NORTH AMERICA

Rockies

Mississippi

1576 Frobisher searches for a northwest passage to China

1534 Cartier explores Canada

1588 A Spanish fleet, or "Armada," tries to conquer England and fails

1519–21 Cortés and his Spanish troops destroy the Aztec Empire in Mexico

Panama •

1513 Balboa crosses Central America and sees the Pacific Ocean

1519 Magellan sails south across the Atlantic to Rio de Janeiro

Andes

SOUTH AMERICA

1532–33 Pizarro, with fewer than 200 soldiers, brings down the Inca Empire

Rio de Janeiro •

1500 Portuguese explorer Cabral lands in Brazil on his way to India

PACIFIC OCEAN

1520–21 Magellan sails across the Pacific

1520 Magellan is the first European to sail around the tip of South America

NEW DEVELOPMENTS in ship design and the expanding science of navigation allow European navigators to venture far from their coastlines and brave the open ocean. The earlier voyage of Christopher Columbus across the Atlantic, the circumnavigation of the world by Ferdinand Magellan in 1519–22, and many other voyages of exploration reveal to the Europeans more of the coasts of Africa, Asia, and the Americas, and bring every continent within reach of European interference.

Strong rulers

Throughout this period, many of the world's nations experience lengthy periods of strong government. In Europe, despite the turmoil created by the religious controversies of the Reformation, Russia, France, and England are all ruled by a succession of powerful monarchs, while the Hapsburg family control Spain, the Holy Roman Empire, and much of Italy. However, the destruction of Philip II's Armada opens the way to overseas expansion by both the English and the Dutch. Throughout Asia, the same picture emerges. The Ottomans dominate Turkey, while new rulers control Persia, Burma, and Japan, and the Moghul Empire is founded in India.

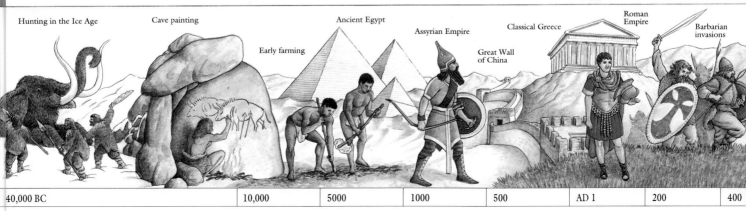

Hunting in the Ice Age

Cave painting

Early farming

Ancient Egypt

Assyrian Empire

Great Wall of China

Classical Greece

Roman Empire

Barbarian invasions

| 40,000 BC | | 10,000 | 5000 | 1000 | 500 | AD 1 | 200 | 400 |

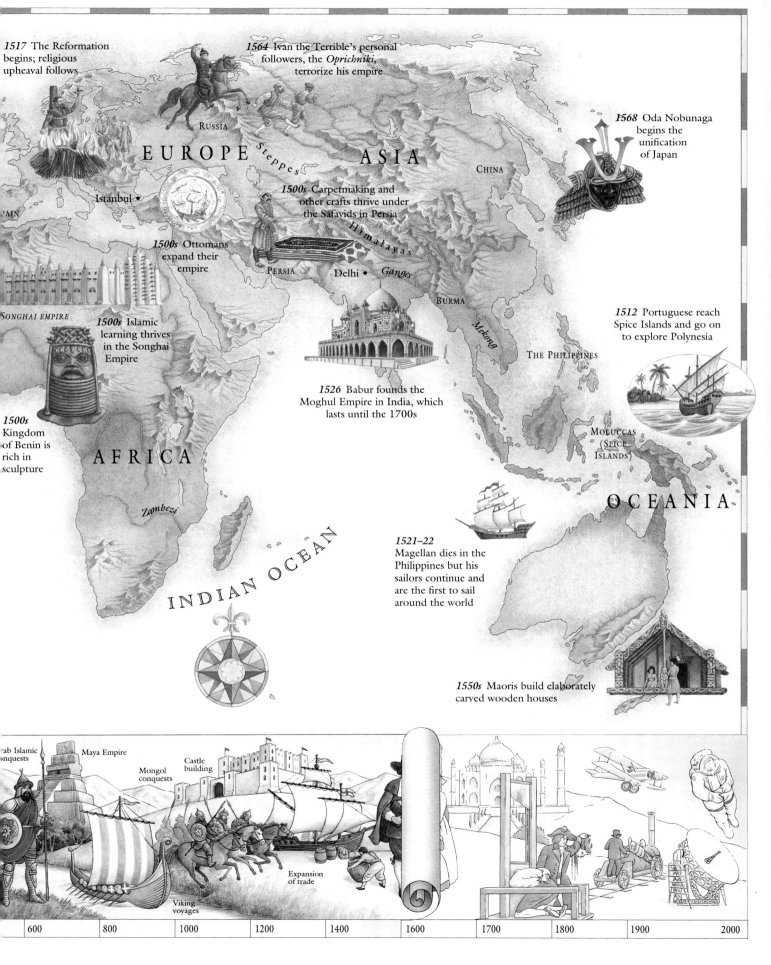

1517 The Reformation begins; religious upheaval follows

1564 Ivan the Terrible's personal followers, the *Oprichniki*, terrorize his empire

1568 Oda Nobunaga begins the unification of Japan

EUROPE

Steppes

ASIA

RUSSIA

CHINA

Istanbul •

1500s Carpetmaking and other crafts thrive under the Safavids in Persia

Himalayas

SPAIN

1500s Ottomans expand their empire

PERSIA

Delhi •

Ganges

BURMA

Mekong

1512 Portuguese reach Spice Islands and go on to explore Polynesia

SONGHAI EMPIRE

1500s Islamic learning thrives in the Songhai Empire

THE PHILIPPINES

1526 Babur founds the Moghul Empire in India, which lasts until the 1700s

1500s Kingdom of Benin is rich in sculpture

AFRICA

MOLUCCAS (SPICE ISLANDS)

Zambezi

OCEANIA

INDIAN OCEAN

1521–22 Magellan dies in the Philippines but his sailors continue and are the first to sail around the world

1550s Maoris build elaborately carved wooden houses

Arab Islamic conquests

Maya Empire

Mongol conquests

Castle building

Expansion of trade

Viking voyages

| 600 | 800 | 1000 | 1200 | 1400 | 1600 | 1700 | 1800 | 1900 | 2000 |

1500

1525

AFRICA

1500s Songhai Empire in West Africa enters period of greatest expansion and power under Askia Mohammed Turré*

1500s Trade encourages growth of Hausa states in West Africa

1505–07 Portuguese capture Sofala on east coast and found Mozambique; they begin to trade with Africans

1507 Nzinga Mbemba, Christian and Portuguese ally, becomes king of Kongo kingdom in Central Africa

1517 Ottomans defeat Mamluks and conquer Egypt

This Hausa beaded snuff taker was made from woven leather

1529 Muslims defeat Christian Ethiopian forces at the Battle of Shimbra Kure and overrun the kingdom until 1543, when Portuguese troops help to defeat them

c.1530 Beginning of transatlantic slave trade organized by Portuguese

Some African kings and merchants sold slaves to the Europeans

ASIA

This elaborate dagger belonged to Sulayman the Magnificent

1501–24 Reign of Ismail, first Safavid Shah of Persia*

1520–66 Reign of Sulayman the Magnificent; Ottoman Empire at its peak*

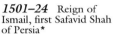

1526 Babur (a descendant of Mongol ruler Genghis Khan and of Tamerlane) first Moghul emperor, invades India*

1546 Tabinshwehti conquers Pegu from the Mons and assumes title of King of all Burma

1549–51 Mission of Jesuit St. Francis Xavier to Japan

Christians were tortured by Japanese rulers who feared European influence

EUROPE

1 1500 Black lead pencils used in England

1506–1612 Construction of Basilica of St. Peter's in Rome

1517 Martin Luther, German monk, publishes 95 objections to Catholic practices*

1519 Charles, archduke of Austria (and king of Spain), elected Holy Roman Emperor (retires in 1556)

1519 Death of Italian Renaissance artist Leonardo da Vinci

Michelangelo Buonarroti designed the dome of St. Peter's Basilica in Rome

1527 Troops of Charles V, Holy Roman Emperor, sack Rome and capture Pope Clement VII

1534 Henry VIII of England breaks with Rome; makes himself head of English church*

1541–64 Leadership of reformer John Calvin in Geneva, Switzerland

1545–63 Council of Trent, Italy; Catholics' efforts to reform

1547 Tsar Ivan IV the Terrible (reigns 1533–84) takes power in Russia*

Anne Boleyn was the second wife of Henry VIII

AMERICAS

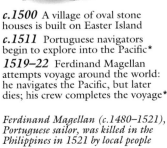

Cihuacoatl was an Aztec snake woman earth goddess

1500 Portuguese explorer Pedro Cabral reaches Brazil

1502–04 Columbus's fourth voyage: reaches Honduras, Nicaragua, Costa Rica, Panama, and Colombia

1513 Vasco Núñez de Balboa, Spanish explorer, first sights the Pacific Ocean

1519–21 Hernando Cortés, Spanish soldier-explorer, brings down the Aztec Empire in Mexico*

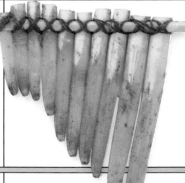

These Inca pipes were made with the quills of the condor

1532–33 Francisco Pizarro, Spanish soldier, invades and destroys Inca Empire in Peru*

1534 French explorer, Jacques Cartier, makes first expedition to settle in Canada*

1540s Spanish arrive in California

OCEANIA

c.1500 A village of oval stone houses is built on Easter Island

c.1511 Portuguese navigators begin to explore into the Pacific*

1519–22 Ferdinand Magellan attempts voyage around the world: he navigates the Pacific, but later dies; his crew completes the voyage*

Ferdinand Magellan (c.1480–1521), Portuguese sailor, was killed in the Philippines in 1521 by local people

1525 Diego Ribeiro, official mapmaker for Spain, makes first scientific charts covering the Pacific

1525 Portuguese probably visit Caroline Islands, northeast of New Guinea, and nearby Palau Islands

1526 Portuguese land on Papua New Guinea

This box from southern New Guinea contains a red pigment which was used to paint the face and body

1550

1560s First Portuguese diplomatic missions in Timbuktu, West Africa

1562 Sir John Hawkins starts English slave trade, taking cargoes of slaves from West Africa to the Americas

c.1570–c.1610 Kanem-Bornu kingdom in west central Africa at its most powerful; alliance with the Ottomans brings it firearms, military training, and Arab camel troops

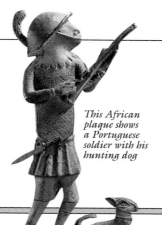

This African plaque shows a Portuguese soldier with his hunting dog

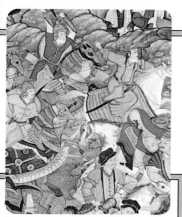

Scenes of Genghis Khan's battles were painted at Akbar's court

1551 Bayinnaung succeeds to the throne of Burma and overruns Thailand*

1556–1605 Reign of Moghul emperor Akbar in India

1568–c.1600 Period of National Unification in Japan begins when feudal lord, Oda Nobunaga, captures capital, Kyoto*

Philip II of Spain was a deeply religious man

This Flemish saddle of c.1570 shows a central figure of Victory

1556–98 Reign of Philip II of Spain

1558–1603 Reign of Elizabeth I of England*

1559–84 Building of palace of Escorial outside Madrid

1560s–90s French Wars of Religion: Protestant minority in conflict with Catholic majority as leading nobles struggle for power under weak Valois kings

1564–1616 Life of English playwright, William Shakespeare

1568–1648 Dutch fight for independence from Spanish rule

1571 Don John of Austria smashes Ottoman fleet at battle of Lepanto*

1572 Massacre of St. Bartholomew: 8,000 Protestants die in Paris, France*

1572 Dutch Sea Beggars take Brill*

The carved prow of this Maori canoe resembles the head of a moa bird

1550s Maoris on both the North and South Islands of New Zealand build fortified enclosures called *pa**

1567 Alvaro de Mendaña, Spanish sailor, sets sail from Callao in Peru westward across the Pacific; he reaches the Ellice Islands and Solomon Islands, east of New Guinea; in 1569 he arrives back in Callao

1575

c.1575 Portuguese begin to colonize Angola; more than a century of warfare follows

1590–91 Songhai Empire overthrown by Moroccan army

c.1598 First Dutch trade posts set up on Guinea coast, West Africa

1573–1620 Reign of emperor Wan Li in China: period of great paintings and porcelain making; imperial kilns at Jingde zhen produce vast quantities of china

1587–1629 Reign of Shah Abbas I (the Great) of Persia: he consolidates and expands territories

1592–98 Korea succeeds in repelling Japanese invasions

c.1590–1605 Burma breaks up into small states

During the reign of Shah Abbas the Great of Persia, the Safavid Empire was at the height of its power

1575–86 Stephen Batory, Prince of Transylvania in Romania, is elected King of Poland

1577–80 English seaman Francis Drake sails round the world

1580–1640 Spain united with Portugal

1588 Defeat of Spanish Armada off south coast of England

1598 Henry IV, first Bourbon king of France, grants toleration to Protestants

The shape of this Polish helmet of c.1580 shows oriental influence

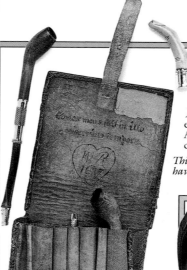

1576 Martin Frobisher, English explorer, sets out to find a northwest passage to China; he reaches the Canadian coast, and Frobisher Bay is named after him

1584 Sir Walter Raleigh sends an exploring party to Virginia in North America, followed a year later by a colonizing expedition, which fails

This leather tobacco pouch is said to have belonged to Sir Walter Raleigh

Marquesas Islanders carved wooden clubs which they used for ceremonial purposes

1595 Mendaña visits Marquesas Islands and then Nderic (Santa Cruz)*

Ankle bracelet
The wealth and sophistication of the kingdom of Benin were expressed in its art, which often had royal or religious purposes.

1500-1600 AFRICA

The Songhai Empire dominated old Mali and much else under a great emperor, Mohammed Turré. After his death, internal quarrels weakened the empire. It was conquered by Morocco in 1590–91. The African continent began to attract European interest, especially from Portuguese explorers and traders, who broke into long-established African trade networks along the east coast, setting up trading posts, and making contact with the interior. On the west coast, they began shipping slaves to America.

1500s
Songhai greatness

After Sonni Ali, ruler of the Songhai Empire, died in 1492, one of his generals, Mohammed Turré, began the Askia dynasty based at Gao in Mali. He formed an efficient administration, created a police force, introduced regular taxation and standard weights and measures, built a canal system on the Niger which improved agriculture, and formed a standing army. With his army he extended the empire north to take in the rich Sahara salt mines, and also expanded it eastward. He lived grandly. It took seventy leopard-skin bags to contain his robes. On a pilgrimage to Mecca, he is said to have given away more than 250,000 gold coins.

WEST AFRICAN ART

The art of West Africa was widely admired. Dutch visitors of the time compared Benin City to Amsterdam. The craftwork of the coast included carvings, ivory saltcellars, spoons, forks, bracelets, hunting horns, and woven goods. Inland, Benin's carvings, castings, and sculptures in ivory, wood, stone, terracotta, brass, and bronze were the most famous of all.

The pillars of the king
Plaques such as this were used to adorn the wooden pillars in the palace of the oba, or king, of Benin. This one shows a ceremonial presentation.

Benin sword
The oba and his chiefs carried ornamental weapons on ceremonial occasions.

Jenne – ancient Islamic city
Jenne was one of the most important trading cities along the river Niger. The mud-brick mosque above, first built in the 1300s, has permanent wooden scaffolding so that it can be continually renewed.

1 The lost wax process of casting began with the shaping of a clay core

2 A wax model was built over the core, and then an outer mold around it

3 The mold was heated, the wax melted, and brass was poured in to replace it

1500-1600 ASIA

The 16th century in Asia was an age of strong empires and outstanding rulers. The vast Turkish Ottoman Empire reached the height of its power under Sultan Sulayman. A dynasty of Muslim rulers, the Moghuls, descendants of Tamerlane and Genghis Khan, dominated India. They constructed splendid buildings and organized extensive trading networks. After centuries of division, Persia was united under new rulers, the Safavids. In Japan, Oda Nobunaga and his successor Toyotomi Hideyoshi unified the country, providing sound government there for the first time for many years.

Shah Abbas
The most remarkable Safavid ruler, Shah Abbas I (1587–1629) formed a regular army and drove his enemies from Persia. He created a splendid court at Isfahan, the wonder of visitors from East and West alike. Cruel, too, he had his children blinded, fearing them as rivals.

Persian empire
The Safavids united Persia and extended their empire into neighboring countries. Shi'ite Muslims, they were continually in conflict with the Sunni Ottomans and Uzbeks. The striped area shows land disputed with the Ottomans.

1501

Shah Ismail founds Safavid capital

The Safavids were Shi'ite Muslims of northwest Persia (now Iran), whose leaders claimed descent from Ali, a cousin of Mohammed. In 1501, their ruler, Shah Ismail, took Tabriz and made it his capital. He conquered all Persia and parts of Iraq, converting the people to Shi'ism. Only the Ottomans defeated Shah Ismail, in Azerbaijan to the north of Persia in 1514, after which it is said he never smiled again. Shah Ismail died in 1524, but despite constant attacks by Turks and Uzbeks that beset his successors, Persian unity held. For the first time, the people felt they were one nation.

Persian carpets
Safavid rulers set up factories to make beautiful carpets, which became famous worldwide. Carpets were handwoven from wool and silk by workers sitting at a loom. Intricate patterns included flowers, animals, and scrolls. Carpets were washed in rivers, and sold to merchants who took them via Turkey to Europe, where they were called Turkish carpets. Workers' salaries increased every three years. When they retired, wages were paid to their children, who started work at the age of 12.

600	800	1000	1200	1400	1600	1700	1800	1900	2000

1520

Sulayman I becomes Ottoman sultan

By 1500, the Ottoman Empire was one of the most powerful in the world. Fired by religious duty to convert their neighbors to Islam, Ottoman sultans had conquered large parts of western Asia and southeast Europe. Sulayman I (1520–66), who was called "al-Qanuni," the Law-giver, by his people, and "the Magnificent" by Europeans, brought the empire to its height. In 1526, he invaded Hungary, and three years later he besieged Vienna. He went on to invade parts of North Africa and Iraq, and his fleets dominated the Mediterranean Sea.

Poetry in steel

This steel blade is inlaid with lines of verse by the poet Nejati. Not a war dagger, it would have been worn by an Ottoman gentleman at court in the Topkapi Palace in Istanbul.

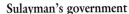

Between three worlds

The Ottoman Empire stretched across three continents: Asia, Europe, and Africa. In the time of Sulayman, it reached from Budapest in Hungary, to Baghdad in Iraq, to Aswan on the Nile River in Egypt.

Sulayman's government

Sulayman was the supreme authority in his lands; he alone made major decisions. His top administrators were slaves. Every five years, talented Christian boys were taken from their families, converted to Islam, and trained for important government jobs. Unrelated to the Turkish aristocracy, the slaves had no reason to ally with them against the sultan. In conquered lands, Ottoman ministers divided the people into groups, or millets, according to their religion. The leader of each millet represented its members before the Ottoman government.

Sulayman's mosque

The Ottomans had conquered Constantinople in 1453, massacring its inhabitants. The city was slowly transformed into the great Muslim capital, Istanbul. Sulayman built mosques, hospitals, bridges, and public baths. After he died, a beautiful mosque was built in the city to house his tomb, a fitting burial place for its famous ruler.

Ottoman women

Islamic law allowed men to have as many as four wives and total authority over them. The women lived in a separate section of the house, called a harem. Sulayman had a harem but was devoted to his Russian consort, Roxelana.

Iznik pottery

As the Ottoman Empire expanded, the influence of foreign cultures crept into the work of its artists. Pottery made in the town of Iznik combined blue and white colors used by Ming artists and high standards of Safavid craftsmanship.

OTTOMAN EMPIRE

c.1300 Osman founds Ottoman dynasty of rulers in northwest Turkey

1359–1451 Ottomans conquer much of Turkey and the Balkans

1453 Ottomans capture Constantinople (Istanbul), joining their lands in Asia and Europe

1520–66 Empire reaches greatest extent during rule of Sulayman the Magnificent

1571 Christian navy destroys Turkish fleet at Lepanto

c.1600 Ottoman Empire begins to decline

1918 Peace treaties ending World War I dissolve empire

1923 Turk republic emerges under President Kemal Ataturk

| 40,000 BC | | 10,000 | 5000 | 1000 | 500 | AD 1 | 200 | 400 |

Imperial gardener

Babur disliked his home in India; he wrote that it was cursed by "heat, dust, and wind." He tried to establish beauty there by creating gardens. These peaceful places, filled with trees, flowers, and streams, reminded him of his Samarkand homeland and of the Muslim paradise. Here he directs his gardeners.

1526
Moghuls invade India

In 1500, India was divided among warring Hindu and Muslim states. Babur, a Muslim Turkish descendant of Genghis Khan and Tamerlane, came to power in the kingdom of Kabul in Afghanistan. An ambitious ruler, he invaded India, defeated the sultan of Delhi in 1526, and marched to the frontier of Bengal. His territory came to be known as the Moghul Empire, a variation of the word Mongol, to reflect Babur's ancestry. Babur died in 1530, leaving behind a weak administration. His son, Humayun, could not keep the empire together. Sher Khan Suri, an Afghan chief, captured Agra and Delhi in 1540, and Humayun did not recover them until 1555. His son Akbar transformed the Moghul state, extending frontiers in all directions. He won the support of Hindus by letting them worship freely and of peasants by fixing a low tax rate. He reorganized the administration to allow high officials to hold military and civil rank. They were well rewarded but were not allowed to settle permanently in a specific territory.

MOGHUL EMPIRE
1504 Babur, first Moghul emperor, captures Kabul
1526 Battle of Panipat: Babur defeats sultan of Delhi
1540 Afghan Sher Khan Suri seizes power from Babur's son Humayun; rules until 1555
1556–1605 Rule of Akbar, who reforms government
1628–58 Arts flourish under emperor Shah Jahan
c.1664 Hindu Marathas challenge Moghuls in west
1720s Moghul Empire begins to break up
1739 Nadir Shah of Persia plunders Delhi
1858 Last Moghul emperor exiled by British

Indian empire

Babur conquered the central part of north India. Akbar enlarged his Indian empire until it stretched from Gujarat in the west to Bengal in the east, and south to the northern parts of the Deccan.

Tiger hunt

Moghul armies were famous for their ferocity in battle. Akbar kept his best soldiers exercised by organizing vast hunts. The men formed a circle, closed in on their prey, and the emperor and his nobles killed the animals.

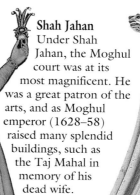

Shah Jahan

Under Shah Jahan, the Moghul court was at its most magnificent. He was a great patron of the arts, and as Moghul emperor (1628–58) raised many splendid buildings, such as the Taj Mahal in memory of his dead wife.

Dagger

The hilt of this Moghul dagger has two gold tiger heads studded with gems.

SIKHISM
A new religion, Sikhism, grew up in India in the early 16th century. Its founder and first guru, Nanak (left), taught that God is one and denied the need for caste distinctions. The tenth and last guru, Gobind Rai (1675–1708), gave some Sikhs a common surname, Singh, and in the face of Muslim Moghul hostility, militarized the Sikhs. He introduced the custom of wearing a dagger and comb and never cutting the hair.

1551
Bayinnaung rules Burma

In the 16th century, two strong rulers tried to build an empire in Burma. At the start of the century, Burma was a collection of small states. In 1531, Tabinshwehti became king of one of these, Toungoo, in the southeast. From 1535 he conquered the people of the Irrawaddy river delta, took Pegu, capital of the southern Mon kingdom, and made it his capital. Soon he overran the kingdom of Pagan in the north, but failed in invasions of Thailand before he died in a Mon rebellion. In 1551 his brother-in-law Bayinnaung crushed the rebellion and inherited the throne. Bayinnaung was the greatest of all Burmese conquerors and overran Thailand, but his absence from Pegu while he waged war led to a revolt, and much of the city was destroyed. He put down the revolt and rebuilt the city in lavish style.

Green demons
Tabinshwehti celebrated his success by decorating Buddhist temples. These elephant-headed demon warriors, who tried to disturb Buddha as he meditated under a tree, adorn a temple of the time.

Defense against guns
Powerful firearms from Europe made it necessary for warlords to build elaborate castles. Bustling towns grew up around them.

JAPAN UNIFIED
1560 Oda Nobunaga routs Imagawa clan at Okehazama
1568 Nobunaga enters capital, Kyoto; begins a series of major government reforms
1570s Nobunaga's general Toyotomi Hideyoshi and ally Tokugawa Ieyasu overcome resistance in east and west
1571 Nagasaki becomes a major port as Japan opens up to European trade
1582 Death of Nobunaga; succeeded by Hideyoshi
1580–98 Land survey to assess farmland for tax rates
1588 Weapons are seized from all classes except the samurai in great Sword Hunt
1598 Hideyoshi dies
1600 Tokugawa Ieyasu wins battle of Sekigahara; he becomes first Tokugawa shogun in 1603

1568
Japanese unification begins

In the early 16th century, Japan was wracked by civil war between the great lords. Finally, strong military leaders emerged to reorganize and unify the country. Oda Nobunaga, an ambitious minor lord, took the capital Kyoto in 1568, and in 1573 deposed the last Ashikaga shogun, or military ruler. He attacked the lords of nearby provinces and forced them to obey him. He died in 1582, and his general, Hideyoshi, became kampaku, or civil dictator, in 1585. Hideyoshi extended his power until, by 1591, he was the undisputed master of Japan. His goal was to gather all Asia into a great empire. He invaded Korea, but his armies were driven back when China intervened. In Japan, Hideyoshi attempted to establish order by enforcing class divisions. New laws forbade samurai to leave their lords and peasants to leave their farms.

Europeans in Japan
Portuguese merchants visited Japan in the mid 1500s. Jesuit missionaries followed to make converts to Christianity. The reforming Japanese rulers welcomed the foreigners who brought new wealth through trade. Ideas and products were exchanged. Japanese lords competed fiercely to buy one new product, the musket.

The first reformer
Once in power, Oda Nobunaga (right) began a program to create a strong government and bind the country together. He took control of currency and increased internal trade by banning tollbooths and repairing roads. Nobunaga did not allow any challenge to his authority. He ordered the brutal massacre of Buddhist warrior-monks who opposed him. In 1582, a rebel lord attacked Nobunaga, who committed suicide rather than be killed.

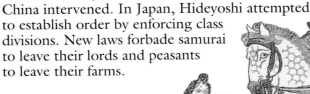

Henry VIII's stirrups
These stirrups belonged to King Henry VIII of England. Henry devoted his youth to hunting, dancing, and other pleasures.

1500-1600 EUROPE

The key event of the century was the Reformation, a movement to reform the Catholic church. It began in Germany, and then spread throughout northern Europe. Although the Catholic church responded by introducing reforms from within, violent conflict between Catholics and the reformers (called Protestants) followed.

1517
Religious revolution

Widespread discontent with the state of the church was set alight by Martin Luther (1483–1546), a German theologian and religious reformer. His criticisms of church practices sparked off a storm of protest that swept most of northern Europe away from the Pope and the Roman Catholic church. New Protestant churches sprang up, inspired by Luther, Swiss reformer Ulrich Zwingli, French theologian John Calvin, and others. They aimed to follow only the teachings of the Bible, getting rid of church traditions. Several powerful kings and princes supported them.

THE REFORMATION

1517 Martin Luther attacks church abuses

1520–21 Luther writes influential books proposing church reform

1526 William Tyndale, English theologian, translates New Testament into English

1534 Henry VIII breaks with Roman Catholic church

1536 John Calvin, French reformer, begins program of reform in Geneva, Switzerland; its influence spreads across Europe

1545 Roman Catholic Council of Trent (1545–63) meets in Italy to begin Counter-reformation

The 95 Theses
In 1517, Luther nailed 95 arguments (theses) to a church door to protest against the sale of indulgences. Indulgences promise God's forgiveness in return for money. Luther's act began a revolution.

Art, the Bible, and religious quarrels
Both sides used illustrated pamphlets and books to promote their views. The new technology of printing spread their ideas around. This is an illustration from Luther's translation of the Bible, c.1530. The reformers, who wanted the Bible to be available to everyone, produced new translations of it and boosted overall literacy. Luther's German Bible and the Authorized (King James) Version in England were so influential that they helped to shape the development of the German and English languages.

1534
Henry breaks with Rome

Henry VIII (1491–1547) took the helm of the English church because the Pope would not let him divorce his first wife. He dissolved the monasteries and took over their property but allowed church services to continue in their old form. In the reign of his son Edward VI (1537–53), a Protestant government brought the Reformation to England. Church services were changed and church decoration was simplified. After Edward's death his half-sister Mary, a devout Catholic, tried to restore her church's authority in England, executing many Protestants in the process. After "Bloody" Mary's death in 1558, Elizabeth I backed a moderate form of Protestantism against both Catholics and radical Protestants, such as the Puritans, for whom the Church of England was not reformed enough.

Henry VIII
Handsome and popular when young, as Henry grew older he became renowned for his tyrannical ways.

| 600 | 800 | 1000 | 1200 | 1400 | 1600 | 1700 | 1800 | 1900 | 2000 |

1547
Ivan IV takes power in Russia

Ivan IV succeeded as Grand Prince of Muscovy in 1533 at age three. A period of misrule first by his mother and then by the Boyar (nobles) Council followed, which lasted until 1547 when Ivan crowned himself Tsar of Russia. He ruled for several years, supported by his chosen council, which was made up of landowners and boyars. He reformed the army and the legal system, expanded foreign trade, and conquered the Tatar khanates of Kazan and Astrakhan. But his first wife's death in 1560 seemed to derange his mind. He split the country into two parts; one was governed by the Boyar Council, the other tyrannically by himself assisted by a much-feared force of armed followers (the *Oprichnina*). He introduced a reign of terror which earned him the name "the Terrible" and devastated the country. Much territory was lost to Poland and Sweden, although the conquest of western Siberia shortly before Ivan's death in 1584 partly balanced these losses.

Ivan "the Terrible"
Ivan was a very complex man who could be unspeakably cruel. He married seven times and suggested that Elizabeth of England should marry him. She did not pursue this course.

The Virgin Queen
Elizabeth never married. She attracted to her service able and adventurous men such as Sir Francis Drake.

1558
Elizabeth I of England

The Protestant princess Elizabeth came to the throne of England in 1558. She chose as her chief minister a middle-class civil servant, William Cecil, who became one of the best advisors any monarch of England ever had. They declared England Protestant but allowed Catholics to hold their beliefs as long as they were loyal to the crown. For years, the queen's position was threatened by the Catholic claimant to the throne, Mary, queen of Scots. There were also dangers from other rulers, in particular the Catholic champion, Philip II of Spain, who in 1588 sent a great fleet, the Armada, against England, but it was completely defeated. When Elizabeth died in 1603, an exciting period of English history died with her.

Unfit for a queen
These fine gloves were a gift to Elizabeth but were too large.

SHAKESPEARE'S THEATER

William Shakespeare (1564–1616) is thought to be the greatest playwright in the English language. He often acted at the Globe Theater in London, where many of his plays were produced. His mastery of language, characterization, and humor have ensured that his plays are as relevant today as when they were first written and performed.

The Spanish Armada
Sir Francis Drake was reportedly playing bowls when the Armada of 130 ships was sighted, but he coolly finished his game. The English fleet under Admiral Howard and Drake engaged the Spanish and drove them to the North Sea, where a storm destroyed them.

1571
The Battle of Lepanto

For much of the 16th century, the Muslim Ottoman Empire fought with Christian powers for control of the important trading routes and cities in the Mediterranean. A "Holy League" of Rome, Venice, and Spain was formed by the Pope. Don John of Austria, half-brother to Philip II of Spain, was given command of a vast fleet of some 200 ships. The Turkish fleet, of about the same size, was drawn up in Lepanto Bay near Corinth in Greece. On October 7, 1571, the fleets met and fought furiously. After three hours, the Turks were beaten and more than 200 ships lost. The jubilant League believed the Turks crushed forever, but they soon regained control of almost all the Mediterranean.

Sea battle
At Lepanto, the ships of both fleets were mostly galleys with rowers, like those of ancient Greece and Rome. The battle was a brutal affair of boarding parties and hand-to-hand fighting.

THE HAPSBURGS

The Hapsburgs were a noble Austrian family. In 1273, one of them, Rudolph I (1218–91) was chosen as Holy Roman Emperor. The family influence grew and from 1438 to 1806, with one exception, every Holy Roman Emperor was a Hapsburg. Their power reached its peak during the reign of Charles V (1519–56), who was also king of Spain. When Charles abdicated in 1558, his lands were divided between his son Philip (Philip II of Spain) and Charles's brother Ferdinand. The family dominated Europe until Napoleon I of France abolished the Holy Roman Empire in 1806.

Hapsburg drinking flagon
This flask bears the arms of Spain and Austria.

The Escorial
The Escorial palace just outside Madrid was built for Philip II. The vast complex, made up of palace, monastery, and church, was built around a series of courtyards. Philip regarded it as a refuge from the demands of the outside world, retiring to it in times of crisis, such as the failure of the Armada.

Emperor's shield
This shield may have belonged to the emperor Charles V. Although hostile to Protestantism, Charles eventually allowed Protestant worship in his empire.

Philip II
Philip, son of Emperor Charles V, was born in 1527. When Charles divided his empire between Philip and Philip's uncle Ferdinand, Philip became ruler of Spain, the Spanish Netherlands, and Spanish colonies in the Americas. Philip was a conscientious and religious man, but he was also bigoted and humorless. Many of his projects failed, especially his efforts to stop Dutch independence and his vain attempt to conquer England with the Spanish Armada. He died in 1598.

600	800	1000	1200	1400	1600	1700	1800	1900	2000

1572

St. Bartholomew's Day Massacre

When the Reformation swept through Europe, France, like many other states, was divided between Protestants (mainly Calvinists known as Huguenots) and Catholics. The king, Charles IX, and his mother, Catherine de Medici, were both Catholics, but the allegiance of the nobility was divided. Soon the country was plunged into bitter civil conflicts. In 1572, all the Huguenot leaders came to Paris for the wedding of the Protestant claimant to the throne, Henry of Navarre (later Henry IV of France). With Catherine's approval, most of the Protestant leadership, including the overall leader, Admiral Coligny, and several thousand other Protestants, were killed in a terrible massacre. When Henry became king in 1589, he tried to end the conflict. He had become a Catholic, but by the Edict of Nantes in 1598, he granted religious toleration throughout France.

Slaughter in the streets
Protestant men, women, and children were slain when the ordinary people of Paris joined in the massacre. Soon it spread to the rest of France and thousands more died.

Wedding gift
This gold and mother of pearl dagger was given by the City of Paris to Henry IV on his marriage to Margaret of Valois.

1572

The Sea Beggars take Brill

The Netherlands in the 16th century were made up of 17 thriving, self-governing provinces (now the Netherlands and Belgium). They were part of the Spanish empire and paid huge taxes to Spain. The Netherlanders (or Dutch) resented this, and when Philip II decided to rule directly from Spain, they rebelled. The rebels were led by William, Prince of Orange, who organized guerrilla warfare. In 1572 rebel sailors, known as the Sea Beggars, captured the Spanish-held Netherlands port of Brill. William was assassinated in 1584, but the struggle continued under his son Maurice, who in 1597 defeated a large Spanish army at the battle of Turnhout. In 1609, Spain appeared to recognize the independence of seven northern provinces (United Provinces) in a Twelve Year Truce, but fighting broke out again.

William the Silent
William of Orange was known as William the Silent. In fact, he was a talkative man but could hide his true feelings and opinions when necessary.

DUTCH INDEPENDENCE

1568 Dutch begin revolt against Spanish rule
1572 Sea Beggars take Brill
1576 Pacification of Ghent; Dutch agree, whatever their religion, to drive out Spanish
1579 Union of Utrecht: seven northern provinces become United Provinces
1597 Battle of Turnhout
1609 Twelve Year Truce between Spain and Provinces
1648 Peace of Westphalia confirms Dutch independence

The Massacre of the Innocents
Philip II sent a huge army under the Duke of Alba to crush Netherlands resistance. Thousands were slaughtered. The artist Pieter Brueghel (1564–1637) used a biblical subject (Herod's massacre of the innocents) to illustrate the situation. *The Massacre of the Innocents* shows Dutch country people being killed by Spanish soldiers. The grim commander is Herod or the Duke of Alba.

40,000 BC		10,000	5000	1000	500	AD 1	200	400

1500-1600 AMERICAS

The lure of gold
Many adventurers were lured to the Americas by the prospect of finding gold. This nose ornament of beaten gold was found in Colombia.

The European belief that gold existed in abundance in the Americas, coupled with a European population explosion, encouraged explorers to sail across the Atlantic in search of wealth and new lands. The ancient Aztec and Inca empires in Central and South America immediately fell to the Spanish, while in the north, the French and English, also spurred by the desire to find gold and to claim profitable lands for their crowns, decided to attempt permanent settlement.

1500s
French explore Canada

Following Columbus's voyages to the Caribbean (1492–1504), many European mariners explored the Americas over the next century. They went in search of gold and other resources, and also to found colonies. In 1534, Jacques Cartier (1491–1557), a brave French navigator, explored the Straits of Belle Isle on Canada's east coast and claimed Canada for France. He made a second voyage up the St. Lawrence River, previously explored by French fishermen, and visited two Huron villages which later became Quebec and Montreal. The French tried unsuccessfully to found a colony at Montreal in 1541. French colonization of Canada began in the next century.

Happy landing
When Cartier sailed up the St. Lawrence River, he met and made friends with the native Huron people. The Huron word for village is *kanata*, and it is from this word that the French took the name Canada.

Kidney beans

Peppers

Pineapple

Peanuts

Sweet potatoes

Potatoes

Tomatoes

New fruits from a new world
European explorers found foods in the Americas which they had never seen before. These included pineapples, tomatoes, and peppers, which they took home with them.

Northwest Passage
Many European explorers sailed westward across the Atlantic to try to find a northwest passage to Asia. Instead they encountered the large land mass of North America.

Balboa	→
Cabot	→
Cabral	→
Cartier	→
Frobisher	→
Hudson	→

EXPLORING AMERICA

1494 Treaty of Tordesillas: Pope divides the New World between Spain and Portugal

1497–98 Italian John Cabot leaves England for North America and reaches Newfoundland

1500–01 Pedro Cabral, Portuguese navigator, lands in Brazil and claims it for his native Portugal

1502–04 Christopher Columbus reaches Honduras and Panama in Central America

1513 Vasco de Balboa of Spain sights and sails in Pacific Ocean

1534–35 French explorer Jacques Cartier sails up St. Lawrence River in Canada

1577–80 Englishman Francis Drake, explorer, sails around the world

| 600 | 800 | 1000 | 1200 | 1400 | 1600 | 1700 | 1800 | 1900 | 2000 |

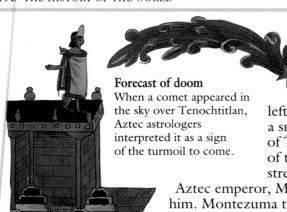

Forecast of doom
When a comet appeared in the sky over Tenochtitlan, Aztec astrologers interpreted it as a sign of the turmoil to come.

1519
The end of the Aztec Empire

Hernan Cortés (1485–1547), a Spanish soldier and explorer, left Cuba in February 1519 bound for Mexico. He was accompanied by a small force of about 500 armed men. They reached the Aztec capital of Tenochtitlan in November. Cortés was amazed at the sight of the huge capital, with its palaces, temples, and wide streets, and as he descended into the city, the great Aztec emperor, Montezuma, was carried out in a litter to welcome him. Montezuma treated the visitors royally, but Cortés betrayed him, quickly put him under arrest, and slaughtered hundreds of the Aztec nobility. Shocked at what was happening, the remaining Aztec leaders organized a revolt in 1520, when Cortés was away. Many Spaniards were killed, but Cortés managed to marshal neighboring peoples against the Aztecs. Montezuma was killed, Tenochtitlan was destroyed, and Cortés became governor of Mexico.

Guns and horses
The Spanish warriors carried guns and fought on horseback, both of which were unknown to the Aztecs. Despite these Spanish advantages, the Aztecs put up a fierce fight.

1532
Inca Empire falls

The Inca emperor, Huayna Capac, died in 1525. His sons fought over the succession, and Atahualpa took it in 1532. As he marched to Cuzco for his coronation, Atahualpa and his followers were set upon by 168 armored knights on horseback, led by the Spanish conquistador, Francisco Pizarro. The entire Inca company was killed, apart from Atahualpa, who was spared on condition that he pay a huge ransom to the Spaniards. Atahualpa delivered the goods – a huge room filled with gold and silver – and was promptly strangled. His death signaled the end of the great Inca Empire.

Gold armlets
The Incas adorned their bodies with gold and silver.

AFTERMATH OF THE INVASIONS

After Cortés invaded Tenochtitlan, the world of the Aztecs collapsed. Many Aztecs were tortured, killed, or enslaved by their conquerors. Diseases such as smallpox, brought by the Spanish, killed many Aztecs. Likewise, the powerful Inca Empire fell into disorder soon after Atahualpa's death.

Conqueror's hat
The Spanish soldiers wore open helmets like this one.

40,000 BC		10,000	5000	1000	500	AD 1	200	400

1500-1600 OCEANIA

Europeans powers began to organize voyages to explore the Pacific. The Portuguese reached some of the Pacific islands, such as New Guinea, and Spanish mariners also traveled there. Ferdinand Magellan, a Portuguese in Spanish employment, navigated the Pacific and reached the Philippines, where he was killed by angry islanders. Meanwhile, unaware of these expeditions, the Maoris in New Zealand built fortified enclosures, and the Tonga people founded two new dynasties.

Marquesas figure
This figure was carved from a sperm whale's tooth and worn around the neck on a string.

c.1511
Portuguese search for a legend

The Portuguese took the great trading center of Malacca, in Malaysia, in 1511 and made it their main base in the region. They then explored the islands eastward, finding their way across Indonesia and into the Pacific. As they did so, legends grew up that the Biblical land of Ophir, source of King Solomon's gold, lay in the southwest Pacific, in the Spanish hemisphere. This may have encouraged them in their exploration. They soon reached a number of island groups, including, in 1512, the Moluccas, the famous Spice Islands, whose lucrative trade they wished to control. One of the navigators, Diego Gomez de Sequeira, probably visited the Caroline Islands and the nearby Palau Island group in 1525. Other Portuguese ships reached New Guinea in 1526.

Wall hanging
This painted wood ceremonial shield from New Guinea was probably hung on the wall inside a temple for decoration.

Yap Island
Yap Island, one of the more important islands within the Caroline Island group, was visited by the Portuguese during the early 16th century.

Magellan's ship
This painting is from Antonio Pigafetta's 1525 manuscript of Magellan's voyage. Pigafetta, an Italian, accompanied Magellan on his voyage and lived to tell the tale.

1521
Spanish sail across the Pacific

Three ships from the Spanish round-the-world expedition led by the Portuguese navigator, Ferdinand Magellan (c.1480–1521), succeeded in navigating the vast Pacific Ocean. They passed two small Polynesian islands on their way, including the island of Pukapuka. Finally, with a somewhat depleted crew, Magellan reached Guam, the largest of the Mariana Island group. On March 16, 1521, Magellan landed on the Philippine island of Samar but was killed a few weeks later by angry islanders. Only one ship, captained by Sebastian del Cano, one of Magellan's lieutenants, returned home to Spain in September 1522, thus completing the first circumnavigation of the globe.

Magellan's patron
Magellan's voyage around the world in the Spanish ship *Victoria* was sponsored by the Holy Roman Emperor, Charles V.

600	800	1000	1200	1400	1600	1700	1800	1900	2000

1550s
Maoris build fortified enclosures

The Maoris on both the North and South Islands of New Zealand built enclosures, or *pa*, for their activities. These varied in size from less than a fifth of a hectare (half an acre) to 40 hectares (100 acres). Many of these *pa* were fortified. The larger *pa* were used as residential areas for communities. Fortifications appear to have been of three kinds: enclosures with terraces, enclosures on a ridge or promontory, and also enclosures surrounded by rings of ditches. Several of these *pa* have been excavated, revealing traces of weapon stores, pits for storing crops, raised fighting platforms, and long wooden houses with hearths and gabled roofs. When Europeans first visited New Zealand in the late 18th century, they found Maori communities still living in *pa*.

Wooden trumpet
Maoris may have used trumpets when hunting.

Maori war dance
This scene shows Maori warriors performing a war dance in front of the heavily fortified great *pa* of Ohinemutu, at Rotorua on the North Island.

1595
Mendaña reaches the Marquesas Islands

The Marquesas Islands, in eastern Polynesia, were first settled by emigrants from Samoa in the second century BC. At that time they lived on fish, turtles, and sea birds, and later grew crops. They built houses on stone platforms and worshiped in temples nearby. The Marquesas were the first Polynesian islands to be explored by Europeans. In 1567, Spanish explorer Alvaro de Mendaña set sail from Callao in Peru to search for Pacific islands, reaching the Solomon Islands the following year. He planned to make further discoveries with a view to colonizing and returned to the Americas to organize an expedition. Finally, in April 1595, he set sail with about 380 men and women. His chief pilot was the Portuguese navigator Pedro Fernandez de Quiros. In July the expedition landed on the Marquesas Islands, where they quarreled with the local people and killed many of them. Sailing on westward, Mendaña searched in vain for the Solomon Islands and arrived at Santa Cruz. Mendaña's attempt to colonize was a failure, and before the year was out, he died of fever, along with many others.

Alvaro de Mendaña (1542–95)
Mendaña was a Spaniard living in Peru. He was only 25 years old when he set sail from Callao for the first time.

Social gathering
Solomon Islands natives lived together in close-knit communities and were unfriendly to strangers, of whom they were suspicious.

Carved canoe god
This wooden statue from the Solomon Islands was fixed to the canoe prow to keep evil spirits away.

| 40,000 BC | | 10,000 | 1000 | AD 1 | 400 | 800 | 1200 | 1600 | 1800 | 2000 |

Chapter 13

1600 – 1700

Commerce and Colonies

Statue of Dutch East India Company officer from Gujarat

1600-1700
THE WORLD

I N THE 17TH CENTURY, European commerce spreads to many parts of the world. In their quest for gold, spices, and other prized commodities, Portuguese, Spanish, Dutch, English, and French merchants establish trading posts on every continent of the world. In the Americas, people from Europe – often fleeing religious persecution or economic hardship – follow the merchants and set up colonies. By 1700 the major European powers, enriched by the proceeds of international trade, govern worldwide economic and territorial empires many times their own size.

The independent world

Not every country is affected by the growing influence of Europe. In 1683, the powerful Ottoman Turks come very close to overrunning central Europe when they attack Vienna, while the Chinese, under the strong rule of the Manchus, enter a period of prolonged economic prosperity helped by the lucrative export trade in ceramics and silk. Japan concentrates on internal affairs and begins a period of comparative isolation from Europe that lasts for more than 200 years. In India, the Moghul emperors achieve their greatest glory, but by the end of the century their empire is greatly overstretched and ready to crumble. Many African kingdoms flourish, although West Africa and Angola are increasingly damaged by the slave trade.

NORTH AMERICA

Rockies

Mississippi

• Quebec

c.1608 French settlers in Quebec trade guns for furs with Native Americans

1629 English ships blockade French ships on the St. Lawrence river, starting a conflict between the nations for control of the fur trade

1621 Pilgrim settlers in Massachusetts prepare a thanksgiving feast to celebrate their first harvest

c.1600 Dutch ships arrive in Venezuela where their crews mine and load cargoes of salt

Andes

SOUTH AMERICA

ATLANTIC OCEAN

PACIFIC OCEAN

N

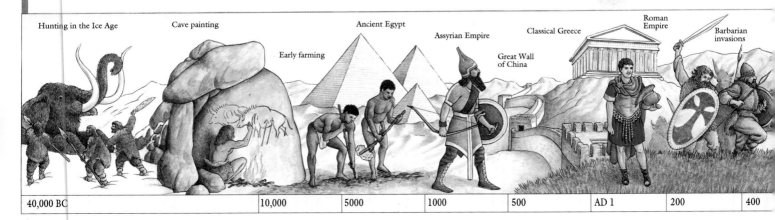

Hunting in the Ice Age

Cave painting

Early farming

Ancient Egypt

Assyrian Empire

Great Wall of China

Classical Greece

Roman Empire

Barbarian invasions

| 40,000 BC | | 10,000 | 5000 | 1000 | 500 | AD 1 | 200 | 400 |

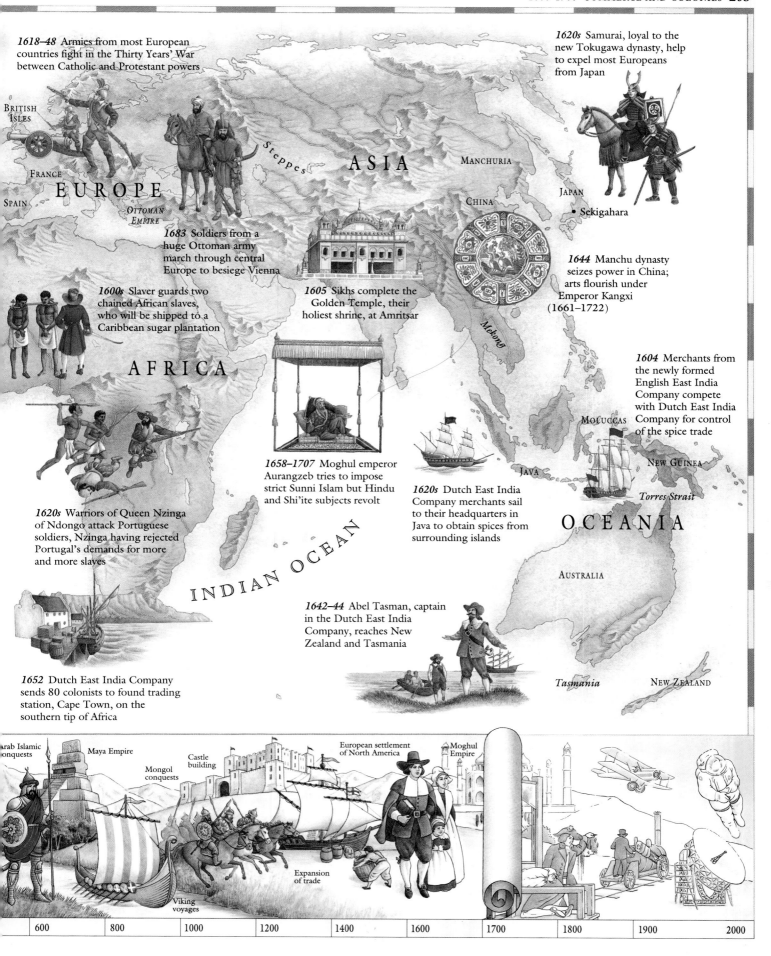

1618–48 Armies from most European countries fight in the Thirty Years' War between Catholic and Protestant powers

1620s Samurai, loyal to the new Tokugawa dynasty, help to expel most Europeans from Japan

BRITISH ISLES

FRANCE

SPAIN

EUROPE

Steppes

ASIA

MANCHURIA

CHINA

JAPAN

• Sekigahara

OTTOMAN EMPIRE

1683 Soldiers from a huge Ottoman army march through central Europe to besiege Vienna

1605 Sikhs complete the Golden Temple, their holiest shrine, at Amritsar

1644 Manchu dynasty seizes power in China; arts flourish under Emperor Kangxi (1661–1722)

1600s Slaver guards two chained African slaves, who will be shipped to a Caribbean sugar plantation

AFRICA

Mekong

1604 Merchants from the newly formed English East India Company compete with Dutch East India Company for control of the spice trade

MOLUCCAS

NEW GUINEA

1658–1707 Moghul emperor Aurangzeb tries to impose strict Sunni Islam but Hindu and Shi'ite subjects revolt

JAVA

Torres Strait

1620s Warriors of Queen Nzinga of Ndongo attack Portuguese soldiers, Nzinga having rejected Portugal's demands for more and more slaves

1620s Dutch East India Company merchants sail to their headquarters in Java to obtain spices from surrounding islands

OCEANIA

AUSTRALIA

INDIAN OCEAN

1642–44 Abel Tasman, captain in the Dutch East India Company, reaches New Zealand and Tasmania

Tasmania

NEW ZEALAND

1652 Dutch East India Company sends 80 colonists to found trading station, Cape Town, on the southern tip of Africa

Arab Islamic conquests

Maya Empire

Mongol conquests

Castle building

European settlement of North America

Moghul Empire

Expansion of trade

Viking voyages

| 600 | 800 | 1000 | 1200 | 1400 | 1600 | 1700 | 1800 | 1900 | 2000 |

1600

1625

AFRICA

1600s Kalonga kingdom, north of the Zambezi River, becomes rich through ivory trade

1600s Hausaland dominates trade routes to Sahara

1600s Great Zimbabwe replaced by several regional capitals in Transvaal, Botswana, and Zimbabwe

1620s Queen Nzinga of Ndongo fights Portuguese in Angola*

Many elephants were slaughtered to obtain ivory for trading

1627 Manchus overrun Korea, which later becomes vassal state

c.1628 Kingdom of Burma breaks up into small states

1632–48 Shah Jahan builds Taj Mahal at Agra in India

1641 Dutch capture Malacca on the Malay peninsula

1644 Qing (Manchu) dynasty takes over in China*

Shah Jahan built the exquisite Taj Mahal in memory of his dead wife, Mumtaz Mahal

ASIA

The Dutch began to trade in modern-day Indonesia; many objects like this kris (dagger) ended up in Europe

c.1600 Abbas I reigns in Persia; introduces reforms and expands territory

1600 Battle of Sekigahara, Japan; Tokugawa Ieyasu defeats rivals, takes power, and the Tokugawa or Edo period begins*

1600–14 English, Dutch, Danish, and French East India Companies founded*

1607 Confucianism begins to be main force in Tokugawa politics and society

1612–39 Japanese persecute Christians

1619–24 Dutch establish virtual monopoly of spice trade in Moluccas and other Indonesian islands

1620s Beginning of Japan's restriction of contact with the outside world*

This Spanish monstrance was a container used to display the Host during the Roman Catholic Mass

EUROPE

1605 End of Boris Godunov's reign in Russia

1605 Gunpowder Plot fails

1609 Italian Galileo Galilei confirms that the sun is the center of the universe

1611–32 Reign of Gustavus Adolphus of Sweden

1613 Michael becomes Tsar of Russia; Romanov dynasty begins

1613–29 Reign of Bethlen Gabor in Hungary

1618–48 Thirty Years War involves almost all Europe*

[1] **1619–28** In London, England, William Harvey discovers the circulation of the blood

1624 Cardinal Richelieu becomes chief minister in France

The Gunpowder Plot was a Catholic conspiracy to blow up the English Parliament; one of the chief plotters, Guy Fawkes, was found in the cellars carrying this lantern

1625 Dutchman Hugo Grotius publishes *De Jure Belli ac Pacis*, which becomes the basis of international law

1627–28 Catholics besiege Huguenots in La Rochelle on western coast of France

1628 Petition of Right, England; parliament curtails king's powers

1629–40 British king Charles I tries to rule without parliament

1632–54 Reign of Queen Christina of Sweden

1640 Portugal gains independence from Spain

Charles I of England

1642–47 Civil war in England, Scotland, and Ireland*

[1] **1643** Italian physicist Evangelista Torricelli invents the barometer

1643 In Thirty Years War, French defeat Spanish at Battle of Rocroi

1643–1715 Reign of Louis XIV of France*

1645–69 Candian War between Venice and Ottoman Turks

1648 Treaty of Westphalia ends Thirty Years War

1648–53 The Frondes (revolts) against Mazarin's rule in France

1649 Charles I of England and Scotland executed

AMERICAS

Quebec is the oldest and one of the most beautiful cities in Canada

1607 Jamestown Colony, first permanent English settlement in North America, founded in Virginia

1608 Quebec in Canada founded by French settlers*

1610 Hudson Bay explored by Henry Hudson

1620 Pilgrims sail to America in the *Mayflower**

1625 French settlements in the Caribbean (St. Christopher) begin

1626 Dutch found New Amsterdam in North America

1629 Massachusetts founded

[1] **1638** First printing press reaches America

1642 Montreal, Canada, founded

1646 The Bahamas colonized by the English

By the early 17th century, tobacco use was commonplace throughout Europe; the tobacco trade was booming and tobacco graters, like this Dutch ivory man, were very popular

OCEANIA

1600s Beginning of building of *tupa*, stone towers with inner chambers, on Easter Island

c.1600 In Tonga, dominant political leadership passes from Tu'i Tonga dynasty to Tu'i Kanokupulu dynasty

1606 Luis Vaez de Torres from Spain sails around New Guinea and reaches the straits now named after him*

This carving tool comes from the island of Tonga

1642–44 Abel Tasman reaches Tasmania and New Zealand*

1650

1650s Portuguese clash with Muslims in Zambezi region

c.1650 Ethiopia expels Portuguese missionaries and diplomats

1652 Dutch found Cape Town in South Africa*

1660s Mawlay-al-Rashid restores sultanate of Morocco

1670s French settle in Senegal

1670s Fulani pastoralist people gain control of Bondu in southern Senegal

This drum of West African, possibly Senegalese, origin is made from a single piece of wood, hollowed and fitted with membranes and lashings of elephant hide

Ceramic production developed in China

1657 Tokugawa Mitsukuni begins compilation of *History of Japan*

1658–1707 Emperor Aurangzeb is the last great Moghul emperor; after 1707 the empire begins to break up

1661–1722 Reign of the Kangxi emperor in China; Chinese territory extended and books and scholarship developed

1664 Dutch force King of Siam to give them monopoly of deerskin exports and seaborne trade with China

1650s Dutch prosperity leads to new achievements in art*

1652–54 First Dutch war with England

1653–58 Protectorate of Oliver Cromwell in Britain

1654 Portuguese drive Dutch out of Brazil

1659 Treaty of the Pyrenees between France and Spain

1661 Death of Cardinal Mazarin; Louis XIV of France rules personally

1665 Great Plague of London

1666 Great Fire of London

1670 Secret Treaty of Dover between England and France

1674–96 John Sobieski reigns in Poland

Charles II of England was restored to the throne in 1660; his pleasure-loving life-style was popular after the strict Puritanism of Cromwell's Protectorate

In their stepped gable roofs, the oldest houses of New York clearly show the influence of the city's Dutch founders

1655 English capture Jamaica from the Spanish

1664 English capture New Amsterdam from the Dutch; it is renamed New York

Tasman found a flourishing culture on Fiji, with many crafts workers creating striking pieces of jewelry; this Fijian necklace is made from carved and polished pieces of sperm whale tooth

1675

1680s Rise of Asante kingdom in West Africa

1680s Butua kingdom flourishes in Zimbabwe plains; Portuguese are driven into Zambezi valley and also eastward

1686 Louis XIV of France officially annexes Madagascar

1698 Portuguese expelled from Mombasa on eastern coast

This Asante hunter, made of dark gold, carries a dead monkey while at his feet is a trapped antelope

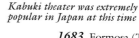

Kabuki theater was extremely popular in Japan at this time

1683 Formosa (Taiwan) becomes Chinese territory

1690 English East India Company official Job Charnock founds the city of Calcutta, on a swamp by the Hooghly River in Bengal, northeastern India

1678 Imaginary "Popish Plot" to overthrow Charles II of England invented by Titus Oates

1679 Habeas Corpus Act in England ensures no imprisonment without court appearance first

1682–1725 Reign of Peter the Great of Russia

1683 Turks besiege Vienna; beaten off by John Sobieski*

1685 Revocation of the Edict of Nantes in France

1688 Revolution in England against James II brings William of Orange to the throne

Peter I (the Great) traveled around Europe in disguise, picking up cultural and technical knowledge of benefit to Russia. Here he is dressed as a ship's carpenter

Louis XIV of France was probably France's greatest king; he made France Europe's most powerful nation and the center of culture

1689 Formation of Grand Alliance of Hapsburgs, the Dutch, and the English against France

1697 Treaty of Ryswick between France and Grand Alliance

1697–1718 Rule of Charles XII of Sweden

1697–98 Peter I (the Great) of Russia travels through western Europe in disguise

1699 Treaty of Karlowitz; Hapsburgs gain almost all Hungary

1679 Father Hennepin reaches Niagara Falls in Canada

1681 Territory granted in North America to Quaker William Penn; becomes known as Pennsylvania

1681–82 Frenchman La Salle explores Mississippi River from source to mouth and founds Louisiana

Louis Hennepin, a Jesuit missionary, was the first European to reach the spectacular Niagara Falls

1680s Statue building ends on Easter Island; resources and then population decline, and this leads to civil war

| 600 | 800 | 1000 | | 1600 | 1700 | 1800 | 1900 | 2000 |

1600-1700 AFRICA

The European slave trade in Africa, begun in the early 1500s, now gathered momentum. African leaders became alarmed at the number of people seized by Europeans for slavery. The ruler of the kingdom of Ndongo, Queen Nzinga, fiercely resisted, partly because of reports of terrible conditions under which slaves were shipped to America. Inland, strong states still prospered, such as the growing empire of Oyo in West Africa. Near the southern tip of Africa, the Dutch began a settlement which grew rapidly. In East Africa, Portuguese power declined as Omani Muslims from the Persian Gulf allied with northern trading centers along the coast.

Pale strangers
This ivory carving is an African view of the Portuguese.

Many kingdoms, much destruction
Many African kingdoms were raided for slaves by the Portuguese from Luanda and later Benguela.

1620s
Queen Nzinga's fight

In 1623 the king of the Ndongo kingdom in Angola died and the next year his sister Nzinga became queen. She was soon at war with the Portuguese because she refused to supply as many slaves as they wanted for shipment to their colonies in Brazil. She made alliances against them with neighboring states. After the Portuguese forced her out of Ndongo she took over the neighboring kingdom of Matamba and fought on. At her death in 1663, Matamba was still independent.

A royal seat
When Nzinga went to negotiate with the Portuguese, she was refused a chair, so she sat down on one of her attendants.

1652
Cape Town founded

Van Riebeeck claims the Cape
The modern state of South Africa began here. For nearly 150 years the Dutch East India Company ran the colony to suit its commercial interests.

In 1652 the Dutch East India Company sent 80 colonists, led by Jan van Riebeeck, to establish a trading post on the southern tip of Africa to supply provisions for ships traveling from Europe to Asia and back. They called it Cape Town. At first the settlement struggled but in the 1680s French Huguenot refugees arrived to strengthen it. From the first, relations between Africans and Europeans were unequal and unhappy. To meet their need for labor the settlers soon began to use local people as servants and laborers, and to buy slaves from Guinea, Angola, and Madagascar. By the 1690s, some 200 ships were stopping at Cape Town every year. The port became known as the "Tavern of the Two Seas."

European farms, African workers
The colonists used African labor to develop their farms.

| 40,000 BC | | 10,000 | 5000 | 1000 | 500 | AD 1 | 200 | 400 |

THE SLAVE TRADE

The practice of slavery, the buying and selling of people against their will, goes back to ancient times. Slaves have no rights or freedoms but are owned entirely by their masters. Selling African people as slaves was begun on a large scale by Arabs when they dominated vast areas of Africa about 1,000 years ago. Fresh demands for slaves arose when Europeans wanted them to work on their plantations and in mines in the Americas. Africans were skilled in tropical farming and mining. Slave traders shipped slaves across the world to lives of toil and suffering, in the Americas, the Caribbean, Asia, and Europe. The Portuguese were the first in the slave markets, but other Europeans soon followed.

Slavers' stronghold
In 1482 the Portuguese in Ghana asked a local ruler for land on which to build "a house," then built this castle as a base for slaving and trading. It was just one link in a chain of fortified bases stretching around the coasts of Africa and far beyond.

Convoy of misery
Arab and European traders, African "kings, rich men and prime merchants," all grew rich from the slave trade.

Africa bleeds
The lives stolen from Africa enriched other lands. By 1800 half the population of Brazil was of African origin. In parts of Africa, entire kingdoms were ravaged by the trade, while other states rose to power on its corrupt profits.

Less spacious than a coffin
An overhead view of the hold of an English slave ship.

Slave conditions
The full details of how many people were sold into slavery may never be known, but it is estimated that over seven million Africans were shipped to the Americas between 1701 and 1810. More than a million died on the way because of the appalling conditions under which they traveled. They were herded into very cramped quarters, packed in narrow holds only 3.3 ft (1 m) high. They might be unable to move for days. This encouraged the spread of disease, especially when there was often no fresh food or water. The ships' crews, who were themselves badly treated, were hardened by their inhuman work.

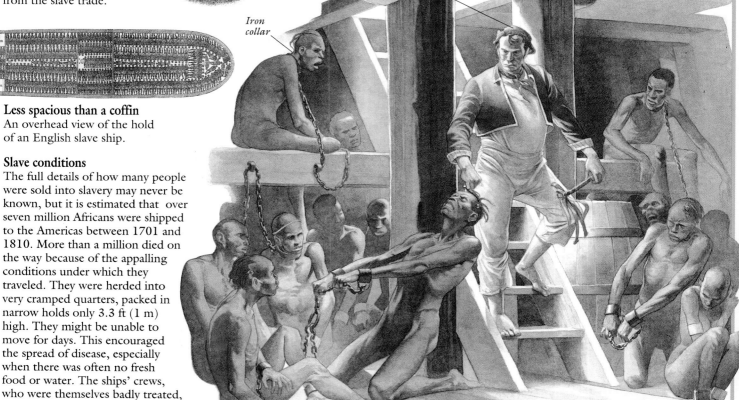

Sailors were often made brutal by the trade

Iron collar

1600-1700 ASIA

After years of dominating trade with Asia, the Portuguese were forced to let stronger European nations in. These included the English, French, and Dutch, who founded new East India companies. In China, the Manchus, a vigorous new power from north China, took over in the 1640s and ruled for nearly 300 years. The first four Manchu emperors were able rulers, and China thrived under them. In Japan, the great Battle of Sekigahara ended a series of civil wars and was followed by a period of national isolation.

East India Company
All the East India companies had their own coats of arms, such as the British one above.

1600
English East India Company founded

After the Portuguese pioneered the sea route to India and eastern Asia, they seized and fortified bases in places like the Moluccas (Spice Islands), Macao in China, and Goa in India. From there they monopolized a lucrative spice trade with Europe, where spices were in great demand, for nearly a century. The English, and also the Dutch, were aware of the profits to be made from this kind of enterprise and decided to challenge Portugal's trade monopoly with eastern Asia. In 1599, 80 London merchants came together to form the East India Company, which was chartered by Elizabeth I in 1600, giving the company exclusive trading rights in the East Indies. Two years later, the Dutch East India Company was founded. Rivalry between the Dutch and English East India companies reached a climax at Amboyna in the Moluccas in 1623 (one of the bases taken by the Dutch from the Portuguese), when ten English merchants were executed for trading there. The Dutch tightened their control of the spice trade, and in 1638 they persuaded the Japanese to let them take over Portuguese trading in Japan. The English were diverted to India, where they soon set up a lucrative trade in textiles.

East India ports
Trading stations, or factories, were sited on the coasts of India. The three main English ones were at Madras, Calcutta, and Bombay.

Storeroom
The East India merchants stored their merchandise in large warehouses.

Dutch headquarters
The Dutch built Batavia (now Jakarta) in Java as their headquarters in the east because of its deep and spacious harbor.

Dutchman
This painted wood figure was probably modeled on a Dutch East India officer and would have been used as an ornament in a nobleman's house.

1600
The Battle of Sekigahara

When the Japanese dictator Hideyoshi died after several months of illness, there was a struggle for power. Tokugawa Ieyasu, who had been a close ally of Hideyoshi, was the leading contender, and his main adversary was Ishida Mitsunari, an able favorite of Hideyoshi's, who harbored grudges against Ieyasu. Mitsunari encouraged hostility towards Ieyasu by stirring up his enemies, and in October 1600 a civil war broke out. A great battle was fought in the pass of Sekigahara, in central Japan, and Ieyasu won an overwhelming victory. It marked the end of a series of civil wars and the beginning of the Tokugawa, or Edo, period in Japan. Mitsunari was soon executed, and Ieyasu was made shogun in 1603. He was the first of the Tokugawa shoguns.

THE OFFICE OF SHOGUN

In theory, shoguns were military leaders appointed by the emperor to maintain peace and order. In reality, most emperors were politically weak and were forced to select the most powerful military leader as shogun. The first effective shogun was Minamoto Yoritomo, who ruled from 1192. After the Minamoto line died out, puppet shoguns were selected from various families. Hideyoshi was prevented by birth from becoming shogun, but Ieyasu (left) was able to claim the title through his Minamoto ancestry. He and his descendants held the office until 1868.

Battle of Sekigahara
Each side had 100,000 men at the Battle of Sekigahara, but Ieyasu's superior military planning won him the day.

1620s
New Japanese foreign policy

When Tokugawa Ieyasu died in 1616, his son, Hidetada, continued as shogun until 1623. He stepped up his father's policy of persecuting Christians, and for the first time European missionaries were arrested and executed. The Christians were persecuted because the shoguns feared that Japan would be invaded or infiltrated by a foreign power. Hidetada's successor, Tokugawa Iemitsu (1623–51), took affairs even further, and gradually all missionaries, and most traders, were expelled from Japan. This persecution was accompanied by a vigorous policy of restricting relations with foreign states. The Japanese were not allowed to travel abroad, and those who were abroad were forbidden to return. The building of large ships for trading over great distances was banned. The only foreigners who were allowed to continue living and trading in Japan were the Chinese and the Dutch; trade with Korea also continued. This restrictive foreign policy encouraged stability and unity within Japan. Buddhism, for centuries the dominant faith, was brought under the shogun's control, and a revival of Confucianism, with its emphasis on learning and loyalty to one's superiors, helped to prevent revolt and civil war.

Crucifixion
In 1622, at Nagasaki, 55 Christians were crucified. Their influence was felt to be a threat to the power of the shoguns.

Dutch allotments at Deshima
The Dutch traders were confined to a small post on the artificial island of Deshima, in Nagasaki Bay. They occasionally went to the mainland of Japan to pay homage at the shogun's court.

Thumb protectors
Manchu archers wore
jade thumb rings to
protect their thumbs;
the skin could be
rubbed raw if the bow
was much used.

Foreign figure
This Chinese cloisonné
figure of a foreigner
was made during
the 17th century.
Trade with
Europeans
was welcomed
by Manchu
governments.

1644
Manchu dynasty founded in China

In 1643, bandits rebelled against the Ming dynasty and
captured the capital city, Beijing. As a result, Ssu Tsung, the
last Ming emperor, committed suicide. A Ming general, Wu
Sangui, asked Dorgon, regent of Manchuria, north of
China, to help him drive out the rebel forces. Dorgon did
so and then, in 1644, he placed his own nephew on the
Chinese throne. This marked the beginning of the Manchu,
or Qing, dynasty. There was strong resistance to it in some
parts of China. The Manchus, for their part, tried to be fair
and friendly to the Chinese, adopting some of their customs
and policies and giving Chinese people top provincial jobs.
The first of these emperors, who had adopted the dynastic
title "Qing" and was known as Shunzhi, died in 1661 and
was succeeded by his seven-year-old son, known as the
Kangxi emperor. Kangxi spent the early years of his
reign trying to crush continuing Ming resistance,
and he also won campaigns against the Mongols.
Kangxi was a very able ruler of China. He strove to
unite the Manchus and Chinese and made tours of
inspection to see his government
at work. He encouraged people
to work for the common good.
Kangxi ruled for 61 years,
one of the longest reigns
in Chinese history.

MANCHU DYNASTY
1644 Shunzhi becomes first Qing emperor of China
1661 Shunzhi succeeded by his son Kangxi (to 1722)
1736 Qianlong, grandson of Kangxi, becomes emperor (to 1796)
1736–50 Development of *famille rose* porcelain at imperial kilns in Jingde zhen
1759 Turkestan in central Asia, later known as Xinjiang, taken into Chinese empire
1839–42 Opium War between China and Britain
1850–65 Taiping Rebellion almost brings down Manchu dynasty
1895 Treaty of Shimonoseki: China recognizes independence of Korea and surrenders Taiwan to Japan
1911 Manchu dynasty overthrown by national revolution; Sun Yat-sen is elected president

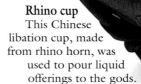

Rhino cup
This Chinese
libation cup, made
from rhino horn, was
used to pour liquid
offerings to the gods.

Packing porcelain
This scene shows people packing porcelain for export. Emperor Kangxi was an
enthusiastic patron of all arts, crafts, and learning and encouraged porcelain
manufacture, painting, literature, and other scholarly activities.

1600-1700 EUROPE

Thirty years of war rocked Europe after 1618, bringing few benefits to any country except France, which emerged triumphant. Britain was not involved in the Thirty Years War, but civil war broke out there. The king was executed, and a great soldier and politician, Oliver Cromwell, came to power. Another able leader, Polish king John Sobieski, stopped the Ottoman Turks' advance into southeast Europe.

Sword of God
The inscription on this 1630s German rapier tells that its owner fights for God.

"Lion of the North"
Gustavus II Adolphus of Sweden (1594–1632) spearheaded the Protestant campaign in the first half of the war. He won victories and persuaded Catholic France to help the Protestants. He was killed just after the Battle of Lutzen in 1632 and mourned in Sweden as a great general and government reformer.

1618
Thirty Years War breaks out

After the Reformation, the Catholic Hapsburg family, who dominated Europe, tried to reimpose Catholicism on Protestant states in their empire. In 1618 Bohemian Protestants, tired of Catholic oppression, threw the deputies of Matthias, Hapsburg Holy Roman Emperor, out of a window. This started a war that lasted 30 years and involved nearly all Europe. Hapsburg armies crushed the Bohemians, then defeated Protestant German rulers and their allies, led by the king of Denmark. Gustavus II Adolphus of Sweden and finally France, although Catholic, joined the German Protestants to curtail Hapsburg power. After several French victories, the war ended with the Treaty of Westphalia. States that were Catholic remained so, but Protestant states were guaranteed independence.

THIRTY YEARS WAR

1618 Imperial governors in Bohemia tossed from window

1620 Imperial forces defeat Protestant Bohemians at Battle of White Mountain

1629 Protestant Danish king Christian IV withdraws from war after defeats

1631–32 Gustavus II Adolphus routs Catholics at Breitenfeld and Lutzen

1635 France declares war on Hapsburg Spain

1643 French defeat Spanish forces at Battle of Rocroi

1648 Treaty of Westphalia

Deserters were hung in public as a warning to the other soldiers

Soldiers stole livestock from peasants to keep for milk and meat during campaigns

Some foot soldiers carried muskets which were not very reliable weapons; others wielded pikes up to 18 ft (5.5 m) long

Some women followed their soldier husbands; they often looted dead bodies after battles or raids on villages

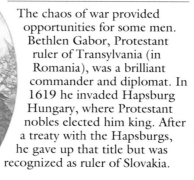

BETHLEN GABOR
The chaos of war provided opportunities for some men. Bethlen Gabor, Protestant ruler of Transylvania (in Romania), was a brilliant commander and diplomat. In 1619 he invaded Hapsburg Hungary, where Protestant nobles elected him king. After a treaty with the Hapsburgs, he gave up that title but was recognized as ruler of Slovakia.

Following an army
Throughout the war, large straggling armies marched through Germany. Soldiers were often mercenaries who had not been paid. They plundered villages and farmland in their path, burning and looting, leaving the inhabitants to starve. The war devastated Central Europe. Starvation and disease caused by the fighting reduced Europe's population from 22 million to 17 million.

1642
Britain plunges into civil war

The strong rule of Queen Elizabeth I (1558–1603) and her ministers, with the consent of parliament, gave way to mismanagement under James I (1603–25) and Charles I (1625–49). These kings believed they were appointed by God, not answerable to parliament or the people. When parliament's members (MPs) demanded that Charles grant them more power, including approval of taxation, the king dissolved parliament and attempted to rule on his own. Also, the king's apparent support for Catholics made him more deeply unpopular with Protestant parliamentarians. In 1640, desperate for funds to quell a Scottish revolt, Charles recalled parliament. He agreed to some reforms but in 1642 tried to arrest five MPs. The attempt sparked off civil war. The king left London for the Midlands to gather support. After royal victories, Oliver Cromwell, a member of parliament, forged a professional army and smashed the king's forces at Naseby in 1645.

Death warrant
This document, agreeing to kill the king, was signed by 59 high court commissioners.

Headguard
This hat was worn in the civil war by the parliamentarian John Bradshaw. It was lined with metal to protect his head.

Beheading the king
After losing the war, Charles negotiated with one faction after another until the army imprisoned him in 1648. Army leaders allowed only 60 MPs to attend parliament. They appointed a High Court, which condemned the king to death. He was executed in 1649 in London before a shocked crowd. His heir, Charles, escaped to France. After Cromwell's death, he returned to Britain in 1660 as Charles II.

THE PROTECTORATE

After Charles's execution, for the only time in its history, Britain became a commonwealth, or republic. Oliver Cromwell, the great parliamentarian commander, was given new powers by parliament as Lord Protector of England, Scotland, and Ireland. In a revolutionary period of government until his death in 1658, he worked to reform the law, increase Britain's trade, and encourage the toleration of all kinds of Protestant belief.

Cromwell
Though a strict Protestant, Cromwell loved music, dancing, and hunting. He was described as "of majestic deportment and comely presence."

1650s
Dutch trade and arts prosper

In 1609 seven Protestant provinces in the northern Netherlands won independence from the Hapsburg empire. By the 1650s the new state was immensely rich from the profits of trade with Asia and the Americas. Skilled Jewish and Protestant refugees flocked to it from Catholic Spain and France. The openness of Dutch society encouraged the free exchange of ideas. Christiaan Huygens put forward the theory that light travels in waves; Antonie van Leeuwenhoek discovered the structure of blood. Merchants built tall, gabled houses and commissioned works of art to decorate them by superb artists such as Rembrandt and Vermeer.

Tulip pot
In the town of Delft, potters began to use a tin glaze and paint in blue and white. The style is still popular today.

Woman weighing gold
This painting by Vermeer shows a calm indoor scene in glowing light. Pictures of everyday life are typical of Dutch art of the time.

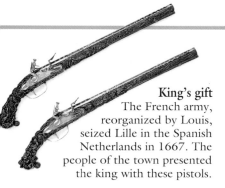

King's gift
The French army, reorganized by Louis, seized Lille in the Spanish Netherlands in 1667. The people of the town presented the king with these pistols.

1660s
Louis XIV strengthens French monarchy

Louis XIV's long reign (1643–1715) marked the triumph of the monarchy in France. He successfully put into practice his belief in the divine right of kings: he was God's glorious representative on earth, and no subject could challenge him. Louis built a splendid palace at Versailles, away from the political intrigues of Paris. Important people flocked there. Elaborate ceremonies kept them busy while Louis made the key decisions of state. He appointed capable ministers but let none grow too powerful. Jean-Baptiste Colbert increased trade, creating French colonies abroad and building canals and roads throughout France to make transport easier. François de Louvois reorganized the French army, winning land on France's northeast frontier. But from 1701 to 1713, Louis involved France in an expensive war against Britain and her allies. Taxes to fund it were forced on ordinary people, many of whom came to resent the extravagant lifestyle of the king.

Louis XIV's tour of Versailles
Work began on Versailles in 1661. More than 36,000 crafts workers were employed. Conditions were dangerous. Workmen died every day, and their bodies were removed at night by cart.

Revolving around the Sun King
Versailles impressed the majesty of the king upon the world. The ornate furniture was soon copied throughout Europe. The palace became overcrowded with nobles and their servants, all crammed into tiny rooms without toilets. They jostled to see their splendid monarch, called the Sun King, who gave pensions and positions to his favorites.

MAKERS OF ABSOLUTE MONARCHY

Two cardinals laid the foundations of royal power in France. Richelieu (1585–1642), shown left, chief minister of Louis XIII, reduced the strength of great nobles by operating through regional officials, called *intendants*. Through clever diplomacy, then armed intervention, he supported Protestant states fighting the mighty Catholic Hapsburgs in the Thirty Years War. His successor Mazarin (1602–61), running France for young Louis XIV, ensured the victory of French forces.

1683
Polish king defeats Ottomans at Vienna

In 1665 a Polish noble, John Sobieski, became commander-in-chief of the Polish army. He was a huge man with tremendous energy. Central Europe was under constant threat of invasion by Ottoman Turks. In 1673 John smashed the Turkish army at the Battle of Choczim. This victory led to his election as Polish king, and Polish prestige rose throughout Europe. In 1683 a vast Turkish army, led by grand vizir Kara Mustapha, marched to Vienna and besieged the city. John raced there with a small but well-trained force and drove the Turks away, inflicting dreadful losses. Turkish danger to Europe evaporated.

Siege of Vienna
About 100,000 Turkish troops camped outside Vienna. They assaulted the city walls and dug tunnels to get in from underneath. The Viennese defended heroically until the Poles relieved them.

Ruler's hat
This large hat was worn by John Sobieski.

| 600 | 800 | 1000 | 1200 | 1400 | 1600 | 1700 | 1800 | 1900 | 2000 |

1600-1700 AMERICAS

In North America, French traders and missionaries explored widely and established a presence in Canada. English merchants and religious dissenters founded colonies along the Atlantic coast, including Jamestown (1607) in Virginia and Plymouth (1620) and Massachusetts Bay (1630) in New England. Swedish and Dutch colonists also began to arrive. To the south, the Spanish explored California, founded New Mexico, and expanded their empire in Mexico and Peru. Portugal continued to colonize Brazil.

Helpful farming hints
Friendly Native Americans showed the newly arrived European settlers how to plant and grow suitable crops. They grew wheat, beans, peas, pumpkins, and large quantities of corn.

"Father of Canada"
Samuel de Champlain (1567–1635) was the son of a naval captain. He dedicated his life to creating a French empire in Canada, which he called "New France."

1608
Samuel de Champlain founds Quebec

Soon after Jacques Cartier explored the site of Quebec on the St. Lawrence River in Canada, several unsuccessful attempts were made to set up a colony there. In 1593, a Frenchman, Samuel de Champlain, joined an expedition to Canada and explored the St. Lawrence as far as the Lachine rapids. Returning to France, he persuaded the king, Henry IV (1553–1610), to fund an expedition to colonize along the St. Lawrence. He set sail with 28 followers, went up the river, and early in July 1608 founded a trading station. This became Quebec, the first city in Canada. He continued to explore the area, and remained in Canada for virtually the rest of his life. In 1663, 28 years after his death, Quebec became the capital of New France.

Fur trapper
Native American hunters exchanged wild animal pelts with the colonists in return for European guns, rum, and other goods.

The Mayflower *was originally a cargo ship, and not designed to carry people*

1620
The voyage of the *Mayflower*

In the early 16th century, many English Protestants were dissatisfied with the Church of England. One group of religious dissenters, the Separatists (who later became known as the Pilgrims) decided to settle in North America, where they hoped to live and worship in peace. In September 1620, about 100 Separatists left England aboard the ship *Mayflower*. Intending to land in Virginia, they instead reached the coast of New England after a stormy voyage. Before landing, the Pilgrims drew up an agreement, the Mayflower Compact, establishing a government for their colony, which they named Plymouth Plantation. Half the settlers didn't survive their first winter in America, and the colony might have failed without help from nearby Native Americans. But Plymouth survived and eventually prospered. Ten years after the landing of the Pilgrims, English Puritans began to arrive in New England in large numbers.

The *Mayflower*
This is a model of the ship that brought the settlers to North America.

SETTLERS IN AMERICA

Many settlers from the British Isles, France, Holland, and other nations came to North America in the 17th century. Some, hoping for quick riches, looked for gold and silver. They didn't find any. A few newcomers grew rich through commerce, especially the fur trade. Others came seeking religious freedom – Puritans in Massachusetts, Baptists in Rhode Island, Quakers in Pennsylvania, and Roman Catholics in Maryland. In England's southern colonies, plantations grew tobacco and other crops for export. These plantations were worked by indentured servants – immigrants "bound" to a planter until they had paid for their passage to America. Unwilling immigrants – slaves from Africa – also arrived in England's colonies.

1 New Hampshire
2 New York
3 Massachusetts
4 Rhode Island
5 Connecticut
6 Pennsylvania
7 New Jersey
8 Delaware
9 Maryland
10 Virginia
11 North Carolina
12 South Carolina
13 Georgia

Settling the East Coast
Thirteen colonies were founded along the eastern coast of North America, the last being Georgia in 1733.

Harvard University
The first university in the present-day United States was founded by Puritans in Massachusetts in 1636.

The first settlements
The first European settlers built simple homes to live in, on land that they had cleared. Each settlement was surrounded by a protective fence. They lived a harsh life, and many settlers died from disease, exposure, and lack of food. The 1587 settlement on Roanoke Island, North Carolina, consisting of 117 men, women, and children, vanished almost without a trace.

POCAHONTAS

Pocahontas (c.1595–1617) was a young Native American woman who reportedly saved the life of Captain John Smith, leader of the Jamestown colony in Virginia. She married another colonist, John Rolfe, and went to England with him. She longed to go home, but died on the voyage back.

Cabins were built with wood from surrounding forests

Tobacco crops were grown for export to Britain

Settlers reared turkeys for food

1600-1700 OCEANIA

The 1600s saw the first Dutch landings in Oceania, as they searched for more sources of trade. Abel Tasman reached Tasmania, New Zealand, Tonga, and Fiji. Willem Jansz charted part of northern Australia's coast. Spanish and Portuguese sailors also ventured deeper into the Pacific. Quiros arrived at Vanuatu, and Torres sailed between New Guinea and Australia.

Magical islands
This New Guinea charm from the island of West Britain contains dried herbs thought to have magical powers.

1606
Torres navigates New Guinea coast

Spanish and Portuguese exploration among the islands of Asia and Oceania, which had begun in the 1500s, continued into the 17th century. In 1605, Pedro de Quiros (1560–1615), a Portuguese pilot who had sailed with Mendaña in 1595, reached Vanuatu while searching for new southern lands. One of his captains, Luis Vaez de Torres (died c.1615), sailed on westwards. He reached New Guinea's south coast in 1606, exploring the strait separating New Guinea from Australia, which today bears his name. Meanwhile a Dutch navigator, Willem Jansz, sailed into the Gulf of Carpentaria in northern Australia and mapped some of the coastline, thinking it was part of New Guinea.

Pacific charm
This necklet from Mangaia in the Cook Islands bears charms made of teeth or bone.

→ Torres
→ Tasman (1642–43)
--→ Tasman (1644)
→ Quiros

Charting fragments
None of the navigators of the 1600s could make a complete map of the southern lands.

1642
Tasman explores uncharted lands

In the early 1600s the Dutch built up their power in Asian and Oceanian seas. They were more interested in trade than exploration, but their route from Cape Town to Indonesia took them very close to the west coast of the unexplored continent of Australia. In 1616 Captain Dirck Hartog went ashore, and a number of other chance landings followed. In 1642 Anthony van Diemen (1593–1645), governor-general of the Dutch East India Company, based at Batavia (now Jakarta) in Indonesia, decided to send Abel Tasman to lead

The Tasmans at home
Abel Tasman (1603–59) spent much of his life far from his family.

A Polynesian canoe
Tasman took this sketch home to Holland.

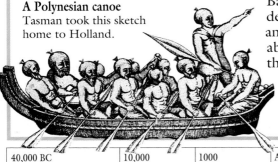

an expedition to Australian waters. The aim was to try to find out more about the extent of the great southern continent that was believed to exist there, and to find a shorter route to South America. Tasman first came to the island now called Tasmania, which he named Van Diemen's Land. Then he reached New Zealand, Tonga, and Fiji. In 1644, on a second voyage, he charted the northern coasts of Australia. The rest of the vast Australian continent remained unknown to all but its native inhabitants.

| 40,000 BC | | 10,000 | 1000 | AD 1 | 400 | 800 | 1200 | 1600 | 1800 | 2000 |

CHAPTER 14

1700 - 1750

THE AGE OF ENQUIRY

An ornate farrier's tool kit from Persia

1700-1750
The World

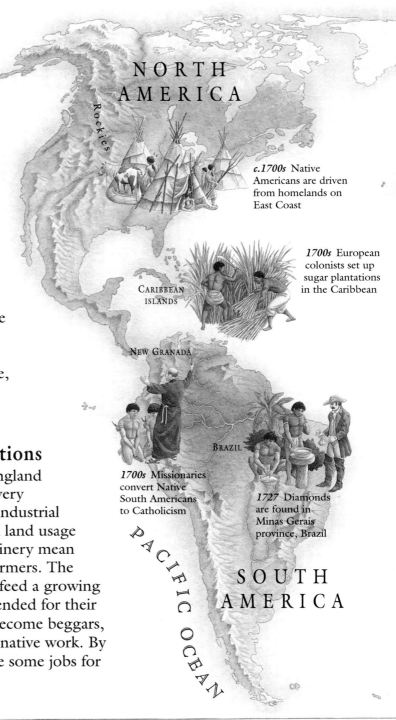

AROUND THE WORLD, the 18th century is marked by a quest for new ideas and new ways of thinking. Across Europe, people have changed ideas about how they wish to be governed, and mathematicians and scientists make huge advances in scientific knowledge. For the first time ever, a system is devised to classify the plant and animal world, and scientists begin to understand the fundamentals of physics, such as gravity and motion. In China, the Manchu emperors commission vast encyclopedias of knowledge, while the Japanese begin to copy and adopt European developments in technology and science to help enrich their own country.

Agricultural and Industrial revolutions

In the early 1700s, a revolution occurs in England that is to have profound effects on almost every country in the world and paves the way for industrial progress. New techniques in agriculture and land usage coupled with the development of new machinery mean that more food can be produced by fewer farmers. The rise in food production makes it possible to feed a growing population, but poor villagers who had depended for their livelihood on common lands are forced to become beggars, or move to towns and cities to look for alternative work. By the end of the century, new factories provide some jobs for displaced rural workers.

NORTH AMERICA

Rockies

c.1700s Native Americans are driven from homelands on East Coast

1700s European colonists set up sugar plantations in the Caribbean

CARIBBEAN ISLANDS

NEW GRANADA

1700s Missionaries convert Native South Americans to Catholicism

BRAZIL

1727 Diamonds are found in Minas Gerais province, Brazil

PACIFIC OCEAN

SOUTH AMERICA

Hunting in the Ice Age

Cave painting

Early farming

Ancient Egypt

Assyrian Empire

Great Wall of China

Classical Greece

Roman Empire

Barbarian invasions

| 40,000 BC | | 10,000 | 5000 | 1000 | 500 | AD 1 | 200 | 400 |

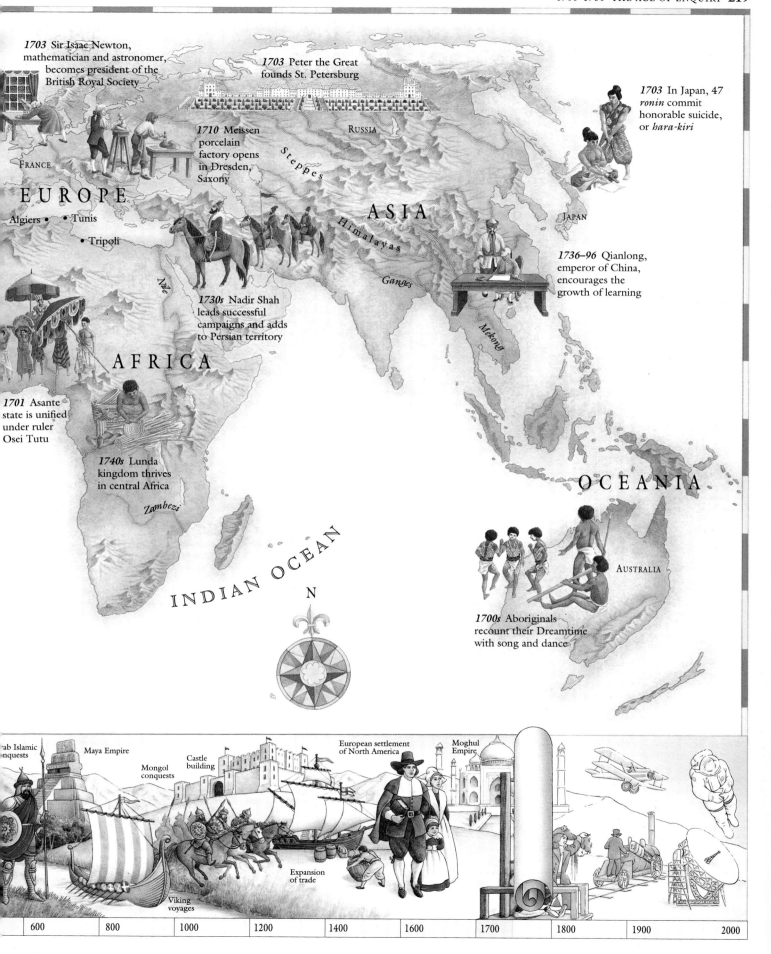

1703 Sir Isaac Newton, mathematician and astronomer, becomes president of the British Royal Society

1703 Peter the Great founds St. Petersburg

1703 In Japan, 47 *ronin* commit honorable suicide, or *hara-kiri*

1710 Meissen porcelain factory opens in Dresden, Saxony

RUSSIA

FRANCE

EUROPE

Algiers • • Tunis

• Tripoli

ASIA

Steppes

Himalayas

Ganges

JAPAN

1736–96 Qianlong, emperor of China, encourages the growth of learning

Nile

1730s Nadir Shah leads successful campaigns and adds to Persian territory

AFRICA

Mekong

1701 Asante state is unified under ruler Osei Tutu

1740s Lunda kingdom thrives in central Africa

Zambezi

OCEANIA

INDIAN OCEAN

N

AUSTRALIA

1700s Aboriginals recount their Dreamtime with song and dance

Arab Islamic conquests

Maya Empire

Mongol conquests

Castle building

European settlement of North America

Moghul Empire

Expansion of trade

Viking voyages

| 600 | 800 | 1000 | 1200 | 1400 | 1600 | 1700 | 1800 | 1900 | 2000 |

1700

1712

AFRICA

1701 Osei Tutu creates free Asante nation in West Africa*

c.1705 Bey (army commander) Husain ibn Ali founds dynasty at Tunis in North Africa

c.1705 Kongo prophetess Dona Beatrice founds new religious cult and helps to end civil war

1710 Dey (military leader) becomes pasha in Algiers, controlling northern Algeria*

Luba stool; in southern Zaire, migrants from the Luba states have great influence over prosperous Lunda kingdom

1714 France captures the island of Mauritius in the Indian Ocean

1720s Yoruba state of Oyo still dominates region west of the Niger River in West Africa

1722–23 Asante conquer kingdom of Bono-Mansu north of the forest area of Akan region of West Africa

Around 1750, probably 200,000 or more muskets were imported into West Africa each year

ASIA

1703 In Japan, forty-seven *ronin* commit suicide

1707 Death of Moghul emperor Aurangzeb followed by breakup of empire

1709 Ghilzai tribesmen under Mir Vais defeat Persian army; Afghanistan no longer obedient province of Persian Empire

1709 Death of Shogun Tsunayoshi of Japan

Five different types of wooden mask were used for Japanese Noh plays

A Tibetan statue of Vajvapani, symbol of law and order

1716–45 Reforming shogun Tokugawa Yoshimune rules Japan*

1716 Manchu emperor Kangxi sends troops to expel Junkar tribe from Tibet; in 1720 Kangxi enthrones seventh Dalai Lama as tributary ruler of Tibet

1722 Death of Kangxi, enlightened Manchu emperor

1722–35 Rule of Manchu emperor Yongzheng; Treaty of Kiakhta signed with Russia; Siberian-Mongolian border defined

EUROPE

1700s Age of Enlightenment introduces revolutionary new ideas to Europe*

1700s Agricultural Revolution begins in Britain; later spreads across Europe*

1700–21 Great Northern War: Russia is victorious and becomes dominant in northeastern Europe

1701–13 Much of Europe involved in War of Spanish Succession; French routed at Battle of Blenheim, 1704*

1703 Peter the Great, Tsar of Russia, founds St. Petersburg*

1707 Act of Union unites England and Scotland as Great Britain

Detail from the Blenheim tapestry, woven to celebrate the Duke of Marlborough's military success

▢ **1712** In England, Thomas Newcomen invents a practical steam pump for use in mines

1712 Religious warfare in Switzerland

1713–40 Reign of King Frederick William I of Prussia*

1715 First Jacobite rising in Britain attempts to restore exiled Stuart dynasty to throne

1720 South Sea Bubble – financial scandal in England

1721–42 Robert Walpole is first and longest-serving British prime minister

The telescope of Isaac Newton (1642–1727), wh[ich] revolutionized physics and mathematic[s]

AMERICAS

1700s Sugar plantations flourish in the Caribbean*

1700s North American colonies begin to prosper

1701 Detroit founded in North America by Antoine de Cadillac to control passage between lakes Erie and Huron

1711 Tuscarora War between settlers and Native Americans in North Carolina

Europeans arriving in North America founded new towns

This shaman's (priest's) necklace comes from Panama, one of the countries which formed the Viceroyalty of New Granada

1715 Yamasee nation attacks South Carolina colony, killing hundreds of settlers

1716 French build fortress, one of the strongest in North America, at Louisbourg in Canada

1717 Spain establishes Viceroyalty of New Granada in South America*

1718 City of New Orleans is founded on Mississippi River

1718 Death of William Penn, the Quaker founder of the state of Pennsylvania

1718–20 Dispute between French and Spanish over territory of Texas; Texas becomes Spanish possession

OCEANIA

A Tahitian tiki, which represents a god; several of these little figures were carried back to Europe

1700s First contact between Tahitians and Europeans; they meet in Opunohu Valley on Moorea Island

1722 Dutch navigator Roggeveen reaches Samoa Islands and Easter Island in the Pacific

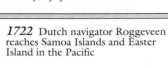

40,000 BC		10,000		1000	500	AD 1	200	400

1724

1724–34 King Agaja of Dahomey in West Africa temporarily disrupts slave trade; it is reintroduced in the 1740s

c.1725 Fulani Muslim cleric Alfa Ibrahim appointed "Commander of the Faithful" in Futa Jalon in West Africa

1727 Death of Mulai Ismail followed by 30 years of anarchy in Morocco

China produced large amounts of ceramics to export to Europe

Asante golden figures often refer to creatures in folktales

1724 Asaf Jah, a minister of the Moghul emperor, retires to the Deccan; he becomes an independent ruler and is declared first Nizam of Hyderabad

1725 *Gujin tushu jicheng*, the largest encyclopedia ever printed, in 10,000 chapters, commissioned by Qing emperor Yongzheng

1729 Yongzheng sets up Grand Council, an informal and flexible body of military advisers

1735 Nadir Shah, chief adviser and general to last Safavid ruler in Persia, defeats Turks in great battle at Baghavand and captures Tiflis

1724 Peter the Great founds Russian Academy of Sciences

1726–43 Cardinal Fleury governs France*

1733–35 France and Austria fight War of Polish Succession to make their candidates Polish king

Russian men, except priests and peasants, had to shave off their beards

Coffee was first found in Ethiopia; Arabs took it to Europe and Europeans brought it to Brazil

1726 Spanish found city of Montevideo in Uruguay to stop further Portuguese colonization southward from Brazil

1727 Coffee first planted in Brazil

1727 First discovery of diamonds in Brazil in the Minas Gerais area where gold is already successfully mined*

1730s Vitus Bering, Danish explorer employed by Russia, reaches the strait between Asia and North America named after him

1735 Libel trial of John Peter Zeuger in New York helps establish freedom of the press in North America

Comb from Samoa; in Samoan political life, achievement was more important than birth

1736

1740s Lunda creates new kingdom*

1746 Mazrui dynasty in Mombasa, East Africa, becomes independent from Oman

Persian powder flask; the Persians were often at war, especially with the Ottomans, long before Nadir Shah's conquering reign

1736–47 Nadir Shah reigns as shah of Persia*

1736–96 Rule of Qianlong, as Qing emperor; boundaries of empire reach farthest limits; population increases greatly; frequent rebellions crushed ruthlessly*

1739 Nadir Shah invades India and sacks Delhi, taking away peacock throne of the Moghul emperors and vast wealth

1740s Power of Hindu Marathas of central India expands into northern India

1740–86 Frederick the Great rules Prussia; he greatly expands its territory, and Prussia becomes a major power in Europe

1740–48 Prussia attacks Austria and drags much of Europe into War of Austrian Succession

1741–61 Reign of Elizabeth I of Russia, daughter of Peter the Great; she founds Russia's first university at Moscow

1745–46 Second Jacobite rising in Britain led by Bonnie Prince Charlie attempts but fails to restore exiled Stuart dynasty to British throne

The second Jacobite rising met defeat at the Battle of Culloden Moor and was stamped out ruthlessly by the king's forces

The fortress of Louisbourg was built to guard the Atlantic approach to France's Canadian lands. It was taken in 1745 by a mixed force of New England settlers and a British naval expedition

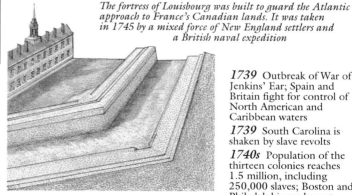

1739 Outbreak of War of Jenkins' Ear; Spain and Britain fight for control of North American and Caribbean waters

1739 South Carolina is shaken by slave revolts

1740s Population of the thirteen colonies reaches 1.5 million, including 250,000 slaves; Boston and Philadelphia are largest cities

1742 Juan Santos takes name Atahualpa II and leads Native Americans of Peru in revolt against Spanish

1745 British capture French fortress of Louisbourg in Canada

1 **1736** Natural rubber discovered in the humid rain forests of Peru

1736 Academic schools of São Paulo and São José founded in Rio de Janeiro, Brazil, by Portuguese Jesuits

1740s Aboriginal culture continues to flourish*

| 600 | 800 | 1000 | 1200 | 1400 | 1600 | 1700 | 1800 | 1900 | 2000 |

1700-1750 AFRICA

The slave trade continued to expand during this half-century. By the 1730s more than 50,000 slaves were being transported each year to plantations in the Americas. In West Africa, the new Asante kingdom became overlord of its immediate neighbors. In Angola, European traders continued to obtain slaves who came originally from inland kingdoms such as those of the Luba and the Lunda.

Emerging states
Asante in West Africa and Lunda in Central Africa emerged as powerful kingdoms in this period.

1701

Osei Tutu creates free Asante nation

Toward the end of the 17th century, new states such as Denkyira, Dahomey, and Asante emerged in West Africa. They were well organized to bring trade to the coast, thus keeping European traders out. Asante and Denkyira were situated in the Akan region of the Gold Coast. To escape domination by Denkyira, various groups of people moved north and gained control of Tafo, a trading town. By about 1680, one Asante chief, Osei Tutu (c.1680–1717), created a new kingdom called Asante with a new capital at Kumasi; he was known by the title of "Asantehene." He created a national army which in 1701 defeated Denkyira and freed the Asante from paying tribute. In 1717 Osei was killed in a border war, leaving Asante a united nation. His successors continued to expand the kingdom through conquest and skillful commercial enterprises.

Asante effigy
A golden stool, which was believed to have come down from the sky, was the symbol of Asante unity. It was hung with gold effigies of generals, like the one above, who had been defeated by Asante.

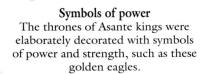

Asante pottery pipe
Everyday objects were often decorated. This pottery pipe was modeled in the shape of a tortoise.

Symbols of power
The thrones of Asante kings were elaborately decorated with symbols of power and strength, such as these golden eagles.

Asante festival
Every year the Asante people gathered for a festival in Kumasi to celebrate the strength of the Asante nation.

40,000 BC		10,000	5000	1000	500	AD 1	200	400

1710
The military take over Algiers

The Ottoman Empire of Sulayman I (1520–66) and his successors was so large that it had to be governed on a provincial basis. Local pashas (governors) were appointed by the sultan at Istanbul. Over the years, provinces became more independent, and officials competed for control, especially in the North African provinces. Algiers was notorious as a stronghold of corsairs (pirates) on the North African coast, sometimes called the Barbary Coast. They raided European ships and held the passengers for ransom. Tunis and Tripoli also profited from piracy, although they were less dependent on it than Algiers. By 1700 piracy was in decline, and power shifted from the corsairs to the soldiers who defended the town. These soldiers were originally the elite Ottoman troops, the Janissaries, but they had settled down, married local women, and formed their own community, a kind of ruling class within Algiers. They governed themselves and chose their own commander, called the dey. In 1710 the dey assumed the title of pasha, thus confirming his independence from the sultan. He raised money by forcing interior tribes to pay huge sums in tribute and encouraging the corsairs. Algeria was, in effect, no longer part of the crumbling Ottoman Empire.

Staff of history
An Algerian Ighil ali Kabyle ceremonial staff. Algerian culture has deep and varied roots, both Islamic and pre-Islamic.

Pendant beauty
This Algerian silver and coral pendant comes from the Atlas Mountains. The people of the interior of Algeria had their own ancient Berber culture, very different from that of the city-dwellers along the coast.

Corsairs' city
In the 1500s, the great corsair (pirate) leader Khair-al Din, known as Barbarossa, made Algiers his base. Thereafter it grew rich and famous on trade and piracy.

Fashion pillow
This Luba wooden headrest from Zaire is carved with male and female figures facing each other. They show the elaborate hairstyles of the area. Headrests such as this were used to ensure that dressed hair remained undisturbed during sleep.

1740s
Lunda creates a new kingdom

By the end of the 1600s, two Bantu-speaking peoples dominated Central Africa, the Luba and the Lunda. Their wealth was based on regional trade, especially iron, salt, and copper. The original Lunda kingdom was ruled by a dynasty of kings called Mwata Yamvo, who sent out expeditions under leaders called kazembes to conquer and exploit neighboring areas. These became satellite kingdoms. By the 1740s, one kazembe had established himself on the lower Luapula river (now a border between Zambia and Zaire). This Lunda kingdom demanded tribute in copper and salt from the west and gained control of iron deposits to the east. By the 1780s, Kazembe was exporting slaves westward, via Mwata Yamvo; he also exported copper and ivory eastward.

600	800			1600	1700	1800	1900	2000

1700-1750 ASIA

When Aurangzeb, the last great Moghul emperor, died, the Moghul Empire broke up. By 1740 major cities such as Delhi, Lahore, and Kabul had been overrun by a revived Persia under Nadir Shah. China prospered in the closing years of Kangxi's reign and in the early years of the reign of his grandson Qianlong. The Japanese, under shogun Tokugawa Yoshimune, started to encourage the study of selected European ideas and technology, while home-based improvements in agriculture created wealth.

Imperial seals
These seals belonged to Qianlong, fourth emperor of the Manchu dynasty, who ruled China from 1736 to 1796. The mark of his imperial seal on documents showed that they were authentic.

1716

Yoshimune becomes shogun

In 1716 the eighth Tokugawa shogun, Yoshimune (1684–1751), was appointed. He was a particularly capable administrator and aimed to dominate the *bakufu* (military government) in his period as shogun. He introduced economic reforms and did much to stimulate agriculture, introducing mechanical devices to raise water levels and improve irrigation. Towards the end of his rule, he had the law codified so it could be better understood by judges. Yoshimune also began to open Japan to outside influences. European theories in subjects such as science, medicine, military tactics, artillery, and astronomy were increasingly studied in Japan. Yoshimune retired in 1745 and died in 1751.

An economy based on rice
Rice was the staple fare of many Japanese, so there was much unrest among ordinary people and officials alike when there were bad harvests as in 1732. Yoshimune aimed to improve this explosive situation by introducing reforms that increased the amount of land available for rice cultivation and by stabilizing the price of rice.

The legendary *ninja*
The samurai, Japan's military class, were noble warriors, fiercely loyal to their lord and fearless in battle. Rather than face dishonor and shame, they chose to commit suicide (*hara-kiri*), which was considered an honorable death. The *ninja*, in contrast, were spies and assassins for whom honor meant nothing. They were used in warfare by lords throughout the period of civil wars. Black-clad *ninja* warriors became legendary heroes who were thought to have semi-magical powers.

The forty-seven ronin
In 1701 a much-respected lord, Asano Naganori, was forced to kill himself as punishment for wounding an official who had insulted him. Forty-seven of Asano's samurai became *ronin* (samurai without a master) and swore revenge. In 1703 they murdered the official. Such acts of revenge were normally punished by execution, but because of the Confucian teaching that it is honorable to avenge a lord's violent death, they were allowed to commit suicide. The event later became the subject of plays, books, and films.

1736

Qianlong reigns

The long reign of Emperor Qianlong (1736–96) of the Qing dynasty was as remarkable as that of his grandfather, Kangxi. During this time, Manchu China reached the height of its power. The emperor himself was a hard-working, serious, and very able ruler who loved ceremony and made many tours of his huge domains to impress his subjects. He was a successful general who destroyed Mongol power in central Asia, incorporated Turkestan, and forced Nepal to accept Chinese sovereignty. On the domestic front, he championed major agricultural and industrial developments which made China extremely prosperous. European trade increased dramatically. During his reign, China's population grew quickly, and millions of people moved from the countryside into a host of new towns established with imperial help.

A patron of arts and literature, Qianlong particularly enjoyed sponsoring huge literary works, such as a 36,000-volume library of classical works, history, and philosophy, among other subjects.

Imperial scepter
One of Qianlong's scepters has the shape of a sacred fungus at one end. It was said to give its owner long life and virility.

Qianlong's court
During Qianlong's reign, the administration of the empire reached a new degree of strength and efficiency. A magnificent and luxurious way of life prevailed in the imperial palace.

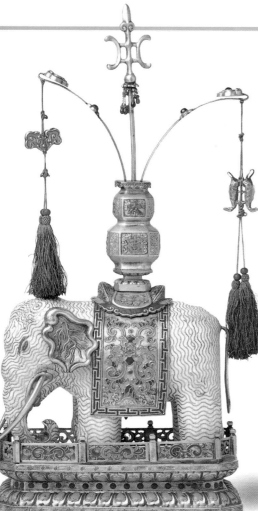

Patron of the arts
Qianlong took a great interest in many of the arts, which thrived during his reign. This ornate elephant is made of copper gilt with enameled decoration.

1736

Nadir Shah rules Persia

Shah Tahmasp II (1722–31) of Persia was greatly helped for much of his reign by Nadir Kuli, chief of the Afshar tribe. In 1732 Nadir deposed Tahmasp, whose baby son became Shah Abbas III. When he died in 1736, Nadir became shah. For the next 11 years, he fought many campaigns to add to Persian territory. He conquered Afghanistan and invaded India, capturing Kabul, Lahore, and Peshawar and finally sacking Delhi. Nadir now virtually ruled India north and west of the river Indus.

Priceless booty
Nadir Shah's troops looted huge amounts of treasure from Delhi, including the Koh-i-noor diamond. This huge gem was eventually acquired by the British and became part of the crown jewels of Britain.

The empire collapses
Nadir Shah's military successes were based on his use of light cavalry. Although he was a brilliant commander, Nadir Shah was no statesman and did not develop his empire. In 1747 he was murdered by one of his own tribesmen. This led to the collapse of his empire.

600	800	1000	1200	1400	1600	1700	1800	1900	2000

1700-1750 EUROPE

Peter the barber
Peter the Great cut off the long beards traditional for the ruling class as a sign of change. Aristocrats and merchants were first banned from wearing beards, then allowed them again on payment of a tax. They remained unfashionable. Peasants and clergy could still wear them free of charge.

At first, much of Europe was involved in the War of the Spanish Succession (1701–13) for control of Spain and its empire. Then a long period of peace allowed great advances in agriculture, beginning in Britain. A burst of scientific and philosophical ideas opened up new ways of looking at most aspects of life, in what is now called the Age of Enlightenment. Even traditional forms of government were questioned. France remained powerful, but less so than under Louis XIV. Tsar Peter the Great made Russia an important force on the new European scene.

1703

Peter the Great founds St. Petersburg

Peter the Great, ruler of Russia with his half-brother Ivan V, 1682–96, and sole ruler until 1725, transformed his isolated, backward nation into a major European power. He picked up ideas from an 18-month tour of western Europe (1697–98) and used them as a basis for restructuring Russia's institutions and ways of life. Peter replaced old systems of government, promoted education, reorganized the church, and made promotion in state service more merit-based. He sent young Russians to western Europe to study military, naval, and industrial techniques and formed a professional army of 300,000 men, as well as Russia's first navy. He fought against and defeated Sweden (1700–21), which gave him access to the Baltic Sea. In 1703 he built a new city, on the edge of the Baltic, which he called St. Petersburg. In 1712 he made it Russia's capital. Peter the Great made himself emperor of all the Russias in 1721.

Russian empire
Peter's conquests in the Baltic were crucial to Russia's development. St. Petersburg linked the country more firmly to Europe than ever before.

PETER THE GREAT

Almost seven feet tall, Peter's physical presence matched his unforgettably powerful character. An energetic and strong-willed man, he could also be terrifyingly brutal. Those who opposed him found no mercy. His enthusiasm for doing things himself extended to learning practical skills such as shipbuilding (he was fascinated by boats), watch-mending, gunnery, woodcarving, bootmaking, and tooth-pulling. He succeeded in reshaping Russia forever.

Russia's first navy
Peter's Baltic fleet defeated the Swedish navy at the Battle of Hango in 1714. He also built a fleet on the Black Sea but lost it to the Ottomans in 1711.

St. Petersburg
Thousands of Russian serfs died in the marshes by the banks of the river Neva during the course of building the city of St. Petersburg. Peter the Great called it his "window on Europe."

SPANISH SUCCESSION WAR

1701 Outbreak of War of Spanish Succession; prince Eugene of Savoy invades Italy

1704 Battle of Blenheim, first of Marlborough's great victories over French armies

1706 Battle of Ramillies, Marlborough's second victory

1708 Battle of Oudemarde, Marlborough's third victory

1709 Marlborough's fourth victory at Battle of Malplaquet

1711 Grand Alliance of powers against France dissolved; Marlborough dismissed by Queen Anne

1712 French army under Marshal Villars gains a victory at Denain

1713 Treaty of Utrecht; war ends with an equal redistribution of territory and power in Europe

1713 Philip V, grandson of Louis XIV of France, confirmed as king of Spain; Louis agrees that France and Spain should never be united under the same ruler

1704
The Battle of Blenheim

Charles II of Spain (1665–1700) had no direct heir. When he died, he left his throne to the French prince Philip of Anjou, who was Louis XIV's grandson. Other European nations, who did not want the powers of France and Spain to be united in this way, formed a Grand Alliance, and in 1701 the War of Spanish Succession broke out. One of the chief Alliance commanders, John Churchill, Duke of Marlborough, won a great victory against the French at Blenheim in 1704, followed by three further victories. Despite these defeats, France remained powerful and by the Treaty of Utrecht, which ended the war in 1713, Philip of Anjou was allowed to remain on the Spanish throne.

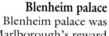

French baton
This commander's baton was used on the French side in the War of Spanish Succession.

Duke of Marlborough
John Churchill (1650–1722) was a British soldier and statesman who was made commander-in-chief of the allied forces in 1702.

Blenheim palace
Blenheim palace was Marlborough's reward for his victory at the battle of Blenheim in 1704.

1713
Frederick William rules Prussia

In 1701 Frederick III, Elector of Brandenburg, was crowned as Frederick I, king of Prussia. His son, Frederick William (1688–1740), succeeded him as the Prussian king in 1713. Two major achievements marked his reign which were to form the basis of a strong state. First, he developed the Prussian government into a strong centralized organization, personally taking over the principal offices of central and local government. Second, he created a powerful Prussian regular army, which he doubled in size to 80,000 soldiers, making it one of the largest in Europe. He also introduced measures to improve the Prussian economy by active reform of agriculture and made education compulsory for all children.

The rise of Prussia
Frederick William continued the expansion of Prussia which his father, the Elector of Brandenburg, had begun.

Tobacco assembly
King Frederick William held smoking parties, to which he invited Prussian army officers and other important people. They were forced to sit smoking and discussing policy, although many of them actually hated tobacco.

Porcelain from Prussia
The first Meissen factory was opened near Dresden in 1710, after Johann Friedrich Böttger, a German chemist, found a way of reproducing the clear, shiny quality of Chinese porcelain using local clay. This jug is made from Meissen porcelain.

Sèvres porcelain
The success of the royal porcelain factory at Sèvres was largely due to the patronage of Louis XV's mistress, Madame de Pompadour. She owned a beautiful chateau at Sèvres.

1726
Fleury governs France

France needed time to regain prosperity following the War of Spanish Succession. When Louis XIV died in 1715, he left a five-year-old heir, Louis XV, and an unstable period of regency government ensued. On reaching the age of 16, Louis XV appointed his tutor, Cardinal Fleury, as chief minister. Fleury's government encouraged industrial and commercial growth, reform of the state's finances, and codification of the law. He made sound alliances with foreign powers and built up the French navy. Above all, Fleury's administration provided stability. However, his ignorance of working class problems caused growing resentment in this period.

Chief minister
Cardinal Fleury was 73 years old when he began to govern France. He was cautious, peaceable, and a great diplomat. He did much for France during his 17 years in office.

THE AGE OF ENLIGHTENMENT

"Dare to know" could have been the motto of the Enlightenment, a period covering the late 17th and 18th centuries, when new ideas about government, personal liberty and responsibility, and religious belief developed among European philosophers. These new thinkers discarded past beliefs and relied instead on personal intellect. Some of their ideas stemmed from writings by the English philosopher John Locke (1632–1704), who said that all men are equal and independent, and that the authority of government comes only from the consent of the governed. This was, and still is, the basis of modern democracy. The movement was very active in France, where philosophers such as Voltaire and Rousseau challenged the idea of absolute monarchy and the tradition that the nobility and clergy were entitled to special privilege. They also believed that education should be available to all. The Enlightenment affected many aspects of European life.

Voltaire (1694-1778)
French philosopher Voltaire played a leading role in the Enlightenment. His liberal views twice landed him in the Bastille prison in Paris.

Wonders of the solar system
The Enlightenment inspired people to take an interest in the natural world. Here, a family pores over a model of the solar system.

Scientific developments

The thinkers of the European Enlightenment were influenced by the growth of scientific knowledge which had begun in the 17th century, when traditional beliefs began to be questioned. Knowledge acquired a much more practical value, and all branches of science advanced. In England, Isaac Newton, who proved the existence of gravitational force and stated the three laws of motion, introduced new approaches to scientific enquiry that were followed by many scientists. Switzerland's Hermann Euler produced the first systematic textbook of mechanics, and in France, chemist and physicist Antoine Lavoisier put forward a new combustion theory.

ENCYCLOPÉDIE,
OU
DICTIONNAIRE RAISONNÉ
DES SCIENCES,
DES ARTS ET DES MÉTIERS.
PAR UNE SOCIETE DE GENS DE LETTRES.

TOME PREMIER.

A PARIS,

M. DCC. LI.

Weighty tome
French writer and critic, Denis Diderot (1713–84), compiled the *Encyclopédie*. Its emphasis on reason embodies the spirit of the French Enlightenment.

Swedish botanist
Carl Linné, or Linnaeus, (1707–78) was a Swedish botanist who classified the plant and animal kingdoms for the first time. He wrote much on the subject.

| | | 10,000 | 5000 | 1000 | 500 | AD 1 | 200 | 400 |

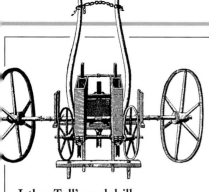

Jethro Tull's seed drill
One invention that helped to make crop planting easier was the seed drill invented by Jethro Tull (1674–1741). This drill enabled farmers to plant in rows and to weed between them. Before this, seeds were sown by hand.

THE AGRICULTURAL REVOLUTION

In 18th-century England, a revolution occurred in agriculture that greatly improved farming. Farmers introduced a successful new Dutch method of growing crops, called crop rotation, which enabled them to grow bigger, better crops. New scientific techniques also helped them produce improved breeds of farm animals. New machines, such as Jethro Tull's seed drill and better types of plough, helped to make farming more efficient and less labor-intensive. Along with these changes came a sharp increase in the practice of enclosing fields with walls or hedgerows. New, smaller, enclosed plots replaced the large open fields that had been inefficiently farmed in separate strips. Common land for grazing animals was also removed from public use and enclosed. These changes were unpopular because poor peasant farmers were driven from the land and forced to seek jobs in the expanding cities.

Crop rotation
Crop fields had formerly been left fallow once every three years in order to keep the soil fertile. Now, by rotating crops, fields were sown with a different crop each year so as not to drain the fertility out of the soil. They were planted with wheat one year, root crops (such as turnips) the next, and clover the third, greatly increasing productivity.

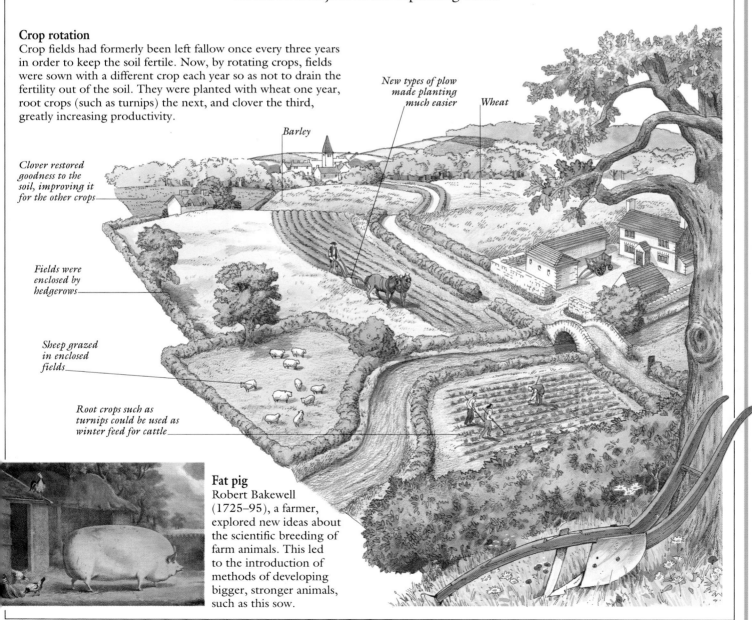

New types of plow made planting much easier

Wheat

Barley

Clover restored goodness to the soil, improving it for the other crops

Fields were enclosed by hedgerows

Sheep grazed in enclosed fields

Root crops such as turnips could be used as winter feed for cattle

Fat pig
Robert Bakewell (1725–95), a farmer, explored new ideas about the scientific breeding of farm animals. This led to the introduction of methods of developing bigger, stronger animals, such as this sow.

Body stamp
Little remains of those people that lived in the Caribbean before the Spanish invasion. This stamp was filled with earth containing the red pigment ocher and pressed onto the body to make patterns.

Suffering for sugar
Native Caribbean people were massacred by Europeans or died from European diseases. As the sugar industry flourished, laborers were needed, and hundreds of thousands of slaves were brought from Africa. Many were killed by the brutal work schedule, the poor food, and the inadequate housing conditions on the plantations. But those Africans that survived came to be in the majority on many islands. Many thousands of slaves took part in frequent rebellions. Other slaves escaped and set up thriving communities of their own.

1700-1750 AMERICAS

I n North America, European settlers continued to colonize land, destroying the inheritance of Native Americans. In South America, Spain united some of its territory into one province, New Granada, under the control of a viceroy. Portuguese settlers in Brazil rushed to make money in mining after gold and diamonds were found. Other Europeans brought African slaves to the Caribbean to work on sugar plantations.

European takeover
By 1750 the Spanish, French, English, and Dutch had taken control of Caribbean islands.

Florida

Bahamas (ENGLAND)

Cuba (SPAIN)

Atlantic Ocean

Hispaniola (FRANCE) (SPAIN) *Puerto Rico (SPAIN)*

Jamaica (ENGLAND)

Guadeloupe (FRANCE)

Caribbean Sea

Martinique (FRANCE)

Curaçao (NETHERLANDS)

Grenada (FRANCE)

Trinidad (SPAIN)

SOUTH AMERICA

1700s
Europeans exploit Caribbean

In the 16th century, Spanish colonists settled on many Caribbean islands. Other European nations grew jealous of Spain's wealth from colonial trade, so in the 17th century, with the unspoken approval of their governments, English, Dutch, and French pirates captured Spanish Caribbean towns and settled islands for themselves. They set up sugar plantations to satisfy increasing demand for sugar in Europe, with slaves imported from Africa as laborers. By the 1700s, the Caribbean produced most of the world's sugar. As Spanish power declined in Europe, other nations seized more trade advantages overseas. In 1713 Britain obtained from Spain the monopoly of the slave trade with remaining Spanish Caribbean colonies.

NATIVE AMERICANS OF THE EASTERN WOODLANDS

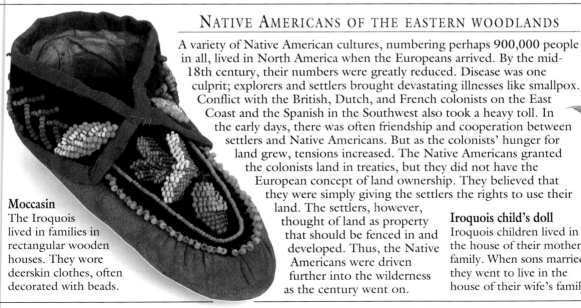

A variety of Native American cultures, numbering perhaps 900,000 people in all, lived in North America when the Europeans arrived. By the mid-18th century, their numbers were greatly reduced. Disease was one culprit; explorers and settlers brought devastating illnesses like smallpox. Conflict with the British, Dutch, and French colonists on the East Coast and the Spanish in the Southwest also took a heavy toll. In the early days, there was often friendship and cooperation between settlers and Native Americans. But as the colonists' hunger for land grew, tensions increased. The Native Americans granted the colonists land in treaties, but they did not have the European concept of land ownership. They believed that they were simply giving the settlers the rights to use their land. The settlers, however, thought of land as property that should be fenced in and developed. Thus, the Native Americans were driven further into the wilderness as the century went on.

Moccasin
The Iroquois lived in families in rectangular wooden houses. They wore deerskin clothes, often decorated with beads.

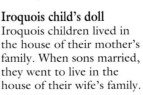

Iroquois child's doll
Iroquois children lived in the house of their mother's family. When sons married, they went to live in the house of their wife's family.

1717

Viceroyalty set up in New Granada

After Spain colonized much of South America, the territories were placed under the control of the Spanish crown. A Council of the Indies was set up to make laws and supervise finance. Viceroys, representatives of the Spanish king, were sent to govern vast regions. In 1717 the viceroyalty of New Granada was created, made up of what are now Panama, Ecuador, Colombia, and Venezuela. Viceroys were responsible for regional courts, or *audiencias*, which exercised legal, financial and administrative powers locally. Viceroys and *audiencia* officials were Spanish. They were resented by rich estate owners of Spanish ancestry, born in South America, who were excluded both from political power and trade privileges.

Overseas empires
The Spanish colonized an area more than twice the size of Europe. The Portuguese colonized what is now Brazil.

Members of the audiencia *carried a canopy over the viceroy as he rode in the procession*

A splendid welcome
A viceroy was received with great ceremony when he arrived from Spain. The city's streets were cleaned and hung with tapestries. He rode through them at the head of a long procession of officials, clergymen, and soldiers. Bullfights and feasting took place in his palace for days afterward.

Christian mission
European Catholic priests went to South America to convert Native Americans. One Catholic order, the Jesuits, set up towns in Paraguay in which local people were converted to Christianity and produced goods in exchange for food and clothing. The wealth and power of the Jesuits worried the Spanish king, Charles III, who did not like this "empire within an empire." In 1767 he banished Jesuits from Spain and its dominions. This scene from the film, *The Mission*, shows the burning of a Jesuit village.

South American silver chain
Workers in silver mines carried heavy loads up steep ladders, in tunnels lit only by a candle. Many were injured or died in the mines.

1727

Diamonds found in Brazil

Europeans came to South America in search of gold and silver. By the 1700s, most of the world's silver came from Spanish mines in Peru and Mexico. At the end of the 17th century, a band of Portuguese slave traders found gold in Minas Gerais province, in eastern central Brazil. People rushed there from the sugar plantations on the Brazilian coast. In 1727 diamonds were also discovered in Minas Gerais. So many people rushed there from the plantations that the sugar industry almost collapsed. The mines were worked by Native Americans who were paid low wages and African slaves. Workers died from disease, lack of food, and injuries in the mines.

Hair pin
Macaw feathers were worn in the hair of Brazilian Native Americans. These birds were common in South American rain forests.

600	800	1000	1200	1400	1600	1700	1800	1900	2000

Europeans continued to look for quicker, easier routes through the Pacific, touching land by accident rather than by design. Jacob Roggeveen, the Dutch navigator, landed at Easter Island in 1722 and wrote about the statues there. There had already been landings in Australia, but its vast size was still not realized, nor did Europeans understand that it was a separate continent. Meanwhile, in parts of Australia, Aboriginals continued their peaceful way of life undisturbed, as they had since about 40,000 BC.

Dilly bag
The Aboriginals believed illness was the result of wicked sorcery. This bag, containing charms, was carried to protect the owner from evil.

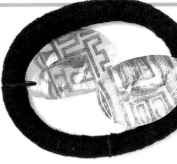

Aboriginal belt
This waistband, made from human hair, bears shells marked with clan signs.

1700s
Aboriginal life

Over thousands of years, the Aboriginals had evolved a way of life that was peaceful and well adapted to the land. Although they did not grow crops, rear livestock, or build cities, their nomadic existence of hunting and gathering was a successful and untroubled one. There is no evidence that, in their long history, they fought any wars, and the tribes, and clans within them, coexisted harmoniously. The clans, which were like extended family groups, went about their daily business of hunting, fishing, and gathering fruits and nuts, and only came together for important occasions such as initiation ceremonies.

Wooden spoon
This Aboriginal spoon shows a turtle pushing a canoe. The turtle figures in some of the Dreamtime legends.

DREAMTIME

The Aboriginals believe that they have animal, plant, and human ancestors who created the world and everything in it. This process of creation is known as the Dreamtime. The Aboriginals have composed many songs and myths about the Dreamtime, which have been passed down orally through many generations and which are believed to keep the spirits of the original creators alive today. The events of the era of creation are enacted in ceremonies and danced in mime form. The songs that the Aboriginals sing refer to features of the landscape that have been created by, and are sacred to, their spiritual ancestors, and they go on long journeys past these features to keep in touch with these ancestors.

Recreating history
Aboriginal people recreated the deeds of their ancestral heroes through song and dance, accompanied by the didgeridoo and clapsticks.

Kangaroo painting
The striped areas on this kangaroo bark painting represent different Aboriginal clans and also refer to legends of the Dreamtime.

CHAPTER 15

1750 – 1800

THE AGE OF REVOLUTION

Medallions of Louis XVI of France and Queen Marie Antoinette

1750-1800
THE WORLD

THE WORLD IS TURNED upside down by two revolutions that occur in this period. The first, in the thirteen British colonies in North America, leads to the creation of the United States of America, the first nation in the world to gain independence from its European colonial rulers. The second, in France, leads to the execution of the king and the declaration of a republic based on the principles of liberty, equality, and fraternity. The shock waves from these two violent revolutions, and from the agricultural revolution already under way in Europe and a peaceful industrial revolution which is slowly gathering pace, dominate the next century.

Mapping the globe

In Africa, Europeans begin to explore the interior for the first time. On the other side of the world, Cook, Bougainville, and other navigators map the Pacific islands in detail. In 1788, the first permanent European colony in the region is established in Australia. The British destroy French power in Canada and take control of the European colonies there. In the Indian subcontinent, Robert Clive's victories lay the foundations of future British rule. By 1800, many nations in Asia and Africa feel the influence of Europe; exceptions include Japan, which continues to be relatively isolated, and China, richer and more powerful than ever but suffering from increased corruption and decadence among the ruling classes. By the end of the century, the Manchu dynasty has reached and passed its greatest height.

NORTH AMERICA

CANADA

Quebec

Boston

Rockies

1759 French general Montcalm and British general Wolfe are both killed in the battle for Quebec

1776 Patriot colonists sign the Declaration of Independence

1773 The Boston Tea Party: patriots empty tea from British ships into Boston Harbor

1790s Toussaint L'Ouverture leads revolt against French plantation owners in Haiti

1780 Tupac Amaru leads Peruvians to revolt against colonial rulers

ATLANTIC OCEAN

PACIFIC OCEAN

Andes

SOUTH AMERICA

Hunting in the Ice Age | Cave painting | Early farming | Ancient Egypt | Assyrian Empire | Great Wall of China | Classical Greece | Roman Empire | Barbarian invasions

| 40,000 BC | | | 10,000 | 5000 | 1000 | 500 | AD 1 | 200 | 400 |

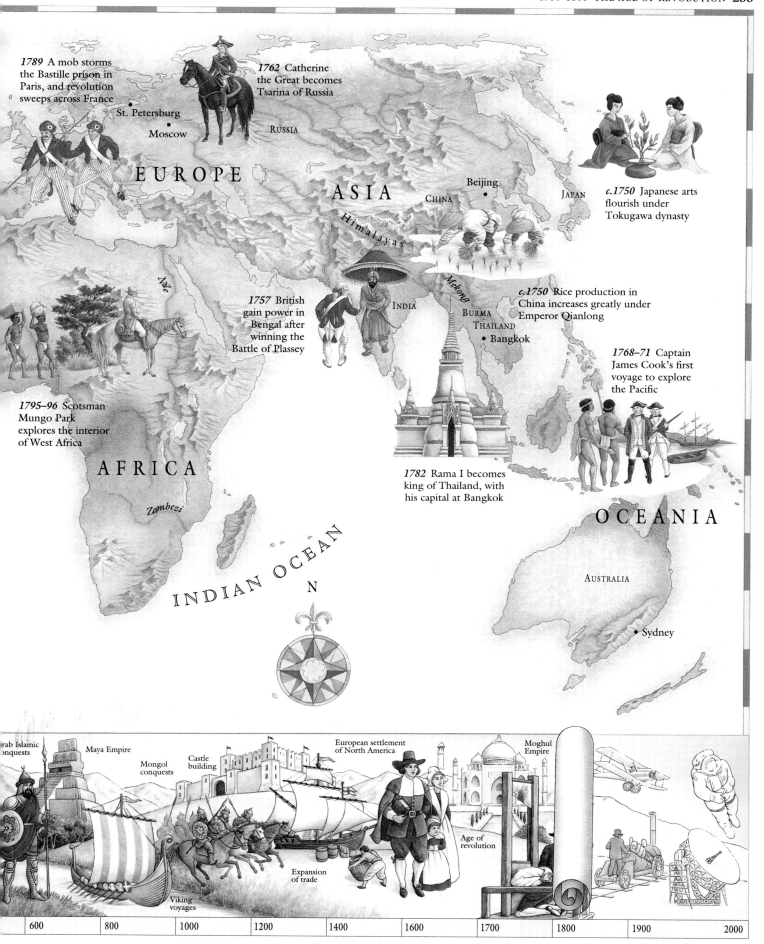

1789 A mob storms the Bastille prison in Paris, and revolution sweeps across France

1762 Catherine the Great becomes Tsarina of Russia

St. Petersburg

Moscow

RUSSIA

EUROPE

ASIA

Beijing

CHINA

JAPAN

c.1750 Japanese arts flourish under Tokugawa dynasty

Himalayas

Nile

1757 British gain power in Bengal after winning the Battle of Plassey

INDIA

Mekong

BURMA

THAILAND

Bangkok

c.1750 Rice production in China increases greatly under Emperor Qianlong

1795–96 Scotsman Mungo Park explores the interior of West Africa

AFRICA

Zambezi

1768–71 Captain James Cook's first voyage to explore the Pacific

1782 Rama I becomes king of Thailand, with his capital at Bangkok

OCEANIA

INDIAN OCEAN

N

AUSTRALIA

Sydney

rab Islamic onquests

Maya Empire

Mongol conquests

Castle building

European settlement of North America

Moghul Empire

Age of revolution

Expansion of trade

Viking voyages

| 600 | 800 | 1000 | 1200 | 1400 | 1600 | 1700 | 1800 | 1900 | 2000 |

1750

1762

AFRICA

1755 The first outbreak of smallpox in Cape Town, brought by sailors, spreads rapidly inland; it kills many Khoisan hunters and herders

These bellows belonged to the Lozi tribe in Zambia

1764–77 Reign of Osei Kwadwo, Asante ruler, West Africa

1768–73 Scottish explorer James Bruce travels in Ethiopia*

1768 Ali Bey, a Mamluk army officer, makes himself ruler of Egypt

1770s Tukolor kingdom gains power in former Songhai region of West Africa

1773 Ali Bey dies a week after being wounded in a battle with rebels led by Abu'l-Dhahab

Asante gold weight

ASIA

This Tibetan ceremonial mask was worn to frighten away evil spirits

1750 Chinese capture Lhasa and take over state of Tibet

1750–79 Karim Khan is dictator of South Persia

1752 Ahmad Shah Durrani (1747–73), who united Afghanistan, invades India, takes Lahore; plunders Delhi in 1755

1753 Alaungpaya reunites Burma; founds last Burmese dynasty, the Kombaung (to 1885)

1756 "Black Hole" of Calcutta

1757 Robert Clive defeats Siraj ud daula, Nabob of Bengal, at Battle of Plassey*

1758 Aoki Konyo, Japanese scholar, who introduced the sweet potato into Japan, completes Dutch/Japanese dictionary

1761 Battle of Panipat between the Marathas and Ahmad Shah Durrani of Afghanistan; great Afghan victory*

Diamonds, rubies, and an emerald adorn this Indian Moghul snuffbox

1762 British fleet captures Manila in Philippine Islands from Spain

1763 Britain becomes dominant power in India as a result of the Treaty of Paris

1767 Burmese invade Thailand, destroy its capital, Ayudhya, and force Thais to accept Burmese overlordship, but the Burmese have to withdraw to repulse Chinese invasion of Burma

EUROPE

1750–77 Sebastian de Carvalho (later Marquis of Pombal) appointed foreign secretary and acts as chief minister to José I of Portugal; introduces reforms*

1754 Concordat with Vatican gives Spanish Church independence from Rome

1755 The great Lisbon earthquake in Portugal; many thousands killed

1756–63 Seven Years War; Prussia and Britain versus France, Austria, and Russia

1757 Battle of Rossbach: Frederick the Great of Prussia defeats French and Austrians*

After the Seven Years War ended many soldiers were forced to find other work; some became tinkers, as shown in this silver statue

1762 Publication of French philosopher Jean-Jacques Rousseau's *The Social Contract*

1762–96 Reign of Russian empress Catherine the Great*

1764–95 Reign of King Stanislas Poniatowski, the last king of Poland

1772–95 Poland is divided between Russia, Austria, and Prussia

1773–75 Emelian Pugachev leads uprising of Cossacks and peasants in Russia

Catherine the Great's Sèvres porcelain ice-cream cooler

AMERICAS

1753 French occupy Ohio Valley in North America

1754–63 French and Indian War in North America

1759 General James Wolfe defeats French at battle of Quebec*

1759 Jesuits expelled from Brazil by Portuguese authorities

1760 All Canada passes into British hands

This jaguar claw necklace with red feathers comes from Brazil

1762 British expedition against Cuba seizes Havana from Spain

1763 Rio de Janeiro becomes capital of Brazil

1763 Pontiac Conspiracy: Native Americans rise against British in North America

1765 Stamp Act imposed on British colonies in America

1773 Boston Tea Party: colonists in America rebel against British taxes*

OCEANIA

French General Montcalm met his death at the battle of Quebec

1767 British Captain Samuel Wallis is the first European to reach Tahiti; six months later, French navigator Bougainville visits the islands

1768–71 First of British Captain James Cook's three voyages to Pacific*

1770 Spanish sailors reach Easter Island

1772–75 Captain Cook's second voyage to the Pacific

Cook's ship was named Endeavour

1774

1777 Sidi Mohammed, ruler of Morocco (1757–90), abolishes Christian slavery

1779 Dutch farmers in Cape Colony clash with organized Xhosa resistance

1781 Militant Tijaniyya Islamic order set up in Algeria

1785 Omani rulers reassert influence in Zanzibar

Boer farmers encountered Xhosa opposition along the Great Fish River

1774–85 Warren Hastings is governor-general of British India

1777 Christianity introduced to Korea by Chinese Jesuits

1782–1809 Rama I reigns in Thailand; founds Chakri dynasty*

1783–88 Severe famine in Japan

1784 United States begins to trade with China

Japanese elephant incense burner

1774–92 Reign of Louis XVI, king of France

1777 Accession of Maria as queen of Portugal; she exiles Pombal but continues his work

1778 War of Bavarian Succession between Prussia and Austria

1780 Joseph II, co-ruler of Austria with his mother Maria Theresa until 1780, becomes sole ruler on her death; ten-year period of important reforms

1783 Russia annexes the Crimea

1783–1801 William Pitt the Younger is prime minister of England

One of a set of six, this chair was made for Louis XVI's card room at Fontainebleau

Paul Revere, folk hero of the American Revolution

1775 American Revolution breaks out with skirmish at Lexington, Massachusetts

1776 Declaration of Independence (July 4)*

1776 Spanish create Viceroyalty of La Plata in South America

1777 Treaty of San Idelfonso defines borders of Brazil

1780–82 Revolt of Tupac Amaru, Inca descendant, in Peru*

1781 Lord Cornwallis surrenders at Yorktown; last major battle of American Revolution*

1783 U.S. independence formally recognized at Treaty of Paris

1776–79 Cook's third voyage; on his way through the Pacific he lands in Hawaii and is clubbed or stabbed to death by angry islanders

1785 Comte la Pérouse, French navigator, leads expedition to Pacific and northwest America; touches Japan; he is lost at sea in 1788

This butterfly was found in Australia in 1770 by Joseph Banks, a naturalist who explored the Pacific with Captain Cook

1786

1787 Tuaregs, nomads in Sahara, abolish Moroccan pashalik of Timbuktu

c.1788 Usuman dan Fodio, a Fulani cleric, stirs holy war against a Hausa king*

1788 African Association founded in England to explore interior of Africa

1795 British seize Cape Colony from Dutch for the first time

1795–96 Scottish explorer Mungo Park travels through Gambia and reaches Niger

Tuareg saddle

This gold sword hilt bears the East India Company crest

1792 Chinese army marches into Nepal and dictates terms to Gurkhas who had been raiding Tibet

1792 Sheikh Mohammed Ibn Abdul Wahhab, founder of Saudi Arabia, dies

1794 Aga Mohammed founds Kajar dynasty and unites all Persia

1796 Emperor Qianlong of China relinquishes power but still directs government (to 1799)*

1799 Ranjit Singh founds Sikh kingdom in India

1787–92 Turkey fights Russia to regain the Crimea but is defeated

1788–90 Sweden attacks Russia, but peace treaty confirms prewar borders

1789 Outbreak of French Revolution; Bastille stormed in Paris on July 14*

1795 France overruns Netherlands; creates dependent Dutch republic

1798–99 Wolfe Tone organizes Irish revolt against English rule

Turkish sultan Selim III (1780–1807) owned this gold watch

This bag from northern Quebec was made from caribou skin and the throats of two loons

1787 Drafting of United States Constitution

1789 Conspiracy of Tiradentes in Brazil; revolt in Minas Gerais gold mines

1789–97 George Washington is first president of the United States

1790s Revolt in Haiti against French rule, led by Toussaint L'Ouverture*

1791 Canada Act divides Canada into Upper and Lower Canada

1793 Trinidad captured from Spanish in Caribbean

1787–89 Voyage of Lieutenant William Bligh in the *Bounty* to the Pacific to find breadfruit plants; the crew mutinies and sets him adrift

1788 First British convicts shipped to Botany Bay, Australia

1790 Bligh returns to England

1793 First free British settlers reach Australia

1798 Strait between mainland Australia and Tasmania navigated by Bass and Flinders

1799 Major civil war in Tonga

Breadfruit plant

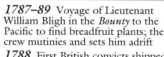

1750-1800 AFRICA

In West Africa, an Islamic revival occurred among the Fulani people that affected the entire region. In southwestern Nigeria, the Oyo Empire was at its height. Further west, Asante dominated Ghana. By the 1780s, 90,000 African slaves were shipped across the Atlantic each year, large numbers from Angola. In East Africa, Zanzibar's trade rivaled that of Mombasa. Europeans probed the African interior to increase knowledge and trade. In South Africa, the Dutch clashed with African peoples; in 1795 the British seized the Cape of Good Hope from the Dutch.

Hungry for fame
Mungo Park (1771–1806) was an ambitious Scotsman who reached the Niger in 1795; he later died trying to follow its course to the sea.

Ethiopian style
An Ethiopian woman's silver leg ornament such as James Bruce might have seen on his journeys in search of the source of the Nile.

1768

Europeans explore the interior

After centuries of confining their interest in Africa to coastal trade, particularly the slave trade, Europeans began to investigate the interior of the continent. They had a variety of motives – scientific, geographical, and commercial. From 1768 to 1773 the Scot James Bruce explored Ethiopia. He thought he had found the source of the main Nile River when he reached that of the smaller Blue Nile. In 1788 a group of British scientists and interested patrons, headed by Sir Joseph Banks, formed the Africa Association to promote the exploration of Africa and search for new trade outlets. In 1795 the association sponsored the first journey of Mungo Park to West Africa; he explored the Gambia River and reached the Niger, showing that it flowed eastward.

→ Mungo Park (1795–96)

→ Mungo Park (1805–06)

→ James Bruce (1768–73)

First steps
By 1750 European knowledge of the African interior had hardly improved since the time of the Roman Empire. Bruce and Park made the first small steps to advance it.

c.1788

First stirrings of a holy war

The Fulani people grazed their herds across large parts of West Africa. Many settled in Hausaland in northern Nigeria. Some were drawn to towns, adopted Islam, and even became Muslim scholars and clerics. In about 1788 Usuman dan Fodio (1754–1817), a Fulani cleric living in the Hausa state of Gobir, challenged its king, saying he was not governing according to strict Islamic law. Usuman gathered a following which by the 1790s had become a serious threat to the Gobir state. In 1804 Usuman left Gobir and declared a jihad (holy war) against all Hausa kings. By 1812 most of Hausaland had been brought into a new empire of Fulani-ruled states. Usuman took the title of caliph, and on his death this passed to his son Mohammed Bello, who ruled from a new town, Sokoto.

Animal charm
This Hausa charm case was worn around its owner's neck.

A Fulani woman
The Fulani were the only West African people whose way of life was mobile pastoralism (moving with their herds). They spread eastward from Senegal as far as northern Nigeria and Cameroon.

40,000 BC		10,000	5000	1000	500	AD 1	200	400

1750-1800 ASIA

Indian sabre
This magnificent sabre, used in the Battle of Plassey, has a hilt of watered steel decorated with a fine gold design.

As the Moghul Empire declined, the British and the French took advantage of its weakness to pursue their commercial and military rivalry in India. Robert Clive beat the Nabob of Bengal in battle and brought the province under British rule. Meanwhile, a brilliant Afghan general, Ahmad Shah, seized huge areas of northern India. In southeast Asia, Rama I strengthened the kingdom of Thailand. China continued to flourish under Qianlong.

1757

The British control Bengal

The east Indian region of Bengal, independent from Moghul rule since the early 18th century, was a powerful state. Both the British and the French East India companies had interests in Bengal. In 1756 the Nabob (ruler) of Bengal drove the British out of Calcutta, their principal base. The next year Robert Clive, an East India Company official turned soldier, recovered Calcutta and then routed the Nabob Siraj ud daula at Plassey. This brought Bengal under the control of the company. Over the next decades, the British strengthened their control over this rich trading region. By the end of the century, however, British interests were seriously threatened again by a strong revival of French ambitions in India.

Elephant armor
This suit of elephant armor was used to protect elephants in battle. It was acquired by Lady Clive in India.

The *Diwani* of Bengal
The British strengthened their power in Bengal following the Battle of Plassey. After defeating a Muslim coalition at Buscar in 1764, they were granted the *Diwani*, or right to collect imperial revenue from the state of Bengal, by Moghul emperor Shah Alam. This painting shows Clive receiving the Bengal *Diwani* from Shah Alam.

1761

Victory for Ahmad Shah at Panipat

When Persian ruler Nadir Shah was assassinated, one of his Afghan generals, Ahmad Shah, took over Afghan provinces that had been under Nadir Shah's control. He established a dynasty, the Durrani. He invaded India no less than nine times, claiming sovereignty over the regions Nadir Shah had conquered. In the late 1750s, Ahmad Shah clashed with the Marathas, a confederacy of states in central India. In 1761 he won a victory over a large Maratha army at Panipat near Delhi. His troops then mutinied, and he lost some territory but kept control of his conquests in northwest India. He died in 1773.

The battle of Panipat
At Panipat, Ahmad Shah's troops drove the Maratha army back to its own lands.

| 600 | 800 | 1000 | 1200 | 1400 | 1600 | 1700 | 1800 | 1900 | 2000 |

Thai earrings
Rama I patronized the arts, especially literature. These exquisite earrings, made of animal skin and painted in gold, are a fine example of the elaborate jewelry made at this time.

1782
A new king for Thailand

In the later 1760s, a Thai general, P'ya Taksin, began to drive back the Burmese, who had invaded Thailand and destroyed its capital, Ayudhya. By 1776–77, Thailand was united with a new capital at Bangkok. But the struggle exhausted P'ya Taksin, and he became mentally ill. His leading general, Chakri, took over the government. In 1782 Chakri was declared king, and P'ya Taksin was put to death. Chakri then became Rama T'ibodi, or Rama I. Much of his reign was spent struggling with Burma, whose new and ambitious ruler Bodawpaya invaded Thailand unsuccessfully in 1785. Rama then concentrated on strengthening his kingdom, appointing as ministers in his government trusted men who had served with him in the long wars. He died in 1809.

Burmese spear
Invading Burmese armies suffered many crippling defeats and were reduced to making ineffectual border raids. Rama I did not retaliate.

Thai dye
During the reign of Rama I, crafts workers produced intricately decorated works of art such as this porcelain bowl.

1796
Qianlong's reign ends

In 1796 Qianlong completed 60 years as Chinese emperor and abdicated, but even in retirement he dominated the government. The first two-thirds of his reign had been almost constantly successful and prosperous. Food for a growing population (said to have doubled from 150 to 300 million people in the 18th century) was provided by the introduction of shorter growing seasons for rice (as little as 30 days per crop in some areas, three times a year) and by increasing imports of new crops such as maize and sweet potatoes from the Americas. But after about 1770, Qianlong began to surround himself with flatterers, especially a handsome but incompetent favorite, He shen (1750–99). He shen rose in rank quickly, relying on corrupt methods, which reduced the efficiency of the imperial government. There were rebellions in the provinces, one of which in northern China was still going on when Qianlong died in 1799.

Decorative arts
This tiny white glass snuff bottle, made during Qianlong's reign, is decorated with the gemstone cornelian.

British ambassador meets emperor
In 1793 Qianlong received the British ambassador, Lord Macartney. Britain was hoping to negotiate a trade agreement with China. However, Qianlong was unimpressed by the British delegation and was not interested in trading with European powers. No agreement was made between the two countries.

40,000 BC		10,000	5000	1000	500	AD 1	200	400

ART AND CULTURE IN JAPAN

From the early 17th century until the mid-19th century, Japan had relatively little contact with the rest of the world. This gave the Japanese a great opportunity to develop new art forms, which reflected their way of life, prosperity, religions (Buddhism and Shintoism), and understanding of the natural world. At the new Bunraku puppet shows, puppets were moved so skillfully that audiences almost believed they were alive. Other new arts included the Kabuki theater, musical plays about modern society or historical events performed in colorful costume. In the late 17th century, Japanese artists began to produce woodblock prints, as well as individual paintings. Some prints were copies of classical works, others were vivid, original scenes from everyday life, known as *ukiyo-e*. Some *ukiyo-e* artists, such as Katsushika Hokusai (1760–1849), became world-famous.

Art of wrestling
Sumo tournaments were first held, along with drama and dancing, at ancient Shinto religious ceremonies. In Sumo wrestling one wrestler tries to throw the other out of the ring or forces him to touch the ground other than with the soles of his feet. Sumo wrestling remains a very popular sport in Japan.

Swords
A samurai's sword was the symbol of his honor. Swordsmiths were regarded as supreme artists taking part in an almost religious ritual. The blade had to be perfectly forged. Fittings were works of great intricacy, often with precious metal inlays.

Nature in miniature
The Japanese used many skills to show their understanding of the beauty of nature. One was the art of bonsai ("tray planting"), in which certain trees were specially grown in trays as miniature copies of full-size trees. They were cultivated to grow indoors and outdoors. Many people all over the world grow bonsai trees today.

The Wave
Hokusai's famous print *In the Hollow of a Wave off the Coast at Kanagawa*, from the series *Thirty-six Views of Mount Fuji*, appeared in the 1830s. It contrasts the smallness of human beings with the majesty of nature, showing ships and their crews flung about by huge waves with clawlike ends.

Tea ceremony
Tea drinking is an elegant ritual, still performed today. Masters of the art of the tea ceremony aim to bring peace and calm to all those taking part. The ceremony is sometimes held in the open air, but is usually held in specially built, small, simple wooden tea houses. Once inside, the guests behave according to precise rules. They look at beautiful bowls, utensils, and flower arrangements and make admiring comments. After sipping a bowl of special green tea, a guest wipes the bowl and passes it to the next person. The ceremony originated among Buddhist priests more than 500 years ago.

1750-1800 EUROPE

Frederick the Great 1712–86
Frederick II of Prussia was an enlightened ruler who brought Prussia to prominence.

Portugal, financed by newly found diamonds from Brazil, flourished under a strong ruler, Pombal. Europe suffered several wars, notably the Seven Years War in which Frederick the Great of Prussia nearly lost his kingdom yet proved himself the greatest of generals. France lost in the war and was also driven out of Canada. Another great ruler, Catherine the Great of Russia, tried to model her country on France, yet continued to rule autocratically. Towards the end of the century, the French Revolution affected almost every European country.

The Marquis of Pombal 1699–1782
Pombal's first major achievement was his energetic response to the destruction of Lisbon by earthquake. When others panicked, he kept his head and set about organizing the rebuilding of the city.

1750

Pombal governs Portugal

Portugal, a great seafaring nation with colonies in Africa, South America, and Asia, recovered its independence in 1640 after 60 years of Spanish rule. In 1750 Portugal's king, José, appointed Sebastian de Carvalho (later Marquis of Pombal) to high office and made him prime minister in 1756. Pombal was perhaps the greatest statesman of Portugal's modern history. In a ministry lasting more than 20 years, he reorganized Portugal's finances, army, and educational system, stimulated industry and colonial development, reduced the nobles' power, broke the Inquisition, expelled the Jesuits, and revived agriculture. But he ruled with an iron hand and punished opposition cruelly. When King José died in 1777, Pombal was driven from office.

EARTHQUAKE IN LISBON

The 1755 earthquake in Lisbon, Portugal's capital, was the worst natural disaster of the 18th century. As thousands of citizens packed the churches for Mass on All Saints' Day (November 1), tremors shook the city to its very foundations for a dreadful 15 minutes. Two-thirds of the buildings, great and small, collapsed in ruins, and as many as 50,000 people lay dead or injured beneath. It was Pombal who directed the capital's rebuilding. He used gold and diamonds from the rich Portuguese colony of Brazil to finance the work.

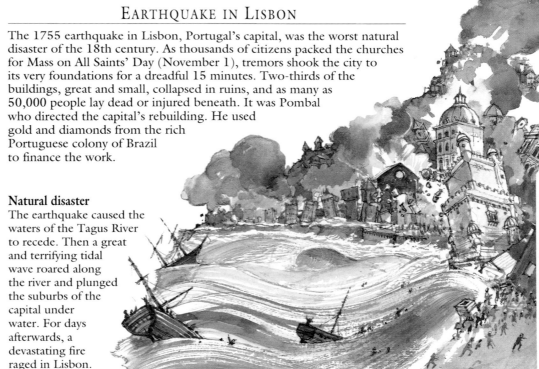

Before the earthquake
Lisbon was a large, wealthy port city. After the devastation of the earthquake, it took decades to rebuild the city to its former glory.

Natural disaster
The earthquake caused the waters of the Tagus River to recede. Then a great and terrifying tidal wave roared along the river and plunged the suburbs of the capital under water. For days afterwards, a devastating fire raged in Lisbon.

40,000 BC		10,000	5000	1000	500	AD 1	200	400

1757
The Battle of Rossbach

When Frederick II of Prussia became king in 1740, he inherited a well-organized state with an efficient army. He used both to increase Prussia's power in Europe. He was a cultured man, but Frederick's real genius was for military campaigning. In the War of the Austrian Succession (1740–48) and in the Seven Years War (1756–63) he won land for Prussia. His greatest victory was at Rossbach when, with 30,000 troops, he routed a combined French and Austrian army of more than 80,000. Prussia emerged from the war as a major power, and Frederick decided on a peaceful policy from then on. At home, he ruled as an enlightened despot. He believed that only a monarch with absolute power could improve the situation of the people. With this aim, Frederick introduced economic reforms, abolished torture, and granted religious freedom. The peasantry, however, remained subject to feudal restraints.

Pointed end of linstock used for defense

A piece of string soaked in saltpeter was passed through the dragons' mouths and then lit

1762
Catherine the Great becomes empress of Russia

Catherine the Great became empress of Russia in 1762 after deposing her husband Peter III. She was an intelligent and energetic ruler who was influenced by the Enlightenment philosophers Voltaire and Montesquieu. Her main achievements included the expansion of Russian territory, development of industry and trade, reform of local government, and the spread of education, particularly for women. A writer herself, Catherine encouraged literature, the arts, the press, and Western culture generally. The actions for which she has been most criticized include the retention of serfdom and her role in the partitioning of Poland. Her achievement was to carry on the work of Peter the Great, transforming Russia into a powerful state.

French linstock
This linstock, a long staff used to light cannons, dates from the Seven Years War.

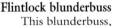

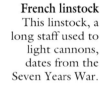

Flintlock blunderbuss
This blunderbuss, from Catherine the Great's armory, was used during her many foreign wars to expand Russia's territory.

Ruler of power
Catherine (1729–96) was autocratic but not enough to overcome landowners' objections to the abolition of serfdom. Her lively intelligence attracted artists and intellectuals from all over Europe and made her court a cultural center.

EMELIAN PUGACHEV 1726–75

In 1773, a revolt broke out among Ural Cossacks as a result of their long-standing economic grievances and miserable living conditions. Emelian Pugachev, a Don Cossack, led the rebellion. Claiming to be the Emperor Peter III (Catherine's dead husband), who had been murdered by Catherine's supporters in 1762, Pugachev set up a mock court and gave his illiterate followers the names of Catherine's ministers. He was soon joined by other discontented peasants, and his revolt spread through the region of the Ural River and the lower Volga. Pugachev was captured in 1775 and executed.

| 600 | 800 | 1000 | 1200 | 1400 | 1600 | 1700 | 1800 | 2000 |

Storming the Bastille
The Bastille prison in Paris was a symbol of tyranny, but it held only seven prisoners when a mob attacked and captured it in 1789. This scene was sketched by one of the revolutionaries.

1789
The French Revolution

The French Revolution was a deep-rooted revolt by many classes against the whole order of society. It stemmed from long-standing grievances. The country was impoverished as a result of three major wars since 1740, and harvest failures had pushed up food prices. Political power was centered in the royal court at Versailles and criticism of the regime was illegal. The country aristocracy still ruled like feudal lords, extracting ever higher dues from poor farming peasants, who also bore the main burden of taxation. The middle classes, stirred by their readings of the Enlightenment philosophers, had also begun to agitate for reform. In 1789 the king, Louis XVI, called the Estates General (the French parliament) for the first time in nearly 150 years to try to obtain national agreement on some reform. This acted as a catalyst for change, and unrest reached a climax in Paris on July 14, when an angry mob stormed the Bastille prison. After this, the king and his ministers were forced to implement changes. The Estates General became the National Assembly, a Declaration of the Rights of Man was issued, and a new democratic constitution agreed to. In 1792 the monarchy was abolished, and a republic was established. The old order of society disappeared, and a new one, based on liberty, equality, and fraternity, was set up in its place.

The Tricolor, a three-colored flag of red, white, and blue, was the new flag of republican France

RADICAL LEADERS

Moderates tried to govern France at first but were pushed out by more radical leaders like Georges Danton and Jacques Hébert. Then the radical party itself split, and Danton and Hébert were put to death by the extremist Maximilien Robespierre (1758–94), seated right. He, in turn, was guillotined after introducing the Reign of Terror. His regime was eventually followed by a moderate board of governors, called the Directoire, or Directorate.

Victims were led up the steps of the scaffold, hands tied behind their backs, to await their turn on the guillotine

Supporters of the revolution included traders, workers, ordinary soldiers, and peasants, all of whom felt they had been ill-treated by their rulers

Louis XVI of France
Louis XVI (1754–93) succeeded his grandfather, Louis XV, as king of France in 1774. He had married Marie Antoinette, daughter of the Austrian empress Maria Theresa, at the age of 16. Louis was a well-meaning man who, when revolution threatened, tried to make concessions to all classes. This did not save his throne, which he lost in 1792, nor his life. He was guillotined in January 1793.

Among the spectators were tricoteuses, women who sat and knitted beside the guillotine each day

40,000 BC		10,000	5000	1000	500	AD 1	200	400

Place of death

Introduced to France by Dr. Joseph Guillotin, originally as a humane way of executing criminals, the guillotine became the symbol of the French Revolution. It stood in what is now the Place de la Concorde in central Paris. During the Reign of Terror, executions were a gory spectacle which drew crowds of spectators.

Release of the rope caused the blade to fall onto the neck of the victim

The sharp blade of the guillotine enabled the quick execution of thousands of accused "enemies of the people"

The heads and bodies of the victims of execution were carried away in baskets and buried in unmarked mass graves

Marie Antoinette

Marie Antoinette (1755–93), the wife of Louis XVI, was never popular in France. She became despised for her carefree and extravagant lifestyle, especially during the early years of her royal marriage. She has been quoted – probably wrongly – as saying, when she heard that Parisians were rioting over bread shortages, "Let them eat cake," which showed her ignorance of the plight of the common people. She was guillotined by the revolutionaries nine months after her husband.

Effects of the revolution abroad

The revolution affected other European countries, too. In Ireland, Wolfe Tone, who campaigned for separation from Britain, obtained promises of French support for a rising against the government. It failed, and Tone was captured and took his own life. British prime minister William Pitt (1757–1806), shown at right, conscious that French forces might attack Britain via Ireland, forced through a union with the Irish Parliament, uniting the two countries formally in 1800.

THE FRENCH REVOLUTION

1789 July 14; angry Paris mob storms Bastille prison and sparks off revolution

1789 Declaration of Rights of Man

1790 Louis XVI accepts new democratic constitution

1791 Louis XVI and Queen Marie Antoinette try to escape from France but are stopped and brought back to Paris

1792 National Convention abolishes the monarchy

1793 Execution of Louis XVI in January; Marie Antoinette follows in October

1793–94 Robespierre's Reign of Terror

1794 Hébert guillotined in March; Danton follows in April

1794 Robespierre arrested and guillotined in July; end of the Reign of Terror

1795 Formation of Directoire

| 600 | 800 | 1000 | 1200 | 1400 | 1600 | 1700 | 1800 | 1900 | 2000 |

1750-1800 AMERICAS

In North America, Britain took control of Canada from France with help from the British colonists on the Atlantic coast. The British government then tried to strengthen its authority over the colonists by imposing new taxes. The colonists rose in revolt and won independence, creating the United States of America. In South America, major revolts against Spanish and Portuguese rule broke out.

1759

British defeat French in Canada

Before the 1750s there were several conflicts between the British and French in North America over trade and as an extension of quarrels in Europe. In 1753 the French moved south from Canada to occupy part of the Ohio River Valley. British troops and colonists from the East Coast were sent against them. Both sides won battles, but there was no conclusive victory. Then the French sent a new commander, the Marquis de Montcalm, to Canada in 1756 and in 1758 General James Wolfe arrived from Britain. The

British attacked French territory including Quebec, capital of French Canada. In 1759 Wolfe defeated Montcalm near Quebec, and the British took the city. Britain's control over all Canada was confirmed in the Treaty of Paris of 1763, which had ended the Seven Years War (1756–63).

Algonquian war club
Algonquian-speaking Native American tribes were often raided by the powerful Iroquois, allies of the British colonists.

French and Indian War
The British suffered some terrible defeats in North America before Wolfe's victory. In 1754 the French and their Native American allies ambushed British forces. This scene from the 1992 film *The Last of the Mohicans* shows Mohican allies of the British fighting Huron warriors, who supported the French.

Soldiers scaled 175 ft (53 m) cliff

One of the first of 30 landing craft, which together carried 1,700 of Wolfe's men

Wolfe discusses the operation with a fellow officer

Surprise attack
In August 1759, Wolfe was camped east of Quebec. He planned a surprise nighttime landing upstream of Quebec at the foot of steep cliffs. At 1 a.m., on September 13 he and his men set out. They reached the landing place at 4 a.m., scrambled up the cliffs, and by dawn were moving toward the Plains of Abraham outside the city. They soon defeated the astonished French but both Wolfe and Montcalm were mortally wounded

| 10,000 | 5000 | 1000 | 500 | AD 1 | 200 | 400 |

1775
Lexington and Concord

To pay for the French and Indian War of 1756–63, the British government imposed a series of taxes on its North American colonies. Many Americans claimed Britain had no right to do so as they weren't represented in parliament. Colonial resistance forced Britain to withdraw all the taxes except a duty on tea. When Bostonians destroyed the cargoes of several tea ships, parliament responded by closing the port of Boston and sending in troops. Protest against British rule spread throughout the 13 colonies. Patriots – colonists opposed to Britain's policies – formed a Continental Congress. In April 1775, Patriots fought British troops at Lexington and Concord, Massachusetts. This was the beginning of the Revolutionary War.

Stamp Act

The tea tax was one of a series of British measures that infuriated colonists. The Stamp Act of 1765 raised money on legal documents. Colonists argued that only their own assemblies had the right to tax them. Delegates from nine colonies called on merchants to stop selling British goods. Merchants in Britain lost business, and in 1766 the act was repealed. In this cartoon Bostonians force tea down a British tax collector's throat. The Stamp Act is nailed on a "Liberty Tree."

Boston Tea Party

Three bands of 50 men, "disguised" as Native Americans, passed cheering supporters on their way to the tea ships and threw the cargo overboard. Other ports followed Boston's example and held "tea parties" of their own.

1776
Congress declares independence

After fighting broke out, Congress appointed George Washington of Virginia commander-in-chief of the Continental Army, the chief Patriot fighting force. Washington forced the British out of Boston, but the Patriots were defeated in New York City and had to retreat into New Jersey. Although some Patriots had hoped for reconciliation with Britain, the movement for independence gathered strength, and on July 4, 1776, in Philadelphia, representatives from the 13 colonies signed the Declaration of Independence, which declared the colonies "Free and Independent States."

The ideas of independence

Brilliant young Virginian Thomas Jefferson (in the red waistcoat) wrote the Declaration of Independence. He restated the theories of philosopher John Locke, who thought that governments had a contract with the people to protect their rights to life, liberty, and, Jefferson added, the pursuit of happiness. He listed the crimes of the British king, whom he said had broken his contract with the colonists. Not all colonists wanted independence. Many of these "loyalists," or Tories, emigrated to Canada. The idea of liberty for all prompted some colonists to campaign strongly to free slaves. Slavery was abolished by the northern states in the early 19th century.

Molly Pitcher

Women did jobs in the war that had traditionally been men's. "Molly Pitcher" took water to men at the Battle of Monmouth Court House and took her husband's place at a field gun when he died.

Molly Pitcher used a ramrod to load gunpowder into a cannon

| 600 | 800 | 1000 | 1200 | 1400 | 1600 | 1700 | 1800 | 1900 | 2000 |

THE REVOLUTIONARY WAR

1775 First clashes at Lexington and Concord

1775 Patriot army besieges British in Boston

1776 British evacuate Boston; colonists declare independence

1777 British general John Burgoyne surrenders at Saratoga, New York

1778 France forms alliance with the United States

1780 In South Carolina, British troops under Cornwallis defeat Americans at Battle of Camden

1781 British victory at Guilford Court House, North Carolina; Cornwallis withdraws to Yorktown

1781 British surrender at Yorktown, ending the war

1781
British surrender at Yorktown

Following a major Patriot victory at Saratoga, New York, in 1777, France began supporting the Patriot cause with money, weapons, and troops. After 1778, the focus of the fighting shifted to the South, until British general Lord Cornwallis's surrender at Yorktown, Virginia, ended the war. In 1783, the Treaty of Paris recognized the independence of the United States of America. The new nation suffered from the lack of an effective central government, so in 1787, representatives from the 13 states met in Philadelphia to work out a new plan of government. The result was the Constitution of the United States.

The road to Yorktown
Washington (center) trapped the British at Yorktown with a perfectly timed plan. A French and Patriot army marched from New York to join French commander Lafayette at Yorktown. A French fleet sailed into nearby Chesapeake Bay and up the York River. Surrounded by land and sea, the British surrendered. As they threw down their weapons, an American band underlined their defeat by playing "The World Turned Upside Down."

Redcoats
Most infantrymen in the Revolutionary War wore long-tailed coats, though in different colors. Generally, Continental soldiers wore blue; the British wore red and became known as redcoats.

The U.S. Constitution
The framers of the Constitution wanted to make sure no person or group held too much power. Thus, the Constitution set up a federal system, with power shared between the national and state governments. The national, or federal government itself was divided into three branches — executive (the Presidency), legislative (the Senate and House of Representatives), and judicial (the Supreme Court) – with a system of checks and balances on each others' power. After ratification (approval) by the required number of states, the Constitution went into effect in 1789. In 1791, 10 amendments, together known as the Bill of Rights, were added; they guaranteed such basic rights as freedom of religion, speech, the press, and trial by jury.

GEORGE WASHINGTON

The great-grandson of an English settler, Washington (1732–99) was born in Virginia. After serving as a militia officer in the war against the French and Indians, he became a planter. Active in colonial politics on the eve of the American Revolution, he was named commander of the Continental Army when fighting broke out. In 1789 he was elected as the first U.S. president and served two terms. The last years were marred by disputes between two new parties, the Federalists, who favored strong central government, and the Republicans, who stressed individual and state freedom.

| 1000 | 500 | AD 1 | 200 | 400 |

1782
Spanish crush rebellion in Peru

The first serious revolts against Spanish rule in South America took place in the 18th century. In Peru, Native Americans of the Andes Mountains, forced to work in terrible conditions in Spanish-run mines and factories, rebelled in 1780. They were led by José Gabriel Condorcanqui, a wealthy Spanish-American who claimed descent from a 16th-century Inca emperor, Tupac Amaru, whose name he had taken in 1771. The rebels overran much of the highlands and attacked the city of Cuzco. They secretly sent news of the revolt to sympathizers in Bolivia using the ancient Inca method of quipus, knots in strings, to convey information. In March 1781, the Spanish captured Tupac Amaru and tortured him to death. But the revolt continued and was only finally crushed in 1782, after rebels had twice attacked the Bolivian city of La Paz.

Spanish soldiers surround Tupac Amaru
Tupac Amaru and about 100,000 followers were killed by Spanish soldiers to put down revolts. Some Peruvians, particularly those who were Spanish or had Spanish ancestors, remembered the rebellions as an uncontrolled lashing out against Spanish Americans. They became more loyal to Spanish rule.

Feather coronet
Native Americans rallied around Tupac Amaru remembering the strong rule of the Inca emperors. They used feathers in their costumes as their Inca ancestors had done.

Native American baton
Rebellion forced Spanish rulers to make some reforms. The *repartimiento*, in which Native American leaders and their people were given as a workforce to a Spanish landowner, was ended. This baton was used by Native American leaders at ceremonies.

1790s
Toussaint L'Ouverture leads slave revolt

In the 1790s Caribbean slaves rebelled against the government in Haiti, the French-held western part of the island of Hispaniola. An educated slave, François Breda, who called himself Toussaint L'Ouverture, emerged as their leader. In 1795 he came to an agreement with the French government which gave him control of most of the island. He then abolished slavery. In 1801 Toussaint declared the island independent. The French ruler Napoleon sent an expedition to reimpose French authority. Toussaint was captured and taken to France where he died in 1803. His colleague Jacques Dessalines drove out the French, declaring Haiti independent again in 1804.

Leader for liberty
News of the success of the revolutionaries in France, with their message that all people are created free and equal, stirred Toussaint (left) and his followers into revolt against their French slave masters.

Haiti in flames
Nighttime gatherings of slaves sent out drumbeats across the island to signal to their allies that revolt had begun. They burned the sugar cane fields on which they had labored and killed plantation owners and their families. The Haitian sugar industry never recovered.

UNITED STATES OF AMERICA

Atlantic Ocean

Bahamas (BRITAIN)

Cuba (SPAIN)

REPUBLIC OF HAITI

Santo Domingo (SPAIN)

Jamaica (BRITAIN)

1750-1800 OCEANIA

I n this period, the British navigator, James Cook made his three famous voyages to the Pacific (1768–79), passing by or landing on many Polynesian islands, sailing around New Zealand, and mapping the east coast of Australia. After Cook, convicts, many of them convicted for petty crimes, began to be shipped out of Britain to serve their sentences in settlements established in southeast Australia.

A chief's ceremonial headdress from the Cook Islands

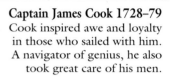

Captain James Cook 1728–79
Cook inspired awe and loyalty in those who sailed with him. A navigator of genius, he also took great care of his men.

1768
The South Seas explored

Between 1768 and 1779, Captain James Cook led three expeditions to the Pacific, doing more to enlarge European knowledge of Oceania than anyone else. He was a brilliant sailor, explorer, and leader, of humble origins from Yorkshire in England, who had first made his name charting parts of Canada during the Seven Years War. There and in the Pacific, he mapped more accurately than anyone before him. Stern but greatly respected, he kept his crews healthy by strict concern for diet and hygiene, and always attempted to establish good relations with the Polynesians he visited. The scientists and artists he took with him observed and recorded the peoples, animals, and lands they visited, both adding to scientific knowledge and increasing European interest in Oceania.

New Plant
This plant was named *Banksia serrata*, after Joseph Banks who led the scientific party on Cook's first voyage.

The three voyages
In 1768–71 Cook sailed first to Tahiti, then right around New Zealand, charting it and the east coast of Australia. Both had been thought part of *Terra Australis*, "South Land," a vast imaginary continent. On his second voyage (1772–75) Cook searched Antarctic waters south to the ice barrier and, finding nothing, proved that this imagined continent could only exist in polar latitudes. He also reached almost every major South Pacific island group. His third voyage (1776–79) was to look for the northwest passage (from Europe north of Canada and Alaska to Asia). On the way he explored Hawaii, where he was killed in 1779.

Unhappy ending
The members of Cook's third expedition were the first Europeans to reach Hawaii. When they arrived, Cook was greeted as a god, but on his second visit relations soured, and he was killed in a quarrel.

ASIA

North Pacific Ocean

Alaska

CANADA

NORTH AMERICA

Cook's third voyage, 1776–79

Hawaii

Cook's first voyage, 1768–71

Fiji

Tahiti

Cook Islands

AUSTRALIA

South Pacific Ocean

NEW ZEALAND

Cook's second voyage, 1772–75

CHAPTER 16

1800 – 1850

INDEPENDENCE
AND INDUSTRY

A model of George Stephenson's *Rocket*

1800-1850
THE WORLD

THROUGHOUT THIS PERIOD, the impact of the American Revolution is felt the length and breadth of the Americas. The newly independent United States rapidly extends its territory westward. Acquiring the vast Louisiana Territory from France in 1803, the young nation fights first Britain and then Mexico, until by 1848 it acquires Oregon and California and reaches the Pacific Ocean. In Central and South America, the Spanish and Portuguese colonies revolt against their European colonial masters and establish their independence. By 1850 European control of the Americas is restricted to Canada and the islands of the Caribbean.

Industrial growth

In Europe, Napoleon establishes his power in the aftermath of the French Revolution and dominates the continent until his defeat in 1815. The old royalist order then tries to reassert its authority, but the twin effects of industrialization and nationalism give rise to increasing tension that eventually explodes in 1848, when revolutions sweep across Europe. By then, the Industrial Revolution has affected almost every aspect of daily life. Huge industrial cities spring up, and railroads are laid across the continent. In their search for raw materials to supply the new industries, the major European nations continue to establish colonies in both Africa and Asia.

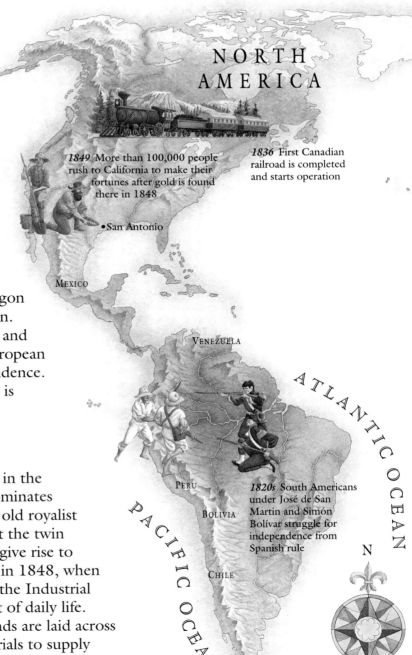

NORTH AMERICA

1849 More than 100,000 people rush to California to make their fortunes after gold is found there in 1848

1836 First Canadian railroad is completed and starts operation

• San Antonio

MEXICO

VENEZUELA

PERU

BOLIVIA

CHILE

1820s South Americans under José de San Martin and Simón Bolívar struggle for independence from Spanish rule

ATLANTIC OCEAN

PACIFIC OCEAN

N

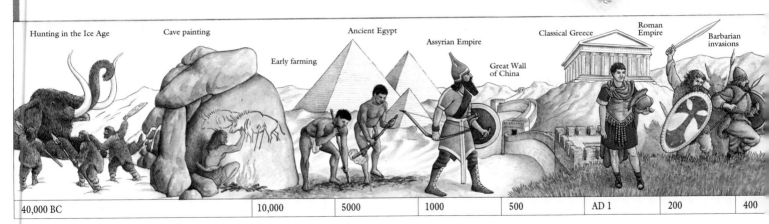

| Hunting in the Ice Age | Cave painting | Early farming | Ancient Egypt | Assyrian Empire | Great Wall of China | Classical Greece | Roman Empire | Barbarian invasions |

| 40,000 BC | | 10,000 | 5000 | 1000 | 500 | AD 1 | 200 | 400 |

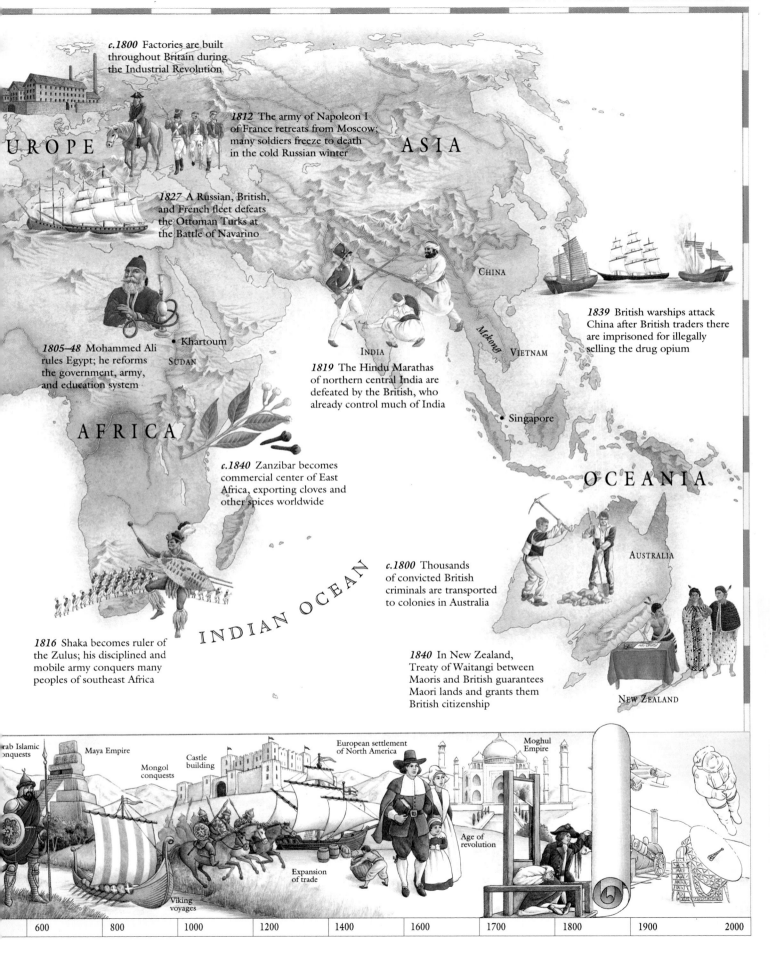

c.1800 Factories are built throughout Britain during the Industrial Revolution

1812 The army of Napoleon I of France retreats from Moscow; many soldiers freeze to death in the cold Russian winter

EUROPE

ASIA

1827 A Russian, British, and French fleet defeats the Ottoman Turks at the Battle of Navarino

CHINA

1839 British warships attack China after British traders there are imprisoned for illegally selling the drug opium

1805–48 Mohammed Ali rules Egypt; he reforms the government, army, and education system

• Khartoum

SUDAN

INDIA

VIETNAM

Mekong

1819 The Hindu Marathas of northern central India are defeated by the British, who already control much of India

• Singapore

AFRICA

c.1840 Zanzibar becomes commercial center of East Africa, exporting cloves and other spices worldwide

OCEANIA

c.1800 Thousands of convicted British criminals are transported to colonies in Australia

AUSTRALIA

INDIAN OCEAN

1816 Shaka becomes ruler of the Zulus; his disciplined and mobile army conquers many peoples of southeast Africa

1840 In New Zealand, Treaty of Waitangi between Maoris and British guarantees Maori lands and grants them British citizenship

NEW ZEALAND

Arab Islamic conquests

Maya Empire

Mongol conquests

Castle building

European settlement of North America

Moghul Empire

Expansion of trade

Age of revolution

Viking voyages

| 600 | 800 | 1000 | 1200 | 1400 | 1600 | 1700 | 1800 | 1900 | 2000 |

1800

1812

AFRICA

1804 Fulani begin jihad (holy war) in northern Nigeria

1805–06 Mungo Park explores Niger River, West Africa

1805–48 Mohammed Ali rules Egypt; Egypt breaks away from Ottoman Empire*

1807 Asante invade Fante confederacy of states

1808 Fulani invade Bornu near Lake Chad

A Zulu woman's comb

1814 Cape Colony in South Africa formally ceded to Britain by Netherlands

c.1816–28 Career of Zulu ruler Shaka in South Africa

c.1820 Fulani emirate founded in Adamawa, West Africa

1820–64 Fulani in Mali, West Africa, found and rule Hamdallahi caliphate

1822 Liberia in Africa founded as home for freed U.S. slaves

Mbutudi, a village in Bornu, central Africa; British explorers Denham and Clapperton explored Bornu and Hausaland in 1823–25

ASIA

This bull's head mace was made in Persia, for use in processions, not battles

1802–20 Emperor Gia-Long unites Vietnam*

1803–05 Second Maratha War disrupts Central India

1804 Russian envoy visits Nagasaki in Japan, tries but fails to negotiate commercial treaty

1811–18 Mohammed Ali overruns much of Arabian peninsula; ends first Saudi empire

1815 Java restored to Dutch by British

1817–19 Last Maratha War; Marathas lose; British rule India except Punjab, Sind, Kashmir*

1819 Singapore founded by Stamford Raffles*

1820 Peace treaty ends piracy and leads to 150 years of British supremacy in the Persian Gulf

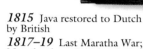

A Japanese matchlock pistol

1820–41 Minh Mang, emperor of Vietnam, reverses Gia-Long's policies and expels Christians

c.1820s Development of North Pacific whaling industry; Japanese authorities clash with ships' crews

EUROPE

1 **1800** Italian scientist Volta invents electric cell

1801–25 Reign of Tsar Alexander I of Russia

1 **1804** First oil lamp made in England, designed by Frenchman Argand

1804 Napoleon becomes Emperor of the French*

1805 Battles of Trafalgar (British naval victory) and Austerlitz (French army victory)

1806 Napoleon brings the Holy Roman Empire to an end

1807 Britain abolishes slave trade; slavery continues until 1833

1808–14 The Peninsular War in Spain

This full dress coat was worn by Britain's greatest admiral, Horatio Nelson

1 **1812** First tin cans produced in England for preserving food

1812 Napoleon reaches Moscow and is forced by partisan warfare and burning of Moscow to retreat to France*

1813 Napoleon defeated in the Battle of the Nations, Leipzig

1815 Battle of Waterloo; final defeat of Napoleon*

1815 Congress of Vienna follows defeat of Napoleon; map of Europe decided

1821–29 Greek War of Independence, against Turks

A miniature of the young Napoleon

AMERICAS

19th-century surveyors used linen measuring tapes like this one

1801 Thomas Jefferson becomes third U.S. president

1803 Louisiana Purchase; United States buys vast tract of western land from France

1804–06 Lewis and Clark explore the Louisiana Territory

1807 Portugal's John VI flees to Brazil; his son Pedro declares it independent under him in 1822

1808–09 Rebellions against Spain begin in South America

1810 Hidalgo begins revolts against Spanish rule in Mexico

Antonio José de Sucre, who defeated the Spanish at the Battle of Ayacucho in Peru in 1824

1812–14 United States at war with Britain; White House burned

1816 Bolívar defeats Spanish in Venezuela; independence confirmed in 1821

1817–18 San Martin defeats Spanish army at Chacabuco in Chile and wins independence*

1820 The Missouri Compromise maintains balance between free and slave states in the U.S.

1821 San Martin wins independence for Peru*

OCEANIA

1801–03 Matthew Flinders circumnavigates, then names, Australia

1810 Kamehameha I becomes king of all Hawaii*

Honolulu in Hawaii c.1850

1815 Russia tries to make landings in Hawaiian Islands

1819 Pomare II establishes Society Islands' first legal code

1819 Death of Kamehameha I of Hawaii; Kamehameha II, his heir, abolishes kapu system which restricted contact between men and women

1821 Protestant missionaries arrive in Cook Islands

This Tahitian drum has a shark skin membrane

1824

1825 Egyptians found the city of Khartoum in Sudan

1828 Basel mission to Ghana (then called Gold Coast), West Africa

1828 Shaka, Zulu ruler, assassinated by his half-brother Dingane who takes over as ruler of Zulu nation

1830 French invade Algeria; they gradually occupy the country

1832–47 Abd-al-Kadir leads Arab resistance to France in Algeria

This mounted antelope skull from Ghana was used as a charm

1836

1836–37 The Great Trek of Boers (Dutch farmers) away from British in South Africa; they found the Republic of Natal in 1838 and the Orange Free State in 1854*

1840 Imam Sayyid Said, ruler of Oman (1806–56), makes Zanzibar, a small island off the east African coast, his capital

1843 Britain takes over Natal from the Boers as a British colony

Trekkers at rest during the Great Trek of the South African Boers, 1836

In 1824 British troops storm a fort in Rangoon in the First Burmese War

1824–26 First Burmese War with Britain

1825–28 Persian-Russian War; Russia captures Tabriz

1825–30 Javanese revolt against Dutch

1828 Indian Hindu Raja Ram Mohan Roy founds reforming Hindu society, Brahmo Samaj

1829 Practice of suttee (widow burning) made illegal in India

1831 Mohammed Ali of Egypt seizes Syria; he rules it until 1840

1835–63 Dost Mohammed rules in Afghanistan

This wooden Japanese ornament depicts a snail on a mushroom

1837–53 Shogunate of Tokugawa Ieyoshi in Japan

1838 Nakayama Miki founds faith-healing Tenri sect in Japan

1839 Ottoman sultan Abdul Majid starts the "Tanzimat," a program of modernization

1839–42 First Afghan War with British; a British army annihilated

1839–42 Opium War in China*

1844 Cambodia becomes a Thai protectorate

1845–49 Sikh Wars with Britain; Britain annexes Punjab

1848 Accession of Nasir ud-din, ablest of the Kajar dynasty of Persia

1 **1827** Frenchman Nicéphore Niépce takes the first photograph

1827 Battle of Navarino Bay; British, French, and Russian navies destroy Turkish fleet*

1830 Russians suppress Polish revolt

1830 Revolution in France

1830–31 Kingdom of Belgium is founded

1832 First Great Reform Bill gives more men the vote in Britain

1833 Abolition of slavery in British Empire

A Russian cartridge case; the Russians supported the Greeks in their struggle for independence

1 **1840** Penny postage stamp introduced in Britain; postage stamps transform postal systems

1841 Nationalist leader Lajos Kossuth founds Hungarian liberal reform newspaper

1844 First effective Factory Act in Britain

1847–48 Civil war leaves Switzerland a federal state

1848 Publication of the *Communist Manifesto*

1848 Year of revolutions throughout Europe*

Storming of the barricades, Vienna 1848

A small South American lute called a charango; the back is made from the carapace (horny skin) of an armadillo

1825 Bolívar founds new state of Bolivia*

1828 Uruguay becomes independent

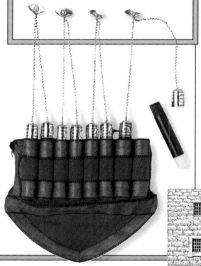

The Alamo in San Antonio where a small but gallant Texan force was defeated by a larger Mexican army in 1836

1836 Texas wins independence from Mexico; siege of the Alamo*

1838 Trail of Tears in the United States: thousands of eastern Native Americans are forced to move west; many die on the way

1846 U.S. and Britain agree to share the huge Oregon Territory

1846–48 U.S. war against Mexico; California and New Mexico ceded to United States

1848 Meeting in Seneca Falls, New York, calls for equal rights for American women

1849 California Gold Rush*

1824 Kamehameha II of Hawaii visits England and dies there

1825 Dutch annex Irian Jaya, western part of New Guinea

1830 Tahitian Protestant missionaries arrive in Fiji

1830 Malietoa Vaiinupo of Savai'i becomes king of Samoa

An Aboriginal ornament of hair strings with fur tassels

1831 Charles Darwin sets out on five-year voyage to Pacific for scientific research

1834 French Catholic missionaries arrive in Mangareva in Tuamotu Islands

1837–40 Frenchman Jules Dumont d'Urville attempts to chart coast of Antarctica; from 1838–42, Lt. Charles Wilkes leads U.S. exploring expedition to Antarctica

1840 British and Maoris in New Zealand sign Treaty of Waitangi *

1840 Kamehameha III begins constitutional monarchy in Hawaii; first written Hawaiian constitution

1842 France annexes the Marquesas Islands and makes Tahiti protectorate

1848 Hawaiian King Kamehameha III gives his people shares in the islands

A Maori whalebone club from New Zealand, with a design of birds' heads

| 600 | 800 | 1000 | | 1400 | 1600 | 1700 | 1800 | 1900 | 2000 |

South African flask
This beaded fruit flask was made from the dried, hollowed-out case of a gourd fruit and was used to store and carry liquid.

1800-1850 AFRICA

The early 19th century saw the breakaway of Egypt from Ottoman dominion and its conquest of the Sudan. West Africa was affected when many European countries abolished the slave trade. Fulani kingdoms continued to flourish in the interior. In the south, during British and Boer clashes over territorial rights and slavery, the Zulus built an empire, frustrating Boer settlements in the southeast.

1805

Mohammed Ali breaks with Ottomans

Mohammed Ali was an Albanian officer in the Turkish army. In 1805 he became Ottoman viceroy of Egypt, despite opposition from the nominal ruler of Egypt, Mahmud II, Ottoman sultan of Turkey. Six years later, opposition from the Mamluk faction in Cairo, encouraged by Mahmud II, was growing, so Mohammed Ali invited the Mamluk leaders to a ceremony and had them murdered. He was free to govern Egypt. He reformed the army, increased government revenue, and promoted education. Cotton became the chief export, and Egyptian power was extended to the Sudan.

Massacre of the Mamluks
Mohammed Ali (1769–1849) was a subtle and ruthless man. He organized a massacre of the Mamluk leaders in Cairo Citadel.

Boer leader
Andries Pretorius was one of the Great Trek leaders.

1836

Boers set out on the Great Trek

Britain formally took over Cape Colony from the Dutch in 1814. There were then 40,000 Dutch-speaking white settlers, mostly farmers, or "Boers." Many lived far from Cape Town, in the eastern Cape. These Boers were upset by British reforms, including the abolition of slavery, and in 1836–37 over 6,000 left the colony for the interior. After much hardship, the Boers formed two republics; one was the mineral-rich Transvaal. These were recognized by Britain in the 1850s.

Beyond the Cape
The Boers moved into South Africa's interior to escape British control. Britain cut off their access to the sea by annexing Natal in 1843. The trekkers then formed two republics, the Transvaal and Orange Free State.

The wagons were called jawbone wagons, because they were shaped like the lower jawbone of a horse or ox

Mass exodus
The Boer farmers and their African servants set out on their epic journey in ox wagons.

THE ZULUS

The northeast of the province of Natal is the land of the Zulus, relatives of the Nguni people in southeast Africa. From 1816 they were ruled by Shaka, originally head of the small Zulu chiefdom. Shaka's military genius enabled him to bring many of the northern Nguni into a huge new Zulu state. In 1828 Shaka's half-brothers had him murdered and one of them, Dingane, became king. When the Boers arrived in Natal at the time of the Great Trek, Dingane attacked them. The Boer leader, Retief, was killed. The Boers retaliated in 1838, defeating Dingane, who fled north. In 1879 the British defeated the Zulus, and in 1897 Zululand was incorporated into Natal, by then a self-governing British colony.

Zulu jewelry
This Zulu necklace was woven with colored beads. The Zulu king's highest award for bravery was a necklace of olive wood.

Food was stored in raised huts to keep it out of the reach of animals

The homestead
A Zulu homestead was usually located on an eastern slope near water, fuel, and grazing. The hive-shaped living huts were arranged in a circle around a central cattle pen. Each hut was made from a framework of woven saplings covered with grass thatching. The entrance was a low door, through which Zulus scrambled on hands and knees. They cooked in earthen pots over open fires and slept on grass mats which were rolled up during the day.

A protective fence surrounded the homestead

Zulu king
The great Zulu warrior king, Shaka, was renowned for his military skills. He introduced new ideas to the Zulu army, such as employment on a regular basis, with discipline, drill, troop mobility, surprise tactics, and a new type of stabbing spear which made a slurping noise like its name, *iklwa*, when drawn out of the victim's flesh. Shaka was a ruthless man and became increasingly dictatorial and cruel. His Zulu nation remained the most powerful African state in South Africa for half a century after his death.

Fires lit inside the huts provided warmth and light, but also made the atmosphere very smoky

Body protector
Warfare was an important aspect of Zulu life. The Zulu shield, an essential item of defense during bloodthirsty campaigns, was made from oxhide. First the oxhide was stretched and pinned out on the ground. It was then cut to the required shape, slits were cut in the center, and a wooden pole was threaded between the slits to make a handle. Animal tails might be tied to the top of the pole for decoration.

1800-1850 ASIA

Power struggles in Afghanistan threatened British interests in northern India. In Thailand, the new Chakri dynasty expanded trade activities with European nations. A united Vietnam emerged under Emperor Gia-Long, and the port city of Singapore was founded by Stamford Raffles. In China, illegal trading in opium by the British caused a war between China and Britain.

Procession of the Nabob of Oudh
The Nabob of Oudh, in northern India, is seen here riding with a British official at Lucknow, flanked by soldiers dressed in British East India Company uniform.

Firm footholds
In the 1800s European powers, particularly the British, French, and Dutch, began to consolidate their interests in India and Southeast Asia.

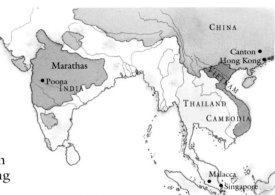

1802
Gia-Long unites Vietnam

In 1777 Nguyen Anh (1762–1820), heir to the state of Annam, a region of present-day Vietnam dominated by the Chinese, was driven into hiding following a revolt. After a struggle lasting nearly 25 years, he was crowned king of Annam in 1801. With French aid, he overran Tongking in the north, thus reuniting Vietnam. He was proclaimed emperor as Gia-Long and was soon recognized by China. He reformed the country, placed governors in Vietnam's regions, improved the central administration, and negotiated peaceful relations with Cambodia and Thailand. He tolerated Christians in Vietnam until his death in 1820, a policy reversed by his successor.

Vietnamese capital
This scene shows the main street of Hué, the capital of Gia-Long's new kingdom. His dynasty of emperors lasted for about 150 years.

1817
Last Maratha war begins in India

The Marathas, from the Deccan region of India, were Hindus opposed to Moghul Muslim dominance in the country. When the Maratha leader, Shivaji (1627–80) died, Moghul emperor Aurangzeb seized the Maratha city of Poona, but failed to crush guerrilla resistance. Maratha power grew so that by the 1720s it was a principal power in India. In 1761 Afghan leader Ahmad Shah Durrani (1747–73) won a victory over the Marathas at Panipat near Delhi, allowing the British to expand their territory. The 1770s saw the first Anglo-Maratha war, which ended in a peace lasting about 20 years. A second war erupted in 1803 ending in British victory. In 1817, the third Maratha war broke out when one Maratha chief attacked the British at Poona. The British retaliated and defeated other hostile Maratha chiefs. By 1819 the British dominated India as far north as the Indus River.

Sindhia's camp
This bazaar was in the camp of Daulat Rao Sindhia, ruler of Gwalior. Sindhia was one of the foremost Maratha chiefs fighting the British. He was defeated in the second Maratha war (1803–05).

Marquess of Hastings
As governor-general of India, he finally defeated the Marathas.

40,000 BC		10,000	5000	1000	500	AD 1	200	400

1819
Stamford Raffles founds Singapore

Singapore, an island, was first occupied by Indonesians in the 11th century. Later, merchants from China and Thailand founded trading posts there. By the 16th century, the recently created port of Malacca on the Malay Peninsula had taken over most local trading. Malacca eventually became a very prosperous outpost of the Dutch East Indies, until in 1795 it was taken over by Britain when the Netherlands were conquered by French armies. In the early 1800s, when Britain was expanding its interests in southeast Asia, a young British administrator, Stamford Raffles, was appointed lieutenant-governor of Java. There he introduced land reforms and tried to ban slavery. After the return of Java to the Dutch in 1815, Raffles was eager to establish a new port that would attract Chinese traders and international tea traders. In 1819 he arranged with the Sultan of Johore in Malaya for Singapore to be formally ceded to Britain.

Founder of Singapore
Sir Thomas Stamford Raffles (1781–1826) was an East India Company employee. His successful appeal in 1808 against the British plan to destroy Malacca gained him recognition.

Singapore port
Raffles obtained a grant of land from a Malay chief in order to found the new port city of Singapore on the site of an old 14th-century town.

1839
First opium war in China

Although Chinese governments were weak and inefficient, they continued to restrict trading with Europeans, confining them to ports like Canton and Shanghai. From about 1800, more and more Chinese were smoking the widely used addictive drug, opium. The British supplied opium grown in India, and the Chinese paid in silver, tea, and silks. The Chinese government became alarmed at the outflow of silver but was mainly concerned with the effects of opium consumption upon its people; however, it failed to control the trade effectively. In 1839 the Chinese government sent a commissioner to Canton, who burned some 20,000 chests of opium there, and then banned all British trading. This led to war between China and Britain.

Opium raid
During the opium war, the British merchant steamer *Nemesis* attacked and destroyed Chinese junks near Canton. Finally, superior British naval power forced the Chinese to sue for peace. The Treaty of Nanking in 1842 ended the war and Hong Kong was ceded to the British.

Drug addicts
This wooden model depicts two opium smokers from Shanghai. They are lying at a table, with their heads on headrests, smoking opium through long pipes. Opium dens were widespread and the Chinese government was very worried about the effects of this dangerous drug on Chinese society, but its efforts to fight the menace were foiled.

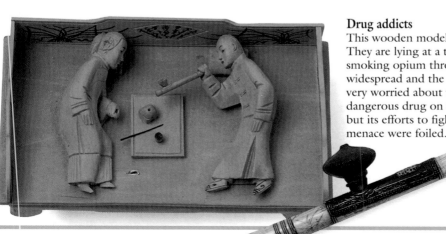

Engraved ivory opium pipe
Opium was placed in the metal bowl of the pipe, which was heated over a flame. The smoke given off was inhaled through the end of the pipe.

600	800	1000		1400	1600	1700	1800	1900	2000

1800-1850 Europe

The first 15 years of the century were dominated by the military campaigns of Napoleon I, the French emperor. The Industrial Revolution, which had begun in mid-18th-century Britain, spread to Europe, bringing wealth to the few who owned factories and mines, and hardship to many workers who labored in them. After Napoleon was defeated, Europe's rulers tried to restore order by ignoring hard-won rights. This led to calls for political and social reform, and the emergence of radical ideas throughout Europe.

French lancer's cap
A brilliant military strategist, Napoleon divided his army into semi-independent corps. They moved fast, living off what they could find or steal. In battle, they fought in massed columns, which broke enemy lines.

From soldier to emperor
Son of a lawyer, Napoleon made his name as a soldier. In 1793 he seized the port of Toulon from British occupying forces; in 1797 he drove Austria from much of northern Italy and negotiated a peace before going to Egypt. Many thought he could bring strong rule after the instability following the revolution and were glad to see him become emperor.

1804
Napoleon crowns himself emperor

In 1799 the ambitious, Corsican-born general of the French army in Egypt, Napoleon Bonaparte, returned to France. He was determined to abolish the Directoire, or committee, ruling France, and govern the country himself. Within two years, he helped throw out the Directoire and became "first," or most powerful, of three ruling consuls, then sole consul. In 1804 Napoleon declared himself Emperor of the French. From 1804 until 1812, his armies marched through Europe from Portugal in the west as far as the Russian border in the east. Some powers collapsed, others resisted; his attempt to dominate Spain was frustrated by Spanish guerrilla fighters as well as Spanish and British troops. The high point of Napoleon's success was his victory over the Austrians at Wagram in 1809, after which he married Marie Louise, the Austrian emperor's daughter.

Men and women of France
The code gave husbands total authority, taking from wives property rights granted during the Revolution.

NAPOLEONIC CODE

Napoleon was determined to reorganize France. In 1804 he introduced a new legal code, the "Code Napoleon," drafted by a committee of lawyers over which he often presided. It enshrined in law some of the principles of the French Revolution. The code protected property rights, established the equality of all people before the law, and allowed people to practice their religion freely. All 2,281 articles were published in a single book. The code was carried through Europe by French armies and remains the basis of the legal systems of many European countries today.

Family fortunes
Napoleon used his relatives to control his empire, appointing them to thrones of kingdoms he had won or marrying them to members of ruling families. Napoleon married his first wife, Josephine (above), in 1796, captivated by her beauty and wit. The marriage ended when she failed to have a son.

40,000 BC		10,000	5000	1000	500	AD 1	200	400

1812
Retreat from Moscow

In 1806, unable to overpower Britain, Napoleon I introduced a trade blockade of the British Isles, forbidding other European countries to import British goods. This "Continental system" was effective but became unpopular when it brought hardship to European countries that relied on this trade. When Russia tried to avoid it, Napoleon launched an invasion with an army of 675,000 men (the Grand Army) and in 1812 defeated Tsar Alexander I's forces at Borodino. He pressed on to Moscow, expecting to capture a wealthy city. Instead, he found the Russians had set it on fire, and the population had fled. Those who remained refused to surrender. Napoleon ordered his army to withdraw. The cold Russian winter came early and wrecked the French army in weeks. Only a few thousand soldiers remained fit to fight again.

Napoleon's empire
Napoleon aimed to dominate all Europe and to turn the continent into a market reserved for French goods. He also wanted to spread administrative reform and the Napoleonic code. In 1800, in his first major campaign as French ruler, his army crushed the Austrians at Marengo. From 1805 to 1807 Napoleon inflicted shattering defeats on the great European powers; on Austria at Austerlitz in 1805, on Prussia at Jena in 1806, and on Russia at Friedland in 1807, although he failed to defeat the British, who won the sea battle of Trafalgar in 1805. By 1809 his empire (shaded green) covered most of western Europe.

Grand army frozen
One French general wrote about the retreat: "The road is littered with men frozen to death. Men throw away their guns because they cannot hold them; both officers and soldiers think only of protecting themselves from the terrible cold." Marshal Ney (center) defended the rear against the attacks of Russian soldiers and peasants. Those in front competed to cross the Berezina River, gateway to Poland and safety.

1815
Battle of Waterloo

The French army's disastrous retreat from Russia started a general European uprising against French power. Britain's Duke of Wellington drove the French out of Spain and by 1814, had crossed into France. At Leipzig in 1813, Napoleon was defeated by the forces of Austria, Prussia, and Russia. He abdicated in 1814 and was exiled to the island of Elba. A brother of Louis XVI was welcomed as French king but became so unpopular within three months that Napoleon was able to leave Elba, gather an army, and drive him out of Paris. Napoleon ruled again for about 100 days. But near Waterloo in Belgium, on June 18, 1815, a British army under Wellington and a Prussian army under Marshal Blücher defeated him. Napoleon abdicated again and was exiled to a South Atlantic island, St. Helena, where he died in 1821.

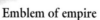

Emblem of empire
Each French regiment had a bronze eagle, symbol of their honor, and of the empire's. This eagle of the 105th regiment was captured by British soldiers at Waterloo.

Loss of life and limb
Many thousands of men died fighting on the battlefields of the Napoleonic wars. Medical aid was limited, so thousands more died from their wounds. Shattered limbs were quickly amputated. When the Earl of Uxbridge, who led the British cavalry, was hit by a cannonball at Waterloo, this saw and glove were used to amputate his badly damaged leg.

600	800	1000	1200	1400	1600	1700	1800	1900	2000

INDUSTRIAL REVOLUTION

In the early 19th century, a revolution in industry transformed life in Britain and eventually the world. It had its origins in the 16th and 17th centuries, when rich businessmen organized large numbers of workers producing textiles at home. In the mid-18th century, machines were invented that mass-produced textiles. Businessmen invested money in factories to house new machines and workforces to labor in them. Ironworks and coal mines were set up to produce raw materials to make and power machines. Gradually many industries were mechanized. Mass-produced goods were sold at low prices at home and abroad. Families moved to find jobs in the towns that grew up around mines and factories. They lived in small, crowded houses, and men, women, and children labored 12 hours or more a day, six days a week. The workers were poor, while factory owners grew rich. The need to move goods and people led to a transportation revolution: railroads were developed.

Spun thread *Fiber to be spun* *Bobbin* *Drive wheel*

Textile factory

For centuries, textile workers spun and wove thread by hand on spinning wheels and looms in their cottages. This was called the domestic system of production. Machines invented in the mid-1700s greatly increased the speed of spinning and weaving, but they were too complex for domestic workers. Businessmen set up machines in factories and employed workers to perform a single task in operating them. This was called the factory system.

Speedy spinning machines

One new textile machine was the spinning jenny, a frame with a number of spindles that spun several threads at once, although operated by one person. It was invented in England by James Hargreaves in the 1760s and was soon followed in 1769 by Richard Arkwright's water frame (above). Driven by water power, thread was quickly drawn out and spun around several bobbins. Ten years later, Samuel Crompton introduced his spinning "mule," worked by steam or water power, which could spin up to 1,000 threads at a time.

Rage against the machines

Mill and factory owners grew wealthy even in times of economic slump, when workers' wages fell. Some workers rioted. The earliest riot was started by an apprentice, Ned Ludd, in Nottingham in 1812, and thereafter rioters were called Luddites. They attacked the new machines which they felt were the cause of their miseries.

Little laborers

In the early years of the Industrial Revolution, employers used child labor. Children worked for up to 16 hours a day doing hard jobs such as pulling heavy coal wagons along tracks in mines.

George Stephenson's *Rocket*

In the 1760s, Scottish inventor James Watt devised a condensing steam engine, more efficient than earlier steam engines. At first, these engines were used in factories to operate mills, cranes, and other machines. Richard Trevithick in 1803 and George Stephenson in 1814 used steam engines in locomotives to pull wagons along tracks. Stephenson then adapted the locomotive to pull carriages with passengers. By 1855 thousands of miles of railway covered Britain, and the great age of railway travel had begun.

World's first iron bridge

For thousands of years iron was extracted from iron ore by heating the ore with charcoal. This required large supplies of timber, burned to obtain the charcoal. In the early 18th century, the English ironmaker Abraham Darby and his son discovered how to make iron using coal, which was more easily obtained than wood. This led to rapid growth in the production of iron to make tools and machinery. Darby's grandson constructed the first iron bridge, over the Severn River in western Britain.

Steel-making factory

The hardened type of iron, known as steel, was invented more than 2,000 years ago, but the process of making it was costly. In the 1850s, an English engineer, Henry Bessemer, introduced a cheap way to make steel. The process had many industrial applications, as steel was longer-lasting than iron. Its use spread rapidly throughout Europe.

Railroad trains transported raw materials and fuel, such as coal, to and from the factory

Workers lived in overcrowded, small houses

Barges on canals carried goods between towns

New towns

Iron-making and steam power needed readily accessible coal supplies. New industries in Britain were set up near coal seams, mainly in South Wales, central Scotland, and northern England. People in search of jobs moved from rural areas to housing estates built close to mines and factories. Small market towns grew quickly into great factory-dominated cities, such as Birmingham, Liverpool, and Manchester.

Steaming across the sea

In the late 18th century, shipbuilders learned to use steam engines to propel ships. Probably the first successful steamship was the *Charlotte Dundas*, launched in 1801, used as a tugboat in Scotland. By the 1840s hulls were made of iron, which led to the development of fast, large, ocean-going liners. Large cargoes were quickly carried from port to port and were vital to expanding worldwide trade routes. Raw materials were imported from colonies of the British Empire, which were a lucrative market for finished goods.

| 600 | 800 | 1000 | 1200 | 1400 | 1600 | 1700 | 1800 | 1900 | 2000 |

1827

Turkish fleet smashed at Navarino

By the 1800s the Greeks had been under Ottoman Turkish rule for nearly 400 years. For the last half-century, they had prospered through expanding trade, especially with Russia, and they wanted freedom. Encouraged by the success of the French Revolution, a secret society was formed to work for independence. In 1821 two revolts broke out. The first failed but the second was more successful, and by 1824 the Ottoman sultan could not suppress it. He appealed to his viceroy Mohammed Ali in Egypt for help. Ali sent an army to Greece, which won some victories. This alarmed the nations of Europe. In 1826 Britain and Russia agreed to threaten war against the Turks. France joined them in 1827. Together, they destroyed the Turkish-Egyptian fleet in 1827 at Navarino Bay. The next year Russia declared war on Turkey and won several victories. In 1829 the Treaty of Adrianople ended the war. The victorious powers decided to grant Greece independence under a king approved by them. In 1832 the crown was offered to Prince Otto of Bavaria.

European power triumphant
Britain, Russia, and France began by trying to stop Turkish reinforcements getting through to Greece. At Navarino harbor in 1827, a combined British, French, and Russian naval force under Admiral Codrington annihilated the Turkish and Egyptian fleet. This was the beginning of the end for Turkey's once-vast European empire: within a century, only Istanbul would remain.

Elegant but deadly
This Turkish miquelet musket is inlaid with brass and mother of pearl and has silver brackets around the barrel. The Turks were too strong for the Greek rebels alone but could not resist the combined power of Britain, France, and Russia.

Romantic hero
George Gordon, Lord Byron, was one of England's leading poets. He sympathized with radical causes and offered to join the Greek rebels in 1823. He wrote and campaigned to raise support for them in the rest of Europe, sailed to Greece, and died there of malaria in 1824. In Greece, and among liberals throughout Europe, he became revered as a symbol of the romantic life and the love of freedom.

COMMUNISM

The huge profits made by factory and mill owners who led the Industrial Revolution contrasted with the difficult working conditions and low wages of workers who manufactured the goods. Throughout Europe, people demanded political and social reform. Chief among these was German philosopher, Karl Marx (1818–83). Marx believed that economic forces shape all history. At any time, one group or class of people controls the production of goods. Marx called factory and mill owners the capitalist class. Marx called the industrial workers – who did the work but got little reward – the proletariat class. He believed that the capitalists were responsible for bad working conditions, and that a struggle would occur between them and the workers. He predicted that workers all over the world would revolt against capitalists and take power. Then they would build a classless society based on common ownership of property and production, called a communist society. Marx set out his ideas in the *Communist Manifesto*, published in 1848 by himself and Friedrich Engels (1820–95).

Karl Marx
Marx's radical views led to him being exiled from Germany by the Prussian government. From 1849, he lived in England, devoting his time to writing.

New movement
Marx helped set up an International Working Men's Association, known as the First International, to spread his views. His name is signed on this card as the German secretary.

1848
The Year of Revolutions

During 1848 there were revolutions in many European countries. Although they occurred independently, they had sprung from problems common to all European countries, such as bad harvests and famines, and discontent and unemployment in towns made worse by trade recession. Alongside this were conflicts between rising movements for constitutional and social reform stimulated by writers, poets, and philosophers and a conservative reaction among national leaders such as Austria's Metternich and France's Guizot. Among the countries which had revolutions at this time were France, Austria, Hungary, many German and Italian states, Ireland, Switzerland, and Denmark. By the end of 1849, all the revolts had been quashed, but the victorious governments had been forced to listen to the voice of the people and to realize the importance of nationalist movements.

France at the forefront
Reformers all over Europe took heart from France's successful revolution in February. The middle classes joined the workers to overthrow Louis Philippe, an uninspiring king who had tried to keep the rich powerful. Napoleon I's nephew, Louis Napoleon, was elected president in 1848 and in 1852 became emperor.

Brief hope burns in Italy
The Italian revolutions began with a revolt in Palermo, Sicily, in January. Fuelled by the desire for a united Italy, the spirit of rebellion spread northward. King Charles Albert of Sardinia-Piedmont led Italian forces which challenged Austrian control of northern Italy. After initial Italian successes, however, the Austrians won. A revolt in Rome forced the Pope into exile, but he was restored by French troops in July 1849.

Radical dreams on the Danube
In March Lajos Kossuth, Hungarian revolutionary writer and lawyer, claimed Hungarian independence from Austria and started a revolution. His rebel Hungarians raised an army 100,000 strong. The Austrians needed a year and Russian help to crush them. Nationalist feeling inspired other revolutions in the Austrian empire. Czechs, Austrian democrats, Romanians, Poles, and Italians also rebelled against imperial domination. Because of their nationalism, they did not unite and the emperor's armies defeated them one by one.

Rebels feel Prussian iron
A successful rising in Prussia in March was followed by a wave of revolts throughout Germany. The rebels were motivated by a mixture of liberalism and nationalism. Their desire for German unification led to an assembly at Frankfurt which began to plan a united Germany. But riots in Berlin in October led King Frederick William to unleash the Prussian army, which crushed the reformers. The Frankfurt assembly soon dissolved.

YEAR OF REVOLUTIONS

February King Louis Philippe of France abdicates; Second Republic is established

February-March After risings in Sicily and Naples (southern Italy) some Italian states grant liberal constitutions

March Revolution in Hungary led by Lajos Kossuth, claiming independence from Austria

March Uprising in Vienna; Austrian Chancellor Metternich resigns and flees to London

April Large demonstration in London by Chartist protesters urging political reforms; it disperses quietly

July A rising by the Young Ireland movement in Tipperary, Ireland, is overpowered

| 600 | 800 | 1000 | 1200 | 1400 | 1600 | 1700 | 1800 | 1900 | 2000 |

1800-1850 AMERICAS

E ncouraged by the American and French revolutions, the Spanish colonies in the Americas began to fight for independence, especially after Spain's King Ferdinand VIII was replaced by Joseph Bonaparte, Napoleon's brother, in 1808. Under the leadership of Simón Bolívar and other patriots, independence was achieved throughout Central and South America by 1830. Brazil, a Portuguese colony, won independence in 1825. In North America, the United States and Britain went to war (1812–15) over several issues. Neither side won a clear victory, but the war confirmed American independence. British Canada, which resisted U.S. invasions during the War of 1812, was organized as a single dominion in 1840, following a rebellion by French-speaking Canadians in 1837–38.

Peruvian soldier
This soldier carries his boots tucked into his poncho, which is tied round his waist in typical Peruvian style. His female attendant follows behind, laden down with luggage.

☐ Spanish colonies (with independence dates)

☐ Dutch, French, and British colonies

Spanish rule in South America
In 1800, large areas of South America were ruled over by Spain. By 1830, Spain no longer controlled any part of the American continent.

1817

The Battle of Chacabuco

The Spanish captain-general of Chile was deposed in 1810, and a junta, or political committee, took power in the name of the Spanish king, Ferdinand VII. It was soon overthrown by José Miguel de Carrera, a republican leader. Carrera governed badly, and in 1814 was replaced by another republican, Bernardo O'Higgins, who was half Irish, half Chilean. The quarrel weakened the republican movement and royalist troops soon reasserted Spanish authority. Then, in January 1817, José de San Martin, one of the two greatest of the South American independence champions (the other was Simón Bolívar), together with O'Higgins as his second-in-command, brought an army of 5,000 men across the high Andes Mountains, trekking over mountain passes more than 2 miles (3 km) above sea level. They took the Spanish completely by surprise in February, when they won a decisive victory over the royalist army at Chacabuco, near Santiago. A second victory at Maipu enabled Chile to declare independence in 1818. O'Higgins became its first dictator, and governed for five years. In 1823 he was deposed and retired.

Street party
Joyful Chileans celebrated their independence by dancing beneath the flag of their newly liberated country.

Bernardo O'Higgins
Son of Ambrosio O'Higgins, an Irishman who became first governor of Chile, Bernardo in his turn was hailed as the hero of Chilean independence.

1821
San Martin wins independence for Peru

After leading armies in Argentina's fight for independence, San Martin devised a plan to liberate Peru, the center of Spanish authority in South America. He built up a Chilean battle fleet, and in 1820 organized a combined sea-and-land invasion. As he marched on the capital, Lima, he gained the people's support and tried to negotiate with the Spanish viceroy to surrender without more fighting. When his troops entered Lima in 1821, the viceroy did withdraw. San Martin became Protector of Peru and declared the colony independent. He retired a year later, as he was unwilling to take part in disagreements among the republican leaders.

General José de San Martin
Born in Argentina in 1778, San Martin was taken to Spain to train for a military career. He returned home when he heard about the fight for independence.

1825
Bolívar creates the new state of Bolivia

Simón Bolívar was born in Venezuela in 1783. He traveled around Europe when the effects of the French Revolution were spreading and became inspired to fight for independence for all South America. He became leader of the Venezuelan republicans in 1812. He led a revolt in 1816 and established Venezuela's independence, although it was not recognized by Spain. In 1819 Bolívar carried the struggle into Colombia, defeated the Spanish, and became its first president. He returned to Venezuela, defeated the Spanish at Carabobo in 1821, and captured Caracas. This confirmed Venezuela's independence. He then went south to help other colonies in revolt. When San Martin resigned as Protector of Peru in 1822, the republicans asked Bolívar to help expel the remaining Spanish forces from the country. This he did, and in 1824 was made dictator. He moved to Upper Peru the following year and founded a republic, later named Bolivia after him.

The Liberator
Simón Bolívar (1783–1830) was a man of great talent. He dreamed of uniting all Spain's American colonies in a political federation, but his ambitions were doomed to failure.

Carabobo
In 1821, Bolívar's army won a great victory for Venezuela on the plains of Carabobo near Valencia.

THE MONROE DOCTRINE

James Monroe (1758–1831), fifth president of the United States, declared in a message to Congress in 1823 that the two American continents, North and South America, were no longer to be considered as regions in which Europeans could attempt to found colonies. The doctrine has since come to mean that the United States regards any outside interference in South America as a situation which could potentially lead to war.

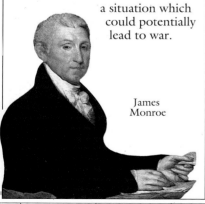
James Monroe

1836
The Siege of the Alamo

After winning independence from Spain in 1821, Mexico invited Americans to settle in its sparsely populated northern territory, Texas. About 25,000 Americans moved to Texas over the next 15 years. They were soon in conflict with the Mexican government, especially over slavery, which was outlawed in Mexico. In 1835, the Texans rebelled, and Mexican dictator Antonio de Santa Anna led an army to crush them. In February 1836, about 200 Texans took refuge in the Alamo, a fortified mission church in San Antonio. After a two-week siege, the Alamo fell to Santa Anna; all the defenders were killed. In April, however, the Texan Army, led by Sam Houston, defeated Santa Anna at the Battle of San Jacinto. Texas became an independent republic, with Houston as president. Texas wanted annexation to the United States, supported by the many Americans who championed "Manifest Destiny" – the idea that the U.S. should expand across the continent to the Pacific. Shortly after Texas was annexed in 1845, the U.S. and Mexico went to war; the conflict ended with Mexico's defeat in 1848.

Bowie knife
Inventor (with his brother Rezin) of the famous Bowie knife, James Bowie (c.1796–1836) became a colonel in the Texan Army and died at the Alamo.

A Texan rebel
Legendary Tennessee frontiersman Davy Crockett (1786–1836) was another famous figure who lost his life defending the Alamo.

"Remember the Alamo!"
The Alamo was besieged by a Mexican force of 4,000 men, who wiped out the Texan defenders. The Texan army retaliated at San Jacinto, where their rallying cry was "Remember the Alamo!"

1849
The California Gold Rush

Many Americans wanted to acquire the Mexican province of California. In 1846, American settlers in California declared independence; soon afterward, U.S. forces arrived to take control. In February 1848, Mexico ceded its northern territories – including California and New Mexico – to the U.S. in the Treaty of Guadelupe Hidalgo, which ended the Mexican-U.S. War. Gold was discovered in California only days before the treaty was signed, and by 1849 thousands of fortune-seekers were arriving. The "Gold Rush" created an urgent need for civil government, so California was admitted to the Union as the 31st state in 1850.

Panning for gold
Gold was first found on land owned by John Sutter, a former officer in the Swiss army. Prospectors quickly overran his vast property, and Sutter, bankrupt, eventually moved to Pennsylvania. Most gold hunters relied on panning – swirling earth from a stream bed in a pan to separate flakes of gold from gravel and sand.

San Francisco
The Gold Rush turned San Francisco from a small seaside town to a thriving port almost overnight. With the arrival of newcomers from all over the world, the city took on a cosmopolitan air.

40,000 BC		10,000	5000	1000	500	AD 1	200	400

1800-1850 OCEANIA

The 19th century saw a steady increase in European interference in the island kingdoms, with Britain, Germany, and France all annexing or forming protectorates over some of them. Hawaii became united under a new dynasty. New Zealand, inhabited by the Maoris for many centuries, began to be settled by British colonists, who later went back on their agreements to respect the Maori people.

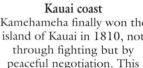

Feathered scepter
This ceremonial feathered scepter, called a *kahili*, was found in the Hawaiian Islands.

Ruler of Hawaii
Kamehameha I (c.1758–1819) was an innovative and ambitious ruler. He came to be known as Kamehameha the Great.

KAMEHAMEHA

1810
Kamehameha I unites all Hawaii

For centuries the Hawaiian Islands were ruled separately by many chiefs. Kamehameha I, the son of a chief, was born on the island of Hawaii. As a young man in the 1770s, he was employed by his uncle, King Kalaniopu'u, as negotiator with Captain James Cook. Kamehameha saw the advantages of uniting the islands under his rule, and in the early 1790s invaded Maui, one of the largest. By 1795 he had overrun most of the islands. There was still some resistance from the remainder, especially from the island of Kauai, which he finally won in 1810. This made him ruler of all the Hawaiian Islands. From then on, Kamehameha pursued a policy of peace, forming councils of local chiefs whom he consulted on a regular basis. He created a government trade monopoly in sandalwood, which was much in demand in other countries. He also encouraged other nations to visit the islands and supported the development of local industries. He died in 1819.

Kauai coast
Kamehameha finally won the island of Kauai in 1810, not through fighting but by peaceful negotiation. This gave him control of all the Hawaiian Islands.

1840
The Treaty of Waitangi

European traders arrived in New Zealand in the 1790s. The Maoris, who had inhabited the country for centuries, took little notice of them, but by 1800 traded with them. In 1840 the first British colonists settled in New Zealand and founded the town of Wellington on land bought from the Maoris. Britain proclaimed sovereignty over New Zealand and sent out a governor, Captain William Hobson. Hobson came to an agreement with Maori chiefs, guaranteeing them land rights and offering them British citizenship. This, the Treaty of Waitangi, was not met in full. Violations of Maori rights led to a major war (1843–48).

The signing of the treaty
On February 6, 1840, 46 Maori chiefs signed the Treaty of Waitangi, guaranteeing them land rights and giving them British citizenship. Their rights were not protected.

| 600 | 800 | 1000 | 1200 | 1400 | 1600 | 1700 | 1800 | 1900 | 2000 |

CONVICTS IN AUSTRALIA

Among the earliest foreigners to settle Australia were convicts transported from Britain to relieve overcrowding in prisons. The British government believed that their arrival would stop other nations claiming the territory. The first expedition, under Captain Arthur Phillip, sailed from Britain in 1787 with 759 convicts. Eight months later, in 1788, the fleet arrived in Botany Bay. There were prisoners of both sexes. Some had committed serious crimes, but many were petty criminals, forced into crime by hunger. Life in the new settlements was hard, and many convicts fell sick. Drunkenness and stealing were rife. When their sentences expired, many ex-convicts stayed in Australia and obtained land grants. Before the transportation of prisoners ended in 1868, 137,000 men and 25,000 women had been brought to Australia.

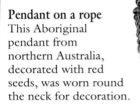

Pendant on a rope
This Aboriginal pendant from northern Australia, decorated with red seeds, was worn round the neck for decoration.

Hard labor gang
Convicts were forced to work extremely hard as a punishment for their crimes. Free farmers and pastoralists were assigned convict laborers, like these ones from Tasmania, whom they were free to treat well or badly.

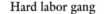

Culture clash
The convicts and settlers clashed with the Aboriginals living in Australia and waged war against them. Because they had superior weapons, the settlers invariably won, and victory was followed by wholesale massacre of Aboriginal men, women, and children. By 1821, the Aboriginal population had been reduced by about half, and those that survived were scattered.

Prisoners walked 30 miles (50 km) each day carrying 56 lb (25 kg) of wooden tiles

Whaling
When convict fleets sighted whales on Australia's southeast coast, whalers from Britain and America quickly took advantage of the situation. Their slaughter of the peaceful animals brought huge profits to many of the new settlements. Soon the whalers living in Australia greatly outnumbered the convicts.

Compassionate captain
When Captain Arthur Phillip (1738–1814) arrived in Australia in 1788, he founded a penal colony at Port Jackson. His kind attitude toward the Aboriginals ensured the colony's survival.

40,000 BC	10,000	1000	AD 1	400	800	1200	1600	1800	2000

CHAPTER 17

1850 – 1900

THE RISE
OF NATIONALISM

An Asante drum

1850-1900
THE WORLD

T HE SECOND HALF of the 19th century sees a great rise in nationalism – a belief in the power and importance of one's own country – as an important political force. Italy and Germany emerge as single nations, while the peoples of southeastern Europe begin to achieve independence from the Ottoman empire. France and Britain, rulers of vast worldwide Empires, remain the most important industrial and economic powers in the world, but their position is challenged first by the United States and then, in the closing years of the century, by Germany.

International empires

The need for European nations to establish colonies to provide raw materials for their industries and markets for their finished goods reaches its peak in this period. Between them, the European powers carve up almost all of Africa, southeast Asia, and the islands of Oceania. India becomes part of the British Empire. Japan increases its contacts with other countries and modernizes its economy and government. After enduring a costly civil war, the United States becomes a major economic power and even establishes colonies of its own. Amid the nationalism and imperialism of the period, there are also reforms. Russia ends serfdom, the United States and Brazil abolish slavery, and New Zealand is the first country in the world to give women the vote.

NORTH AMERICA

1860s Increasing European settlement threatens Native Americans

CANADA

1861–65 American Civil War: northern and southern states fight over slavery and state rights

MEXICO

ATLANTIC OCEAN

Andes

SOUTH AMERICA

BRAZIL

PACIFIC OCEAN

URUGUAY

ARGENTINA

1865–70 Paraguay attacks neighboring countries and is almost annihilated

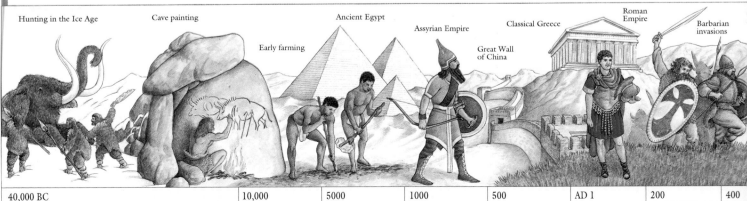

Hunting in the Ice Age

Cave painting

Early farming

Ancient Egypt

Assyrian Empire

Great Wall of China

Classical Greece

Roman Empire

Barbarian invasions

| 40,000 BC | | 10,000 | 5000 | 1000 | 500 | AD 1 | 200 | 400 |

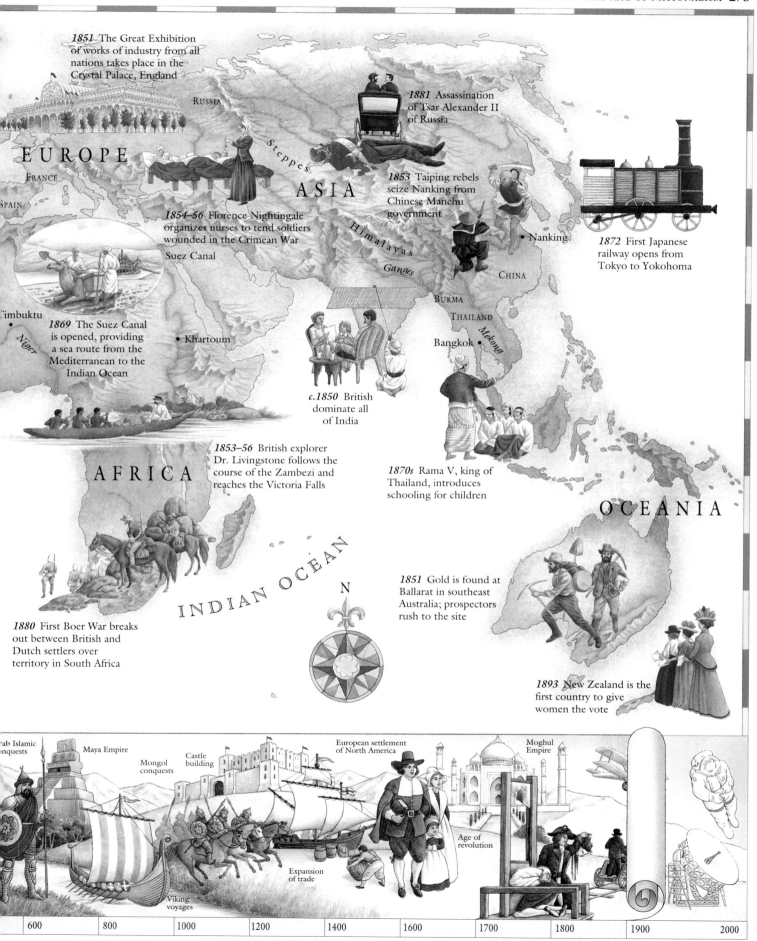

1851 The Great Exhibition of works of industry from all nations takes place in the Crystal Palace, England

RUSSIA

1881 Assassination of Tsar Alexander II of Russia

EUROPE

Steppes

ASIA

FRANCE

1853 Taiping rebels seize Nanking from Chinese Manchu government

SPAIN

1854–56 Florence Nightingale organizes nurses to tend soldiers wounded in the Crimean War

Himalayas

Suez Canal

Ganges

Nanking

CHINA

BURMA

1872 First Japanese railway opens from Tokyo to Yokohoma

Timbuktu

1869 The Suez Canal is opened, providing a sea route from the Mediterranean to the Indian Ocean

Niger

THAILAND

• Khartoum

Mekong

Bangkok •

c.1850 British dominate all of India

AFRICA

1853–56 British explorer Dr. Livingstone follows the course of the Zambezi and reaches the Victoria Falls

1870s Rama V, king of Thailand, introduces schooling for children

OCEANIA

INDIAN OCEAN

N

1851 Gold is found at Ballarat in southeast Australia; prospectors rush to the site

1880 First Boer War breaks out between British and Dutch settlers over territory in South Africa

1893 New Zealand is the first country to give women the vote

Arab Islamic conquests

Maya Empire

Mongol conquests

Castle building

European settlement of North America

Moghul Empire

Expansion of trade

Age of revolution

Viking voyages

| 600 | 800 | 1000 | 1200 | 1400 | 1600 | 1700 | 1800 | 1900 | 2000 |

1850

1862

The Victoria Falls, also called "Mhosi oa Tunya" (The Smoke That Thunders)

AFRICA

1852 Tukolor leader al-Hajj 'Umar launches jihad along Senegal and upper Niger Rivers to establish Islamic state

1852 In South Africa, Britain recognizes Transvaal's independence

1853–56 Dr. David Livingstone crosses Africa; follows course of Zambezi River, reaches Victoria Falls

1855–68 Reign of Emperor Theodore of Ethiopia

1863 Al-Hajj 'Umar takes Timbuktu*

1865–68 Wars between Orange Free State and Moshweshwe's Basuto people in South Africa

1867 Diamonds discovered at Kimberley in South Africa

1869 Suez Canal opened

1872 Cape Colony in South Africa granted self-government by Britain

1873–74 War between Asante kingdom and Britain

This Asante drum was taken from the palace of King Prempeh in Ghana

ASIA

This Persian lacquer pen case depicts lovers in a garden

1850–64 Taiping rebellion in China; Nanking falls in 1853*

1851–68 Rama IV rules Thailand

1852 Nasir-ud-Din (1848–96) takes personal power in Persia; major reforms of administration by Vizier Mirza Taki

1853–78 Mindon Min reigns in Burma; able, modernizing king

1854 Treaty of Kanagawa; United States opens Japan to trade

1857–58 Indian Mutiny shakes British rule in India; East India Company abolished by India Act of 1858

1860 In China, British and French forces loot and burn down the emperor's summer palace on the outskirts of Beijing

1862 French begin to occupy Indochina (southeast Asia)

1865–70 King Kojong persecutes Christians in Korea; reform of traditional institutions

1868–1910 Reign of Rama V, founder of modern Thailand*

1868–1912 Meiji period in Japan: great leap forward in industrialization; 1868, capital moves to Edo (renamed Tokyo), shogunate abolished; 1875–88, civil legal code drawn up*

1872 First Japanese railway opens (Tokyo to Yokohoma)

A Chinese rabbit, carved out of the stone known as tiger's eye

EUROPE

1851 The Great Exhibition in England

1852 Louis Napoleon becomes Emperor Napoleon III of the French*

1853–56 Crimean War: Russia fights Turkey, Britain, France, and Sardinia*

1860 Italian parliament meets in Turin; Garibaldi takes southern Italy; most of Italy unified*

1861 Tsar Alexander II abolishes serfdom in Russia

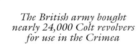

The British army bought nearly 24,000 Colt revolvers for use in the Crimea

1862–90 Career of Bismarck as chief minister of Germany

1863–64 Poles rebel against Russian rule

1866 Prussia defeats Austria at Sadowa in Seven Weeks War

1867 Disraeli introduces Second Reform Bill in Britain*

1868–74 Gladstone is British prime minister for first time

1870–71 Franco-Prussian War; Napoleon III abdicates, Third Republic established in France (to 1940)

1871 Unification of Germany: Prussian king William I becomes emperor of Germany*

A French military cap, called a kepi

AMERICAS

A Union officer's dress hat from the American Civil War

1850 Australian Colonies Government Act transfers some powers from Britain to the four major Australian colonies; they achieve self-government by 1856

1851 Gold found in southeastern Australia

1853 France annexes New Caledonia

1854 Eureka stockade; brief miners' revolt at Ballarat*

1860 R. O. Burke and W. J. Wills cross Australia from south to north

1860–70 Second Maori War in New Zealand

1861 Gold discovered in Otago, New Zealand

1850 Compromise in U.S. Congress over expansion of slavery fails to resolve growing tension between North and South

1850–89 Pedro II's reign sees great national progress in Brazil*

1856 Antislavery Republican Party formed in United States

1858–61 Benito Juarez becomes Mexican president*

1859 John Brown tries to start slave revolt, alarms whites in southern United States

1861 Southern states secede to form Confederate States of America

1861–65 Civil war in United States*

1862 U.S. land given to European immigrants to farm*

1862–90 Last wars against Native Americans in western United States

1863–67 French invade Mexico and set up Austrian archduke Maximilian as emperor of Mexico

1865 Thirteenth Amendment to U.S. Constitution outlaws slavery

1867–77 Radical Republicans in U.S. Congress impose harsh reconstruction policies on the South, causing white backlash

1867 Britain makes Canada a dominion*

1869 U.S. Transcontinental Railroad completed

1870–88 Antonio Guzman rules Venezuela; major reforms

Aboriginal kangaroo tooth necklace from Queensland, northeastern Australia

This tomahawk pipe is said to have been made by the great Apache leader Geronimo while in exile in Florida after his final defeat

OCEANIA

1864 First French convicts sent to New Caledonia

1865 First Chinese laborers arrive in Hawaii

1865 New Zealand seat of government transferred from Auckland to Wellington

1869 Germany acquires land in Caroline Islands

1870s Gold Rush in New Caledonia

1871 Cakobau, most important leader of Bau, one of the Fiji Islands, establishes a national monarchy in Fiji

This bamboo nose flute comes from Fiji; it has a blowhole at each end and three fingerholes; players blow with one nostril, blocking the other

1874

1874 Beginnings of Mande state in old Mali under Samori Turé*

1879 Zulu war with British; British defeated at Isandlwana but victorious at Ulundi

c.1880 Beginning of the European "Scramble for Africa"

1880–81 First Boer War; Transvaal defeats Britain

1885 Conference in Berlin on Scramble for Africa

1885 In Sudan, Muslim leader, the Mahdi, takes Khartoum from Egypt; General Gordon killed*

English soldier's belt and bullet pouch, found among Zulu king Cetshwayo's possessions after the ZuluWar of 1879

The seated, marble figure of a Burmese Buddha

1876 Queen Victoria of Britain is proclaimed Empress of India

1876 Japanese pressure forces Korea to open ports to trade

1876–78 Famine in the Deccan, southern India; over five million die

1877 Satsuma rebellion in Japan: last stand of traditional samurai class is defeated

1878–79 Second Afghan War: British invade Afghanistan to counter Russian influence

1884 Dowager Empress Cixi fires Grand Council of China

1885 Foundation of Indian National Congress; campaign for home rule*

1885–86 Third Burmese War; Britain annexes Burma

1874–80 Disraeli's second and last government in Britain

1876 Turks put down Bulgarian rising with great cruelty

1878 Congress of Berlin ends Russo-Turkish War (1877–78); freedom for some Balkan countries

1881 Assassination of Tsar Alexander II of Russia

1882 Triple Alliance between Germany, Austria, and Italy

[1] 1885 German Karl Benz is first to sell automobiles

The pioneers of the Californian Gold Rush needed tough clothes, so Oscar Levi Strauss invented blue jeans

Benjamin Disraeli, British politician and novelist

[1] 1876 In United States, Alexander Bell invents telephone

[1] 1877 U.S. inventor Thomas Edison invents the record-player

1876–1911 Rule of President Diaz of Mexico: period of great expansion

1879–84 The War of the Pacific between Chile, Peru, and Bolivia

[1] 1883 Edison invents the light bulb

1885 Canadian Pacific Railway opens

1874 Prince David Kalakaua becomes ruler of Hawaii (to 1891)

1878 New Caledonian peoples rebel against French

1879 Britain establishes a naval station in Samoa

1880 Australia's most famous bushranger, Ned Kelly, captured by the police, is hanged

1880 France annexes Tahiti as a colony

1885–86 Goldfields opened up in Papua New Guinea

A dog's tooth necklace from Papua New Guinea; the teeth were used as money

1886

1886 Gold found in Transvaal

1894 French set up protectorate in Dahomey (Benin), West Africa

1895–96 Jameson Raid into Transvaal*

1896 France takes Madagascar

1896 Ethiopian ruler Menelik crushes Italian army at Adowa

1897 Slavery banned in Zanzibar

1899–1902 Second Boer War in South Africa

Haile Selassie's father, Ras Makonnen, helped defeat an Italian invasion

Japanese decorative art here uses lacquered wood, coral, and shell

1887 Bulgaria elects Ferdinand of Coburg king; it becomes leading Balkan state*

1888–1918 Kaiser (Emperor) William II reigns in Germany

1891–94 Franco-Russian agreement

[1] 1895 In France, the Lumière brothers invent the film projector

1895 Assassination of Bulgarian prime minister Stambuloff

[1] 1895 Marconi invents wireless telegraphy, or radio

1889 New Meiji constitution for Japan; first general election in 1890

1894–95 War between Japan and China; Japanese win, occupy Korea

1896 British persuade Malay states to form federation

1898 In China Dowager Empress Cixi crushes attempts at reform

1899 France proclaims protectorate in Laos, southeast Asia

An early film projector; the Lumière brothers used a powerful lamp behind the camera to project films

Emperor Pedro II ruled Brazil from 1840 to 1889

1886 American Federation of Labor (AFL) established

1888 Slaves freed in Brazil

1889 First Pan-American Conference held at Washington

1889 Pedro II deposed by army revolt; Brazil becomes a republic

1891 Civil war in Chile

1898 Spanish-American War; Spain gives Cuba independence, United States takes Puerto Rico, Guam, and Philippines as colonies

1889 Malietoa Laupepa, king of Samoa, is recognized by Britain, United States, and Germany, "joint supervisors" of Samoa

1893 Votes for women introduced in New Zealand*

1897 New Zealand introduces eight-hour working day and old age pensions in 1898

1898 United States annexes Hawaii

1899 Australian and New Zealand troops sent to Boer War

Richard John Seddon was prime minister of New Zealand, 1893–1906; his government gave women the vote and began one of the world's earliest welfare states

Powerful Muslim rulers in West Africa expanded their territories and, during the course of their campaigns, clashed with French and British troops in the area. In southern Africa, British and Boers came into conflict as mineral discoveries gave the region great new economic value. Europeans from many countries carved out African empires in a process which came to be known as the Scramble for Africa, until by the end of the 19th century almost the whole of the continent was controlled by European powers.

Zimbabwean snuffbox
This container was used to store tobacco, or snuff, which acted as a stimulant when inhaled through the nostrils.

1863

Al-Hajj 'Umar takes Timbuktu

Al-Hajj 'Umar (1795–1864) was a learned Muslim from Futa Toro, on the middle Senegal River. In Futa Jalon, near the sources of the Niger, he joined the Tijaniyya brotherhood and then set out on pilgrimage to Mecca: he was away for many years. On his way home, in Egypt he observed the reforms of Mohammed Ali in the face of European pressures. In Sokoto, from 1821 to 1837, he studied the effects of the recent Fulani jihad, or holy war. By 1840 he was back in Futa Jalon, determined to create an Islamic state of his own. With guns from French traders, he conquered local rulers between the upper Niger and Senegal. He then clashed with the French in the Senegal valley, and in 1862 defeated the Hamdallahi caliphate in nearby Masina. 'Umar's troops invaded Timbuktu, but there was widespread resistance, and in 1864 'Umar was killed. His son and successor, Ahmadu, struggled with great difficulty to keep the empire together.

View of Timbuktu
Timbuktu had been a town of much commercial and intellectual activity during the 15th and 16th centuries, with many Islamic scholars living there. It declined thereafter, and bad administration laid the city open to attacks. 'Umar and his followers invaded Timbuktu in 1863.

Distinguished warrior
Achieving military distinction early in life in the service of a local ruler, Samori Turé (c.1830–1900) went on to create his own army. He conducted military campaigns with great energy and built a vast empire, which lasted over 20 years. He later died in exile.

1874

Samori Turé creates trading empire

In the late 1860s, Samori Turé, a military adventurer from Konyan, in present-day Guinea, built a Mande empire in the upper Niger region. By 1874 it was based on the trade of gold and ivory for guns from the coast. By 1885 Samori's power extended from Sierra Leone in the west to Bamako in the east. This posed a challenge to the French military advance, and from 1886 Samori also faced internal unrest provoked by his plans for an Islamic state. He commanded a large army and obtained guns from Sierra Leone, but in 1892 the French forced him to move eastwards, into the northern Ivory Coast. Further east, his way was blocked by British troops. In 1898 Samori was captured by the French and exiled to Gabon, where he died in 1900.

Omdurman water carrier
The Sudan was largely desert country. This water bottle would have been vital for hot journeys across the dry terrain.

1885
General Gordon dies at Khartoum

The Sudan in North Africa, through which much of the Nile River flows, was conquered in the early 1820s by Mohammed Ali of Egypt. Mohammed Ali built a capital at Khartoum in 1825. In 1874 his grandson, Khedive Ismail, appointed Englishman Charles George Gordon (1833–85) administrator of the southern Sudan; in 1877–79 Gordon was governor-general. Gordon did much to reduce slavery. By 1882 the British controlled Egypt. In the same year, a Sudanese religious leader, who called himself the "Mahdi" (messiah), led a rebellion against Egyptian occupation of the Sudan. The British government, realizing that the Egyptian occupying forces would not be able to withstand the rebellion, sent Gordon to get the Egyptian troops out of the Sudan. Soon after he entered Khartoum, the Mahdi laid siege to the city. Khartoum fell at the end of January 1885 and Gordon was killed. His death was avenged by Sir Herbert Kitchener at the Battle of Omdurman in September 1898, when the Sudan was reconquered and became jointly governed by Britain and Egypt.

The death of Gordon
General Gordon was killed outside the governor's palace by the Mahdi's soldiers. British relief forces arrived two days too late to save him.

THE OPENING OF THE SUEZ CANAL

In 1856 the ruler of Egypt, Sa'id Pasha, granted the French diplomat Ferdinand de Lesseps (1805–94) permission to cut a canal linking the Mediterranean Sea with the Indian Ocean. De Lesseps founded the Suez Canal Company in 1856. The canal was opened to traffic in 1869 and provided Europe with a quick ship route to the east. In 1875 the then ruler of Egypt, Ismail, Sa'id's nephew, sold his shares in the Canal Company to the British government.

1895
The Jameson Raid

In 1886 gold was discovered at Witwatersrand in the Boer republic of Transvaal, South Africa. Transvaal's president, Paulus Kruger, employed foreigners to mine the gold but refused them any political rights. In 1895, secretly supported by Cecil Rhodes who had designs on the wealth of the Transvaal, Dr. Leander Starr Jameson (1853–1917), a Scottish-born South African politician, led a force into the Transvaal, supposedly to help the foreign workers overthrow Kruger's government. It was a disaster. Jameson and his men were captured by Boer forces. Rhodes was disgraced and relations between the British and the Boers, always bad, deteriorated into war.

The Boer War 1899–1902
In 1902 the Boers surrendered, and their republics were reduced to colonial status. During this time, the African peoples were caught between the warring whites, and suffered greatly.

Capitalist and imperialist
Cecil Rhodes (1853–1902), prime minister of Cape Colony from 1890, dreamed of uniting all South Africa under British rule.

600	800	1000	1200	1400	1600	1700	1800	1900	2000

THE SCRAMBLE FOR AFRICA

During the last quarter of the 19th century, several European powers sent armed expeditions into Africa to claim exclusive rights over African territory. They were motivated by the knowledge, brought to them by explorers, of the vast, untapped resources of the African continent. These resources could provide cheap raw materials for the new industries that had spread across Europe since the Industrial Revolution. Despite resistance from African nations such as the Asante and Zulu, the European forces, foremost among whom were France, Britain, and Germany, gained possession of the land. They had the advantage of far superior weapons, and by 1900 most of Africa was under European control.

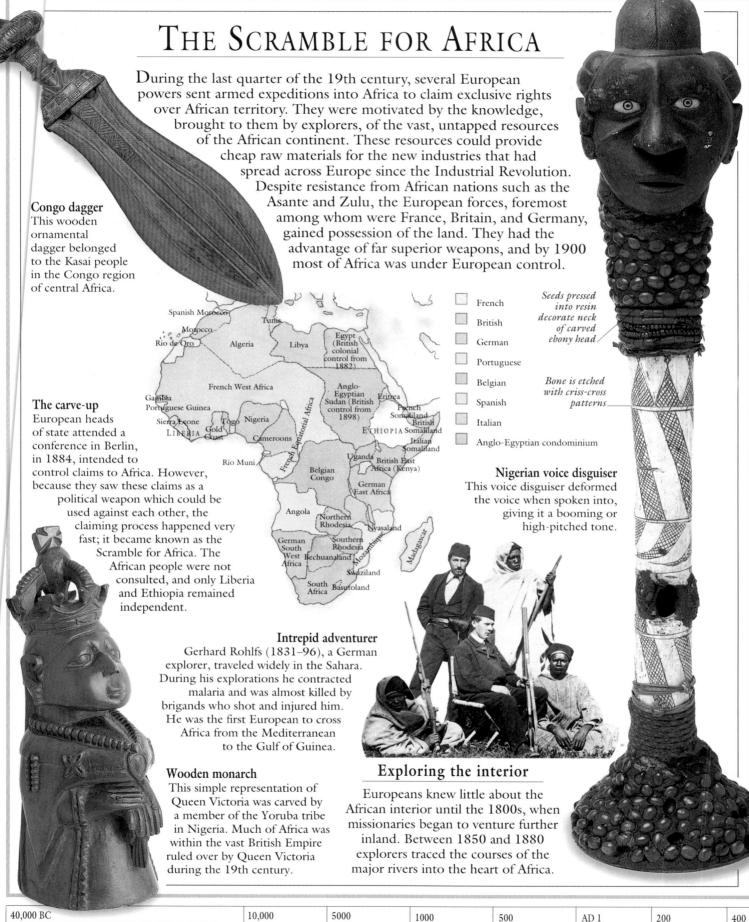

Congo dagger
This wooden ornamental dagger belonged to the Kasai people in the Congo region of central Africa.

The carve-up
European heads of state attended a conference in Berlin, in 1884, intended to control claims to Africa. However, because they saw these claims as a political weapon which could be used against each other, the claiming process happened very fast; it became known as the Scramble for Africa. The African people were not consulted, and only Liberia and Ethiopia remained independent.

Seeds pressed into resin decorate neck of carved ebony head

Bone is etched with criss-cross patterns

Map legend:
- French
- British
- German
- Portuguese
- Belgian
- Spanish
- Italian
- Anglo-Egyptian condominium

Map labels: Spanish Morocco, Morocco, Tunis, Rio de Oro, Algeria, Libya, Egypt (British colonial control from 1882), French West Africa, Gambia, Portuguese Guinea, Sierra Leone, LIBERIA, Gold Coast, Togo, Nigeria, Cameroons, Anglo-Egyptian Sudan (British control from 1898), Eritrea, French Somaliland, British Somaliland, ETHIOPIA, Italian Somaliland, French Equatorial Africa, Rio Muni, Belgian Congo, Uganda, British East Africa (Kenya), German East Africa, Angola, Northern Rhodesia, Nyasaland, Mozambique, Madagascar, German South West Africa, Southern Rhodesia, Bechuanaland, Swaziland, South Africa, Basutoland

Nigerian voice disguiser
This voice disguiser deformed the voice when spoken into, giving it a booming or high-pitched tone.

Intrepid adventurer
Gerhard Rohlfs (1831–96), a German explorer, traveled widely in the Sahara. During his explorations he contracted malaria and was almost killed by brigands who shot and injured him. He was the first European to cross Africa from the Mediterranean to the Gulf of Guinea.

Wooden monarch
This simple representation of Queen Victoria was carved by a member of the Yoruba tribe in Nigeria. Much of Africa was within the vast British Empire ruled over by Queen Victoria during the 19th century.

Exploring the interior
Europeans knew little about the African interior until the 1800s, when missionaries began to venture further inland. Between 1850 and 1880 explorers traced the courses of the major rivers into the heart of Africa.

Geisha girl
Japanese men could relax for an evening in the company of professional companions, or geisha women, schooled in singing, dancing, and conversation.

1850-1900 ASIA

These years began in China with the utterly devastating Taiping rebellion, which cost millions of lives. In Japan, the shogunate was overthrown when the Meiji emperor took power for himself and welcomed contact and trade with western Europe and North America. By 1900 Japan had grown into one of the world's industrial and imperial powers. In the 1850s the British government took control of India in a period known as the British Raj, or rule.

1853

Taiping rebels seize Nanking

By the 1800s the prestige of the Manchu rulers of China had declined. The administration was corrupt and inefficient. Secret anti-government societies flourished. One such society was begun in South China by a religious fanatic, Hong Xiuquan. In 1850 he led a force towards Nanking, capturing it in 1853. The revolt spread throughout 15 provinces. The leaders introduced important social policies, such as outlawing private property, and giving equal rights to women. The Manchu government was given help in their fight against the rebels by some European powers. In return, it granted them better port facilities for trade, and legalized opium sales. Hong died in 1864, and Manchu forces retook Nanking the same year. The Taiping rebellion, as it became known, finally came to an inglorious end.

Civil war disaster
Hong declared himself ruler of the "Heavenly Kingdom of Great Peace," "Taiping tian guo" in Chinese, hence the name "Taiping." But the rebellion was the most destructive civil war in world history. Hundreds of towns and villages were destroyed, and between 20 and 30 million people killed.

Fighting ship
Rapid population increase had led to famine, and peasants suffering economic hardship joined the rebels. War junks were often used in the fighting.

1868

Rama V reforms Thailand

Rama V became king of Thailand in 1868, when he was 15. A regent governed for him while he traveled abroad, and when he began to rule for himself in 1873, he knew more about European politics and culture than anyone else in Thailand. He embarked on a series of reforms to make his country more like modern Europe. He established government by cabinet, or body of ministers, abolished slavery, educated his nobles' children, reorganized taxes, and introduced a railroad system.

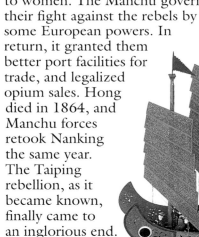

Visible monarch
Rama V's predecessors left their palace in the Thai capital, Bangkok, (left) once a year for a ceremonial tour. But ordinary people had to cover their windows so they would not see their king. Rama V was more accessible to his subjects. He traveled and talked to his citizens, as did European monarchs.

| 600 | 800 | 1000 | 1200 | 1400 | 1600 | 1700 | 1800 | 1900 | 2000 |

Industrial revolution

The Japanese feared that unless they could match the military and technological power of the United States and Europe, these powers would threaten their national independence. Meiji leaders hired Europeans and Americans to pass on knowledge of agriculture, engineering, and military technology. They set up mills, factories, dockyards, and railroads. A national education system was established.

1868
Meiji rule begins in Japan

In 1853 and 1854, Commodore Matthew Perry, representing the U.S. government, visited Japan to establish relations between the two countries. A treaty, signed in 1854, opened two Japanese ports to American trade. Treaties between Japan and other countries, including Britain and Russia, followed. By 1868 these concessions had greatly weakened the shogunate. Many samurai wanted real power to be given back to the emperor. A coalition of lords overthrew the shogunate and persuaded the young emperor, Mutsuhito, to move his capital from Kyoto to Edo, which was renamed Tokyo. "Meiji," meaning "enlightened rule," was chosen as the name of Mutsuhito's reign. Radical political, social, and economic changes were made, enabling Japan to modernize and become a major world power.

Footsoldier's parade hat
In 1894–95 Japan tested its European-style forces, defeating China in a dispute over Korea.

1885
Indian National Congress founded

In 1857 Indian troops mutinied because they believed that the British were violating their religious laws. After the mutiny was crushed, the British disbanded the East India Company and took direct control of India. In 1876 Queen Victoria was declared empress and a viceroy was appointed to represent her. Indians were excluded from senior government and army posts. In 1885 the Indian National Congress was founded to force the British to employ more Indians in the civil service. It was the start of a nationalist agitation within British rule. Some Muslim Indians supported Congress, but fear of Hindu domination of new institutions led to a Muslim breakaway.

A memsahib, or official's wife, at home
Each Indian district had a headquarters with a community of British officials and their families, living apart from local people, with many Indian servants. They recreated a wealthy British lifestyle, attending balls and picnics and playing polo, a sport learned in the days of the Moghuls.

Burmese golden lion
The British controlled much of southern Burma by 1852. In 1885–86 they overran the north, and Burma became a province of the Indian empire. Armed bands of Burmese carried on guerrilla warfare against the British, inflicting heavy losses.

Hindu advancement
By the late 19th century, Indians, especially upper-caste Hindus, saw the English language and European education as keys to advancement and supported the growth of their own schools and universities. Congress was the pressure group for this new Indian elite.

A Hindu temple plaque

40,000 BC		10,000	5000	1000	500	

1850-1900 EUROPE

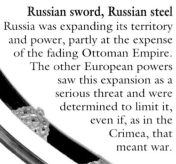

T he growing might of the emergent German nation caused great concern throughout Europe, especially in Germany's neighbor, France. The gradual breakup of the once-powerful Ottoman Empire led to independence for some Balkan states. The destructive Crimean War of 1853–56 between Russia, and Britain, France, and Turkey had resulted in an uneasy peace. Italy's self-governing states united to form an Italian kingdom with its capital the city of Rome.

Splendid city
Napoleon used public works to enhance his public image. He had much of Paris rebuilt in magnificent style.

1852
Another Napoleon reigns in France

Louis Napoleon (1808–73) was the nephew of the great Napoleon Bonaparte. In the confusion of the year 1848, Louis Napoleon had himself elected to the French National Assembly. Then he ran for president of the new Second Republic and was elected by a huge majority. In 1851, in a national vote, he persuaded the French to give him dictatorial powers, and in December 1852 he was made Emperor Napoleon III. In his 18-year reign, he promoted manufacturing, industry, and public works, and gradually liberalized the government. His ventures in foreign affairs were less successful, particularly the attempt to make an Austrian archduke emperor of Mexico. Finally, in 1870, he declared war on Prussia, but was soon defeated and captured by the Prussians. His regime collapsed.

1853
War in the Crimea

The Crimean War (1853–56) was fought between Russia on one side and Turkey, France, Britain, and Sardinia on the other. The war arose from a dispute over protection of Christian shrines in Palestine, then under Ottoman Turkish rule. The Turks declared war on Russia in October 1853. Britain and France feared Russian domination of the route from the Black Sea to the Mediterranean, so they chose to help Turkey. When a Turkish fleet was destroyed by Russia, French and British fleets sailed into the Black Sea; their armies landed in the Crimea in September 1854 and laid siege to Sebastopol. Military administration was hopelessly incompetent on both sides and 700,000 lives were wasted. Sebastopol fell in September 1855, and early in 1856 Russia accepted peace terms.

Bloodshed beside the Black Sea
The allied armies twice defeated Russian attempts to relieve Sebastopol at the Battles of Balaclava and Inkerman.

The lady of the lamp
More men died of disease than combat, until English nurse Florence Nightingale arrived. She organized the first modern wartime nursing service. The Crimean War was also the first war to be photographed, and the first in which the telegraph allowed modern-style news reports.

Wasted bravery
A mix-up in orders sent the British cavalry's Light Brigade at Balaclava on a famously courageous but suicidal charge.

1860

Italian parliament meets in Turin

For centuries Italy had been made up of several self-governing states. Much of northern Italy was controlled by the Austrians. Count Camillo di Cavour, the chief minister of King Victor Emmanuel II of Sardinia, with the help of Napoleon III of France, succeeded in driving the Austrians from Italy. Soon Parma, Tuscany, Lombardy, and Modena united with Sardinia, and in 1860 Victor Emmanuel opened an Italian parliament at Turin. The Pope and the hated Bourbon ruler of the Kingdom of the Two Sicilies did not want Italian unity. Giuseppe Garibaldi (1802–82), a veteran revolutionary, assembled a force of about 1,000 men, dressed them in red shirts, and sailed for Sicily. They quickly conquered the island and the rest of the Sicilian kingdom. Only the Papal States remained against union. Cavour, fearful of Garibaldi's power, sent an army south and defeated the Pope's forces. Garibaldi was persuaded to bring his conquered states into the union.

Fit for a king
When Italy was united, Victor Emmanuel became its king. In this British cartoon, Garibaldi is shown helping Victor Emmanuel to power.

One Italy
The unification of Italy took just over ten years. Venetia joined the union in 1866, the Papal States in 1870. In 1871 Rome became the capital of a united kingdom.

Architect of Italian unity
Many Italian liberals were also nationalists. They advocated a constitutional monarchy based upon the Kingdom of Sardinia. Count Camillo di Cavour (1810–61) became Sardinia's prime minister in 1852. A supreme statesman, Cavour used practical and diplomatic means to obtain his goal.

1867

More British gain the right to vote

Britain had the leading liberal government of 19th-century Europe, but it was a very unrepresentative one. New towns which had sprung up during the Industrial Revolution had no seats in parliament, and many rural seats could be won by buying votes. Only wealthy men had the right to vote. In 1832 the government, worried that the republican aims of the recent French Revolution could spread to the British people, gave the vote to more middle-class men, but millions still could not vote and demand for further reform grew. In 1867 future prime minister Benjamin Disraeli (1804–81) introduced a Second Reform Bill. It redistributed seats and gave the vote to another million men. However, women still had no vote.

The labor aristocracy
Increasing industrialization allowed a growing number of skilled men and women to command reasonably high wages. They believed in education and self-help and supported cooperative societies and trade unions founded on their behalf. *The Dinner Hour, Wigan* by Eyre Crowe (1824–1910) shows well-paid textile mill workers.

The Great Exhibition in London in 1851
The hugely successful Great Exhibition was the brainchild of Prince Albert, husband of Queen Victoria. It celebrated industry and technology throughout the world and was the first international exhibition. It was housed in a glass building known as the Crystal Palace.

| 40,000 BC | | 10,000 | 5000 | 1000 | 500 | AD 1 | 200 | 400 |

1871

German states unite under William I

After Napoleon's defeat in 1815, many Germans wanted a united Germany. A loose confederation of states was formed, but attempts in 1848 to achieve real unity failed. In 1861, King William I came to the throne of Prussia, the largest German state. His chief minister was Otto von Bismarck (1815–98) who was convinced that a united Germany, dominated by Prussia, could only be brought about by war. In 1864 Bismarck's offensive began. He attacked and decisively defeated first Danish and then Austrian armies, increasing German territory. He next courted northern Germans with a new liberal constitution. Then in 1870 Bismarck goaded Napoleon III of France into war. German forces soon routed the French, captured Napoleon, and gained land in eastern France. In 1871 Bismarck proclaimed William German kaiser, or emperor.

New Germany
At the end of the Franco-Prussian war in 1871, at Versailles in France, William I was proclaimed German emperor. Bismarck stands in the front to the left.

Steel and arms
In the 1870s German industry and commerce expanded rapidly. The Krupps works at Essen in the Ruhr region was one of the leading steelmakers in Europe, employing 8,000 people.

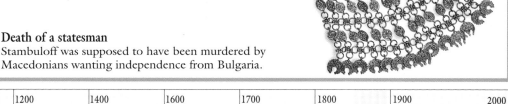

Harnessing power
Germany was in the forefront of car manufacture in Europe.

1886 German Benz "motorwagon"

1887

Bulgaria becomes leading Balkan state

Bulgaria, which was once an important empire, was overrun first by the Byzantines and then by the Ottoman Turks. In the 1870s the Bulgarians began to demand independence. The Turks suppressed the independence movement with great cruelty, which angered European powers, especially Russia. In 1877 Russia went to war with the Ottoman Empire. When the British supported the Ottoman Turks, the Russians made peace at the Treaty of San Stefano in 1878. Part of the peace agreement was a much-enlarged Bulgaria, but soon afterward the south was returned to the Ottoman Empire. In 1887, led by Stefan Stambuloff (1854–95), the Bulgarians reunited northern and southern Bulgaria and elected Prince Ferdinand of Coburg, a relation of Queen Victoria, as their ruler. But for seven years Stambuloff was the real ruler of Bulgaria, now the leading Balkan state, and generally regarded as the main bulwark against Russian expansion. Stambuloff worked hard for reconciliation with Turkey, Russia's old enemy. This angered Prince Ferdinand, who dismissed Stambuloff in 1894 and probably conspired in his assassination in 1895.

An intricate Bulgarian necklace

Death of a statesman
Stambuloff was supposed to have been murdered by Macedonians wanting independence from Bulgaria.

	1200	1400	1600	1700	1800	1900	2000

1850-1900 AMERICAS

A terrible civil war between the northern and southern states tore the United States apart and claimed 600,000 lives. The war ended slavery, and African-Americans won some political rights in the decade of Reconstruction that followed, but their gains proved temporary. Western settlement continued, with the Native American nations defeated and driven onto reservations. Immigrants from overseas swelled the growing cities of the East and Midwest. In Central and South America, there were major political and social reforms.

Water transport
Newly invented steamships, as well as rafts, carried people and goods along rivers.

Rubber tappers
Brazil was the world's biggest rubber exporter. Workers flocked to the Amazon forest to tap the rubber trees.

1850
Pedro II reforms Brazil

Pedro II began to rule Brazil in 1840. Capable, liberal, and scholarly, he spent the first years dealing with rebellions, but by 1850 had established his authority throughout the country. Over the next 40 years agriculture, business, and industry expanded rapidly. With government encouragement railways were built, and coffee, sugar, and rubber production greatly increased. The population grew from about eight million in 1850 to over 14 million by 1889. Pedro abolished slavery over the years 1870–88. In the last years, his freeing of remaining slaves without compensation to owners turned landlords against him, and they finally forced him to abdicate. The monarchy was abolished, and Brazil was proclaimed a republic. Pedro died in exile in 1891.

Emperor and his generals
In 1854 Pedro II (seated) sent a force to Uruguay to support the ruling party and increase Brazil's influence abroad. The War of the Triple Alliance (1865–70) broke out when Paraguay attacked Brazil, Uruguay, and Argentina in an unsuccessful attempt to force the Brazilians to evacuate Uruguay. More than half of Paraguay's people died in the war.

Foreign Legion
The French force in Mexico included 8,000 members of the Foreign Legion. These were men from all over the world who volunteered to fight for France. Based in the deserts of Algeria in Africa, they were tough, capable soldiers. Few questions were asked about their backgrounds, giving them an air of mystery and romance.

1858
Juarez is president of Mexico

In 1858 civil war broke out in Mexico between conservative and liberal forces. Liberal leader Benito Juarez, a Native American lawyer, became president. In 1860 his forces defeated the conservatives but only by borrowing money from foreign powers. France, Spain, and Britain invaded Mexico to enforce payment of their loans. Spain and Britain withdrew, but in 1863 a French army captured Mexico City. Napoleon III of France set up Archduke Maximilian of Austria as Mexican emperor. Juarez' forces defeated the French in 1867 and executed Maximilian. Juarez was reelected president, holding office until his death in 1872.

1861
The war between the states

In 1861, tensions between the free, industrialized North and the agricultural, slave-owning South exploded into civil war. When Abraham Lincoln – Republican Party candidate, which opposed the spread of slavery – won the presidency in 1860, Southern states seceded from the Union to form the Confederate States of America. Confederate shelling of Fort Sumter, South Carolina, in April 1861 started the war. Despite the Union's superiority in population and resources, it took four whole years to defeat the Confederacy – largely due to the Confederacy's able generals, including Robert E. Lee and Thomas J. "Stonewall" Jackson. The conflict came to an end after Lee surrendered to Union commander Ulysses S. Grant in April 1865.

Lincoln first said the war was about the preservation of the nation, and not the abolition of slavery, but then in 1862 he proclaimed slaves in the seceded states free; the Thirteenth Amendment to the Constitution (adopted in 1865) ended slavery throughout the U.S.

King Cotton
Cotton was the South's chief crop, and before the war planters relied on slaves to raise it. The war freed the South's 2.5 million slaves, but many former slaves wound up as sharecroppers – tenant farmers – in conditions little better than slavery. Postwar Reconstruction laws were passed to protect freed slaves' rights, but white resistance was such that by 1877 Reconstruction was mostly abandoned.

Union cartridge box
The chief weapon of both sides was the rifled musket, which fired a heavy lead bullet. The noise and smoke of these black-powder firearms made battle a deafening and terrifying experience.

Union vs. Confederacy
Eleven southern states (orange) seceded from the Union. Four border states (purple) stayed in it but permitted slavery; one new state, West Virginia, was created in 1863.

1 Vermont
2 New Hampshire
3 Massachusetts
4 Rhode Island
5 Connecticut
6 New Jersey
7 Delaware
8 Maryland

A modern war
Many aspects of 20th-century conflict had their first widespread use in the Civil War. Troops moved by railroads and steamship; the telegraph improved communications; and reporters and pioneering war photographers captured soldiers' lives and deaths. Sanitation, medicine, and care of prisoners, however, were primitive; more soldiers died of disease than combat; thousands died in prison camps.

Abraham Lincoln 1809–65
Kentucky-born but a longtime resident of Illinois, Abraham Lincoln is considered one of the greatest U.S. presidents. He was shot by a pro-Confederate actor during the last days of the war.

CIVIL WAR BATTLES

1861 Confederates defeat Union forces at Bull Run, near Washington, D.C.

1862 Lee halts Union advance on Richmond, Virginia, the Confederate capital, in the Seven Days Battle

1862 Confederate invasion of North stopped at Antietam, Maryland

1863 Jackson killed after victory at Chancellorsville

1863 Confederates defeated at Gettysburg, Pennsylvania; lose Vicksburg, Mississippi

1864 Grant named Union commander, advances on Richmond

1864–65 Union forces under Sherman take Atlanta, Georgia

1865 Richmond falls, April 4; Lee surrenders to Grant

NATIVE AMERICANS

For thousands of years, Native American nations lived in the Great Plains between the Mississippi River and the Rocky Mountains. The Plains peoples – including the Dakota, or Sioux, Cheyenne, and Arapaho – followed buffalo herds, their main sources of food and materials. War between groups was common, to preserve favored hunting grounds and prove bravery. The arrival of white settlers' in the 19th century led to the slaughter of buffalo and the end of the traditional way of life.

Supporting poles

Smoke flap

Nothing wasted

Sioux people used every part of a buffalo. Apart from eating the meat, they made spoons from the horn, chiseled the bones into scrapers or knives, cooked and stored food in the bladder, and used the skull in religious rituals. Buffalo hides were sewn together to make shelters called tepees.

Women scraped buffalo skins to remove flesh and hair

Sledges called travois carried heavy loads

The Sioux

By 1850 the Sioux numbered about 30,000, making them the largest and most powerful of the Plains peoples. There were three main Sioux groups, each divided into small bands based on kinship. Horses, which reached the plains from the Spanish colonies to the south in the 1700s, gave the Sioux great mobility in hunting and warfare. They believed in a Great Spirit and religion was an important part of Sioux life.

1862

The Homestead Act

Between 1850 and 1900, millions of people settled lands west of the Mississippi; thirteen new western states were created during this time. Some pioneers were lured by the mineral wealth of Colorado and Nevada; others established cattle ranches on the plains. Most of the pioneers were farmers attracted by the Homestead Act of 1862, which granted 160 acres of land to anyone willing to settle on it for five years. Railroads speeded up settlement; the first transcontinental railroad, built mostly by Chinese and Irish laborers, was completed in 1869.

Wagons roll west

Early settlers traveled in canvas-topped wagons along the westward trails.

Tepees could tower over 20 ft (6 m) high

Hides were skillfully sewn together to make tepees

Volunteers depart to join a "war party", or band of Sioux warriors

Warrior's bow and arrows

War against the intruders

Conflict with the Native Americans was inevitable as white settlers moved westward after the Civil War, fencing in the plains, overrunning hunting grounds, and slaughtering buffalo – often just for sport. Plains peoples, especially the Sioux, resisted and sometimes defeated the troops sent to force them out of the path of settlement. Sioux leader Red Cloud forced the army to withdraw from the Black Hills of South Dakota in the late 1860s, and in 1876, warriors led by Sitting Bull and Crazy Horse killed 250 soldiers under Lieutenant Colonel George Custer at the Little Bighorn in Montana. The army finally overcame the Native Americans with great brutality. The last conflict ended with U.S. troops shooting down between 200 and 300 Sioux, including many women and children, at Wounded Knee, South Dakota, in 1890.

Warriors' feathers had patterns showing what they had done in war

Most men had long hair

The reservations

By 1890, most surviving Native Americans were confined to reservations, lands allocated by the federal government. Today, about one-fourth of the United States' 2 million Native Americans live on reservations. In recent years, Native Americans have sought compensation and revived aspects of their traditional culture. At rituals, they often wear traditional costume, like the headdress shown here.

Good luck charm
Made of lizard skin, this beaded amulet was sewn by a woman and worn to ward off evil.

1867

Canada becomes a dominion

The British took control of all Canada in 1763 after defeating the French in the Seven Years War. In 1840 they united the English-speaking province of Upper Canada and the French-speaking province of Lower Canada. English- and French-Canadians argued bitterly. Both groups worried that the United States might invade. It became clear that Canada needed strong national government. In 1867 the British North America Act made Canada a dominion, a self-governing nation of the British Empire. A British governor-general was appointed. Most of modern-day Canada was absorbed into the dominion by 1905.

Mountie
In 1873 a semimilitary police force was formed to maintain law and order in northwest Canada, where traders clashed with Native Americans. Nicknamed "mounties," they traveled thousands of miles on horseback, in the heat and dust of summer and the cruel blizzards of winter. Young British men joined the mounties, looking for a life of daring adventure.

600	800	1000	1200	1400	1600	1700	1800	1900	2000

1850-1900 OCEANIA

Australia and New Zealand underwent a time of great social and political change during the second half of the 19th century. They developed democracy, gave women the right to vote in the 1890s, and granted old-age pensions as a statutory right. Both countries also moved toward dominion status and began to build a cultural awareness separate from their British origins.

The Eureka flag
This flag was flown over the miners' stockade at Ballarat. It became a powerful symbol of radical nationalism.

Striking it rich
Thousands of prospectors rushed to Victoria in 1851 when they heard that gold had been found there. As a result, Victoria's population quadrupled from 77,000 to 333,000 by 1855.

The Eureka stockade
Miners at the Eureka lead mine shut themselves inside a wooden stockade for four days, defying government troops sent to arrest them. The stockade fell on December 3, 1854.

1854
Miners rebel at Eureka mine

Colonial development in Australia in the 19th century was slow until 1851, when gold was discovered in the states of New South Wales and Victoria. Then it rapidly accelerated. One strike, at Ballarat in Victoria, attracted huge numbers of fortune-seekers from as far away as Britain and the United States. The government tried to control the rush by making the miners buy licenses to search. This caused resentment, and in November 1854 at the Eureka mine in the Ballarat goldfields, about 150 miners rebelled. Government troops killed about 30 men and arrested the leaders. They were later released, and the license was abolished.

1893
Women in New Zealand get the vote

For much of the period 1870 to 1890, New Zealand suffered deep economic depression under a Conservative government that favored the rich landlord class. After some bitter agitation, in 1889 the government finally granted the vote to all men over 21. A general election held the following year produced a Liberal government which immediately began to introduce social reforms. These included factory laws regulating working conditions and hours, progressive income tax rates, industrial arbitration boards, old-age pensions, and in 1893 votes for women. This was the first time any country in the world had given the vote to women.

Leading suffragette
Katharine Sheppard was the head of the franchise department of the Women's Christian Temperance Union. The Union was formed to uphold Christian values and to combat the excessive drinking habits of many local people.

Rolls and scrolls of signatures
A number of petitions were presented to parliament from the early 1880s to 1893. The largest one comprised 546 sheets of paper glued together as one large roll 900 ft (274 m) long, with 25,519 signatures from 179 different places. The electoral bill was passed by two votes.

WOMEN'S RIGHT TO VOTE	
1893	New Zealand
1894	Australia
1907	Norway
1917	Russia
1918	Britain
1920	United States
1944	France
1971	Switzerland

40,000 BC	10,000	1000	AD 1	400	800	1200	1600	1800	2000

Chapter 18

1900 – 1919

The World Goes to War

An imperial German officer's helmet

1900-1919
THE WORLD

THE OPENING YEARS of the new century see increasing competition between the world's great empires. Britain, shaken by near defeat in a war in South Africa against the Boer states, and France, weakened by the Dreyfuss scandal, face stiff economic and military competition from the newly united Germany. Faced with this threat, France and Britain put aside long-standing colonial rivalries and begin to work together. As German power increases, new alliances are formed that by 1914 divide the continent into two armed camps. Outside Europe, the once-mighty Chinese empire collapses in 1911. A major new force in the region, Japan, inflicts the first defeat in modern times by an Asiatic power on a European one when it sinks the Russian fleet in 1905. The Ottoman Empire continues to decline and by 1913 loses almost all its European territory. In the Americas, the United States continues its industrial and economic growth.

Technological revolution

In 1903 the world's first powered flight takes place when the Wright brothers lift off above the sand dunes of North Carolina. The real impact of this momentous event is felt when the European powers go to war in 1914. For the first time in human history, a war breaks out that involves entire nations in the war effort as it uses the latest technology for human destruction. Aeroplanes, tanks, submarines, and chemical weapons are used against soldiers and civilians alike in a war involving every continent.

1903 Wilbur and Orville Wright make world's first powered flight in North Carolina

1908 Henry Ford's motor company mass-produces small, inexpensive cars

New York

1914–15 Pancho Villa controls the most powerful military force during a long civil war in Mexico

1917 German submarines torpedo Allied merchant ships during World War I

c.1900 Argentinian gauchos, or cowboys, work in rapidly expanding cattle industry

1914 German naval force sunk by British cruisers in Battle of Falkland Islands

NORTH AMERICA

UNITED STATES

PANAMA

COLOMBIA

SOUTH AMERICA

ARGENTINA

ATLANTIC OCEAN

PACIFIC OCEAN

Hunting in the Ice Age | Cave painting | Early farming | Ancient Egypt | Assyrian Empire | Great Wall of China | Classical Greece | Roman Empire | Barbarian invasions

| 40,000 BC | 10,000 | 5000 | 1000 | 500 | AD 1 | 200 | 400 |

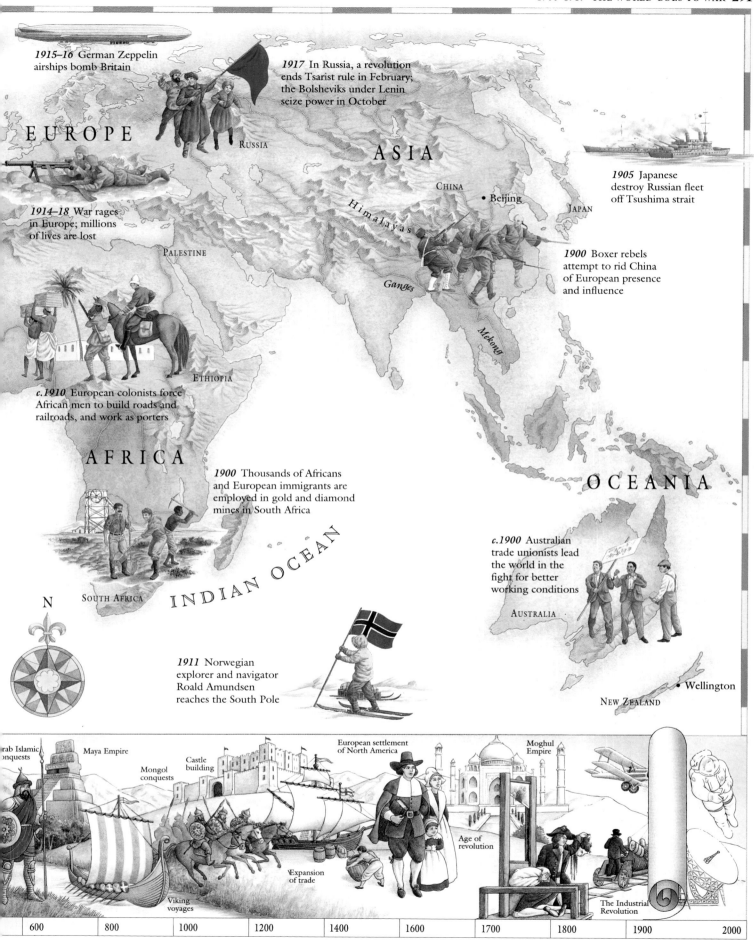

1915–16 German Zeppelin airships bomb Britain

1917 In Russia, a revolution ends Tsarist rule in February; the Bolsheviks under Lenin seize power in October

EUROPE

RUSSIA

ASIA

CHINA

• Beijing

JAPAN

1905 Japanese destroy Russian fleet off Tsushima strait

Himalayas

1914–18 War rages in Europe; millions of lives are lost

PALESTINE

Ganges

Mekong

1900 Boxer rebels attempt to rid China of European presence and influence

ETHIOPIA

c.1910 European colonists force African men to build roads and railroads, and work as porters

AFRICA

1900 Thousands of Africans and European immigrants are employed in gold and diamond mines in South Africa

OCEANIA

SOUTH AFRICA

INDIAN OCEAN

c.1900 Australian trade unionists lead the world in the fight for better working conditions

AUSTRALIA

N

1911 Norwegian explorer and navigator Roald Amundsen reaches the South Pole

• Wellington

NEW ZEALAND

Arab Islamic conquests

Maya Empire

Mongol conquests

Castle building

European settlement of North America

Moghul Empire

Expansion of trade

Age of revolution

Viking voyages

The Industrial Revolution

| 600 | 800 | 1000 | 1200 | 1400 | 1600 | 1700 | 1800 | 1900 | 2000 |

1900

1905

AFRICA

1900 Buganda, East Africa, is ruled by the kabaka, or king, with British advice

1900–01 Rising in Asante, West Africa; Britain annexes Asante

1902 Treaty of Vereeniging ends second Boer War in South Africa; defeated Boers remain bitter and determined to regain power

1903 Sokoto caliphate in Hausaland taken over by Britain

1904 French create federation of French West Africa

This Asante sword-bearer's cap is made of monkey skin and decorated with painted shells

1905 Kaiser William II of Germany visits Tangier and provokes crisis with France

1905 Maji-Maji rebellion begins in Tanzania (German East Africa)*

1906 Tripartite pact (Britain, France, Italy) seeks to preserve integrity of Ethiopia

1907 Government of Mozambique organized

1908 Belgium takes over Congo Free State

1909 Franco-German agreement reached on Morocco

1909 Liberia calls on United States for financial assistance

Moroccan lute with feather plectrum

ASIA

1900 Boxer Rebellion in China*

1900 Russia annexes Manchuria

1902 Anglo-Japanese Alliance agreed

1902 Resistance to U.S. rule in the Philippines ends

1902 Ibn Saud captures Riyadh, beginning the creation of Saudi Arabia

1903 British Viceroy of India (Lord Curzon) sends an expedition into Tibet

This Tibetan Kyelang instrument was said to cure madness

This brightly painted demon mask comes from Korea

1905 Japan presses Korea to sign a treaty whereby Japan "protects" Korea

1905 Japanese navy routs Russian fleet in Tsushima strait*

1907 Emperor Kojong of Korea abdicates; succeeded by son Sujong

1908 Death of Chinese empress dowager Cixi and of the Guangxu Emperor

EUROPE

1900 German naval law introduces 20-year building program for a high seas fleet to compete with the British navy

1901–05 Separation of the church from the state in France

1901 Foundation of Russian Social Revolutionary Party (Bolsheviks)

1903 Assassination of Alexander, King of Serbia

1903–05 Scandal breaks in Belgium over Belgian rule in Zaire

1904 *Entente Cordiale* between Britain and France*

1904–05 Russo-Japanese War

Japanese and Russian mounted patrols clashed near the Korean border in the Russo-Japanese War

1905 Revolution in Russia

1905 Norway breaks away from Sweden; elects King Haakon VII

1906 Liberal government elected in Britain: extensive reforms

c.1906 Naval arms race escalates*

1908 Young Turk Revolution

1908 Carlos I of Portugal assassinated

1908 Austria annexes Bosnia and Herzegovina

1908 Ferdinand I proclaimed emperor of Bulgaria

This Bosnian silver gilt cross was made to contain a piece of the true cross from Jerusalem

AMERICAS

Railways helped the United States become a great industrial power

1901–09 Theodore Roosevelt is president of United States: works to reform business, railroads, child labor, conserve natural resources*

1903 Panama secedes from Colombia with U.S. backing

1903 Boundary dispute over Alaska between Canada and United States settled

1904 Final settlement between Bolivia and Chile after the War of the Pacific

1904–09 Presidency of Ismael Montes in Bolivia; period of social and political reforms

1905 Provinces of Alberta and Saskatchewan formed in Canada

1906 San Francisco, California, devastated by earthquake and fire

1906 Cuba occupied by U.S. forces following a liberal revolt

1907 Run on American banks checked by J. P. Morgan

1908 Henry Ford produces first Model T car*

This carved ivory Inuit model of a sperm whale was found in western Alaska

OCEANIA

1900 Phosphate-rich Ocean Island annexed by British

1900 New Zealand annexes the Cook Islands

1901 Britain gets control over Tonga's external relations

1901 Commonwealth of Australia formed*

1902 Votes for women introduced in Australia

1904 Fijian delegates sit in legislative council for Fiji

Australian Commonwealth coins were first minted in 1910

1905 British New Guinea becomes the possession of Australia and is named Papua

1906 Britain and France rule over New Hebrides

1907 New Zealand becomes a dominion*

1907 First elections for national assembly in Philippines

1909 Creation of separate Labour Party in New Zealand

Government buildings in Wellington, New Zealand

1910

1910 Union of South Africa

1912 New loans to Liberia coupled with U.S. control over customs revenue

1912 French make Morocco a protectorate at Treaty of Fez

1913 South African government introduces laws to reserve 87% of land for whites*

1914 Britain and France occupy German colonies in West Africa

This Egyptian coin and bead necklace has a central crescent and star charm

1915

1917 Ras Tafari (later, Haile Selassie) becomes regent of Ethiopia*

1916 Boer leader Jan Smuts leads an anti-German drive from Kenya into East Africa

1916 British and Belgian troops take Yaounde, the capital of the German Cameroons

1917 German forces in German East Africa withstand British and Portuguese at Mahiwa; Germans withdraw into Mozambique

This gourd with an incised pattern of cattle was made in Madagascar

This Chinese smiling figure is carved of wood

1911–12 Chinese rebellion against Manchus; republic is established, Sun Yat-sen first president, but warlords gain power

1912–26 Taisho period in Japan

1912 Japan constructs its first dreadnought battleship

1913 China recognizes Outer Mongolia as independent

1913 Indian poet, Rabindranath Tagore, awarded Nobel Prize for Literature

Revolts broke out against the Manchu government throughout the southern provinces of China

1916 Beginning of Arab revolt against Ottoman Turks in Hijaz

1916 Hussein proclaims himself King of the Arabs

1917 Balfour Declaration promises homeland for Jews in Palestine*

1917 British troops capture Baghdad and Jerusalem

1917–25 Sun Yat-sen struggles for leadership of Chinese Republic

1918 Emir Faisal proclaims Syrian state; becomes king in 1920

1910 Portuguese revolution brings about the end of the monarchy

1912–13 Balkan Wars *

1913 Coup d'état of Young Turks in Turkey

1914 Assassination of heir to Austrian throne leads to outbreak of World War I

1914 Battle of the Marne

1914 Battle of Tannenberg between the Germans and the Russians; German victory

A British soldier on observation duty in a trench on the western front

The 1917 Russian revolution was publicized with dramatic posters like this one

1915 Dardanelles Campaign; British try to force passage to Constantinople

1915 Germans start submarine campaign to blockade British Isles

1916 Battle of Jutland between British and German fleets; stalemate

1916 Easter uprising against British government in Ireland*

1917 Russian revolutions: Liberal revolution (February); Bolshevik revolution (October)*

1918 Armistice ends World War I

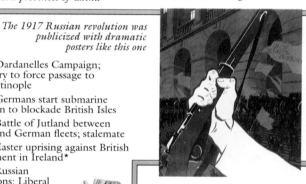

1911 President Diaz of Mexico overthrown

1912 Alaska granted territorial status in United States

1912 Arizona and New Mexico become U.S. states

1912 Secret ballot and universal suffrage introduced in Argentina

1913–21 Woodrow Wilson is president of United States

1914 Panama Canal opened

1914 Completion of Grand Trunk Pacific Railroad in Canada

Woodrow Wilson (1856–1924) was the 28th president of the United States

1916–22 Hipólito Irigoyen elected president of Argentina: extensive reforms*

1917 Mexico adopts a new constitution

1917 Brazil declares war on Germany

1917 United States declares war on Germany

1918 Venezuela oil fields opened

1918 President Wilson puts forward "Fourteen Points" for settling World War I

Mexicans used fans made of tule reeds to stir up their charcoal fires

1910 First victory for Labour Party under Andrew Fisher in Australian general election

1911 Universal military training established in New Zealand

1913 Wallis Islands become a French protectorate

1913 Foundation of United Federation of Labour and Social Democratic Party in New Zealand

These men are dryblowing for gold in Murchison, Western Australia

1915 Britain annexes Gilbert and Ellice islands

1916–18 Efforts to introduce national army conscription in Australia defeated in referenda

1917 Filipino National Guard organized in Philippine Islands

1918 Queen Salote becomes queen of Tonga

1918 Influenza epidemic kills one fifth of population of West Samoa

Queen Salote ruled the island of Tonga for 47 years

| 600 | 800 | | 1600 | 1700 | 1800 | 1900 | 2000 |

1900-1919 AFRICA

Resistance to European rule continued across Africa. At the start of the new century, the Maji-Maji and Herero rebellions in Tanzania and Namibia and unrest in South Africa highlighted African resentment against their new overlords. In spite of their discontent many Africans fought for their colonial rulers in World War I. The South African government worked to ensure that white domination continued; Africans, and Asian immigrants too, organized campaigns of peaceful protest. Ethiopia was still independent and thriving. Its empire had been doubled in size by the brilliant Emperor Menelik.

African sadness
This mask is from Zaire, which King Leopold of Belgium controlled with ruthless brutality from 1885 to 1908. His rule was so barbaric that entire areas were depopulated, and up to half of all Zaireans may have died. The king became very, very rich.

Graceful snuff
This carved antelope head snuffbox comes from Tanzania. Africans were often forced to labor for Europeans, sometimes to build roads or railroads, sometimes to produce cotton or coffee or rubber for export, meeting European desires, not African needs.

1905
Water against bullets in Tanzania

Across the continent, Africans protested against the taking of their land, new taxes, humiliating treatment, forced labor, corruption and unpunished violence, rape, and exploitation from Europeans. In German East Africa (now mainland Tanzania), people particularly resented heavy taxes, forced labor, and being forced to grow cotton for the government to export. Then a spirit medium claimed the power to provide magic water which could protect against bullets, and across the country many peoples rose in revolt. (The Swahili word for water is *maji*, and so the revolt came to be called the Maji-Maji rebellion.) The colonial government crushed the rebels by killing their leaders and creating a famine. Its soldiers burned crops, grain, and villages. They did their work most thoroughly: more than 200,000 people died.

WAR AFTER WAR

1896 Ethiopian army under Emperor Menelik destroys a 17,000-strong invading Italian army at Battle of Adowa

1896–97 African peoples of Zimbabwe rise in revolt against the British

1900s German campaigns to subdue Cameroon and British campaigns in Nigeria continue

1902–03 People of the Ovimbundu kingdoms in Angola fight the Portuguese

1904–08 Herero and Nama uprisings in Namibia

1905 Rebellion in Tanzania

1914–18 Germans and Allies use African troops to fight for them in Africa; 41,000 Kenyans die; 169,000 West Africans fight for France in Europe

c.1920 Wars of resistance against British in Sudan and Somalia, and French in Niger

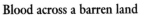

Blood across a barren land
In January 1904 the Herero people of central Namibia rose up against their German rulers. An army was sent from Germany. It drove the rebels into the Kalahari Desert and shot all who tried to return. Later, Herero survivors were sent to forced labor camps, where more than half of them died. Shocked, the Nama cattleraisers of southern Namibia rebelled in October. They were skilled horsemen, and their leaders were brilliant guerrilla fighters; it took 14,000 German troops to crush them. When captured, they, too, were sent to the forced labor camps. Before the uprisings, there had been an estimated 20,000 Nama and 80,000 Herero; in 1911 only 9,800 Nama and 15,000 Herero remained.

Pioneers of freedom
The African National Congress (ANC) was founded on January 8, 1912, to create national unity and defend Africans' rights. Pixley Seme, one of its founders, started the first national newspaper for Africans. In 1914 the ANC sent a delegation to London (pictured above) to plead, eloquently but unsuccessfully, for help.

Pass book for poverty
Pass books were used to control African men in South Africa, who had to carry them. They could only travel or get a job if their pass books showed that they had permission. When, in 1913, the Orange Free State tried to make African women carry pass books, too, there was such resistance that it was forced to give up. Women did not have to carry pass books until the 1950s.

1913
Laws to keep land for whites only
In 1910 the British government united Cape Colony, Natal, Orange Free State, and Transvaal as the independent Union of South Africa, without insisting that the rights of the nonwhite peoples of South Africa should be upheld. Instead, those rights were trodden down still further as the white minority strengthened its hold on wealth and power. The Natives Land Act of 1913 reserved 87 percent of land for whites. Vast numbers of Africans were made homeless. They were left with no choice but to work for Europeans on farms, in homes, and down mines, for very low wages. In the same year the government tried to restrict immigration by Indians and curb their freedom on arrival. A well-organized protest campaign forced it to back down.

The Johannesburg Pass Office

Necklace
This necklace from Natal is made with tiny beads strung together.

THE RELIGION OF RAS TAFARI
Ras Tafari, or Haile Selassie (1892–1975), ruled an ancient and powerful African empire at a time when countless people of African origin across the world were oppressed. For many in the Caribbean he was a symbol of hope. They mixed biblical stories with their own wishes and dreams and came to see black people as a chosen race, suffering now but destined to be saved and led to a better life back in Africa by Ras Tafari himself, their messiah. They named themselves Rastafarians, after him. Since the 1970s reggae music, inspired by Rastafarianism, has spread their ideas worldwide.

The faithful
Rastafarianism is strongest on the Caribbean island of Jamaica, but Rastafarians are found in many other countries, dreaming of liberation to a better life. These true believers are celebrating Haile Selassie's birthday.

1917
A new ruler in Ethiopia
For much of the 20th century, Ethiopia was the only major independent black nation in Africa, ruled from 1889 to 1913 by Emperor Menelik. At a time when Europeans were taking over most of Africa, he doubled the size of his empire, defeating an Italian invasion at Adowa in 1896. In 1917 a relative, Ras (Prince) Tafari, took power. He acted as regent for Menelik's daughter Judith until 1930, then became emperor as Haile Selassie ("Light of the Trinity"). He modernized Ethiopia, especially the army, and abolished slavery. In 1935–36 Italians invaded the country but in 1941 the British drove them out and the emperor returned to rule until 1974.

Haile Selassie

1900-1919 ASIA

The large fortunes that European merchants had been making on Chinese territory for some decades provoked anger and protest, as seen in the Boxer Rebellion. This eventually led to the collapse of the Manchu dynasty and the formation of a Chinese republic. Japan became the first Asian power to defeat a European power in war, winning a great victory over a Russian fleet in the Tsushima strait, and became a force to be reckoned with. Although China and Japan were hardly involved in World War I, the Arab areas of western Asia were wrested from the Ottoman Empire by European powers.

Qing dynasty frog
This turquoise frog-shaped snuff bottle dates from the time of the Qing dynasty.

1900

Boxer Rebellion in China

China failed to regain strength after the Taiping rebellion (1850–64), and in the following years European powers extended their commercial activities throughout the country. Many Chinese people resented these intrusions. A group of young discontents secretly formed the Society of Harmonious Fists (hence the name Boxer for their uprising), whose aim was to expel the foreigners. The movement gained support. By 1900 the rebels were burning foreign missions, slaughtering Chinese Christians, and besieging foreign legations (embassies). The German minister to China was murdered in June, and European powers, Japan, and the U.S. sent troops to China to retaliate. They arrived in Beijing in August to relieve the besieged legations. The empress dowager, Cixi, who supported the Boxers, fled to Xian. She soon accepted a demand from several European powers, the United States, and Japan to end the uprising.

Western intrusion on the Qing Empire
By 1900 foreign powers had severely encroached on China. Some countries even acquired special trading facilities in the "Treaty Ports," chiefly in Shanghai, and finally in at least 15 other towns. The Boxers attacked foreign embassies in Beijing and killed many Europeans and Chinese Christians.

Propaganda print
Issued by Boxer rebels, this print shows them besieging foreigners at Tianjin (Tientsin) in northeast China.

SUN YAT-SEN 1866–1925

Sun Yat-sen (shown right with his wife) was born the son of a peasant near Macao. In 1905 he founded the Kuomintang (KMT), or Chinese Nationalist Party. His main aim was to unify China under a democratic, representative government. As early as 1894, he had been organizing a secret revolutionary society which aimed to overthrow the crumbling Manchu dynasty. His first attempt in 1895 failed, and he swiftly fled China and traveled to various parts of the world, including Britain, the United States, and Japan, to gather support for his cause. Finally, in 1911, the revolutionaries overthrew the Manchus, and Sun was elected provisional president of the new Chinese republic.

40,000 BC		10,000	5000	1000	500	AD 1	200	400

1905
Russian defeat at Tsushima

In the early 1900s Japan clashed with Russia over conflicting interests in Korea and in Manchuria, a northeastern province of China increasingly dominated by Russia after 1898. After discussions broke down in 1904, the Japanese navy attacked the Russian eastern fleet at Port Arthur, a naval base in the Liaotung province leased to Russia by China. War followed. The Russians were badly organized, and the Japanese defeated them in a series of battles on land and at sea. In May 1905 the Russian Baltic fleet, sent earlier by Tsar Nicholas II to reinforce the eastern fleet, reached the Tsushima strait between Korea and Japan. The Japanese almost totally destroyed it, effectively ending the war. Peace was agreed to in September 1905 at a meeting in the United States organized by President Roosevelt.

Japanese victory at sea
Russian battleships were attacked by Japanese torpedoes in the Tsushima strait in May 1905. It was the first time in history that an Asian fleet defeated a European fleet.

Admiral Togo
Admiral Togo Heihachiro led the Japanese fleet. In a bold maneuver in the Tsushima strait, he turned his battle fleet around and changed direction to engage the Russians coming out of the mist. His strategy was to stop them from breaking through on the last stage of their 18-month voyage.

1917
Jewish people are promised a homeland

After the Romans reasserted power in Palestine in the 1st century AD, Jewish communities grew in other parts of the world. Jewish people settled in many European countries, and later in the United States, but they never lost their Jewish identity. Other races often persecuted them. In the 19th century, this persecution, or anti-Semitism, led to a movement for the Jews to have their home once again in Palestine. The movement, called Zionism, had much support in Britain, and in 1917 A. J. Balfour, the British foreign secretary, formally declared the government's support in a letter to Lord Rothschild, a leader of Britain's Jewish community. It became known as the Balfour Declaration. After World War I, Palestine, which had been part of the Ottoman Empire for four centuries, became a British-run territory. Almost at once, there were clashes between immigrant Jews and indigenous peoples – mostly Arabs – who had been living in Palestine for centuries. These conflicts set the tone for much of the trouble that exists there today.

The Zionist Commission
This photograph shows members of the Zionist Commission, the official Zionist organization, arriving in Palestine in 1918. Chaim Weizmann (1874–1952) was the head of the Zionist Commission.

The hand of God
This Jewish silver hand ornament from Jerusalem, Israel, is a symbol of strength and power.

1900-1919 EUROPE

The problems in Europe that brought on World War I in 1914 were festering in 1900. France, anxious about growing German militarism, allied itself with Russia and later Britain. Balkan states, which had recently won independence from the Ottoman Empire, began to fall out among themselves, leading to the great powers taking sides. In the four-year war, massive casualties were suffered by all sides in a huge conflict that left Germany, the economic superpower of Europe, devastated and bankrupt. Three revolutions in Russia, meanwhile, changed the country completely, making it the world's first Communist state.

German helmet
Dating from around 1912, this imperial German officer's helmet bears the eagle which represents the ruling house of Prussia.

THE DREYFUS AFFAIR

Alfred Dreyfus (1859–1935), a Jewish captain in the French army, was wrongly imprisoned for life in 1894 for treason in passing military secrets to Germany. He was a victim of anti-Semitism. His case caused international outrage, and in 1906 he was retried, cleared, and restored to the army.

1904
The *Entente Cordiale* is signed

There had been friction between France and Britain since the 1890s over territorial claims in West Africa and the Pacific, fishing rights in Newfoundland, and developing interests in Egypt and Morocco. In 1904, following a successful visit to Paris by the British king Edward VII, statesmen on both sides made a friendly agreement, the *Entente Cordiale*, in which the two countries settled overseas disputes and agreed not to interfere in each other's empire building. This was the first step in British alignment with France against Germany.

Artistic interpretation
The *Entente Cordiale* was often represented by cartoonists as a French woman flirting with an English soldier.

Thriving German industry
The buildup of German militarism was accompanied by the growth of industry and armaments. This scene shows workers at a shipyard in northern Germany.

1906
Naval arms race escalates

One threat hanging over Europe during the early 1900s was the rise of German militarism. Otto von Bismarck (1815–98), the architect of the German empire, had worked hard to keep good relations with the main European powers. When he was fired in 1890 by the new German emperor, or kaiser, William II, this cautious policy was dropped. The kaiser set about making Germany one of the world's most powerful nations. He encouraged Grand Admiral Alfred von Tirpitz to build a German navy to match the British one, and in 1906 Tirpitz resolved to build ships that would compete with British dreadnoughts. This created tension throughout Europe and shifted the balance of power. Russia, France, and Britain formed alliances; other countries looked to their national defenses.

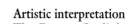

1912
The Balkan states go to war

In 1912 Bulgaria and Serbia laid claim to parts of Macedonia, a part of the Ottoman Empire populated by Bulgarians, Serbs, Macedonians, and Greeks. Greece and Montenegro allied with Bulgaria and Serbia to form the Balkan League. They attacked and defeated Turkey, leaving its European territory vastly reduced. A temporary peace was made, but the four League states fell out over the settlement, and war erupted again in 1913. Serbia hoped to gain Albania, but Austria-Hungary, fearing an increase in Serbian power, established Albania as an independent state. Serbian anger against the Austrians reached boiling point.

Bulgarian armies
By the end of the First Balkan War, Bulgaria's territory reached the Aegean Sea. In 1913 Bulgarian forces attacked the Greeks and Serbs, but they were defeated. A peace was made in which all states gained land apart from Bulgaria.

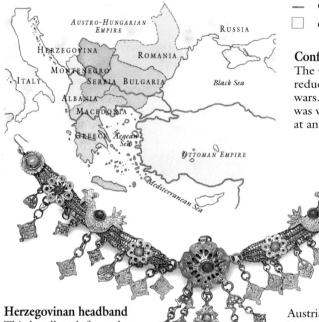

— Ottoman Empire before the Balkan wars

☐ Ottoman Empire after the Balkan wars

Conflict in the Balkans
The Ottoman Empire was vastly reduced as a result of the Balkan wars. The great empire was virtually at an end.

Herzegovinan headband
This headband, from the Balkan state of Herzegovina, was worn as a magic charm.

The final straw
Austrian archduke Ferdinand and his wife were assassinated by a Serbian in 1914. This was the spark that ignited the conflict of World War I.

Liberty Hall, Dublin
About 500 people were killed in the Easter uprising, and many Dublin buildings were ruined. The British government was unmerciful in its revenge, and 15 Irish leaders were executed.

1916
Easter uprising in Ireland

The Irish had wanted independence from British rule for centuries. In 1914 an Irish Home Rule bill was passed by the British government, but it was stopped by the outbreak of World War I. The republican Sinn Fein party decided to campaign for separation at once. They planned an uprising in Dublin for Easter Monday 1916 and proclaimed an Irish republic. After a week of fighting they surrendered. The British government's bloodthirsty reprisals created powerful support for independence, and in the 1918 general election Sinn Fein won a huge majority.

Irish Nationalist
John Redmond (1856–1918) was the head of the Irish Nationalist Party. Unlike Sinn Fein, his party wanted to achieve its aims peacefully. He was deeply distressed by the Easter uprising.

600	800	1000	1200	1400	1600	1700	1800	1900	2000

1917
The Russian Revolution

In January 1905 thousands of demonstrators in St. Petersburg, demanding higher wages and shorter hours in the local factories, were fired on by troops. This led to strikes in many cities, including a general strike in St. Petersburg. The demonstrators later demanded an end to the war with Japan, a constitution, free and universal education, and tax reforms. Peasants rose against landlords and there were military and naval mutinies. The tsar was forced to grant a constitution providing for a duma (parliament), but disorders and strikes continued for some time. Meanwhile the Russian army in World War I lost over 5 million men by 1917. Renewed disturbances in St. Petersburg (by now renamed Petrograd) led to the tsar's abdication in March 1917 and the formation of a liberal (so-called provisional) government. It soon found itself opposed by Lenin's Bolshevik party. In September the provisional government declared Russia a republic, but in October Lenin organized a coup, seized power, and established the Soviet Union.

Discredited ruler and son
Tsar Nicholas II (1868–1918) was disliked by many of his people. He was forced to abdicate in March 1917.

RUSSIAN REVOLUTION

January 1905 Workers' protest march to the Winter Palace, St. Petersburg

1914 Russian empire is drawn into World War I

August 1915 Nicholas II assumes supreme command of the armed forces

February 1917 Workers' protest marches sparked off by local bread shortages in Petrograd

October 1917 Lenin orders capture of the Winter Palace; Bolsheviks take power

July 1918 The tsar and his family are murdered by revolutionaries

Revolutionary weapon
This Japanese naval rifle, bought by the Russians in World War I, was used in the 1917 revolution.

Storming the Winter Palace
In October 1917 the Bolsheviks seized the Winter Palace in Petrograd, formerly St. Petersburg, which the moderates had been using as a Parliament House, and took power.

LENIN 1870–1924

Vladimir Ilyitch Lenin was born in Simbirsk on the Middle Volga. Politically minded from an early age, he was expelled from a university for political agitation, spent 14 months in prison in 1895, and three years in exile in Siberia for subversive behavior. In 1903 he became leader of the Bolsheviks. The Bolsheviks, or "members of the majority," were the extremist wing of the Russian Social Democratic Party. After the Winter Palace was captured in 1917, an all-Russian congress of soviets (councils) met to give executive power in Russia to the Bolsheviks, later called Communists, who offered the country "Peace, Land, and Bread." Power in the factories was given to the workers, an agreement at Brest-Litovsk in 1918 ended the war with Germany, and a new Soviet constitution was declared. Lenin was master of the biggest country in the world.

1900-1919 AMERICAS

The United States saw great industrial expansion. Although sympathetic to Britain and France, it kept out of World War I until German submarine attacks forced it to declare war in 1917. In South and Central America a number of regimes showed increasing resentment at U.S. influence on their countries. In Argentina, attempts at radical reform foundered amid government corruption.

Welcome to New York
New York's Ellis Island was the first taste of America for most immigrants.

1901

The Rough Rider in the White House

Theodore Roosevelt (1858–1919) was at different times a rancher, big-game hunter, and explorer, as well as a politician. He learned politics as a reforming Republican in New York, then became popular leading the volunteer "Rough Riders" in the Spanish-American War of 1898. Later that year he was elected governor of New York, and in 1901, became vice-president. When President McKinley was assassinated in September 1901, Roosevelt became president, and he won a second term in 1904. His administration embarked on a long program of reforms. Major achievements included curbing the power of big business and introducing the first measures for conserving U.S. natural resources. He regulated abuses in the expanding railroad industry and limited the hours children were allowed to work in factories. Abroad, he supported Panama when it broke away from Colombia and won the right to build the Panama Canal.

The right man at the right time
Brilliant, flamboyant, and energetic, Theodore Roosevelt was immensely popular. His mediation at the end of the 1904–05 Russo-Japanese War earned him the Nobel Peace Prize.

The Railroad Age
The railroads linked the far reaches of the United States. By 1900 there were 250,000 miles (402,500 km) of track.

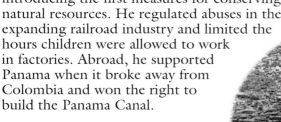

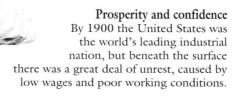

Prosperity and confidence
By 1900 the United States was the world's leading industrial nation, but beneath the surface there was a great deal of unrest, caused by low wages and poor working conditions.

The "American Dream"
By 1904 a million immigrants a year were arriving in the United States. These included many people from Central, Eastern, and Southern Europe seeking "the American Dream" of progress from abject poverty to wealth and happiness.

| | 1400 | 1600 | 1700 | 1800 | 1900 | 2000 |

1908
Ford puts the world on wheels

Henry Ford, the U.S. industrialist, developed mass production in order to make motor cars more cheaply. He used standardized parts, which could be put together quickly by unskilled workers; and he began to build cars along a moving assembly line, with each worker repeating one small job. This cut the production time for a car from several days to 12 hours or less. His production techniques have since been copied around the world. Ford founded his motor company in Detroit, Michigan, in 1903.

Five years later, in 1908, he introduced a new small car, the Model T, which was tough, reliable, and easy to buy. It heralded a revolution in transportation. By 1914 Ford had 45 factories producing cars on continuous assembly lines in the United States and abroad. By 1920 half the cars in the world were Model T Fords. He was also an innovative employer. In 1914 he introduced a basic wage of five dollars for an eight-hour day and brought in profit-sharing schemes for his employees.

Henry Ford (1863–1947)

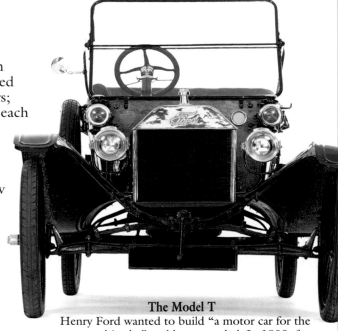

The Model T
Henry Ford wanted to build "a motor car for the great multitude," and he succeeded. In 1908, fewer than 200,000 people in the United States owned cars; by 1930 over 15 million Model T's had been sold at home and abroad. People had a mobility unknown to even the very rich 50 years before.

Riders wild and free
The gauchos, horsemen of the great grasslands of Argentina and southern Brazil, are national heroes. Modern farming techniques made Argentina one of the world's great exporters of food, especially meat, but made the gauchos largely redundant.

The other side of Argentina
Those who made fortunes exporting beef and farm products had leisure to enjoy the fine boulevards of Buenos Aires. But there were very many poor.

1916
Irigoyen, "the father of the poor"

In 1912 Argentina began to enjoy some form of democracy when a series of electoral reforms was introduced. One of the main politicians behind the reforms was the radical lawyer, Hipólito Irigoyen, a very talented and talkative democrat who in 1916 was elected president of Argentina. Known as "the father of the poor," he introduced a range of social reforms, such as compulsory pensions, regulation of working hours, and improvement of factory conditions; but he was not helped by aides who mismanaged the economy. Irigoyen refused to take sides in World War I. Afterwards, Argentina became a member of the League of Nations but pulled out in 1921 and Irigoyen lost power in 1922. Elected president again in 1928, he took on too many powers and provoked a military coup. Hopes of further reform died.

A mixed blessing
Hipólito Irigoyen (1850–1933) was a brilliant political organizer, loved by the poor. But he ruled dictatorially and, although he was honest, the governments he led were chaotic and corrupt.

	AD 1	200	400

1900-1919 OCEANIA

I n 1901 the Commonwealth of Australia was formed when six British colonies united under a federal government. New Zealand became a dominion, or self-governing state, of the British Empire in 1907. Its governments introduced pioneering social and political reforms but Australian Aboriginals and New Zealand Maoris continued to be oppressed by the white populations.

Headgear
This Aboriginal brow band is made of red seeds and shells.

Trade unionists on strike
While rich Australians thought of themselves as British, poorer workers' loyalty was often to Australia. Powerful trade unions representing the workers promoted nationalist policies as well as workplace reforms.

1901

Australian colonies unite

By 1880 Australia was divided into six colonies, each with its own administration, but subject to British sovereignty. Many families had lived there for four generations. Australians began to shed cultural ties with Britain and take on a national identity, creating their own arts and even fielding cricket teams to play English teams. Trade unions held their first congress to press for reforms such as a maximum eight-hour working day. The colonies finally agreed to unite. In 1901 a government was established with overall power over the so-called Commonwealth of Australia, although each colony kept a regional administration. The Commonwealth government was still subject to British sovereignty but over the years became increasingly independent.

National hero
Australian "Breaker" Morant fought for the British in the Boer War. He was shot for killing prisoners in 1902, inciting anti-British feeling in Australia.

1907

New Zealand becomes a dominion

The British colony of New Zealand was given a constitution in 1852, dividing it into six provinces. A government with real responsibilities over the provinces was established in 1856, and New Zealand remained self-governing for half a century. In these years its social policies were among the most advanced in the world. It was the first country to give women the vote, and one of the first in which old people became entitled to pensions. In 1901 New Zealand refused to join the new Commonwealth of Australia, and in 1907 it was given official dominion, or self-governing, status within the British Empire.

Parliament building
Wellington was the capital city of New Zealand. Parliament was held there.

Leisure time
Industrial and agricultural growth meant prosperity for many. New leisure pursuits included going to see silent films in newly built cinemas. People traveled by motor car, bus, and railroad to rugby games, the races, or picnics on the beach.

| 600 | 800 | 1000 | 1200 | 1400 | 1600 | 1700 | 1800 | 1900 | 2000 |

RESTORING LOST RIGHTS

Aboriginals lived in Australia for 40,000 years before British settlers arrived in the late 18th century. The settlers hunted down and killed Aboriginal men, women, and children and confiscated the survivors' lands. The first Commonwealth governments of the 1900s excluded Aboriginals from welfare laws. Aboriginals were segregated from white Australians in public places. A turning point came in 1967, when vigorous campaigners persuaded the government to hold a referendum on Aboriginal rights. Nearly 90 percent of Australians voted to give government powers to make laws for Aboriginals, making them full citizens for the first time. In 1992 Prime Minister Paul Keating apologized on behalf of white Australians for 200 years of injustice. In June 1992 the High Court made it possible for Aboriginals to reclaim land seized by settlers as far back as 1788.

Feeding funnel
In an elaborate ceremony, a Maori leader is fed a special liquid through a funnel before being tattooed.

Maoris campaign for equal rights

Ill-treatment of native peoples was also a major issue in New Zealand. Maoris lived there for nearly 1,000 years before European settlers came in the late 18th century. By 1900 broken land treaties and conflict left most Maori land in settlers' hands. Government welfare programs of the 1890s and 1900s were mostly limited to European families. Maoris pressed for self-government and inclusion in legislation, but in the 1930s differences in living standards were still marked. Nearly half the unemployed were Maori, and nearly three times as many Maoris died of disease as did white people. Today, Maoris demand better treatment. Some land seized by settlers has been returned. In 1987 Maori was recognized as an official language of New Zealand.

Bringing the past to life
Aboriginals have revived their ancestors' customs. Women wear armlets like this one during traditional mourning ceremonies.

Community meeting
Maori friends give each other a traditional greeting, *hongi*, or pressing together of noses. They are gathered in front of a sculpture carved with ancient Maori patterns by a modern artist.

Native knife
By 1900 colonists' demand for land still affected many native Pacific Island communities. On Tahiti, where this knife was made, French colonists grew cash crops on land traditionally held by Tahitians. Tahitians demanded that their land should be restored to them. The cry "Tahiti for Tahitians" went up on the island.

APIRANA NGATA 1874–1950

Talented lawyer Apirana Ngata was a leading campaigner for Maori rights. He became secretary of the Young Maori Party, which aimed to revive Maori society by introducing a public health service and modern farming methods into the community. In 1905 Ngata became a Member of Parliament, elected to one of four Maori seats, and remained an MP for nearly 40 years, becoming Minister for Native Affairs in 1928. He ceaselessly fought for higher living standards for his people and was very active during an economic depression in the 1930s. Jobless Maoris, who were not entitled to state unemployment benefits, were forced to eat wild animals to avoid starvation. Ngata developed large farms which provided jobs and helped to restore the dignity of many Maoris. His work was recognized by the British government and he was knighted in 1927.

WORLD WAR I

In June 1914 a Serbian nationalist murdered Archduke Ferdinand, heir to the Austrian throne. Austria declared war on Serbia on July 28. The alliances between European powers drew them quickly into the crisis. Russia mobilized forces along its Austrian and German borders to help Serbia. Germany declared war on Russia and Russia's ally, France. To get to France, German troops invaded Belgium. Britain had agreed to protect Belgian neutrality and declared war on Germany and Austria on August 4. The war soon spread to European colonies all over the world.

Telling the people
In Europe's streets, news of war was greeted by patriotic crowds. Few dreamed of the horrors that would follow.

Carving out the western front

The Germans quickly overran most of Belgium, pushed British forces back at Mons on August 23, and crossed into France. On September 5, in a decisive battle, the Allies counterattacked on the Marne River, north of Paris, forcing the Germans back to the Aisne River. The Germans never fully recovered their initiative. By the end of the year both sides had dug lines of trenches stretching 400 miles (650 km) from Nieuport on the Belgian coast to the Swiss frontier. The area of fighting became known as the western front.

Bravo, Belgium!
In an exemplary invasion operation, more than 550 German troop trains sped into Belgium each day. This British cartoon praises the Belgian army's stiff resistance.

Hail of bullets
For four days, German machine gunners mowed down wave after wave of Russian troops at the Battle of Tannenberg.

Guns blaze on the eastern front

While the German army attacked France, Russia launched an offensive into the German province of East Prussia but was defeated in August 1914 at Tannenberg. The Russians never again invaded Germany, although they did overrun and hold for a time the Austrian province of Galicia. But heavy losses helped spark the Russian revolutions of 1917. The new Bolshevik government soon sued for peace.

☐ Central Powers
☐ Allies
☐ Neutral nations

A continent divided
During the war, most European nations joined one of the opposing sides, which came to be called the Central Powers and the Allies. Young people from all over Europe prepared to fight.

1914

August 1 Germany declares war on Russia
August 3 Germany declares war on France and invades Belgium
August 4 Britain declares war on Germany
August 23 Germans push back at Mons, Belgium

August 26–30 Germans under Hindenburg defeat Russians at Tannenberg, taking 125,000 prisoners
August 30 German planes bomb Paris for the first time
August 30 New Zealand forces occupy German Samoa
September 5–13 Battle of the Marne River: British and French defeat Germans

September 6–15 Germans defeat Russians at Battle of Masurian Lakes
September 21 Australians occupy German New Guinea
October 20–November 11 Allies withstands German attack at Battle of Ypres
November 5 Germans win victory over British in German East Africa (now Tanzania)

November Turkish sultan proclaims a *jihad* (holy war) against all enemies, including Britain, France, and Russia
December 8 British win naval victory over Germans at Battle of Falkland Islands
December 17 Turks attack Russian-Armenian town, Kars
December 21 First air raid on England, at Dover

| 600 | 800 | 1000 | 1200 | 1400 | 1600 | 1700 | 1800 | 1900 | 2000 |

Entrenching tool
This implement was used to dig trenches.

Living and dying in the trenches

Trenches were lines of defense works resembling large ditches with earth ramparts. Opposing sides were never far apart, and neither side ever advanced more than a few miles beyond the central no-man's-land. Living conditions in the trenches were appalling. Soldiers endured food shortages, lice and rats, attacks of poison gas, cold and damp, and the constant stench of dead troops who could not be moved quickly. Heavy rainfall turned the trenches into quagmires through which the soldiers had to wade up to their knees while performing their duties.

Gas alarm whistle

Gas alert!
This respirator was worn during poison gas attacks. Air was inhaled through a filter which neutralized the dangerous gas.

Going over the top
Soldiers faced almost certain death when they were ordered to go "over the top" of the trench to attack the enemy.

Barbed wire provided defense against the enemy

Soldiers crawled over the top and ran across dangerous no-man's-land towards the enemy

Next, please
After enlisting, recruits had to line up and have their measurements taken for their new uniforms.

Conscription and propaganda

At first, men on both sides volunteered by the hundreds of thousands to fight for their country. Governments appealed for more to come forward with war propaganda in the form of persuasive posters glorifying war. After about two years, it became necessary to introduce conscription – men were made to enlist in the forces by law. Some pacifists refused and were jailed.

Sandbags reinforced the walls of the trench

Join up!
Posters, like this one advertising for recruits to the U.S. Navy, portrayed war in a heroic and patriotic light.

1915

January First German airship raids on England
February German navy begins submarine campaign against shipping to and from Britain; *Lusitania* sunk on May 7; nearly 1,200 killed
April 22–May 25 Second battle of Ypres

April 25 Australian, British, and New Zealand forces land in Gallipoli as part of an unsuccessful attempt to take Constantinople
May 2 Austro-German attack begins in Galicia; Russian Poland overrun by September 2
October British and French forces land in Macedonia to help Serbs and Greeks

1916

February 21 Long battle begins for fortress town of Verdun in eastern France; lasts nearly a year, but Verdun is not captured by the Germans
May 31–June 1 Naval battle of Jutland, off northwest Denmark, between British and German fleets ends in stalemate

June 4 Major Russian offensive under General Brusilov begins; after initial successes, it peters out, but not before a million Russians die in the fighting
July 1 Battle on the Somme River in northwest France begins; lasts several weeks, with huge British losses on the first day

Horrific new weapons of war

Both sides unleashed terrifying new weapons of war. The Germans first released poison gas into Allied trenches in spring 1915 and used flamethrowers that sprayed burning fluid at the siege of Verdun in 1916. Planes were specially built to drop bombs on towns and frontline positions or shoot down enemy planes in the air. The Germans introduced U-boat submarines that fired torpedoes, mainly at British merchant ships bringing much-needed food and supplies across the Atlantic from North America. In the last months of 1916 a British invention, tanks, appeared on the front lines in France. These movable armored fortresses could withstand the heaviest machine-gun fire, as well as crumple barbed wire entanglements. Soldiers stationed inside the tanks fired powerful guns.

"Red Baron" rules the skies
The first really successful fighter planes were German Fokkers, introduced in 1915, which had a machine gun at the front. The German LVG CV1 (left) also had a rear machine gun. Daring pilots such as Manfred von Richthofen, nicknamed the "Red Baron," became popular heroes.

Lumbering landships
One horrified German described tanks as "those monsters crawling along the top of the trench, filling it with machine-gun fire."

Women join the workforce
The demand for troops in the war zones left few men to work in supply factories. This led to the large-scale employment of women for the first time, in factories, farms, and public services such as post offices and ambulance driving.

Hardship on the Home Front

It was not only the men in the front line who took risks and suffered. Those left at home endured danger and deprivation. Civilians were bombed from the air; those in coastal towns were shelled from the sea. Destruction of supply ships led to severe food shortages. Shops had little to sell to growing lines outside them. Soon people were only allowed fixed amounts, or rations, of food. Wives and families of those at the front lived in fear that their men were dead or wounded. The involvement of the whole population in the conflict was called total war.

SINKING THE *LUSITANIA*

In May 1915 a British liner, the *Lusitania*, was sunk by a German U-boat. Over 1,200 died. More than 190 were American, including famous figures such as millionaire Alfred Vanderbilt. The U.S. public was outraged. U.S. intervention in the war became more likely.

1917

April 6 United States enters war on Allied side
July Russian troops move into Galicia in major offensive that soon peters out
July–November British offensive near Ypres achieves little; 400,000 casualties, many at Passchendale

July 6 British Colonel T. E. Lawrence leads Arabs against Turks and captures Aqaba
October–December Italians defeated by Austrians in the Caporetto campaign
November 20 Attack by nearly 400 British tanks at Cambrai on the western front
December 15 Armistice between Russia and Germany

1918

January 8 U.S. president Wilson proposes a peace plan based on "Fourteen Points"
May–July Germans under Ludendorff launch last great offensive on western front
July British, French, and U.S. forces, led by Foch, begin a successful counteroffensive

October 24–November 4 Battle of Vittorio Veneto: Italians defeat Austrians
October 28 German fleet mutinies at Kiel
October 30 Turks surrender after defeats by British under Allenby
November 11 Armistice agreed between Germans and Allies; war ends

---

| 600 | 800 | 1000 | 1200 | 1400 | 1600 | 1700 | 1800 | 1900 | 2000 |

Victors dictate a peace

By November 1918 Germany was exhausted. In a revolution, the fleet mutinied, and the kaiser abdicated and fled to Holland. The government of the new republic arranged an armistice for November 11. A series of peace treaties followed which redrew the map of Europe by heavily penalizing the defeated powers. The treaty between the Allies and Germany, signed at Versailles, near Paris, in 1919 dictated that Germany surrender all overseas colonies and some European land to Allied powers, as well as pay reparations to countries devastated by its troops, especially France. Its army was limited to 100,000 men, with no modern weapons.

Paris peace conference
Decisions at the peace conference were made by politicians from the major victorious powers: the U.S., Britain, France, and Italy.

Counting the cost in human lives

World War I had lasted for more than four years. During that time, about 10 million people were killed in action, in air raids, or at sea, and twice as many again were wounded. Over 6 million troops, sailors, airmen, and civilians were taken prisoner, many of whom returned to their homes afterward sickened by their experiences. Germany and Austria-Hungary suffered by far the greatest number of casualties, some 3 million dead and nearly 8 million wounded – nearly a whole generation of young men. Some of the most memorable moments were of protest and mutiny, as well as victory and defeat. In 1917, for example, some French soldiers marched bleating loudly like sheep, knowing they were being led like innocent lambs to the slaughter.

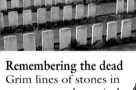

Remembering the dead
Grim lines of stones in war graveyards remind today's visitors of the number of precious lives lost in battle.

Collective security
The League was the first example of a permanent international organization. The United Nations replaced it in 1945.

A difficult homecoming
Soldiers who survived the war often found it hard to adjust to normal life. Many suffered from an illness called shell shock, a loss of sight or memory, resulting from the mental strain of fighting.

A league of nations

After the war was over, the League of Nations was founded in 1920. Its aim was to keep peace throughout the world and settle disputes by negotiation. The United States refused to ratify the Treaty of Versailles or to join the League. This was a bad start for the future of the League as a peace enforcement agency. Although it settled minor disputes, it failed to solve major issues, such as the Japanese invasion of China in 1931, or the Italian invasion of Ethiopia in 1935. It collapsed in World War II and was dissolved in 1946.

1919

January–July Treaty of Versailles worked out between Allies and Germany
April Geneva in neutral Switzerland becomes League of Nations headquarters
June German navy scuttled by its crews at Scapa Flow, off the coast of Scotland

September Treaty of St. Germain between Allies and Austria, which recognizes Yugoslavia, Poland, Hungary, and Czechoslovakia as independent states; Austrian Empire reduced by two thirds
November Treaty of Neuilly between Allies and Bulgaria: Bulgarian land is given to Greece, Romania, Yugoslavia

1920

January Dutch government refuses to surrender German ex-kaiser to Allies for trial
June Treaty of Trianon between Allies and Hungary: Hungary reduced to a quarter of its size; its lands go to Romania, Czechoslovakia, and Yugoslavia

July Spa conference: Germany agrees to pay huge reparations to Britain, Belgium, France, Italy, and smaller powers
August Treaty of Sèvres between Allies and Turks whereby Turkey loses much of its land; the treaty is unacceptable to Turkish nationalists and not ratified

CHAPTER 19

1919 – 1946

PEACE AND WAR

Bren machine gun used in World War II

1919-1946
THE WORLD

THE ENDING OF WORLD WAR I brings
an uneasy peace to the world. War-
torn Europe is exhausted after
four years of fighting, while Russia is
consumed by the civil war that follows
the Communist revolution of 1917.
The collapse of the Ottoman empire
creates instability throughout western
Asia, while Japan emerges resentful of
the few colonial rewards obtained for
fighting on the Allied side. Only the
United States is strengthened by the
war, establishing itself as the world's most
prosperous nation. Throughout the period,
China and India struggle to assert their
independence. China fights against Japanese
invasion, and India resists the continuance of the
British Raj. African nations, too, remain under colonial
rule, and in South Africa, white power is strengthened.

The world economy

A postwar economic boom soon gives way to
slump, and many countries are gripped by high
inflation. In 1929, the U.S. economy plummets after
the New York Stock Exchange crashes. World economic
confidence collapses, leading to severe economic depression
and political instability. The extreme nationalist Nazi party
led by Adolf Hitler comes to power in Germany in 1933,
pledged to reverse postwar settlements and restore
German power. In alliance with Italy, and later Japan,
Nazi Germany leads the world back to war in 1939.

NORTH AMERICA

1930s Drought in the central
United States turns fields into
"dust bowls" and forces
many farmers to
leave their land

• New York

MEXICO

1943 The Allied convoys begin
to win the Battle of the Atlantic
against German submarine warfare

1938 The Mexican
government takes
over British and
U.S. oil interests
on its territory

SOUTH AMERICA

Andes

PERU

BRAZIL

ATLANTIC OCEAN

PACIFIC OCEAN

1932 Chaco War;
Bolivia and Paraguay
fight over disputed
territory

CHILE

Hunting in the Ice Age | Cave painting | Ancient Egypt | Assyrian Empire | Classical Greece | Roman Empire | Barbarian invasions

Early farming | Great Wall of China

| 40,000 BC | 10,000 | 5000 | 1000 | 500 | AD 1 | 200 | 400 |

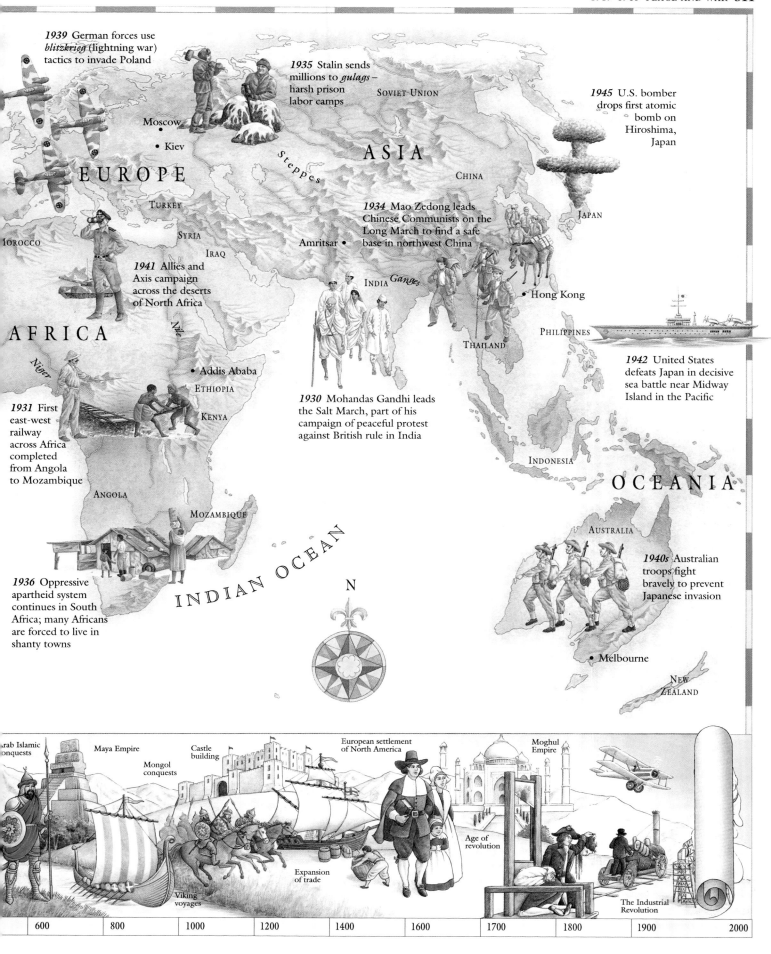

1939 German forces use *blitzkrieg* (lightning war) tactics to invade Poland

1935 Stalin sends millions to *gulags* – harsh prison labor camps

SOVIET·UNION

1945 U.S. bomber drops first atomic bomb on Hiroshima, Japan

Moscow

Kiev

ASIA

EUROPE

CHINA

TURKEY

1934 Mao Zedong leads Chinese Communists on the Long March to find a safe base in northwest China

JAPAN

SYRIA

IOROCCO

IRAQ

Amritsar

1941 Allies and Axis campaign across the deserts of North Africa

INDIA *Ganges*

Hong Kong

PHILIPPINES

AFRICA

THAILAND

Nile

Addis Ababa

ETHIOPIA

Niger

1942 United States defeats Japan in decisive sea battle near Midway Island in the Pacific

KENYA

1931 First east-west railway across Africa completed from Angola to Mozambique

1930 Mohandas Gandhi leads the Salt March, part of his campaign of peaceful protest against British rule in India

INDONESIA

OCEANIA

ANGOLA

MOZAMBIQUE

AUSTRALIA

INDIAN OCEAN

N

1940s Australian troops fight bravely to prevent Japanese invasion

1936 Oppressive apartheid system continues in South Africa; many Africans are forced to live in shanty towns

Melbourne

NEW ZEALAND

Arab Islamic conquests

Maya Empire

Castle building

European settlement of North America

Moghul Empire

Mongol conquests

Age of revolution

Expansion of trade

Viking voyages

The Industrial Revolution

| 600 | 800 | 1000 | 1200 | 1400 | 1600 | 1700 | 1800 | 1900 | 2000 |

1919

1926

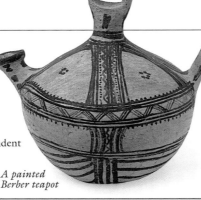

*A painted
Berber teapot*

*This pendant
cross is from
Ethiopia*

AFRICA

1919 ANC demonstrates against pass laws in Transvaal

1920s More British and Indians settle Kenya*

1921–26 Abd-el-Krim leads Berbers and Arabs against Europeans in North Africa*

1922 Egypt becomes independent from Britain under King Fuad

1923 Ethiopia admitted to League of Nations

1930 White women given the vote in South Africa

1930 Ras Tafari crowned emperor of Ethiopia and takes the name Haile Selassie

1931 First trans-African railway completed from Angola to Mozambique*

ASIA

After 1919 Gandhi told Indians to resist British rule passively but firmly

1919 British troops massacre over 300 Indian civilians at Amritsar*

1920 Palestine becomes British mandate

1920 Indian leader Gandhi launches peaceful non-cooperation movement against British rule

1923 Mustafa Kemal becomes president of new republic, Turkey*

1924 Chinese nationalist party, Kuomintang, holds first national congress

This toy was made in the Thai capital, Bangkok

1927 Kuomintang leader Chiang Kai-shek establishes government at Nanking; Communists challenge his rule

1928 Japanese troops murder military ruler of Manchuria

1930 First Round Table Conference between British government and Indian parties

1931 Japanese occupy Chinese province of Manchuria*

1932 Absolute rule of Thai king ends; he agrees to new constitution

EUROPE

[1] **1919** Ernest Rutherford splits atom for first time

1921 Lenin introduces New Economic Policy (NEP) in Russia

1922 Irish Free State founded*

1922 Mussolini becomes Italian prime minister; dictator from 1925

1923–30 Dictatorship of Primo de Rivera in Spain

1924 First British Labour party victory at a general election

1924 Death of Vladimir Lenin

1925 Locarno Agreements between major European powers aim to maintain peace and stability

Benito Mussolini was the Fascist dictator of Italy, 1925–43

[1] **1926** In Britain, John Logie Baird develops the television

1928 French begin to build fortification, the Maginot Line, on German border

1928 Stalin launches five-year plan to expand Soviet industry*

1931 Republic declared in Spain after King Alfonso XIII abdicates

1931 Statute of Westminster makes dominions of British Empire self-governing

Soviet farms were brought under the control of peasant collectives

AMERICAS

Police seized alcohol, banned in the U.S. 1920–33 in a period called Prohibition

1919–20 U.S. Congress refuses to ratify the Versailles Treaty

1919–30 Great material progress in Peru during presidency of Augusto Leguiá

1920 Nineteenth amendment to U.S. Constitution is adopted, giving all U.S. women the vote

1920–33 Prohibition against sale of alcohol in United States

1921–25 Progressive government of President Juan Bautista Saavedra in Bolivia

Necklet from the Gran Chaco plain

1926 Panama and United States agree to protect Panama Canal in wartime

1929 Wall Street Stock Exchange crashes; Great Depression follows*

1930 Getulio Vargas becomes Brazilian president and assumes dictatorial powers in 1937*

1932 Democrat Franklin D. Roosevelt becomes U.S. president

1932–35 Chaco war between Bolivia and Paraguay*

OCEANIA

1919 Dry dock completed at Pearl Harbor in U.S. territory of Hawaii

1920 New Zealand given mandate over Samoa

1920 Formation of a federal Country Party in Australia

1920 New Zealand becomes member of League of Nations

1921 Australia given mandate over German New Guinea

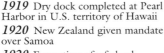

Typical comb from Samoa

1927 Canberra becomes federal capital of Australia

1929 Uprising of Mau people of Samoa against New Zealand government

1931 Founding of United Australia Party (UAP)

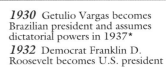

This Fijian club is bound with coconut fiber

1933

1939

1934–36 British colonial government of Ghana suppresses radical African critics

1936 Representation of Natives Act denies black South Africans any chance of political equality*

1935–36 Italians under Mussolini invade and annex Ethiopia

Kenyan artists were making carvings for tourists by the 1930s

1939 South Africa declares war on Germany at start of World War II

1941 German army under Rommel attacks British in North Africa

1941 Ethiopia liberated from Italians by Ethiopians and British, and recognized as independent

1942 British defeat German army at Battle of El Alamein in Egypt

1943 Germans and Italians driven from North Africa

This necklace combines glass and brass beads with teeth from one of the big cats, perhaps a lion

1934 Communists go on Long March through China, led by Mao Zedong and Zhu De*

1934 Opening of British oil pipeline from Kirkuk (Iraq) to Tripoli (Syria)*

1935 Government of India Act passed; provinces of British India granted autonomy and self-government from 1937

1936 General strike in Syria; French grant Syria home rule

1937–45 Undeclared war breaks out between China and Japan

1937–38 Conflict between Jews and Arabs in Palestine

Japanese sword

1941–42 Japanese overrun much of southeast Asia

1945 World Zionist Conference calls for Jewish state in Palestine*

1945 United States drops atomic bombs on Japanese cities of Hiroshima and Nagasaki

1933 Nazi leader Hitler appointed German chancellor; Nazis begin organized persecution of Jews*

1934 Mussolini meets Hitler*

1936 Germany occupies Rhineland region on French-Belgian border

1936–39 Civil War in Spain*

1937 Eamonn de Valera becomes prime minister of Ireland (Eire)

1938 Hitler compels Austria to form union (*Anschluss*) with Germany

1938 Munich crisis: France and Britain agree to let Germany partition Czechoslovakia

Worn by a Nazi political director, this uniform has a swastika, the Nazi emblem, on the armband

The atomic bomb killed nearly 80,000 people in Hiroshima

1939 Stalin and Hitler agree to divide Poland between them

1939 Germany invades Poland; this leads to World War II

[1] **1940** British scientists develop radar

British soldiers used this machine gun during World War II

1940 France surrenders to Germany

[1] **1941** Jet aircraft developed in England and Germany

1943 German Sixth Army fails to capture Stalingrad (present-day Volgograd) in Soviet Union and surrenders

1944 Allies invade France and begin to reconquer Europe

Vargas rebuilt many areas of his capital, Rio de Janeiro

1933 Peruvian president Sanchez Cherro assassinated by an *aprista**

1933 U.S. "New Deal" laws, such as National Industrial Recovery Act, promote economic recovery

1935 U.S. Social Security Act – first step in creation of welfare state

1937 U.S. National Labor Relations Act

1938 Mexico takes over U.S. and British oil companies in Mexico*

This Guatemalan headcloth was worn by important members of the Catholic church

1941 Congress passes Lend-Lease Act; billions of dollars' worth of military hardware is loaned to Allies

1944 First free presidential elections in Guatemala

[1] **1945** U.S. scientists build first atomic bomb

1933 Australia takes control of large sector of Antarctica

1935 First Labour government elected in New Zealand; many reforms follow*

1936 Arbitration court of New Zealand fixes basic wage for man with wife and three children

1937 Formation of New Zealand National Party, in opposition to Labour Party

M. J. Savage became New Zealand's first Labour prime minister

1939 Robert Menzies becomes Australian prime minister*

1941 Japanese attack U.S. fleet in Pearl Harbor, Hawaii; United States enters World War II

1942 U.S. naval victory over Japanese fleet off Midway Island in the Pacific

Australians fought in Allied forces all over the world; here Australian troops embark for Palestine

1919-1946 AFRICA

Between the two world wars, the colonial powers tightened their hold over Africa, despite various movements of African resistance. Production for export greatly increased; many people went to work for wages in towns, which grew fast. A small but important group of educated Africans began to make itself heard. By the end of World War II some African leaders were pressing for self-government or independence.

Competing for control
Both France and Spain were eager to colonize Morocco, where this ornament was made. In 1912 they agreed that the south become a French protectorate and the north a Spanish protectorate.

Displaced wanderers
In the early 20th century nomadic Masai cattle herders were barred from large areas in Kenya to make room for settlers' farms. Many Masai resisted the influence of white culture and still live much as their ancestors did.

1920s
Conflict over land in Kenya

By 1905 Kenya was largely under British control. White settlers from Britain and South Africa were given much farmland and pasture in the fertile highlands, at the expense of the Masai, Nandi, and Kikuyu peoples. These settlers soon gained much influence over the British colonial administration. Meanwhile, many Indians settled in Kenya as shopkeepers and traders. They resented white settlers' land rights and increasing political power. The British government did not wish to see either white settlers or Indians grow too powerful, and the colonial secretary declared in 1923 that the interests of Africans should be paramount. But the government failed to introduce a program of economic development for Africans, and white settlers strongly resisted any change to land distribution.

Kikuyu bead-covered gourd
In the early 1920s a Kikuyu association campaigned against land loss, forced labor, and tax increases imposed on them by the white administration.

1921
Disaster for Spain in Morocco

Spain had two outposts on the Mediterranean coast of Morocco from the 16th century. These became the basis of a Spanish protectorate in 1912, and the Spanish then moved into the Rif Mountains to the south. They were opposed by Muslim Berbers who lived in the Rif. Under Mohammed Abd-el-Krim the Riff Berbers defeated a Spanish army at Anual in 1921 and occupied two ports, which enabled them to obtain guns and other military help. It was only after Riff Berbers attacked French-controlled Morocco, in 1925, that French and Spanish forces combined to defeat them.

Battle of Anual
Abd-el-Krim wrote that bullets flew like grain at Anual. Over 12,000 Spanish troops were killed or injured, and their commander committed suicide.

| 500 | AD 1 | 200 | 400 |

1931
A railroad crosses Africa

After the Scramble for Africa, European powers built roads and railroads through their territories to help trade and communications. Engineers dreamed of a line from Cape Town in South Africa to Cairo in Egypt. But the powers did not integrate their rail networks, not even agreeing to use the same rail gauge. As a result, lines laid in different territories did not link up. However, in 1931 a railroad was completed between Benguela, on the coast of Angola, and the copper mines in Zaire. These were already linked by a line through Zambia and Zimbabwe to Beira on the coast of Mozambique. For the first time, a railroad spanned the continent from east to west.

Manual labor
The railroad building projects provided work for thousands of Africans. In Uganda, contractors also employed Asian workers who returned to Asia after the railroad was completed.

Balamba drum
The trans-African railroad was not profitable. It ran through vast areas inhabited only by African peoples such as the Balamba, who had little need for it.

JAN SMUTS 1870–1950

Smuts became a Boer general during the Boer War (1899–1902). He helped to create the Union of South Africa in 1910 and was prime minister in 1919–24 and 1939–48. During World War I he fought German forces in East Africa and afterward helped establish the League of Nations. His support for the Allies during World War II antagonized many white South Africans. Other whites deplored his occasional efforts to improve conditions for nonwhites, and he was defeated in 1948 by the pro-white National Party.

1936
Black Africans lose political power

From the first, the government of the Union of South Africa aimed to segregate the country's so-called "races": whites, Indians, "colored," and black Africans. In 1912 the Natives Land Act restricted African land ownership to 13 percent of the country. Much of this land was unproductive, and many Africans had to work for whites for low wages – whether on farms, in houses or in industry. Outside their "reserves," Africans had to carry passes, and their presence in towns was strictly controlled. Many jobs done by whites were closed to Africans. From 1936 the few Africans still allowed to vote in Cape Province could only do so in special elections, which sent three white representatives to parliament. The South African Party led by Jan Smuts, which passed this law, lost power in 1948 to the National Party, which was determined to enforce an even more strict system of racial segregation, which came to be known as *apartheid*.

Industrial revolution
South African industry, based on gold and diamond mining, grew by 600 percent between 1930 and 1950. This was only made possible by the use of cheap African labor.

Protecting privilege
In 1922 mine owners threatened to employ Africans as skilled workers but at lower wages than whites. They backed down after a well-organized strike by white workers determined to maintain control of skilled occupations.

	600	800	1000	1200	1400	1600	1700	1800	1900	2000

1919-1946 ASIA

Peace arrangements after World War I created problems in the eastern Mediterranean, particularly in Palestine. The prospect of making a Jewish national home there caused violence between Jews and Arabs. In Turkey, the overthrow of the Ottoman sultanate led to a period of radical westernizing rule under Kemal Ataturk. The Japanese sought to control large areas of China, culminating in war with the Chinese. British rule in India was threatened as the independence-oriented Congress Party grew more powerful under the inspired leadership of Mohandas Gandhi, the architect of passive resistance.

Dancing Shiva
This bronze carving from southern India represents Shiva as Lord of the Dance, one of the chief Hindu deities along with Brahma and Vishnu. Under another guise, Shiva is also the great god of Time. Many of the young followers of Gandhi were dedicated to Shiva.

The Salt March
In 1930 Gandhi set out with a band of chosen followers to collect salt from the sea. This was a symbolic action taken because it was in defiance of government laws and was the first step in a civil disobedience campaign. As he had hoped, it drew worldwide attention.

1919

Amritsar massacre in Punjab

The British government in India introduced antiterrorist laws to combat continued threats by Indian nationalists during World War I. This offended many Indians and Mohandas Gandhi (1869–1948), a nationalist leader, urged his supporters to stop work. In March 1919 a strike was planned in Amritsar, but the ringleaders were arrested. This provoked angry rioting. As a result, General Dyer, the local army commander, banned public meetings, but a large crowd assembled in a walled area, the Jallianwallah Bagh. Dyer took 50 soldiers there and ordered them to fire into the crowd. More than 300 people were killed. This massacre led to violent rioting throughout the Punjab. Gandhi was a key figure in the Indian National Congress enquiry into the Amritsar massacre. By June 1920 Gandhi had convinced himself that British policy in India must be opposed by passive resistance.

The Golden Temple at Amritsar
The town of Amritsar in the Punjab housed a Sikh religious shrine.

Hand spinning
Gandhi encouraged village communities to be self-sufficient. People began to spin their own cloth, which was cheaper than purchasing imported material.

Dyer disgraced
General Reginald Dyer was severely reprimanded for his conduct over the Amritsar massacre. He was removed from active service in 1920.

40,000 BC		10,000	5000	1000	500	AD 1	200	400

1923

A Turkish republic is proclaimed

The great reformer
Mustafa Kemal Ataturk (1881–1938) was born in Salonika in Greece. As a talented soldier, he served in Macedonia, Libya, Syria, and in the Balkan Wars (1912–13). During World War I he commanded the Ottoman forces which repelled the Allied attack on Gallipoli (1915). As the president of the new republic, he was both ruthless and dictatorial. His policy of reform came to be known as Kemalism.

World War I spelled the end for the once-mighty Ottoman Empire. Its Arab provinces were granted independence, it lost all of its lands in southeast Europe apart from Constantinople, and in 1923 the last of the Ottoman sultans, Mohammed VI, abdicated and fled from his capital. In October 1923 a republic was proclaimed and an army officer, called Mustafa Kemal, who had helped to form a nationalist movement at the end of the war, was chosen as first president. He was reelected in 1927, 1931, and 1935. In those years, Mustafa Kemal, who was given the additional name of Ataturk, which means "Father of the Turks," modernized his country with a series of sweeping reforms. These included introducing a new constitution, new civil and criminal law codes, abolishing polygamy, giving women the vote, adopting the Latin alphabet, encouraging Turks to wear European-style clothes, and initiating a four-year economic plan. He died in 1938.

1931

Japan goes to war with China

After the fall of the Manchu dynasty in 1911, China was divided by rival factions trying to take power. In Manchuria, in the northeast, the Japanese wielded great influence through their huge spending on industrial development. The military governor, Zhang Zuolin, encouraged this and also let them keep troops to protect railways and installations. In 1928 some Japanese officers murdered Zhang Zuolin because they thought he was going to surrender Manchuria to the Kuomintang, which wanted to reunite China. The Japanese government took no action against the officers because by then the army was very powerful in Japan. Three years later, in September 1931, following a bomb explosion on the railway near the Manchurian capital, Mukden, Japanese troops seized the city and overran the province, setting up a republic of Manchukuo in 1932. By 1937 Japan and China were at war, which lasted until 1945 when Japanese forces in China formally surrendered.

The last emperor
Henry Puyi (1906–67) was the last Manchu ruler of China, becoming emperor at the age of two. He was installed as the puppet emperor of Manchukuo in 1934 but was never more than a figurehead sovereign.

Puppet state
In 1932 Japan created the puppet state of Manchukuo and consolidated its control over Manchuria. This lasted until the end of World War II.

Japanese advance on Shanghai
Hundreds were reported dead in a Japanese bombing raid on Shanghai in January 1932. In November 1937 Japanese forces took Shanghai, and by December they were in possession of Nanking, the Chinese Nationalist capital.

Chinese symbolic padlock
This padlock was worn by a child during the first years of life to lock in the child's spirit and stop evil spirits from stealing it.

1934
The Long March

During the unstable period in China in the 1920s before the Kuomintang, or KMT (Chinese Nationalist Party) established a government, there were millions of Chinese without any means of earning proper livings. Many were in the Jiangxi province and in the neighboring Fujian province. In 1931, under their leaders Mao Zedong and Zhu De, they seized land and created a Chinese Communist republic in Jiangxi. They resisted many Kuomintang attempts to dislodge them, but in 1934 they were finally forced to give up the province. About 100,000 people marched some 6,000 miles (9,700 km) westward into China's wilder regions, hoping to find sanctuary. They reached Shaanxi province in 1935, where Mao Zedong set up Communist headquarters and continued to resist the Kuomintang. In 1937 both sides agreed to join together to fight the Japanese, who in that year overran northern China. This was the beginning of the Sino-Japanese War.

Nationalist leader
Chiang Kai-shek (1887–1975) was an early supporter of Sun Yat-sen, the founder of the Kuomintang, and took over leadership after his death. In 1934 Chiang led an army to Jiangxi and forced the Chinese rebel Communists out of the area.

Roundabout route
Only 20,000 of the original 100,000 marchers reached Shaanxi province. They seized 62 cities, scaled 18 mountain ranges, and crossed 24 rivers on their way. Kuomintang troops pursued them almost daily.

Mao Zedong

Mao Zedong (1893–1976) was the son of a Hunan peasant. After fighting in the revolutionary army in 1911, he developed an interest in Marxism and helped found the Chinese Communist Party. He set up his own rural-based branch with followers in Hunan and Jiangxi and, having gained stature within the party, was chosen as party leader in 1935. The success of the Long March enabled him to eliminate his internal opposition and rally his people to "go forth and fight the Japanese."

Perilous journey
The marchers' worst battles were with nature. Dangerous swamps, high mountains, and harsh weather conditions claimed many lives.

1934
Oil pipeline opened from Kirkuk to Tripoli

The oil resources of western Asia were known in ancient times, but it was not until the beginning of the 20th century that oil became a vital commodity in the industrial world and methods for extracting it were developed. The first major oil strike (a find of large quantities of oil under the earth's surface) was in Iran in 1908. Vast oil resources were also discovered in Iraq, but these were not developed until after World War I, when the Iraq Petroleum Company began to drill for oil; in 1927 huge deposits were found in the Kirkuk region. Part of the oil production process entailed laying oil pipelines from Iraq and other areas to ports on the Mediterranean. A pipeline from Kirkuk to the Syrian port of Tripoli was opened in July 1934, followed by another from Kirkuk to the Palestine port of Haifa in January 1935. Despite this progress, Asian oil production was slow to develop; by 1939 it was still only 6 percent of world production. After World War II there was a huge expansion in the oil industry in the Arab states. They grew rich and powerful, using their economic power to achieve political ends throughout the region.

Oil carrier
Caravan mules, a common method of transport in Iraq, were used to carry cases of oil for domestic use.

Oil-rich city
Baghdad, situated on both banks of the Tigris River in Iraq, grew rich on the profits of the oil industry. Today it is the capital and largest city of Iraq.

1945
World Zionist Conference

After the Balfour Declaration of 1917 that called for the Jews to have a national homeland in Palestine, Palestine became a British mandated territory (1920). A long period of unrest, rioting, and terrorism followed as Jews and Arabs clashed. In 1937 the British suggested dividing Palestine into two states, one for Jews and one for Arabs, but this was rejected by the Arabs. Then World War II intervened, during which millions of Jews in Europe were systematically murdered in prison camps and gas chambers in Nazi Europe. When the war ended in 1945, the World Zionist Conference, a congregation of leading Jews from around the world, asked that Palestine be made available to one million Jews, many of whom were refugees. U.S. president Harry Truman urged Britain to open Palestine to the first 100,000 Jews at once. Britain, willing to create a Jewish state but frightened by threats of war from the Arab states, such as Egypt, Iraq, and Syria, played for time, but this resulted in renewed terrorism in Palestine. Britain submitted the Palestinian problem to the United Nations, and in 1948 the British mandate was ended.

Terrorism in Jerusalem
In 1946 Jewish terrorists bombed British headquarters at the King David Hotel in Jerusalem, killing 91 people.

First president of Israel
Chaim Weizmann (1874–1952) was a committed Zionist. He was made president of Israel when the Jewish state became independent in 1948.

Home at last?
Jewish refugees from Nazi Europe who had survived the holocaust arrived in Palestine on crowded ships. The British refused to let some of them land.

	1200	1400	1600	1700	1800	1900	2000

1919-1946 EUROPE

The years that followed the horrors of World War I brought a great yearning for peace, which the League of Nations did not secure. Some nations experimented with new forms of government, such as Communism in Russia, Nazism in Germany, and fascism in Italy and Spain. In all these, dictators imposed their rule on every aspect of life, silencing opposition using brutal secret police, torture, and prison camps. German dictator Adolf Hitler, leader of the Nazi party, was bent on creating a powerful German empire. Small states such as Czechoslovakia and Austria were threatened by German expansion. France and Britain observed this without interfering but were forced into war to halt German aggression in 1939. The world was caught up in another disastrous conflict.

Selling success
Advertisements like this appeared in the 1920s to persuade consumers to buy products from home and abroad.

Nation divided
The 26 predominantly Catholic counties of Ireland became the Irish Free State. Six predominantly Protestant counties of northeast Ireland (purple) stayed in the United Kingdom. The political division of Ireland is still the cause of tension and conflict in the region.

1922
Home rule for Ireland

The question of Irish independence from Britain became critical after World War I. Members of Sinn Fein, the Irish republican party, won the majority of Irish seats in the British general election of 1918. They set up their own parliament, the Dail, in Dublin and declared Ireland independent. War broke out between Sinn Fein and the British. Michael Collins, a leader of the military wing (later to be called the Irish Republican Army) of Sinn Fein, built up an intelligence network and directed guerrilla warfare so effectively that in 1921 the British agreed to terms which the Dail accepted in 1922. Six counties of northeast Ireland kept their own parliament but joined Britain. Together, they became the United Kingdom. The rest of Ireland was granted dominion status and became the Irish Free State. In 1949 the Irish Free State severed all ties with Britain and became the Republic of Ireland.

Armed support
Sympathizers in the United States sent money to Sinn Fein to help them buy weapons, easily come by in postwar Europe.

Black and Tans
The British sent troops to Ireland in 1920 known as the Black and Tans because of the color of their uniforms. They became the most hated symbol of British oppression after committing several bloody atrocities.

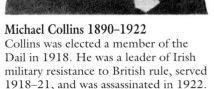

Michael Collins 1890–1922
Collins was elected a member of the Dail in 1918. He was a leader of Irish military resistance to British rule, served 1918–21, and was assassinated in 1922.

BETWEEN THE WARS

After the peace celebrations of 1918, Europeans felt uncertain about the future. Trading had almost ceased during the war, and overseas markets such as India had developed their own industries. Allied nations owed the United States enormous sums of money borrowed during the war. As a result, unemployment and inflation dominated Europe in the 1920s. The German economy collapsed under the added burden of reparations. Some blamed leaders and political systems, and social unrest increased across the continent, especially when governments tried to lower the price of goods and increase exports by reducing wages. In Britain, this led to a general strike in 1926. Then in 1929 the U.S. economy crashed, resulting in a worldwide depression. Banks collapsed, factories closed, unemployment soared throughout Europe. Sick of poverty and insecurity, Europeans turned to authoritarian leaders promising to restore national prosperity.

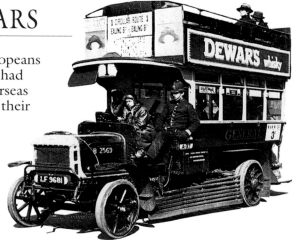

General strike
In 1926 British coal mine owners threatened to cut miners' low wages. The miners went on strike. Many other workers went on strike in sympathy, and Britain came to a virtual standstill. Volunteers ran essential services. Here policemen guard a volunteer bus driver.

GERMAN ECONOMIC CRISIS
By 1922 Germany could not afford to keep up reparations payments. Its main creditor, France, occupied the Ruhr industrial region along the Rhine River in 1923. The German economy was destroyed. Money became worthless, and millions of banknotes were needed to buy a loaf of bread. The reparations debt was finally rearranged on easier terms, and the currency stabilized. But in the 1930s all Europe was hit by depression, and Germany suffered especially badly. By 1932 nearly half the labor force was unemployed.

Consumer society
In the mid-1920s U.S. investors poured millions of dollars into European industry. Europeans made and bought for the first time consumer goods many Americans took for granted – washing machines, telephones, and hair dryers. When the U.S. economy crashed, investors withdrew European loans. European banks and businesses failed. Throughout the continent the standard of living rapidly declined.

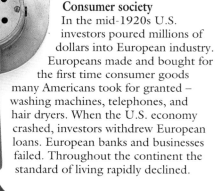

Increasing mobility
One flourishing industry was motor car manufacture. Cars were mass produced in the United States before the war. After it, European factories imitated their methods, producing small cars such as Citröens in France, Austins in Britain, and Fiats in Italy.

Working women
While men fought in the war, women took over their jobs at home successfully, and began to demand careers in many professions traditionally closed to them. Fashions were more practical: hemlines were higher and haircuts shorter.

Faith under attack
The Communists under Lenin constantly attacked organized religion. Priests were persecuted, and church property seized. Families hid their religious items, such as this household icon.

1928
Five-year plan for Soviet Union

The Bolshevik (soon called Communist) takeover in Russia led to civil war. Russian leader, Lenin, used terrible violence to suppress opposition and started to transform Russia in line with Marxist principles of common ownership, putting private industry and land under state control. The Communists won the civil war, but many found Lenin's measures too severe. In 1921 Lenin began the New Economic Policy (NEP), which allowed some free trade. A new constitution replaced imperial Russia with the Union of Soviet Socialist Republics. After Lenin died in 1924, three party leaders took control, including Joseph Stalin, but excluding Lenin's ambitious colleague Leon Trotsky. By 1928 Stalin held supreme power. He launched a five-year plan to expand farming and industry under state management. Industry probably developed faster than at any other time in Russian history.

Leon Trotsky 1879–1940
Trotsky's priority was world revolution, while Stalin's was a strong Communist Soviet Union. By the time of Lenin's death, Trotsky's influence was in decline. Stalin was able to exercise great influence after becoming the Communist Party's General Secretary in 1922. In 1928 Trotsky was banished to Kazakhstan in Central Asia and later exiled from the Soviet Union. In 1940 he was murdered in Mexico by an agent of Stalin.

Collective farming
Posters showing Stalin (center) among peasants promoted his agricultural plans. Farms, including their livestock, were combined in large units. On huge, state-owned farms peasants were paid wages, or they owned the farms collectively. Peasants resisted giving up land and livestock, most of all in the Ukraine. Millions were shot or sent to labor camps. The chaos, and government seizure of grain, led to famine and millions of deaths in the early 1930s.

Wave of terror
Stalin's effort to remove all possible enemies peaked in the purges of 1935–38. Intimidated people denounced neighbors as traitors to show loyalty to the state. Famous Communists were forced to admit to crimes in public trials. Over 10 million people were sent to labor camps (left) or executed.

State takes over
Five-year plans demanded vast increases in production in heavy industry (coal, steel, and machinery). Workers' lives were hard, and conditions sometimes dangerous. Victory celebrations were held when quotas were surpassed, but workers who did not perform well or criticized the system were punished as criminals. Production of everyday goods, such as this plate, was relatively neglected.

1933
Hitler becomes German chancellor

After Germany was defeated in World War I, the Versailles Treaty reduced its territory and armed forces. Many in Germany regarded this as a national humiliation. One was Adolf Hitler, president of the National Socialist German Workers (Nazi) party. Nazis blamed the Jews for most problems. Recession and unemployment devastated the country in the late 1920s. The Nazis gained massive support by promising to restore national pride and create jobs. In 1933 President Hindenburg made Hitler his chancellor; when he died in 1934 Hitler became *führer* (leader) of the German *reich* (state). He rebuilt the economy, pouring money into the army and public works. The Nazis imposed total control, banning political parties, introducing a violent secret police, and persecuting racial and social minorities, especially Jews.

Adolf Hitler 1889–1945
Austrian-born Hitler fought for Germany in World War I, then joined the German Nazis and became their leader. In 1923 he tried to overthrow the Bavarian state government in southern Germany and was briefly jailed. In prison, he wrote *Mein Kampf* (*My Struggle*) describing his dream of a German empire.

Nazi propaganda
The radio, newspapers, and art were all used to impress Nazi beliefs on Germans. The Nazi emblem, the swastika, appeared everywhere – even on children's toys. Nazis burned any books that praised democracy, denounced war, or were written by Jewish authors. Nazis produced "science" books claiming that Germans of "Aryan" descent, blonde haired and blue eyed, were a "master race."

New religion
Prosperity brought Hitler the lasting loyalty of workers and industrialists. The middle classes believed he would protect them from big business and from Russian-style Communism. At mass rallies his hypnotic speeches filled people with intense dedication to the Nazi cause.

Volkswagen "Beetle"
Hitler took a personal interest in developing Volkswagens, or people's cars, as part of his program to revive German industry. The "Beetle," as it later became known, became one of the most popular cars in the world.

Anti-Semitism
In 1935 laws deprived Jews of their German citizenship. Jews were publicly taunted and thrown out of schools and jobs. In 1938 Nazis vandalized Jewish homes and shops and set fire to synagogues. Thousands of Jews were killed or arrested in this *Kristallnacht*, or "night of broken glass."

600	800	1000	1200	1400	1600	1700	1800	1900	2000

1936
Rome-Berlin Axis

Italy fought with the Allies in World War I but gained little from the peace treaties. Many blamed the government, and the country neared civil war. A new movement, Fascism, grew up in the cities, led by Benito Mussolini. Fascists were bands of workers set on change, who believed in national pride and obedience to their leader. They attracted the upper and middle classes by attacking Communism. In 1922, 50,000 Fascists marched on Rome, and Mussolini became prime minister. He took dictatorial powers and pursued an aggressive foreign policy. He was at first hostile to Hitler, the German dictator, fearing a German invasion of Austria. But he sought Hitler's support after invading Ethiopia in 1935, and in 1936 the two made a pact, the Rome-Berlin Axis.

Two dictators
This poster celebrates a meeting between Mussolini and Hitler in 1938. Both rulers had dictatorial powers, crushed all political opposition, and embarked on grand public building programs to glorify themselves and the movements they led. But in Italy, industrialists, the church, and the army kept much control, and Jews were not ferociously attacked, as they were in Nazi Germany.

Fascist aggression
The Fascists strongly believed in expanding Italy's power abroad. In 1935 Italy invaded Ethiopia in East Africa and annexed it, despite protests from the League of Nations. This gun was made for the Italian viceroy of East Africa in 1939.

1936
Civil war breaks out in Spain

In 1931 Spanish republicans forced King Alfonso XIII into exile. A new republican government introduced socialist policies, such as nationalizing land, and limited the power of the church and army. Spanish army officers, some of whom supported the Fascist Falange party, revolted in 1936. General Franco became their leader and carried the revolt through Spain, which became locked in terrible civil war. Fascist Italy sent troops, and Germany sent aircraft, to aid Franco. Communist Russia sent money and arms to help the republican government, but by the end of March 1939 Franco had won most of Spain. He became a dictator allowing only one party, the Falange, to govern.

Taking sides
This poster shows Fascism as an Angel of Death. It was designed during the war to persuade Spaniards to fight Franco. Spain's republican government had the support of the workers, Communists, and those from the Catalan and Basque regions who wanted independence. Army officers, landowners, and clerics, as well as Fascist Falange members, supported Franco.

Republican pistol
Thousands of idealistic young Europeans and Americans, seeing the war as a Fascist attack on democracy, flocked to Spain to join a republican force, the International Brigade. The war was brutal; over 1 million people were killed, more than 10,000 from the International Brigade.

Francisco Franco 1892–1975
An excellent organizer, Franco rose through army ranks to become chief of staff in 1935. After joining the 1936 revolt, he arranged Italian and German aid for the rebels and for this was made army commander-in-chief and head of state. He planned the offensives that brought the rebels victory, and afterward ruled Spain as a dictator.

Going cheap
After the Wall Street Crash, many people were ruined. Cars and other assets were sold at ridiculously low prices in order to raise cash.

1919-1946 AMERICAS

After World War I the United States enjoyed a decade of material progress, although farmers suffered from a slump in crop prices resulting from overproduction of grain and other commodities. Then, in 1929, the New York Stock Exchange collapsed and a depression followed that reverberated around the world. In Latin America, countries like Mexico and Peru tried to break free from U.S. domination, while other countries introduced far-reaching economic and social reforms. Brazil, badly hit by the slump in its two main resources, coffee and rubber, tried to resolve its difficulties under the dictatorship of Getulio Vargas.

1929
The Great Depression

The United States emerged from World War I as a great power. After a brief postwar recession, the U.S. economy went into high gear, making the 1920s a decade of prosperity for many Americans. (The nation's farmers, however, suffered from a serious drop in crop prices.) The boom was fueled by widespread speculation on the mostly unregulated stock market. On October 29, 1929, a panic began on the New York Stock Exchange. Millions of shares were sold, and many investors were ruined overnight. The stock market collapse was followed by the failures of many banks and businesses; by 1933, 16 million Americans were unemployed. The panic spread and soon the whole world was in the grip of a great depression. In Europe the depression was dealt with in different ways by the national governments. In Germany, recession and rising unemployment produced increasing support for Adolf Hitler and his Nazi Party.

AL CAPONE 1895–1947

In 1920 Prohibition (prohibiting alcohol to be made or sold) was made law in the United States. Bootlegging (selling illegal drink) and gang wars resulted. Police turned a blind eye as gang fought gang for control of the markets. Gang leader Al Capone controlled the Chicago illegal liquor trade for years without police interference. He was finally jailed in the 1930s – for tax evasion.

Feeding the nation
The Great Depression caused mass unemployment and homelessness. In many big cities, soup kitchens serving free food, like this one in Chicago, were set up to feed the hungry.

In celebration
After years of gang violence, Prohibition was ended in 1933. The nation erupted in celebration.

600	800	1000	1200	1400	1600	1700	1800	1900	2000

ROOSEVELT'S "NEW DEAL"

In the presidential election of 1932, Democrat Franklin Delano Roosevelt defeated incumbent Republican Herbert Hoover. Roosevelt took office promising a "new deal" to an American people ravaged by the Depression. In his first months in office – a period often called the "Hundred Days" – the new president took swift action to stabilize the nation's shaken banking and financial systems and to bring relief to the millions of unemployed and impoverished Americans. The president later introduced many reforms and set up a number of agencies – a program known collectively as the New Deal – to bring about economic recovery. New Deal programs helped many Americans survive the miseries of the Depression, but the U.S. economy didn't return to pre-1929 levels until the coming of World War II. Franklin Roosevelt was reelected in 1936 and went on to win unprecedented third and fourth terms in 1940 and 1944.

Franklin Delano Roosevelt (1882–1945)

Tennessee Valley

The Tennessee Valley Authority (TVA) developed the river system for agricultural purposes, navigation, flood control, and to create hydroelectric power. More than 20 publicly owned dams were built. By the 1960s the system supplied 6 percent of U.S. electricity.

The Grapes of Wrath

In the West, drought and winds turned fields into "dust bowls" and thousands of farmers, forced from their land by debt, headed to California in search of work. John Steinbeck wrote of them in his book, *The Grapes of Wrath*, which was made into a film.

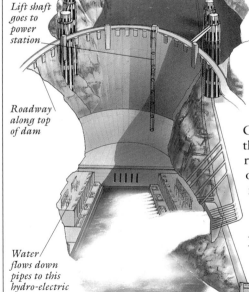

Lake Mead

Lift shaft goes to power station

Roadway along top of dam

Water flows down pipes to this hydro-electric power station

New Deal Programs

Many New Deal programs were aimed at helping the nation's farmers; these included the Agricultural Adjustment Act (1933), which paid farmers to limit cultivation. Industrial workers benefited from the 1935 Labor Relations Act, which strengthened labor unions. Millions of Americans found employment with the Work Projects Administration or the Civilian Conservation Corps. Other reforms of the New Deal years included increased regulation of businesses and the creation of the Social Security system. There was much public support for the New Deal, although the Supreme Court declared some measures unconstitutional.

Dam building

Hydroelectric projects helped to restart the nation's economy. The huge Hoover Dam on the Colorado River was completed in 1936.

THAT'S ENTERTAINMENT

The onset of the Great Depression coincided with the coming of the talkies in the movies. For many people, movies were an inexpensive way of escaping a hard and joyless daily life. Movie magazines also flourished. Their largely fictional accounts of the glamorous lives of the great stars were very popular with the moviegoing public.

New camera

The weighty three-strip Technicolor camera was used to shoot the first really successful color films.

1930
Revolution flares up in Brazil

Brazil's domination of the world rubber trade was badly affected by Asian competition. Then world coffee prices slumped sharply during the late 1920s. Population, however, was on the increase, and social unrest began to spread rapidly throughout the huge country as businesses foundered and food shortages followed. In 1930 a revolution broke out and Getulio Vargas, governor of the province of Rio Grande do Sul, seized power and was declared president. At first he acted with moderation, but gradually he became more dictatorial. In 1938 he suspended elections and formally proclaimed a dictatorship which lasted until 1945. In that time, he ruled with an iron fist in a velvet glove and did much to modernize Brazil and improve conditions for the poor. In 1942 he declared war against the Axis powers and in 1943 sent a Brazilian army to join the Allies in Italy.

Too much coffee in Brazil?
Coffee was introduced into Brazil in the early 1700s and soon became vital to the country's economy. By 1900 Brazil supplied more than 75 percent of world demand. The fertility of the land around the city of São Paulo, the center of the Brazilian coffee industry, and the cheapness of the labor force, who lived in dire poverty, encouraged constantly increasing production. Two bumper crops were grown between 1927 and 1929, and efforts of the Brazilian Coffee Institute to restrict sales failed. Coffee flooded world markets; prices plummeted.

Coffee beans

Getulio Vargas 1883–1954
Vargas fell from power in 1945 but returned for a short inglorious term in 1950. The one-time idol of his people was condemned for corruption and his mishandling of the economy, and in 1954 he committed suicide.

1932
The outbreak of the Chaco war

Since the mid-1800s, Bolivia and Paraguay had disputed the sovereignty of the Chaco region, a 96,525 sq-mile (250,000 sq-km) wilderness situated between the nations of Bolivia and Paraguay. By the 1920s there was international interest in the region, as it was believed to be rich in oil deposits. In 1928 armed clashes broke out between the two countries, and Paraguay, a smaller and much less populated country than Bolivia, appealed to the League of Nations to arbitrate. All negotiations failed, and in 1932 a full-scale conflict erupted. Paraguay, regarded by many as the innocent party, soon began to gain ground. After three years of war "at the cost of about three Bolivians and two Paraguayans for each square kilometer," according to a commentator, the Paraguayans controlled most of the region. Both sides were exhausted and a truce was made through international mediation, followed by a treaty in 1938. The Chaco was divided, with the larger share going to Paraguay.

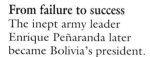

From failure to success
The inept army leader Enrique Peñaranda later became Bolivia's president.

A costly war
The terrain of the region made battle conditions appalling. At times, 50,000 men on each side were fighting in heavy jungles and scrub or in flooded swamps. In the dry season, there was scarcely a drop of water to be found. Malaria and dysentery killed as many men as the guns, and the poisonous snakes which are very common in the area added to the heavy death toll.

| 600 | 800 | 1000 | 1200 | 1400 | 1600 | 1700 | 1800 | 1900 | 2000 |

1933

Peruvian president assassinated

The War of the Pacific between Peru and Chile (1879–84) was disastrous for Peru, and it took the country many years to recover. During the 1920s, a new revolutionary movement sprang up in Peru led by José Carlos Mariátegui (1895–1930) and Victor Raul Haya de la Torre. Haya was exiled in 1923 for his activities, and in 1924 in Mexico he founded the American Popular Revolutionary Alliance (APRA), which aimed to fight U.S. imperialism, to nationalize land and industry, and to integrate Native Americans throughout Latin America. APRA cells were founded in many South American countries but the movement only caught on in Peru. In 1930 Haya returned to Peru and stood as APRA candidate in the presidential election. His opponent Sanchez Cherro won but he was killed in 1933 by an *aprista* (an APRA supporter). Conflict between successive governments and APRA went on for years.

Old campaigner
Haya de la Torre (1895–1979) continued to fight elections into the 1960s. Although they came close, APRA never won a presidential election in Peru.

Outlawed
From its conception, APRA achieved huge popularity in Peru, but it was outlawed for several years and was opposed by both army and police who saw it as a threat to stability. Nevertheless it was to become the most enduring political party in the history of Peru.

Lima, capital of Peru
The people of Lima, a city of wide and ornate boulevards and squares, supported José Luis Bustamante, the candidate backed by APRA, in the 1945 presidential election. He was successful. Haya de la Torre, although not in office, dominated the government for two years, the nearest he came to real power in his long career.

1938

Mexico takes over U.S. oil interests

After the end of World War I, the governments of Latin American countries began to feel nervous about the growing power of the United States and U.S. government and big business, industrial, commercial, and social pressures. In Mexico U.S. oil companies had such huge investments in Mexican oil production that they were able to restrict Mexican government land reform programs, and even had the power to threaten military intervention in Mexican internal affairs. In 1934 a new Mexican president, Lázaro Cárdenas, came to power and carried through a massive program of land reforms, which included distributing 40 million acres (162,000 sq km) in village communal holdings. In 1938 Cárdenas took over the properties of the U.S. and British oil companies, a very popular move throughout Mexico. Despite diplomatic retaliation and requests for compensation from Britain and the United States, Cárdenas stood firm and instead negotiated to trade oil with other countries like Italy and Germany.

Lázaro Cárdenas 1895–1970
Cárdenas was a great social reformer. Born of a poor village family, he never forgot his roots. Agrarian land reforms and an extensive building program of country schools helped better the lot of the rural poor.

On guard
After the oil wells were seized and placed under Mexican control, there were fears of reprisals from the U.S. and Britain.

1919-1946 OCEANIA

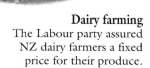

Australia was initially badly affected by the Great Depression but recovered rapidly because it was rich in gold resources. Robert Menzies, the new prime minister, encouraged continued ties with Britain. In New Zealand, great social distress resulting from the depression was partly relieved by a new Labour government, which took daring remedial measures. Limited forms of power-sharing were introduced by colonial powers in many of the Pacific islands such as Fiji.

Dairy farming
The Labour party assured NZ dairy farmers a fixed price for their produce.

Horohoro Native School
The new Labour government argued that Maoris should have the same rights as everybody else in education, housing, and social benefits. The Minister of Native Affairs is pictured here with Maori pupils in front of their school.

1935

New Zealand Labour party wins election

The world depression which began in the late 1920s upset New Zealand's economy dramatically. Export prices fell by almost half, the country could no longer borrow the money it needed, and unemployment soared. The government in power seemed unable to remedy the situation. As a result, at the 1935 general election, the New Zealand Labour party won power for the first time. It was an overwhelming victory, spurred by promises to relieve the country's distress. Immediately big loans were made to the government, an act of parliament gave farmers guaranteed prices for their products, and the 40-hour work week was introduced. In 1938 the Social Security Act was passed, ensuring all citizens a minimum standard of living.

Success story
Robert Menzies (1894–1978) was a successful lawyer from Melbourne. He was elected prime minister when only 44.

1939

Menzies is elected Australian prime minister

Increases in the price of gold, and after 1933 of wool, enabled Australia to recover more quickly than some countries from the world depression. In 1931, a new United Australia party, made up of members of the older Labour party and the National party, formed a government. Three years later, the United Australia party joined with the Country party to form a coalition government. In 1937 the coalition won a safe victory in a general election, and in 1939 Robert Menzies was elected prime minister. By this time, it was clear that Britain was going to war with Germany. The main concern of the new prime minister was to assist the "mother country," and he devoted his early months in office to developing Australia's forces and improving defense arrangements. World War II finally broke out in early September, and Australia immediately joined in on the British side and made generous offers of help.

Going out to fight
Australian soldiers helped the British to combat German forces at Tobruk, in North Libya, during World War II.

| 600 | 800 | 1000 | 1200 | 1400 | 1600 | 1700 | 1800 | 1900 | 2000 |

WORLD WAR II

The causes of World War II lay in Adolf Hitler's expansionist military and foreign policies. In 1936 he reoccupied the Rhineland, a demilitarized zone between France and Belgium. In March 1938 he forced Austria to unite with Germany and then took over part of Czechoslovakia. Each time, Britain and France did not resist. Their policy of nonintervention came to be called appeasement. On September 1, 1939, Hitler invaded Poland, having agreed with the Soviet Union to divide the country between them. He did not think that Britain and France would help Poland, but on September 3 they declared war. Two years later Japan came in on Germany's side.

Last charge of the Polish cavalry
Poland had a large army but its equipment and tactics were no match for Germany's.

Instruments of terror
Stuka divebombers were greatly feared.

Lightning war, lightning victories

The assaults of the German forces involved powerful thrusts by columns of tanks and other armored vehicles deep into enemy territory, followed up by linking or sweeping movements by infantry coming up from behind which surrounded large pockets of enemy forces, the whole operation supported by powerful air cover. This method of warfare was called *blitzkrieg*, which means "lightning war," and using it the Germans were unstoppable. Poland collapsed before the end of September 1939. After a lull of six months, Hitler turned on Belgium, Holland, Denmark, Norway, and France. By mid-June 1940, all had fallen. Britain stood alone.

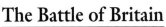

The Battle of Britain

Hitler planned to invade Britain in 1940, and from July to September he launched a series of heavy air attacks against shipping, airfields, ports, and towns to "soften up" the British before sending in the landing craft. But the Royal Air Force, although smaller, destroyed two German planes for every one British plane lost and forced Hitler to abandon his invasion scheme.

Lived to fight another day
Just before France's collapse, French and British troops, cut off by the German advance, massed on the beaches of Dunkirk in Belgium. A massive evacuation was organized. Every available British boat, including small pleasure craft, was used to rescue more than 200,000 British and 120,000 French troops.

Leaving all behind them
All over Europe, families were broken up and millions were displaced by the war. In England, children were evacuated from the cities.

1939

August 23 German-Soviet Nonagression Pact signed in Moscow
September 1 German forces invade Poland
September 3 Britain and France declare war on Germany
September 17 Soviet forces invade Poland

1940

April 9 Germans invade Denmark and Norway, which, after a determined resistance, surrender in May
May 10 German forces invade Belgium and Holland; Churchill becomes British prime minister and forms coalition government

May 12 German armies enter France; French to surrender after seven weeks (on June 22)
June 4–5 After rapid German advance, British and French (some 320,000 men) evacuated from Dunkirk to England but lose all their equipment
June 10 Italy under dictator Benito Mussolini declares war against France and Britain

August German air force directs major bombing offensive against British airfields and towns in the Battle of Britain
September 13 Italians attack British-controlled Egypt; in December, the British drive them back and enter Libya
October 28 Italians invade Greece but are defeated; they abandon stores and munitions

---

40,000 BC		10,000	5000	1000	500	AD 1	200	400

War of the world

By June 1941 the Axis (Germany and Italy) had conquered Yugoslavia, Albania, and Greece and persuaded Romania, Hungary, and Bulgaria to assist them. Then, on June 22, Germany launched a massive invasion on its former ally, the Soviet Union. In September Hitler's armies besieged Leningrad (now known as St. Petersburg). When the Russian winter set in, a stalemate followed. In December the Japanese, who had already overrun much of China, attacked Pearl Harbor, and the United States declared war. Germany and Italy, Japan's allies, declared war on the United States a few days later. Japan swiftly overran all Southeast Asia, threatening Australia and India.

Flying cap
This distinctive cap was worn by a member of the U.S. Army Air Force.

Unprovoked attack
On December 7, 1941, without first making a declaration of war, the Japanese attacked Pearl Harbor, the main U.S. naval base in Hawaii. Five U.S. battleships and 15 other ships were sunk or crippled.

Rain of fire
These German bombs are incendiaries, designed to start fires.

Death from the sky

Aerial bombing played a large part in the warfare of World War II. Large aircraft carrying several tons of bombs smashed enemy factories, railways, electrical and oil installations, dams, dockyards, and airfields; but they were used against civilians as well as troops. The Germans bombed many of Europe's major cities. The Allies began raids on German cities in 1942, using as many as 1,000 bombers in a single raid. In the bombing of Dresden in 1945, some 80,000 civilians were killed in one night.

Nowhere to run
Bombers were turned against civilians in their homes and workplaces.

1941

March United States grants lend-lease arrangement to help Britain fight Germany
April 3 German General Rommel launches attack on British forces in North Africa; reaches Egypt at end of May
April 6 Allies capture Addis Ababa in Ethiopia from Italians

April 6 German forces invade Yugoslavia and move into Greece; brave resistance no match for German weaponry
May 27 British sink German battleship *Bismarck* in Atlantic; most of the 1,000 crewmen die
June 22 Massive German army of over 3,000,000 men invades Soviet Union along 2,000-mile (3,200-km) front

September 4 Germans begin siege of Leningrad in Soviet Union; the city defies attack for 900 days until the besiegers are driven back
September 19 Germans take Kiev, Soviet Union
October German armies begin assault on Moscow, anxious to take it before winter; Soviets counterattack in December

December 7 Japanese attack U.S. fleet in Pearl Harbor, Hawaii; United States immediately declares war on Japan
December 25 Hong Kong, a British colony, falls to Japan; in next few months Japanese take all Southeast Asia, including Singapore, Burma, and the Philippines

"The Desert Fox"
In 1941 Erwin Rommel (1891–1944) became commander of the Afrika Korps. He grew increasingly sceptical about Hitler's direction of the war and in 1944 became involved in a plot to overthrow the leader.

The two sides in the war
By November 1942 most of Europe was in the hands of Germany and Italy. The Soviet Union and United Kingdom were hard pressed to hold out until the United States entered the war on their side at the end of 1941.

- ▢ Axis states
- ▢ Areas controlled by Axis
- ▢ Allied states
- ▢ Areas controlled by Allies
- ▢ Neutral states
- ▢ Extent of German military occupation

War in the African desert

By 1940 the war had spread to North Africa, where Italian forces in Libya attacked Egypt, which the United Kingdom was committed to defend. The British drove back the Italians, prompting the Germans to send the Italians military aid. Under General Rommel, the Germans pushed the British back to Egypt. The struggle continued until British forces, led by General Montgomery, won a decisive victory at El Alamein in Egypt in October–November 1942. Montgomery then advanced swiftly across Libya to meet a British and U.S. force which had landed in Algeria and Morocco. The Axis armies were trapped between the Allied armies and surrendered in May 1943.

Hitler's "Final Solution"

In 1943, the incessant Allied bombing attacks on German cities and factories severely hampered the German war effort. Still, horrifying killings and torture continued on an ever-increasing scale in the concentration camps (camps for the confinement and mass murder of Jewish and other prisoners) throughout Germany and occupied Europe. The camps were the terrible centerpiece of Hitler's program, known as the "Final Solution," to eliminate the Jewish people.

Jewish yellow star
Germans forced Jews to wear identity badges.

Jewish uprising in the Warsaw ghetto
Germans took Warsaw, the Polish capital, in 1939. Jews were forced to live in a small area of the city (ghetto) and were terrorized daily by the Nazis. In 1943 they rose up and fought back. Almost all the 40,000 Jews in the ghetto were killed.

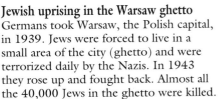

Holocaust victims
Millions of Jews were used for slave labor in the concentration camps, where they suffered starvation, torture, and ultimately death.

1942

February 15 Japanese take Singapore from Britain
April 18 U.S. planes bomb Tokyo
June 3–6 Battle of Midway; U.S. warplanes defeat Japanese naval force
July 2 Germans capture Sebastopol in the Crimea

July 17 Germans open offensive against Volgograd (then Stalingrad); Soviet forces counterattack in November
October/November British Eighth Army drives Germans from El Alamein and pursues them across North Africa
November 8 British and U.S. forces land in French North Africa

1943

January 23 Allied troops take Tripoli, last remaining Italian-held city in Africa
February 2 Starving German Sixth Army trapped in Stalingrad surrenders; liberation of Soviet cities begins

May Germans and Italians expelled from North Africa
July Soviet forces win massive tank battle at Kursk
July 10–11 Allies invade Sicily; Sicily falls in August
July 25 Italian dictator Mussolini forced to resign
September 2 Allied forces invade Italian mainland

Japan and the war in the Pacific

War in Europe left British, French, and Dutch colonial possessions in Asia and the Pacific unprotected. In 1941–42 the Japanese exploited this situation and overran many countries and Pacific islands. The first Allied successes were achieved at sea, starting with two important victories by the U.S. Navy in the Battle of the Coral Sea and the Battle of Midway, both in 1942. This frustrated Japan's plans to capture Australia and the Hawaiian Islands and so deprive the United States of bases from which to counterattack Japan.

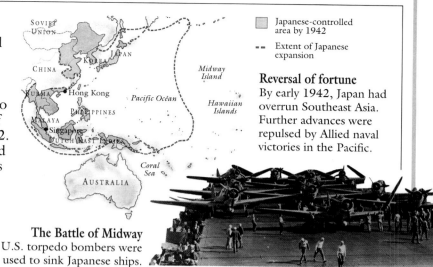

Japanese-controlled area by 1942

-- Extent of Japanese expansion

Reversal of fortune
By early 1942, Japan had overrun Southeast Asia. Further advances were repulsed by Allied naval victories in the Pacific.

The Battle of Midway
U.S. torpedo bombers were used to sink Japanese ships.

Soviet partisans meet in a forest
The Allied campaign had been greatly assisted by local and national resistance movements in Belgium, Czechoslovakia, Yugoslavia, Greece, Poland, and behind the lines in the Soviet Union.

Allied troops land on Normandy beaches

By 1944 the German hold on Europe was weakening. The Allied invasion of Europe began on June 6, 1944, with a massive assault on the beaches of Normandy by British, U.S., Canadian, and other troops, masterminded by U.S. General Eisenhower. A bridgehead was soon established and, after hard fighting, U.S. and British soldiers broke through German defenses. In August a force landed in southern France and moved north. The people of Paris drove out the German occupiers. A month later nearly all France was free. By April 1945 U.S. and British troops were well into central and southern Germany.

Hiroshima and the beginning of the end

In 1943, the tide began to turn in the Pacific when U.S. forces retook some islands; in 1944 several U.S. and British land campaigns led to the recovery of the Philippines and Burma. Early in 1945 U.S. forces took the Japanese islands of Iwojima and Okinawa. Then, on August 6, the U.S. Air Force dropped the first atomic bomb on the Japanese city of Hiroshima, devastating the inner city and killing about 150,000 people. Three days later, a second bomb was dropped on Nagasaki. In addition, the Soviet Union declared war on Japan. These three calamities forced the Japanese to surrender. On August 14, 1945, they laid down their arms.

D-Day landings
D-Day was the code name given to the first day of the Normandy landings, June 6, 1944.

Remnants of Hiroshima
Heat from the atomic blast destroyed buildings within a 4-mile (7-km) radius.

1944

January 22 Allied troops land at Anzio on Italy's coast
May 12 Soviet army completes liberation of Crimea
June 4 Anglo-American forces enter Rome, left unharmed by the retreating German forces
June 6 Allies invade Normandy

August Soviets break into east Prussia and Poland
August 24 Citizens of Paris rise against German occupying forces and drive them out
October 20 U.S. troops begin reconquest of the Philippines
December 16–25 German forces attack U.S. armies in the Ardennes, France; action fails after Allied bombing offensive

1945

April 1 U.S. forces invade Japanese island of Okinawa
April 30 Adolf Hitler commits suicide in Berlin
May 8 Formal declaration of the end of the war in Europe
August 6 First atomic bomb dropped on Hiroshima, Japan, causing massive destruction

August 8 Soviet Union declares war on Japan
August 14 Japanese surrender to United States and Allies: World War II over

The road to victory and peace

Germany surrendered unconditionally to the United States, Britain, France, and the Soviet Union in May 1945. Control of the German nation was put into the hands of an Allied control committee headed by the three leading Allied commanders: Eisenhower (United States), Montgomery (Britain), and Zhukov (Soviet Union). Germany was split into four zones of military occupation under the four Allied powers. A peace conference was held at Potsdam in July to decide the country's future.

The millions who died

The total number of victims of World War II amounted to about 50 million. The Soviets suffered the greatest losses – about 20 million died (one tenth of the whole Soviet population). Millions of civilians were killed in bombing raids, and at least 10 million died in the Nazi death camps, of whom six million were Jews. Many others, made homeless, became refugees.

Death a reality
The bodies of some dead soldiers were wrapped up and brought back from the battlefields to be buried on home soil.

London celebrates victory
The British prime minister, Winston Churchill, officially proclaimed VE (Victory in Europe) Day, May 8, 1945, as the day of celebration of the end of the war in Europe.

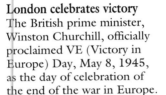

Red Army enters Berlin
Soviet troops finally reached the center of Berlin on April 30, 1945, where they planted their Red Flag on top of the ruined Reichstag (parliament) building.

The dividing of the German capital

After the Germans surrendered, Berlin was totally devastated. Hitler had committed suicide in his bunker. Soviet troops occupied most of eastern Germany and Allied troops the west. Berlin, which was in eastern Germany, was divided up among the four Allied powers. It was soon clear that dissension was growing in the Allied ranks between the Communist Soviets and the others.

Nuremberg trials in Germany

In November 1945, 21 leading Nazis were put on trial at Nuremberg before an international tribunal. They were indicted on one or more of four counts: conspiracy to make war, war crimes, crimes against peace, and crimes against humanity. There were also trials for less important German officials, particularly commandants and principal officers who had served in the concentration camps.

Final verdict
Of the 21 Nazis prosecuted, 11 were sentenced to death by hanging. Others were imprisoned, and only two were acquitted. Many other Nazi war criminals escaped punishment.

1945

September 1 British troops take Hong Kong, and then Singapore on September 5
September 2 Formal terms of Japanese surrender signed; Japan put under control of U.S. army of occupation, but Emperor Hirohito remains head of state

September 8 Korea divided into zones controlled by Soviets and United States
October 24 United Nations formally established
November 20 Trial of 21 Nazi war leaders by British, French, Soviet, and U.S. judges, begins at Nuremberg; 11 Nazis are sentenced to death by hanging

1946

January 7 Allies formally recognize foundation of an Austrian republic within its 1937 borders, after Austria divided into four zones of Allied occupation (between United States, Britain, France, and Soviet Union)

July–October Paris peace conference between 21 nations which fought Germany; treaties signed in February 1947
October 15 Nazi Hermann Goering kills himself hours before planned execution
November 4 United States and China sign a pact of friendship

CHAPTER 20

1946 – 1990s

ONE WORLD

View of the earth from space

1946-1990s
THE WORLD

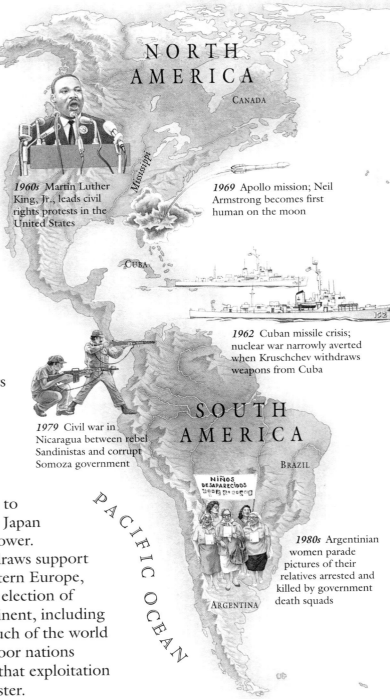

THE DROPPING OF THE atomic bombs on the Japanese cities of Hiroshima and Nagasaki in August 1945 brings World War II to an abrupt end. The peace that follows is fragile as the two main victors of the war – the United States and the Soviet Union – struggle for supremacy. Both superpowers develop massive arsenals of nuclear and other weapons and construct worldwide military and economic alliances. The uneasy balance that exists for 40 years between the two is known as the Cold War, since neither side fights the other directly. However, both powers help rival sides in wars that erupt in Korea, Vietnam, the Middle East, and Africa.

The end of the Cold War

Maintaining a constant state of military readiness costs both the United States and the Soviet Union dearly. The United States begins to retreat from its international responsibilities as Japan overtakes it as the world's leading economic power. By 1989, an impoverished Soviet Union withdraws support from satellite Communist governments of Eastern Europe, leading to the unification of Germany and the election of democratic governments throughout the continent, including in Russia itself. Yet throughout this period, much of the world remains poor, and the gap between rich and poor nations widens. For the first time, concerns are raised that exploitation of the planet could lead to environmental disaster.

NORTH AMERICA

CANADA

1960s Martin Luther King, Jr., leads civil rights protests in the United States

1969 Apollo mission; Neil Armstrong becomes first human on the moon

CUBA

1962 Cuban missile crisis; nuclear war narrowly averted when Kruschchev withdraws weapons from Cuba

1979 Civil war in Nicaragua between rebel Sandinistas and corrupt Somoza government

SOUTH AMERICA

BRAZIL

NIÑOS DESAPARECIDOS

1980s Argentinian women parade pictures of their relatives arrested and killed by government death squads

ARGENTINA

PACIFIC OCEAN

Mississippi

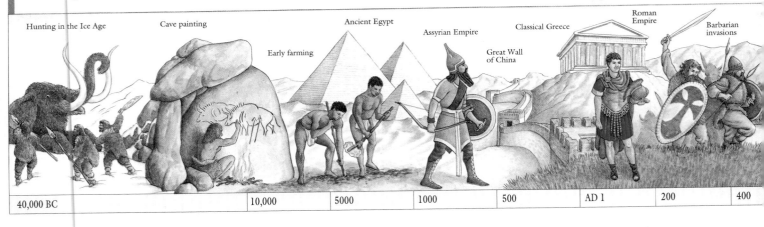

Hunting in the Ice Age

Cave painting

Early farming

Ancient Egypt

Assyrian Empire

Great Wall of China

Classical Greece

Roman Empire

Barbarian invasions

| 40,000 BC | | 10,000 | 5000 | 1000 | 500 | AD 1 | 200 | 400 |

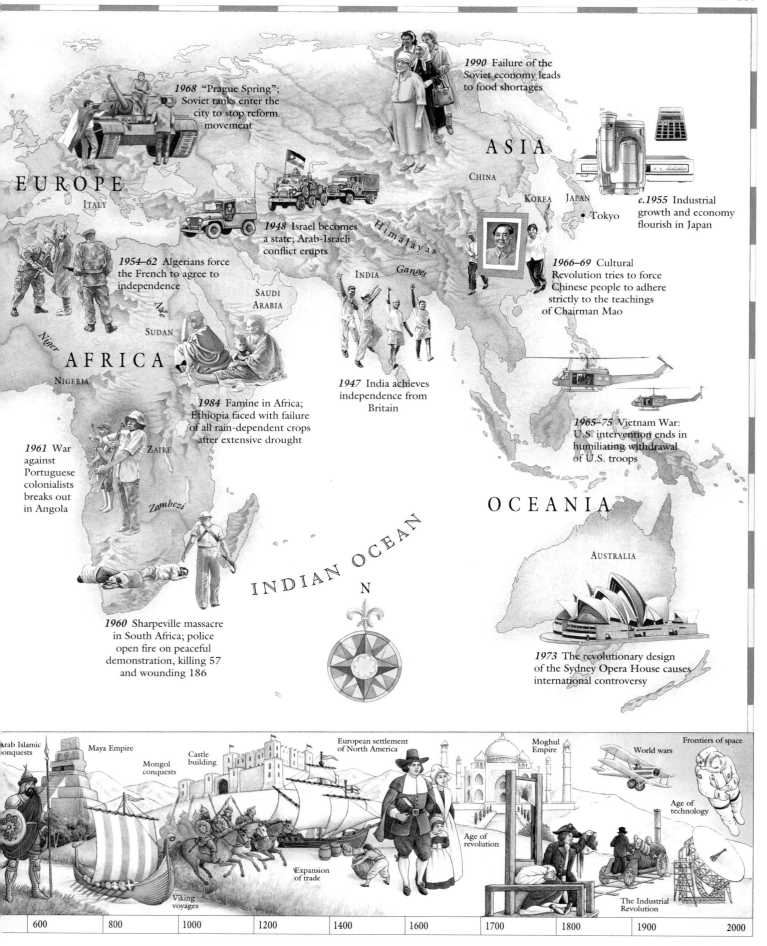

ASIA

1990 Failure of the Soviet economy leads to food shortages

1968 "Prague Spring"; Soviet tanks enter the city to stop reform movement

EUROPE

ITALY

CHINA

KOREA JAPAN

• Tokyo

c.1955 Industrial growth and economy flourish in Japan

1948 Israel becomes a state; Arab-Israeli conflict erupts

1954–62 Algerians force the French to agree to independence

Himalayas

SAUDI ARABIA

Nile

SUDAN

INDIA Ganges

1966–69 Cultural Revolution tries to force Chinese people to adhere strictly to the teachings of Chairman Mao

Niger

AFRICA

NIGERIA

1984 Famine in Africa; Ethiopia faced with failure of all rain-dependent crops after extensive drought

1947 India achieves independence from Britain

ZAIRE

1961 War against Portuguese colonialists breaks out in Angola

Zambezi

1965–75 Vietnam War: U.S. intervention ends in humiliating withdrawal of U.S. troops

OCEANIA

INDIAN OCEAN

N

AUSTRALIA

1960 Sharpeville massacre in South Africa; police open fire on peaceful demonstration, killing 57 and wounding 186

1973 The revolutionary design of the Sydney Opera House causes international controversy

Arab Islamic conquests

Maya Empire

Mongol conquests

Castle building

European settlement of North America

Moghul Empire

World wars

Frontiers of space

Age of technology

Age of revolution

Expansion of trade

Viking voyages

The Industrial Revolution

| 600 | 800 | 1000 | 1200 | 1400 | 1600 | 1700 | 1800 | 1900 | 2000 |

1946

1958

AFRICA

1948 Afrikaner National party wins power in South Africa

1951 Libya gains independence

1952–59 Mau-Mau guerrilla war against British in Kenya

1954–70 Colonel Nasser rules Egypt

1954–62 War for independence in Algeria; freedom won in 1962*

1956 Suez crisis; Britain and France attempt but fail to regain control of Suez Canal from Egypt

1956 Morocco, Tunisia, and Sudan gain their independence

1957 Ghana is first country in sub-Saharan Africa to become independent*

A Ghanaian farmer; many Africans left their farms for the cities

1958–60 Independence for Zaire, Nigeria, Somalia, and 12 of France's 13 sub-Saharan colonies

1960s Civil war in south Sudan

1960–65 Civil war in Zaire, formerly Belgian Congo

1961–67 Independence for Tanzania, Uganda, Kenya, Sierra Leone, Rwanda, Burundi, Malawi, Zambia, Lesotho, Botswana, Gambia, and Swaziland

1963 Organization of African Unity (OAU) founded

1965 White regime in Zimbabwe declares independence

1967–70 Biafran War, Nigeria

Idi Amin ruled Uganda by terror, 1971–79, killing perhaps 100,000

ASIA

Woman soldier in the Israeli army

1947 India gains independence*

1947 Japan's new democratic constitution comes into effect

1948 Israeli independence leads to the first Arab–Israeli war*

1949 Mao Zedong proclaims People's Republic of China

1950–53 Korean War

1951 United States and 48 other countries sign peace treaty with Japan in San Francisco

1953 Mao Zedong introduces first five-year plan in China*

1954 Vietminh defeat French troops at Dien Bien Phu*

c.1955 Start of period of fast economic growth in Japan*

Camouflaged soldiers advance across country in the Vietnam War

1961 Troops from Saudi Arabia and other Arab states take over defense of Kuwait from British in face of Iraqi threat

1964 Tokyo Olympic Games; first Olympic Games in Asia

1965–73 Vietnam War

1964 Arab leaders set up Palestine Liberation Organization to unite Palestinian refugees

1966 Indira Gandhi becomes prime minister of India

1966 Beginning of Cultural Revolution in China

1967 Six Day War between Israel and neighboring Arab states

EUROPE

1948–49 The Berlin Airlift *

1949 Britain recognizes the independence of Ireland

1951 Sir Winston Churchill forms his first peacetime government in England

1953 Death of Stalin in Russia; Nikita Khrushchev takes power

1 **1953** DNA discovered

1955 The Warsaw Pact is signed

1956 Soviet troops invade Hungary and quash revolt*

1957 Russians launch Sputniks; Laika, a small dog, becomes the first living creature in space

1957 The Treaty of Rome ushers in the EEC*

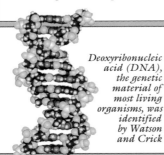
Deoxyribonucleic acid (DNA), the genetic material of most living organisms, was identified by Watson and Crick

1958 Charles de Gaulle brings strong presidential rule to France

1 **1961** Russian Yuri Gagarin becomes first human in space

1961 Berlin Wall built to stop East Germans fleeing to the West

1961 Female oral contraceptive pill comes onto the market

1964 Leonid Brezhnev takes over from Khrushchev as ruler in Russia

1968 Paris erupts into student riots followed by general strike*

1968 Czechoslovakia tries to initiate internal reforms; Soviet troops enter Prague and end "Prague Spring"*

Soviet troops entered Prague to enforce Soviet rule

AMERICAS

Police guard buses of black students

1947 In Truman Doctrine U.S. government promises aid to any country resisting Communism

1948–51 Under Marshall Plan, United States dispenses aid to Europe to help postwar recovery

1949 United States and West European nations set up North Atlantic Treaty Organization (NATO) for collective security

1950s Black Americans campaign for civil rights*

1955 Army officers seize power from Argentinian president Perón*

1962 Cuban missile crisis*

1963 U.S. president John F. Kennedy assassinated

1963 Thousands march on Washington D.C. to press for civil rights for black Americans

1964 Military leaders seize power in Brazil

1964 U.S. Civil Rights Act bans racial discrimination in federal funding and employment

1968 Major protests in United States against Vietnam War

1 **1969** U.S. astronauts Neil Armstrong and Edwin Aldrin land on the moon*

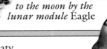
Astronauts were carried to the moon by the lunar module Eagle

OCEANIA

1946 United States tests atomic bomb at Bikini Atoll in Marshall Islands; continuing U.S. and French nuclear testing on Pacific islands causes massive resentment

1940s Immigration of non-English-speaking Europeans to Australia begins to change national ethnic makeup

Atomic bombs were tested at Bikini Atoll

1959 The Antarctic Treaty limits exploitation of Antarctica

1962 Western Samoa becomes independent

Penguins in Antarctica left alone to get on with their own affairs

1970

1970s Severe droughts in northeastern Africa and the lands on the southern edge of the Sahara

1974 Nigeria becomes leading oil producer in Africa

1974–91 Revolutionary regime in Ethiopia; civil war spreads

1974–75 Portuguese colonies gain independence after long struggle

1976 African schoolchildren spark uprisings in Soweto in South Africa

1980 Zimbabwe gains independence after guerrilla war

When famine struck in the midst of Ethiopia's long-running civil war, the results were devastating

Oil was purified in refineries such as this one at Yanbu in Saudi Arabia

1972 "Bloody Sunday" in Londonderry, Northern Ireland; troops fire on civil rights marchers

1972 Munich Olympics; Israeli athletes killed by Arab "Black September" organization

1976 Helsinki convention on human rights adopted

1977 240 Czech intellectuals sign Charter 77 stating that democratic freedoms are still denied

1979 Britain elects first female prime minister, Margaret Thatcher

1980 Independent trade union, Solidarity, formed in Poland*

Computers contained silicon chips

1970 Tonga and Fiji gain independence from Britain

1975 Papua New Guinea becomes independent from Australia*

1975 Political crisis in Australia as governor-general, appointed by British monarch, controversially dismisses elected government, causing considerable resentment

Mid 1970s Asian immigration to Australia increases sharply; it continues to be high, making Australia more multicultural

1970 Communist Khmer Rouge forces take over Cambodia

1971 After a brief Indo-Pakistani war, East Pakistan declared independent as Bangladesh

1973 Yom Kippur War between Arabs and Israelis begins

1973 Cut in Arab oil production and increased prices cause oil crisis in United States and Europe

1976 Zhou Enlai and Mao Zedong die; fall of "Gang of Four"

1978 Vietnam invades Cambodia and forces out Khmer Rouge

1979 Ayatollah Khomeini adopts Islamic constitution for Iran

1980 Iran-Iraq war breaks out

Solidarity began in Gdansk

1972 U.S. Congress passes Equal Opportunity Act in response to growing women's rights movement

1972–74 Watergate scandal in U.S.; Republican presidential aides are found to have "bugged" Democratic headquarters: President Richard Nixon resigns (August 1974)

1973 Elected Chilean president Allende killed in a military coup led by General Pinochet

1978 Camp David summit between Egypt and Israel hosted by the United States

1979 Sandinistas seize power in Nicaragua*

Children in Papua New Guinea

1982

1983– Conflict in Sudan; so far more than 1.5 million people have died

1983– Increasing numbers of African countries adopt IMF (International Monetary Fund) plans for managing their economies

1989– Zambia and other countries see changes of government by democratic election

1990 Namibia gets independence

1990 Nelson Mandela freed in South Africa; process of dismantling apartheid begins*

1993 Eritrea (in north Ethiopia) breaks away from Ethiopia; first successful secession in Africa

A defenseless student protests among soldiers in Tian'anmen Square

1985 Mikhail Gorbachev elected Soviet Communist party leader; introduces reforms*

1986 Nuclear power disaster at Chernobyl in Ukraine

1989 Berlin Wall dismantled

1990 East and West Germany are unified as one nation

1990 Solidarity's Lech Walesa is elected president of Poland

1991 Breakup of the Soviet Union, resignation of Gorbachev; Yeltsin takes power in Russia

1992 Yugoslavia breaks up and erupts into bloody civil war

Sandinista guerrillas won a civil war against government forces

1980s Australia and New Zealand go through economic recession; both later develop trade links with Asia

1984 New Zealand declared a nuclear-free zone; in 1985 *Rainbow Warrior* sunk by pro-nuclear agents

1986 Treaty of Rarotonga sets up South Pacific nuclear-free zone

Nelson Mandela, freed in 1990 after 27 years in prison

1982 Israeli forces invade Lebanon; massacre of Palestinians in Beirut refugee camp

1984 Indian prime minister Indira Gandhi assassinated by Sikhs

1988 Cease-fire in Iran-Iraq war

1989 Mass demonstrations for democracy in Tian'anmen Square, Beijing, China, ends in massacre

1989 Vietnamese troops withdraw from Cambodia

1990 Iraq invades Kuwait; United States and allies send forces to the Gulf region; Gulf War begins

1991 Allied forces liberate Kuwait

1991 Japan becomes world's largest donor of foreign aid

In 1989 the border between East and West Berlin opened

1980–92 Civil war in El Salvador

1982 Falklands war between Argentina and Britain

1982 Mexico fails to repay foreign loans, provoking international financial crisis

1989 U.S. forces invade Panama and depose ruler, General Noriega

1990 Sandinistas defeated in Nicaraguan elections

1993 Palestinian leader Arafat and Israeli prime minister Rabin sign agreement in United States; terms include self-rule for Palestinians in some territories occupied by Israel

The Rainbow Warrior, a Greenpeace ship, was sunk in Auckland harbor

| 600 | 800 | 1000 | | 1600 | 1700 | 1800 | 1900 | 2000 |

1946-1990s AFRICA

Most African countries gained their independence in just 12 years, from 1956 to 1968, as a tide of political and economic change swept through Africa. Almost universal in 1950, European rule had disappeared by 1978, although the struggle against white minority rule in southern Africa took longer. The new nations had high hopes, but they also had few educated people, underdeveloped economies, and fast-growing populations. There was no stable framework within which political life could take place peacefully. Often, leaders became dictators or the army seized power; many governments were corrupt and oppressive. Wars devastated a number of countries. But there was also progress, most of all in education.

North African cloak pin
Libya was the first country in Africa to gain its freedom after World War II, in 1951.

Charismatic and visionary
Kwame Nkrumah (1909–72) led Ghana's campaign for independence. He called for a united Africa, a vision which has inspired many but still seems as far from being realized as ever.

1954
War in Algeria

In 1950, there were about a million European settlers in Algeria, far more than in any other African country except South Africa. Because of them the French colonial government blocked Algerian attempts to move towards independence. This provoked Algerian nationalists to form the FLN (National Liberation Front) and launch an armed rebellion. France tried to crush it with an army 500,000 strong, using such brutal methods that more than a million Algerians perished. The French government finally collapsed in 1958, when the army in Algeria demanded that General de Gaulle take power. De Gaulle decided to negotiate, and freedom for Algeria was agreed to in 1962.

Celebration time
Algeria's independence day jubilation did not last. Its leaders proved less able at peace than they had been at war. Angry and poor, many Algerians turned to Islamic militancy, in spite of increasingly brutal military repression.

1957
Independence for Ghana

In 1948 Ghana (known at the time as the Gold Coast) was shaken by riots against the British colonial government. A new constitution was introduced, offering Africans limited self-government. This was eventually accepted by the Convention People's party, led by Kwame Nkrumah, which won the election held in 1951. Nkrumah formed an African government and led his country to full independence six years later. Development in Ghana was difficult, however, and Nkrumah became increasingly dictatorial. In 1966 the army took over and, apart from one more brief spell of civilian government from 1969 to 1972, soldiers have been in power ever since.

INDEPENDENCE DAYS

1956 Independence for Tunisia and Morocco; Algeria follows in 1962

1957 Ghana is first country in sub-Saharan Africa to gain its freedom; Britain's other colonies free by 1968

1958–60 12 of France's 13 sub-Saharan colonies gain independence

1974–75 Portugal's five colonies win freedom, after much bloodshed

1980 Zimbabwe free, after guerrilla war against white minority regime

1990 Namibia achieves independence from South Africa; end of a long war

1994 South Africa holds its first multiracial election

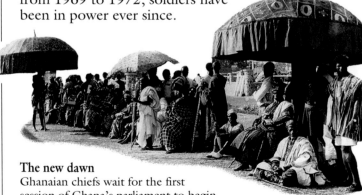

The new dawn
Ghanaian chiefs wait for the first session of Ghana's parliament to begin.
Chiefs were the traditional African leaders, and after independence they often continued to have great influence over the new nations.

40,000 BC		10,000	5000	1000	500	AD 1	200	400

DIFFICULT BEGINNINGS

African countries achieved freedom damaged by colonial misrule. Hasty attempts had been made to set up European-style forms of government, but democracy had had no chance to establish deep roots. National borders, drawn by colonial rulers, usually left countries very divided, with their citizens' first loyalty to one of the many ethnic groups living within those borders, not to the new country. Partly in response to this, many new governments tried to control every aspect of national life and crushed all opposition. As their power became complete, such governments became more and more corrupt. Interference by the rich nations often hindered progress. Drought, famine, and war struck hard. Population growth threatened to outrun economic growth. Many plans for economic development did more harm than good, and by 1991, 17 of the world's 20 poorest countries were in Africa. But there were also triumphs, and democracy has brought hope for change.

Lords of misrule

Jean-Bedel Bokassa seized power in the Central African Republic in 1965. In 1976 he had himself made emperor (left), and in 1979 he was overthrown. Others who came to power by force and ruled by terror included Idi Amin, who ravaged Uganda in the 1970s, and Mobutu Sese Seko, whose misgovernment of Zaire has made him fabulously rich and his country famously poor. They, and other dictators, were backed by non-African states playing power games whose cost was counted in African lives.

EDUCATION FOR A CONTINENT

Population growth has been so fast that in the 1980s half of all Africans were under age 16. Education has expanded even faster as governments across Africa have made it a top priority. In the 20 years after 1960 the percentage of children receiving primary education in sub-Saharan Africa more than doubled. There was equally remarkable progress in both secondary and university education.

African enterprise

This scene in Lusaka, in Zambia, could be repeated endlessly across the continent. Old and new live side by side. Traditional products are sold in the shadow of the skyscrapers that now rise above growing cities. In spite of the failure of many hopes, and new tragedies such as the massive death toll caused by the disease AIDS, the enterprise of the citizens of Africa remains greater even than the obstacles confronting their nations.

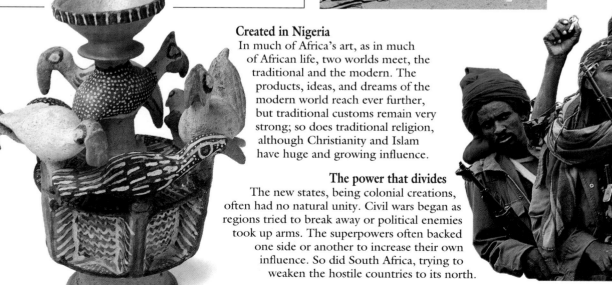

Created in Nigeria

In much of Africa's art, as in much of African life, two worlds meet, the traditional and the modern. The products, ideas, and dreams of the modern world reach ever further, but traditional customs remain very strong; so does traditional religion, although Christianity and Islam have huge and growing influence.

The power that divides

The new states, being colonial creations, often had no natural unity. Civil wars began as regions tried to break away or political enemies took up arms. The superpowers often backed one side or another to increase their own influence. So did South Africa, trying to weaken the hostile countries to its north.

DROUGHT, FAMINE, AND WAR

Parts of Africa have suffered severely from drought in the years since independence. The lands along the southern edge of the Sahara have been particularly affected. The effects have been made worse by the rapid increase in population, which has led to the widespread erosion of overcrowded lands. Wars, too, in Angola and elsewhere, have created hunger on a massive scale, even where there is plenty of rain. Famines in Sudan and other countries have shown how utterly devastating it is when drought and war strike together. However, efforts to fight erosion are increasing in a number of countries, and in southern Africa governments and people overcame a series of droughts in the 1980s, without loss of life on the same scale as in the north.

Harvesting guns instead of grain
Civil wars in Sudan, Ethiopia (above), and Somalia in northeast Africa had already disrupted farming before those countries were struck by drought. The wars made the famines that followed much worse.

The suffering of the innocent
Untold numbers of children have died in Africa's famines. Television pictures beam their suffering around the world.

Fighting the desert
When land at the edge of the Sahara becomes dusty and eroded, the desert reaches out to swallow it. This is happening more and more. Here, villagers in southern Sudan plant seedlings to protect their land from the advancing sand.

1990
The beginning of the end for apartheid

Throughout the 1980s pressure to end South Africa's apartheid system grew, both inside and outside the country. In 1989 the ruling National party chose a new leader, F. W. de Klerk. In February 1990 he released Nelson Mandela, the leader of the African National Congress (ANC), the country's biggest opposition group, from jail and legalized the ANC and more than 30 other political groups. Talks to agree on a path to multiracial democracy then began, and in 1991 de Klerk began to dismantle the laws of apartheid. Progress was obstructed by political violence, which rose to very high levels, and there was disagreement between the ANC, the government, right-wing white extremists, and regionally based parties, notably the Zulu Inkatha Freedom party. But a draft constitution was completed in November 1993 and in December a multiparty Transitional Executive Council took power alongside the government to oversee the last months before multiracial elections in 1994.

New hope for a new South Africa
Nelson Mandela's release, after 27 years as a political prisoner, made him the focus of hope in South Africa. His bravery, wise leadership, and selfless dedication have inspired countless people throughout the world. As he himself put it, "the struggle is my life." Mandela and de Klerk shared the Nobel Peace Prize in 1993.

Power without justice
Apartheid was created and upheld by force. But, in the end, even ruthless repression by police and army could not turn back the tide of protest that rose throughout the 1980s.

1946-1990s ASIA

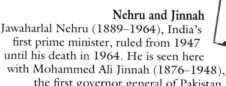

World War II brought independence for the Asian colonies. India was freed from British rule and divided into two nations, India and Pakistan. The Communist regime in China struggled to raise living standards and rekindle the economy. Japan became a world economic leader. The creation of the state of Israel led to an Arab-Israeli conflict which drained the economies of all nations involved. The exploitation of oil in the Middle East gave wealth to those living there and led superpowers to vie for influence in the area.

Nehru and Jinnah
Jawaharlal Nehru (1889–1964), India's first prime minister, ruled from 1947 until his death in 1964. He is seen here with Mohammed Ali Jinnah (1876–1948), the first governor general of Pakistan.

1947

India becomes independent

Indian National Congress leaders like Mohandas Gandhi wanted an independent, united India, with Hindus and Muslims living in harmony together, but most Muslims wanted a separate state. After World War II, in which Indian troops had fought the Japanese, the British finally decided to grant India independence. The original plan was for a united India, but the communal violence that broke out between Hindus and Muslims proved that this would not work. The British government and Indian leaders agreed that the British would leave India in August 1947, and the country would be divided into two nations. Jawaharlal Nehru became prime minister of a mainly Hindu India, Mohammed Ali Jinnah the first governor general of a Muslim Pakistan. The territory of Pakistan was in two parts, West and East Pakistan, with India in the middle. The East resented rule from the West, which was richer and more powerful, and relations worsened. In 1971 civil war erupted, and East Pakistan broke away with Indian help to become Bangladesh.

Industrial plant at Bhopal
Gandhi's dream of a self-sufficient India based on a simple peasant way of life was not shared by Nehru, who wanted to make the country more like the industrialized nations of the West. In the 1950s, with the assistance of Britain, West Germany, and the Soviet Union, three enormous steelworks were constructed, and by the 1970s nuclear energy powered parts of the subcontinent. By the 1980s India was the tenth largest industrial producer in the world. In 1984 leaks at a massive pesticide plant in Bhopal killed 2,000 people in India's worst industrial disaster.

Muslims surround a Hindu corpse
When the boundaries for the partitioning of India were drawn up, millions of Hindus and Muslims suddenly found themselves living in the "wrong" country. Massive migrations followed as some 5 million Hindus and Sikhs moved eastward out of Pakistan and as many Muslims fled westward from India. Atrocities were inflicted by both sides, and a probable half a million lives were lost. Mohandas Gandhi was killed by a Hindu extremist who was angered by his policy of pacifism towards the Muslim community.

Rajiv Gandhi greets Mikhail Gorbachev
Rajiv Gandhi became prime minister of India after the assassination of his mother, Indira (Nehru's daughter), in 1984. Rajiv continued to develop Indo-Soviet relations during his short premiership. He was assassinated in 1989.

| 600 | 800 | 1000 | 1200 | 1400 | 1600 | 1700 | 1800 | 1900 | 2000 |

1948
Jewish state founded in Palestine

In 1947 the United Nations agreed to the founding of independent Jewish and Palestinian Arab states in Palestine. On May 14, 1948, the Jewish state of Israel was established. Nearby Arab states, tired of foreign powers dictating Arab affairs, attacked Israel the next day. Over 600,000 Palestinians lost their homes in the war. Peace treaties left Israel with the areas allotted to it in 1947, and many areas allotted to Palestinians. Israel's refusal to acknowledge Palestinian claims, and the refusal of Arab states to recognize Israel, led to further wars in 1956, 1967, and 1973. In the 1967 war, Israel occupied the West Bank of the Jordan River and Gaza, inhabited by over a million Palestinians. Years of unrest in these areas led to a Palestinian campaign against occupying forces from 1987, which was harshly repressed. In 1993 the Palestinians recognized Israel's right to exist in exchange for Israeli concessions, including limited self-rule.

Refugee camp
Homeless Palestinians fled to refugee camps in Lebanon, Jordan, Gaza, and Syria. Some set up the Palestinian Liberation Organization (PLO) in 1964 to press for their own state, by violence if necessary.

Kibbutz farmer
To grow food in their dry land Israelis organized *kibbutzim*, farms on which people lived and worked and shared everything together.

- Border disputed in Iran-Iraq war (1980–88)
- Israeli-occupied territories, September 1993
- Area disputed in the Gulf War (1991)

World trouble spot
Nationalism, oil, and the struggle between Arabs and Jews has made the Middle East the scene of many bitter conflicts.

The peace process
In September 1993 PLO chairman Arafat (right) and Israeli prime minister Rabin (left) signed a declaration in front of U.S. president Clinton (center) agreeing in principle to Palestinian self-rule in Gaza and Jericho, the election of a Palestinian council, and economic cooperation.

CONFLICT OVER OIL

Israel's Arab neighbors were major oil producers. In 1960, 13 mainly Arab nations formed the Organization of Petroleum Exporting Countries (OPEC) to set oil prices jointly. Oil profits soared; OPEC nations became immensely rich. The Soviet Union and the United States gave arms and financial aid to Arab nations in a competition for influence in the area. During the 1973 Arab-Israeli War, OPEC cut supplies to the United States and Europe, which supported Israel, and quadrupled prices, causing worldwide economic chaos. U.S. politicians sought peace in the region, partly to stabilize the world economy. One success was to negotiate the 1978 Camp David peace treaty between Egypt and Israel.

Ayatollah's funeral
Searching for Arab allies, the United States sent aid to Iran in the 1960s. Ayatollah Khomeini led strict Muslims opposed to U.S. influence to power in 1979. He died in 1989. Thousands of mourners attended his funeral.

Burning oil wells
In August 1990 Iraqi president Saddam Hussein sent his army into oil-rich Kuwait. UN troops freed Kuwait in February 1991 in what was called the Gulf War. Over 25,000 Iraqis were killed in the fighting; 200 UN soldiers were killed or missing. Retreating Iraqis set fire to oil fields; pollution will affect the local environment for years.

| 40,000 BC | | 10,000 | 5000 | 1000 | 500 | AD 1 | 200 | 400 |

1953
Mao introduces five-year plan in China

After the Sino-Japanese war ended in 1945, civil war broke out between Mao Zedong's Communist troops and the Chinese Nationalist party. By 1949 the Communists had control of the mainland, leaving the Nationalists to rule the island of Taiwan, and on October 1, Mao declared the birth of the People's Republic of China. War had left the country in financial chaos, so in 1953 Mao began a five-year plan for economic recovery. The government took over factories and began land reforms. Land was taken from landlords and redistributed among the peasants, who were put to work on collective farms. The economy improved, but Communist leaders were not satisfied, and in 1958 they initiated a second plan, the Great Leap Forward. Its goal was to increase industrial and agricultural production rapidly, but the plan failed and resulted in widespread famine. By the 1960s, Communist rule had brought great social change, but Mao was still not content. So in 1966 he launched the Cultural Revolution to purge China of old traditional ways. This caused great disorder and weakened his influence. New leaders turned to longer-term plans for the future of Communist China.

Female factory worker
Mao set up many small industries in the countryside in the hope that industrial production would double, but the factories could not cope with the heavy demands placed on them.

The Korean War 1950–53

In 1945 Korea was divided into Soviet-occupied North Korea and U.S.-occupied South Korea. From 1948 both countries claimed sole legality as the government of Korea. When the occupying troops withdrew in 1949, border clashes grew, leading to full-scale fighting in June 1950. Forces of the United Nations (UN) were sent to the aid of South Korea, while thousands of Chinese troops fought on behalf of the North. The UN forces' commander, General Douglas MacArthur, demanded an all-out attack on China, but UN officials wanted to limit the war and began peace talks. In July 1953, by which time more than three million people had been killed or made homeless, peace terms were finally agreed.

Tank advance
These UN forces are advancing through a street in Pyongyang, the former capital of North Korea.

Red Guard demonstration
The Red Guards were young followers of Mao who campaigned throughout China against anyone who sympathized with traditional ideas. They eagerly supported the Cultural Revolution, which appealed to their youthful idealism and ambitions, and used violence to oust people in authority who did not show enough revolutionary zeal. This caused disorder, and Mao finally called an end to the revolution in 1976. Here, the Red Guards brandish posters of their revered leader at a mass demonstration.

Student gathering in Tian'anmen Square
In 1989 hundreds of thousands of students gathered in Beijing's central Tian'anmen Square to express their discontent with the country's leadership and to voice their demands for democratic reform. The Chinese government sent soldiers in to deal with the situation. Possibly 1,000 people died in the ensuing massacre.

| 600 | 800 | 1000 | 1200 | 1400 | 1600 | 1700 | 1800 | 1900 | 2000 |

1954

Vietminh crush French at Dien Bien Phu

By 1893 the French had colonized Cambodia, Laos, and Vietnam. After the Japanese occupation of the area in 1941–45, the Communist Vietminh movement, founded in 1941 by Ho Chi Minh, declared Vietnam independent. The French soon reasserted their control over southern Vietnam and tried to force the Vietminh to accept a French-led federation of all three countries. Fighting broke out in 1946 between the two sides and continued until the Vietminh under General Giap won a decisive victory against the French at Dien Bien Phu in May 1954. In the peace treaty signed in Geneva, Switzerland, in July 1954, France granted independence to Laos and Cambodia. Vietnam was divided between the Communist government of Ho Chi Minh in the North and an increasingly repressive government in the South backed by the United States. Relations between the two Vietnams deteriorated as Vietminh guerrillas attempted to overthrow the South Vietnamese government.

French troops at Dien Bien Phu
In November 1953 French troops set up a strongpoint at Dien Bien Phu, in the heart of Vietminh territory. From March to May 1954 they were besieged by the Vietminh.

c.1955

Japan enters a period of fast economic growth

Japan was left impoverished by years of war. From 1945–51 U.S. General Douglas MacArthur, as commander of the occupation forces in Japan, was responsible for helping to reform and rebuild the ruined country. It was necessary to rekindle the Japanese economy in order to protect Japan from Communism and reduce the cost of the occupation to American taxpayers. When war broke out in Korea, the United States turned to Japan to supply war materials. Japanese manufacturing industries rose to the task of supplying military equipment, and the economy began to take off. Japan continued to create wealth through industry, and the domestic economy grew rapidly. During the 1970s Japan became the second largest economic power in the world, and it remains so today. The economies of Hong Kong, Singapore, Taiwan, and South Korea also grew and became known as "the Four Dragons" or "the New Japans."

Tokyo by night
Tokyo was largely demolished by air raids in World War II. The center was rebuilt in the style of Western European and U.S. commercial cities, with bright neon lights and huge, modern high-rise buildings.

THE VIETNAM WAR 1965–75

In 1961 the U.S. government, worried about the spread of Communism in Southeast Asia, began to send military aid to South Vietnam to help it repulse the Communist Vietminh (or Vietcong) guerrillas supported by North Vietnam. U.S. troops landed in the south early in 1965, and by the end of 1966 almost 400,000 men were fighting in Vietnam; bombing against the north averaged 164 raids a day. Two years later, in 1968, the Vietcong launched a major Tet offensive on South Vietnam. It failed, but it did prove to many Americans that the war could not be won. A year later U.S. troops began to withdraw; a cease-fire was agreed in 1973. In April 1975 the North Vietnamese united the country under their control.

Vietnamese soldier
The North Vietnamese were well adapted for guerrilla warfare. They wore sandals and carried rice in scarves around their necks.

Japanese technology
Japan's passenger car industry is now the second largest in the world. Factories are highly automated, and robots are used on assembly lines. Having invested heavily in the microchip, the Japanese electronics industry now manufactures a wide variety of computers, radios, televisions, and other electronic equipment, which are exported in vast quantities all over the world.

40,000 BC		10,000	5000	1000	500	AD 1	200	400

1946-1990s EUROPE

B y 1950 an ideological and political conflict had arisen between the Soviet Union and the United States which became known as the "Cold War"; it divided Europe and the world. In the next 40 years several Eastern European nations tried to loosen the Soviet grip. But independence did not come until 1989 when European Communist regimes were overthrown.

Berlin Airlift
The airlift continued for 15 months.

1948
Soviets isolate Berlin

In 1945 Germany was divided into four zones each administered by one of the Allies, Britain, France, the United States, and the Soviet Union. Berlin, too, was divided four ways but lay in the zone controlled by the Soviets. In 1948 the Soviet Union blockaded Berlin's western sectors in protest against the unification of the western zones under one authority. The United States, Britain, and France frustrated the blockade by airlifting essential supplies to their sectors, to prevent the whole city falling into Soviet hands. The three western zones and West Berlin later formed the Federal Republic (West Germany) with Bonn as its capital. The Soviet zone became the Democratic Republic (East Germany) with East Berlin as its capital.

The Berlin Wall
In 1961 the East German government built a high wall to separate East and West Berlin. Thousands of East Germans lost an escape route to the West.

Signing the Pact
The pact signed at Warsaw established military alliances between Communist members.

MILITARY ALLIANCES

NATO The 1949 North Atlantic Treaty Organization was a militarily supportive alliance between several Western European countries and Canada and the United States against aggression from any outside nation.

The Warsaw Pact In 1955 in response to the setting up of NATO, the Soviet Union formed an alliance of European Communist states called the Warsaw Pact. It authorized the stationing of Soviet troops in pact states.

1956
The Hungarian uprising

In World War II the Soviet Union suffered crippling losses of both people and resources. Afraid of invasion and needing new industrial bases, it was determined to retain its power in Eastern Europe. By a mixture of political pressure and military might, it established "people's republics" sympathetic to the Soviet regime. In 1956 Poland and Hungary demanded greater self-rule. In Poland military threats and promises of liberalization quieted the situation, but in Hungary the demands grew into general anti-Communist feeling and attempted secession from the Warsaw Pact. On November 4, Soviet troops entered Budapest, suppressing the liberation movement with great brutality and executing the leaders. NATO countries were outraged but did nothing.

March for freedom
The bravery of the Hungarians aroused the sympathy of the world.

1957
Europeans unite

On March 25, six nations, France, West Germany, Italy, Belgium, the Netherlands, and Luxembourg, signed a treaty in Rome which set up the European Economic Community, or Common Market. The Treaty of Rome abolished tariffs between the nations and established free movement for workers, capital, and goods between the member states. Over the next 30 years, several other countries, such as Britain, Denmark, and Ireland, and later Spain and Portugal, joined the community, making it a powerful trading force.

Parliament buildings
The parliament of the European Economic Community (EEC), now the European Union, elected for the first time in 1972, meets in Strasbourg in France. Since 1973 Spain, Portugal, Greece, Britain, Ireland, and Denmark have joined the original members.

Barricades in the streets
Students of Paris's Sorbonne University marched and made barricades in the streets. De Gaulle lost support due to his handling of the riots. A year later he resigned from office.

1968
Students riot in Paris

After World War II, university enrollment increased rapidly in many European countries. The new student population pressed for educational and social reforms and challenged traditional values. In France, serious unrest occurred. Students took to the streets in protest against high government spending on defense and demanded greater spending on education and a modernized curriculum. Demonstrations in Paris were suppressed by the police and riots followed. Workers supported the students, and there was a general strike against the policies of French president General de Gaulle. De Gaulle was forced to make concessions, promising the students reforms and the workers a new minimum wage.

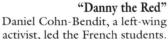

"Danny the Red"
Daniel Cohn-Bendit, a left-wing activist, led the French students.

1968
The "Prague Spring"

Early in 1968 Alexander Dubcek (1921–92) became first secretary of the Communist party in Czechoslovakia, a central European country controlled by the Soviet Union. Dubcek gradually began to reform the government, reorganizing the administration, pursuing an independent foreign policy, and encouraging a new growth in intellectual life. In spite of his assurances to Moscow that Czechoslovakia was not trying to leave the Warsaw Pact, Soviet tanks rumbled into the capital, Prague, in August 1968. Citizens' demonstrations were suppressed by the Soviet Red Army.

Banished leader
After the Soviet tanks had entered Prague, Dubcek was banished. He returned in 1989.

Resistance
The people of Prague had no weapons to resist the tanks.

40,000 BC		10,000	5000	1000	500	AD 1	200	400

Solidarity's struggle
Solidarity's majority in parliament was short-lived. They were unable to produce economic reforms and were ousted from government.

1980
The rise of Solidarity

During the 1970s, countries in Eastern European were growing increasingly resentful of Soviet interference in their internal affairs. In Poland an independent trade union known as Solidarity was established under the leadership of a Gdansk shipyard electrician, Lech Walesa (b.1943). Supported by the Catholic church, Solidarity organized workers' strikes which brought the country to a standstill. The government was forced to agree to some reforms but on December 14, 1981 imposed martial law, banned Solidarity, and put Walesa and other leaders in prison for a short time. Over the next ten years confrontation between Solidarity and the Polish government continued, until in 1989 the ban was lifted and Solidarity's candidates achieved spectacular success in the general election. The break up of the Soviet Union allowed Solidarity to take power, and in 1990 Walesa was elected president of an independent Poland.

1985
Gorbachev leads the Soviet Union

In March 1985 Mikhail Gorbachev (b.1931) became general secretary of the Communist party of the Soviet Union. He wanted to reform Soviet social and economic life. He promised a major reconstruction of the Soviet state (*perestroika*) and introduced a policy of openness (*glasnost*) to tell the Soviet people what changes were taking place. Under Gorbachev's regime, relations with Western powers improved and a historic agreement was signed in 1987 with U.S. president Ronald Reagan to limit some nuclear missiles. Major constitutional changes led to the release of some dissidents, and old-style Communist party members were ousted from the Congress of People's Deputies. Gorbachev was elected Soviet president in 1989; by this

Thawing of the Cold War
During the 1980s the mutual suspicion between the Soviet Union and the United States relaxed. Gorbachev's prestige abroad was higher than at home.

time there was growing unrest in the Soviet republics, many of whom wanted total independence. The failure of the economy and increasing food shortages weakened Gorbachev's position at home. He survived an abortive Communist coup in 1991 with the support of powerful Russian Federation president Boris Yeltsin, but later resigned. Most of the republics declared their independence, and the Soviet Union ceased to exist on December 21, 1991. It was replaced by the Commonwealth of Independent States.

REUNITED

There was growing discontent among the satellite states of the Soviet Union during the 1980s. Germany eventually erupted in 1989 and the Berlin Wall, a longtime symbol of the divided nation, was dismantled, and friends and families were reunited with each other. A year later, with the support of the people, there was full political unification of East and West Germany. Berlin has once again become the capital city of a united Germany.

CONFLICT IN THE BALKANS

In June 1991 the republics of Slovenia and Croatia declared their independence from federal Yugoslavia. In 1992 Bosnia followed suit and within months Yugoslavia had split into independent states, the most powerful of which was Serbia, and erupted into the bloodiest war in Europe since World War II. In spite of international peace efforts, many atrocities occurred on all sides. Serb forces pursued a policy known as "ethnic cleansing," expelling Muslims and other non-Serbs from their homes in towns and villages.

Refugee crisis
The war has left thousands starving and homeless. So far all peace efforts have been defeated by mutual hatred.

1946-1990s AMERICAS

While the nations of Latin America searched for new methods to build strong economies, the United States became the richest nation in the world. It competed with the Communist Soviet Union for worldwide power and influence. Billions of dollars were spent on the manufacture of weapons and on economic and military aid to foreign allies, including in Latin America.

Chilean cloak pin
This cloak pin was made from silver mined in Chile. In 1970 Dr. Allende became Chilean president. He took over U.S.-owned mines so profits from them would stay in Chile. Allende was ousted in a coup in 1973 led by General Pinochet.

1955
Military coup in Argentina

From colonial times on, Latin American economies depended on the sale of a single product in the world market. Between 1940 and 1960 some nationalistic governments launched industrialization programs to produce a great variety of manufactured goods and make their economies self-sufficient. A class of rich industrialists formed, and the working classes grew stronger. Political power was taken by "populist" alliances between workers and industrialists, held together by energetic leaders such as Argentinian president Perón (1895–1974). Landowners lost out as governments kept agricultural prices low to keep food cheap. New industry relied on money and tools from the United States and from Europe. Latin American nations could not repay foreign debts when world prices for their traditional exports dropped. In times of depression, the interests of industrialists and workers clashed, and populist alliances collapsed. Military coups brought the army, backed by landowners, to power, in Argentina (1955), Brazil (1964), and Chile (1973).

Photographs of the missing
Military governments often repressed opposition. From 1976–82, 20,000 Argentinians disappeared, probably killed by military rulers' death squads. Relatives paraded pictures of the lost.

Heroine of the people
Perón married a flamboyant radio actress, known as Evita, who was hugely popular with workers and the poor. From her vast, marble headquarters, she dispensed cash to the needy who queued to see her. She began reforms in education and won the right to vote for Argentinian women. Her death in 1952, age only 33, greatly diminished support for her husband.

GUERRILLA WARFARE

By the 1960s some political groups in Latin America decided that only guerrilla warfare could destroy military dictatorships and stop foreign powers from supporting them. Guerrillas kidnapped foreign diplomats, demanding the release of political prisoners as ransom, and attacked U.S. property. "Che" Guevara, an Argentinian Communist, helped Cuban guerrillas overthrow the Cuban dictator in 1959. He then went to Bolivia to rouse support for revolution there, but was killed by the army. He was revered as a martyr by revolutionaries worldwide.

Brazilian street children
From 1960 to 1980 the Latin American population grew by over 3 percent a year. Neither agriculture nor industry expanded fast enough to provide work for all. Millions live in poverty today; thousands of children live on the streets, without adequate food or clothing.

MARTIN LUTHER KING, JR.

Born in 1929 in Atlanta, Georgia, King became a clergyman and powerful public speaker. Inspired by Gandhi, he persuaded black Americans to make protests peacefully and with dignity. His personal participation in demonstrations and his willingness to go to jail (more than 16 times) for his cause made him the most highly regarded defender of black rights. After his assassination in 1968 an outbreak of rage and protest led to riots in 125 cities.

1950s
Black Americans demand equality

In the 1950s black Americans stepped up their fight for civil rights and an end to segregation – forced separation of races in education, public transportation, etc. Millions participated in peaceful protests. One noted action was a year-long boycott of segregated buses in Montgomery, Alabama in 1955–56, led by Baptist minister Martin Luther King, Jr. In 1963, King and his followers marched daily on the city hall in Birmingham, Alabama, despite being attacked by city authorities with dogs and hoses. Later that year, in the biggest protest in the capital's history, 200,000 campaigners marched on Washington, D.C. Bowing to public pressure, Congress passed civil rights acts in 1964–65 outlawing racial discrimination in employment, education, and public housing, and protecting black voting rights.

Equality remains a dream
Millions of black people moved to cities in the northern and western United States during and after World War II. They rarely got good jobs, and inner city areas where they settled became run down. Some turned to leaders like Malcolm X, who believed blacks should take control of local businesses and schools and counter police brutality. Riots shook many cities (1965–68), but matters did not improve. Black groups today continue to campaign for equality. Above, protesters ask that King's birthday be made a nationwide holiday, recalling his words: "I have a dream that one day this nation will rise up and live out the true meaning of its creed: 'We hold these truths to be self-evident, that all men are created equal.'"

Trouble in Little Rock
In 1954, the Supreme Court ruled that black and white children should attend the same schools – a decision that angered many white southerners. In 1957, the governor of Arkansas threatened to use force to stop the desegregation of Little Rock's Central High School. President Dwight Eisenhower sent federal troops to Little Rock to enforce the court's ruling.

WOMEN'S MOVEMENT

During the 1960s the fight for black equality led others to protest against injustice. After the National Organization for Women (NOW) was founded in 1966, women united to campaign for equal pay and job opportunities, better health care, and the right to abortion. New laws banned sex discrimination at work and by 1970, 47 percent of women were employed. But most held junior posts earning less than men doing the same work, and a 1972 Equal Rights Amendment prohibiting sex discrimination failed to win ratification by enough states to become part of the Constitution.

Mothers in the workforce
Women campaigned for better childcare facilities so they could continue their careers after having children.

Gay rights
From the late 1960s lesbians and gays campaigned for equal rights. In 1987, half a million marched on Washington, D.C., to protest against lack of progress and government inaction on gay issues.

1962
Cuban missile crisis

In 1945 the United States dropped atomic bombs on Hiroshima and Nagasaki in Japan, devastating both cities and proving the terrifying power of the new weapons. World War II ended immediately, but peace was soon threatened by growing hostility between the United States and the Soviet Union. The Americans watched the Soviets take control of Eastern Europe with deep suspicion and in 1947 pledged to support any country resisting Soviet pressure. Both powers built expensive nuclear weapons so destructive no other nation would dare attack. This "balance of terror" helped to keep the peace. In 1959 Fidel Castro took power in Cuba, allied the island nation with the Soviets, and asked for their protection after U.S.-trained Cuban exiles tried to invade in 1961. In 1962 U.S. intelligence found Soviet nuclear missiles in Cuba. President Kennedy sent the U.S. Navy to blockade the island. The world held its breath, fearing a new world war, but the Soviets agreed to remove the weapons. World leaders realized bad relations were too risky and in a step toward peace signed a treaty to limit nuclear tests in 1963.

A dangerous cargo
This photograph was taken by U.S. surveillance aircraft a week after the missile crisis. It shows a ship carrying eight missile transporters and canvas-covered missiles from Cuba back to the Soviet Union.

John F. Kennedy (1917-63)
Handsome, charming, and wealthy, Kennedy was the youngest man ever to be elected president of the United States (1960). He energetically declared a major reform program, a "New Frontier" for his country, although much new legislation got held up in Congress. Kennedy devoted the most time to foreign affairs, taking a firm stand against Communism during the Cuban missile crisis and helping South Vietnam's rulers to fight the Communist guerrillas. His assassination in 1963 stunned the world, and his vision and vigor have never been forgotten.

1969
Astronauts land on the moon

For centuries humans have dreamed of traveling in space. From the 17th century, scientists studied the universe through telescopes, but it was only after World War II that the development of rockets made space exploration possible. In 1957 the Soviets sent the first artificial satellite, *Sputnik I*, into orbit to observe the world from space. This was a major blow to U.S. national pride and Americans feared that the huge rocket that carried the satellite could deliver a nuclear bomb across the Atlantic Ocean. A "space race" between the two powers began. Soviet cosmonaut Yuri Gagarin became the first man to orbit the earth (1961), but in 1969 U.S. astronaut Neil Armstrong became the first person to land on the moon. Since then, U.S. scientists have concentrated on launching satellites to perform tasks such as observing the weather, surveying military activity, and sending pictures of news events from around the world to television screens.

Voyager probe passes Saturn
Space probes are unstaffed spacecraft sent to gather information about the solar system. Two U.S. *Voyager* probes were launched in 1977. Each flew past Jupiter and Saturn. *Voyager I* traveled on to the edge of the solar system to explore interstellar space.

Giant leap for mankind
On July 21, 1969, watched by millions of television viewers, Neil Armstrong stepped off his lunar module onto the moon. "That's one small step for a man, one giant leap for mankind," he said. He and fellow astronaut Edwin Aldrin collected dust and rock samples and planted the U.S. flag before returning to the module.

40,000 BC		10,000	5000	1000	500	AD 1	200	400

THE AFFLUENT SOCIETY

Between 1945 and 1970 the U.S. economy grew fourfold, and the real income of the average U.S. family more than doubled. Americans could afford to buy more of everything. Over a million houses were built each year, particularly in suburban areas of major cities. Car sales doubled, and Congress approved the construction of thousands of miles of highway. Americans bought billions of dollars' worth of consumer goods, such as washing machines, televisions, dishwashers, and cameras. But not all citizens benefitted from the prosperity. Every city had a slum area that housed the poor and unemployed, and declining farm incomes created rural poverty.

Information revolution
By 1990 a hundred million U.S. families owned a television, and the average person spent four hours a day watching it. Television enabled viewers to see for themselves important political, sporting, and entertainment events. The world seemed a smaller place now that people could look into every corner.

Fashionable hippies
In the late 1960s, some young people refused to work like their parents to earn money for a house, car, and consumer goods. Instead "hippies" chose to lead a life of peace and love, based on drugs, sex, and music. Their ideas influenced millions. Other young people channeled their energy into political groups, such as Students for a Democratic Society (SDS), protesting against sending U.S. troops to Vietnam.

Silicon chip
Wealthy U.S. companies invested millions of dollars in developing new products. In the 1970s scientists learned how to etch thousands of electronic circuits, which could store and process vast amounts of data, onto tiny silicon chips. Chips were cheaply produced and were used in machines that revolutionized life at home and work, such as computers, industrial robots, and fax machines.

1979
Sandinistas govern Nicaragua

Central American nations shared many problems: single-product economies, limited industry, dependence on foreign capital, and extremes of wealth and poverty. They became battlegrounds for conflicting forces for change and key areas in the global conflict for influence between the United States and the Soviet Union. In Nicaragua, guerrillas known as the Sandinistas overthrew dictator Anastasio Somoza Debayle in 1979. They redistributed land from the rich to peasants and provided better education and health care. U.S. politicians saw the Sandinistas as Communists, sent arms and aid to rebels (the contras), and enforced a trade boycott, pushing the Sandinistas into dependence on the Soviet Union. In the chaos, the Sandinistas lost power in the 1990 election.

Sandinista guerrillas
In the 1970s a small number of rich families owned most of the land in Nicaragua; the Somoza family alone owned 20 percent. The Sandinistas drew support from rural peasants, urban workers, and city intellectuals opposed to the unequal distribution of resources. As there were no democratic institutions in Nicaragua through which to voice opposition, Sandinistas turned to guerrilla warfare.

One-product economy
Many Central American economies relied on coffee or banana exports. When world prices for these crops dropped, job losses led to poverty. To decrease Nicaragua's dependence on coffee sales, the Sandinista government developed a variety of crop industries.

Conflict in El Salvador
In the 1970s demands for land and jobs for the poor became widespread in El Salvador, supported by the Catholic Church led by Archbishop Romero. In 1979 some army officers seized power, promising reform but cruelly repressing opposition. Romero was assassinated in 1980. Civil war broke out between U.S.-backed government forces and guerrillas, during which 75,000 died. Peace terms were agreed to in 1992.

| 600 | 800 | 1000 | 1200 | 1400 | 1600 | 1700 | 1800 | 1900 | 2000 |

1946-1990s OCEANIA

I n the years after World War II, most of the nations of Oceania gained their freedom, although France and the United States kept control over many islands. Their nuclear testing, and nuclear dumping by the United States and Japan, caused great resentment. Immigration from many different countries changed Australia. Aboriginal people were granted civil rights. Australia and New Zealand became less tied to Britain and developed economic links with Asia.

1975

A new nation in New Guinea

Papua New Guinea (PNG), home to three million people and more than 700 languages, gained independence from Australia in 1975. Since then it has developed quickly, but traditional ways of life remain strong; most land is owned by communities, not individuals. PNG is heavily forested, mountainous, and thinly populated. It has large amounts of copper and gold. On the island of Bougainville, site of a massive copper mine, there are efforts to break away from the rest of the country.

A world apart
Until recently the more remote parts of New Guinea were completely isolated from the rest of the world. Now the modern world has crashed in upon their lives.

Stepping out into the future
Modern communications, especially films and radio, bring to young Papua New Guineans the ideas and images of the modern world, but not the technology or the money which make the rich world's ways of life possible. Growing frustration has led to increased violence, especially in the towns.

Australian Chinatown
Australia is now home to people from many lands. It has big Greek and Italian minorities and has begun to receive large numbers of people from Asian countries. Refugees from Vietnam, exiles from Lebanon, businessmen from Hong Kong, all find a home in the land sometimes called "the lucky country."

CHANGING TIMES FOR AUSTRALIA

In the years after World War II a wave of non-English-speaking immigrants arrived, mainly from southern and eastern Europe, and began to make society more diverse. A "White Australia" immigration policy kept non-Europeans out until the 1970s, when Asian immigrants started to arrive in large numbers, changing the face of Australia. Meanwhile, Aboriginal people had finally been granted civil rights. Their campaigns for land rights met with increasing success. Australia forged new economic links with Asia as its old ones with Britain withered. Australians still enjoyed a famously relaxed lifestyle but questioned their place in the world more. Awareness of the environment grew. By the 1990s there was a move to make the country a republic, severing the last official ties with Britain. The Australian economy struggled during much of the 1980s and into the 1990s but today there is a sense that the nation has finally come of age.

Cultural flower
Sydney Opera House, opened in 1973, symbolized a growing interest in the arts in Australia. Australian films, especially, and filmmakers, many of them female, have become world famous.

| 40,000 BC | | 10,000 | 5000 | 1000 | 500 | AD 1 | 200 | 400 |

GLOBAL CHALLENGE

As the 20th century nears its end many people believe that the world is in crisis. Economic growth has brought benefits but also many problems. Industrial pollution and the careless use of the world's natural resources are damaging fragile environments, harming the atmosphere, destroying animal and plant species, and possibly threatening human survival. At the same time the gap between rich and poor nations widens daily. There are more hungry and homeless people than ever before. Today more than five billion people live in the world; by 2100 the number will have doubled, and most will live in dire poverty.

Urban predicament
Bombay's slum area is typical of many overcrowded cities. Soon more than half the world's people will live in cities, many without adequate housing or clean water.

Sea pollution
Oil spills and waste dumping kill sea birds and marine life.

This cormorant is covered in oil as a result of the *Exxon Valdez* disaster off Alaska in 1989.

Traffic threat
Cars pump out carbon dioxide and other poisons which pollute the air.

Pollution

Pollution is a by-product of modern industrial life and affects the whole world. Agricultural chemicals have poisoned the soil and entered food chains; industrial and chemical wastes have been dumped into seas and rivers; poisonous gases from factories and power stations and exhaust fumes from cars have entered the atmosphere causing acid rain that has destroyed forests, lakes, and buildings. Pollution in the atmosphere has also damaged the ozone layer, the protective layer that blocks out the sun's ultraviolet rays that can cause cancer in humans and animals. Increased use of fossil fuels and rapid deforestation have led to a build up of "greenhouse" gases causing global warming and possible climate change.

Deforestation

Throughout the world tropical rain forests are rapidly being destroyed. The main reasons for this are the growth of logging industries, the clearance of land for mining, and the constant need for more land for farming or for cattle grazing. Since 1945 nearly half the world's rain forests have been destroyed, and the rate has doubled since the 1980s. Trees which have taken 200 years or more to grow can be felled in minutes. As forests are destroyed, so are unique animal and plant species. Loss of tree cover and the destruction of complex root systems can also lead to soil erosion and to flooding.

Desertification
Somalia in East Africa has been badly affected by desertification. Poor peasant farmers burned forests to create crop or grazing land. Without time to replant they exhausted the soil, turning the land into desert and destroying the resources they need to survive.

Forest clearance
In the 1970s, the Brazilian government cleared vast areas of rain forest for farmland, and started to build a huge highway, but the project failed leaving the region bare of forest and ecologically devastated.

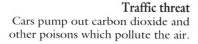

TOWARD SOLUTIONS

The United Nations held its first conference on the Human Environment (UNEP) in 1972. Since then, "green" pressure groups and the public have increasingly demanded that the world's governments make environmental problems a priority. There has been some progress. In 1987, 33 countries agreed to phase out emissions of CFCs (Chlorofluorocarbons) responsible for damage to the ozone layer. In the same year, the UN Brundtland Report proposed sustainable development (meeting current needs without trespassing on the rights of future generations to enjoy the world's natural riches) as the way forward. But solutions are complex and change is slow. Since the 1980s, some of the most promising developments have been community initiatives arranged at local level.

Green groups
Campaigning groups such as Greenpeace, seen here in the Antarctic, have won much public support and made environmental issues front-page news.

Safe technology
Technology can help toward a sustainable future. In Nepal, micro hydroturbines (above) provide energy for local people without damaging the environment. Wind farms in California (right) are used increasingly to provide power.

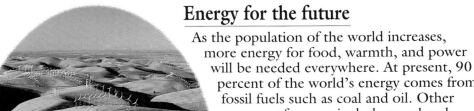

Energy for the future

As the population of the world increases, more energy for food, warmth, and power will be needed everywhere. At present, 90 percent of the world's energy comes from fossil fuels such as coal and oil. Other sources of energy include wood and nuclear power. But these sources have already caused serious environmental damage. In addition, world stocks of coal, oil, and fuel wood are rapidly running out. The search is on for nonpolluting sources of energy that can accommodate the needs of future generations. More and more people, and some governments, believe that a sustainable energy future will involve greater energy conservation and efficiency plus the use of safe, renewable sources of energy such as sun, wind, water, and tidal power.

Food security

In 1985, the world produced nearly 1100 lb (500 kg) of cereals and root crops per head, and yet some 800 million people are malnourished, most of them in Africa and Latin America. Increasing food production for a growing and hungry world without damaging the environment is a severe problem. To achieve food security, the Brundtland Report recommended the redistribution of land, the increased use of organic and sustainable farming methods based on need rather than want, and the practice of traditional techniques such as terracing and irrigation in local, community-based projects.

Women's cooperatives
In parts of Africa such as Niger in West Africa, women are forming local cooperatives to manage and farm land in a sustainable way to meet the food needs of the local community. Many such projects are great success stories.

REFERENCE PAGES

14th-century psalter from England

EMPIRES AND CIVILIZATIONS

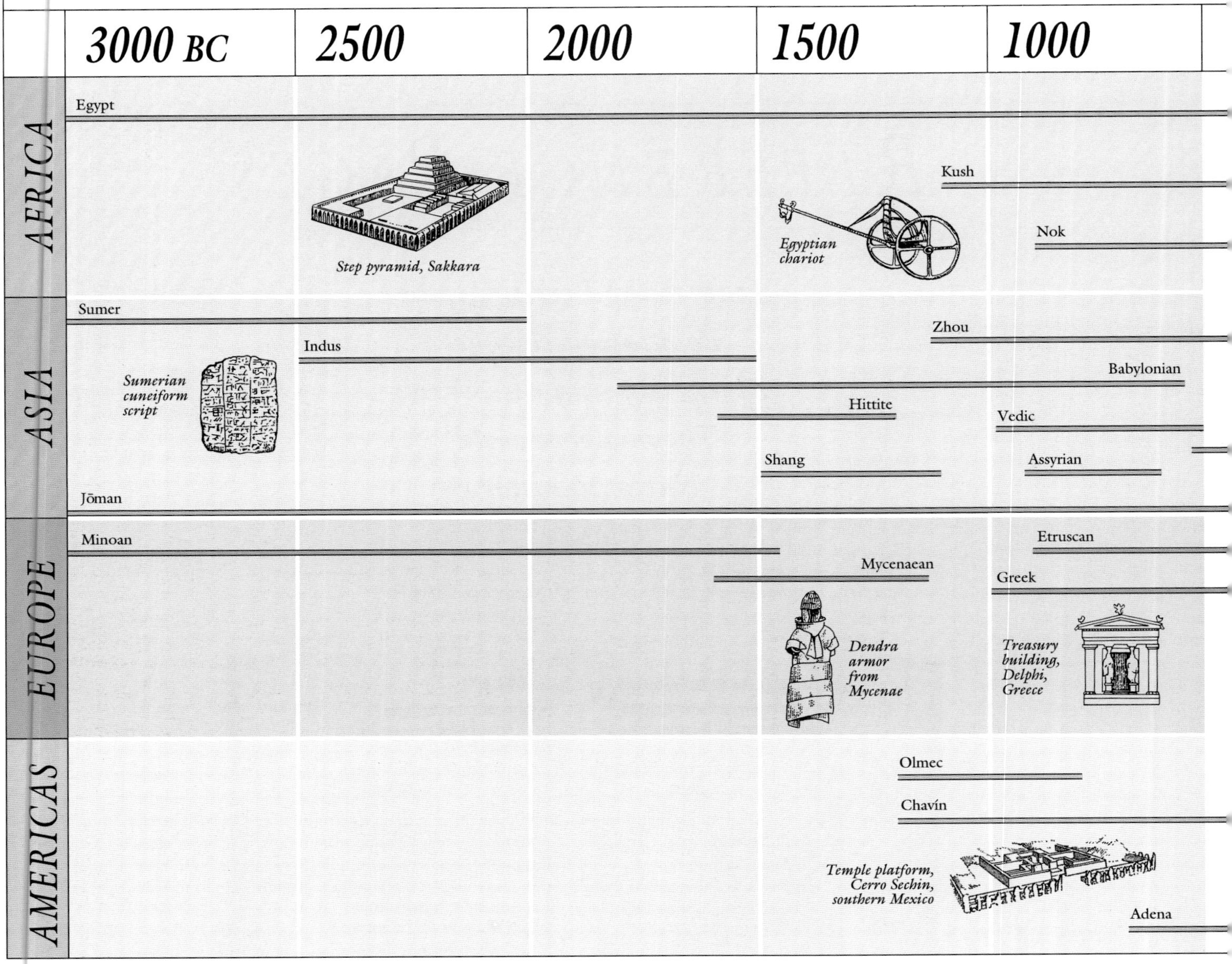

	3000 BC	2500	2000	1500	1000

AFRICA

Egypt

Step pyramid, Sakkara

Egyptian chariot

Kush

Nok

ASIA

Sumer

Sumerian cuneiform script

Indus

Zhou

Babylonian

Hittite

Vedic

Shang

Assyrian

Jōman

EUROPE

Minoan

Mycenaean

Etruscan

Greek

Dendra armor from Mycenae

Treasury building, Delphi, Greece

AMERICAS

Olmec

Chavín

Temple platform, Cerro Sechin, southern Mexico

Adena

The history of buildings

From the simplest animal-skin shelters to the most ornate places of worship, buildings have been around since the earliest humans. Styles of architecture – the design of a building – vary greatly over the centuries and differ from one culture to another, changing according to the climate and the needs of the local inhabitants. Architecture continues to develop as people endeavor to create buildings that are attractive, functional, and comfortable.

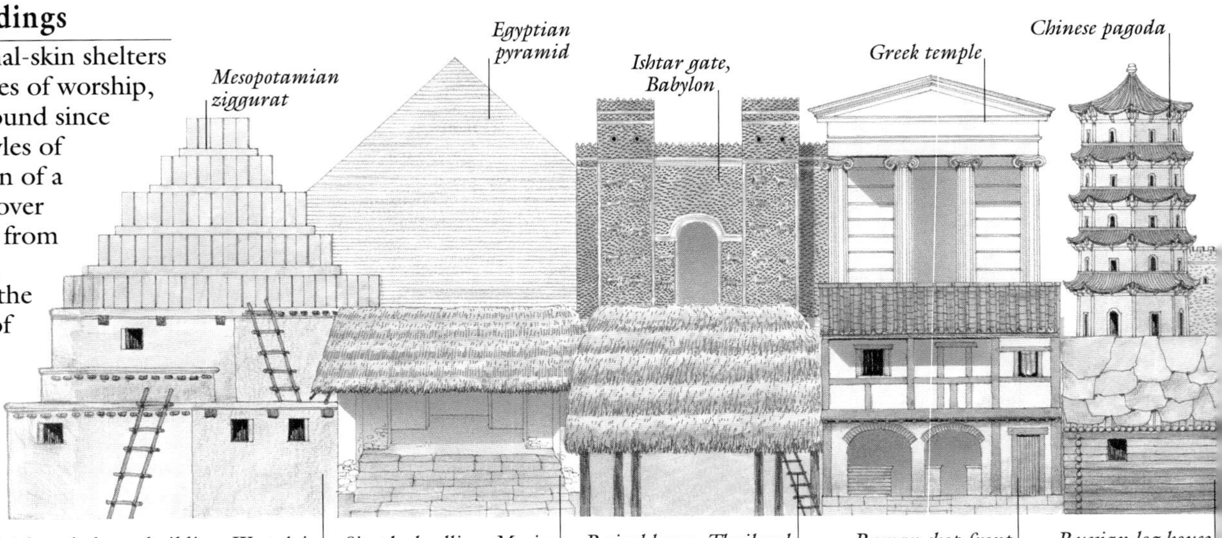

Mesopotamian ziggurat

Egyptian pyramid

Ishtar gate, Babylon

Greek temple

Chinese pagoda

Brick and plaster building, West Asia | *Simple dwelling, Mexico* | *Raised house, Thailand* | *Roman shop front* | *Russian log house*

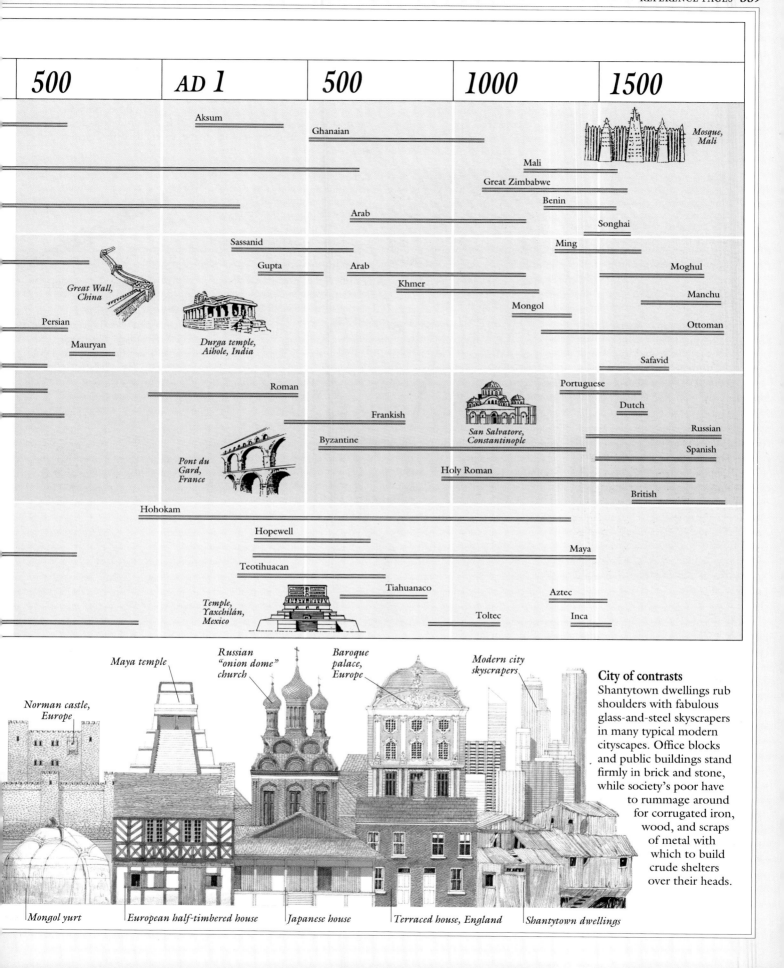

500	*AD 1*	*500*	*1000*	*1500*

Aksum

Ghanaian

Mosque, Mali

Mali

Great Zimbabwe

Benin

Arab

Songhai

Sassanid

Ming

Gupta

Arab

Moghul

Great Wall, China

Khmer

Manchu

Mongol

Persian

Ottoman

Mauryan

Durga temple, Aihole, India

Safavid

Roman

Portuguese

Frankish

Dutch

San Salvatore, Constantinople

Russian

Byzantine

Spanish

Pont du Gard, France

Holy Roman

British

Hohokam

Hopewell

Maya

Teotihuacan

Temple, Yaxchilán, Mexico

Tiahuanaco

Aztec

Toltec

Inca

Maya temple

Russian "onion dome" church

Baroque palace, Europe

Modern city skyscrapers

Norman castle, Europe

City of contrasts

Shantytown dwellings rub shoulders with fabulous glass-and-steel skyscrapers in many typical modern cityscapes. Office blocks and public buildings stand firmly in brick and stone, while society's poor have to rummage around for corrugated iron, wood, and scraps of metal with which to build crude shelters over their heads.

Mongol yurt   *European half-timbered house*   *Japanese house*   *Terraced house, England*   *Shantytown dwellings*

POPULATION CHANGES

Diseases through the ages

Through time, disease has changed the balance of population across the world. In the 19th century, tuberculosis (TB), and cholera were leading killers in the so-called developed countries; today they have been replaced by noninfectious "diseases of civilization" such as heart disease. In poorer nations many people still die from starvation.

Black Death Deadly plague carried by fleas on rats. Spread through world on ships trading between Asia and Europe. Three bouts, in 542 (25 million dead), 1346–53, and 1894 (12 million dead in India but only 91 people in Europe). Cause identified and vaccine produced in Europe

Smallpox Ancient disease that killed or disfigured thousands every year. At its height in 17th–18th centuries. Disease eradicated by 1978

Cholera Bacterial disease spread through infected food and water. In the 19th century it spread across the world in 20 years. Six world epidemics

In 1796 a cowpox vaccination for smallpox was invented. The last case occurred in Bangladesh in 1975

Malaria Ancient disease caused by *Anopheles* mosquito. Still one of world's greatest killers

Influenza After World War I, in 1918, the most widespread influenza epidemic killed 20 million men, women, and children worldwide

AIDS Acquired Immune Deficiency Syndrome may be the result of infection by a virus known as HIV. First cases appeared in 1970s. Has now reached epidemic proportions and as yet there is no cure (1994)

Heart disease Accounts for more than half of deaths in affluent nations, where the disease is related to lifestyle – diet, smoking, etc.

Louis Pasteur (1822–95) set up the Pasteur Institute in Paris, a research center for the study of contagious diseases

Medical advances

As the human body has become better understood, so too have the diseases and ailments associated with it. In time, cures have been found for many illnesses. The 20th century began an era of technological innovation in medicine, particularly in diagnosis, and today doctors are able to save many lives.

c.1543 First accurate anatomical drawings by Andreas Vesalius enabled real understanding of the body

1628 William Harvey understood heartbeat and blood circulation, laying foundations for modern physiology

1796 Vaccination discovered, starting with smallpox vaccine. Big effect on eradication and prevention of diseases such as polio

1840s Anesthetics pioneered by Americans Horace Wells and William Morton, leading the way to pain-free surgery

1847 Antiseptics developed by Hungarian Ignaz Semmelweiss for use in childbirth, one of the first doctors to connect disease and hygiene

1860 French chemist Louis Pasteur demonstrates bacterial cause of disease. From 1875–1906 more than 20 diseases made preventable through immunization

1867 Modern mercury thermometer developed

c.1885 Psychoanalysis pioneered by Sigmund Freud

The syringe was devised to inject drugs straight into the blood system

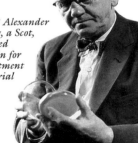

1895 X-rays used for the first time

1950s Ultrasound used to screen pregnant women

1954 Contraceptive pill developed to aid birth control

1958 Heart pacemaker developed; first implants 1960s

1960s–70s Development of laser surgery

1964 Chemotherapy developed to treat illnesses, particularly cancer

1967 First successful heart transplant

The stethoscope was invented in 1816 to enable doctors to listen to the heart and lungs. This version dates from 1855

In 1928 Alexander Fleming, a Scot, discovered penicillin for the treatment of bacterial diseases

The growth of cities

Cities usually grow up on rivers, lakes, or coasts, natural arteries for trade and communication. A few grow up around mineral resources, such as Johannesburg, on South Africa's gold fields. The proportion of the world's population living in cities is increasing rapidly. In 1980, 35 percent of the population lived in cities, and by the year 2000, 60 percent of the world's population will be urban inhabitants (according to one estimate). Then the biggest cities will be Mexico City, with 26 million people, and São Paulo in Brazil, with 24 million, followed by Tokyo, with 17 million, and Calcutta and Bombay in India, with 16 million each.

City	1890	1950	1990
Mexico City	330,000	2,943,000	20,900,000
São Paulo	35,000	2,449,000	17,113,000
New York	1,513,000	7,892,000	14,600,000
Calcutta	840,000	2,071,000	10,916,000
Paris	2,344,000	4,775,000	9,063,000
Beijing	1,650,000	1,603,000	6,920,000
Cairo	375,000	2,100,000	6,325,000
Sydney	386,000	1,484,000	3,657,000
Cape Town	84,903	383,830	1,911,000

Rush hour in Beijing
Beijing is the political, financial, educational, and transportation center of China, a country which has more than 1 billion people and over 30 cities with more than 1 million inhabitants.

Natural disasters

Volcanoes, earthquakes, floods, famines, fires, and disease have all taken their toll on the lives of people throughout the world. Preventive measures, such as reinforced buildings in the event of earthquakes and barriers to stop flooding, go some way toward alleviating the damage caused by natural disasters.

365 Earthquake at Knossos, Crete – 50,000 killed

1347 Bubonic plague (Black Death) – over 30 percent of European population died; millions more in Asia

1664–65 Great plague of London – 70,000 died

1669 Volcanic eruption, Etna, Italy – 20,000 killed

1703 Earthquake in Tokyo, Japan – 200,000 killed

1737 Earthquake in Calcutta, India – 300,000 killed

1755 Earthquake in Lisbon – 60,000 killed

On September 19, 1985 a large area of Mexico City was wrecked by a huge earthquake

1883 Krakatoa volcano, Indonesia – 36,000 killed

1894 Canton and Hong Kong plague took between 80,000 and 100,000 lives

1902 Volcano, Mount Pelée, West Indies – 26,000 killed

1976 Earthquake in Tang shan, China – 240,000 killed

1980 Volcano, Mount St. Helens, Washington State – 66 people killed

1985 Earthquake in Mexico City, Mexico – 10,000 killed

This body was found preserved in the ashes of Pompeii after Mt. Vesuvius erupted in AD 79

Deaths caused by humans

There has always been human conflict in the world, as nations seek to destroy one another. Over the years, weapons have become more and more deadly, and the power to kill has grown. The invention of nuclear arms now burdens humankind with the prospect of a force too dangerous to use.

This painting shows the Battle of Pea Ridge, March 6–8, 1862, in the American Civil War

1398 Tamerlane massacred about 100,000 Hindu Indians before he sacked Delhi

1572 Massacre of St. Bartholomew in Paris and other towns left nearly 20,000 Protestants dead in France

1618–48 Thirty Years War in Europe: about 20 percent of German population killed, or died from wounds

1641–52 618,000 Irish people killed in Ireland during the Civil Wars (about 41 percent of the population)

1861–65 American Civil War: over 600,000 killed

1914–18 World War I: about 10,000,000 killed on all sides

1939–45 World War II: about 55,000,000 killed on all sides, including about 22,000,000 Russians, military and civilian

February 13–14, 1945 Allied air attack on Dresden in Germany; between 60,000 and 130,000 people killed

August 1945 Atomic bombs dropped on Japanese cities of Hiroshima and Nagasaki killed more than 78,000 and more than 73,000 people, respectively

Florence Nightingale nursed soldiers in the Crimean War (1853–56) and reduced the death rate from 50 to two percent. Her lamp is shown here

World population growth

World population has risen and fallen over the years as health and food supplies have changed. When there has been plenty of food, the number of people living rose, and it has fallen when famine or disease took many lives. Until about AD 800 the world's population stayed below 200 million, but since then it has risen dramatically, the most rapid rise occurring in the 20th century. The graph shows population growth in billions.

NORTH AMERICA

EUROPE

ASIA

AFRICA

SOUTH AMERICA

OCEANIA

☐ Less than 10 people per sq km

☐ 10 to 100 people per sq km

▨ Over 100 people per sq km

Population density

The areas of the world with the highest population densities are in South and East Asia and Europe. The highest rates of population increase are in Africa and the Muslim world. Population growth tends to decline as wealth increases, and health and education become available to a nation's people.

1
2
3
4
5
6

| 1500 | 1600 | 1700 | 1800 | 1900 | 2000 |

INVENTIONS
AND
DISCOVERIES

Since the beginning of time, a
continuous flow of new inventions and
discoveries has changed, and usually
improved, the human condition.

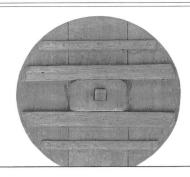

c.4000 BC Bricks first
made in Egypt and Assyria
c.3000 BC Wheel appeared
in Mesopotamia
c.3000 BC Plough used in
Egypt and Mesopotamia
c.3000 BC Glass first made
in Egypt

*This early wheel was made by
fastening planks together with
wooden or metal cross-pieces*

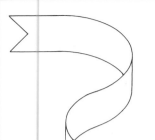

4000 BC ▶

1827 First successful photograph
taken by Niépce in France
1831 Discoveries which form
the basis of electrical engineering
made by Faraday in England
1834 Reaping machine invented
in the United States
1836 Gun with a revolving bullet
chamber – a revolver – invented by
Samuel Colt in the United States

*This 1870's model of a disk generator
demonstrates one of Faraday's
electrical experiments of 1831*

1800 Electric cell battery invented
by Alessandro Volta in Italy
1805 High-pressure steam engine
perfected by Cornish engineer,
Richard Trevithick in England
1815 Miner's safety lamp invented
by Sir Humphry Davy in England
1816 Bicycle invented by Karl von
Sauerbronn in Germany

Trevithick's steam engine

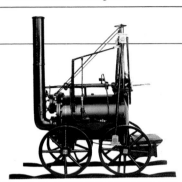

◀1820

1837 Electric telegraph printing
messages in code invented by
Samuel Morse in United States
1846 Successful sewing machine
invented in United States
1849 Safety pin invented by
Walter Hunt in United States
c.1850 Jeans created by
Oscar Levi Strauss, for pioneers
in the Californian gold rush

*This telegraph
transmitted
messages in code*

*The Bunsen
burner has
aided many
scientific
experiments
right up to the
present day*

1853 Aspirin invented by
Charles von Gerhardt in Germany
1855 Bunsen burner invented
by Robert Bunsen in Germany
1857 First passenger elevator for
public use began operation in
United States
1860 First internal combustion
engine to operate successfully
invented by Lenoir in France

◀1800

1840 ▶

1924 Freezing food invented
by Birdseye in United States
1926 Television working
system invented by John
Logie Baird in Scotland
1927 First talking movie,
The Jazz Singer, produced by
Warner Brothers in United States
1928 Penicillin discovered by
Alexander Fleming in England

*An early
television
receiver*

1901 Vacuum cleaner invented
by Booth in England
1903 Airplane achieving first
sustained flight made by Wright
brothers in United States
1909 Bakelite, invented by Leo
Baekeland in United States
1915 Tank with caterpillar tracks
invented by Swinton in England

First flight by the Wright brothers

◀1920

◀1900

*Sheer nylon
stockings
were hugely
popular
in the
1940s*

1930 Whittle began first design
of turbojet engine in England
1934 Cat's-eye reflectors, used
on roads, invented by Percy Shaw
in England
1935 Polyamide fibers (including
nylon in 1937) invented by W. H.
Carothers in United States
1937 Grocery carts developed
in United States

*Sputnik I was
successfully launched
in the Soviet Union*

1944 Automatic calculator
invented by Howard Aiken in
United States
1945 Microwave oven invented
by Percy Spencer in United States
1954 Contraceptive pill invented
by Gregory Pincus and John Rock
in United States
1957 Space satellite, *Sputnik I*,
launched by Soviet Union

1930 ▶

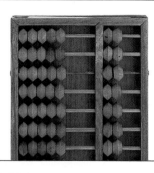

The abacus is still used in China

c.747 BC Calendar invented by Babylonians

c.700 BC Dentures first worn by Etruscans using human or sometimes animal teeth

c.600 BC Coins first made in Lydia (in Turkey)

c.500 BC First working bead frame abacus made in China

c.400 BC Saddle invented in Asia

Chinese bronze inkstone: solid ink was rubbed on to an inkstone with water, then a brush was used to apply the resulting ink

AD 105 Writing with ink on paper made from pulp in China

c.120 Seismograph invented by Zhang Heng in China

c.350 Stirrup invented in China

c.650 Windmills used in Iran

c.1000 Chinese perfect gunpowder

c.1000 Magnetic compass invented in China

1500 BC ▶

100 BC ▶

1710 First real piano created by Bartolomeo Cristofori in Italy

1712 First successful steam engine built by Newcomen in England

1757 Sextant developed by John Campbell in England

1769 Mechanical cotton spinning invented in England

1795 Food preserved in airtight jars by Nicolas Appert in France

A sextant

1455–56 First Bible printed in Europe by Gutenberg

1592 Thermometer devised by Galileo in Italy

1594 Flush toilet invented by Sir John Harrington in England

1608 Telescope invented by Hans Lippershey in Netherlands

1620 Submarine invented by van Drebbel in the Netherlands

Gutenberg used hard metal punches carved with letters

◀ AD 1400

Early typewriters were cumbersome machines

1860s Antiseptics used in surgery for the first time; pioneered by Joseph Lister in Scotland

1866 Dynamite discovered by Alfred Nobel in Sweden

1870 Margarine invented by Mège-Mouriès in France

1870 First truly marketable typewriter made in Denmark by Malling Hansen

This box telephone is one of Bell's early designs

1874 Bulk production of barbed wire invented in United States

1876 Telephone invented, partly as the result of an accident, by Alexander Graham Bell

1877 Phonograph invented by Thomas Edison in the United States

1879 Saccharine (sugar substitute) invented by Constantin Fahlberg in United States

1860 ▶

1870 ▶

1893 Zipper invented by Judson in the United States

1895 Wireless telegraphy and radio invented by Guglielmo Marconi in Italy

1895 Safety razor invented by King Gillette in United States

1895 First seaworthy submarines invented by American John Holland, ordered by U.S. Navy

Zippers revolutionized the clothing industry

1880 Baked beans, perhaps the most famous canned food, first canned in the United States

1880 Ballpoint pen developed by John Loud in United States

1889 First truly modern car invented by Gottlieb Daimler and Wilhelm Maybach in Germany

1889 Pneumatic tire invented by Scottish vet John Boyd Dunlop

Ink reservoir for early ballpoint pen

◀ 1880

Tiny silicon chips can hold a huge amount of information

1960 Laser constructed by Theodore Maiman in United States

1970s Silicon chip invented in the United States; it revolutionized the electronics industry

1973 Mountain bikes, able to scale mountains, made in United States

1975 VHS (Video Home System) launched by Japanese company JVC

A compact disc

1979 Compact disc codeveloped by Dutch company Philips and Japanese company Sony

1979 Portable stereo, the Walkman, invented by Sony chairman Akio Morita in Japan

1979 Mobile or cellular telephone invented in Sweden

1990 Virtual reality (computer simulation) created in United States

1960 ▶

1980 ▶

THE MODERN WORLD

NORTH
AMERICA

United States

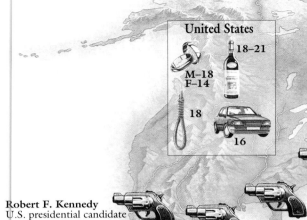

18–21

M–18
F–14

18

16

Malcolm X
Black Muslim leader
New York 1965

Robert F. Kennedy
U.S. presidential candidate
Los Angeles 1968

Martin Luther King
Civil rights leader
Memphis 1968

John F. Kennedy
U.S. president
Dallas 1963

Leon Trotsky
Russian revolutionary
Mexico City 1940

NORTHERN IRELAND
Republicans seeking a united
Ireland independent from
British rule clash with
Unionists and British troops

France

15

M–18
F–15

N/A

18

Nigeria

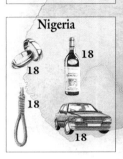

18

18

18

18

HAITI
Military rulers suppress
opposition as brutally as did
dictators "Papa Doc" Duvalier
(president 1957–71) and his
son "Baby Doc" (1971–86)

PERU
"Sendero Luminoso"
(Shining Path) Maoist
guerrillas fight government
security forces

Brazil

21

18

N/A

16

SOUTH
AMERICA

WORLD FIGURES

Twentieth-century history has
been shaped by the actions of
the superpowers, the Soviet
Union and the United States,
and their influential leaders.

RUSSIAN AND SOVIET LEADERS

1894–1917	Tsar Nicholas II
1917–24	Vladimir Lenin
1924–53	Joseph Stalin
1953–55	Georgi Malenkov
1955–58	Nikolai Bulganin
1958–64	Nikita Khrushchev
1964–82	Leonid Brezhnev
1982–84	Yuri Andropov
1984–85	Konstantin Chernenko
1985–91	Mikhail Gorbachev
1991–	Boris Yeltsin

US PRESIDENTS

1897–1901	William McKinley
1901–09	Theodore Roosevelt
1909–13	William Howard Taft
1913–21	Woodrow Wilson
1921–23	Warren Harding
1923–29	Calvin Coolidge
1929–33	Herbert Hoover
1933–45	Franklin Roosevelt
1945–53	Harry Truman
1953–61	Dwight Eisenhower
1961–63	John F. Kennedy
1963–69	Lyndon Johnson
1969–74	Richard Nixon
1974–77	Gerald Ford
1977–81	James Carter
1981–89	Ronald Reagan
1989–93	George Bush
1993–	William Clinton

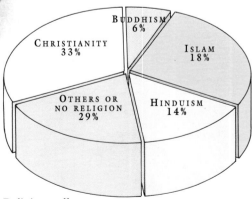

BUDDHISM
6%

CHRISTIANITY
33%

ISLAM
18%

OTHERS OR
NO RELIGION
29%

HINDUISM
14%

Religious adherence
Conquerors, colonists, and missionaries have
spread Christianity and Islam across the
world. In India, Hinduism remains dominant.
Many formerly Communist countries have
recently seen a resurgence of religious activity.
However, growing numbers of people,
particularly in Europe, have no religion.

E U R O P E

A S I A

Francis Ferdinand
Archduke of Austria
Sarajevo 1914

GEORGIA

TAJIKISTAN
Ethnic and political
conflicts have erupted in
many republics of the
former Soviet Union

ARMENIA/
AZERBAIJAN

AFGHANISTAN

BOSNIA

ISRAEL

IRAQ

KASHMIR

Japan

20

M–20
F–16

M–17
F–18

16

India

N/A

M–21
F–18

18

18

Park Chung Hee
South Korean president
1979

Mahatma Gandhi
Indian nationalist leader
New Delhi 1948

BURMA
Military regime
brutally suppresses
opponents who
demand democracy

Egypt

N/A

18

18

18

Anwar el-Sadat
Egyptian president
Cairo 1981

Indira Gandhi
Indian prime minister
New Delhi 1984

SRI LANKA
Thousands die in civil
war between Tamil
Tiger guerrillas and
Sinhalese people

SOMALIA
Food shortages
and civil war lead
to many deaths

SUDAN

S. W. R. D. Bandaranaike
Sri Lankan prime minister
Colombo 1959

ANGOLA

Melchior Ndadaye
President of Burundi
1993

A F R I C A

INDONESIA
People of East Timor
(absorbed by Indonesia in
1976) are harshly controlled
by Indonesian army

Christopher Hani
South African Communist
Johannesburg 1993

SOUTH
AFRICA

Australia

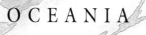

18

16–18

N/A

16–18

Hendrik Verwoerd
South African prime minister
Cape Town 1966

O C E A N I A

N

KEY TO WORLD MAP

Minimum legal age
for **drinking alcohol.**
The U.S. age varies
between states. N/A
means alcohol is
illegal for all.

Minimum legal age
for **marriage.** "M"
refers to males and
"F" to females.

Minimum legal
age for **driving.**
This is 16 or 18
in most countries.

Minimum legal age
for the **death penalty.**
N/A means there is
no death penalty in
this country.

Assassination
has silenced
many prominent
community and
political figures.

**Violent political
conflict,** causing
great suffering,
engulfs many
parts of the world.

INTERNATIONAL ORGANIZATIONS

ASEAN	Association of Southeast Asian Nations
CACM	Central American Common Market
COMECON	Council for Mutual Economic Aid
EFTA	European Free Trade Association
EU	European Union (formerly European Community)
LAIA	Latin American Integration Association
NATO	North Atlantic Treaty Organization
OAS	Organization of American States
OAU	Organization of African Unity
OECD	Organization for Economic Cooperation and Development
UN	United Nations
GATT	General Agreement on Tariffs and Trade
IMF	International Monetary Fund
UNESCO	United Nations Educational, Scientific, and Cultural Organization
UNICEF	United Nations Children's Emergency Fund
WHO	World Health Organization

Arab League
promotes inter-Arab cultural, economic, and military cooperation
Amnesty International
works to secure the release of those imprisoned for their beliefs
The Commonwealth of Nations
association of sovereign states that are or were ruled by Britain
Greenpeace
environmental conservation organization
International Red Cross and Red Crescent
provides medicine and aid for victims of war and natural disaster
World Wide Fund for Nature
works to protect endangered species

THE HISTORY OF CANADA

The first people in North America were hunters who came from Asia via a land bridge now covered by the Bering Sea, and they arrived between 80,000 and 12,000 years ago, during the last Ice Age. There is debate as to when Canada was first settled, but artifacts between 12,000 and 17,000 years old have been found at the Bluefish Caves in the Yukon Territory.

As the glaciers retreated, the first Canadians spread settlements across Canada and developed lifestyles based on their environments. They obtained food by hunting, fishing, gathering, and in the case of Eastern Woodland tribes, by farming. By the time explorers from Europe reached Canada, the native people had well-developed trading patterns, arts and crafts, languages, writing, religious beliefs, laws, and government.

The first Europeans

The claim that an Irish monk arrived around 550 AD has not been proven, but the existence of a Viking settlement in Newfoundland around 1000 has been confirmed by archeologists working at L'Anse aux Meadows.

In the 15th and 16th centuries the search for a route to the Far East led explorers to the New World. Giovanni Caboto (John Cabot) first landed on the Canadian coast in 1497, although Europeans had been visiting the fishing grounds on the Grand Banks since the early 1400s.

c.1000 Leif Ericson and other Vikings visit Labrador and Newfoundland

1497 John Cabot (Giovanni Caboto) claims Cape Breton Island (or possibly Newfoundland or Labrador) for Henry VII of England

1534 Jacques Cartier visits the Strait of Belle Isle (Newfoundland), and charts the Gulf of St. Lawrence

1576 Martin Frobisher of England makes the first of his three attempts to find a northwest passage, sailing as far as Hudson Strait

1600 King Henry IV of France grants a fur-trading monopoly in the Gulf of St. Lawrence to a group of French merchants

1605 Samuel de Champlain and the Sieur de Monts found Port Royal (Annapolis, NS)

1608 Samuel de Champlain founds Quebec

1610 Étienne Brûlé becomes the first European to see Lakes Ontario, Huron and Superior. Henry Hudson explores Hudson Bay

1617 Louis Hébert, the first habitant (farmer), arrives in Quebec

1634-40 The Huron Nation is reduced by half by European diseases. A smallpox epidemic in 1639 is particularly devastating

1642 Montreal is founded by the Sieur de Maisonneuve

1663 Quebec becomes a royal province

1665 The Carignan-Salières regiment is sent from France to Quebec to protect the colony. Jean Talon becomes Quebec's intendant

1667 Canada's first census counts 3,215 non-native inhabitants in 668 families

1670 The Hudson's Bay Company is formed and granted trade rights over all territory draining into Hudson Bay

1673 Marquette and Jolliet explore the Mississippi to its junction with the Arkansas

1682 La Salle explores the Mississippi to its mouth

1697 After years of raiding, the Treaty of Ryswick restores the status quo in the struggle between England and France. All captured territory is returned

1710 Francis Nicholson captures Port Royal for England

1713 The Treaty of Utrecht confirms British possession of Hudson Bay, Newfoundland, and Acadia (except Cape Breton Island). France starts building Fort Louisbourg (Cape Breton)

1739 La Vérendrye's expedition explores Lake Winnipeg

1749 Britain founds Halifax to counter the French presence at Louisbourg

1754 Beginning of French and Indian War in America. This marks the final phase in the struggle between France and Britain in North America

1755 Britain expels the Acadians from Nova Scotia, scattering them throughout her other North American colonies

1756 The Seven Years' War in Europe pits Britain against France in Europe and North America

1758 The British under Generals Amherst and Wolfe take Louisbourg

1759 Wolfe takes Quebec, defeating Montcalm on the Plains of Abraham

1763 France cedes its North American possessions to Britain in the Treaty of Paris

1774 The Quebec Act provides for British criminal law but restores French civil law and guarantees religious freedom for Roman Catholic colonists

1775 American revolutionary forces capture Fort Ticonderoga and Crown Point, opening the way for an invasion of Quebec. Richard Montgomery leads American forces, capturing Montreal and attacking Quebec City

1776 Under Governor Guy Carleton, Quebec City withstands the five-month American siege until the appearance of a British fleet in May

1778 Captain James Cook

NEW FRANCE

Jacques Cartier mapped the Gulf of St. Lawrence in 1534 and established settlements for France in the 1540s. Samuel de Champlain furthered the cause of New France by founding a colony at Quebec in 1608 and building a fur-trading network with local Algonquins and Hurons.

The fur trade was the economic foundation of New France, and until the 1660s efforts at settlement were sporadic, interrupted by wars between England and France. In 1663 New France became a crown colony with a governor (defence), an intendant (industry, trade, and administration) and a bishop (religion and education) to oversee the colony. Jean Talon, the first intendant, boosted population and industry, while Governor Frontenac extended the fur trade as far as the Gulf of Mexico. The vast territory claimed by France was thinly populated and impossible to secure. Increasing pressure from the English and their native allies resulted in a series of wars in the 18th century and the loss of New France in 1763.

BRITISH RULE

A Royal Proclamation in 1763 attempted to establish Protestant schools, the Church of England, and elected assemblies in New France. Under British law Roman Catholics could not hold office, and the first two British-appointed governors refused to call elections because the result would be unfair to the majority of the colony's inhabitants.

The Quebec Act of 1774 brought back appointed councils that could include Catholics and guaranteed both French civil law and the seigneurial system of land tenure. The Quebec Act also expanded the borders to include the lands of the Ohio valley. This preferential treatment of the Canadians angered the citizens of the Thirteen Colonies to the south and an American army invaded and captured all of Canada except Quebec City in 1775.

Citizens wishing to retain allegiance to the British crown arrived in Nova Scotia, New Brunswick, and Quebec in the years after the American War of Independence and in 1791 the colony was divided into Upper and Lower Canada.

The fur trade continued and both the Hudson's Bay Company and the North West Company led expeditions west and north in search of supplies. The surveyors and adventurers crossed the country to reach the Pacific Ocean, the Beaufort Sea, and eventually the Arctic Ocean.

anchors in Nootka Sound, Vancouver Island

1783 The American Revolutionary War ends; the border between Canada and the US is settled in the area between the Atlantic Ocean and Lake of the Woods. 7,000 United Empire Loyalists arrive in the Saint John River area

1784 New Brunswick becomes a separate colony with its own council and elected assembly

1786 St. John Island (Prince Edward Island) is declared a separate colony from Nova Scotia

1789 Alexander Mackenzie journeys to the Beaufort Sea, from Fort Chipewyan to the Arctic Delta

1791 The Constitutional Act (Canada Act) divides Quebec into Upper and Lower Canada along the Ottawa River

1792 George Vancouver begins his explorations of the Pacific coast

1793 Alexander Mackenzie travels from the Peace River across the Continental Divide and reaches the Pacific

1808 Simon Fraser, a North West Company employee, travels the river named after him to the Pacific

1811 David Thompson charts the Columbia River to the Pacific coast

1812 The US declares war on Britain, beginning the War of

1812. The Red River settlement is begun in Canada's northwest

1816 Agents of the North West Company kill the governor of the Hudson's Bay Company's Red River colony, and 20 others during the Seven Oaks Massacre. The settlers abandon the colony until Lord Selkirk brings forces to recapture the territory

1818 The 49th parallel is accepted as Canada's border with the US from Lake of the Woods to the Rocky Mountains

1821 The Hudson's Bay Company and the rival North West Company are amalgamated as the HBC

1825 Population surveys report 479,288 inhabitants in Lower Canada and 157,923 in Upper Canada

1832 Cholera epidemic kills 3,800 at Quebec City and 4,000 at Montreal

1834 The Assembly in Lower Canada passes the "Ninety-two Resolutions" setting grievances against the colonial administration. William Lyon Mackenzie becomes the first mayor of Toronto after Reformers gain a majority on city council

1836 Canada's first passenger train runs from St. Johns, Quebec, to La Prairie, Quebec

1837 Reformers in Upper and Lower Canada, led by William

Lyon Mackenzie and Louis-Joseph Papineau, stage unsuccessful rebellions

1839 Lord Durham's Report recommends union of Upper and Lower Canada and the establishment of responsible government

1841 The Act of Union unites Upper and Lower Canada as the Province of Canada, with its capital in Kingston, Ontario and a united parliament

1842 The Ashburton-Webster Treaty settles the Maine-New Brunswick border dispute

1843 Fort Victoria is built to bolster Britain's claim to Vancouver Island

1846 Great Britain ends a preferential trading policy with the British North American colonies and enters into a limited free trade agreement with the United States

1847 90,000 immigrants, mostly from Ireland, arrive in Canada. 5,000 die of cholera at Grosse Ile while in quarantine; 15,000 die after moving to Quebec City, Montreal, Toronto and Kingston, where the

epidemic spreads to townspeople

1848 Responsible government is achieved in the Canadas and in the Maritimes, due to the efforts of Robert Baldwin, Louis-Hippolyte La Fontaine, and Joseph Howe

1849 The boundary of the 49th parallel is extended to the Pacific Ocean. Lord Elgin approves the Rebellion Losses Bill to give compensation for property damage in 1837 in Canada East. Demonstrations are held in Toronto to protest and riots in Montreal lead to the burning of the House of Assembly

1854 The Reciprocity Treaty between Canada and the US is signed

1864 The Charlottetown Conference (Sept. 1–9) takes the first steps toward Confederation. The Quebec Conference (Oct. 10–27) sets out the basis for union

1866 The London Conference (Dec. 4) passes resolutions which are redrafted to become the British North America Act. The American government allows the Reciprocity Treaty of 1854 to lapse

THE WAR OF 1812

American resentment over Britain's interference with American ships and suspicions that the British were arming native people in American territory led the US to declare war on Britain in 1812.

American invaders expected Canadians to join their cause, however Canadians remained loyal to the British Crown and the Americans were driven back by the combined British and Shawnee forces under British-born General Isaac Brock and Chief Tecumseh. American General William Hull invaded Canada from Detroit in 1812, taking over present-day Windsor, but was forced to retreat, and surrendered Detroit after a brief siege. The battle of Queenston Heights was a Canadian victory, but General Brock was killed during the battle.

In 1813 the Americans attacked and burned York (Toronto), but were defeated at Stoney Creek. The battle of Beaver Dams was also a Canadian victory after Laura Secord eluded American sentries and walked 32 km through dense bush to warn of an American attack. The battle of Put-in-Bay gave the Americans control of Lake Erie and Tecumseh was killed during the Canadian loss at Moraviantown. The Canadians won battles at Chateauguay and Crysler's Farm.

In 1814 the Americans again invaded the Niagara district, but were stopped at Lundy's Lane. A Canadian force based in Halifax succeeded in occupying most of Maine and another launched an attack on Washington where government buildings were burned. A British offensive against Plattsburg on Lake Champlain failed and the two sides negotiated the Treaty of Ghent to end the stalemated war in 1814.

Fathers of Confederation

Delegates to three conferences [Charlottetown: Sept. 1, 1864; Quebec: Oct. 10, 1864; London: Dec. 4, 1866] preceding the formation of the Dominion of Canada were known as the Fathers of Confederation:

Adams G. Archibald, George Brown, Alexander Campbell, Frederick B.T. Carter, George-Étienne Cartier, Edward B. Chandler, Jean-Charles Chapais, James Cockburn, George H. Coles, Robert B. Dickey, Charles Fisher, Alexander T. Galt, John Hamilton Gray (of New Brunswick), John Hamilton Gray (of Prince Edward Island), Thomas Heath Haviland, William A. Henry, William P. Howland, John M. Johnson, Hector L. Langevin, Jonathan McCully, A.A. Macdonald, John A. Macdonald, William McDougall, Thomas D'Arcy McGee, Peter Mitchell, Oliver Mowat, Edward Palmer, William H. Pope, John W. Ritchie, J. Ambrose Shea, William H. Steeves, Sir Étienne-Paschal Taché, Samuel Leonard Tilley, Charles Tupper, Edward Whelan, R.D. Wilmot.

1867 Confederation. Britain's North American colonies are united by means of the BNA Act to become the Dominion of Canada and Sir John A. Macdonald is Canada's first prime minister

1870 Louis Riel leads the Métis in resisting Canadian authority in Canada's northwest

1876 The Intercolonial Railway linking central Canada and the Maritimes is completed. The Indian Act of 1876 defines special status for aboriginal people living on land reserves and sets out land regulations

1879 Macdonald introduces protective tariffs as part of his National Policy

1885 Métis and the NWMP clash at Duck Lake; the Métis are defeated at Batoche. The last spike of the transcontinental railway is driven at Craigellachie, BC. Louis Riel is convicted of treason and hanged in Regina (He is pardoned in 1992)

1896 Canada's minister of the interior, Clifford Sifton, develops an immigration plan to bring farmers from central and eastern Europe to settle on the Prairies

1897 Gold Rush begins in the Klondike

1899 The first Canadian troops ever sent overseas are dispatched to the Boer War

1903 Canada loses the Alaska Boundary dispute with the US

1914 Canada is at war with Germany when Britain declares war. Parliament passes the War Measures Act, allowing suspension of civil rights

1915 Canadians face German gas attack at Ypres, Belgium

1916 The Manitoba government grants women the right to vote and hold office. 24,713 Canadians and Newfoundlanders are killed in the Battle of the Somme

1917 Income tax is introduced as a "temporary wartime measure." The Military Service Bill is introduced, leading to the Conscription Crisis. Canadians take Passchendaele, Belgium; 15,654 are killed or wounded. Explosion of a munitions ship in Halifax harbour wipes out 5.2 sq km of the city, killing almost 2,000 and injuring 9,000

1918 Armistice ends World War I

1919 A general strike paralyzes Winnipeg; an armed charge by the RCMP kills one person and injures 30

1920 Federal legislation makes women eligible to sit in the House of Commons

1921 Postwar economic depression puts 300,000 men and women out of work–more than 15% of the work force

1922 Sir Frederick Banting, Dr Charles Best, Dr J.J.R. MacLeod and J.B. Collip share Nobel Prize for the discovery of insulin

1927 The Diamond Jubilee of Confederation is marked by Canada's first coast-to-coast radio network broadcast. The government passes Canada's first Old Age Pension Act

1928 The Supreme Court of Canada rules that, according to the British North America Act, women are not "qualified persons" who can sit in the Senate. This decision is reversed by British Privy Council in 1929

1929 The Great Depression begins

1935 Ten percent of Canadians rely on welfare or "relief." The "On to Ottawa Trek" by young men from government work camps ends in a riot at Regina

1939 Canada declares war on Germany. Quebec Premier Maurice Duplessis, who opposed Quebec participation in the war, is defeated in a provincial election

1940 Unemployment insurance is introduced

1942 Canadian forces overseas suffer losses of 2,200 killed or captured in the raid on Dieppe. Canadians of Japanese descent are moved inland from the coast of British Columbia as "security risks"; their property is confiscated

1944 Canadian troops push further inland than any other Allied unit on D-Day

1945 War in Europe ends. One million Canadians fought in World War II; 42,042 were killed. Igor Gouzenko defects from the Soviet Embassy in Ottawa and reveals the existence of a Soviet spy network in Canada. Canada's first nuclear reactor begins operations at Chalk River, Ont.

1947 Imperial Oil discovers the Leduc oil field

1949 Under Premier Joey Smallwood, Newfoundland becomes Canada's 10th province

1950 The Korean War begins; Canadian troops participate in the conflict as part of a United Nations force

1951 The midcentury census reports a population of 14,009,429. Immigration to Canada exceeds 100,000 annually during the 1950s

1952 Vincent Massey becomes the first native-born Governor General of Canada. Canada's first television stations begin broadcasting in Montreal and Toronto

1954 An economic slump interrupts the postwar boom. The Geneva Conference on the Far East invites Canada to join in supervising peace in Indochina. This peacekeeping commitment continues until 1973

THE LEGACY OF THE GREAT DEPRESSION

The depression that was felt world-wide in the 1930s was particularly hard on Canada because one-third of the GNP was based on exports. World prices for resource-based commodities dropped, beginning with falling wheat prices in 1929, and the subsequent collapse of the stock market ruined many investors.

In Western Canada the reliance on wheat and the added effect of a severe drought devastated the prairie provinces. In Saskatchewan, provincial income fell by 90% and two-thirds of the population had to go on welfare. Business leaders and politicians assumed that the Depression was temporary and would be followed by a recovery, and declined to intervene with the exception of the creation of work camps for single, unemployed men.

The failure of the established political parties to help economic recovery led to the rise of reform parties such as the Co-operative Commonwealth Federation, the Social Credit Party and the Union Nationale during the war years and pressure for some form of income protection. As early as the 1920s a small group of Progressives paved the way by making the creation of the Old Age Pension in 1927 the price for their loyalty to the minority Liberal government. By 1945 unemployment insurance and family allowance legislation had been passed. In the 1960s Medicare, the Canada Pension Plan and the Canada Assistance Plan were introduced to complete an extensive social safety net that remained unchanged until the economic downturn in the 1990s.

How Canada Grew

The ten provinces and two territories joined or were created between 1867 and 1949:

Alberta (1905), British Columbia (1871), Manitoba (1870), New Brunswick (1867), Newfoundland (1949), Northwest Territories (1905), Nova Scotia (1867), Ontario (1867), Prince Edward Island (1873), Quebec (1867), Saskatchewan (1905), Yukon Territory (1898).

1957 Lester B. Pearson wins Nobel Prize for his role in resolving the Suez Crisis. Canadian supply and services troops are sent to work with a multinational UN force around the Gulf of Aqaba. They stay until 1967 and return in 1973

1958 Coal mine disaster at Springhill, NS results in death of 74

1959 The St. Lawrence Seaway is opened

1960 Liberals under Jean Lesage win provincial election in Quebec, inaugurating the Quiet Revolution. A Canadian Bill of Rights is approved by Parliament

1962 The Saskatchewan government introduces the first Canadian Medicare plan

1964 Canada ends difficult peacekeeping duties in the Congo (Zaïre) after four years of service with heavy casualties. Canadian troops join UN forces in Cyprus, a posting which continues until 1993

1965 Canada gets a new flag. Failure of an Ontario Hydro relay device at Queenston plunges eastern North America into a power blackout

1966 The Canada Pension Plan is established

1967 The Canadian army, navy and air forces are unified to become the Canadian Armed Forces. Montreal hosts a world's fair, Expo '67. Canada celebrates its Centennial

1969 English and French become official languages of federal administration

1970 The FLQ kidnaps British trade commissioner James Cross, precipitating the October Crisis. Quebec labour and immigration minister Pierre Laporte is kidnapped and murdered. The federal government invokes the War Measures Act

1971 Canadian Gerhard

Herzberg wins the Nobel Prize in chemistry for his studies of chemical reactions that help produce smog

1977 Quebec government passes Bill 101, restricting English-language schooling to children whose mother or father had attended English elementary school in Quebec

1979 Antonine Maillet wins the prestigious French literary prize, the Prix Goncourt, for her novel *Pélagie-la-Charette*

1980 Canada's ambassador to Iran arranges the escape of six American Embassy staff from Tehran while their colleagues are held hostage. Quebec votes "no" to "sovereignty-association" (separatism) in a referendum

1981 The federal government and every province except Quebec reach agreement on a method for patriating Canada's constitution

1982 The Quebec Court of Appeal rejects the Quebec government's claim of veto power over constitutional change. Canada gains a new Constitution and Charter of Rights and Freedoms. The charter entrenches bilingualism within federal jurisdictions and provides for minority language education rights across Canada

1984 Conservatives under Brian Mulroney win federal election with 211 seats, the largest majority in Canada's history

1986 Canadian John Polanyi shares the Nobel Prize for chemistry

1987 The Meech Lake Accord, proposing major constitutional amendments, is agreed to by the prime minister and the 10 provincial premiers. A free trade agreement between Canada and the United States is reached

1989 The federal government announces a new goods and

services tax (GST) to take effect Jan. 1991. Fourteen female university students are killed by an anti-feminist gunman in Montreal

1990 The Meech Lake Accord dies when both Newfoundland and Manitoba fail to ratify the constitutional agreement by the deadline. A land dispute leads to a 78-day armed confrontation between Mohawk warriors and government forces at the Kanesatake reserve near Oka, Quebec

1991 Yukon First Nations members sign agreement on land claims and self-government; agreement also reached on creation of Nunavut in Northwest Territories

1992 Crisis in the Atlantic fisheries results in a virtual shutdown of the industry. A national referendum on the Charlottetown Accord for constitutional reform rejects the deal

PRIME MINISTERS

Sir John A. Macdonald (1867-1873)
Alexander Mackenzie (1873-1878)
Sir John A. Macdonald (1878-1891)
Sir John Abbott (1891-1892)
Sir John Thompson (1892-1894)
Sir Mackenzie Bowell (1894-1896)
Sir Charles Tupper (1896)
Sir Wilfrid Laurier (1896-1911)
Sir Robert Borden (1911-1920)
Arthur Meighen (1920-1921)
Mackenzie King (1921-1926)
Arthur Meighen (1926)
Mackenzie King (1926-1930)
Richard B. Bennett (1930-1935)
Mackenzie King (1935-1948)
Louis St. Laurent (1948-1957)
John Diefenbaker (1957-1963)
Lester Pearson (1963-1968)
Pierre Trudeau (1968-1979)
Charles Joseph Clark (1979-1980)
Pierre Trudeau (1980-1984)
John Turner (1984)
Brian Mulroney (1984-1993)
Kim Campbell (1993)
Jean Chrétien (1993–)

CANADA'S GOVERNORS GENERAL

The Imperial Conferences of 1926 and 1930 decreed that the Governor General could only act on the advice of the Canadian prime minister and Cabinet and was not an agent of the British government, reducing the office to a symbolic and ceremonial one. The Governor General is now selected by the Prime Minister and formally appointed by the reigning British monarch to act as the monarch's representative in Canada.

Sir Charles Stanley, Viscount Monck (1867)
Sir John Young, Baron Lisgar (1869)
Frederick Temple Hamilton Blackwood, Earl of Dufferin (1872)
John Douglas Sutherland Campbell, Marquess of Lorne (1878)
Henry Charles Keith Petty-Fitzmaurice, Marquess of Lansdowne (1883)
Frederick Arthur Stanley, Baron Stanley of Preston (1888)
John Campbell Hamilton-Gordon, Earl of Aberdeen (1893)
Gilbert John Elliott Murray-Kynynmound, Earl of Minto (1898)
Albert Henry George Grey, Earl Grey (1904)
His Royal Highness The Prince Arthur, Field Marshall Duke of Connaught (1911)
Victor Christian William Cavendish, Duke of Devonshire (1916)
Julian Byng, General Baron Byng of Vimy and of Thorpe (1921)
Freeman Freeman-Thomas, Baron Willingdon of Ratton (1926)
Vere Brabazon Ponsonby, Earl of Bessborough (1931)
John Buchan, Baron Tweedsmuir (1935)
Alexander George Cambridge, Major General Earl of Athlone (1940)
Sir Harold George Alexander, Field Marshall Viscount Alexander of Tunis (1946)
The Right Honourable Vincent Massey (1952)
General the Right Honourable Georges P. Vanier (1959)
The Right Honourable Daniel Roland Michener (1967)
The Right Honourable Jules Léger (1974)
The Right Honourable Edward Richard Schreyer (1979)
The Right Honourable Jeanne Sauvé (1984)
The Right Honourable Ramon John Hnatyshyn (1990)

GLOSSARY

abdicate to give up power or a throne

absolute ruler or **monarch** a ruler or monarch whose power has no legal limits

administration the government, especially the executive part of government which carries out laws and runs government business

alliance an official agreement between two or more countries to achieve a particular aim

ambassador a person representing the interests of one country in another country

anarchy lawlessness and disorder, in the absence of any strong government authority

apartheid in South Africa, the government policy of racial separation and white supremacy

appeasement the policy of giving in to the demands of an aggressor to maintain peace

armistice an agreement to halt fighting while negotiating peace

Asia Minor the peninsula where Europe and Asia meet, in modern Turkey, at the eastern end of the Mediterranean Sea

blitzkrieg a sudden, rapid military attack; from the German for "lightning war"

bourgeoisie the prosperous middle classes of society

caliph the title of a monarch who rules, or claims the right to rule, the Islamic world

Capitalism an economic system based on the private ownership of property and free and competitive conditions for business

caste in Hinduism, the unalterable place in society into which a person is born

censorship policy of stopping writings that the authorities find objectionable from being published and distributed

charter a document granting a group of people certain rights and privileges

chivalry the code of behavior followed by feudal European nobles and knights

citizen a member of a state, city, or other political community

city-state an independent state consisting of a city and the surrounding territory

civil disobedience the use of nonviolent resistance to defy laws thought to be unjust; also called passive resistance

civil rights or **liberties** the personal rights of the individual citizen

civil service the nonpolitical service which administers a country for the government

civil war a war fought between groups from and in the same country or region

civilization a human society that has reached a high state of cultural, political, social, and intellectual development

class one of the groups into which society is divided by social, economic, and other factors

code of laws a set of laws arranged in a systematic way

colonialism the policy of powerful nations which take control of weaker peoples; also sometimes called imperialism

colony a group of people settled in a land outside their homeland but still bound to it; or the land in which they are settled (and may rule)

commune a large farm or other social unit in which property is, theoretically, owned by the community

Communism a political and economic philosophy that calls for violent revolution, followed by total state control of society in the name of the people

confederacy an alliance of several people, communities, states, or cultural groups

conquistador one of the Spanish conquerors of Native American civilizations

coup from the French phrase "coup d'état"; a sudden violent or illegal seizure of government

crusade one of the European campaigns to recover Palestine from Muslim rule; any similarly dedicated campaign

culture the knowledge, values, and way of life of the people of a country or region

delta the land area (often triangular) formed by soil deposited at a river mouth

democracy a form of government based on rule by the people, usually through elected representatives

depression a period of drastic decline in economic activity, marked by widespread unemployment and hardship

despot a ruler who uses power in an unjust, oppressive way

dictator a ruler with absolute power, usually unelected and ruling by force

diplomacy relations between governments, especially in respect to making agreements, treaties, and alliances

divine right the theory that monarchs receive their power from God and so should not be questioned or disobeyed

domestication the taming of wild animals to make them useful to human beings

dominion a self-governing nation within the British Commonwealth of Nations

dynasty a series of rulers from the same family

economy the system by which a society produces and distributes its goods and services

edict an official order or decree

elite the most powerful, rich, gifted, or educated members of a group or community

embassy or **diplomatic mission** the business, or mission of an ambassador

empire a state and the conquered lands that it rules

Enlightenment, the or the Age of Reason: a period of European history (in the 1700s) when radical thinkers tried, in the name of reason, to reach a new understanding of society, government, and humanity, and then to transform them

entente agreement, from a French word meaning "understanding"

entourage a group of people around an important person

epic a long poem that tells the adventures of a hero or heroes

Fascism an ideology stressing dictatorship and nationalism and placing the strength of the state above individual citizens' welfare

federal system a two-level system of government made up of a supreme national government and states retaining strong local powers

feudalism a political system which developed in Europe from the 700s onward; under it, lords granted land to other nobles in return for loyalty, military assistance, and services; similar systems elsewhere are sometimes known as feudal

free trade international trade that is free of government interference

genocide the systematic murder of an entire people

ghetto a section of a European city where Jews were required to live; a similar urban area

glasnost the Russian word for "openness"; used by Mikhail Gorbachev of his policies in the Soviet Union in the late 1980s

guerrilla warfare a type of warfare in which small groups of fighters make surprise attacks

guild a medieval organization formed by merchants of the same trade or by skilled workers of the same craft to protect its members and control business

gulag the system of forced labor in the Soviet Union

Hellenism the culture of ancient Greece, particularly as it spread beyond Greece

heresy the holding of beliefs by a member of a religious group that are considered in conflict with that group's established beliefs

hieroglyphics the ancient Egyptian writing system that used pictures to symbolize words or sounds

humanism in the Renaissance, a cultural movement that looked to ancient Greek, Roman, and sometimes biblical knowledge to find how best to live; it had far-reaching effects on society

icon a religious image, especially one painted on wood

ideology a set of ideas, especially political, embodying the beliefs and interests of a person, group, or nation and influencing their actions

illuminated manuscript an ornately decorated handwritten book

imperialism the policy of building or extending a nation's control over other lands to gain economic and political advantages

irrigation supplying land with water, usually to help the growth of food crops

isolationism a policy of not taking part in international affairs

jihad Arabic word meaning "holy war"

judiciary the judges in a country, considered as a group

junta a small ruling group, especially in a Latin American country

kaiser the common title of the German emperor between 1871 and 1918

Latin America the areas of the Americas whose official languages are Spanish or Portuguese (both Latin languages): South America, Central America, parts of the Caribbean, and Mexico

legation a diplomatic mission headed by a minister, or such a minister's residence in a foreign country

liberalism a political philosophy that emphasizes progress and reform

looting robbery during war or riots; the robbers often cause much damage as they steal

mandate a country or region that is assigned by some official authority to be administered by another nation

mercenary a soldier, usually of foreign background, fighting solely for pay or other gain

migrate to move from one region or country and settle in another

missionary someone who travels with the goal of making converts to a particular religion

monopoly the control of all (or nearly all) production and trade of a certain product

native belonging by birth or origin to a place

Nazism the ideology of the National Socialist German Workers' party, based on state control of the economy, racist nationalism, and national expansion

Neolithic of the later Stone Age, during which improved stone and flint tools and weapons were produced and primitive farming was practiced

neutral not supporting or assisting either side in a war or dispute

nomad one of a group of people who have no fixed home and wander from place to place in search of food and water

oust to force a person or group out of a position or place

parliament an assembly of the representatives (usually chosen by election) of a nation or other group

partisan a member of a fighting group that attacks the conquering forces in an occupied country or region

patrician one of the class of wealthy landowners to which the leaders of the Roman republic usually belonged

peasant in many traditional societies, a member of the class of ordinary working people living in the rural areas

perestroika Russian word meaning "reconstruction," used of radical political and economic change, especially in communist or ex-communist countries

plebeian one of the ordinary people of ancient Rome

policy a plan of action

Papacy the office of the Pope, the bishop of Rome and head of the Roman Catholic church

populist a politician or other person who claims to support the interests of ordinary people

private ownership the right of individuals to own and control capital (money and property); a major characteristic of capitalism

propaganda news and information designed to persuade people to adopt a particular point of view

protectorate a country protected and partially controlled by a stronger country

racism the belief that one's own racial or national group is superior to others

radical extreme

raze to demolish buildings, villages, towns, or cities

rebellion or, revolt: organized resistance or opposition, usually violent, to a government or other authority

Reformation in 16th-century Europe, the movement that rebelled against the authority of the Roman Catholic church

regent someone who rules a country during the childhood, absence, or illness of its monarch

regime a particular government or system of government

reich the German word for "empire"; especially the German nation formed in 1871 by the uniting of several states under a strong central government

Renaissance a period of European history, beginning in the 14th century, when far-reaching changes occurred in the arts and intellectual life

reparations payments made by one nation to another in compensation for property destroyed in war

republic in ancient Rome, government by some citizens and not a monarch; in modern times, a democracy in which citizens choose their leaders

revolution the overthrow of a government by the people

ronin in Japanese society, a samurai or warrior who had no lord to serve

royalist a supporter of a monarch or monarchy

sack to take and loot a city or major building

satellite kingdom or **state** a kingdom or state which is dependent on a foreign power

samurai the warrior class of feudal Japan

secede to withdraw formally from an alliance, organization, association, country, or other political entity

serf in Europe, from late Roman times until, in places, the 1800s, a peasant farmer who was legally bound to remain on the estate of a lord

shogun one of the military leaders who ruled Japan in the name of the emperor from the 1100s to the 1800s

siege the attempt to capture a fortified place or a city by surrounding, isolating, and attacking it

socialism a political and economic philosophy that calls for government or worker control and operation of business and industry for the benefit of society

sovereignty supreme and unrestricted power, as possessed by independent states

steppes vast plains stretching from eastern Europe across central Asia

suffrage or **franchise** the right to vote, especially for representatives in a legislative body or assembly

superpower an enormously powerful state with influence around the world; usually used of the United States and the Soviet Union

technology the development of methods, materials, and tools used in doing work

terrorism the use of violence, especially against random civilian victims, to win demands or influence the policies of a government

totalitarian a government in which unified action is achieved through the complete authority of the leader

tsar the title of the male rulers of Russia from the 15th century until 1917; female rulers were titled tsarina

vassal in feudalism, a noble who pledged loyalty and services to a feudal lord in exchange for a grant of land and serfs

viceroy in some colonial systems, a representative of the monarch in a colonized land

vizier a high official in certain Muslim countries

welfare state a system in which the government has major responsibility for the social and economic security of its people

Zionism the movement to create and maintain a national homeland for the Jewish people in Israel

This illustration comes from an eighth-century Maya painted vase from Central America; it shows the Maya rabbit god as a scribe, writing with a brush pen on a manuscript with jaguar skin covers

INDEX

D

T

ACKNOWLEDGMENTS

Additional design, editorial, production, and picture research: Peter Bailey, Louise Barratt, Jacqui Burton, Simon James, Lisa MacDonald, Sandy Ransford, Julia Ruxton, Linda Stevens, Adam Thomas, Christine Webb **Index DTP**: Jillian Somerscales **Cartography**: Roger Bullen **Specially commissioned photography**: Peter Anderson, Andy Crawford, Geoff Dann, Ranald MacKechnie **Additional photography**: Geoff Brightling, Martin Cameron, Philip Dowell, Mike Dunning, Christi Graham, Peter Hayman, Alan Hills, Chas Howson, Colin Keates, Dave King, Liz McAulay, Andrew McRobb, Nick Nicholls, Stephen Oliver, Roger Phillips, Tim Ridley, Steve Shott, James Stevenson, Harry Taylor, Kate Warren, Barbara Winter, © Jerry Young, Michel Zabé. Also, additional photography at: The British Library, The British Museum, The Hunterian Museum, The Museum of Mankind **Specially commissioned illustrations**: Simone Boni, Stephen Conlin, Peter Dennis/Linda Rogers Associates, Luigi Gallante, Nick Harris/Virgil Pomfret Agency **Maps**: World maps, Russell Barnett; small maps, Sallie Alane Reason **Additional illustrations**: Elaine Anderson, Graham Corbett, Fiona Bell Currie, Chris Forsey, Ray Grinaway, Nick Hewetson, John Hutchinson, Sergio Momo, Anthony Morris/Linda Rogers Associates, Tony Smith/Virgil Pomfret Agency, Peter Visscher, John Woodcock. Dorling Kindersley would like to thank the following museums and their staff for their invaluable help: **The Ashmolean Museum of Art and Archaeology,** Oxford; **Cambridge University Museum of Archaeology and Anthropology,** Cambridge; **The Imperial War Museum**, London; **Musée des Thermes et de l'Hôtel de Cluny**, Paris; **National Army Museum**, London; **The Oriental Museum**, University of Durham; **The Pitt Rivers Museum**, Oxford, with special thanks to Sandra Dudley; **The Royal Museums of Scotland**, National Museums of Scotland, Chambers Street and Queen Street, Edinburgh; **The Wallace Collection**, London. The author acknowledges with great gratitude the valuable and long-term assistance of: Cambridge City Library; Suffolk County Libraries, especially Ipswich Library and Bury St. Edmunds Library; the following Cambridge University department libraries: Oriental Studies, African Studies, Haddon Library (Archaeology & Anthropology), Classical Archaeology Museum Library, Latin-American Studies Library, Faculty of Modern and Medieval Languages Library, South Asian Studies Centre Library, Latin-American Studies Centre Library, and Wolfson College Library. The biggest debt of all, however, is owed to the Cambridge University Library, to whose staff it is impossible to express enough gratitude.

Picture Credits:
Abbreviations: t = top; b = below; c = center; l = left; r = right.
Ancient Art and Architecture Collection: 41tl, 43cl, 44bl, 46c, 57ctr, 62/3, 73bl, 74tl, 78ctr, 79ctr, 79br, 85c, 86cbl, 90cbl, 94br, 95tl, 106cr, 111bl, 120c, 120bcr, 136tr, 138tl, 139ct, 150ct, 152tl, 154br, 157tr, 186ctl, 189tr, 190cl, 190cr, 225bl, 244cr, 245cr; / D.F.Head 162bl; /L.Sower 145cbl Aquarius Picture Library: 303ctr Ashmolean Museum, Oxford: 46bl Associated Press: 340br Arxiu Mas: 136bl Auckland Institute and Museum: 288cbr Australia House, London: 232bl Barnaby's Picture Library: 123c Bildarchiv Preussischer Kulturbesitz: 278cb, 305cl Bridgeman Art Library: 47cbr, 58cl, 59br, 62bl, 74bcl, 76bc, 79bl, 88cr, 89t, 101ctl, 108bl, 125cl, 134ctr, 138tr, 141cr, 146tl, 150cbr, 177r, 178bl, 191c, 194cbl, 193br, 193bl, 208tl, 213br, 220tc, 224br, 225cr, 226br, 229bl, 239bl, 240cr, 240bl, 241bl, 244cl, 248c, 248bc, 255ctr, 255cr, 257cr, 257cr, 258tl, 259tl, 260bl, 263cl, 264bl, 269br, 270cr, 274tc, 274ctl, 274ctr, 275ctl, 275ctr, 277ctr, 279tl, 280ctr, 280bc, 280br, 280ctl, 282bc, 285tr, 292c, 293ctl, 293cbl, 294tr, 296tl, 316tl;/Bibliotheque Nationale 121cr, 150ctl, 151cr; /Bodleian Library, Oxford 154tr; /British Library 104cr, 105tl, 105bl, 135tr, 194bl, 225cr, 230cl; /Department of the Environment 156cl; /Derby Museum and Art Gallery 228cr; /Fitzwilliam Museum, University of Cambridge 199br, /Giraudon 120cbl, 174tl, 190bl, 228cl, 248c, 260cr, 281ctl, 360cl; /Giraudon /Musée Condé Chantilly 106bl, /Hermitage, St.Petersburg 226cr; /House of Lords, London 212tr, 212tc; /Philip Mould Historical Portraits, London 195cr; /Musée des Beaux-Arts, Rouen 213cr; /National Gallery of Art, Washington 212br; /National Maritime Museum, London 195tl, 255ctl, 259cr, 307cbr; /Royal Geographical Society 195bl, 200tr; /Science Museum, London 214bl; /Staatliche Schlosser und Garten, Potsdam 227bl; /Walker Art Gallery, Liverpool 194c British Library, London: 151cl, 239cr, 258bl, 258br, 259tcr, 241cr British Petroleum Company: 319tr Courtesy of the Trustees of the British Museum, London: 90cr, 142tr, 159br, 206cr J. Allan Cash: 101tr Central Zionist Archive: 297bl Channel 4: 295bl Jean-Loup Charmet: 162tr, 173cr, 211bl, 276bl Peter Clayton: 38c Bruce Coleman: 16cbr, 16bc /Peter Darcy 16bc; /RIM Campbell 16cbr; Colorific: 344cr, 354cbl, 354tr; /John Moss 338tc Comstock: 351bl Coo-ee Historical Picture Library: 288tr, 292br, 293bc, 303ctl, 304cb, 313br, 329tr, 329tcl, 329cbl, 329br Crown Copyright: 225br C.M.Dixon: 38ctl, 58br, 100cbr, 103tl, 109tr, 113tr ET Archive: 101cb, 108cl, 109cr, 110tl, 111bcr, 194tl, 196tr, 212bl, 213bl, 214tr, 216cbr, 222bl, 228bc, 236bl, 249tl, 250tr, 250c, 254cbr, 256cr, 263bc, 264tl, 267tr, 279cl, 280tl, 280cbl, 282c, 298c, 299tr; /Victoria and Albert Museum, London 208cbl Mary Evans Picture Library: 134cr, 137br, 140tl, 143tl, 154bl, 156cr, 156bl, 158tl, 158bl, 158br, 166cr, 170cr, 182br, 186ctr, 186cr, 187ctr, 196cr, 199cr, 200bl, 205ctl, 207c, 207cl, 207ctl, 207cbl, 209bl, 216cbr, 228bl, 242bl, 244tl, 254bcl, 258c, 264cr, 265cr, 270cl, 270br, 275c, 275br, 277c, 277cr, 282c, 283ct, 283bl, 284cr, 293cr, 294br, 298ctr, 298bl, 302cbl, 306br, 312ctl, 315tl, 317bl, 318tr, 320tr, 321tr, 322tr, 323c, 324tr, 324c, 324br, 325br, 327cbr, 332tr, 333cl, 362cbr J.Filochowski/APA: 353ctr Dr.Josephine Flood: 23bl, 27bl Werner Forman Archive: 53tc, 69cl, 96br, 101bcr, 102br, 103cr, 120cl, 145ctl, 152c, 156cr, 156bl, 166tr, 167ct, 192cl. 205ctr, 207tl, 238br; /Art Institute, Chicago 192cr; /Courtesy David Bernstein Fine Art New York 80cr; /Dallas Museum of Fine Arts 64tl, /Musee National du Bardo, Tunis 122cbl; Arizona State Museum 129tl, 129tr, 129c, 129cr; Auckland Institute and Museum, New Zealand 187bl; /Biblioteca Nacional, Madrid 137 bl; /Biblioteca Nazionale Marciana, Venice 110br; /British Museum 52ct, 187tc; /Courtesy of Entwistle Gallery, London 54tr; /Field Museum of Natural History, Chicago 166cbl; Gulistan Library, Tehran 187ctl; /Museum fur Islamische Kunst, Berlin 121tr; /National Museum, Lagos 52tr, /Peabody Museum, Harvard University 113tl; /Statens Historika Museet, Stockholm 127bl; /Sudan Museum, Khartoum 54c, /University Library, Prague 159tr Fotomas Index: 151tl, 198tl, 206br, 210br, 223cr, 240br, 308cr, 308tl Giraudon: 142bl Ronald Grant Archive: 179bl, 231c, 326ctr Greenhill-S.A.C.U.: 296br, 318cr Sonia Halliday: 30br, 102cl, 104cl, 104bc, 120tc, 175tl; /Laura Lushington 75bl; /Jane Taylor 54br Robert Harding Picture Library: 22bl, 25tl, 25ctr, 34tl, 36cbl, 38bl, 38br, 40cr, 52bl, 61bl, 68ctl, 70tl, 72cb, 88br, 90cl, 91br, 92tr, 96 tr, 101bl, 102tl, 114tr, 130ctl, 135cb, 136c, 138bc, 166ct, 166ctl, 168br, 169bc, 171cr, 171cbr, 173tl, 173tr, 188bl, 191tl, 241br, 279bc, 341c; /Mohamed Amin 107tc; /ASAP/Israel Talby 75 /Bildgentur Schuster/ Scholz 241br; /Robert Cundy 52bl; /Robert Francis 286tl; /F.Jackson 54tl; /M.Jenner 120tr; /Victor Kennett 155cl; /Paola Koch 345bl; /Photri 53tr, 70ctr, /Sassoon 124bl, 137ctl, 150/151, 171tr; /Michael Short 43tr; /Adina Tovy 113bl, 269cl; /Adam Woolfitt 44cr, 45ct Hikone Castle Museum: 209cr Michael Holford: 27cr, 30tr, 60tl, 71tr, 75cbr, 77cbl, 80tl, 84tr, 86cr, 94tl, 94bl, 100tcl, 100cr, 101ct, 101ctr, 101cr, 107cbr, 110cr, 123tl, 130bl, 134tr, 134cbl, 135ctl, 135ct, 136br, 139bc, 142c, 144cl, 167tr, 179tr, 205cr, 206tl, 220c, 223bl, 227cr, 237br, 263tr Lucy Horne: 123bl Hulton Deutsch: 18bl, 243bc, 277bc, 282br, 295br, 299cr, 299br, 300tl, 301br, 302br, 306cr, 308cb, 308cbl, 313ctr, 313bc, 317tl, 317cr, 319bl, 320bl, 328ctr, 330bl, 332cl, 332bc, 333cbr, 334ctr, 334cbr, 338bc, 343tr, 343bl, 352ctl, 353tl Robert Hunt Picture Library: 319br Hutchison Library: 106tr, 204tc, 276cr; /Sarah Errington 107tr, 342cr, 353bc; /R Francis 80c INAH c: 35bc Illustrated London News: 316cbr, 316br Images: 56/57 The Image Bank: 354br; /Amanda Clement 269cr; /Steve Dunwell 215tr; /Proehl 356c; /Russell 355cbr; /Weinburg/Clark 107cl; Simon Williamson 339br; /Sam Zarenber 205br Images Colour Library: 45tr, 45bl Imperial War Museum: 333br Jiji Press, Tokyo: 241tl David Keith Jones: 170tl Keystone: 347tr David King: 264br, 312cr, 322cl Kobal Collection: 42bl, 70bl, 109tl, 140bl, 174cr, 316bl Kon Tiki Museum: 116bc Kunsthistorisches Museum, : 121cl, 128tcl Life File: 114br, 116tl; /Selwyn Taylor 105tr Magnum Photos: Bruno Barbey 141cl; /Bruce Davidson 351c; /Stuart Franklin 356tr; /Burt Glinn 354ctl; /John Hillelson 135tc, 141cl; /Thomas Hoepker 360bc; /David Hurn 304cl; /Susan Meiselas 361ctl; /M.Rio Branco 355bl; /Paul Rusco 355cl; /Steele-Perkins 355cbr Mansell Collection: 110tr, 122bl, 178tr, 216bl, 221c, 226cbl, 242cl, 247ctr, 249bl, 262br, 275cbr, 282tr, 305tr, 312cl, 316cr, 320br, 315cl, 316cr; /J.Thompson 124cr Mayibuye Centre, Belville, South Africa: 295tl, 315cbr Moviestore: 246ctl NASA: 338cb, 352cbr, 352bl National Archives and Museum, Wellington, New Zealand: 288bl National Archives of Zimbabwe: 168br National Cultural History Museum, Pretoria, South Africa: 256cl National Museums of Scotland: 158tr National Palace Museum, Taiwan: 172tr National Portrait Gallery of Scotland: 125c Natural History Museum, London: 15cl Peter Newark's Pictures: 144tr, 204cl, 209cl, 211tl, 214cl, 214cr, 215cr, 226tr, 229tl, 238tl, 247tl, 247cbl, 247br, 248bl, 250bl, 255tr, 257bl, 262cl, 267bl, 268tr, 268cl, 268cbr, 270bl, 281bl, 281bcl, 283tl, 285bl, 285br, 287br, 292cbl, 293cl, 297tr, 301tl, 301ctr, 301c, 301bl, 307cbl, 308cr, 308cl, 330cr, 331tl, 333ctr, 334c, 360tc, 361ctr North Wind: 284cl Christine Osbourne: 319ctl Panos Pictures: 314cl; /Ron Gilling 356tr; /Jeremy Hartley 356cl; /Rui Vieira 89cbr Pictor International: 60bl, 88bl Ann and Bury Peerless; 91c, 191bl Pictor International: 60bl Philadelphia Museum of Art: 170tr Popperfoto: 293br, 297cl, 299bl, 312cbl, 313cbl, 319cl, 322bl, 325tl, 325cr, 325bl, 326tl, 326c, 327tl, 327cr, 327bl, 328c, 328cbr, 328bcr, 330tl, 330br, 334tl, 340cr, 345cl, 345cr, 347cb, 346cl, 350bl Public Records Office, crown copyright: 142br Rex Features: 338ctl, 339bc, 341cl, 342cl, 346bl, 348cl, 354tr; /Action Press 339cr; /Nina Berman 351br; /Pete Brooker 339tr; /Tim Page 338ct, /Sergio Penchansky 350cl; /Sipa Press 338tr, 341tr, 341br, 342tr, 348cl, 351tr; /Sipa/CTK 338cr Michael Roaf: 90bl Royal Armouries: 239cl Royal Collection, Windsor Castle, copyright Her Majesty the Queen: 177tl St. Louis Art Museum: 160cr Scala: 39cl, 40tr, 61cbr, 61c, 63br, 76cr, 95bl, 176cbl, 177br, 196bl, 265cl; /Biblioteca Marciana, Venice 179tl Science Photo Library: 16tr; /Philippe Plailly 338c; /St. Mary's Hospital Medical School 360cr South American Pictures: 112bl, 114/115, 130tr, 267cr, 267br; /Kimball Morrison 112tr South African Library: 206bl Frank Spooner: 346br; /Esais Bartel 344tl, 344tr/Gamma 338br, 343cl, 350cr, 350br, 353cbl; /Gamma /Novosti 128br; /Ferry Liaron 349bl; /N.Pye 339cbl, /John Reader 16tr;/Eslami Rad 344cbr; /L.van der Stock 344bl John Massey Stewart: 155cbl Sygma: 339tl, 340cbl, 342bl, 347cl, 347br, 348cr, 348bl, 348br, 351tl; /Bisson 349tl, /Fabian 339c, /John Jones 349cr; /J.P.Laffont 351tl; /J.Langevin 339ct, 343br, 345br; /Gus Ruelas/LA Daily News 349cr; /A.Tannenbaum 342br Syndication International: 134ct, 186bc, 199bl, 296bl, 268bl, 296bl, 300cr, 302ctl, 338cbl, 352tr Telegraph Colour Library: 89bl, 95br, 353ctr; /Bill Gentille/ Picture Group 339cb; /Masterfile 339cbl Trinity College Library, Dublin: 140ctr Ullstein Bilderdienst: 305tl Courtesy of the Trustees of the Victoria and Albert Museum, London: 191bc, 192br, 224cl Wallace Collection: 213cl, 227br, 228tl, 236cr Zefa Picture Library: /Neville Presho 181ctr; /Starfoto 56br

Jacket: front, Fotomas Index: ctl INAH: ctr Peter Newark's Pictures: br; back, INAH: ctl Syndication International: br; front flap, Bridgeman Art Library: cbl C.M. Dixon: cr Fotomas Index: br

Every effort has been made to trace the copyright holders and we apologize in advance for any unintentional omissions. We would be pleased to insert the appropriate acknowledgment in any subsequent edition of this publication.